CW01501178

SHOLOM MORDECHAI RUBASHKIN: THE INSIDE STORY אמת

TWO BOOKS IN ONE:

Book 1: **Trials, Tribulations, and a Triumph of Trust**

Book 2: **A Jew in "A Place Called Prison"**

By Getzel Rubashkin

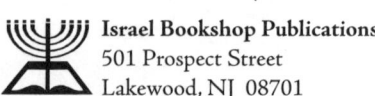 Proceeds of this book will go to support
the work of Aleph Beis Gimmel in helping
Yidden apply *emunah* and *bitachon* to challenges in life.
alephbg@gmail.com | alephbeisgimmel.com

Cover Photo:
Chaim Bhatia Photography | (732) 966-3910

Book & cover design by:

VIVIDESIGN
SRULY PERL | 845.222.1967
srulyperl.com | info@srulyperl.com

Published and distributed by:

Israel Bookshop Publications
501 Prospect Street
Lakewood, NJ 08701
Tel: (732) 901-3009
Fax: (732) 901-4012
www.israelbookshoppublications.com
info@israelbookshoppublications.com

Printed in the USA

Distributed in Israel by:
Tfutza Publications
P.O.B. 50036
Beitar Illit 90500
972-2-650-9400

Distributed in Europe by:
Lehmanns
Unit E Viking Industrial Park
Rolling Mill Road,
Jarrow, Tyne & Wear NE32 3DP
44-191-406-0842

Distributed in Australia by:
Gold's Book and Gift Company
3-13 William Street
Balaclava 3183
613-9527-8775

Distributed in South Africa by:
Kollel Bookshop
Ivy Common
107 William Road, Norwood
Johannesburg 2192
27-11-728-1822

This book is dedicated in loving
memory of our beloved father

ר' אברהם אהרן בן ר' שניאור זלמן ישׂשׂכר געציל הלוי ע"ה

He lived with pure faith and trust in *Hashem
Yisbarach*. Throughout our family's *nisayon*, he
inspired us and so many others to follow in his
way with *simchah*. He always reminded us that "*der
Oibershter bleibt nisht kein ba'al chov*," and he was
right. Tatty, we love you! Our hope to G-d Almighty
is that, by telling the inside story, this book will be
another step toward correcting the terrible injustice
done against you and your family.

Yaakov Yitzchok ע"ה *and* יבדל"ח *Gutel & Family* שיחיו
Yehoshua and Shterna Sara & Family שיחיו
Yosef and Rochel Leah & Family שיחיו
Yosef Yitzchok Halevi and Bella & Family שיחיו
Moshe Yaakov Menachem Halevi and Faigy & Family שיחיו
Sholom Mordechai Halevi and Leah & Family שיחיו
Yosef Yitzchok ע"ה *and* יבדל"ח *Chaya & Family* שיחיו
Tzvi Hersh Halevi and Basya & Family שיחיו
Sholom Ber and Chana Zelda & Family שיחיו

Dedicated in loving memory of our dear parents,

Berish and Saba Zolty *a"h*

שיינדל בת שאול   דוב בן יוסף

21 Adar Beis   **24 Av**

Although they suffered through the Holocaust, their steadfast belief in the Ribono Shel Olam never wavered. They understood that Hashem's ways are simply beyond human comprehension, and for the rest of their lives, they would refer to Hashem only with immense love, speaking about His kindnesses and the many blessings which He showered upon them.

Our parents channeled their pain into triumph, establishing a family steeped in Torah and *chessed*, and becoming leaders of their community, where their names were synonymous with charity and kindness. They still remain a beacon of light and hope to their children and to the many whose lives they've touched.

יהי זכרם ברוך

Dedicated as well in loving memory of our cherished husband, father, and brother,

Yoseph (Joey) Zolty *a"h*

יוסף בן דוב

הלך לעולמו בל"ג בעומר

18 Iyar

He personified kindness in every sense of the word, dedicating his life to bringing joy and happiness to his family and to others. Joey had the knack to see what no one else saw, and he would specifically befriend those who were silently suffering. He was a devoted friend and confidant to countless people. Whether you needed a ride to the other side of town ("C'mon, I'm going that way anyway!"), or a good word or *dvar Torah* to lift your spirits, Joey was your man. He was brilliant, exquisitely sensitive—yet incredibly modest. His example will always be a guide and an inspiration to his beloved family and to all those who loved him.

יהי זכרו ברוך

How fitting it is that a book about Reb Sholom Mordechai Rubashkin, the Yid who taught all of Klal Yisrael how to respond when faced with adversity, should be published in the *zechus* of our dear parents and their beloved son.

May Reb Sholom continue to inspire others in the area of *emunah* and *bitachon* in Hashem, and may this book be a vehicle in helping all of us become more connected to our loving Father in Heaven.

Atara Zolty & Family
Bentzy and Phyllis Friedman & Family

To watch a man, bound and chained in the physical world, have the inner strength and true faith to be so completely, emotionally free, is an inspiration. It is an example for us all to strive toward—*emunah* in its purest form!

David Huebner and Family

Thank you to our dear friend
Reb Shmuel Bodansky
for his dedication and warmth, both before the *nes* and following the *nes*, toward furthering the work of teaching *emunah* and *bitachon*. May it bring the *Geulah Sheleimah, b'meheirah b'yameinu!*

אנו אסירי תודה על החיזוק וקידוש השם
שהמחבר נותן לכלל ישראל

חזק ואמץ
מידידים ובני ידידים

We were so touched by the story of faith and trust,
which shows the true strength of the Jewish people.

With feelings of love,
David Edelstein and Family

It is a true *zechus* to be a part of this amazing story,
which gives so many people the *chizuk* they need.

May our participation be a source of
brachah for our whole family.

Gideon Gratsiani and Family

גדעון מנחם בן מירה ומשפחתו
שלי בת תמר וכל משפחתה
חי'ה מושקא סימי בת שלי שתחי'
דובער בן שלי שיחי'
יוסף יצחק בן שלי שיחי'
שירא–ל בת תמר שתחי'
וכל אוהבינו שיחיו

TABLE OF CONTENTS

BOOK TWO
A Jew in "A Place Called Prison"

Foreword

By Rabbi Pinchos Lipschutz

WHEN I TRAVELED TO POSTVILLE, IOWA, THE FIRST TIME, ALL I KNEW was that a person named Sholom Mordechai Rubashkin was indicted on some serious charges. We were told that he ran a decrepit plant, took advantage of his workers, harbored illegal aliens, cut corners, and deserved to be put away for a long time.

I didn't get to meet him that day; he was too busy running the plant. But I met his father and his brother Yossi and they impressed me as really fine people.

The plant was cutting edge, the workers had no complaints, and everyone sang the praises of the Rubashkins. As the visit went on, I realized that the media narrative was a lie. I was hurt and affronted that good people were being maligned, their business was being destroyed, and the town they had breathed life into was going to be put on life support.

Upon my return, I wrote about the visit and my impressions. I resolved to do what I could to help them. Little did I know that this cause was going to take over my life. I came to know Sholom Mordechai on a personal level as well. We would speak often on the phone while he was in "a place called prison," as he called it. We came from different worlds—he from Samarkand, me from Lithuania—but our conversations were of Torah, where all Jews can meet and converse. We studied *Chovos Halevavos*. He went on to live it as his case took challenging and unforeseen twists.

As time went on, I watched a travesty unfold, and there was little we could do about it. The charges began piling up against the fine man who had built a beautiful plant to supply Jews with kosher beef and donated the majority of his income to charity. My heart and soul drove me to work to help him defend himself against the charges and the accompanying avalanche of negative publicity.

Everything about this case was extraordinary—the man, the charges, the surprises and turns, the ups and the many downs, and the way Klal Yisrael eventually rallied around him. Everything that could never happen happened. Things that never happened to anyone else happened to Sholom Mordechai.

I wrote many words about the saga and enlisted others to do the same. We laid out the truth of the story and spoke of Sholom Mordechai's faith. People were inspired, and many asked when "the book" was coming out. I told them that I was waiting for the happy ending. They laughed.

We hear amazing stories of faith from hundreds of years ago, from the Holocaust period, and about great people throughout Jewish history. We think that such stories could not happen in our time, because we are not on a high enough spiritual level to possess the belief of giants of years past. If nothing else, the saga of Sholom Mordechai teaches us that a regular person in our day can be in an awful situation and maintain steadfast faith.

When a *frum* Jew is targeted by the Fake News and corrupt prosecutors force a business into bankruptcy, collapse its assets, and then collude with a witness and a judge to send a fine person to jail for bank fraud, everyone takes notice. When Sholom Mordechai was found guilty and sentenced to twenty-seven years in prison, there was almost no one who did not see a vendetta and excessive punishment.

When even after finding incriminating documentation against the judge and prosecutors, appeal after appeal is denied, people feel that there is some kind of agenda at work. This led leading legal and ethics experts, people who spent their lives prosecuting criminals, judging, teaching, and living justice, to sign petitions, write letters, and participate in the campaign to free Sholom Mordechai. Despite it all, he was never broken and publicly maintained his belief in Hashem through all the curious curves, turns, and negative decisions in his case.

Jews of all types came together at public gatherings in an unprecedented fashion to hear from *rabbanim* and advocates for his cause, to *daven* for him and donate to help cover his enormous legal fees.

When he was freed in dramatic, miraculous fashion on Zos Chanukah, Jews around the world burst out in emotional song. They danced in the streets, in shuls, in *batei midrash*, and in stores across the Jewish world, because it was historic.

We saw history. We experienced history. We saw Hashem save a person who had *emunah* and *bitachon*. We saw *achdus*. The night he was freed, we got a small taste of what it will be like when *sinas chinam* is banished once and for all.

Through it all, the man at the center of the storm, the target as it were, was tranquil. He preached simple faith and sang the song of the believer even when to outsiders the realities appeared so different. He looked at everything with a brain, heart, soul, and eyes fueled with faith.

He became a friend and inspiration to a nation. His faith was rewarded. The *tefillos* of thousands were answered.

As we mourn those who lost their lives in tragedies, recently and in times past, and as people *daven* for salvation for themselves, their loved ones, and others who seek *yeshuos*, his story inspires us to hope that the end will be bright, the end will be joyous, and when it seems that there is only darkness, light will break through.

The book you are about to read is not just Sholom Mordechai's story. It is our story as well. It is the story of a Jew in *galus*. And it has a happy ending.

May our stories, as well, have happy endings, and may we merit the coming of Mashiach speedily in our day.

Rabbi Pinchos Lipschutz
Menachem Av, 5781

A Story That's Not a Story

By Reb Sholom Mordechai Rubashkin

THERE ARE NO STORIES IN THE TORAH.

Well, technically, there *are* stories in the Torah, but they're clearly not included in the Torah to provide a historical account. If that were the goal, *all* the stories would be included in Chumash, but they're not. Many details of the lives of our *Avos* and subsequent generations are left out, and only some of those gaps are filled in the Gemara or midrash. Only some events are described, which begs the question: Why are these particular stories included in the Torah?

The clue is in the name. The word "Torah" is from the word *hora'ah*—instruction or guidance. These specific stories are included in the Torah not to tell stories but because they have something important to teach us. They're instruction and guidance in the *form* of stories.

The Ba'al Shem Tov extends this even further, saying that *everything* a Yid sees or hears is a lesson in his *avodas Hashem*. In the Torah, Hashem tells stories to the whole Jewish nation, but Hashem also tells stories specifically and directly to you, by writing experiences into your life or by orchestrating that you hear the experience of another, and for the same reason: to teach you something.

I lived with that teaching of the Ba'al Shem Tov throughout my ordeal, opening my heart and my mind to the message Hashem was teaching me in each instance. The central lessons I learned by living through my experiences, and which I hope you will learn by reading about them, are the following:

1. You Are a *Neshamah*

Powerful people and institutions had targeted me, systematically destroyed everything I'd built, and torn me away from my family. They had imprisoned me and thrown away the key, deaf to every attempt to argue in my favor. I was powerless and doomed. That was the natural narrative, the perspective of my body.

Our body and soul are so seamlessly integrated that we sometimes overlook this, but they are, in fact, two separate entities, rooted in two very different realities.

The reality, as far as my *neshamah* was concerned, was very different. I was precisely where Hashem wanted me to be. The people and institutions who had played a role in my ordeal were powerless puppets enacting the will of my Creator. Everything they had done and were doing was something Hashem wanted me to experience for my own benefit in properly serving Him, realizing my potential and illuminating the world.

I was *not* imprisoned indefinitely by a malicious power—I was on a temporary assignment from Hashem, Who would return me to my family as soon as His purpose was complete.

This clarity alleviated terrible emotional suffering and enabled me to respond the right way, rise to the challenge, and complete my assignment—after which I was promptly released from my difficulty despite all the threats and promises of those who thought *they* had imprisoned me.

> **Embrace and constantly remind yourself who and what you truly are. If you identify with the body and its perspective, you are imprisoned, body and soul, even if you're a king. Identify with your soul and *its* perspective, and you will be truly free, body and soul, even in prison.**

2. The Importance of Learning

We have a lifetime's worth of lived experiences from the body's perspective and very little instinctive understanding of the truth as the *neshamah* (correctly) sees reality. It is only by learning Torah, which illuminates the world with Divine truth and clarity, that we can orient ourselves correctly.

> **Open a *sefer* and see the world correctly through the eyes of the Torah.**

3. Access *Emunah* and *Bitachon*

As I've described, it's critical that we see through the natural perspective of the world and perceive the truth—but our logic and intellect is not always up the task, whether because of its own shortcomings or because you face a particularly dense facade.

As *Yidden*, we're not limited to working with our intellect. We're gifted with a much more perceptive faculty—the power of *emunah* and *bitachon*. Our *emunah* tells us of Hashem's presence and His benevolence, and our *bitachon* assures us that we will experience this benevolence in our lives in the positive outcomes we hope to see.

Develop and nurture your faith and trust in Hashem. Developing your *emunah* and *bitachon* will transform your attitude toward the past and present and your outlook on the future. This will help you through troubled times, and, in this merit, you will also see Hashem's salvation.

4. See *Hashgachah Pratis*

Events may seem random or, perhaps worse, shaped by others, but everything that happens in this world down to the most minute detail is being created and carefully orchestrated by Hashem. Sometimes we can see the benefit from a given occurrence—it advances our interest in some way or plays an important role in fulfilling our purpose. Other times, we see no apparent benefit to an occurrence, or it may even seem to be detrimental.

The Torah assures us that this is nothing more than the limitations of our perception. Everything that happens is the will of the ultimate good, Hashem Himself, and it is for a beneficent purpose.

Learn to see Hashem's hand in the events that happen to and around you. This brings the Torah reality to life in a very real way, bringing it out of the realm of books, out of your mind and heart, and into the tangible world. If you can't see the good or when it appears bad, remind yourself that it is certainly *hashgachah pratis* and for the best—for *your* best.

5. Be Happy

The Torah instructs us to serve Hashem with joy. This is a critical element, not a nice suggestion. Even if you have the clarity, ability, and strength to prevail in a struggle, depression and lethargy invite failure.

Our emotional reactions to the events in our lives flow from our perspectives. By consciously choosing and cultivating the perspective of our *neshamah*, our *emunah* and *bitachon*, and our perception of *hashgachah pratis*, all based on the direction and clarity of the holy Torah, we are not dragged down to depression by adversity. Instead, we see it accurately, in a positive light, and can face it with energy and enthusiasm.

Find joy in the life and the task Hashem has given you.

6. Mitzvos Are a Lifeline, Not a Burden

Our instinct, courtesy of the *yetzer hara*, paints our obligations to Hashem as burdens to be borne when necessary and lightened when possible. Particularly in times of adversity, such as in a place called prison, the temptation is strong to limit our involvement and exertion in Torah and mitzvos to the minimum and take advantage of any possible leniency, lightening the load. This is a tragic mistake.

In truth, Torah and mitzvos are what *lift* us to a different reality, connecting us to Hashem and enabling us to rise above the adversity we face. Diminishing them in any way only weakens their effect on us, making us that much more aligned to the world which is so full of the challenges we seek to overcome.

Go the extra mile in doing mitzvos—it will connect you to Hashem and make your burden *lighter*, not heavier.

Throughout this book, these lessons and others will emerge from the stories I've experienced. I consider them the keys to survival. I hope you can internalize them, as I have, and that they transform and elevate your connection with Hashem and your fellow Jews, making my stories much more than just stories.

I want to take this opportunity to give a special mention to my son Shneur Zalman Yissachar Getzel Halevi and his wife and family, for all the efforts he invested in writing this book.

Sholom Mordechai Rubashkin
Chodesh Nissan, *Chodesh HaGeulah*, 5781
Jackson, NJ

Author's Foreword

MY FATHER'S STORY HAS INSPIRED MANY PEOPLE—TO GREATER FAITH and trust in Hashem, to greater strength in the face of adversity, to greater and more joyous expression of Torah and mitzvos. All this, despite the fact that his story has never really been told.

So powerful is the truth and the clarity of perception which he represents that even the general outlines and the incomplete snippets, fragments, and anecdotes gleaned from the Jewish media and the grapevine have had this great effect.

In the years since his miraculous release, he has traveled the country and the world, filling in some of the blanks in the context of *shiurim* and speeches on the topic of strengthening and applying *emunah* and *bitachon*, but those are obviously not the place for a thorough recounting of a story which spanned decades.

In this book, I set out to finally tell the story. The book reflects my own recollections of events refreshed by documents in my possession and expanded on through lengthy conversations and correspondence with others involved. It represents my best efforts to publish a true version of what transpired. The legal details that are included reflect my understanding of the legal case and my best efforts to summarize and convey them accurately.

For practical reasons, the story is told from my father's perspective and in his voice. I've made every effort to accurately reflect my father's spirit and attitude, but the responsibility for framing and for word choices, and any unintended nuance or implication that results, rests entirely with me.

If I do become aware of any factual errors or other corrections or clarifications that should be made, those will be posted on a website[1] created for this book. That's also where you can find a more comprehensive list of

---

1. Rubashkinbook.com.

people who are deserving of credit for helping my father but could not be included in the book simply for lack of space.

I use quotes throughout the book. Some are direct quotations and others are indirect, merely paraphrasing or imagining the wording used in a given circumstance. I trust the reader to distinguish between the two based on context.

Writing this book has been an enormous undertaking. The time, resources, and any ability that I've been able to apply to this task are all a gift from Hashem. I wholeheartedly thank Hashem for all of them.

For her patience, support, and practical contributions, I have to recognize and wholeheartedly thank my *eishes chayil*, Chana. I mean that literally. I have to. I can't not. As an author, it's expected of me. That's a problem in this case, because an obligatory statement doesn't get the presumption of honesty and sincerity. I can only say that, in my case, the recognition is completely honest and the gratitude completely sincere. Thank you.

In addition, I have to also sincerely and actually thank: My father for sharing the values and ideas described in these pages and for subjecting himself to countless hours of interrogation relating to various factual or philosophical aspects of this book; my mother for her strength and fortitude in all those long, trying years during my father's and our family's lengthy ordeal; my sister Roza Hindy Weiss for being the force of nature she proved to be and for her willingness to help with the book; my brother Yossi who helped in the research phase; my siblings Meir Simcha, Shmuly, Chaya Mushka Zaltzman, Moishie, Mendel, Menucha, and Uziel to whom I'm grateful for just being my family; my children Rashi, Menucha Rochel, Mendel, Yossi, Shterna, and Levi who are the pride and joy of my life; and all of Klal Yisrael who proved time and again that *Yidden* are not a nation comprised of families but a family the size of a nation.

As this book goes to print, I'd also like to thank the dedicated team at Israel Bookshop that helped turn the manuscript into a finished book. Their hard work is apparent throughout the book—the capable editing by Mrs. Weiss, the careful proofreading by Mrs. Sonenblick, the meticulous layout by Sruly Perl of ViviDesign—all ably managed by Mrs. Gendelman and Mrs. Delmar and led by R' Moshe Kaufman. They were patient and accommodating to what must have been a deluge of questions, requests, and suggestions and worked very hard to meet a difficult deadline. Thank you all—individually and as an incredible group.

It is my sincere hope that this book gives you the inspiration, strength, and clarity that my father gave and continues to give me, filling us all with the true and pure *emunah* and *bitachon* that will carry us all straight to the *Geulah Sheleimah* with Mashiach Tzidkeinu.

Getzel Rubashkin
Chodesh Nissan, *Chodesh HaGeulah*, 5781
Brooklyn, NY

THANK YOU, KLAL YISRAEL!

When describing how we merit Hashem's salvation, the Rambam tells us to think of our deeds as being measured on a scale. This is a telling *mashal*, because no matter how much weight is needed, every ounce is indispensable to tipping the scale.

Every single mitzvah to free Sholom Mordechai Halevi ben Rifka, large or small, was critical. We owe *hakaras hatov* to each and every one of you.

So, THANK YOU:

- To those who had me in mind by "*Matir Assurim*" or said an extra *kapitel* of Tehillim on my behalf…
- To the *kollel* couple who gave up their vacation money for me…
- To the elderly Yid who waited in line to sign a petition for me…
- To those who ran lemonade stands and carnivals to raise money for my benefit…
- To the dedicated Otisville volunteers who kept the kosher vending machine full…
- To all the *Yidden* who wrote letters, shared their *kabbalos*, and had me in mind during *hafrashas challah* and *Shabbos licht*…
- To the volunteers from Dror who took my children on Chol Hamoed trips when I could not…
- To all of you who didn't sleep with a pillow and drank coffee without sugar as a *zechus* for me…
- To the lady who organized pizza every Thursday for my family for eight and a half years…
- To all those amazing performers who took time to perform and give *chizuk* to me in Otisville—always an uplifting experience…
- To the rabbis and *askanim* who contacted politicians…
- To the *bachur* who made my release his "Make-a-Wish" request…
- To the volunteers who came from far and wide to help us make a weekly *minyan* in Otisville. You can't imagine how much *chizuk* it gave all of us…
- To the donor who was also a cheerleader…
- To the donor who gave $150,000 when my daughter asked for $15,000…
- To the women who sold their jewelry to raise funds…
- To the people who joined in the *simchah* on the big day…

The list goes on and on.

Thank you to my dear family, Klal Yisrael!

It is my hope that these acts continue for those awaiting their own release, and may they tip the scale of our national merit and bring about the true miraculous salvation with Mashiach Tzidkeinu.

שלום מרדכי הלוי (ס) בן רבקה אסתר ימ"ש

BOOK ONE

Trials, Tribulations, and a Triumph of Trust

CHAPTER ONE

The Beginning

The True Beginning

MY FATHER, REB AVRAHAM ARON HALEVI A"H, ALWAYS INSISTED THAT a story be told from the beginning, but finding the beginning of stories from our lives isn't always easy. After all, our lives are a seamless and overlapping series of many events, some large and some small, which combine in many different ways and tell many different stories. We have to be very clear about what story we're telling in order to figure out where to start.

The milestone dates in my life are clear. To name some of the obvious ones: I was born in 1959. I moved to the Midwest to work at my father's kosher meat plant in 1990. The attack that upended my life and that of my family occurred in the summer of 2008. Any one of those is a reasonable place to start *a* story, but none of them is the right beginning for *my* story—because my story isn't really about what happened to me.

Those events and experiences, dramatic though they were, are only the backdrop for the *true* story. The true story is the strength and clarity a Yid possesses—when he taps into his *Yiddishe neshamah*—to persevere over, and even grow from, the difficult experiences that Hashem puts him through.

I'm in no way unique, nor can I take any credit, for having the strength to overcome the challenges to my connection to Hashem. That strength is intrinsic to the *neshamah*, the natural inheritance of every Yid from our first forefather, Avraham Avinu. Through the generations, even simple, unlettered *Yidden* have defied attempts to separate them from Hashem, to the point of *mesiras nefesh*.

An obvious demand that we abandon Hashem, *chas v'shalom*, will naturally awaken this innate strength of our *neshamos*, and there is no challenge we can't face once it's awakened.

However, it is when such demands are *less* obvious, when the efforts to separate us from Hashem are more subtle, that it can be difficult to recognize them as such and to access this innate strength. The ability to recognize and resist even those less obvious attacks and to infuse daily life with the light of the *neshamah* is what sparked many people's interest in my story, but I can't even take any credit for *that*.

I am proud to live in the real world—the world as defined and described by the Torah and as perceived by my *neshamah*—but I didn't get there on my own. From my earliest youth, I was surrounded by immediate and extended family and a community who not only learned Torah but *lived* Torah. There was never a question about whether what I learned in *cheder* and yeshivah was purely academic or if it was the actual, practical reality of life. The world was the way it is described in Torah and *chassidus*. That was a simple statement of fact to my father and my mother, and this was demonstrated in everything they did.

This truth that they passed on to me also wasn't something that *they* discovered. They got it from their parents—and their parents, in turn, from *their* parents. The reality of Torah and the power of the *neshamah*, central to Jews in every generation, was embraced in my family by generations of Jews whose steadfast connection to Hashem and His Torah were tested and strengthened in the crucibles of Czarist and Soviet Russia.

They passed their strong, single-minded, and pure commitment to *Yiddishkeit* to each successive generation through education and example. I was raised on the stories of three centuries of grandparents *yirei Shamayim*, stories that were echoed in living color in the quiet, yet awe-inspiring, lives of my parents themselves.

Clearly, the beginning of my story stretches back to a time before the trial, before the raid, before Agriprocessors, before even my childhood. In fact, to tell my story from the beginning, I need to start well before I was even born.

For over a century, the Rubashkin family lived in Nevel, a small city of around fifteen thousand people near the border of Belarus, about 130 miles from Lubavitch. It was home to a long-established community of Lubavitcher chassidim who lived the teachings of *chassidus* with such pure simplicity and sincerity that the Rebbe Rashab once remarked, "A butcher from Nevel is more precious to me than a scholar from Kremenchuk," which was a city renowned for its great scholars of *chassidus*.

When Communism first gained popularity in Russia, it was as an ideological revolution, a philosophy. The new world it offered promised Russian Jews true equality and the destruction of all the old prejudices and barriers, "freeing" the *Yidden* to leave their old ways and fully integrate into the wider society.

My father described its appeal and effect on the Jews of Russia as an immense tidal wave, an overwhelming surge that washed away many communities, root and branch. Spiritual leaders did their best to shield their congregations, and parents tried to shield their children, but the spiritual casualties among Russian Jewry were staggering, particularly among the youth.

My grandfather, Getzel Rubashkin, was a young teenager when this bewitching new philosophy was at a fever pitch, but he simply and stubbornly resisted its call, staying true instead to his proud heritage. With so many of his peers running in new circles, young Getzel spent much of his time with the older generation. Other Jews his age called him "old man" and "backward." When speaking of those years, he recalled those mocking insults with pride that he'd found the strength to withstand the crushing peer pressure of the time.

My father's father, Zaideh Getzel Rubashkin

Instead of fading into history like the Communists who mocked him, he merited to see and participate in the continuation of our holy and eternal nation. He raised his children—and they, their children—as true *yirei Shamayim*.

A short story that my father told on occasion demonstrates how Zaideh Getzel fostered his children's inherent connection to Hashem and His Torah. At the young age of ten, my father had gone to the barber for a simple haircut. The barber, who was not Jewish, didn't stop when he reached my father's *peyos*. Feeling the scissors cut through his precious *peyah*, he clapped his hands to his ears. "Stop!" he cried out in panic, but it was too late. One of his proud *peyos* now lay on the barber's floor. Now on guard, he made sure that no harm would come to his other *peyah*.

When the barber finished the haircut, the young boy went home and showed his father what had happened. Without a word, Zaideh Getzel got some shoe polish. Dipping a cloth in, he daubed black polish in front of his son's ear, where his *peyah* should have been. He went over his first stroke a few times. "*Dos iz peyos, dos iz peyos*—This is *peyos*, this is *peyos*," he repeated with each stroke.

When his father was finished, the young boy jumped off the chair and walked away—a black stain where one *peyah* should have been and a memory that stayed with him his whole life. A Yid has *peyos*, and he is a Yid—it was as simple as that. Until his hair grew back, this would be a reminder. It wasn't a logical response, not even according to the logic of halachah, but it reflected, expressed, and cemented in his young mind the fundamental and uncompromising bond of the Yid with Hashem.

Eventually, the ideological revolution escalated to actual violent revolution and ultimately, a new regime. Drunk with power, zealous Jewish adherents formed the *Yevsektzia*, the "Jewish section" of the Communist party, with the explicitly stated mission of destroying traditional Jewish life. This group was the true impetus behind the aggressive and violent persecution of *Yidden* and *Yiddishkeit* in the new Soviet Union.[1]

The Iron Curtain closed around Russia, and the Jews were left to choose between the poisoned carrot of assimilation and the deadly stick of persecution. Miraculously, the *Yidden* in Nevel withstood the Communists and the *Yevsektzia* until the very end, which came with World War II in 1941. Zaideh Getzel would remember their triumph with a warm smile: "Sholom Mordcheh," he would tell me, "Nevel was a city of *ehrliche Yidden* right up until the Nazis *ym"s* destroyed it."

In 1941, the German army launched a surprise attack on their erstwhile ally, Russia. Within weeks, they were approaching Nevel, and the local Jews had a decision to make. Misled by memories of the Great War in which the German armies were liberators from centuries of cruel and oppressive Czars—and themselves suffering under the cruel and oppressive Soviets— many of the Jews of Russia doubted reports of Nazi atrocities as just more Soviet propaganda. There was much debate in Nevel about whether to flee or

---

1. As I experienced a hundred years later, the government as a whole had other things to focus on and it was individuals using the raw power of the government for their own personal agendas that were driving the persecution. Of course, the anti-Semites in the government, going all the way to the top, were only too eager to empower and support them.

welcome the advancing Germans. My *zaideh* and his family came to the right conclusion and fled just in the nick of time along with a group of other Jewish families—only twenty-four hours ahead of the invading Nazis.

Like many fleeing Jews in that region, their destination was the distant city of Samarkand, in Uzbekistan. Pressed by the advancing Nazis, they took whatever they could and fled on foot, under repeated bombardment by German warplanes who fired indiscriminately on innocent refugees. Later, by Hashem's kindness, they were able to find a train to take them the last leg of the arduous two-and-a-half-thousand-mile journey.

My mother's family was also from Nevel, and they also fled to Samarkand, but they had left earlier and traveled in comfort. My mother's father, Zaideh Uziel Chazanov, had been in no doubt whatsoever about the German atrocities, even though his family had directly experienced the Germans as liberators in World War I. Recalling his clarity in those critical moments, he would say with a sad smile, "*Az ich her az a goy helft a Yid, hub ich sfeikois, az ich her az a goy harget a Yid, gloib ich dus mit emunah peshutah*—When I hear that a *goy* is helping a Yid, I have doubts, but when I hear that a *goy* is killing *Yidden*, I believe it with simple faith."

My mother's father,
Zaideh Uziel Chazanov

This was an extension of the clarity that protected him from the allure of Communism. Like his future *mechutan* Zaideh Getzel, he too, had seen through their false promises. A distant family member asked him, years later, how he had known. He pointed to Avraham Avinu's words to Avimelech: "*There is no fear of G-d in this place, and they are liable to kill me over my wife.*" The Soviets had proudly and emphatically rejected G-d, and he knew that that path leads not to a People's Paradise but to oppression and murder.

My parents' *shidduch* was made in Samarkand during those terrible wartime years. They were married in the shared courtyard of their parents' homes in true chassidic form. The wedding *seudah* was celebrated as a joyous *farbrengen,*[2] punctuated by dancing, which lasted until 7:30 the next morning.

---

2. A gathering of chassidim to strengthen themselves in their *avodas Hashem*. The participants share words of insight and inspiration and stories of old, exhorting each other to improve in

When the war ended, Soviet Russia announced that it would be repatriating Poles who had fled to Russia during the war. That was "Soviet-speak." What they were really doing was expelling native Poles from Polish lands which Russia invaded and annexed during the war. To the Jews of Russia, facing persecution and destruction, this was a Heaven-sent crack in the Iron Curtain. Many made their way to the border city of Lemberg (Lvov), where *askanim* helped them blend in with the steady stream of Polish emigrants.

Seeing so many *Yidden* taking this opportunity, my mother insisted that they go along. Her father, Zaideh Uziel, was also eager to leave, seeing no future in Russia for his family, particularly for his son Meir Simcha, for whom there were no proper *chadarim* or yeshivos. They all set out for Lemberg together—both of my grandparents and all their children, including my newly-married parents.

They arrived in Lemberg with all their worldly possessions in tow. Upon arrival, they discovered that the local committee organizing the minting of new Polish citizens was strapped for cash. It was a matter of life or death, particularly for the many who were being actively hunted by the KGB, and the *rabbanim* had *paskened* that everyone must give all their valuables to the committee to save as many people as possible.

Hashem had blessed Zaideh Getzel with success in the preceding years, and he was carrying a large amount of money. This was the money that would enable them to start over in their new home, but, hearing the instruction of the *rabbanim*, he didn't think twice. He marched straight to the specified address and handed over every penny he owned. He didn't even remove a handful of bills for his own needs. "The only thing I ask," he said, "is that you provide papers for my family."

When their turn came, and they received their papers from the committee,[3] the family gathered with other "Polish" refugees, in the wee hours of the morning, in a field near the train tracks. A freight train passed through this secluded spot, right on schedule, and the conductor slowed and stopped the train, as he'd been paid to do. They all jumped on board and, hours later, with tremendous *siyata d'Shmaya*, they were safely across the border in Poland.

It turned out to be one of the last trains that made it out under this

---

their *avodas Hashem* and *ahavas Yisrael*. They sing *niggunim* that reflect the topic and tone of their *farbrengen*, stirring or joyous, and say *l'chaim*, blessing each other with all good things.

3. They were actually one passport short, but that's a story for another time.

arrangement. The Russians discovered and shut down the homespun "Polish consulate," executing some of those involved and exiling others to Siberia.[4]

From Poland, the family made their way west, heading toward France, a common destination for Jewish refugees at that time. Along the way, they spent some time at the Hallein Displaced Persons Camp, where my parents welcomed their first child—my sister Gutel.

They eventually made it to Paris, where the Jewish community was beginning to rebuild and there was already a Chabad presence. My father was a skilled *menaker*.[5] His father-in-law, Zaideh Uziel, had been a *shochet* in Nevel and had secretly continued this holy work in Samarkand, *shechting* in backyards under cover of night for fear of the Communist police. During that time, he trained his son-in-law to perform the *nikur*, so that they could give the *Yidden* of Samarkand fully *kashered* meat.

Now in France and in need of *parnassah* to support his fledgling family, my father partnered with another Jewish refugee and opened a butcher store. The family remained in Paris for six years.

With the destruction of the Old World, the center of Jewish life shifted decisively to the New World. More directly relevant to the Rubashkins and Chazanovs, the previous Lubavitcher Rebbe had relocated to New York when he miraculously escaped the Nazis in 1940, and the center of the Lubavitch world was now Brooklyn, New York.

They applied for a visa to immigrate to the United States. By Hashem's kindness, it was granted, and they arrived in New York in 1953. My grandfathers both settled near the Rebbe in Crown Heights. My father wanted to live there as well, but the Rebbe instructed him to settle in Boro Park instead. My father and his partner, Alter Lieberman, had opened a butcher shop there, where they pioneered the self-service butcher store for kosher consumers. The Rebbe said it was important for him to live close to his work for the sake of his wife and his growing family.

My Early Life

I was born in Boro Park in 1959. My father wanted to name me after his

---

4. For example, Reb Mendel Futerfas, for his role in this affair and for other counter-revolutionary activities, was sentenced to twelve years of hard labor in the frozen North—although he was miraculously freed after eight years.

5. An expert in removing forbidden veins and fats, an important part of *kashering* meat.

My father's grandfather and my namesake, Reb Sholom Rubashkin

paternal grandfather, Sholom. My mother, in the meantime, had heard of a legendary chassid, Reb Mordechai Dubin. As a minister in the Latvian government, he had stood in direct opposition of the mighty Soviet empire and played a key role in saving the previous Lubavitcher Rebbe's life. In revenge, the Soviets later arrested him and exiled him to Siberia. The Nazis killed his only son, and there was no one to carry on his name, so my mother wanted to name her son after him.

Unable to reach a consensus, they turned to the Rebbe for advice. Although the Rebbe generally did not intervene in these matters, and said so, he nonetheless noted that, "There is room on the head [for two names][6] ... both sides can be satisfied." That's how I got my name, Sholom Mordechai.

Like many children, my formal education didn't begin until the age of four or five, but *chinuch* doesn't wait until a certain age. Everything children see, hear, or experience in those early formative years is, as the term implies, formative. Children notice and absorb every decision, every interaction, every word or gesture, and my parents' daily lives made a profound impact on me.

I grew up in a modest two-story house in Boro Park. Including the basement, the house had three floors, but our family made do with only one of them. My father rented the second floor, for far less than the going rate, to a childless couple who'd survived the war. This was a respectful way of helping *Yidden* who had been through so much.

He didn't rent out the basement, but he often invited people in need to live there for extended periods of time. A family whose house burned down stayed there for months; three teenagers rescued from Iran during the violent revolution in the late seventies stayed for *years*. That left the first floor, with two and a half bedrooms, for my parents and their nine children.

Even on the first floor, my parents hosted a constant stream of guests. At

---

6. This is a phrase from *Shulchan Aruch*, which notes that two pairs of *tefillin* fit on the head and can be worn simultaneously.

a moment's notice, the children would vacate their room for an unexpected guest and relocate to the floor in my parents' bedroom. These guests would also sometimes stay for extended periods of time, and they were always treated like royalty.

One such guest, who was staying in the half-bedroom that was otherwise my sister's room, was a smoker. My mother was very bothered by smoke, and she was very firm with family that there was no smoking in the house. This fellow knew how she felt, but he would still sometimes have a cigarette in his room. He would open the window to let out the smoke and the smell, but that wasn't very effective. The smell of smoke would inevitably waft through the house and we would look to see how my mother would react, but she never said anything to the guest.

My father showed the same sensitivity to their guests. He worked long, grueling days at the butcher store. When he came home, usually after 10:00 p.m., he would settle down for a quiet meal and get some much-needed sleep—unless one particular guest was staying with us; a fellow he knew always wanted to talk with someone about his day. Despite the late hour, on those days, my justifiably tired father would sit at the table with his guest and listen to his stories, responding as appropriate with an appreciative chuckle, sincere sympathy, or honest advice on his plans for the future.

Their selfless love for others extended beyond the home. My mother opened a restaurant on Thirteenth Avenue, called Crowns. She employed a few people, but she was the heart and soul of the place. She arrived every day at the crack of dawn to prepare the food and she personally cared for the many who ate there throughout the day. I called it a restaurant, but my mother didn't run it like a restaurant. If someone couldn't pay, they simply didn't—and often left with more money in their pockets than they had when they'd arrived. The next

My mother's restaurant, an address for all who were hungry or needy. She never bothered to update the original signage, which was good enough for her needs.

time they walked through the door, they were greeted with the same warm welcome, ushered to a table, and fussed over like every other customer.

This quietly non-profit restaurant was financed by my father, who did similar mitzvos in his butcher store—quietly adding items to a needy family's shopping bags or sending a meat delivery to a struggling *cheder*. Of course, his care extended beyond just sharing his wares. He helped wherever he saw a need, such as sending a *kollel* man with a threadbare suit to a local clothing store where he had an account or buying a book of bus tickets for a *bachur* who couldn't otherwise travel home for Shabbos.

Ahavas Yisrael radiated from my father. Walking to shul alongside him on Shabbos, I would (sometimes impatiently) watch him greet every Jew he passed with a warm, heartfelt smile and a *"Gut Shabbos!"* Not satisfied with a generic greeting, he followed up with a few words specific to that individual if he happened to know them—congratulations if they had a mazel tov, a *brachah* for *refuah sheleimah* if he knew someone in their family was unwell, or just regards to someone they both knew.

When we finally made it home, we sat around a Shabbos table that was always beautified with guests. My father's genius in *ahavas Yisrael* was on full display, and he gave each one exactly what he needed. One regular guest was always given the opportunity to share a *dvar Torah*, even though his speech was unclear due to a mild stroke he'd suffered. When I asked my father why he always asked him to speak, he told me that this Yid had been a shul *rav* accustomed to speaking on the *parshah* every week. He no longer had the opportunity to be heard by a shul full of people, but my father saw to it that he was still able to share his thoughts with others.

My parents treated their guests as an extension of the family. Years later, when many of their children were grown and married, my sister Rochel Leah invited them to spend Pesach with her family in their home in Tzfas. My father refused. I thought it would do him and my mother good and tried to persuade him to go. In the course of our conversation, he said, seemingly offhand and with a twinkle in his eye, "And what will be with my guests?!"

Later, thinking over our conversation, it occurred to me that not only was it possible that he was actually serious about that reason, it might actually be the *main* reason he'd refused to go! Sure enough, when I called him up and offered to host his guests for Yom Tov, he reconsidered his decision. He passed the responsibility for the Pesach of his guests on to me, and he and my mother went to *shep* some well-earned *nachas* from their daughter in Eretz Yisrael.

One more aspect of Shabbos and Yom Tov that left an indelible impression on me was the absence of any discussion relating to business or weekday concerns. I intentionally call it absence and not avoidance—the topics just never came into my father's mouth. No matter how difficult the week had been or what kind of issues or challenges were going on at the time, it was as if there had been no workweek. Only Shabbos existed. If someone else asked a question or brought up the topic, it was pleasantly but firmly brushed aside.

This drove home an important lesson about how the world works. During the six days, we work—and we work hard. That wasn't just something my father told us; it was something he demonstrated every day, week in, week out. Then, every Shabbos, he demonstrated where our livelihood actually comes from, despite all that. It comes from Hashem. Talking or even *thinking* about the details or aggravations of our workweek on Shabbos, when we're connecting directly to Him, is getting that backward.

This clarity about where our sustenance truly comes from, taught not through speeches but through his behavior and choices, laid the firm foundations for a life of *emunah* and *bitachon*.

Instead of busing us to Crown Heights, my parents sent my brothers and me to local schools in Boro Park. Up until the sixth grade, I was sent to the Karlin-Stolin yeshivah on Fourteenth Avenue.[7] Guided by the Lubavitcher Rebbe's position on secular studies, my parents arranged for us to leave school at two o'clock, when those studies began. My father made this decision despite his involvement in the world of business, where such studies are claimed to play a role in success, once again teaching and *demonstrating* to his children that success is really only from Hashem.

At two o'clock every day, my brother Moishie and I walked the few blocks to the Kopyczynitzer *beis midrash*, where we learned Torah with the Kopyczynitzer Rebbe's *gabbai* until the end of the day. This insulation from secular ideas and perspectives during my formative years stood me in good stead throughout my life. As Rabbeinu Bacheye writes, exposure to these ideas is one of the *mafsidei bitachon*—things which undermine proper trust in Hashem.

For the sixth, seventh, and eighth grade, I was enrolled in Yeshivah Torah

---

7. I fondly remember many of my teachers from that time, including Rabbi Meir Pilchik, Rabbi Chaim Kugelman, and Rabbi Yitzchok Perris, among others.

Vodaath of Rabbi Margolis,[8] after which, at the age of twelve[9] I was enrolled in Tomchei Temimim on Ocean Parkway.[10]

My class picture from sixth grade in Yeshivah Torah Vodaath with Rabbi Klang. I am sitting on the floor, fourth from left.

At around that time, I went to live with my Zaideh Uziel and Bubbeh Hindeh, who lived in Crown Heights. Living in such close quarters with my *zaideh* at such a young age and observing his Torah, mitzvos, and *yiras Shamayim* was an important experience. When Bubbeh Hindeh passed away around a year later, at the young age of sixty-six, I decided to stay with my *zaideh* to take care of him and provide him the company he needed to keep his spirits up and his mind off his tragic loss.

When it came time to go to *yeshivah gedolah*, I went to Tomchei Temimim in Morristown,[11] after which I returned to Crown Heights to continue my studies there. During this time, I had the opportunity to study in the *chassidus shiur* of Reb Yoel Kahan, a *chozer*[12] for the Rebbe. He was renowned for his unique ability to bring abstract concepts to concrete reality through his deep understanding of the *nefesh* and his precision with fitting *meshalim*. These *shiurim* helped me see through the reality that the world presents and live

---

8. Where I studied in the classes of Rabbi Klang, Rabbi Nosson Scherman, Rabbi Finkel and others.

9. In those days we began first grade at four years old, hence, ninth graders were twelve.

10. Where I was taught by Rabbi Marlow *a"h*.

11. Where I had the *zechus* of studying with and observing the well-known *gaon* and chassid Reb Meilech Tzvibel *a"h*.

12. An individual tasked with memorizing the Rebbe's words during the *farbrengens* (especially on Shabbos and Yom Tov) so they could be transcribed later.

instead with the reality of *emunah* and *bitachon*, something which I leaned on very heavily throughout my life.

At the age of twenty, I merited to be sent on *shlichus*. The Rebbe would send chassidim to communities across the globe as emissaries—*shluchim*—tasked with doing whatever necessary to strengthen *Yiddishkeit* and support the local Jews in their *avodas Hashem*.[13]

In addition to the *shluchim* with which people are most familiar—those who move as a family to all parts of the globe, with no return ticket, and transform their destination into a place of Torah and *kedushah*—hundreds of yeshivah *bachurim* are also sent on *shlichus* each year. After they've completed their years of structured yeshivah learning, around the age of twenty, selected *bachurim* are sent for one year, usually in groups, to support existing communities and yeshivos. I was sent to Buenos Aires, Argentina, with a group of nine other *bachurim* to establish a new yeshivah and help with other efforts to strengthen and support the Jewish community.

I found the community there to be as united as it was diverse. They were *Yidden* with different ways of serving Hashem—Ashkenazi, Sephardi, *Yekkishe*, *chassidishe*—but the unity and *ahavas Yisrael* between them was remarkable. It resonated with everything my parents had taught me and reinforced my earlier experiences of the unique brotherly bond within our nation. Seeing it on a community level made a powerful impression on me.

Our time there was very successful and we sowed seeds that went on to blossom and flourish. The yeshivah we founded started with thirteen local boys in a single-family home which blossomed and grew over the years into a yeshivah of hundreds, housed in an appropriately magnificent multi-story building.

When my time in Argentina came to an end, I returned to Brooklyn to continue learning in 770,[14] with a focus on studying *Shulchan Aruch*.

---

13. This was not a new concept. The Ba'al HaTanya would send his senior chassidim to distant hamlets to teach and inspire the simple Jews, and the Rebbe of every subsequent generation followed suit. Usually, these were accomplished chassidim, but upon his arrival to America, the previous Rebbe expanded this corps to include yeshivah students. The Rebbe, after accepting the leadership in 1950, broadened and developed this initiative even further.

14. 770 Eastern Parkway, the Rebbe's shul and *beis midrash*, the center of the Chabad Lubavitch world. Among other things, it hosts the central Lubavitch yeshivah.

In 1981, I married and settled in Crown Heights, where my first five children were born. I spent the first year after marriage learning in *kollel*.[15]

At the end of *shanah rishonah*, I looked for a *shlichus* posting for our family but without success. Instead, we established our home in Crown Heights in the spirit and practice of *chessed* and hospitality. I combined the need for *parnassah* with the mitzvah of *kibud av* and went to work for my father, helping in his various business ventures.

During that time, I attended many *farbrengens* at which the Rebbe continued speaking about the importance of *shlichus*, moving even to far-flung cities to help *Yidden* come closer to Hashem through the Torah and mitzvos. Inspired, I resumed my efforts to find a place where this need was not being met by others, where I would be fully committed to these activities without distraction.

Despite my renewed efforts, nothing was materializing. During the *hakafos* on Simchas Torah, I pushed through the crowd to kiss the Rebbe's *sefer Torah*. I took the opportunity to ask the Rebbe for his *brachah* to find a place where I could do his holy work. In response, the Rebbe responded, "Amen!" loud enough to be heard above the tumult of the joyous crowd.

The Rebbe's *brachah* quickly materialized. We settled in Atlanta, Georgia, tasked with helping the *shliach* who was already living there, Rabbi Yossi New. I was in my element—meeting new people, teaching, touching lives. We did our part to foster unity in the city, partnering with a rabbi from the *kollel*, which was affiliated with another community, to run programs together, like the joint "Lunch and Learn" program we held at the nearby Emory University.

We also made personal connections in Atlanta that transformed lives. There are a number of *Yidden* whose first experience of Torah *Yiddishkeit* was around our Shabbos table, who went on to become *shomrei Torah u'mitzvos* and have established warm Jewish homes.

Due to local consideration, after only one year I needed to find somewhere else to pursue *shlichus*. A bit disappointed, but still energized by the experience, we returned to Brooklyn and resumed our search for a place we could go on *shlichus*.

---

15. During that time, I finished the necessary sections of *Shulchan Aruch* and received *semichah* from Harav Hagaon Reb Yisroel Yitzchak Pikarski and Harav Hagaon Reb Mordechai Mentlik.

Agriprocessors

The year was 1987. The preceding two decades had brought a lot of change to the national meat industry. Refrigerated trucks had become standard, which allowed meat to be shipped long distances. This allowed producers to centralize in rural areas, where they processed the animals and shipped the finished product to distant population centers. The older, smaller plants, which had been located closer to the cities to allow the meat to be transported without spoiling, began to shut their doors.

This was a big problem for those supplying the Jewish community with kosher meat, my father among them. They needed these small plants so they could carefully *shecht* the small number of animals needed by the neighborhood kosher butcher stores. *Shechting* at the new rural mega-plants was out of the question because the processing speed there would not allow for the careful attention required for kosher meat.

As an individual shopkeeper in need of a supply, my father decided that the surest way forward would be to adopt the same innovations that were causing these changes in the industry. His idea was bold, but not overly ambitious: He would establish a small slaughterhouse in "Cattle Country" designed specifically for *shechitah* and the *kashering* process and use refrigerated trucks to move the meat to Boro Park. Whatever excess supply he created could be sold to other butcher stores dealing with the same supply issues as he was.

He looked for an existing plant where he could launch this project. His search brought him about as far from Brooklyn as you can get—the town of Postville, Iowa, about 1,100 miles west, home to a shuttered meatpacking plant. Run by a national company, the Hygrade plant had operated there for decades and had been a critical part of the town's economy until it was shut down eight years earlier, when the workforce unionized.

The plant was the right size, it had its own freshwater well and three large lagoons for water treatment, and it was within driving distance of many farms and cattle barns where quality corn-fed cows could be purchased. This was all the infrastructure necessary for the modest operation my father envisioned.

He expressed an interest to the town leaders, who strongly encouraged him to make the move. Although there was another plant in town, Iowa Turkey Products ("ITP" to the locals), the town was hurting, and my father's arrival would be a welcome investment for the town, giving a much-needed boost to the local economy.

My father visiting a farm of the type which supplied Agriprocessors with quality corn-fed Iowa cattle.

My father examining industrial machinery for use in the plant.

Before proceeding, my father sought the Rebbe's *brachah* for this undertaking. When he received it, he closed the deal and made the large investment required to purchase, repair, and modernize the plant and customize it to the highest standards of kashrus.

The setup was under the supervision and to the specifications of the Margaretiner Rav, Rabbi Kleineman *zt"l*, but the commitment to *hiddur* in kashrus, despite the cost, was my father's. The plant would be predicated on the iron-clad *yiras Shamayim* and commitment to Torah that had seen my ancestors through centuries of oppression in Russia and through the equally difficult but very different challenges of life in the *goldene medineh*.

As I mentioned earlier, my mother's father, Uziel Chazanov, was a *shochet*. When he arrived with his family in the United States, he'd intended to continue that job, but he had difficulty finding a position in New York. As the entry point for so many refugees, there were plenty of *shochtim* already living and working in the area.

Try as he might, he couldn't find anything close to home. Even looking further afield, it took much searching before he finally found a job in relatively distant Philadelphia. It meant that he would be away from home for extended periods of time, but he had no choice. He bid an emotional farewell to his wife, Hindeh, and his children, and set off for work.

He wasn't expected back for months, so you can imagine Bubbeh Hindeh's surprise when, a few weeks later, he walked through the door. "What happened?!" she asked in surprise.

"*Mein neshamah vel ich nisht farkoifin,*" was his firm reply. "I refuse to sell my soul."

Aerial view of the picturesque city of Postville, a sliver of habitation
in the vast expanse of Iowa farmland. The plant my father built,
one sixth the size of the city itself, is on the left.

He then explained that a short while after his arrival, he'd been called into
the office of the plant owner. "Rabbi Uziel," the owner had said, "the number
of animals you deem kosher is very low."

"I'm sorry," Zaideh Uziel responded, surprised, "that's out of my control.
The animal either is or isn't kosher. There's nothing I can do to change the
numbers."

Over the next couple of weeks, in various interactions, it became clear to him
that they wanted him to bend and break the rules of kashrus and designate
as "kosher" animals that simply were not. Without hesitation, he bid them
farewell, packed his bags, and returned to New York. His family needed the
money, but, as he put it to his wife, he would not barter his soul.

This was the spirit of my father's new endeavor. He built a plant where
the guiding determination wasn't productivity or speed but a spirit of *yiras
Shamayim* and a mission to provide unquestionably kosher meat to every Yid
in the country.

I'm proud to say that we stayed true to that spirit. Throughout the time the
plant was operating, on matters of kashrus, the certifying *rabbanim* were not
only given a seat—they were given the *driver's* seat.

My father made many noteworthy improvements to the standards of kashrus available to the Jewish consumer. For example, he imported a rotating pen from France used to invert the animal for *shechitah*. Inverting the animal allows the *shochet* to perform the mitzvah of *shechitah* by cutting downwards, called *shechitah munachas*, which is the way it was done since Har Sinai, and the way it was done even in the dark days in Communist Russia. In addition to the high cost of buying and importing the equipment, there was also the ongoing cost of slowing down production to *shecht* this way. Nonetheless, *hiddur* in kashrus was the overriding consideration, and the new plant was equipped for *shechitah munachas*, the only place in the United States where this was so.

Years later, the Satmar Rebbe, Rav Aron Teitelbaum, came to observe the kashrus at the plant. He was mesmerized by this part of the process and the higher kashrus standard the machine enabled. After stopping to observe the *shechitah* for a while, he jokingly said to my father, "Reb Avraham Aron, you are causing me to be *over* on *lo sachmod*!" Of course, my father immediately offered to help him acquire such a rotating pen.

When the plant expanded to *shechting* poultry, the same commitment to high kashrus standards was upheld. When we were initially setting up the *shechitah*, the Margaretiner Rav wanted each *shochet* to be assigned a worker

Aerial view of the Agriprocessors complex, which took twenty years to build. The three water-treatment lagoons are visible at the top left of the picture.

who would immobilize the bird. This would free the *shochet* to focus on *shechting* without worrying that the chicken might suddenly flap its wings and hit the knife. This was a costly and unprecedented arrangement, something no other plant was doing. "It isn't strictly required," he told me, "but it would be a great improvement, and I would like to do it." I passed the request along to my father. Despite the substantial cost of adding an additional person for each of the seven *shochtim* on the line, not to mention the production slowdown this would inevitably cause, my father agreed.

Other kashrus enhancements that we made went on to become industry standards, and this elevation of the standard of kashrus across the board is to my father's eternal *zechus*. His well-deserved reputation as someone who was not just a businessman but a *yerei Shamayim* dedicated to kashrus made *rabbanim* from many communities proud to certify the kashrus of his products.

Of course, it wasn't just in the area of Torah standards that my father insisted on going above and beyond. At his insistence, Agriprocessors went well above industry standards in many areas. He made every effort to update the old plant to provide a modern, smooth, and safe work environment. This was an ongoing commitment. Over the years, we continued to invest in improving and updating the facility and ensuring that we had the right equipment, people, and procedures in place.

Baruch Hashem, we succeeded. Agriprocessors earned praise from working professionals and politicians alike. For example, Rod Heston, an industrial refrigeration contractor who worked widely in the industry, testified in court that our plant was in the same league as the top five Blue Ribbon meatpacking companies—giants with revenues measured in the billions.

We were also praised by US Senator Tom Harkin, a member of the Senate Committee on Agriculture, who told a member of the Postville City Council that "Agriprocessors is one of the cleanest and most well-run" meatpacking plants among the many he had visited across the country.

In staffing the plant, my father made a conscious effort that the employment benefits stay in the local community, and the many jobs, both supervising and working on the production line, became a source of income for the locals.

At the time, the minimum hourly wage was $3.35; $7.50 in today's dollars. The other local plant, Iowa Turkey Products, paid minimum wage, but my father wouldn't hear of it. In all of his years doing business, he'd never paid anyone so little for an honest day's work, and he wasn't about to start. Instead, he offered starting employees around $5 an hour, $11.63 in today's dollars. He also offered all employees, even workers on the plant floor, a medical insurance plan and paid vacation, unlike the other employers in the area.

The decision was good-hearted, but in trying to do right by the workers and the town, he earned the enmity of the locally influential owners and managers of ITP who now had to follow suit, raising their costs. They caused us untold difficulties until 2003, when they abandoned the town after a fire at their plant.

The number of workers needed at the plant quickly exceeded the local labor pool, and additional workers were needed. The other plant in town employed Hispanic workers, but my father was cautioned that the townspeople would not look kindly on an influx. He would never turn someone away for a job, but to avoid taxing the tolerance of the locals, who were already dealing with a lot of changes to their town and community, he made efforts to find an alternative labor source. One labor source was the community of Eastern European immigrants in "nearby" Minneapolis who found temporary housing and moved to town.

Postville obviously had nothing by way of Jewish infrastructure, so the Jewish portion of the workforce was not able to move to town so easily. Instead, in an arrangement still common in the industry, the *shochtim, bodkim,*[16] and *mashgichim* flew to the area at the start of each week and flew home to their families and communities for Shabbos. They stayed in a large, white, three-story house on the edge of town, which my father had purchased for this purpose. The locals called it the "Rabbi House."

This wasn't a great arrangement. In addition to the financial burden this entailed, it was not an easy commute. The closest airport was ninety miles away and other airports serving the area were twice as far away. It was also an unreliable arrangement, subject to travel delays common to air travel and endemic to Chicago O'Hare, the local hub. The driving conditions in the snowy Upper Midwest also wreaked havoc in the winters.

To oversee this project of sending the highest quality kosher meat from the rural farm to the urban table, my father asked my brother Heshy, who was then newly married, to move to town. With the Rebbe's *brachah,* he accepted. The day-to-day running of the plant was handled by (non-Jewish) managers with extensive meatpacking experience, and Heshy would monitor it and

---

16. Rabbis trained in the inspection of the lungs to determine the kosher status of the animal.

report back to my father, who remained at the humble butcher store which had prompted this necessary expansion.

Heshy and his fledgling family spent a few lonely years as the only Jewish residents of Postville, Iowa. "You know how, in the stories, the travelers would pass through a small village and find a candle burning in the window of the only Jewish person in town?" Heshy would say. "That's me."

My father by the counter of his butcher store in Boro Park.

Moving West

When I returned to Brooklyn from Atlanta, Agriprocessors had already begun sending the fruits of this undertaking to the East Coast, and I found my father dealing with an excess supply of high-quality, kosher meat. Agri's output was more than he needed to stock his own store, which he'd anticipated, but the plan to sell to the other wholesalers and retailers was off to a slow start. Until then, they'd been fully *kashering* and processing their meat themselves, and they were slow to embrace the idea of buying packaged cuts of meat already de-veined, soaked, and salted.

Fresh from my time away from the great urban concentrations of Jewish life, I saw my father's excess supply not as a problem but as a solution. In Atlanta, I'd seen firsthand how difficult it was to find glatt kosher meat outside of New York and Chicago. Those who were committed to eating only glatt kosher meat outside of those two cities had to forgo the quality and taste of fresh meat and instead import frozen meat from New York. Many families would buy meat in bulk and keep it in a dedicated freezer in their homes.

As sacrifices for religion go, perhaps it doesn't rank so high, but if you hope to inspire and enable people to make the leap and commit to only eating kosher, this was a real obstacle. The reduced quality, additional effort, and increased cost resulted in *Yidden* who would otherwise be willing to commit to keeping glatt kosher settling instead for a lower standard and buying the cheaper and fresher non-glatt meat available in their cities.

It seemed to me that instead of looking to the retailers in the Jewish centers to buy Agri's meat, whatever was not needed for Rubashkin's butcher store could be directed toward the rest of the country as a retail product. I envisioned a future where any Jew in the United States who wanted to keep kosher to the highest standards would be able to walk into a local store and find fresh, high-quality kosher meat, and eventually poultry, at an affordable price.

Making this happen was a full-time job, and not one I could farm out to someone else. It meant setting aside what I'd imagined my role to be—that of a *shliach*, rabbi, and teacher—and entering the world of business, but it was a unique opportunity to improve the availability and affordability of glatt kosher meat beyond what was possible at the time.

This project would require what was, at the time, cutting-edge technology. The company could not invest in the machinery at that time, but I had some personal savings set aside. I could buy the vacuum-packing machine myself—the first small step of many, G-d willing, which would bring that vision to life.

I discussed the idea with my father and, receiving his consent, I asked the Rebbe for his *brachah* to move to the Midwest and for success in my new undertaking. The Rebbe responded in the affirmative and gave me the *brachah* of *"Meshaneh makom meshaneh mazel l'tovah v'livrachah*—One who changes his location changes his fortune, to goodness and to blessing."

My wife, Leah, and I already had school-age children, so instead of moving to Postville, we moved to a Chabad community in Minnesota, which had a *cheder*, although it meant a three-hour commute.

CREDIT: CHAIM B HALBERSTAM / JEM

Receiving a *brachah* from the Rebbe along with a dollar for *tzedakah*.

It was a very difficult time for my family. I woke before dawn each morning to make the long drive and returned home in the late evening. I willingly undertook the grueling daily drives for the precious time it gave me with my family. As my responsibilities grew, I often had to stay overnight and my children only saw me on Shabbos.

There are moments in life that stick with you, lessons that Hashem shows you to prepare you for what lies ahead. One such moment happened during this period, and the lesson I learned that day stood me in good stead in my most difficult hours.

It was Erev Yom Kippur. The rest of the *Yidden* on staff had left as early as possible, but I'd stayed behind to ensure that things were shut down properly and everything was in order. I planned to leave with plenty of time to make it back to Minnesota for the onset of the holy day, but something came up that had to be handled before I could leave. The clock kept ticking, and by the time I was ready to leave, making the three-hour drive would get me home a mere hour and a half before Yom Kippur began.

Although the drive was all on rural highways with no traffic that might prolong the trip, I didn't want to rush my own preparations for Yom Kippur and certainly not the pre-fast *seudah* during which a father *bentches* his children with the *Birkas Habanim*. I needed a quicker way home.

One of the workers knew a farmer just up the road who had a small single-engine plane that could make the flight. The farmer turned out to be willing to fly me to Minnesota and he estimated the flight time at a little over an hour.

When I arrived at his farm, the farmer walked us to a large shed near his house and lifted the door, revealing a small four-seat airplane. He pulled it out of the shed by a thick rope and helped me up into the cockpit. Once I was seated in the plane, he handed me a set of earphones so we could communicate over the racket of the plane's propeller and prepared for takeoff. He adjusted various dials, made radio contact with a flight controller somewhere, and with a yell of "Clear!" we started to move, jolting over his pitted lawn toward a somewhat flat stretch behind his house. Within a few short minutes, we were airborne and headed north.

I'm naturally curious. Once we'd reached our cruising altitude and settled in for the boring part of the flight, I started asking him about the various dials and controls. He explained the altimeter, which shows the plane's altitude, the airspeed indicator, which is pretty self-explanatory, and then I pointed to a dial which was a hollow sphere with a small plastic plane floating inside it. The small plastic plane tilted up and down, matching the tilt of the plane itself.

"Why do you need that?" I asked.

"That's the attitude indicator," he said. "It tells me which way is up and which way is down."

I burst out laughing, certain he was joking. Why would you need a dial to tell you which way is up?! Look out the window and see!

"Don't laugh!" he said, slightly offended. "We're flying in clear conditions, and you can see what's up and what's down, but what about when you're flying through a dark storm cloud, when there's no visible horizon and you're bumping around? It's not so easy then!

"Believe it or not, people relying on their own senses in those conditions get disoriented and get it backward! You think you're flying up and out when you are actually flying straight down to your death. The faster you try to go up, the faster you hit the ground.

"The only way to stay safe is to ignore your senses and look at the dial. Everything in you might be screaming that you need to go one way, but if that dial says that up is the other way, trust the dial and go that way because that's the way to safety."

I later learned that five to ten percent of aviation accidents are attributed to this type of problem, which they call "spatial disorientation." The FAA brochure explaining this phenomenon to pilots has the tagline, "Seeing Is *Not* Believing."

The Ba'al Shem Tov says that a Yid needs to take a lesson in his *avodas Hashem* from everything he sees or hears, and this experience struck me as teaching an obvious and powerful lesson. Even something as simple as determining which way is up, which way is life and good and right, can be impossible for our senses to determine, especially when we're flying through a dark cloud or turbulent times. Our senses might even send us in exactly the wrong direction.

To help us navigate safely, Hashem gave us a clear navigation tool, the Torah, so we'll always know which way is up. When our eyes or minds are pulling us in any direction, we must always consult the Torah before we can be confident about which way to go.

I took this to heart and tried to live by this lesson through the good years, when I was able to focus on building my family and community and my contribution to Hashem's world. When the storm hit, it became all the more critical to survival. In all the years that followed, the lesson I learned in that encounter helped me fly true.

A Little *Shtetl* on the Prairie

Those exhausting commutes continued for three long years, a sacrifice so that my children could grow up in a Jewish community and attend *cheder*. In

1993 things came to a head. Heshy's children were growing up and they needed to attend *cheder* too. He wanted to leave, but we really needed someone living in Postville. It was important for a stable relationship with the locals and for when things came up at the plant after hours. We couldn't both live off-site. That left only one option: If we couldn't both send our families to live in a Jewish community, we would have to build a Jewish community ourselves.

I found a house for my family, and, over the summer, we moved our family to Postville. As the only Jewish family in Postville for years, my brother Heshy and his wife almost couldn't believe their eyes when our family walked into his house, not for a visit, but as their new neighbors, the newest Jewish residents in town. We were quickly followed by another couple of families—other *Yidden* working at Agri brought their families to town to join the new community.

Schooling had prompted our move, and we established a school as soon as we arrived. We approached this task the way we approached everything else that had to do with *Yiddishkeit*—determined to do it right, without compromise, to the fullest degree that the Torah demands.

The older of the two classes in our *cheder*, taught by Rabbi Yisroel Noach Vogel.

We immediately ran into our first decision that tested that commitment. Practically speaking, the only way we could afford enough teachers and space to provide modern class groupings (first grade, second grade, and so on) was by grouping the boys and girls together. Rather than compromising our values and opening a mixed school, we decided to abandon the standard classes and group children of different ages together. Far from being a new idea, this was a very old idea—the tried and true *cheder* that our great-grandparents and many generations before them had attended.

The detached garage of the "Rabbi House" was converted into a two-room schoolhouse, and the boys of

The younger of the two classes in our *cheder*, taught by Rabbi Mendel Raices. Although my sons Shmuly and Meir Simcha are a year apart, they learned in the same class.

our little *shtetl* were grouped into two classes, one for the older boys and one for the younger boys. The children were only roughly the same age and kept the same *rebbi* year after year. Their *melamdim* taught them not only how to learn the holy Torah but how to live in the ways of Torah and *yiras Shamayim*.

When our children outgrew our *cheder*, we started a *mesivta* for boys between the ages of thirteen and sixteen. A handful of *bachurim* from other cities came to study in Postville and, to our satisfaction, we found that our boys were more than capable of keeping up with boys who had studied in the larger city schools.

Our new *cheder* enabled more families with children to move to town, and the community took root. As our budding *shtetl* began to form, the "Rabbi House" dormitory was the most natural place to conduct *minyanim*, and it was reborn as the community shul. In the basement, we'd already built a men's

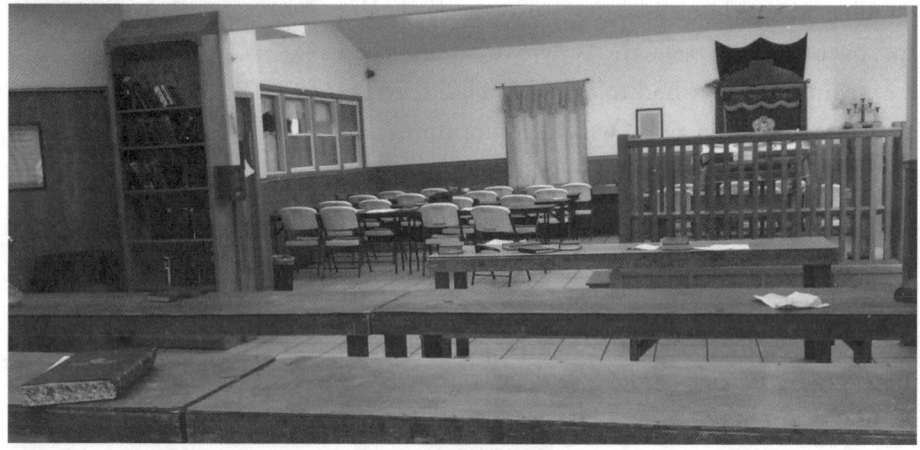

The interior of the shul, the simple but lively heart of our *shtetl*.

Our beautifully diverse community gathered for a
Lag B'Omer barbeque in the field near my house.

mikvah—an important thing in any community but an absolute necessity for *shochtim*.

The factory produced meat and poultry for a wide range of Jewish communities around the country. Each community wanted a *rav* and a *shochet* who followed the standards and customs of their community, which meant that our local community was wonderfully diverse, with *Yidden* of all sorts: Lubavitch, Satmar, Vizhnitz, Gur, Yerushalmi, *Litvish*, and more. We all worked together during the week to provide kosher food for Klal Yisrael, and we all came together on Shabbos to *daven* together.

Achdus is the single most important conduit for Hashem's *brachah*. My father, in his wisdom, had seen this as the key difficulty in building and growing our fledgling community, something which would require great care and attention on my part. For this reason, I insisted that we only have a single *minyan* on Shabbos and Yom Tov, even when the community grew to include one hundred households.

We served Hashem together, celebrated family *simchos* together, and supported each other in times of stress or need. We found ways to make place for the different *nuscha'os* and *minhagim* so everyone could serve Hashem as his father had taught him without diminishing the *achdus* and *ahavas Yisrael* of our community. After *davening* each Shabbos, we gathered around tables for a

The *upsherin* of the son of one of our dear brothers, a Vizhnitzer chassid, which we celebrated together in my home.

kiddush and *farbrengen*, each bringing *divrei Torah*, stories, and *niggunim* from his community as we found strength, inspiration, and guidance in serving Hashem together.

It was in appreciation of this that many years after the community had blossomed, Reb Yisroel Baruch Blum, an elder Vizhnitzer chassid and *shochet*, suggested that we finally name our shul and *kehillah* "Kehillas Achdus

Yisrael." We all embraced the new name as properly representing the spirit of our community.

For the first few years after families began moving to town, we didn't have a *mikvah taharah*. The closest one was in Rochester, Minnesota, about two hours away. When we finally decided to build our own, I had the *zechus* to actually build it with my own hands. I gathered the necessary tools and, together with other *Yidden*, went to work. I can still remember the experience vividly, standing in the large pit we were digging, alternating between the jackhammer and the shovel, pausing once in a while from the heavy exertion to wipe off the *zei'ah shel mitzvah* and renew my energy. Working together on this project was also a bonding and unifying experience, infusing the various individuals with the common goal of building our small community together.

As families moved to town, I had the opportunity to help a few of them find and purchase their homes. Once, while I was making the mortgage arrangements for one of the first houses, the bank manager had some criticism for me. We were paying $25,000 for the house and he felt I was overpaying. As a bit of friendly advice, he suggested that I should have negotiated a better price. I thanked him, but I couldn't imagine negotiating down from $25,000 for a house!

This episode replayed in my mind very often over the years when various rabble-rousers trotted out the antisemitic caricature that we were hard-nosed negotiators "Jewing down" the locals, taking them for everything they had. It also came to mind as I watched the value of real estate more than quadruple over the years and marveled at the animosity of some of the locals (often those who had most profited) despite the tremendous economic benefit we brought with us.

The warm, unified community that grew around the jobs at the plant also attracted others. One family moved to town and sold kosher groceries out of their basement, a business that grew into a proper storefront grocery and an adjoining kosher restaurant. Another example was Aaron Goldsmith, who relocated with his family from California to enjoy the unique Jewish community in small-town America, bringing along his business manufacturing custom electric hospital beds. The families that moved encouraged others to join them and our community grew.

Every year seemed to bring more life and vibrancy to our steadily growing community. As families settled in and grew attached to the community, they invested their time, energy, and money in improving it. One family opened up a Jewish library in memory of a loved one, and numerous *gemachim* were established, offering everything from small loans to baby clothes and accessories and over-the-counter medications.

Community Relations

Our children took to the rural setting like fish to water, biking around town, exploring the surrounding fields and streams, and just all-around enjoying the slower pace of life while settling into our new homes. A small handful of locals were sincerely welcoming but we quickly learned that the famed Iowa friendliness wasn't for everyone. It was reserved for people passing through, long-time residents, or new arrivals that fit in. Despite the neighborly smiles and dutiful hand waving, prominent members of the town immediately began making it clear that we were less than welcome.

As we've experienced so often in our long and difficult *galus*, we were seen by the locals as the barbarians next door, very literally in some cases. My son Meir Simcha, about eight years old at the time, was playing in the park when he was approached by a local child his age. "Hey," the kid called out from the bottom of the slide, "do you guys wear lion-fur underwear?"—referencing popular culture's image of a barbarian in a loincloth; obviously exploring sentiments he'd heard at home. Meir Simcha, sheltered from that "culture" and blissfully unaware of the connotation, was just happy he could answer the kid's question. "No," he answered sincerely, "Fruit of the Loom." Another one of my children was asked by a local kid if his yarmulke was covering his horns.

We had brought industry and employment to a town that desperately needed it, but our "sins" were many. We had different customs and had not yet learned the rules of small-town etiquette. We didn't socialize over meals or drinks in the local restaurant or bar, we didn't join their community swims in the local pool, we didn't cut our lawns to their liking, and someone wearing a yarmulke had once made a U-turn.

A laundry list of petty grievances such as these were the claimed reasons for a shocking level of antipathy and antagonism. It ran the spectrum from small indignities and petty comments to an admittedly smaller group actively obstructing and undermining everything we did. Misled by the famous "Iowa smile," we only realized later that they were actually not smiling—they were just showing their teeth.

We did what we could to live in harmony with our neighbors without compromising our religious values. We reached out to community leaders

"Uncle Moishy" performs for the people of Postville at a cultural food and music festival. The Postville water tower is visible over his shoulder.

and the local newspaper, hoping to ease the tension and friction between the communities. We brought the well-known lecturer Rabbi Manis Friedman to hold gatherings for the Postville community, where he fielded their questions about our culture and religion in an attempt to break down the walls. We brought Jewish musicians, like Moshe Yess and Uncle Moishy, to play at their food and music festivals in the hope that it would help.

At every turn, we did our best to make a *kiddush Hashem* and avoid the opposite. *Yidden* are often held accountable for what their fellow Jews do—only for the negative, naturally. One day, a local fellow barged into the office and demanded that I give him money. Apparently, a Yid had damaged his car somehow, and he insisted I pay for what my "brother" had done. I calmed the man down and assured him that I would make it right, reaching into my pocket for my wallet.

Donald Hunt, an upper-level manager at the plant and a very straitlaced guy, put his hand on my arm to stop me. He started to explain to this guy that whoever had done the damage was definitely not my brother—the only sibling I had in town was Heshy, and Heshy had been in the office all day.

I appreciated what he was trying to do but I asked him to step out with me for a moment. "Donald," I explained to him, once we were alone, "to you, we're individuals, and you judge us each separately. To him, we're one family. If I don't settle the matter, he won't think badly of that one guy—he'll think and speak badly of *all* Jews."

The man received the money he'd demanded and an apology for his trouble. He could no longer claim that "the Jews" had caused him financial loss, which was the best I could do to prevent a *chillul Hashem*. Despite this, it's likely that he, and others like him, still didn't think well of Jews, precisely *because* of my generosity, as another story showed me.

In his kind-heartedness, my father set up a loan fund for employees facing unexpected expenses or emergencies, but I was still approached directly, by employees and sometimes by locals, and asked for loans. I tried to oblige whenever I could, using the opportunity to create goodwill and cause a *kiddush Hashem*. Sometime in the first or second year, an employee came into my office asking for a loan. His roof had been damaged in a recent storm, and he didn't have money set aside for the unexpected expense. He needed $400 to make the needed repairs, which I gave him.

The next day a different employee pulled me to the side and said that I shouldn't lend money to guys like that anymore. They were ungrateful and disrespectful. "I was drinking at the local bar last night, and I heard this guy laughing with his buddies about how he fooled the soft-hearted Jew into giving him money."

At the community level, the company did its part to support local civic and charitable projects. My father made sure

Posing for a picture with my father in the heart of the plant, in front of the industrial deli smoker ovens.

that we went the extra mile to help those in need, supporting all three local charities that assisted the poor, as well as other community organizations, like the community pool and the radio station.

I asked the local dentist, Dr. Kolarich, to reach out to the local public school and proactively identify children who needed dental work but were not going to the dentist because they couldn't afford it. Under our arrangement, he provided dental care and forwarded the bills to Agriprocessors, which paid for the work.

With time and conscious effort, the Jewish community also became more accustomed to the norms of small-town life. The lawns were properly cared for, the friendly greetings were properly initiated or returned, and the slower pace of life took the edge off of the harried and rushed manner some had brought with them from the city. More importantly, the town as a whole was reaping the benefits of our arrival. Slowly, many of the locals stopped fighting us, and we built warm relationships with many of our neighbors.

Many, but not all. The real opposition, the ones who'd been opposing and obstructing from day one, never stopped.

CHAPTER TWO
Exercises in *Bitachon*

On the Job Training

From the day I first set foot in Postville until I left it, G-d willing never to return, I didn't have a single peaceful day. I was part of achieving great things, *baruch Hashem*, but it was always a battle. It seemed like as soon as one issue was resolved, the next one immediately cropped up. Of course, there was nothing on the scale of what I would face during the fight for my life, but it was an intense and difficult time nonetheless.

Looking back at that period, I see it as Hashem's kindness, preparing me for what was to come; a sort of spiritual training—much like the training of childhood—in the development of my *emunah* and *bitachon*.

Scrapes and falls, both literal and metaphorical, are critical to the development of a child. Although in real terms they are usually trivial, they strengthen the child and teach him or her valuable lessons which help them later in life, when the stakes are much higher. When they are reckless and fall off their bikes, for example, they skin their knees and learn a lesson, which later in life ensures that they drive the far more dangerous automobile with the proper care and attention.

In order to confront and overcome the difficulties and outright attacks that I faced in Postville and at Agriprocessors, relatively trivial though they were compared to what came later, I had to fully embrace the reality of the Torah's description of the world. Faced with intractable problems or powerful opponents, when the world said, "You don't have a prayer," I had to find the clarity and strength to realize and insist that I actually *do* have a prayer—to Hashem!

Although the world may bluster and roar, trying to intimidate a Yid into believing that it has independent existence and power, every circumstance is of Hashem's making and for His reasons. He gave me a mitzvah to recognize that and turn to Him for help, assuring me that His help would surely come.

These were real-life situations. I wasn't taking a test in school or teaching someone something it says in the books. There were decisions to be made which had consequences for myself and others, and even in situations where there weren't options to choose from, I needed to restore confidence and tranquility to my heart and to my mind. It wasn't enough to accept these truths in some abstract way. The *facts* about Who and What is the real power in every situation needed to be as real to me as gravity or electricity.

Each of the difficult experiences I had in this period demanded that I walk the path from acknowledging *intellectually* to embracing as *reality* Hashem's power and providence. I had to walk that path many times, each time with increasing difficulty or in a different area. Each time, with effort and with help from Above, I succeeded. As a result of all those "childhood" difficulties, when I faced my steepest climb, I was able to surmount every obstacle. During my long ordeal, I often thanked Hashem for all the experience and exercise which helped me when I needed it most.

I've chosen three examples from the many attacks I faced during my eighteen years in Postville. They include attacks by individuals, business interests, local government, and activists, and clearly show the self-interest, bigotry, and dishonesty that motivated them.

Water Wars

The first organized antagonists we faced were the good ol' hometown boys managing the Iowa Turkey Products plant.

Meat and poultry processors use a lot of water, and by the time they're done with it, it's heavily polluted. The water has to be treated before it can be discharged back into the waterways. For this purpose, three large lagoons were built behind the Hygrade plant, which would later become Agriprocessors' facility. The construction was funded primarily by Hygrade, and they were therefore allocated most of the limited treatment capacity, with the remainder allocated to ITP.

When my father purchased the old Hygrade plant, he also purchased the right to use Hygrade's share of the water treatment capacity. In fact, the plant's freshwater well and access to wastewater treatment were among the key factors in my father's decision to choose the Postville plant.

This was an issue for ITP. When Hygrade had shut down, ITP had simply expanded their use of the lagoon system beyond their allotment. With our arrival, they now had to return to their limited allotment or pay for improvements which would increase the treatment capacity. They came up with a third option: They would just keep the capacity that was rightfully ours.

Agriprocessors was still relatively small and didn't yet need its full allotment, so when they sent over a representative to discuss a neighborly accommodation, we were open to discuss it. We saw the other businesses in town, and certainly the local government, as allies working together to make the town a place where we could all prosper.

They didn't share our cooperative attitude. We were increasing their costs, both by our generous treatment of the workforce and by claiming treatment capacity they wanted, and they were hoping to knock us out entirely, despite the harm this would do to the town. This was an unrelenting campaign they kept up for a decade, but the maneuver they were lining up over the water treatment was our first encounter with them and we didn't see it coming.

They engaged us directly, posing as a cooperative local business, and at the same time, they also secretly recruited their friends on the city council, and others in positions of political or regulatory power, people with whom they had long friendships. Those people were the next to show up at our door. These community leaders encouraged us to make this arrangement and lend the unused capacity to ITP. After all, what's a small loan between neighbors in a time of need?

Eventually, with Hashem's *brachos*, our operations increased to the point that we actually needed that capacity ourselves. When we went to reclaim our loan, however, we found to our chagrin that the city had decided that the loan was, in fact, permanent. It would not be returned, and if Agri exceeded the smaller volume now allotted to it, they would impose fines.

They eventually made good on these threats, issuing violations and fines if we exceeded the individual capacity they set—even though the total treatment capacity of the system was not exceeded, and all pollutants were properly removed before the water was released into the rivers.

To add insult to injury, these technical overruns (the result of the legal theft of our treatment capacity) and the fines assessed were then used to falsely paint us in the media as greedy polluters. It was also used later, when the national spotlight fell on us, as "proof" that we were the ones who had no regard for law and morality—despite the history and details of this issue, and ignoring the monumental investments we made in a first-class treatment facility, as I will detail later.

This began a trend in which our dishonest opponents weaponized regulations, waging near-constant lawfare against us, initially by focusing on environmental regulations. Salt was a favorite target of theirs. Since salt is a key part of the *kashering* process, it was a way of undermining Agriprocessors' ability to do business under the guise of environmentalism. For the closet bigots, it was also a way of targeting the Jews by attacking something that just happens to be critical to Jews.

One day, our general manager, Donald Hunt, received a letter from the city. Attached to the letter was the results of the city's monthly lab test of the plant's wastewater. According to the results, that month there had been a violation: excessive amounts of chloride—a component of salt—in the water.

It seemed like a straightforward issue that needed standard trouble-shooting, all in a day's work for a plant manager. He ran it by my father and they hired a wastewater engineer to review and fine-tune the salt handling procedures, after which they implemented his recommendations and assumed the matter was closed.

To Donald's surprise, he received the same notice of violation the next month, and the next month, and the month after that. This was a real issue. He discussed it with the line managers and, stumped, they brought the problem to my father. No one could understand why the chloride levels were suddenly so high. The engineer was also stumped. There was nothing wrong with our handling of the salt. Without anything to fix, the only thing he could think of to reduce the chloride in the water discharged from the plant was to reduce the amount of salt we were using in the process.

That was a non-starter. Salt is a key part of the *kashering* process, and there was no way to reduce the amount of salt without reducing the amount of kosher meat we produced.

One day, I overheard Donald on the phone with the engineer about yet another violation letter from the city. By this point, the city had begun fining the company $10,000 *each month*. I could hear that Donald was exasperated and out of ideas, so I asked him if I could speak to the engineer myself. He was happy to hand over the phone.

Patiently explaining the problem, the engineer directed me to the line in the lab report that indicated the number of milligrams of sodium per liter of water, which exceeded the allowable amount. My mind struggled with the calculations. We literally purchased salt by the ton and I couldn't put these two scales together in my head. I asked the engineer if he could calculate backward from the per liter amount and determine how much salt was washed into the approximately eight million gallons of water we used in a month.

"Sure," he said, "it's a fairly straightforward calculation. I'll call you back shortly." Twenty minutes later, he called back with his number. About seventy to eighty thousand pounds of salt would result in this level of salt per liter. That was all I needed to hear. I immediately knew that the lab tests were incorrect, and I told him so.

He was skeptical. "How do you know?" he asked.

"Simple!" I answered. "I know how much salt the plant is buying every month. There's simply nowhere *near* that amount of salt in the plant. Eighty thousand pounds is twice as much salt as we *started* with. It's a physical impossibility!"

In those days, people were reluctant to accept that someone wearing a white lab coat could possibly be wrong, or worse, lying. The engineer's first thought was that perhaps the plant purchased and used more salt some months. I invited him to review all the salt purchases for the last year, which he did. He could no longer doubt what I was saying: the amounts of salt the city was claiming we were putting into the water had never been in the plant, never mind in the water! There was something wrong with the tests which were resulting in a mounting pile of monthly $10,000 fines for the Jewish plant and for which the only remedy seemed to be reducing production.

Hesitantly, due to the weight of the charges, our engineer confronted the city manager. The manager initially defended the city lab and insisted its process was accurate, but when shown the documented proof that these numbers could not have been the result of honest testing, he fell silent. It took a few weeks, but finally, the city manager sent a letter acknowledging that there had been some "mistake."

The city dropped their fines, but they never retracted the state and federal violations that were issued. Because of this, their retraction did little to counter the damage done by the false violations. They were dishonestly used by activists and "journalists" to smear Agriprocessors for decades (to this day, in fact) as a brazen polluter.

The truth was that we took our responsibility to the environment we all share very seriously. At one point, we drafted a technical solution to remove ammonia from the wastewater, although that was not required at the time. There was a state grant available that would make the project possible, but when we presented our recommendation to the other stakeholders—ITP and the city water manager—we were mocked. "Our local wastewater permits don't require ammonia to be tested and removed!"

Our engineer acknowledged that this was true, but argued that it *ought* to be required, because the ammonia would kill the fish. We had a workable solution and it was irresponsible to ignore the problem merely because of the regulatory omission. They waved us off, accusing the Jewish company of suggesting a solution in search of a problem just to get our hands on the grant money.

Months later, close to five thousand minnows died in the Yellow River because of ammonia in the water, an event which drew headlines and federal attention. True to form, blame was laid at the feet of Agriprocessors, despite our vigorous but stymied efforts to avoid exactly this outcome.

The federal environmental authority even sued us over this episode. That's a long story and too much of a detour to explore in detail in this book, but one thing is worth recording: The pollution flowed from shared lagoons, yet Agriprocessors, the Jewish company which tried and was prevented from solving the problem, had to endure a lengthy and costly legal battle before the government agreed to settle, and they demanded a settlement that was six times the amount of their settlement with ITP, which Agri granted without a fight.

This new, undeserved, federal lawsuit joined the excessive salt in the list of episodes and allegations that were stitched together and used by our detractors to establish a "pattern" and paint us as arrogant scofflaws who repeatedly and flippantly ignored rules.

The overly restrictive, wrongfully reduced water treatment capacity was an obstacle to the growth of the company. When it became clear that our rightful claim would not be honored, we began work on a fourth lagoon. In their animosity, ITP tried to obstruct it. As construction on the new lagoon was wrapping up, I was notified that ITP had registered opposition with the city. They wanted the city to prevent us from opening the additional lagoon and integrating it into the water treatment system.

Although I had become quite used to their hostility and obstructions by then, the utter ridiculousness of their objection caught me by surprise. They wanted the city to prevent Agriprocessors from adding a fourth lagoon and linking it up to the other because...because...the salt in our wastewater would prevent the use of the water outflow to irrigate hydroponic tomatoes in greenhouses they planned to develop!

Their friends on the council actually treated this ridiculous excuse as a legitimate objection and officially delayed the launch of the fourth lagoon for months. Eventually, ITP realized that they themselves actually needed the additional capacity and we were given the green light for the lagoon.

We had found a way to survive and thrive despite the legalized theft of our share of the lagoon capacity. The fourth lagoon was finally operational and it seemed like we were finally past the water conflicts, but our enemies weren't ready to lay down their arms.

A scheme was hatched in which the turkey plant would take full possession of the lagoons from the city in a backroom sale, authorized by the city council. This would have meant the end of our access to water treatment and the end of our company.

When we caught wind of the plot, we demanded the minutes of the city council meetings related to the sale only to be told that they'd somehow been misplaced and lost. This transparent attempt at concealing their machinations backfired dramatically, in a clear example of Hashem's protection. With no written record to rely on, we pressed for and received the audio recordings of the meetings, which they'd apparently forgotten to "disappear."

On the tapes, the council members could be heard discussing the scheduling of the vote to approve the sale. One of the councilmen was recorded gleefully snickering as he suggested that the vote be scheduled for Friday after sunset (which would, of course, preclude participation by the Jews). If they hadn't concealed or misplaced the written record, the truth of their motivations would not have become as clear—a written record of that exchange would've disguised the malicious intent so obvious in the audio recording.

Miraculous intervention by the state court delayed the sale, but it was only after Agriprocessors sued council members individually that the idea of a unilateral sale was finally dropped and the city agreed to arbitration.

Their efforts stymied, but still trying to honor their promise to their friends at ITP to sell them the lagoons, the city council members pushed Agri to borrow money from the federal government and undertake the construction of a first-class mechanical water treatment plant, at high initial construction costs and a ten-fold increase in operating costs. This would mean we no longer used the lagoons and they could be sold.

Hoping that this effort would alleviate the never-ending conflicts surrounding wastewater treatment, we agreed to participate in the project. It was a tremendous undertaking. The construction alone carried an approximately $10 million price tag, a very significant investment for a company our size, but it was an investment we hoped would pay the dividends of peace.

When it was finally completed, it was a magnificent accomplishment; the water it treated was cleaned so thoroughly that it was practically potable. A ribbon-cutting ceremony was scheduled by the state environmental department, the IDNR, who were eager to share the spotlight on this tremendous investment and achievement. Suddenly and without explanation, they canceled their participation in the event. This was in late 2007. I guess they knew something was coming and wanted to stand clear—but that's a story for later.

There is one more water-related episode that deserves to be highlighted, both because it so strongly echoed old antisemitic libels and for the way in which Hashem helped to uncover the plot in the nick of time.

Agriprocessors *shechted* around sixty thousand chickens every day. We paid other companies until 2004 to raise and deliver the chickens, when we decided to build a few of our own chicken houses. We purchased the necessary land for two structures and built them to industry standards—about sixty feet wide and six hundred feet long with immense fans built into the walls to circulate the air. Each one would house around 49,000 chickens.

Not long after the houses were completed, before they were even put into operation, a formal complaint was filed in court. The owner of a farm in the area claimed that the chicken houses would contaminate the well he used for his livestock. He came in with a complex presentation about aquifers, water tables, and geology, but the whole thing seemed preposterous to me. All the herbicides, pesticides, and other contaminants from agriculture and from the livestock all around were not a problem, but if the Yid is allowed to put an industry standard chicken house—with all the proper precautions and a substantial distance away—it's going to poison his well?!

To settle the matter, he demanded a "dye test." They would seal his well and pour a dye solution on the ground at the chicken house. They would then open the well and see if the dye was present in the water. This would establish whether or not contaminants from the chicken house could reach the well through the ground. The judge accepted this solution and set a date and time when the test would be administered.

I couldn't put my finger on it, but something about this whole thing was off. His demeanor was too confident, as if there was no question that the test would go his way. How was he so sure? He had some sort of information or plan that would assure a favorable outcome, but I couldn't think of what it might be.

Stumped, I requested to be included in the group that would be present when the well was to be sealed. The morning of the test, I arrived to find everyone already clustered around the well—the farmer, an IDNR official, and the company lawyer. With a flourish, the farmer clanged the lid shut and started putting on a padlock.

"Wait a minute," I interrupted him. "I'd like to look into the well." He reopened the lid and I peered down. It was a relatively narrow shaft and I could faintly see flowing water at the bottom of it. I was about to give the go-ahead to close it back up, when I noticed a small pipe running halfway up the wall of the shaft and disappearing into the wall.

"What's that?" I asked.

"Oh, that?" the farmer replied. "It's nothing. Our washing machine runs on this well water."

I'd found the ace up his sleeve. I knew why he was so confident in the results. He was planning to introduce the dye into the "sealed" well through that pipe! The whole group trooped up to his house to see the other end of the pipe, and sure enough, the washing machine had already been pushed aside and the other end of this pipe was exposed, ready for dye to be poured into the well.

With the pipe trick uncovered and the well properly sealed, the dye test came up negative and that was the end of that. Of course, the farmer suffered no consequences for his false and malicious complaint and his attempt to cause us economic harm. I had to be content with establishing that, no, the Jew was not poisoning anyone's well. I chalked it up as a win and thanked Hashem for His kindness in protecting me.

War on *Shechitah*

The Torah tells us that it is our duty to elevate every aspect of creation by using it for its specific purpose in the service of Hashem, or by avoiding it, if its purpose is to be something that proves our commitment to Hashem by not indulging a forbidden appetite.

Food, both from the plant and the animal kingdom, gives us strength and energy. That's one way in which an animal fulfills its purpose. Standing in opposition to this mission that Hashem has given animals is an organization called PETA.

PETA needs little introduction. These are the people who, like normal human beings, could not stay silent when terrorists sent a donkey strapped with bombs to kill Jews in Eretz Yisrael. Unlike normal human beings, what had them upset was the *donkey*. They sent a letter to the terrorists asking that they "leave the animals out of the conflict."

This twisted organization sees animals as equivalent to human beings. It is their position that animals are not to be used by humans *at all*, and certainly not as food, denying animals their place and purpose in Hashem's creation.

Sometime in 2003, Agriprocessors received a letter from PETA demanding that they be granted access to the plant to see the way the *shechitah* was being performed. They claimed that they just wanted to ensure that everything was done as humanely as possible, and perhaps make some recommendations.

The main certifying *rav* at the time, Harav Chaim Kohn, was consulted. He wouldn't even hear of it. Every legitimate concern was represented at the plant. The USDA ensured that everything was done according to the laws of the land, including the robust laws covering humane handling. The *rabbanim, l'havdil*, through their *mashgichim*, ensured that everything was done according to the eternal laws of the Torah. These radicals, committed to the destruction of the industry on whose door they were so politely knocking, had no legitimate reason to be at the plant at all. Access denied.

The Rav wasn't being difficult or paranoid. Their strategy was well-known, perfected by their counterparts across the world, and he recognized their playbook:

1. Open up the definition of *shechitah* and humane handling for debate, manipulated and pressured by ugly propaganda campaigns.

2. Champion the inevitable concessions or distortions of the naive or "progressive" members of the Jewish community as the new definition of halachically acceptable *shechitah*.

3. Attack the traditional method of *shechitah*—now portrayed as unnecessary by Jewish law and therefore not a question of religious

freedom—as inhumane (by their custom-made definitions) and demand that it be restricted or even banned.

Internationally, this strategy has met with some success, even in countries where *shechitah* was once considered sacrosanct as a matter of religious freedom. A number of countries have actually banned *shechitah* outright, while in others there are restrictions and fierce debate—the end result of campaigns that began by introducing these false standards and considerations.

As far as we were concerned, and also by the law of the land, when it comes to kashrus, the *rabbanim* were the final word. We firmly but respectfully responded to PETA's request, declining to allow them access. We considered the matter closed. For them, as we would soon find out, it was just the beginning.

It was a Thursday in November of 2004, the day of the American national holiday of Thanksgiving. Agriprocessors' turkey, which had won various awards for taste, was popular even among non-kosher consumers and the plant had been in high gear to keep up with the seasonal demand. Finally, things were quiet and I was alone in the office getting some work done when I received a call from Nat Lewin, a renowned lawyer and public advocate for *Yidden* and *Yiddishkeit*.

He had been contacted by a *New York Times* reporter working on a story about *shechitah*. More specifically, the reporter had received a video depicting the *shechitah* at Agriprocessors and he was troubled by what he saw.

Before calling the reporter back, Nat was calling me for some background on what issues he could expect to see and how they were best explained. This was the first I'd heard of any video and I couldn't imagine what issues it could possibly depict. We were under constant supervision by both the USDA and multiple *rabbanim*, and we'd ensured the best possible processes and procedures at great cost and effort.

I suggested that he call Harav Kohn. Not only was he the *rav* who was actually in charge of the kashrus and *shechitah* aspects of the plant, he's also a respected authority and distinguished public figure—an *av beis din*, dean of a *beis hora'ah*, and founder of the Business Halachah Institute. He was based in the New York area and he would surely be able to help.

A day or two later, I got an update. Harav Kohn had been equally nonplussed and couldn't offer any insight without first seeing the video, so he'd offered to meet the reporter together with Nat and provide his expertise in real time.

They set a date and time and met with the journalist, who showed them the video which he'd been sent.

Apparently, PETA, the champions of ethics, had deceitfully infiltrated the factory and recorded video of the *shechitah* over the course of seven weeks. In possession of hundreds of hours of footage, they had created a selectively edited thirty-minute clip to include a handful of cases they could cast in a bad light and sent them to this reporter, claiming to have uncovered terrible abuses.

After sitting through the video, they (mainly Harav Kohn, as the expert) calmly explained to the urban fellow that what they had just seen, unpleasant as it was to watch, was simply the act of kosher slaughter. It involves blood and the loss of animal life, exactly like non-kosher slaughter. As a matter of fact, *shechitah* is significantly more humane because it prioritizes a painless death over pretty presentation. There was no scandal here.

With the rabbi so firmly rejecting the claim that something was amiss, the *New York Times* chose not to go to press with the story, but they kept shopping around for analysis that would help them do something with the video. Eventually, about a week later, they found someone who did express (misplaced) alarm over the video and they ran the story.

The *Times* article started an avalanche of coverage, just as the PETA strategists intended when they'd sent them that video, and PETA was ready and waiting to capitalize on the attention. They posted the video on their various websites and platforms and also reached out directly to well-meaning rabbis and community leaders in congregations all across America who had no background in this area, no point of reference for identifying and challenging their deceptions.

For example, at one point in their video it sounded like a cow was mooing (vocalizing) after it was *shechted*. It's distressing to see and hear what you assume is pain or panic from a dying animal—until you realize it is a physical impossibility. As the USDA investigation noted, at this point in the process the animal is physically incapable of making any sounds at all. They either edited the sound in or used the few seconds from their footage in which sounds from the nearby barn lined up with the video to give a false impression to their unsuspecting audience.

Their campaign, designed by Jews who'd abandoned their tradition, paired this standard exploitation of the kind-hearted and sheltered consumer with snippets and fragments of Torah, out of context and distorted. They had the chutzpah to claim that not only were there animal rights to consider, but the kashrus of the meat was in question. Here was a group opposed to all meat consumption, waging war against *shechitah* by claiming to be defending it against respected *rabbanim* and *mashgichim*!

Their carefully crafted message, given credibility and national exposure by an expertly managed press, resulted in the expected outcry from individual consumers and communal leaders. Most of the *frum* community knew better, but here and there, even some *frum* individuals or groups accepted the propaganda that the *rabbanim* had somehow fallen short of the Torah's standards on *tza'ar ba'alei chaim* or kashrus, or both, and that these barbarians had the solutions.

Hoping we would take the noise they'd stirred up as an endorsement of their authority by the public, PETA came back to us, demanding huge changes in the way *shechitah* was performed at Agriprocessors. They wanted us to stop using the revolving pen to invert the animal for *shechitah*, which they labeled inhumane, and also to shoot each animal immediately after *shechitah*, among other "improvements."

Even if this would be an improvement from the scientific perspective (which it's not, more on that soon), it's important to recognize that they were demanding we abandon proper *shechitah*. Inverting the animal is something Jews have been doing since the giving of the Torah. Special equipment was even built into the Beis Hamikdash itself to facilitate this method. It's unequivocally an attack on our religion to portray this as barbaric, cruel, or even just unnecessary.

Their demands also had nothing to do with helping the animals, as laid out by Rabbi Dr. I. M. Levinger, the renowned and respected animal physiologist and veterinary surgeon from Basel, Switzerland, who literally wrote the book on *shechitah* in light of modern scientific understanding. In his book, he shows— from a scientific perspective—that inverting the animal has an anesthetizing effect and makes things a little easier for the animal, while shooting the animal afterwards is pointless at best. Studies done at the Cornell University School of Veterinary Medicine determined that the animal is unconscious within two seconds of the incision done during *shechitah*.

Notwithstanding all the press releases and protestations of PETA's allies and dupes, their aim was not to improve *shechitah*. The very idea is ludicrous—

the kind of comforting lie they tell their victims in order to delay opposition, the kind of comforting delusion their victims cling to as long as possible rather than face the reality that they're under attack.

The cold, hard truth was that they were at war with *shechitah*. Once they established this beachhead and won a seat at the table determining what *shechitah* should look like, the invasion would begin in earnest. They would chip away at it until the only *shechitah* acceptable to the government would be unacceptable to any *frum* Jew and, just like that, a large number of people would no longer eat meat. Mission accomplished. If that sounds crazy to you, look overseas.

This was an incremental step, an initial salvo, but there was no question it was war. What I needed to decide was, is it *my* war?

Many of our large customers, especially chain stores, were calling to express concern, questioning if they could continue to do business with Agriprocessors. There was a furor in the media and political pressure was being exerted by politicians, always conscious of which way the wind is blowing.

Business considerations dictated that, rather than picking an unpopular fight and trying to prove a point, I should demonstrate to the public and to my customers that I accepted the criticism and was working to fix the issues. From a business standpoint, the best thing to do would be to adopt PETA's recommendations, maybe even outdo them in an attempt to show that I was serious. This is what many businessmen targeted by PETA do—it just makes business sense.

But I wasn't a businessman engaged in Judaism—I was a Jew engaged in business. As a Jew there was no question. It *was* my war. It was up to me to fight it and Hashem would grant me victory.

It meant standing up against people who had no regard for decency and morality, who had no compunction crushing a man into the dirt to prove their compassion to an animal, but I am a Yid. I was put in this position by Hashem and it was for a reason. I hadn't asked for this, but I was the first line of defense for *shechitah* in the United States.

If I caved to these demands, kashrus in America would be changed forever. The *rabbanim* would no longer be the final authority on the proper way to *shecht* within the limits of the law. Man-made standards and arbitrary audits, calibrated to the constantly changing sensibilities of the public, would supersede the eternal Torah. It might take time to fully unfold, but the principle would be conceded then and there—all to assuage a band of militant vegans whose ultimate goal is to eliminate meat consumption.

The outcome of this battle would not only affect the US. Our brothers in Europe and Australia were (and still are) fighting for their rights with organizations like PETA. A defeat in the United States of America, the beacon of religious liberty, would reverberate and be magnified across the world.

I chose the more difficult path. Placing my trust in Hashem, I marshaled what resources and allies I had to fight and win this war, defending the mitzvah of Hashem.

On the advice of Harav Kohn, we hired Rabbi Dr. I. M. Levinger himself to audit the processes in place at Agriprocessors. He came in December 2004. He thoroughly reviewed and observed the entire process and concluded that the livestock were being handled most humanely and the *shechitah* was done in a humane manner.

On the legal front, the government regulators did a thorough review of the allegations and cleared Agri of any wrongdoing. It took great effort and extracted a heavy cost, both financial and emotional, but with great *siyata d'Shmaya*, the issue was laid to rest. None of the doom-filled predictions that the industry experts warned about, should we fail to obey these terrorists, came to pass. We thanked Hashem for His kindness in protecting us from evil and evil-doers.

Contrary to their propaganda, we had a real and ongoing commitment to avoid *tza'ar ba'alei chaim*. It was important to the *rabbanim* from the halachic perspective, but it was also something we personally cared about as *Yidden, rachmanim bnei rachmanim*.

A couple of years after this attack, at the recommendation of Rabbi Menachem Genack of the OU, we invited Dr. Temple Grandin to audit the plant. She is a popular proponent of humane handling of animals and a top consultant on this issue for the livestock industries. Dr. Grandin conducted a thorough review and expressed a general satisfaction with our facilities and our methods. She did have some minor recommendations for improvements, which we implemented.

The Union and the Civil War

Not long after Agriprocessors had first begun operations, in the early nineties, the UFCW[1] union came to town and offered to represent the workers. There was enough initial worker interest to trigger a general vote, but when all the workers gathered to vote for or against unionization, the majority voted against. The union accepted the result of the vote and moved on.

In 2005, they came back and tried again. This time, they couldn't even drum up enough interest to trigger a vote. The workers sent them the same message as they had the first time—they were not interested in being represented—but the new and improved union no longer cared about a small thing like that. They approached the management and insisted that they be instated as the workers' representatives with or without their consent. This was an outrageous request and besides, my father had very bad experiences with the union, so we refused. In response, they went nuclear.

They immediately initiated an aggressive, coercive strategy which had come to prominence in the years since their first attempt: the "corporate campaign." It's essentially all-out war, stopping just short of physical violence. In their own words: "Corporate campaigns swarm the target employer from every angle, great and small, with an eye toward inflicting upon the employer the death of a thousand cuts rather than a single blow."

If a company surrenders and unionizes (against the wishes of the workers!) the attacks will stop. Otherwise, they'll keep slashing until the company is dead—collapsing into bankruptcy, isolated and out of funds. This puts the local workers out of a job, but the national union has its own interests. Their "victory" enables them to point to the scalps they've collected when they go to intimidate their next victim, helping them in future unionization efforts.

It was a strategy I'd seen before. As a child, I was in my mother's restaurant one morning when a man came in and approached the register. Without a word, my mother handed him some money and he left. This was not, in itself, unusual. As I described earlier, my mother is the personification of *chessed*. Her restaurant doubled as a discreet soup kitchen and, in addition to food, she often gave money to her "customers." Still, there was something about the way this man was dressed and carried himself that told me this was different.

When I asked my mother about it, she said the money was for "window protection." If the money wasn't paid, the union would come at night and break the big storefront glass, which would cost a lot more to replace than it

---

1. United Food and Commercial Workers; a union that covers the food industry among others.

cost to "protect." They were the perfect solution to the problem because they *were* the problem. The union's corporate campaign was the same racket on a larger scale.

First, they create the problem. Union analysts and strategists identify the vulnerabilities of the company they've targeted for destruction, whether in their supply chain, strategic partnerships, or customer base. Then they methodically identify what would be needed to disrupt each of those relationships.

They use all available mechanisms to create ammunition by filing trivial or groundless claims, complaints, or reports, often to supervising agencies who are required to look into any complaints filed. This has the immediate effect of snarling the company up in costly red tape and oversight, sometimes even disrupting operations. Then, they use transparency laws to gather information the regulators collected in response to their complaints, along with any other information they manage to access, and add that to their ammunition to be used against the weaknesses their strategists identified.

If any of the investigations they cause result in notices or fines, they point to that as proof of their target's shortcomings. If not, they point to the inspections themselves to prove misbehavior—"Where there's smoke, there's fire!" they insist, as they expertly operate their artificial smoke machine.

They attack the target's reputation with their customers and create the impression that the product is unsafe or otherwise unacceptable. They also share their misinformation, along with any customer reactions they've caused, with suppliers, wholesalers, distributors, and so on, calling into question the viability of the business relationships. They underline all of this with sustained harassment through pickets outside stores, pamphlets, and robocalls.

In our case, for example, they compiled and misrepresented regulatory reports used by the USDA to notify management when something needs to be addressed. These reports are really a routine oversight tool, but the union relied on the general public's unfamiliarity with these details and issued dishonest press releases, pointing to these reports as evidence that we were ignoring laws and were flippant about food safety.[2] They reached out directly

---

2. As a matter of fact, in the course of our defense against these claims, we filed Freedom of Information requests for the same type of reports at a plant comparable to ours but represented by that same union. They had reports of the same nature and in even greater numbers—not because they were shady operators but because these were routine reports resulting from normal operations, raising issues to be resolved.

to the wholesalers and retailers of our products with these false claims and even initiated robocalls directly to consumers.

In fact, Trader Joe's, a longstanding client of ours, related that they were being harassed by picketers in their parking lot. In addition, they had been planning on pushing Agri's turkey for Thanksgiving, but due to false allegations spread by the union, they felt they could not even advertise that they carried our products.

All of this is perfect fodder for the media, who are famously willing to put ratings ahead of reality. The corporate campaigners leverage that willingness with expertise born of vicious experience, generating sensational media coverage of their target. They then use the news coverage as more ammunition in their war, increasing pressure on customers, wholesalers, and ultimately, the target company.

Having created this problem for their target, making it all but impossible for them to go about their business, they are always there with the solution. Just instate them as the workers' representatives (without the workers' consent) and they'll be happy to "protect the windows" and business can get back to usual.

Of course, if the union campaign reached this public stage, the cost of protecting your windows has increased exponentially, because there are now so many more people with their hands out. As the target company becomes the popular punching bag of the day, many more people and organizations swarm in to attack. This is part of the union's strategy. It's harder for the public to discount criticism and attacks coming from diverse and unrelated entities, with less of an obvious financial incentive to attack the company than the union has.

In our case, some of these were well-meaning people taken in by their lies. Others were more opportunistic allies, hoping to gain something by jumping on the bandwagon. The occasional politician weighing in was bad, but those were usually hit-and-runs. More damaging were the activists and organizations who joined the fight for the long haul, pursuing their own agendas against a weakened target.

The most hurtful and dangerous example of this in our case was an opportunistic attack that came from our fellow Jews. During my time living in Minnesota I had become close with the *rav* of the Chabad community there, Rabbi Asher Zeilingold. In early 2006, he called me with a request.

Their local kosher meat store had recently shut its doors and his congregants were having difficulty finding kosher meat and poultry. He'd found a solution, but there was a catch. A local supermarket was willing to carry those products if he could show them that there was enough demand, but the Orthodox community there just wasn't large enough. If he could persuade the Conservative community to commit to buying the kosher products, the two communities combined would have enough buying power to sustain a kosher meat department, and that's where I came in to his plan.

The Conservative clergyman had agreed to encourage his community to buy their meat at this supermarket—on the condition that he be granted access to inspect the plant in Postville first.

I wanted to do everything I could to increase the availability of kosher meat, but I was very wary of this demand. The plant was already thoroughly supervised by government regulators and, *l'havdil*, kashrus certifiers, and it underwent annual audits by highly regarded auditing companies. We were just moving on from the PETA attack, during which I'd learned only too well how eagerly and dishonestly agenda groups would twist facts to further their causes. I'd never had a request like this before, and I simply did not trust his motives. My instincts were telling me that this clergyman was using Rabbi Zeilingold to get his foot in the door for his own purposes.

I shared my concerns with Rabbi Zeilingold, but he dismissed them. He ran a kosher certification agency and he had a process in place to prevent such abuse of access: Any rabbi visiting a plant under his certification had to commit to voice any concerns immediately, while they were still at the plant. That way, it was still possible for the concern to be investigated and dismissed or corrected as appropriate. He saw this agreement as an iron-clad protection against self-serving claims that had no basis in reality. He was sadly mistaken, as we would both discover.

Feeling pressure to help this community, I agreed to the visit.

They made the trip down from Minnesota together and were given free rein in the plant. They returned to my office with glowing praise for the factory. The Conservative clergyman took the opportunity to ask about the PETA allegations, and I took the opportunity to set the record straight, showing him the third-party audits and the conclusions of Dr. Levinger. He was satisfied and they left. Upon their return to Minnesota, he wrote a letter to Rabbi Zeilingold praising the plant and agreeing to join in his efforts to bring kosher meat from Agriprocessors to the supermarket in their city.

A few months after this trip, Agriprocessors was the subject of a hit piece in the *Forward*. The *Forward* is a New York-based newspaper founded at the end of the nineteenth century, a Yiddish-language pro-union socialist propaganda rag. It was founded by irreligious, socialist *Yiddishistin*—Jews who championed Jewish culture while vehemently attacking Jewish religion and tradition—and its content reflected that. Promotion of socialism and unions was its primary focus, but it was also a vicious opponent of religious Jews and a source of constant criticism of everything we hold holy.

As the union's campaign against us intensified, the *Forward* jumped into the fray with an article professing to reveal terrible working conditions and abuse at Agriprocessors. The corporate campaign strategy, which called for throwing blood in the water and sparking spontaneous attacks by unaffiliated sharks, served them well here. This defamatory garbage served as the cue for this Conservative clergyman to pile on and try to further his own career and his denomination at the expense of his innocent Jewish brothers.

Troubled by the coverage but interested in the truth, Rabbi Zeilingold arranged a trip to Postville to investigate the article's allegations. He brought along a fluent Spanish-speaking academic and they toured the plant and freely interviewed many employees about the substance of the article. They concluded that the article was absolutely false, a finding which was corroborated by other honest organizations that investigated these claims.

The Conservative clergyman also came to town, but he was interested in something else entirely. He brought his own group of people and went through the motions of investigating at the plant, but this was a deception. The first red flag was that he brought his own group and didn't join Rabbi Zeilingold, as he had in the past. His subsequent behavior made it clear that he simply didn't want objective witnesses who could contradict what he claimed he heard or saw. He also wanted to smuggle his allies into the plant—people in his group were later revealed to be union activists and organizers.

Once he'd toured the plant and could credibly claim to have seen and heard things which corroborated the allegations, it was his turn to tell us his price for "window protection." He wasn't shy. His demands were nothing less than a full seat at the table. Practically every table, as a matter of fact. He wanted to be involved in internal decisions and discussions by the plant management and to have input on various policies. As you can imagine, his demands were not met.

Next, I received a letter from the main office of the Conservative movement in Manhattan. It wasn't just a local clergyman who saw an opening for personal prestige and enrichment. It was the national leadership of their religious movement and they were thinking big, eyeing the whole food industry.

Their letter introduced me to a new kind of kosher certification they were launching. I'd already heard of the concept, since it had already been announced by their clergyman and was being vigorously promoted by falsely vilifying us. This *hechsher* proposed to change the definition of "kosher" to cover ethical considerations and, without seeming to note the irony, they insisted that Agriprocessors be the first to meet their qualification demands and adopt their certification...or they wouldn't be able to "protect" us from the consequences.

As in the case of PETA's attack, I had a decision to make. Again, we were faced with media pressure, political and regulatory considerations, and many large customers and chain stores questioning if they could continue to do business with Agri.

Business considerations dictated that I play ball, that I make the changes and accept the additional certification. In this case there was not just a stick, but a carrot as well. It was an opportunity to expand our market share to the non-Orthodox community.

In the age of social consciousness, it also promised to increase our appeal in general and set us apart from our competitors. We already boasted six certifications for our glatt kosher products from the leading authorities in the various communities we served. The Conservative certification would bolster our position and enable us to expand into new communities.

As I'd determined during the PETA attack, I couldn't look at it from that perspective. I wasn't a businessman engaged in Judaism; I was a Jew engaged in business. From that perspective this all looked very different.

They were offering a "*hechsher*," but it had nothing to do with what the Torah defines as kosher or even other aspects of *Toras Moshe*. They pointed to phrases from the Torah, but all their goals and definitions were based on contemporary values developed with secular "experts."[3] When they eventually

---

3. The fine print revealed that the standards were developed with a company called Social Accountability Accreditation Services. On the advisory board of this noble-sounding organization, crafting this noble-sounding certification, sat none other than Alan Spaulding, the director of Global Strategies for the organization sworn to our destruction, the UFCW union.

released their detailed requirements, in 2010, they included items like carbon footprints and recycling requirements. This was the new definition of "kosher" they wanted us to promote by accepting their certification.

We've all seen the confusion and havoc wrought by their redefinition of *geirus*, which puts often honest, well-intentioned converts through a process other than the one halachah prescribes and results in conversions which are not recognized by the rest of *Am Yisrael*. This was, and continues to be, a source of controversy and strife, which rose to its greatest pitch when the government in Israel took up the question of whether the determination of "who is a Jew" was to be decided by halachah. The damage is still with us today.

They were now poised to introduce that same turmoil into the realm of kashrus by redefining it based on authorities other than halachah. To accept their certification and follow their guidelines would also have the damaging effect of legitimizing their authority and standing in Torah matters.

I knew that turning them down, essentially refusing to pay for "window protection," would mean increased attacks—attacks which would have added credibility because they came from fellow Jews, and clergymen to boot.

I knew that Hashem had not granted us success in the kosher meat industry in order to bring confusion and turmoil into the world of kashrus or to promote as authorities people who do not espouse halachah. I needed to place my trust in Hashem and not allow fear or concern to sway me to the wrong decision, sacrificing truth for (the promise of) personal or professional safety or success.

I discussed the issue with the *rabbanim* who certified the kashrus at Agriprocessors and they concurred. This *hechsher* must not be adopted. One of the *rabbanim* went so far as to vow that he would never allow it to happen and another wrote me a long letter stating, in the strongest possible terms, that it was *forbidden* for me to accept this certification.

We sent an official response to the Conservative movement, informing them that the company had discussed the proposal with its glatt kosher certifiers and they forbade us from accepting the certification.

Although it was the existing certifying organizations who had rejected their proposal, they went on to escalate their attacks on the company and on me personally. The local clergyman even secretly conspired with the Iowa labor commissioner, a former union leader himself, who was exploring ways to

These were the "*mashgichim*" that the Conservative movement chose as authorities over what Jews should eat.

weaponize the regulatory power at his disposal against Agriprocessors. We only discovered this years later, in documents the government had to turn over in preparation for the trial. Among the documents, we found records of the meeting between this clergyman and the labor commissioner, along with correspondence in which the clergyman insisted that his involvement be kept confidential.

This was only one of the battles stirred up by the corporate campaign. The loose alliance between the few big adversaries and countless small ones—anyone who thought making us look bad would make them look good in some way—resulted in an almost constant stream of new allegations, accusations, rumors, and innuendo. A thousand cuts, as promised, painting a false picture for the public of exploitation, abuse, and greed.

Under the slightest scrutiny, this house of cards would fall apart—though the fact that this took place in the twenty-first century meant they had absolutely nothing to worry about. Scrutiny simply doesn't happen, especially for a juicy story delivered through trusted mainstream media sources. New developments came out like clockwork, shifting the focus to a new outrage and neatly sidestepping the question of whether the first one ever even happened. The misrepresentations and outright fabrications slowly built up, each one making the next one seem obvious, almost inevitable.

The few who saw through the hoax were easily dismissed as lone voices, individual conspiracy theorists contradicting the many thousands who were convinced—all of whom had read the same articles written by the same liars.

Scrutiny on many of these stories only came when I was forced to defend myself in court. Then, in front of the world, the dramatic claims all disintegrated under the slightest challenge. For example, the dangerous chemicals and lung irritants to which we were said to have exposed workers were revealed to be refrigerants running inside pipes, and spices like pepper and garlic in the deli kitchen. These revelations were made by the accusers themselves, sheepishly, in response to the unheard of, exotic technique of simply asking the accusers for more details. It could have been done by the media or any of the other consumers of the opposition propaganda, but they were not interested then and, to their eternal shame, the truth of these claims didn't even interest them after they were all disproven under oath.

Even then, the opposition continued defaming me and my family with these decisively discredited lies in order to further their own careers or agendas.

A full hour of a sensationalist television program was dedicated to pushing these discredited accusations, with the full-throated participation of the union organizers and the tireless Conservative clergyman, almost a year after they'd been exposed as hollow and shameless lies.

Postville was idyllic for many people, including my family, but for me it was difficult and exhausting from day one, and that only intensified as time went on. Nonetheless, I put up with the constant crises and attacks and I embraced my role in building and developing this place for them, and in accomplishing what I could for Klal Yisrael.

CHAPTER THREE
The Pogrom

The Infamous Raid

THEN CAME THE ORGANIZED DESTRUCTION AND DEVASTATION OF everything we had built. The perpetrators of the initial attack and sustained aftermath were in some cases motivated, and in other cases felt secure from backlash, by the fact that we were Jews.

My great-grandparents had experienced the pogroms in Russia, during which organized and often state-sanctioned mobs of peasants rampaged through Jewish communities, leaving terrible destruction in their wake. The events in Postville in mid-2008 reminded me of the stories I'd heard as a child. Obviously, they didn't rise to the horror of the historical pogrom, which often resulted in physical injury and even death of many innocents, but wanton destruction of Jewish businesses and communities was at the heart of the historical pogroms.

The word itself, pogrom, is from the Russian word *"gromit,"* which means to destroy, to violently demolish, and, in an only slightly different sense, to raid. In this respect, the infamous raid was a modern-day equivalent.

It started as local gossip. There was some sort of law enforcement buildup happening in Cedar Rapids, ninety miles to the south. Immigration and Customs Enforcement, ICE, had rented a local fairground and were setting up a makeshift detention facility. It seemed like something big was in the works.

The three meat packers based in Cedar Rapids were very worried, and news reports said that many of their workers were staying home. We had no reason to think they were looking at us, but it caught our attention nonetheless.

Like everyone else in our industry, and in most industries involving unskilled labor, we struggled with the results of porous US borders and incoherent immigration policies.

More than ten million people are in the country illegally, most of them unskilled. Many find work that doesn't involve showing documentation, like landscaping, housecleaning, and construction. The ones who seek work in industries that *do* require documentation, get their hands on black market documents and provide them to prospective employers. This makes it hard to identify them and keep them out of the workforce.

To complicate things further, it's illegal to withhold employment, or even ask for additional documentation, if an applicant's paperwork passes standard examination. An employer who does so will face a racism lawsuit from the federal government. The only thing businesses can do is train their hiring staff to better identify the fakes, which we did.

Forced to do the work of trained border agents, the HR personnel faced a constant battle to keep up with those seeking work and those running the black market that serves them, all of whom constantly adapt to survive.

Like every other law-abiding, medium-to-large employer in the nation, we did what we could, with the guidance of (and within the restrictions of) the federal government. In fact, our hiring manager had attended a federal training session on spotting fake documentation only a few months before the preparations in Cedar Rapids got people talking.

We did our best, and regularly turned away applicants, but we had to accept the likelihood that there were some unidentified illegal immigrants on staff at any given time. This heightened our awareness of the increased law enforcement activity, but on balance, it seemed implausible that they would set up in the backyard of three factories which clearly had jumpy workforces, only to drive two hours to hit us. Besides, there wasn't much to be done about it but wait. *Daven* and wait.

A phone call changed all that. A woman who worked in the regional meat industry, a member of a business association to which we belonged, reached out with information and a suggestion. The information was that we were definitely the target. She'd heard this from someone in the know and it was solid. The suggestion was that we get a lawyer, fast. Not just any lawyer. She gave us the name and number of a lawyer who had reached out to ICE on the eve of a raid in Texas earlier that year. He had succeeded in avoiding a traumatic and destructive raid by convincing them that the plant would willingly cooperate. They came into the office like civilized people, identified their concerns to plant management, and the concerns were addressed.

This wouldn't be a new policy for us. We'd always cooperated with the authorities and intended to continue to do so. Earlier that year, we had actually hired a prestigious law firm to review and improve Agri's hiring processes. If we were short of perfection in implementation it was, as far as we knew, due to the impossibility of the task. We were willing to enhance our procedures if ICE had guidance on how to do that. There was definitely no need for aggressive action.

Grateful for the warning and the contact information, we reached out to the law firm that had handled the Texas case and authorized them to act on our behalf. They sent a letter to ICE, making it clear that we were a law-abiding company trying to hire only authorized employees, and we had processes in place to find and address those that slipped through, just like everyone else in the industry and in the nation at large. If they had a list of people they wanted us to fire, they were cordially invited to come to our offices and we would cooperate fully.

The law firm was stonewalled. ICE didn't accept the proposition and wouldn't even admit we were their target. When this failed, I reached out to an Iowa State Senator who lived in town. He knew well the ramifications of a raid on our small town and he reached out to see if a peaceful resolution could be found. He had stature as a part of the state government, but that didn't earn him their cooperation or even an honest answer. They brushed him off the same way they'd brushed off the lawyer.

Monday, May 12, 2008. I arrived at the office as usual, after Shacharis and my morning *shiurim*. A customer had made the trip to Postville to see the beautiful new wastewater treatment facility firsthand. First on my itinerary for the day was to give him the grand tour. We were just wrapping it up and heading back to the office when my cell phone rang. It was one of the plant managers. "ICE is here!"

I heard the helicopter a moment later. *Thwup-thwup-thwup-thwup.* The sound is almost commonplace over major metropolitan areas, but we were hundreds of miles away from that kind of city. I looked up. This was not a commercial or a medical helicopter. It was an attack helicopter. We were under attack. Again.

The sound of my cell phone ringing snapped me back to reality. This time it was one of the office workers. She was panicking. "You'd better get back to your office to open it up or they're going to break down the door." I headed over immediately, watching the scene unfold around me with disbelief. Vehicles were streaming through the security station, faster than was safe. Walking through the security station to the office area, I saw that they'd crashed right through the movable security barrier without waiting for it to open.

Cletus Pladsen, a hardworking and loyal local man who'd worked security for us since the beginning, shrugged at me helplessly as I passed. What was he going to do? Tell the adrenaline-soaked guys with the badges and guns to wait one civilized second and not cause unnecessary damage? Close to six hundred agents had descended on the town, surrounding the plant and swarming the premises wearing bulletproof vests and brandishing guns, their own version of shock and awe.

Looking back, this would have been a moment of intense emotion, but I was focused on what I needed to do to address the situation right in front of me. I walked up the stairs to my office, calmly unlocked the door and walked in, officers flooding in behind me. One of them flashed a badge and a warrant. He handed me the warrant and informed me that they were here executing an "enforcement action" and that I was not permitted to leave my office.

The immigration raid at Agriprocessors.

My office had a second door which opened onto the landing of a staircase down to the large open-plan office area. I opened the door and looked out at the office. The officers had rounded up all the office workers and had them sitting in a small cluster of chairs under armed guard. One woman was crying, terrified.

"What are you doing?!" I demanded of the agent in charge. "These people aren't a danger to anyone. You need hostages? Let them go home!" The agents held a quick murmured consultation amongst themselves and, *baruch Hashem*, agreed to let them leave.

I sat down to read the warrant. Like every aspect of this raid, it was created with a real eye for effect. Leafing through the grounds for this attack, my eyes grew wider with each page.

The way this guy told it, the factory had a meth lab—guns and bombs, either for sale or to trade for drugs—with floor supervisors ("hasidic Jews," no less) duct taping workers' eyes and hitting them, just to mention the "highlights."

All of this was somehow taking place under the constant and complete supervision of the US government, represented by the USDA, and half a dozen other organizations with regulatory or certifier's oversight. The details that comprised this whole lurid hodgepodge were inconsistent, incoherent, or irrelevant.

It wove together preposterous assertions into a narrative that would net flashy headlines but that they clearly didn't even believe themselves. For example, they included the nonsense about a meth lab, but they didn't bring any of the special personnel or follow any of the protocols they would have followed if they truly thought there was one.

Taking a page out of the corporate campaign playbook, they listed routine regulatory health and safety citations issued two months earlier, similar types of OSHA violations, reports and quotes by our avowed enemies such as the union and the *Forward*, and Senate testimony citing Agriprocessors as a bad employer.

Senate testimony sounds impressive, but wait until you hear the rest of the story. The testimony (little more than a recitation at a Senate hearing of the other items that the warrant listed separately) was presented by none other than expert witness Eric Frumin, the health and safety coordinator for "Change to Win"—a collection of labor unions including the UFCW, at the time in open war against us on every front. Including this in the warrant was nothing more than an attempt to appropriate the Senate's credibility to make defamation by an avowed adversary seem respectable.

Many of these flaws are not apparent to the casual reader, presumably including the judge who signed the warrant. Some didn't even occur to me at the time. The cultural respect for authority—especially for the federal government, the formal language, and the seemingly methodical approach deactivates a person's skepticism. This is a version of the facade that nature puts up to give the impression that it's the true reality, when the truth is that everything is dictated by Hashem and nature conforms as instructed.

While I was sequestered in my office, reading all this carefully with the smug agent of destruction guarding the door, the people in the factory itself were going through a harrowing ordeal. My son Getzel was there and gave me a firsthand account later that day.

He had been on his way down the stairs from the old office, heading to the rabbis' room,[1] when he heard the helicopter. He ran into the room and looked out the window. There were already agents running alongside the building and a handful of agents walking along the train tracks. Within moments, a number of armed agents burst into the rabbis' room and instructed everyone to follow them single file down to the employee cafeteria.

They walked through the processing room, huge sides of beef hanging from the overhead tracks, still swaying from the workers handling them, but not a worker in sight. They'd all already been herded downstairs.

Getzel, along with the rabbinical staff, was likewise led downstairs. When they reached the expansive hallway between the cafeteria and the employee locker rooms, all the Hispanic-looking employees were instructed to line up on the right side of the hallway. The others were to stand along the left side. Everyone complied, shuffling to their designated side.

Reports over the next few days detailed just how traumatic all this had been for them. The sounds of the assault, so loud in the stillness outside, had been completely masked by the loud noises in the plant itself. The agents had burst in suddenly and without warning, brandishing their weapons and shouting. "Come on out, rats!" some of them taunted in Spanish. "Pretty soon this place will be swarming with cops and we'll find you and drag you out anyway…"

The Hispanic workers were being ushered into the cafeteria one at a time. Without thinking, Getzel walked over to the cafeteria entrance and peered inside. There was an agent sitting at each of the tables and, upon entering, the Hispanic employees were each sent to a table for one-on-one interviews. Many of the women were crying.

He was helpless to assist them in all ways but one. This is America and everyone is entitled to a lawyer, but not everyone knows it. He doesn't speak Spanish, so he asked one of the rabbis how to say "lawyer" in Spanish. "*Abogado*," he was told. He walked along the line telling each of the employees

---

1. This was the employee nickname for the locker room/break room used by the rabbinical staff, which was also used as a shul and *beis midrash* during breaks.

to request a lawyer, using basic English and mime to fill in everything but the word "*Abogado.*"

In all the commotion, he was walking around for a while. He managed to speak to quite a few workers before one of the agents made him his problem. He asked Getzel who he was and why he was walking around and told him to leave the area, assigning an agent to escort him to the office portion of the complex.

At one point, I was granted permission to collect something from the plant itself and I saw my employees cuffed hand and foot and chained to each other in a long, single-file line. I noticed one of the agents who was walking behind the line of unfortunate arrestees leave his position and move up the line to the middle. Apparently, a guy in the middle wasn't walking straight enough for his liking. Even from the distance I could see that he was verbally abusing the man. Then he reached out and physically pushed him! "Hey!" I shouted out. "Why are you hitting them?!" He looked up, surprised that I was standing there and even more surprised that I was interfering with his "work." *Baruch Hashem*, he decided to de-escalate the situation and just walked back to the end of the line without a word.

Whatever physical pain and discomfort they endured, I'm sure it paled in comparison with the emotional anguish, fear, and uncertainty about what the future held for them, tinged with worry about their families.

The emotional pain of loved ones weighs heavier on a person than their own. More practically, these workers were primary breadwinners for spouses and children, and some were also caring for parents and siblings. Headed for jail, they would no longer be able to provide for the basic needs of their loved ones, who would now probably suffer physical deprivation to one degree or another.

This concern was more immediate than they could have expected. In the days that followed, we tried to pick up the shattered pieces of the company, but we didn't forget the shattered families of those arrested and their needs. I reached out to the payroll department to make sure that at least the outstanding paychecks were getting to the families smoothly. They were not.

State law prohibits employers from giving checks to anyone other than the person on the check. In this case, that meant that paychecks would have to be sent to the workers in detention to be authorized by their signature and only then could they be mailed back to their hungry families. These were real people in real need at a very traumatic moment in their lives. Thinking of my father's way, always putting people first, I stopped what I was doing and reassured them that I would do everything in my power to help.

I called the company lawyer and insisted that a solution be found. Together with another lawyer at his firm, he contacted the state's lawyers with possible solutions, which they discussed back and forth, looping me in from time to time. At one point, they raised the problem of liability if the money went to the wrong person and the rightful recipient sued—a possible liability of $150,000, all told. "Are you guys joking?!" I asked. "If anyone sues, *I'll* take the liability! There are scared and hurting people here with no money for food or rent!"

I shuttled back and forth from the local religious charity to the local bank, trying to negotiate a way to make this happen. When all was said and done, the local bank agreed to cash the checks, if the local charity would vouch for the identities of the people picking up the checks. The local charity agreed to do so. The only piece missing was the sign-off by the state lawyers. The day wore on and closing time approached, but the bank agreed to stay open while we waited for the state's approval.

When they finally called it was not with an approval. The representatives of state law enforcement gave us a firm refusal and a warning: They would actually press separate criminal charges for each and every check that was issued to the wrong party. I couldn't believe my ears. I was stunned. We had offered to take complete liability. Bank officials, community leaders, the company—we were all working together because these women and children were in a desperate situation and the state officials just shrugged callously.

I was furious, but my hands were tied. I went to give the waiting families the bad news along with my promise to continue my efforts to help them in any way I could. They clustered around me and I tried to explain the inexplicable through a Spanish translator. Even after all my explanations, I'm sure it made no sense to them because it made no sense to *me*. It made no sense at all. They left, disappointed and empty-handed.

As a special souvenir of that day, a press photographer had caught some moments on film. For the next little while, a close-up of me talking to a group of Hispanic people, looking grim and a little angry, became their go-to image to accompany every article. Out of context, it made me look aggressive and intimidating, which usually went well with whatever lie or distortion they were reporting in the article. Of course, I didn't like it, but I have to say it fit—an

One picture depicts a man passionately addressing the pain of others, the other is just a mean face. A deceptively cropped picture can lie better than a thousand words.

image implying the exact opposite of what actually happened, accompanying words that did the same.

The pain and suffering caused by these officials, in this and in many similar instances, dishonestly reported and attributed to me by the local and national media, was shaping public opinion. It was actually poisoning the minds and hearts of those in the jury pool, as I would discover at the trial. In fact, the man who became the jury foreman specifically cited the troubles of the workers and their families after the raid as something which prejudiced him against me.

The Aftermath

The raid had hit us hard. The hours, days, and weeks that followed were critical if we were ever going to recover. We threw ourselves into our work, dealing with the fallout of the raid on our company and community. Our opponents, unencumbered by the need to deal with the destruction, rushed straight to the cameras, microphones, and keyboards.

The representatives of the federal government were first in line. First to boast, but also to justify their actions. They knew how the raid looked. It looked exactly like what it was: an overwhelming and unnecessary use of force. Perhaps it was intended to impress the President's anti-immigration base on the eve of the presidential election, but this wasn't an Air Force flyover or some other harmless muscle-flexing. Real people with real lives were hurt in this display. The American people are not cruel and they don't want their representatives to be cruel. They would want an explanation.

The warrant had been prepared as a dramatic, thoroughly absurd soundbitesalad for exactly this reason. No one likes to see bad things happen to good people, but when bad things happen to bad people nobody loses any sleep. They had prepared all the ingredients they would need to convince the public that we were bad people.

The press happily passed along the narrative about what a dangerous and exploitative criminal enterprise the government had attacked in this record-breaking raid. They had a field day with it—the guns, the bombs, the blind-folded abuse victims, the meth lab. Especially the meth lab. It disappeared from the coverage eventually, like the rest of the impossible-to-sustain fairy tales, but it spiced up early coverage.

Not a day went by without negative press. For years, our enemies at PETA and the UFCW had been doing everything in their power to paint us as the bad guys, with the occasional assist from local bigots or that Conservative clergyman. All of their foundation work had new weight now that the federal government raised our profile and made us a national topic for conversation. People and organizations across the nation who were pushing an agenda or looking to make a name for themselves began piling on, and the local and national media was only too happy to give them all a platform.

The battering to our reputation wasn't only an assault on our pride. Suppliers started to balk at doing business with us and banks and leasing companies started to slow-walk or even renege on their commitments. In the immediate aftermath, we couldn't even take a minute to properly respond to the deluge of misinformation and flat-out lies.

The most immediate problem was getting back to work. More than three hundred workers had been arrested and we didn't even have enough people to finish the work that had been interrupted by the raid. We couldn't simply pack the beef into the freezer to be processed later, since kosher meat needs to be fully de-veined, soaked, and salted within three days of *shechitah*.

Family and friends rose to the occasion, working from dawn until dusk to salvage what they could and help the company get back on its feet. My son and daughter-in-law spent their first few months of married life in hard hats and butcher frocks, de-boning chicken on the processing line. People even flew in from New York to do what they could. It was heartwarming, but obviously we needed to find a real solution.

Agri reached out to staffing companies in the state and found one, Labor Ready, which was able to supply 150 workers. It wasn't enough, but it was something. Within two weeks, they very publicly quit, citing concerns about "safety and care afforded to our workers." This was puzzling. It was a slaughterhouse, sure, and one in crisis and under a lot of stress, but, UFCW lies aside, it was no different than other companies in the industry and even had a better than average safety record. Labor Ready worked in the industry and we knew their announcement was bogus, but we couldn't imagine what was really driving their decision.

They were replaced by a company called Jacobson Staffing. Within days of their arrival we got a clue as to why Labor Ready might have left. Shortly after Jacobson Staffing had set up their office, a fellow walked in and nabbed an employee handbook. When they asked him if he was looking for a job, he said, "No. I'm with the UFCW. I have a letter for your boss." In the letter, the union thugs urged the staffing company to "reconsider" their arrangement with Agriprocessors, adding their litany of lies and misrepresentations about health and safety concerns to the general intimidation of finding yourself in the union's cross-hairs.

We had assumed that the union had walked away now that Agri had been knocked down by the federal government itself, but clearly, they were sticking with their corporate campaign, doing their best to make sure we stayed down. *Baruch Hashem*, the manager of the staffing company was having none of it. He had been through the plant himself more than once to collect job descriptions for the positions and he knew the truth. He wasn't intimidated by the union, and Jacobson Staffing stayed with Agri.

These aggressive efforts to undermine our staffing meant that we had to get creative to fill our workforce. Three years earlier, we had opened a small plant near a Native American reservation in Nebraska at their invitation. We asked a number of our employees from there to come to Postville. We also expanded our search as far and wide as we could. We brought in native-born Americans from as far away as Texas, Somali refugees with work permits from Minnesota, and even citizens of the small island nation of Palau, between Guam and the Philippines, which has a treaty under which they are allowed to work in the US.

Our newly raised profile meant that it was open season on Agriprocessors, and the vultures and hyenas were coming out of the woodwork. Among them was a Jewish clergyman, part of an insidious movement claiming to be a version of Orthodox *Yiddishkeit* but which in fact embraces and promotes modern social justice values, going so far as supporting immoral relationships.

At that time, he was still preparing for his "ordination," looking forward to a pastoral career of some sort. He'd already decided it would be in the public eye, with an emphasis on social justice. He was followed by film cameras for over a year as they documented his training and preparations for religious leadership, such as visiting the site of California wildfires. Taking on his fellow Jews in their most difficult moments, under attack and struggling to regain their footing, looked to him and his friends like the perfect opportunity to jump-start their careers.

He joined with some of his "rabbinical" student friends and formed a social justice organization whose first order of business was to issue a public call to boycott Agriprocessors. The Conservative movement had already issued a similar call to their communities, but this new boycott gave our detractors the ability to claim that Orthodox Jews also believed the accusations and were outraged. The group withdrew their call to boycott a few weeks later, after they had milked the moment for what it was worth, but the damage had been done. It made our ability to recover more difficult at a time when not only the company, but the whole region, was beset by difficulties.

The raid and the resulting shutdowns and slowdowns at Agri had been a devastating blow to the whole economic ecosystem. Chicken growers with houses full of chickens suddenly had no place to send them. Cattle sellers saw a solid demand for five hundred heads of cattle a day vanish. Gas stations accustomed to refueling fleets of trucks were faced with quiet pumps and tanks full of gas. Bank loans held by people with stable employment suddenly soured, backed by houses whose values had collapsed overnight. Mom-and-pop retail stores that catered to everyday needs now served a clientele cutting back on expenses, unsure of what the future might bring and when their money might run out.

Millions of dollars pumped into a small rural economy every week were suddenly gone—money whose value was multiplied seven-fold as each recipient spent it at another local business for his own needs.

It wasn't just union hooligans, ambitious clergymen, assorted advocacy groups, and sensationalist media obstructing our efforts to restore Agriprocessors. As we made every effort to recover, conscious of how many people were counting on us, we discovered that this had not been a hit-and-run by the Feds. They stuck around and kept hitting us to ensure we never recovered.

Obviously, money was a big part of the problem. Normally, operating costs are covered by earlier income, but the repeated attacks over the previous few years, coupled with the reduced income caused by the public relations attacks by the union and others, drained whatever reserves we had. When the raid interrupted the flow of business, it crippled the company. We needed a cash infusion if we hoped to ever get back up and running.

We began looking for loans. It's never easy to find loans, especially when you're under attack, but we quickly discovered there was more stacked against us than the standard financial risk assessments. One person who had agreed to lend a large sum of money opened his front door one morning to find FBI agents at his doorstep. "Why are you helping Rubashkin?" they demanded.

"Get off my porch," he responded. "I'll lend money to whomever I want." They left, but obviously didn't consider their visit deterrent enough and he was later subpoenaed to testify before a grand jury.

Others who helped in one way or another received similar treatment.

They were actively undermining our ability to find the money and other resources we needed to carry us through this difficult period—and it wasn't an unintended side effect. The court-appointed trustee brought in seven months later to manage the plant would eventually confide that he'd been told by the prosecutor's office to let the company shut down.

Although the regional economy would suffer terribly if we failed, the state government got in on the action undermining our recovery too, cutting off their nose to spite their face. I got that message outright from Nat Lewin, who met with state officials and told me afterwards, "You won't believe it, but they want you closed down." I also got the message through their actions, which spoke louder than any words.

The state's greatest contribution to the unwarranted destruction was a highly publicized but completely baseless accusation of child labor violations. Some of the employees who'd provided false papers to get hired claimed that not only had they lied about their immigration, they'd also lied about their age and they were actually too young to work. (Not coincidentally, this claim also made them too young to be punished, or be punished severely, and even opened up the possibility of a free visa and eventually, a green card.)

There were thirty-two workers who made that claim, but thirty-two wasn't an impressive enough number. They wanted something astronomical, so they counted each day these people spent at work and multiplied that by the number of restrictions in the law. The law in Iowa allows teenagers to work in certain situations, but it prohibits employing minors to work for longer than specified hours and they can't be exposed to certain dangers like knives or chemicals. Each of these restrictions was counted as an additional charge.

They leveled a record-breaking and sensational 9,311 charges against the company, and against me personally, despite there being absolutely no indication that I had any knowledge at all of their supposedly underage status.

They dramatized these charges by claiming to the press that there were elements of human trafficking, extortion, physical abuse, and forced labor. They never formally made those charges because they would have to back them up, which they couldn't do. It was just designed to contribute to a huge public scandal. (Of course, they couldn't even back up the charges they did make, and I was completely exonerated by the jury of every single charge.)

For close to two critical years, until the trial took place, these accusations were taken at face value by the public, as earnest accusations that would be proven in court, rather than what they actually were; an extra-judicial publicity stunt/character assassination.

The initial announcement earned us a whole new wave of bad press and condemnations. When the media's attention started to wander, the state focused it back again by staging a law enforcement operation at the plant. They ostensibly came in order to pick up some knives as evidence, but they really came in order to pick up some additional press attacking Agriprocessors. Prosecutors manipulating the media as an extra-judicial tactic was something with which I would become very familiar.

Amidst the avalanche of negativity and adversity, we saw the beginnings of our salvation in the response of our fellow Jews. It did take some time. In those first, flailing moments, we felt besieged and alone. It was a personal manifestation of the Gemara's description of the time before Mashiach's arrival. The world had gone mad and there was no one on whom to rely but Hashem Himself. Of course, the Gemara there ends off with the reminder that we can always rely on and place our trust in Hashem.

In time, I realized that this initial isolation was an important gift from Hashem. By teaching us to rely *exclusively* on Him, Hashem gave us a sturdy foundation—the only foundation upon which we could survive what was to come. If we had received immediate support we might have learned to rely, even only partially, on human beings, and that would be a very *weak* foundation, certainly not up to the task.

Baruch Hashem, after a punishing two weeks, the leadership of many *frum* organizations began to stir. The volume of the slander against me was steadily increasing, liberal voices within their own communities and in general society were demanding a redefinition of kashrus, and the prices of kosher meat and poultry were starting to rise.

The Torah obviously forbids condemning someone sight unseen, but the Torah also doesn't consider passive ignorance an excuse for not ruling. They couldn't just abstain and sit on the sidelines. The Torah demands that a judge proactively investigate—*v'darashta v'chakarta heiteiv*, so, led by Rabbi Pesach Lerner of the National Council of Young Israel, they gathered remotely for a conference call meeting.

At this meeting, they heard from numerous people with firsthand knowledge of the situation, including representatives of the plant management and the certifying *rabbanim*. The meeting was informative and persuaded those in attendance that the public perception was far from the truth, but ultimately, they decided it wasn't enough to be able to offer an informed, confident, and full-throated defense.

Rabbi Lerner suggested a fact-finding mission; a visit to Postville to see the plant and meet the workers for themselves. Although it was in the middle of the summer and many of them were spending time with their families, twenty-five rabbis, community leaders, and *frum* media representatives from the US and Canada made the trip.

Like every rabbinical or regulatory representative who visited, they were given free rein to tour the plant and interview the employees, including governmental supervisors and others in supervisory roles. They took their time inspecting the production line, watching the *shechitah* itself, and following the production line through to final labeling and boxing. They interviewed a number of people at different levels of the hierarchy in the plant itself, as well as people around town.

Having seen everything firsthand, they finally felt equipped to set the record straight: we ran a clean, modern plant complying with relevant rules and regulations. The employees worked hard, but they were happy with their arrangements and had good things to say about their jobs and about the people they worked for.

Among the delegation was Rabbi Pinchos Lipschutz, founding editor and publisher of the *Yated Ne'eman* newspaper, a discerning individual with a sensitive *neshamah*. Along with the rest of the group, he went on to take the tour of the plant and talk with the employees and supervisors, but he later told me that it was at the moment he met my father—who'd greeted the delegation as they alighted from the coach bus upon their arrival in Postville—that he realized this was nothing more than a vicious blood libel of upstanding, righteous fellow Jews and, by extension, an attack on all Jews.

An influential publisher and gifted writer, he helped his readers see what he saw. As the attacks intensified over the coming years, Reb Pinchos matched and surpassed them in the intensity of his *ahavas Yisrael* and dedication to setting the record straight. Although this subjected him to criticism from certain quarters, he did the right thing with characteristic self-sacrifice.

Rabbi Pinchos Lipshutz in my Postville home.

I cannot overstate the importance of his involvement. Aside from the impact of this tremendous *ahavas Yisrael* where it really counts, in the Heavenly Court, the effect in earthly terms was enormous. The prosecutors had made every effort to paint me as a monster, successfully isolating me from public and political support. By loudly and publicly setting the record straight, Reb Pinchos and the *Yated* made it acceptable to support me. In a very real way, he has a share in every act of support that followed.

His outspoken support was unflagging, throughout the trial and beyond sentencing. Along with his writers and reporters, among whom Debbie Maimon deserves special mention and gratitude, he kept the spotlight on the injustice well after any case would have naturally faded from the headlines—and that was only in his role as a writer and a publisher.

As an individual, as a caring Jew, he went even further. Together with other *askanim*, he formed a committee which they named the Klal Yisrael

Fund, and jumped in to help organize the unity rallies and other fundraising efforts—going so far as to offer his own address as the destination for mail-in donations. As part of the committee, he helped vet, hire, and advise the lawyers presenting the case in court. He became a close and cherished friend and we spent countless hours (mostly in fifteen-minute increments) in conversation, bonding over *divrei Torah*, inspiration, and discussion of the case.

Getting Personal

In the months following the raid, I began receiving "target letters" informing me that I was the target of an investigation. The terminology is very telling.

You would expect someone who's being investigated to be described as the *subject* of the investigation: Investigators are digging and sifting through information surrounding an incident to determine if wrongdoing was committed, and, if so, by whom.

Instead, they're described as the *target* because that's not what happens at all. The "investigators" have already decided who it is they want to pursue and they look for information that helps them achieve that. They incentivize others to blame that person. They even encourage people who clearly implicated their own misbehavior to shift the blame to the person they've targeted.

It was a twisted version of the famous *mashal*: A person once came across a target range in which every target had an arrow dead center; a perfect bullseye. As he stood there, admiring the marksmanship, the archer returned to the range, so he decided to stay and watch this master at work.

To his surprise, the archer stood at his mark and just shot wildly toward the trees, emptying his quiver haphazardly. He then picked up a small jar of paint, walked over to the small number of trees his arrows had hit and painted a target perfectly centered on each arrow—bullseye!

It goes without saying that the observer was greatly disappointed. Painting a bullseye around your arrow is not marksmanship. In the same way, obviously, painting evidence around your target is not an investigation.

I hired a lawyer and he immediately reached out to the prosecutors to offer appropriate cooperation and discuss any agreements that could be reached, as is usually done in such cases. I vividly remember his call to me after he'd interacted with them for the first time. He had been a federal prosecutor himself before going into private practice, so he knew how these things were normally handled, yet he was thoroughly taken aback by their response, both in substance and tone. Over the ensuing months he reached out a number of times and was repeatedly rebuffed.

The only conclusion he could draw was that they didn't want to work with me toward some *other* goal because I *was* their goal—all they wanted was to throw me into prison. This was a frightening thought and, at first, my emotions threatened to get the best of me.

I saw that processing this development from the worldly perspective would be destructive. I needed to find out how the Torah teaches a Yid to properly process and address such circumstances, and I reached for the *Sha'ar Habitachon* and the *Tanya*. I spent as much time as I could in study and reflection, applying their teachings to my situation. I found myself in a ferocious storm and my own senses were dragging me down, so I turned to the Divine instruments to guide me through safely, as I'd learned from the pilot in Iowa.

Before formally charging an American citizen and dragging him to court, prosecutors are required to gather a group of citizens to act as a "grand jury." The prosecutors present their side of the story to this jury, showing documents and calling witnesses. If the grand jury is persuaded that there's some substance to the allegations, they sign off on an official indictment.

As their interactions with my lawyer showed, the prosecutors had clearly worked out who their target was, but they hadn't quite worked out what their actual allegations were. During the raid, they had carted away a truckload of paperwork from the office and they had collected electronic data as well. They were all set for a fishing expedition, trawling through their haul for things they could use in their indictments.

Almost half a year after the raid, they arrested two of the HR managers and accused them of crimes related to harboring illegal immigrants. I wasn't the subject of that indictment, but I was definitely the target. Both were threatened with years in prison, but allowed a plea deal resulting in only probation in return for cooperation. They were after bigger fish, and the little fish were just needed for building the case.

A little over a month after those little fish were scooped up, I got a call from the office. "Where are you? There are officers at the plant looking for you." I was on my way home at the time. Recent interactions gave me reason to believe that they were there to take me in and there was no telling when I would be home again. I decided against heading back to the office to meet them, and instead let them know they could find me at home.

They already had a vehicle posted near my house. I passed it as I pulled onto my street. I hurried inside and told my wife what was about to happen. This was a moment for *emunah* and *bitachon* and she was equal to the task. She took the news with her characteristic strength and calm, and focused on practical steps that we needed to take next.

As we spoke, three or four vehicles sped up our street and pulled up to the house. Some officers came in and informed me that I'd been formally charged and I was under arrest. My wife reassured me that Hashem would help and they would do whatever was necessary to get me released on bail so I could return home. I was led out of my house in front of my wife and small children, handcuffed and shackled, and placed in the back of their vehicle.

They brought me straight to the courthouse, where I immediately entered a plea of not guilty and we turned to the question of bail. Although there was only a single charge against me—that of harboring illegal immigrants—they demanded the outrageous sum of one million dollars for bail. My wife had been working on finding resources since they'd led me away, and she'd already found a cousin in New York who was willing to put his home on the line as a bail guarantee.

They also demanded that I relinquish my passport and agree to wear an ankle tracker.

Baruch Hashem, I was able to return that very night. My family and friends had feared the worst and were overjoyed at my quick return. Recognizing to Whom we owed thanks for this kindness, we gathered in the *shtetl* shul for a *seudas hoda'ah* organized by the community to praise and give thanks to Hashem.

This innocent expression of gratitude was used by our enemies to increase the *sinas Yisrael* and *chillul Hashem*. They reached out to news outlets and portrayed our happiness as arrogant triumph, as if we were mocking the rule of law.

I'd been "granted" a right promised to every American citizen, under pretty onerous conditions, and I was entitled to a presumption of innocence, but they took the opportunity to demonize me and paint me as a contemptuous Jew. Throughout our ordeal, this continued to be the chosen role of the media, to our pain and dismay.

One particular individual, a small, bitter man, was a constant source of twisted, poisonous portrayals. He presented himself to the world and to the media as a citizen journalist, but the concealed truth is that he was just a hateful man with a petty personal grudge related to a business matter.

In 2004, he shifted his focus to mudslinging. An unrelated issue provoked him into conflict with Chabad Lubavitch and he started a blog to vent his anger. Finding that he had a gift for agitating and an audience for slander, he expanded his site into a broader assault against Chabad and eventually aimed his venom at *frum* people and institutions more generally. His vicious little online tabloid earned him a vocal following of assorted anti-religious and antisemitic types and, unfortunately, a sizable silent readership among the broader public, driven by morbid curiosity.

As he was just settling into his new vocation, PETA launched a sensational attack on his two prime enemies—Torah *Yiddishkeit* and Chabad chassidim— by way of the Rubashkins. He dedicated himself to throwing mud and stirring up trouble during that episode. The public interest in the PETA attack brought readers, and eventually journalists, to his site.

He never let up on his attacks, and when the union and its various allies began smearing and criticizing us, he gleefully joined in, amplifying and embellishing the attacks and allegations. His twisted framing of the news of the day influenced others in the media, and he actively reached out to them with his preferred take. He never disclosed his personal history with us and when he was quoted in articles it was always as a citizen journalist, never as a vindictive personal enemy with a grudge.

Journalists weren't the only ones reading and repeating his distortions. In fact, those who interacted with the prosecutors reported that the prosecutors checked his site daily and read his distortions and fabrications religiously.

As a result of his efforts and the efforts of others, our private and justified feelings of gratitude to Hashem over my release on bail were publicized and cast in a negative light in the local area and was even mentioned that way in the *New York Times*.

These terrible portrayals by this man and the more traditional "journalists" weren't just unpleasant and hurtful. They were part of a feedback loop which made the next article sound more credible, and they were actually used by the government as proof in various court filings.

My arrest threw our personal financial straits into sharp relief. Until then, the scramble for sorely needed funds had focused on saving the company, obviously a benefit for the family, but also something important to Klal Yisrael.

The charges against me personally were the start of a long and costly journey, just when our own funds and those of everyone we knew had been strained to the breaking point. We simply had no money to hire the lawyers I would need to defend myself. Due to the prosecutors' extended campaign against the company after the raid, I'd been disarmed before they had even formally declared war. I don't think that was accidental.

My daughter, Roza Hindy Weiss, threw herself at the problem. She was determined not to let her father face the fight of his life unarmed and she set out to collect whatever money she could. She had no contacts or connections, no grand plan or strategies. She just made her way to Jewish neighborhoods and went door to door.

Her whole life, she'd been blessed to be the one opening the door to help people in need—now she was the one knocking and asking for help. Even people who got their news from honest and empathetic Jewish sources didn't understand the true scope of the crisis and hadn't realized the devastation it had brought to our family or the even greater threat we now faced. Many assumed that even if the company was foundering, we must have a personal fortune squirreled away somewhere and we'd be fine.

Night after night, Roza Hindy went out, putting into words the most painful aspects of what we were living through, the disaster that had struck, and the personal tragedy that we could only hope to avert with their help. It was her dedication and self-sacrifice that enabled us to fight back and survive until the *askanim* and established organizations took notice and got involved.

It was actually during this time that she met Yerachmiel Simmons, an accomplished lawyer and an *askan* who played a pivotal role in the case of the Spinka Rebbe and later spearheaded efforts to protect *bris milah* when it came under attack in New York. Moved by her story, he joined Reb Pinchos Lipschutz as an active *askan* in the case and he became an important advisor on the complex legal decisions throughout.

This also marked my daughter's assumption of the difficult task of coordinating between all the various groups working to defend me and, later on, to extricate me from a place called prison. She was supported in her tireless efforts by her husband, Yaakov Weiss, who also threw himself into the task with diligence. He went on to become a staunch and energetic champion of

Jewish inmates nation-wide and helped many of them individually, in addition to his tremendous achievements in *askanus* that impacted them all as a group.

The prosecutors had issued a formal indictment and charged me with something, but they weren't finished. They continued trawling through their trove of data and leaning on smaller fish, reassembling the grand jury an extraordinary total of seven times to add or expand charges as they tried to decide what exactly it was that they had targeted me for.

When all was said and done, they came up with a whopping seventy-two immigration charges for the presence of the undocumented workers and eighty-six financial charges that recast as bank fraud (and other financial misdeeds) things such as handshake business arrangements, a complex structure of interlinked companies, and disorganized accounting. And then, scraping the bottom of the barrel, they even managed to cook up twenty charges for violating an order of the Secretary of Agriculture for instances of paying cattle suppliers more than twenty-four hours after processing. That law, passed in 1921 under the name Packers and Stockyards Act, had never before been used in a criminal charge. A single violation could carry up to a five-year penalty, so those charges represented a combined consecutive total of a hundred years in prison.

It's worth noting that they weren't claiming suppliers weren't paid, only that they were paid late—delays ranging from two to eleven days. When the time came to show damages at sentencing, the only thing they could come up with was one supplier which claimed damages of $3,600—interest they had to pay on loans—for the simple reason that their checks had been held up by bankruptcy red tape for six to seven months before they were paid in full. To provide an example for context, a case in Northern Iowa in which half a million dollars were not paid *at all* was handled as a strictly civil matter and no criminal charges were filed.

The exaggerated number of charges was achieved in large part by applying different laws to the same underlying actions, and then again for each instance of those actions. This was clearly designed to overwhelm the general public—also known as the jury pool—by sheer volume. The formal announcements were also parceled out slowly over time, increasing their impact.

The prosecutors' extra-judicial PR strategy was largely successful, as the jury selection would show.

CHAPTER FOUR

Under Arrest

Dubuque County Jail

FRIDAY MORNING, NOVEMBER 14, 2008, AT AROUND 7:00 A.M., WE AWOKE to pounding on the door. My daughter Mushka, eighteen years old at the time, went to see who was knocking so early in the morning.

It was a team of federal officers. Flashing a warrant, they barged into the house and on into my bedroom. Mushka was told to stay in the kitchen with the other children. To spare them the trauma of seeing and hearing what was about to unfold, she instead dressed them quickly and took them to school.

They ousted me out of bed. "You're under arrest! Get dressed quickly and you'll be escorted to the car!" Knowing that even in the best-case scenario I'd be detained for many hours until my release could be arranged, I asked for permission to *daven* in *tallis* and *tefillin* before they took me away—a request which they granted. I *davened* in a corner while they began turning over the house, looking for something they could use to hurt me. When I finished, I was handcuffed and led to one of their cars to be taken to the county jail.

CREDIT: DES MOINES REGISTER

My wife was not allowed to follow their car. She waited until they left, then headed to the county jail to see about bailing me out, leaving Mushka to prepare for Shabbos and care for the kids.

Their search continued even after my wife left. Rooting through my closet, they found a bag on a high shelf which held various items out of the reach of the kids. In the bag was a travel pouch with cash in it from my recent trip to Canada, a small pouch with silver coins used for *machatzis hashekel*, cash on hand for family expenses, and my family's important documents such as birth certificates, social security cards, and passports.

I was taken to the federal courthouse in Cedar Rapids, where they requested and received the judge's permission to delay my release on bail until a hearing could be held. The local jailhouse was still damaged from the recent floods, so they transferred me to the Dubuque County Jail. By the time we arrived there, it was only a few hours before Shabbos. Upon arrival, they processed my paperwork and made me change into a bright orange jumpsuit, part of the systemic degradation designed to make a free citizen docile.

I was led into a communal cell which was used for higher-profile prisoners and those with physical disabilities. It had three two-person sleeping areas, separated from each other by thin internal walls. They had expanded the occupancy to seven by placing a mattress on the shared space in the center which was also used for meals.

Each sleeping area had two steel shelves for sleeping, one above the other, each with a thin mat. I was assigned the bottom shelf in one of the sections. The top shelf was already occupied by a man who had been a judge. The neighboring section was occupied by another judge in trouble with the law and an African-American fellow who was physically handicapped.

After they'd given me time to settle in, I was taken to meet the warden. He took his responsibility to safeguard prisoners' constitutional rights very seriously and asked me to list my religious needs. I'd never been in a situation like this and I didn't really know what I needed to request. I thought quickly, trying to anticipate the issues that might come up.

I asked for four things: To be allowed to wear my yarmulke and *tzitzis*, to be allowed to *daven* daily with my *tallis* and *tefillin*, to be given water that wasn't from the bathroom to wash my hands, and to be given proper kosher food. *Baruch Hashem*, the warden graciously agreed to all four.

All the time I was in Dubuque, I was allowed to wear my yarmulke and *tzitzis* without any issues. I was grateful at the time, but only learned to really appreciate it when the same "concession" in other facilities was only obtained with sweat and tears, and in one case, blood.

For the daily *davening*, he instructed the guards to take me from the cell every morning to a small room. There, I was given my *tallis* and *tefillin* and allowed some privacy to *daven*—prison-style privacy, monitored by a one-way mirror. Initially, they limited my time in this small locked room to forty-five minutes, but they eventually lifted that restriction and I was told to just let them know when I was finished. This enabled me to stay in the room and *daven* for hours at a time. On Shabbos, I would *daven* there from seven in the morning until noon. I drew tremendous strength from these hours spent in *tefillah*.

To accommodate my kosher needs, he had food with a few different kosher certifications brought in and asked me which of them were acceptable to me. *Baruch Hashem*, he agreed to use the *hashgachos* that I indicated were acceptable.

Arranging the water for washing was a bit trickier. The only sinks accessible to prisoners were in the bathroom. To meet my religious needs, the warden took an unprecedented step and instructed the guards to take me into the staff locker room, which had the only sink in the facility not in a bathroom. It's difficult to convey the degree to which bringing a prisoner into the guards' locker room violated the rigid hierarchy in a place called jail and I considered this nothing short of a miracle.

A few words on terminology: Instead of simply saying jail or prison, I usually say, "a place called jail/prison." There's a reason for that. While it was simply factual to say that I was in jail or prison, in the sense that I was physically in those locations, there is another meaning conveyed by those phrases which I wanted to firmly reject: Saying that someone is "in prison" is the same as saying they are imprisoned. The warden and the guards are in the same physical location, but you would never describe them as "in prison" because they're not imprisoned. Well, neither was I.

I had been "in-prisoned," but I was emphatically not *imprisoned*. If I couldn't leave my location it wasn't because I was under the control of my so-called jailers. I was where I was because *Hashem* wanted me there and as soon as His purpose was fulfilled, I would leave—without regard to the threats or wishes of those who thought they controlled my fate. I made sure to remind myself of that fact by never describing myself as being in prison. Every time I used that slightly clumsy phrase, I was reminding myself, my family, and my friends of the true nature of my situation.

I also just used the term "miracle" to describe the authorization to use the staff locker room. When I describe this—or other non-supernatural events—as miracles, I sometimes get quizzical looks, but they clearly qualify!

A miracle is any occurrence in which we see Hashem's hand clearly—it doesn't necessarily have to be supernatural to be a miracle. My story was marked by many occurrences that, although not strictly supernatural, were so improbable that only the most stubbornly and willfully blind could fail to see Hashem's direct involvement.

With these four requests, I was successful in safeguarding my connection to Hashem, which our *chachamim* remind us cannot be obstructed even by barriers (or bars) of steel.

My connection to my family was a different story.

Visitors younger than eighteen years old were barred outright, which meant that my younger children, the ones most in need of reassurance and some contact with their father, were entirely excluded. For those who were allowed to visit, visitation was limited to only two twenty-five-minute visits a week.

Forget physical contact, like a hug or a kiss—I wasn't even brought into the same room as my visitors. They would be brought into a room equipped with a closed-circuit video screen. In the corner of the common area of the communal cell, there was a corresponding screen, visible to everyone in the cell, and the sounds of the conversation were broadcast on the speaker for everyone to hear. That was the "visit."

Aside for those fifty minutes a week, the only way to be in contact with my loved ones, or anyone else, was by using the phone. Prisons, where people are held *after* sentencing, heavily curtail phone use, but that was not the case in a place called jail, which is typically a short-term holding facility for those awaiting trial. There were certain hours that the phones were available, and each phone call was limited to fifteen minutes, but there were no other restrictions. If no one else was waiting for the phone, you could just call again.

As a matter of fact, the authorities *want* the person to talk as much as possible. They listen in on every call and use the information to their advantage, both in and out of the courtroom. I learned this the hard way.

Shortly after my arrival, I reached out to some friends and acquaintances, one of whom was a former lawyer of mine. The content of our discussions was important to me, but legally innocuous. There was some discussion of what I was going through on a personal level and reassurances from them that they would testify on my behalf if called upon.

Calls could be made "collect" or the recipient of the call could fund a "call account" which would pay for calls to them. These friends all put money into accounts so I could call them back, but, to my surprise, when I tried to call again a few days later, none of them would accept the call.

It was only after the trial that one of them filled me in. Days after taking that first phone call, he'd been visited by FBI agents. They had noted his connection to me and his willingness to testify, presumably by monitoring my calls. Their visit and the substance of their "conversation" with him left the distinct impression that talking to me was dangerous for him. Frightened, he reached out to his own lawyer, who advised him to cut ties, which he did. It was something he later regretted and apologized for. I found that others who'd mysteriously cut me off had also had similar experiences.

Another way to stay in contact with family and friends was through the mail. Among the packages I received during my stint in Dubuque was one the significance of which would be impossible to overstate. My son-in-law, Yaakov Weiss, sent me a translated pocket edition of the *Chovos Halevavos*, which includes the *Sha'ar Habitachon*—the "*Shulchan Aruch*" on the subject of *bitachon*. I had learned it in the past, but my circumstances prompted me to a more in-depth and practical study of this powerful *sefer*. I learned it every day, going through the whole thing again and again as I absorbed its message and learned how to apply it to my difficult situation.

Yaakov worked tirelessly on my behalf in the ensuing years. He stopped everything in his life and threw himself into every aspect of my case with tenacity and passion—from legal strategy to fundraising, from public relations to political efforts. His dedication was that of a son, not just a son-in-law, and Hashem blessed many of his initiatives with success. I will always be grateful to my dear son-in-law for everything he did, and it all started with sending me the *Chovos Halevavos*. Everything he went on to do was creating a natural means through which the salvation could come—it was studying the *Chovos Halevavos* he sent me that brought the salvation itself.

The Founding Fathers of the United States, all too familiar with the excesses of those in power and their abuses of law enforcement processes, wrote into the US Constitution that "excessive bail shall not be required" of those awaiting trial.

Not only does every citizen, presumed innocent before a trial, have the right to bail, the government is explicitly forbidden from demanding a larger security than is just and appropriate. There are only two reasons to lock a person up before their trial—if they're a danger to others or if there are no measures that will ensure the person doesn't flee. There was never a suggestion that I was a danger to others, which meant the only obstacle would be coming up with an arrangement that ensured I would stick around.

As soon as I was arrested, my family, friends, and community began preparing a financial security that would exceed any conceivable demand the prosecutors or judge might make at the as-yet-unscheduled bail hearing. They were short on cash, obviously, but a respectable amount was mustered from Jews eager to help with *pidyon shvuyim*. This was supplemented by family and friends who were willing to offer the equity they held in their homes as collateral. All told, the value of the bond offered exceeded *three million dollars*.

They even went so far as contacting a security firm they could hire to monitor me personally at all times—in addition to the digital tracking via ankle monitor that the court had agreed to after the first arrest. This was all wildly excessive, but we'd seen that they were being unreasonable and trying to use legal machinations to undermine my ability to prepare for the trial. It was critical that I be returned home to prepare a proper defense, not to mention that every moment in county jail was a torment for both body and soul.

With the financial support of Klal Yisrael, they also arranged for the best possible legal representation at the upcoming hearing. Baruch Weiss, an expert in these matters, based in Washington, DC, was hired and made the trip to the Midwest to provide legal firepower.

It was close to a week of unjustified incarceration before I got my day in court. I was brought back to the federal courthouse in Cedar Rapids for the bail hearing, presided over by a magistrate judge. Although we had expected the prosecution to make wild demands, no one could ever have anticipated the position they actually took. Instead of putting bail out of reach with outlandish or excessive conditions, the prosecutors argued that no conditions *at all* would be sufficient.

The way they saw it, I was not an American citizen—not fully, anyway. Sure, I'd been born in Boro Park, which is in Brooklyn, New York, USA. I didn't hold a passport or citizenship or even have any real estate or business holdings in any other country, but I was Jewish, you see.

As a Jew, the prosecutors argued, I'm not like other citizens of the United States. Jews can travel to Israel and receive citizenship there under Israel's "Law of Return." Even without any ties there or any indication of interest in going there, this made me, quote, "a *de facto* dual citizen" and therefore not eligible for bail.

They bolstered this with other arguments, including the claim that I was likely to flee the country. This was obviously laughable—I'd only recently traveled out of the country to visit a sick friend, and possibly also secure funding for Agriprocessors, and I returned to face their witch hunt. They were insisting that I would use the opportunity to flee, when I'd already successfully crossed the border to Canada, fully aware of my situation due to their numerous and detailed target letters, yet here I was.

Their only counter to that incontestable fact was proof that I owned a travel pouch, the presence of cash in the house (just enough to cover the bills for a family our size for a few months in uncertain times), an assortment of coins worth a couple hundred dollars, and important family documents they considered suspiciously out of place, something for which we readily provided a reasonable alternate explanation.

Even if the judge sided with them that this weak collection of evidence proved that I wanted to flee—despite my recent return—the sheer size of the collateral and the number of people I would have to betray and hurt by forfeiting the security was surely strong enough to outweigh any temptation to flee. Add to that a guard shadowing me and an ankle bracelet, and there was absolutely no reasonable argument to jail an American citizen before his day in court.

The judge issued his ruling the next day. Not only did he side with the prosecutor to deny me bail under any circumstances, he explicitly based his ruling in part on their argument that I am (and by extension ruling that all Jews are) a *de facto* dual citizen of a foreign country and therefore a higher flight risk than non-Jewish citizens.

Jewish organizations raised the alarm over this aspect of the ruling and it garnered some mention in the national media, but this had no immediate effect on my situation and I was returned to a place called jail until the trial would be held.

Aside from the personal unpleasantness of incarceration in a county jail, it was an impossible place to properly prepare my defense against their scheme to bury me alive in the federal prison system. We couldn't allow this denial of bail to stand. My lawyers filed the appropriate appeals, while I *davened* that I be returned to my family. Facing this setback, I strengthened my trust in Hashem that, despite appearance, I would very soon put this whole ordeal behind me.

I was returned to the communal cell for the time being. I met many people during my *nisayon* that I would not otherwise have met. Most were rough characters with no interest in discussion, but there were also a few educated, intellectual people. The other occupant of my sleeping section was one such person, a well-educated fellow with a curious mind. Now that my bail hearing was behind me, he figured I'd be around for a while and tried to strike up a friendship.

Initially, he made small talk, which I politely returned, but fairly quickly he turned the discussion to his Bible, which he studied daily and in which he was pretty well-versed. His religious teachers had encouraged him to think for himself and, as this was his first encounter with a religious Jew versed in the Torah, *l'havdil*, he wanted to discuss his thoughts and his questions with me.

I was usually happy to talk with inmates about life or religion in the hope that I would be able to teach them something about Hashem—His existence, His oneness, and His commandments—but with guys as fervently religious as he seemed to be, my first instinct was to decline. I told him we should probably avoid the topic. He had very specific ideas about religion that he would want to bring up and if my responses would not be to his liking… I didn't know him personally, but if the past two-thousand-odd years were anything to go by, it would probably end badly. I wasn't interested in any visits to the infirmary.

He assured and reassured me that he was open-minded and would be okay with anything I might say, and he was eager to hear my thoughts. In the end, I relented. We had many discussions during my time there, both on abstract and practical subjects.

We spoke about the existence of Hashem and of His unity. We spoke about the creation of the world from nothing and about the concept of *ein od milvado*, there is nothing but Hashem. We also spoke about how one can believe Hashem is good and kind, all powerful, and the only One with power over our lives when there is pain and evil in the world. This wasn't merely an academic issue in our situation.

He was a good listener and very quickly grasped the subjects we discussed, although I noticed that, like all the judges I'd met before and have met since, he wasn't very interested in delving beneath the surface.

One thing that came up early and often was our very different perceptions of Hashem. He was in jail and had been for a while and he was bitter. The worst part of the day, he told me, was waking up. "You open your eyes, realize that you're in hell, and you just want to shut your eyes again and be someplace else." It wasn't just hyperbole. I'd noticed that he was fairly active during the day, but was always very slow to wake up and get the day started. "G-d is vengeful," he would often grumble.

I really love Hashem and didn't like hearing that, so I'd always say something in response, firmly maintaining that Hashem is merciful and kind. He'd usually quote some verse or the other to show that he was right. No matter what he quoted, my first response was always with the way Hashem revealed Himself to Moshe Rabbeinu when Moshe merited a uniquely close perception of Hashem: *"Hashem, Hashem, benevolent G-d, Who is compassionate and gracious, slow to anger and abundant in loving-kindness and truth…"*

Obviously, he wouldn't let me get away that easily and would open his Bible to show me proofs to his position. "Aha! Sholom, see what it says here!" or "Look! Read here!" He would hold out his book and ask me to explain a section or sentence. I didn't want to look into his book, which is *avodah zarah* and also full of mistranslations. Instead, I would ask him where he was reading, look it up in my Chumash, and read and translate that portion out loud. On this issue, and many others that he raised, an accurate and honest translation was all it took to realize that there was really no question or issue at all.

After this—what seemed to him a serious question simply evaporating with proper translation of the original—repeated itself a number of times, I asked my family to send a properly translated Chumash. They sent a very good one called the Gutnick Chumash and I showed it to him. He took it and would sit awake for hours, deep into the night, his book on one side and, *l'havdil*, the Chumash on the other, carefully reading each *pasuk* and comparing the translations.

One day I overheard him on the phone with his son, Jacob. "Jacob," he said, "if you want to know the real story of your namesake, go online, and buy yourself a Gutnick Chumash!"

When he got off the phone, he turned around and saw me sitting there. There was no privacy on the phones and he knew the whole cell had heard his call, so when he looked at me, I asked him directly, "What was that all about?"

"You know the story of Jacob and Esau?" he asked me.

"Of course!" I said. "Why?"

"I studied that story last night. In your translation the story is very benign— it's no big deal. Jacob buys the rights of the first-born from Esau and that's it. The way my guys translated it, it's a totally different story! They make Jacob look like a real sneaky Jew, a devious trickster. I wanted my son to know he could be proud to carry that name."

He really valued our time together. My sister Chayala had heard about him from my emails and phone calls home. When I was transferred out and he lost that human connection, my sister felt bad and sent a letter with some words of encouragement to this suffering individual. He wrote back, expressing great appreciation for her letter. Among the other things he wrote was that he cherished the time we'd spent together. "If I had to end up here just to meet your brother, I think it was worth it."

Although our friendly conversations and interactions continued until I was released on bail, I ended up moving to a different sleeping section in order to help another inmate.

The black handicapped fellow in the next sleeping section was having an issue. His sleeping shelf was near a drafty window. We were having a typical Midwest winter and nightly temperatures often went below zero. He couldn't sleep and complained bitterly about the cold, but the others totally ignored him. His request for an extra jail-issued blanket was also denied.

I couldn't just watch the guy suffer. I slept fully clothed anyway, for *tznius* reasons, and I figured I could handle the cold better than him, so I offered to change places. Thrilled with the offer, he asked for and received permission from the guards and we swapped. The cold was not as easy to tolerate as I had expected but I was happy I had made the switch, warmed by the knowledge that my actions had brought about a *kiddush Hashem*.

Chanukah Behind Bars

Chanukah was fast approaching. While I fully expected a miraculous release, Torah demanded that I make arrangements to do the mitzvah.

I'd long been acquainted with the work of the Aleph Institute, a wonderful

Jewish organization dedicated to helping men and women in prisons and in the US military. Among other things, they help *Yidden* with their religious needs, which are often not granted easily.

Rabbi Mendy Katz, Aleph's director of prison outreach, was someone we came to know very well. He went above and beyond the call of duty to ensure I was able to connect to Hashem through His Torah and mitzvos. Throughout my ordeal, I was surrounded by reminders of his *ahavas Yisrael* in the many mitzvos he helped me fulfill, and I will always be grateful to Aleph and to Mendy himself. I have to also mention the Chabad *shliach* to Iowa City, Rabbi Blesofsky, who helped with these matters and visited me a number of times while I was in Cedar Rapids, which gave me a lot of *chizuk*.

I asked my family to contact Aleph and have them advocate on my behalf in this instance. Specifically, I requested that they get permission for me to light the menorah with olive oil, which is the preferred way to light and how I've always performed the mitzvah.

It didn't take long to hear back. Aleph was willing to do whatever it took, but they foresaw a battle. I'd be very fortunate, they said, to even receive permission to light the menorah at all, for which they could lobby based on precedent and policy at other jails and prisons. They had little hope I'd be permitted to light with olive oil, which had never before been allowed in places of incarceration, but they were still willing to fight for it.

They reported back a few days later that even lighting candles would not be allowed. The warden, who'd been very accommodating when it came to my religious needs, was deferring in this case to the fire marshal, who rejected the request.

I wasn't willing to give up on fulfilling the mitzvah. I suspected that the warden was envisioning something very different than what a menorah actually is, so I asked Aleph to send Rabbi Kalmanson, a Chabad *shliach* in the Midwest who was also a chaplain, to meet with the warden. He could show the warden the pre-filled olive oil cups and demonstrate that the size of the flame in question is not a real fire hazard, especially since it would be monitored at all times.

Baruch Hashem, this approach was blessed with success and the warden reversed his decision—not only about the menorah in general, but about the olive oil as well. He informed Aleph about his decision, adding that he'd identified a fireproof room in which I could light. Aleph was happy to relay the news. I was overjoyed and looked forward to Chanukah with the anticipation of fulfilling its mitzvos properly even under these difficult circumstances.

The Midrash tells us about the obstacles Avraham Avinu and Yitzchak encountered on their journey to the *Akeidah*. As they traveled, the Satan placed a river in their path. There was no way to safely cross the river and fulfill Hashem's direct commandment, but instead of concluding that the mitzvah was impossible, Avraham Avinu concluded that the *river* was impossible.

Avraham and Yitzchak ignored the dangerous-looking river and walked forward, as if unopposed. The waters swelled and threatened to drown them, but they persisted—and the river suddenly vanished as if it had never been there at all.

We often relive this experience, faced with obstacles to doing a mitzvah. It's up to us to react the way our Forefathers did, recognizing that any resistance to a mitzvah is only a test, a moment of truth. Will we be discouraged by fear or discomfort and abandon or compromise on the fulfillment of the mitzvah or will we fix our sights on the mitzvah and push through?

Now that I'd pushed through, the truth was revealed. The initial resistance to the proper lighting of the menorah was not real. It was a scenario contrived by Hashem to test my reaction, and with a little effort and persistence, the "river" vanished.

As it turned out, this was only the first river I would have to cross to do this mitzvah correctly that year.

The first night of Chanukah finally arrived and I was eagerly looking forward to lighting the menorah. An hour and a half before the designated time, the door to the cell opened unexpectedly. A guard came in with bad news. The warden had left the jail for holiday vacation (it was December 21st) and had forgotten to give them the menorah and oil cups, which were in his now-locked office.

I asked if the warden could be contacted and asked to return and open his office. The very idea was so preposterous that their only response was to burst out laughing. The difference in position between warden and inmate is so vast that it would be like calling the President back to the Oval Office because an intern might have dropped his keys there.

This was a real misfortune, so, like any Yid in a bad spot, I turned to Hashem and *davened* that He help me in this time of need. At the same time, I was grateful to Hashem for this relatively early notification, which gave me time to do something to address the situation. I called my family to tell them what had happened and see if there was something that could be done from the outside to channel Hashem's imminent salvation.

Until today, I don't know what channels were made or if Hashem just resolved this one without our involvement. Not much time passed, and the guard returned with good news. The warden had returned to take the menorah out of his office and I'd be able to fulfill the mitzvah after all. The guards were all astonished and impressed—it was a real *kiddush Hashem*.

Sure enough, a few minutes later, two men came and took me out of the cell. One was dressed in a very sharp uniform, clearly a man of rank in the jail. The other wore the simple uniform of a regular prison guard. I followed them through a maze of hallways until we reached a large black steel door.

The door opened with the loud clanging characteristic of prison doors and we entered a large cell. The floor and walls were cement and there were no windows. Attached to each wall were benches, enough seating for fifty people. There was a low, L-shaped partition in the corner of the room. The guard walked over, placed the menorah on this partition with a mock flourish, and said, "Go ahead, do your thing!"

I approached the menorah with great joy and prepared to fulfill the holy mitzvah. Chanukah is a time of miracles and illumination. Lighting the menorah would both metaphorically and literally bring the light and warmth of *kedushah* into this cold and dark place. I was grateful to Hashem that I would merit not only to fulfill the mitzvah in its basic form, but to continue my lifelong *hiddur* to light with olive oil.

I placed a single pre-filled oil cup into the menorah and picked up the beeswax *shamash* and the matches. As I was about to strike a match, I glanced down. It took a second to register what I was looking at. I couldn't believe my eyes. There was a toilet behind the partition! I had been so caught up in my excitement that I didn't realize the obvious purpose of the partition. Of course, they would have a toilet in this cell, as they do in every cell, and they had placed it behind this waist-high partition.

Could I possibly recite a *brachah* with Hashem's holy name and light the menorah on the partition of a toilet?! I dismissed the intellectual gymnastics that sprang to my mind unbidden. Even if there was a *heter*, a way to excuse that decision under the circumstances, I was preparing to do a mitzvah and connect with Hashem. This was not a place where holiness can dwell!

I turned to the guard, who was standing there watching my every move and said, gently indignant, "I can't light the candles *here!*"

He looked puzzled. "Why not?"

"I am about to fulfill G-d's commandment. I need to say a blessing before I do so. Do you think it's respectful to say G-d's holy name in front of a toilet?!"

He didn't immediately respond, but I could see that he understood and possibly even agreed, so I powered on. "Listen, these are holy lights, lights that proclaim and publicize the miracles G-d performed for His people. Do you want me to light these holy lights to shine on a toilet? To proclaim the miracle over a toilet? That would be beyond disrespectful."

He could have easily said, "Rubashkin, you're wearing this bright orange jumpsuit because you're a prisoner. You'll do what we tell you to do!" But he didn't. He simply asked, "Well, what should I do about it?"

Since he asked, I offered a suggestion: "Look, I'm taken every day to pray and to eat my kosher meals in a small side room. Why don't you allow me to light the menorah there? I'll sit near the candles and ensure there's no fire hazard."

His initial reaction was to dismiss the idea. He had his own orders, and due to the legal holiday, there was no one in the office who could sign off on a change. He didn't want to make the call himself. I continued pressing, and he turned to the other guard for his opinion. I said a silent *tefillah* to Hashem that their hearts be opened, although they had nothing to gain and something to lose by taking the initiative.

Miraculously, after a quick consultation, they agreed. The officer picked up the menorah, the guard picked up the olive oil cups, and they led me out.

Seeing that Hashem was helping me to fulfill the mitzvah in the best possible way, with olive oil and in an appropriate place, I worked up the courage to ask for the one thing still missing. As we walked down the hallway, I said, "Officer, I have another issue."

"What's your issue?" he asked, more patiently than I'd expected.

"I'm scheduled to light the candles, recite the prayers, and sit near the candles for thirty minutes. That follows the letter of the Jewish law, and I appreciate the accommodation, but it's the custom in my community to sit by the candles for no less than fifty minutes. Would that be possible here?"

The officer stopped walking in order to process the new information. Each step of this process had only revealed another requirement. First came the initial request to light the menorah, then it needed to be olive oil, then the toilet is causing problems, and now the time allowed is insufficient. Going by prison norms, he should have angrily dismissed my pestering requests, but the hearts of rulers are in the hands of Hashem. He looked at me and said, "Rubashkin, just tell me, how did you do this in your home?"

My heart twisted suddenly at the thought of Chanukah with my family. Each night of Chanukah I would completely clear my schedule, go home, and gather my children around the menorah. Together, we would light the candles, sing the Chanukah songs, and dance in front of the menorah. Then we would sit at the table nearby and eat latkes, play dreidel, and share thoughts about the Yom Tov until the candles burned out, some two and a half hours later.

The words just tumbled out. It was more information than he asked for, but I told him how I did it in my home. Much of it was gibberish to him, I'm sure, but I made sure he understood the important part: At home I would sit by the candles until they went out.

I stood there as he thought about it, fearing I'd gone too far. Perhaps I should have just asked for fifty minutes instead of the half hour. After what felt like an eternity, he reached his decision. He looked at me and said, "Okay. You'll do it here the way you did it in your home."

Grateful that he'd agreed, I was also strengthened by the extra words Hashem had put in his mouth. He didn't just say "okay" or "permission granted." He said, "You'll do it here the way you did it in your home." In those few added words, I heard a message from Hashem. You need to do it, here, there, or wherever you are, the way you do it at home—you need to be an immutable and enduring Yid.

When we're out of our comfort zone, away from home or just out of our element and off balance dealing with life's many adversities, our instinctive thought is often to adjust our behavior. "In my home," we say to ourselves, "when things are stable, I'd *certainly* do the mitzvah in the best possible way, but under the circumstances, it's okay to do less, especially when the *hiddurim* require additional sacrifice and I'm under fire."

Hashem had put the right words into the mouth of this guard. Be the same Yid here as you were in your home. I tried to do exactly that throughout my ordeal, and, *baruch Hashem*, that Chanukah my efforts were successful. Each and every day, I was permitted to light the menorah in that small room and sit by its light as long as the oil burned. When the candles went out, I would bang on the big metal door, the noise echoing through the jail as one last flourish of *pirsumei nisa*, and the guard would open the door and return me to the cell.

This episode was more than just a victory in one specific area—it set me on the right track more generally. When you do your part to fulfill Hashem's mitzvos fully and properly, He will be with you and grant you success.

As Chanukah drew to a close, a very helpful development occurred. Even before trial preparation could begin in earnest, the legal costs were mounting. Due to the prosecutors' continued and unreasonable opposition, something as simple and fundamental as release on bail was already draining our meager coffers. This did not bode well for the costly and drawn-out legal process we could expect when these charges actually came to trial.

A group of Chabad chassidim in Crown Heights gathered to form a *va'ad*, a committee to help. Along with the rest of the world, the Chabad community had seen our business come under attack, requiring every resource we had to stay afloat. Despite our best efforts, things were very publicly not going well on that front. The day after I was formally charged, Agriprocessors' primary lender filed a lawsuit, starting a process which resulted in the company declaring bankruptcy and eventually being placed under the control of a court-appointed bankruptcy trustee.

It was obvious to these good *Yidden* that I'd be unable to pay for proper legal defense for myself, so they stepped up. Led by Rabbi Sholom Ber Hecht, they gathered under the auspices of the NCFJE, a non-profit organization in Brooklyn that has extensive experience in helping *Yidden* facing all sorts of difficulties, including *pidyon shvuyim*. They set up a charitable fund with a board to oversee decision-making and expenditures and began raising the money they knew I would need.

The official announcement of this initiative, so full of *achdus* and *ahavas Yisrael*, was made on *gimmel* Teves. Hashem's response to us is always *middah k'neged middah*, measure for measure, and the power of Klal Yisrael's mitzvah surely influenced the great miracle that would ultimately happen on *gimmel* Teves. Until then, there was another *nes* in store for us, on a different *gimmel*.

The First *Aleph, Beis, Gimmel*

About two weeks after Chanukah, I was notified that a delegation of prominent rabbis would be coming to Dubuque. Troubled by the antisemitism implicit in my case, they were coming to take a public, united stand against the denial of bail. They also wanted to visit me in jail to strengthen and encourage me. This was welcome news. It had been a very long time and I looked forward to spending time with fellow *Yidden* in person.

The group that came included Rabbi Chaim Dovid Zwiebel representing Agudas Yisrael, Rabbi Pesach Lerner representing National Council of Young Israel, Rabbi Yaakov Wasser representing the Rabbinical Council of America, Rabbi Moshe Elefant representing the Union of Orthodox Jewish Congregations, Rabbi Gershon Tannenbaum representing the Rabbinical Alliance of America, Rabbi Shimon Hecht representing the National Committee for Furtherance of Jewish Education, and Rabbi Yossi Jacobson from Des Moines, Iowa, representing Chabad Lubavitch—who was joined by other *shluchim*. The *achdus* this diverse group represented warmed my *neshamah* and gave me tremendous encouragement, knowing that Hashem always listens to us when we are united.

The rabbis were promised fifteen minutes each to visit with me but at the last minute it was changed to a group visit. This gave me an opportunity I hadn't had in far too long—a chance to *daven* with a *minyan*. I even had the *zechus* to lead the *davening*, wearing a borrowed hat and *gartel* wrapped over the garish orange prison clothes. Together, we said, *Ashrei yoshvei veisecha*— "How lucky are we who sit in Your house." Wherever a Yid may find himself, he only needs to do a mitzvah or say a *tefillah* to remind himself that he is always in Hashem's house and he is very lucky indeed.

I truly appreciated their visit and it gave me great *chizuk*, which helped me continue to keep my head and heart clear and in the right place as I waited for Hashem's salvation. After they left, they held a press conference denouncing

The distinguished rabbinical
delegation in a place called jail.

Davening Minchah
with the delegation.

the prosecutors' use of the Law of Return, which was designed to protect *Yidden* from persecution, as an excuse to imprison a Jew until a trial which wasn't expected to begin for close to a year. They spoke words from the heart, which do not fail to enter the heart—provided, of course, that the listener *has* a heart. Their visit and public advocacy was prominently covered by the Iowa media, but I spent another month behind bars before my situation changed for the better.

After more than two months of incarceration, the chief judge agreed to schedule a hearing so evidence and testimony could be offered in our appeal of the bail decision. It was initially set for Thursday, January 22nd, *chaf-vav* Teves, but at the last minute it was rescheduled. The new date was January 26th, Rosh Chodesh Shevat, *aleph* Shevat.

I, along with my family and friends, undertook a half-day fast on Erev Rosh Chodesh, which is an auspicious day for *teshuvah* and forgiveness by Hashem. It's a day referred to in *sefarim* as Yom Kippur Katan, a mini-Yom Kippur, and we *davened* on this special day that I be inscribed by Hashem for a miraculous salvation.

Hearings of this type are typically short, but the judge had to sit on a different trial and split the hearing over two days, to conclude on the next day, *beis* Shevat.

The second day's hearing was brief, and the judge was ready to issue her ruling on the spot. She granted bail under harsh conditions, although not as harsh as what we had offered the first judge. She demanded that I wear a location-tracking ankle bracelet, pay $500,000 in bail money, and relinquish all of my family's passports.

It must be noted that although she overturned the denial of bail, agreeing with us that there was "absolutely no evidence [that I had] made any preparations to flee," she did not reject the hateful argument that Jewish people should be treated differently, nor has any federal judge or US Attorney since. It stands to this day as an argument that was accepted in the US legal system, potentially to be used by other prosecutors as precedent.

I should have been able to walk out of the courtroom with my family then and there, but the prosecutor leapt out of his chair to object. He reserved the right to argue with this decision, and insisted that I remain in their hands until he had a chance to do so. The judge authorized this extension of my unjust incarceration, and I was returned to the county jail in Dubuque.

The next day, I was informed that the prosecutors had decided not to object to my release after all. The only obstacles that remained were a mountain of paperwork and a meeting with the probation officer in Cedar Rapids, which were both required before I could go home. There was no guarantee they could manage it still that day, but despite the uncertainty, my wife started her drive to pick me up, trusting in Hashem that I would be released that day. The lawyers worked hard, but by the time they finished the paperwork, there wasn't enough time to make the seventy-five-mile drive to Cedar Rapids before the probation officer left for the day.

My friends and family were determined that I not spend one night more than necessary behind bars. They managed to arrange a small plane that could make the trip quickly enough, and before I knew it, I was taking to the skies, still not technically freed, but en route to Cedar Rapids to make it so.

As the plane climbed during takeoff, I caught a glimpse of the jail building far below. The words of Dovid Hamelech in *Tehillim* sprang to my mind and gladdened my heart: *Mekimi mei'afar dal, mei'ashpos yarim evyon*—"He lifts the pauper from the dust, from the dung heaps He raises up the needy." That morning, I'd been locked in a cell in that building and now, a few short hours later, I was among the clouds, flying to freedom.

I was taken to the probation office, jumped through all the bureaucratic hoops, and was finally permitted to return home and reunite with my family. My *eishes chayil* was waiting outside with my children. There were tears of joy and hugs all around and we made the two-hour drive back to Postville.

The community gathered again to celebrate my freedom, this time in my home. Coming after an actual and extended incarceration, our gratitude to Hashem was even greater than the first time, but we kept it as quiet as we could. We had learned from the past and took care not to give ammunition to the circling vultures.

The *seudas hoda'ah* ended and the last of the well-wishers left. I was sitting at the dining room table with my wife and children, reveling in the simple joy of sitting with my family when I realized the significance of the timing of my miraculous release. "*Aleph, beis, gimmel!*" I exclaimed.

Seeing the puzzled looks at my outburst, I explained myself. The first day of the hearing had been delayed until the first day of Shevat, *aleph*—for *emunah*. The hearing took more than one day, which is uncommon, and stretched into *beis*—for *bitachon*. Our *emunah* and *bitachon* in Hashem had been rewarded, and I had returned home on *gimmel*—our personal *geulah*!

It may not seem like much, but it was an example of what my wife called Hashem's "winks and smiles." Sometimes, for reasons known to Hashem, we go through a difficult time. If you look closely enough, though, you can see Hashem hinting to His presence. These hints are not always in ways that alter the course of your difficulty, sometimes they can even seem trivial, but they're reminders that you're not on your own. He hasn't abandoned you, *chas v'shalom*, He's with you, and He has orchestrated this experience for your benefit. Make the right decisions and trust that all will be well. Thanks to her reminders, we were seeing His hand everywhere and it really helped us get through the difficult moments.

Any hope for a recovery and restoration of Agriprocessors was gone by that point. Beleaguered by enemies and undermined by prosecutors who should have been pursuing justice instead of destruction, the company had succumbed. It had declared bankruptcy and the court-appointed trustee was already trying to sell it off.

Even this wasn't being allowed. The prosecutors actively interfered with the sale, intimidating potential buyers and warning them of dire consequences if they allowed my father or anyone from my family to continue on in management or even to act as a consultant.

Their actions were increasing the likelihood that the bank and other creditors would suffer a loss, something that could be avoided entirely with a legitimate sale. I'd been part of taking the loans and wanted to do everything I could to ensure that no one got hurt, but there was nothing I could do about it. They had taken the keys to the plant when the bankruptcy was granted and I was barred from any involvement. It was their responsibility now.

Instead, I turned to the personally pressing matter of preparing my defense properly, now that I was free of the restrictions of the county jail. While I had been fighting for my release on bail, my son Shmuly had arranged to hire local attorneys, bringing some hometown advantage to the trial team. He found Guy Cook, a well-respected lawyer who'd been a president of the Iowa Bar Association, to lead the team. He joined the existing team, and set out to prepare for trial alongside the lawyer who was already on the case, attorney Monty Brown.

My true defense was in bolstering my connection to Hashem and strengthening the clarity which allowed me to face my situation as a Yid. I spent every spare moment learning, *davening*, and *farbrenging*, usually with the precious *bachurim* who studied in the yeshivah which we had built with dedication and sacrifice. I started a nightly *chavrusa* in *Maseches Megillah* and we made a festive *siyum* to celebrate when we completed it.

We had recently completed an extension to our home, an oversized dining room and a few additional bedrooms and bathrooms, primarily so that our extended family could come for Yamim Tovim. That Pesach, my parents came to spend Yom Tov with us, as did some of my siblings and their families.

My father was very pained by the threat I faced, and spending time together meant that he was forced to confront it. I noticed that he was visibly disturbed whenever I had to step out to recharge the tracking device on my foot. Nonetheless, he came to spend Yom Tov and we both took strength from our time together.

We had an inspiring and emotional Yom Tov. The whole family was impacted by the destruction of Agriprocessors, but the moment the Yom Tov candles were lit, it was as if nothing was amiss. Even the threat looming over my own head faded away. What was left was a deep, personal appreciation for the freedom which Pesach represents, the true freedom of being Hashem's nation, and heartfelt gratitude, both for the wonders and miracles of the past and for those we were certain were in our immediate future.

A group picture with the precious *bachurim* during one of the
weekly *melaveh malkahs* in my home in Postville.

CHAPTER FIVE
Pre-Trial Tribulations

Invitation to Self-Convict

From the Holiday of Freedom, we turned to the looming threat of incarceration.

I had a very naive understanding of the judicial process, as do many Americans. From the moment the charges had been leveled, I'd been looking forward to disproving them when I finally got my day in court. When I discussed this with the defense lawyers, I learned that although it's a constitutional right and a cornerstone of the justice system, insisting on your day in court is often a very bad idea under the justice system as it stands now.

In most cases, when prosecutors charge someone, the first thing they do is give them a choice: plead guilty without ever presenting your case to a judge or a jury and we'll recommend a relatively light punishment, or meet us in the courtroom and face terrible repercussions if you're convicted. These offers are not between reasonably similar alternatives. For example, they might offer to recommend six months in prison if the accused agrees to self-convict, and threaten them with thirty-five years in prison if they insist on a hearing in court.

One of the guys I met in Otisville was serving an eight-year sentence, five years more than the co-defendants in his case. The difference between him and them was only that they pled guilty and he insisted on his day in court. There's even a name for this—a trial penalty; the penalty an American citizen pays for having his case heard by a judge instead of a prosecutor.

Less than two out of every ten people prevail in court against the prosecutors, so every defense attorney advises their client, innocent or not, to think long and hard before insisting on their day in court. Faced with the near certainty of conviction, and the exorbitant penalty of going to trial to prove their innocence, an astounding and horrifying ninety-eight percent of people who are accused take the "go straight to jail free" card and never get to make their case to a judge and jury.[1]

Prosecutors offer these "deals" for a number of reasons. Sometimes they never intended to defend their charges in court. In their pursuit of their actual target, prosecutors often first charge others, threaten them with severe sentences at trial, and offer a lighter sentence or even just probation—if they agree to cooperate in the case against the prosecutors' real target.

The decision to file an indictment is also not always driven by the facts and the law. Career considerations of individual prosecutors, local political factors, or even national political factors might drive a prosecutor to file charges against someone. These plea deals, made "too good to refuse" by contrasting them with extreme threats, offer speedy resolution of these cases while sparing the prosecutors from having to back up their accusations.

Even relatively strong cases are not unassailable, and prosecutors benefit by "winning" the case without having to defend them, but many cases are also very far from strong. Charges are often based on thin or distorted factual foundations, unreliable witnesses, or a disputed interpretation of the law. Bullying the defendant into conceding the case means the prosecutors never have to test any of those things in court.

As much as the innocent may dream of exoneration through their promised "day in court," a pragmatic plea deal is often their best course of action. Lawyers see a trial as rolling the dice with their client's freedom and failing to at least explore a "deal" is considered professional malpractice.

Shortly after I was finally released on bail, my lead attorney, Guy Cook, asked for authorization to reach out to the prosecution to discuss a plea agreement.

Aside from my confidence that with Hashem's help I would be exonerated, I was reluctant to allow it. These deals are not what they pretend to be. Believe it or not, they only cover what the prosecutors will recommend to the judge and aren't actually binding on the judge! This isn't an academic nitpick. I actually met an inmate who traded his soul to the prosecutor in return for a six-year

---

1. Groups advocating for justice reform even point to a shocking number of people who pled guilty out of fear of the threatened sentences who were later exonerated by DNA or other conclusive evidence.

sentence—only for the judge to ignore the deal and sentence him to eighteen years despite his cooperation.[2]

The prosecutors could also, after the fact and at their sole discretion, decide that their conditions weren't met and void the whole agreement, pocketing whatever advantage their victim gave them and bringing the case to trial in pursuit of a longer sentence than they'd negotiated.

Although I was reluctant, and my wife was also opposed to the idea, the lawyer strongly urged that we at least allow him to look into it. He wasn't alone in this. The *va'ad* had also been pushing the idea for a while, and so had a number of people who'd promised financial support for our struggle.

Under pressure, we allowed the lawyers to meet with the prosecutors. Perhaps there was a way to put all this behind us without going to trial. When I agreed to this approach, I made clear that, whatever the terms, I would consult with *rabbanim* before making a final decision.

Before Mr. Cook went to Cedar Rapids as my representative, I made sure he understood what I was willing to consider and what I was not, in part based on the specifics of the case, and in part based on principle. For example, I would not consider collaborating or volunteering any information relating to other people. As a Yid, this was out of the question, even if it meant paying a heavy price.

He dutifully noted my various positions, and conveyed them at his meeting with the prosecution team. They received him very coldly, heard him out, and said that they would send an offer. We didn't hear from them for a long time. They eventually did send an offer, but apparently, their playbook called for softening up their targets first.

As described above, despite indicting me, arresting me, and fighting dirty to deny me bail, the prosecution hadn't quite settled on their case and repeatedly reconvened the grand jury for superseding indictments. Each additional charge made the threatened penalty of requesting a trial larger, something the media dutifully calculated and discussed. They also aggressively pursued the strategy of threatening other people with charges and using them as weapons against me. The periodic announcements of plea deals reached with others in the case sparked discussion and speculation in the media that they had committed to testifying against me.

---

2. In my own case it also turned out not to be a groundless fear—when the time came, the judge indeed exceeded the sentence that the prosecutors recommended.

When the prosecutors felt they'd softened me up enough with their target letters, indictments, and rumors and leaks to the press about the investigation and cooperating witnesses, they finally reached out to offer a "deal."

I was in Monty Brown's office when their official offer arrived. He perused it first, then handed it to me for review. I went outside to read it. They had totally ignored our position, demanding false confessions not only to the more serious financial and immigration charges but even to the farcical Packers and Stockyards charges. They also demanded that I provide testimony that would lead to arrests or convictions of others, something expressly forbidden by halachah.

As a Yid, it was a non-starter. It was also objectively a terrible deal. In exchange for this false confession and testimony, they magnanimously offered to recommend a sentence of *fifteen years of incarceration*.

There was no reason to believe that in the event of a conviction, *chas v'shalom*, a judge would issue a sentence even close to that. Despite the sensational media coverage, the immigration charges were so weak that there was no chance they would prevail on those charges. Even the more confusing and less predictable financial charges didn't carry sentences anywhere in the *neighborhood* of a decade and a half.

The company assets were valued at close to $100 million when the keys had been turned over to the court-appointed trustee, far more than the amount needed to repay all creditors.[3] There was no reason for there to be any loss to the banks at all, certainly not loss attributable to me, and without any loss the sentencing range was zero to six months.

It was preposterous to even *contemplate* a fifteen-year sentence, much less consider it a bargain.

This was clearly not a good faith offer—it was a mockery. I walked back into Monty's office and handed him the packet. "Would you advise me to sign this document?" I asked.

He didn't hesitate or equivocate. "No," he responded.

Over the next few months, we were contacted a number of times to discuss a plea arrangement. My lawyers kept the dialogue going, but I was always told not to attend these meetings. Based on their observations, my lawyers

---

3. These were our calculations filed in bankruptcy court but even the trustee's evaluations, done after months of erosion due to handicapped operations and adjusting the assets, put the value at close to $70 million, still well over the amount required to repay the creditors.

felt that my presence made it difficult for the prosecutors to be reasonable. That's disgraceful enough, but it seemed to me that it was my existence, not my presence, that was having this effect, because they were no more reasonable in my absence.

They made trivial or cosmetic variations to their offer, but it stayed fundamentally the same. They were still talking about periods of incarceration that surpassed the average time served by *murderers*.

Although they couldn't take issue with this assessment of the merits of the offer, my lawyers began pressuring me to accept it. After each meeting with the prosecutors, none of which resulted in substantial improvements to the offer, my lawyers would press me to accept. They were increasingly annoyed that I stuck to my decision, which was made with the guidance of my *rav* in accordance with *da'as Torah*.

It was a weighty decision, and one which I was constantly pressured to revisit. At the urging of those pushing this deal, the Amshinover Rebbe was also consulted and he concurred that I should not accept the offer.

When they saw I wasn't taking the bait, the government set a deadline after which the offer would be retracted. It was an arbitrary, artificial deadline and it changed nothing. I didn't allow them to manipulate me, and I stuck to the decision that I'd made on the merits of the offer and with the guidance of a *rav*.

After the final deadline on their final offer passed, they reached out to Guy Cook to make another offer, something they admitted made them look foolish. They were clearly very interested that this case not go to trial, which gave me the impression that, despite winning on all the pre-trial questions, their case wasn't as strong as they claimed. That, or they had something to hide that they worried would come out if we went to court.[4]

A meeting was scheduled to discuss this new, post-final offer. It was set for a Friday morning after one of the pre-trial hearings. Unlike the earlier meetings, this time I was present, as was my wife. It was a memorable meeting.

We sat in a cramped, rented meeting room, facing two Assistant US Attorneys, representatives of a global superpower. The first one spoke like a polished professional, trying to persuade me that it was in my best interest to

---

4. Maybe it was their improper contact with the judge, their impact on the loss amount, or their legally indefensible position on forfeiture—all of which we eventually discovered and which will be detailed later—or maybe something else entirely which we never discovered.

play ball. He played up how strong their case was, and suggested that it would be best to avoid a trial. When I mentioned that I was following the guidance of my rabbis, he tried to dissuade me, saying that it's easy for them to give advice but I would be the one to pay for it.

He recognized that they were taking a very hard line, unwilling to negotiate toward a more acceptable arrangement, but he justified that by rebuking me for not cooperating with the investigation. I corrected him. We'd reached out countless times, from the very beginning, only to be rebuffed each and every time. He glanced at his colleague, and seemed genuinely surprised. He had no response to this information, and just changed the subject.

When he had said his piece, the other official, who seemed to be the one in charge, spoke. The difference was jarring. There was no veneer of civilized professionalism. "Mr. Rubashkin," he said callously, "you know how a kill floor[5] works. I know how a courtroom works. We will kill you in there!"

I turned to look at my wife, in shock at his cruel words and sorry she had to hear them. Her reliance on Hashem was so absolute that his menacing words had no impact. She gave me tremendous strength—in that moment and throughout my ordeal.

Moving on from his threat, this would-be "butcher" claimed that although he wanted to make a deal, others in his office wanted to go to trial. This transparent attempt to project confidence in their case actually reeked of desperation. He had already shown that he was not a man of noble character, the type of guy who would go out of his way to be kind to an all-but-defeated opponent. This only strengthened my suspicion that they had a strong motive to avoid a trial. The meeting ended with no real change to their offer and no change at all in my response.

Even this offer was not the last. They kept offering to "allow" me to convict myself by pleading guilty. One of these many "final deadlines" was on Tzom Gedaliah, less than a month before the trial was to begin. An *admor*, who helped many *Yidden* facing the prospect of imprisonment and who had been involved in my case, made the difficult trip to Iowa on a fast day to meet with the prosecutors.

We made a *minyan* for him at a hotel near the airport and I spoke to him

---

5. "Kill floor" is the industry slang for the part of the slaughterhouse where the animal is killed and dismembered.

briefly before he went into the meeting. He told me that Rabbi Genack of the OU had heard he was meeting with the prosecutors, and asked him to make sure they knew that Klal Yisrael was paying attention and that he was not the only rabbi interested in the case.

I joined him in the elevator, but to my shock and dismay, when we reached the meeting room, my lawyer told me that I had to leave and escorted me back down to the lobby. I waited there until the meeting ended and they returned with news:

The prosecutors were still taking a belligerent and aggressive stance. They still insisted that I plead guilty on all charges and their only "concession" was to slightly lower their suggested sentence from fifteen years to a still-unacceptable twelve and a half.

Not only was it an unreasonable position, and one that would not be binding on the judge, this arrangement also left me very vulnerable on the state charges. The state charges, as I will detail later, dealt with underage workers and they were based on the same foundations as the federal immigration charges. Both were falsely claiming that I knew the truth about the ineligibility of certain people (whether in the area of age or of immigration status) and hired them anyway.

Pleading guilty to the federal charges would practically forfeit the state case[6] and since they were charging me with 9,311 violations, that meant serious consequences for me—as well as a tremendous *chillul Hashem*. It would essentially be a false confession that I'd intentionally and callously exploited and endangered children.

I had insisted that any deal with the federal prosecutors would have to include an arrangement with the state to dismiss their charges, but the federal prosecutors refused, maintaining that they could not speak for the state and we would need to make a separate agreement with them.[7]

The trial loomed, and although I had rejected these offers so many times before, this time felt more final, somehow. It obviously wasn't only my decision—it would affect my wife and children and I felt that I needed to talk it over with my wife before I gave my answer.

---

6. Which I eventually won so decisively that the state expunged it from the record as if it never happened.

7. Documents provided during discovery later showed that they were actually in close contact and cooperation over their respective cases.

Baruch Hashem, my wife had come with me that day and I took some time to discuss the matter with her. She reassured me that she and the children had full *bitachon* in Hashem and encouraged me to stand firm. She gave me the strength to calmly respond that this was not the deal we had discussed and it was not one I was willing to take. Looking back years later, she confided that both as a wife and as a mother, this had been the hardest day of the whole ordeal—the pressure that day to accept the "deal" and plead guilty.

An early-morning meeting had been scheduled for the next day in Des Moines, at which I was to inform the attorneys of my answer. We made the trip that evening and checked into a motel so we could attend the meeting without a long early-morning drive. I woke up early in our motel room to say Tehillim, as I always did.

In the hope that I would finally relent, the prosecutors had "graciously" extended the deadline to plead guilty. I could still technically agree and accept the plea deal. I found that, like the prosecutors, my *yetzer hara* was also willing to extend the deadline and my heart was still troubled, second-guessing what we had said was our final decision.

Reciting the words of Dovid Hamelech in the pre-morning hours, alone with my thoughts, I pondered my situation. Experiencing a moment of clarity, I pulled out a paper and wrote down my thoughts so I could refer back to them if I ever wavered:

> Hashem is creating this circumstance, as He creates all things. They're pressing me to endorse lies and do things halachah forbids. If I agree and do so for my own benefit, it will be the opposite of *ratzon Hashem* and the opposite of a *kiddush Hashem*. I need to do the only thing within my power, which is to make the right choices, and have *emunah* and *bitachon* in Hashem to do what is truly only in *His* power—protect me and my family and give us only good.

With the sense of relief that comes from finalizing an agonizing decision and moving on, I *davened* Shacharis and we headed over to the meeting. I told the lawyers that, extensions notwithstanding, my decision stood and I would not be accepting the "deal" that was offered.

They were not happy about it, to put it mildly. This is the terrible situation created by the current system. Even the defense lawyers who were hired and agreed to defend me were pressuring me into a total surrender!

The pressure came from many sides and didn't let up until the trial began and the offers finally expired for good. I stood by my decision with the support of my family and those I'd consulted to determine *da'as Torah*. During this period, a family member in Eretz Yisrael approached the Amshinover Rebbe again, and he said that under *no circumstances* should I plead guilty.

The summer passed and Tishrei arrived, full of momentous and joyous days. Although my *tefillos* were, of course, full of requests that Hashem inscribe me for a year of freedom, I was successful in putting out of my mind and heart the pressures and concerns connected to my own involvement in making that happen. I celebrated a focused Rosh Hashanah and Yom Kippur, and a truly joyous Sukkos, only sporadically interrupted on Chol Hamoed by some (motivated by sincere love and concern, I'm sure) who were still making last-ditch efforts to get me to surrender before the battle even began.

Shaping the Battlefield

While the prosecutors were doing their best to end the trial before it even began, by pressing for a guilty plea, the judge was moving forward with the first phase of the trial—pre-trial hearings on matters of great importance. At issue were all the things which would shape the battlefield on which I would fight for my life: whether the diverse charges would be lumped together in a single trial or split into two, which of these two trials would come first, where they would take place, and so on.

The prosecution was doing their best to gain every advantage and we did our best to counter their arguments. The court ruled against us on every meaningful issue, with the exception of one, which seemed at first glance to have gone our way, but turned out to be their greatest weapon.

The prosecutors had thrown the book at me, charging me with violations in banking and accounting, hiring and harboring illegal immigrants, even paying cattle providers more than a day after delivery. They wanted to get it all in front of a single jury. The defense countered that (almost certainly by design) the sheer volume and variety of the combined charges and the dramatic nature of the immigration testimony would improperly sway the jury. Therefore, we argued, the charges should be separated into two separate trials.

In this one instance, the judge seemed to side with us, agreeing to separate the financial charges from the immigration-related charges. She'd notified the lawyers that she would schedule two separate trials, saying that it would be "impossible for the jury to compartmentalize the charges."

The lawyer was elated. This was critical to our ability to present the facts without the irrelevant and manipulative drama the prosecutors hoped to employ and it seemed like a big win. We were innocent and naive, and we only truly realized the import of this maneuver as it unfolded in later hearings and was weaponized during the trial.

Another important matter handled before the trial was something called a *"Motion in Limine."* I'd been accused of very serious and terrible things and had been looking forward to having my day in court where I could lay this all to rest and end the *chillul Hashem*. I was shocked to learn that having your day in court doesn't mean you can actually make your case.

Prior to a trial, the judge instructs the parties on what pieces or types of information will be excluded. Even entire avenues of defense can be blocked. During the pre-trial phase of my case, the government filed a motion specifying what they wanted the court to exclude in our case, including a lot of arguments and evidence I'd intended to bring. I found the whole concept bewildering in principle, and the actual ruling in this instance was a disgrace which severely handicapped my ability to make my case.

The court's ruling on the *Motion in Limine* came only days before the trial. The lawyers had been working long and hard to prepare for trial and now they received restrictions—a lengthy list of things that could not be used in my defense. Some of them were obvious barriers to an effective defense, some less obvious.

For example, the defense was forbidden from discussing what the bank knew. "The bank is not on trial," the judge repeated more than once—as if what the bank knew was totally irrelevant in a case which alleged that the bank was tricked!

She even blocked expert testimony on that point. At one point, the defense called Abe Roth to testify. A distinguished accountant who leads a prestigious New York accounting firm, Mr. Roth had done work for Agriprocessors and was familiar with its operation.

His testimony was, among other things, that all the activity under discussion at the trial was openly laid out in the filings to the bank and not concealed from the bank at all. In a trial all about accounting, the judge refused to allow Mr. Roth to testify in front of the jury.

On the day of his testimony, the judge allowed him to speak only after dismissing the jury from the courtroom so that his words would have no impact on their verdict. After allowing him to present his testimony, the judge reiterated for the record that the bank "can't be blamed for what occurred" and she would not allow the jury to hear this information. The defense wasn't trying to blame the bank; it was trying to establish, in a case alleging fraud, whether or not anyone was tricked—and the judge was not allowing it!

Another prohibition in the *Motion in Limine* which directly undermined my courtroom defense was the judge's ban on mentioning the involvement of lawyers in the company's implementation of hiring and employment.

Over the defense's objections, the prosecution was permitted to bring testimony about the presence of illegal immigrants at the plant. It was used by the prosecutors to portray me as a scofflaw, totally indifferent to the rules and regulations. The hope was that it would improperly influence the jury to conclude that I'd acted the same way in the financial actions that were the legitimate subject of the trial.

The obvious response was that I had *not* been indifferent to the rules and regulations. In fact, I had, on behalf of the company, hired the top law firm in the state to review the company's practices and to guide and advise it in following all necessary hiring laws.

It was the obvious response, but the defense couldn't make it in front of the jury. The judge ruled before the trial that our involvement of lawyers in these matters was irrelevant and excluded it. This left us muzzled, unable to counter the false portrayal and show that I'd made good-faith efforts to follow the law.

Prohibitions that were less obviously handicaps also ended up playing a large role in undermining our case. The judge forbade us from describing any generosity or charitable activity, on the grounds that it would inappropriately sway the jury. She similarly forbade mention of my son Moishie's special needs to avoid generating sympathy. On the surface, these seem like reasonable efforts to ensure a trial on the facts and they would have been no problem— but the prosecutors continuously abused the rules, mischaracterizing me, misrepresenting facts, and then hiding behind these restrictions to prevent me from properly correcting them.

For example, they told the jury that I'd provided interest-free loans to help employees who'd lost their jobs due to documentation issues, claiming that the only reason I would give them money was to buy fake documents.

The reality was that throughout my time in Postville, following my father's example, I had frequently helped people who'd fallen on hard times with money for bills and expenses. There was a long list of situations we would have brought up to decisively prove that there was nothing unusual or nefarious about my giving money to people in need, but to do so would be to violate the judge's ruling. Instead, the jury was left with the misrepresentations of the prosecutor, which somehow didn't violate any of the judge's rulings.

The prosecutors even found a way to abuse the prohibition against bringing up Moishie's health. With the guidance of experts in treating autism, we had built a safe, sheltered playroom in our home, where it would be easier to form the close emotional bonds that would slowly coax him out of the mental and emotional isolation that is characteristic of autism.

A sweet moment of bonding between father and son in the playroom, so critical to Moishie's development.

For years, I would drive home every day to eat with him, either lunch or an early supper, and spend time one-on-one in his closed playroom. I would also occasionally take him along with me to the office, so he could explore and experience the wider world while staying near me.

Also relevant to this story, I often gave away my car for days or weeks at a time—sometimes to visiting rabbis, but frequently to locals as well—who found themselves without a means of transportation. At those times, I needed a ride from someone in the office.

The prosecution presented testimony by someone who often gave me rides, telling the jury that she'd been asked to drive me one day, along with my son, and I had her stop the car near the barn for a surreptitious meeting. They painted a picture of sinister conspiracy, so secretive and out of the office loop that I didn't want to take my own car and only took along a family member.

On cross-examination, my lawyer tried to correct the impression that this gave the jury. Through questioning the witness, he first demonstrated why I'd asked the worker for a ride—it wasn't because I wanted anonymous transportation, but simply because I didn't have a car at the time, and this was not unusual for me.

Then he tried to address the implied family conspiracy by explaining that my son's presence couldn't possibly be seen in this way. "Are you aware that the defendant's son, Moishie, is a special-needs autistic child?" he asked the witness. The prosecution immediately and loudly objected, insisting that Mr. Cook not be allowed to explain why Moishie's presence was not nefarious. The judge angrily agreed. At the end of the day's proceedings, she revisited the issue, loudly and angrily rebuking Mr. Cook for mentioning a forbidden topic.

The rules allow a response—even on a forbidden topic—if the government "opens the door" by bringing up the story, but when he tried to explain and defend himself, she rudely cut him off and continued berating him, ignoring his explanation entirely. When she finished, he again tried to explain that he had not intentionally violated her rules and believed the topic had been brought "in bounds." She only grew angrier at his response and warned him that he was "on the line" and in danger of being disbarred.

Mr. Cook was not some paralegal or novice fresh out of law school. He was a senior member of his law firm, a serious and successful trial lawyer, a former Assistant US Attorney. He was a president of the Iowa State Bar Association and had sat on the committee that selects candidates for federal magistrate judgeships in the state of Iowa. This unexpected and inappropriate treatment at the hands of a federal judge hit him like a bolt of lightning. The threat silenced him in fear and embarrassment and he took his seat.

Later that day, when I asked him to do something important to my case, he refused, saying, "Sholom! I almost lost my law license today..." The judge's angry outburst in the courtroom had not just been embarrassing for the lawyer—it had a real chilling effect on my legal team and their willingness and ability to defend me.

Actually, seeing the supposedly neutral arbiter livid, publicly berating and threatening the man who was our representative, shook us all. When we returned to the hotel that day, I found that those who had come to support me needed support themselves.

We sat together over a meal in the hotel's conference room and I reached into the depths of my *neshamah* for the pure *emunah* and complete *bitachon* in Hashem that was the correct reaction. I took out my well-worn copy of the *Sha'ar Habitachon* and reviewed with those around me the parts that were relevant to our situation and the day's events.

As we processed the situation through the lens of the holy Torah, our confidence returned. Whatever had happened was for the best, *gam zu l'tovah*, and the future certainly held Divine salvation from the *tzarah* that loomed over me. I could feel the tension and anxiety fade from my own heart and from those gathered around me.

The restrictions on how I could defend myself gave the prosecution all the tools they needed. They were able to cherry-pick evidence and testimony and misrepresent it in ways that made me look like a crafty and greedy criminal who exploited people and duped a bank for personal gain, without worrying about a robust correction by the defense.

While the lawyers made this and other efforts in the federal court, I knew that my fate would actually be decided in the Heavenly Court. The month of Tammuz was approaching and I very much wanted to make the trip to the Ohel of the Rebbe to *daven*. Remember, I was out on bail at the time, the primary purpose of which was to ensure that I didn't flee the country. Now I wanted to make the 1,100-mile trip to New York, a hub of international travel. Miraculously, the court signed off on a quick in-and-out trip.

I was sure they'd jump at the excuse to claim I'd violated the bail conditions if I exceeded the speed limit or changed lanes without a blinker, so I didn't want to do the actual driving. I would need a driver—two, in fact. Because of the small window of time I was granted for the trip, the drive had to be non-stop. Two of the older *bachurim* from the yeshivah volunteered to drive.

The overnight, eighteen-hour trip itself was long but unremarkable. The destination was energizing and uplifting. We arrived in the early morning and went first to the Ohel, where we *davened* Shacharis. I wrote a *pan*[8] asking the Rebbe to intercede on my behalf at the Heavenly Throne.

From there we went to 770, the Rebbe's shul. There was a *hachnasas sefer Torah* in progress, full of joy and festivity. I saw the opportunity to participate in this celebration of the Torah—the source of our strength and our life—as encouragement from Hashem. I was invited to lead one of the *hakafos* and those moments stayed with me for many months to come.

The day was drawing to a close and my time in New York was running out. I took the time and made a quick stop in Boro Park to see my beloved father and mother and, before night fell, we were back on the road for the eighteen-hour trip back west.

---

8. A written request for intercession in prayer.

Sioux Falls

Another important issue that needed to be settled before the trial could begin was the location of the trial, host to the population from which the jury would be selected.

Intentionally hiring illegal immigrants for jobs the locals would otherwise take is an incendiary accusation across the Midwest, regardless of the identity of the alleged perpetrator. My identity made it worse. A chassidic Jew is viewed with suspicion and distaste even under the best of circumstances, as our years of experience in Postville had shown. Combining the two got us off to a very bad start. The public actions and pronouncements of the prosecution and other government representatives, and the sensationalized and toxic media coverage, had made all that even worse.

Hoping to benefit from this, the prosecution resisted our request that the trial be moved, insisting that their behavior and that of the press and others had not poisoned the minds of the local populace. To settle the matter, questionnaires were sent out by the court. The responses soon proved our contention. Many were full of venom and prejudice, some even crossing the line into explicit antisemitism. The percentage of respondents who answered in this way or simply noted that they would be unable to overcome their negative preconceptions made it incontrovertible. It would be impossible to seat an unbiased, impartial jury in Iowa.

There are several metropolitan areas within a reasonable distance that would have been acceptable alternatives, such as Minneapolis or Chicago, which didn't have those problems, and we wanted the trial moved to one of those places. Instead, the judge chose Sioux Falls, South Dakota. It was more than an hour further than the alternatives and, we argued, suffered from all the same problems as Iowa—the same heightened sensitivity to the issues covered in the trial, exposure to regional press, and a parochial bigotry and xenophobia.

These were well-founded and reasonable concerns (and they proved very real during jury selection in South Dakota, which I will describe shortly) but the judge nonetheless insisted on Sioux Falls, calling it the "most similar to Cedar Rapids" in some unspecified way which overrode our concerns. It made no sense, but there was nothing we could do about it. In a way, that's the best indication and reminder that we are watching Hashem openly orchestrating our movements. Clearly, He wanted us in Sioux Falls, South Dakota.

Sioux Falls is the largest city in the state of South Dakota, but it would still be considered fairly small by national standards. Driving there for the first time, the tranquility of the countryside and the calmness of the streets struck me as a bizarre contrast with the ferocious attack I was there to face.

Our "headquarters" in Sioux Falls was at a local hotel about a half-mile from the courthouse, just across the Big Sioux River. The staff were very accommodating and, in addition to the numerous rooms we booked for family and lawyers, they allowed us to use the hotel's conference room. It became our common area, where we ate together at mealtimes and *davened*, learned, or *farbrenged* together at all other times when court was not in session.

The hotel was on the banks of the river. There was a picturesque bike path running along the river where I would often walk with my *Tehillim* during the four difficult weeks that followed. These paths also provided a quiet spot where I could take private walks with my wife to discuss the personal aspects and ramifications of all that was unfolding. My wife was a steadfast and crucial source of support and encouragement, always providing the clarity and pure faith that helped me through the darkest times.

This hotel was minutes away from the courthouse but a full five hours from Postville. The family only had to make the trip once a week because we stayed at the hotel, but for those who wanted to come for one or two days to give moral and public support, the increased distance was a real obstacle. This made me all the more grateful that people did come, despite the time, effort, and expense it entailed.

Not only did many people from Postville attend the trial in support, many people came from much, much further. A close friend named Hilly Alenik paid for a coach bus to drive from far-away New York, and a bus-full of wonderful *Yidden* took time off from their busy lives to offer moral support. *Yidden* from diverse communities traveled close to 1,400 miles, over twenty hours by bus, to show—both before the US court and, more importantly, before the Heavenly Court—that they loved me and supported me.

Other people made their own travel arrangements from many other locations across the country, and a few remarkable people even came from abroad, all for the same reasons and with the same encouraging and supportive effect.

Not that the support had any positive effect on the judge or caused her to question her preconceptions of me. One day in court, after the jury had been dismissed for the day, Rabbi Friedman approached me at the defense table. He gave me a warm *shalom aleichem* and an encouraging hug of support. The judge was still sitting at her table collecting her papers and she looked up. Seeing the long-bearded, distinguished-looking rabbi reassuring and comforting me, her face contorted into an obvious expression of disdain and disapproval.

Another impediment to those who came in support was the very small gallery in the courtroom chosen for the trial. The three benches available in the courtroom were very quickly filled, and most of the people who had traveled to be there were diverted to a separate room. The overflow room had a closed-circuit setup so they could observe the trial on screen, but they could not themselves be observed. This obviously diminished the emotional and psychological benefits they had hoped to give me by their physical presence while I was facing such vile attacks.

Despite the separation during court hours, these supporters were a tremendous source of *chizuk*. Day in and day out, I saw the presence of Hashem in the presence of these precious *Yidden*. Hashem had inspired them to make the arduous journey and spend weeks with me in far-off South Dakota, reminding me that I'm not alone and He is very much with me, even though it was sometimes hard to see.

Davening in our makeshift shul in the Sioux Falls hotel conference room.

I would rise very early each morning, preparing myself for the day ahead by saying the whole Tehillim. I found strength in the words of Dovid Hamelech who not only describes the greatness and the wonders of Hashem, but speaks of turning to Hashem when he faced adversity and conflict, and thanks Hashem for protecting him and granting him victory against all odds. This bolstered my *emunah* and *bitachon*.

Thanks to the special *Yidden* who came from far and wide, we were able to *daven* Shacharis with a *minyan*. *Davening* the proper way was very important to maintaining and strengthening my close connection with *Hashem Yisbarach*.

After *davening*, we would all head to the courthouse. Sometimes I drove the half-mile to and from the courthouse, and other times I walked, just to be in the company of my fellow Jews and supporters. As we each went to our respective seating areas at the start of each day, they would wish me well and reassure me that they would continue to *daven* for me.

The lawyers were always already there, working with the judge on the legal technicalities for the day. If necessary, I would meet with my lawyers in a side room to discuss any decisions and share any information required for the day ahead.

When the court took a break during the day, and after it had adjourned in the evening, my friends and supporters were there to process the day's events together. They offered *chizuk*, but also often sought it for themselves, especially if the day's proceedings had seemed to unfairly go against us, as they often did.

Sometimes they would offer their take on the events of the day, other times they would ask about or even challenge the principles of *emunah, bitachon,* or *hashgachah pratis* in light of something that had happened. In thinking through and answering their questions, I often found more clarity than I had before we talked.

We took every opportunity to sit around the large table in the hotel conference room and learn together. Mostly, we learned from the *sefarim* which dictate how a Yid should process the events in his life, including the *Chovos Halevavos* and the many *sichos*[9] of the Rebbe which address these fundamental questions. We studied, discussed, and debated these very real issues in a very personal way for hours on end, learning to see through the eyes of the Torah, maintaining and strengthening our *emunah* and *bitachon*.

Some days actually seemed to go well. Counter-intuitively, it was even *more* important on *those* days to focus on our *emunah* and *bitachon*. We needed to resist the urge to take comfort or strength from seeing that things seemed to be going our way for natural reasons. Our confidence should come *only* from the kindness and mercy of Hashem. On those days, we would thank Hashem for any seeming victory and *daven* that we would merit to see the complete victory, which we knew comes only from Hashem.

One of the people who had come, a *bachur* from New York, had a gift for seeing the absurd side of the very consequential happenings of the day. He was

---

9. Public talks by a rebbe often explaining or expounding on an aspect of Torah, the Jewish calendar, Jewish life, or how to approach or learn from current events.

constantly reenacting and parodying the latest outrage in the case. Through his humor, he succeeded in breaking the spell the court and the prosecutor worked so hard to create. This allowed us all to see through the menacing facade and reconnect to the truth—that they were simply playing a part in what Hashem wanted us to experience for our eternal benefit. Safe in His hands, we knew that we needed to do whatever He required of us in our situation, and in His kindness, He would surely grant us the victory we needed.

Our small but vibrant pop-up community was more organized *Yiddishkeit* than South Dakota had seen in close to a century. As a matter of fact, it was the only state in the Union at the time that didn't have a full-time Orthodox rabbi or even a Chabad House.[10] Still, there were some individuals and families in the state—press reports from around that time put the number of Jews in the state at around four hundred—and we merited to meet a few of them.

The most amazing encounter with one of the local Jews took place unexpectedly, while we were walking back to the hotel for lunch during the court's midday break. My son Meir Simcha noticed someone walking nearby and, fully aware of how unlikely this was, he asked, "Excuse me, sir... Are you Jewish?"

"As a matter of fact, I am!" came the unexpected answer.

The obvious follow-up question was, "Have you put on *tefillin* today?"[11]

Randomly encountering a not-yet-observant Jew on the street in South Dakota was already so startling and surreal that I don't think our jaws could have dropped lower if he'd answered, "Yes! I have." But no, he hadn't put on *tefillin*. Meir Simcha invited him to accompany us to the hotel to do the mitzvah and join us for a warm, home-made supper.

When we reached the hotel, I helped him put on *tefillin* and say Shema, and then we sat down for a hot meal. Chatting over the meal, he spoke wistfully of his childhood and his limited Jewish education.

The promise that "with *aleph* (*emunah*) and *beis* (*bitachon*), one will merit

---

10. The dedicated *shluchim* in the region did what they could for the Jews there and Rabbi Katzman from Nebraska would travel there during the summer and kept in contact from afar with the Jews that he met there. One of the Jews we met was a woman who had grown up in Brooklyn and her heart's desire was for a rabbi to move to town to bolster their community. Seven years later, in 2016, a *shliach* finally moved to South Dakota.

11. The Rebbe instituted the *tefillin* campaign in 1967, emphasizing the power of this mitzvah to elevate the one who performs it even only once in his life.

gimmel (geulah)" had been a central topic of discussion for days by that point, and had become something of a catchphrase, which is why the next words out of our new friend's mouth brought all other conversation at the table to a sudden halt.

"I did learn a bit as a child, but I can't remember much," he said. "All I remember is '*aleph, beis, gimmel.*'" Everyone turned to look at him in surprise. He hadn't said "*aleph-beis,*" which is usually where people stop. This Jew we'd

 encountered on a South Dakota sidewalk—unexpectedly and by Divine Providence—and invited for a mitzvah and a meal, had said that the only thing he remembered was "*aleph, beis, **gimmel.***" A wink and a smile from Hashem.

Putting on *tefillin* with the Yid we found on our way back from court. *Aleph, beis, gimmel!*

We were so immersed in the topic of Divine Providence, Hashem's detailed involvement and orchestration of every little aspect of our lives and the world as a whole, that it was immediately crystal clear to everyone around the table that this was a message straight from Hashem, encouraging our approach and our clarity: If we embraced Hashem and His will with pure faith and trust that it will be good, we would merit an openly positive outcome.

Other local Jews heard about our arrival through the media coverage of the legal circus setting up in their city, and soon came by the courthouse to offer support. One of the local Jewish families asked me if I had the time to visit their home and speak for a gathering of their friends. The truth was that preparations for the trial were taking up every available moment, but I'd learned long ago that you don't *have* time—you *make* time. This seemed to me a much more important contribution toward receiving Hashem's *brachah* than anything I could do with the lawyers, so I agreed to go.

My wife and I drove to their home and we had a very inspiring evening. Those few hours spent focusing on the light and life of Torah were a welcome and necessary breath of fresh air, for us perhaps more than for them. Returning to the hotel that night—from that oasis of calm and light to the chaos and darkness of battle—was jarring, but I felt more connected to Hashem, and my *bitachon* was stronger. I felt more ready than ever for Hashem's infinite blessing which was sure to come.

We met many fine local Jews that were hungering for more Jewish experiences. It occurred to us that perhaps this was the reason the trial had been relocated there, so that we could bring more *Yiddishkeit* to these sweet people. Shabbos was fast approaching and we thought, "Why not spend Shabbos in Sioux Falls?"

Instead of heading back to Postville, we arranged for everything we would need for Shabbos to be brought to South Dakota, and invited all the people we'd met to join us at the hotel for an impromptu Shabbaton. A few families from Postville joined us as well. The legal drama faded away in the joy and tranquility of Shabbos spent together with our brothers and sisters. We got to know each other better and spent the special day deepening our connection to Hashem, His Torah, and His mitzvos.

We were joined for Shabbos by Rabbi Feller, the head *shliach* of Minnesota and the Midwest, who came together with his son to lead the Shabbaton. He was excited to be there because he'd been given the mission to support *Yiddishkeit* in the whole region and this was the first real gathering he was able to support in South Dakota.

This brought up the question of the long term. We were able to support the local Jews while we were there, but our presence there was only temporary. What could we do to support them after our time in South Dakota had passed? We discussed various ideas. With Agriprocessors well and truly behind us, regardless of the outcome of the trial, we even considered moving to South Dakota to continue what we'd started.

Things didn't quite turn out that way, but the next year, when Chanukah rolled around, I encouraged my family to go back to foster the connections we'd made with the *Yidden* there and help them celebrate Chanukah. In doing so—returning to the place that had been the source of so much pain—they displayed true certainty that everything was orchestrated by Hashem, as well as great commitment to their fellow Jews.

They reached out to the people we'd met there and helped them light their *menoros*, and even lit the menorah in a public place, bringing light to a very dark place as they awaited their very own miraculous victory of the few against the many and the weak against the strong.

A mitzvah and its impact are forever, and, years later, our big *nes* happened on Chanukah, too.

CHAPTER SIX
The Federal Trial

Jury Selection

THE TRIAL BEGAN ON TUESDAY, OCTOBER 13, 2009, *CHAF-HEI* TISHREI. I was encouraged that Hashem had chosen the date of the *yahrtzeit* of Reb Levi Yitzchak Barditchover, well-known as "the defender of *Yidden*." He saw *Yidden* and everything they did in the best possible light, and argued their case before the Heavenly Court.

I had some experience with the legal system in civil cases, but this was my first personal encounter with the criminal legal system. My point of reference for how a court and court case should run were the instructions of Torah, and the contrasts were striking. The most telling difference is that the Torah gives the judge the responsibility to find the truth—through exhaustive inquiry, questioning of witnesses, and so on—while, to my surprise and chagrin, there is *no one* in the modern courtroom whose job it is to find the truth!

In their system, which they call an "adversarial system," the case is a contest between two adversaries, the prosecution and the defense, each trying to persuade the judge or jury to side with them. The problem with this approach is that it doesn't really tell you what the truth is—it only tells you who can best use the process and procedure to convince the jury. This is what the prosecutor meant when he warned me that he would win simply because he knows how a courtroom works, irrespective of anything else.

This problem is magnified by the fact that the two parties are far from evenly matched. For a while, I would give an incredulous chuckle whenever I saw the title of my case: The United States of America vs. Sholom Rubashkin. This "system" for determining the truth was setting up a contest between the world's preeminent superpower and a lone individual—one they had made every effort to systematically strip of resources and support.

(Of course, I wasn't facing them alone. To paraphrase Dovid's words to Golias, they brought the might of a superpower, but I faced them with the strength of Hashem, the G-d of Yisrael. His presence was most obviously represented by the scores of supporters who rallied at my side to help with the financial burden, to offer emotional support, and most importantly, to storm the gates of Heaven with *achdus*, *tefillos*, and mitzvos on my behalf.)

The judge's function in this system is not to find the truth. They are relegated to setting up the battlefield by defining or clarifying the laws in question, and then to merely observing and ruling if one side or the other goes out of bounds. The job of deciding between the two parties is given to a jury, a group of regular citizens, who rule based not on their own inquiries or investigation, but on what is laid before them by the parties.

In my case, a twelve-person jury was required. They were to be selected from a random group of local citizens called in for jury duty. Since they're pivotal to the outcome of the trial, everyone involved is very invested in who, from among the initial pool of potential jurors, ends up on the jury.

In our case, as in all cases, the judge was the first to question the candidates. In keeping with her official role, she kept her questions focused on whether participating would cause them personal hardship and whether they could be impartial, having no animosity or bigotry toward either side and having drawn no conclusions based on personal experience or media exposure. Then, the two sides had an opportunity to question the potential jurors. If any of the answers made it obvious that the candidate was ineligible, the judge would dismiss them. In addition, each side had a handful of vetoes and could dismiss a small number of candidates upon request, without offering a concrete justification.

It was an exhausting process and took up a full day. The trial had already been moved to a different state because of bias, and this process revealed that we'd been right to oppose moving it to South Dakota. Some of the comments by potential jurors, before the case had even begun, were appalling. The prosecutors' charging strategy and their media strategy had been designed to convince the public of my guilt, not on the merits of their case, but by the sheer volume of their allegations and the weight of their authority with the assistance of repetition and dramatization in the media. It had clearly had a large impact.

Although this was a trial on the financial charges, quite a few candidates volunteered their antipathy toward me, based on the negative media coverage of the workers' plight and their difficulties in the aftermath of the raid. The mountain of formal immigration charges against me convinced them that *I* was responsible for those hardships, and therefore they couldn't be impartial.

One candidate actually said, "Well, he's charged with ninety-one counts, so he must have done *something*." Unbelievably, this was not disqualifying!

"If the court instructs you to set that feeling to the side and judge the case on the merits, can you do so?" the judge asked him. His terse, affirmative response was deemed sufficient, and he was seated on the jury.

He was not alone on the jury. Others who made similar comments were also seated. The defense used all six of its vetoes in an attempt to keep the jury impartial, but six was far from enough. A month later, one of the candidates who'd expressed prejudice, and then promised to set it aside when prompted by the judge, was actually selected by the jurors as their foreman, the one who usually leads and guides the jury deliberations.

This low bar for a juror—not lack of prejudice but the claimed ability to set it aside—explains the prosecution's attempt to seat a jury in Iowa. They knew there was no way they would find an impartial jury, in large part due to their own actions, but they didn't *want* to and they didn't *have* to. If the candidates would only claim they could set aside their predispositions, which the judge strongly urged them all to do, they could seat a prejudiced jury and reap the benefits.

The questions were asked and answered and the vetoes exercised. We were left, minutes before the end of the court session, with a jury. Twelve jurors had been selected, along with an additional four as "alternates," potential substitute jurors. In the remaining minutes of the day, they were all formally sworn in as the jury and court was adjourned for the day.

The Prosecutors' Kill Floor

With a jury seated, the presentation of the case itself began. The case was presented over a period of four weeks. Over those four weeks, I often found myself thinking back to the menacing words of the Assistant US Attorney in that meeting in Cedar Rapids: "We know how a courtroom works. We will kill you there." Sitting at the defense table and watching them work, his choice of words made more and more sense.

He hadn't warned me that "we have a compelling case." He had urged me to accept defeat, even if I *knew* their case was actually detached from reality, because they knew how courtrooms work and would be able to use their procedural knowledge and experience in the courtroom to destroy me.

In the aftermath of the raid, I'd already seen their relentless and blind pursuit of a conviction, both through legal maneuvering and extra-judicial tactics and measures. Now, before judge and jury, I watched them use every tool and advantage they could to shape the case, actively and strenuously resisting every effort to allow the straight facts and context to decide the outcome.

Because of their success in these efforts, the trial was fundamentally flawed. Instead of presenting the story as it actually occurred, my lawyers could only offer restricted responses to the distorted account of the prosecutors. Even defense witnesses had to tie in to something the prosecution was saying and only within the lines of defense that the judge authorized.

The technical and legal aspects of the case deserve a detailed review and analysis, but that's for another book by another author. My intention here is only to tell the story of what happened to me, the strength I drew upon to persevere, and the miraculous salvation that I received.

I've only included the legal details for very specific reasons. Some general information is critical to following the story, some details highlight the fiction that the world presents. The degree to which the system proved impervious to every effort to extract a measure of justice also strongly underscores the miracle that occurred when Hashem freed me from my *tzarah*.

The indictment process, the charges, and the trial that weighed their merits were, at their root, so distorted, contrived, and artificial that it's impossible to use them as a starting point or framework to discuss what actually happened. Instead, in addressing the trial, I will focus on a few of my observations as a layman, and exchanges or interactions that, to me, highlighted the farcical nature of the trial.

The prosecutors repeatedly twisted mundane interactions into sinister conspiracies. I mentioned the example with my son Moishie earlier—it was a pattern that repeated itself throughout the trial. In another instance, they put a customer service representative on the stand. After her substantive testimony, they prodded her to also recount that she'd seen me give a mysterious envelope to her manager, a woman named Judy Meyer. They intentionally avoided asking her what was inside the envelope and led the jury to believe it was some kind of shady exchange.

On cross-examination, my lawyer took up the story and prompted the witness to correct that mischaracterization. Judy's son had been killed in a tragic accident not long before that interaction, and the grieving, single mother couldn't even afford to pay for her son's funeral. Since he had been the driver, she was also facing potential legal action from the families of the passengers. The mysterious envelope I had handed her had been financial assistance to a person in need, during a very difficult chapter in her life.

This witness herself knew exactly what the exchange was all about and presumably informed the prosecution when she told them about it. She herself had asked me to help Judy on another occasion, when she'd fallen ill and couldn't afford treatment—something I had readily done. Yet, here they were, eliciting only one part of the story, using her words to twist an act of charity into false evidence of misbehavior on my part, secure in the knowledge that the judge had forbidden the defense from providing context to my—actually charitable—behavior.

It wasn't about the truth. They were my adversaries in an adversarial system and simply used whatever tactics and strategies they could in order to win.

At the prosecutors' prompting, and sometimes all on her own, the judge very strenuously kept the defense team within the very narrow parameters of the case. The prosecution, by contrast, ranged far and wide in their attempts to muddy me up in the eyes of the jury. They threw everything at me, from implying that I was involved in bringing illegals to the country to the infamous PETA allegations. This had nothing to do with determining the truth of the charges they had leveled, but it was helpful in persuading the jury to return a conviction against me—and that was what the prosecution was after.

This was also made clear during my own testimony, toward the end of the trial.

Another thing that jumped out at me again and again during the trial was the underhanded shrewdness that was the "sever-and-switch" maneuver that was pulled during the pre-trial phase. It spared them an immigration trial they wanted to avoid and simultaneously enabled them to claim they'd proven those charges in court—which they "did" by making related claims with a lower legal standard while the judge blocked an effective defense. I mentioned it briefly before, but it deserves some level of detailed explanation.

During the charging stage, the prosecutors had gone all out and had ended up with two general groups of charges against me, immigration and financial.

The initial thought of the prosecutors was to cram them all into one trial and benefit from the number, variety, and drama of the charges.

We were obviously opposed to this, and, to our initial delight, the judge agreed. She separated, or "severed," the cases, purportedly for the sake of justice. Her official position was that combining the cases would improperly sway the jury and it would be impossible for them to compartmentalize the charges, despite any instructions she would give.

It seemed like a big win, but we were innocent and naive. In reality, this was a clever maneuver by the judge in favor of the prosecution, and we didn't have to wait long to realize the true nature of this ruling.

Because the bank charges rested in part on the immigration charges, law and logic dictated that the immigration trial come first. This way, the immigration charges could be dealt with properly and then, if warranted, they could build the other charges on top of them. There was no need to expose the financial case jury to the improper impact of the immigration narratives that the judge herself had so clearly identified. So: Immigration first, financial second—full, thorough, and fair.

That wasn't what they had in mind. Their maneuver called for holding the financial trial first. That way, the prosecution could present a carefully restricted and curated selection of immigration testimony and sidestep the full testing of those facts that would have resulted from a proper trial.

For that to happen, they needed to shuffle things so it was financial first, immigration second—or immigration not at all, as it happens. The perfect vehicle to camouflage their illogical reshuffling of the cases soon presented itself.

Initially, the immigration trial was expected to begin mid-September. A supervisor at Agriprocessors, a co-defendant on the immigration charges, requested a few more weeks to prepare. That would put the start date of the trial in mid-October. Instead of just pushing off both trials by one month, the judge used the delay of the immigration case as the reason to put the financial trial first.

The defense team protested vigorously. The financial charges that I was facing were much more serious and far more complex than the immigration charges of this supervisor. There was no justice in accommodating a simpler trial, with less at stake, at the expense of a more serious one. Besides, as I mentioned before, the bank charges would rest in part on the conclusions of the immigration trial. If this supervisor legitimately needed more time, the reasonable solution was to delay both trials and keep the logical sequencing so justice could be done!

The defense arguments were noted, then completely ignored. The sequencing was finalized and the maneuver was completed. Everything was fully in place.

As events made clear, the extra time needed for this supervisor was only ever a fig leaf of an excuse. When it came time to actually finalize the dates of the trials, the date of the first trial was set for mid-October anyway, which would have satisfied the supervisor's request without changing the subject of the trial.

The immigration trial could have been held and laid the matter to rest, ensuring a fair and untarnished trial on the bank charges. It didn't matter. The request had been useful and it had been used. The subject of the first trial was set to the judge's and prosecutors' satisfaction and there was no revisiting the question.

Before the trial, when the prosecution had to list their witnesses and evidence, they included a significant number dedicated to making the case that Agri had knowingly employed undocumented immigrants. My lawyers obviously and immediately objected, pointing to the separation of the trials and the judge's own rationale.

The prosecution countered that the presence of illegal aliens was actually a component of bank fraud. The standard fine-print on the loan agreements stated that the borrower complies with all relevant laws. If I was actually aware that the company was violating the law by having knowingly hired illegal immigrants, they said, I was lying to the bank.

Maybe the judge had agreed to separate the trials as a way to bypass the immigration trial, where her excessive and improper involvement would undoubtedly come to light and become an issue. Maybe she realized the charges could be jumbled back together to greater effect this way. One thing is certain: Despite what she said, she didn't separate them for her stated reason—to keep the immigration testimony out of the financial trial. We know that because, when the time came to do so, she didn't. Despite her own eloquent explanation of why this would make for an unfair trial, the judge allowed it.

Suddenly, whether or not we were hiring illegals was not a subject for another trial—it was a supporting argument in this one! The prosecution brought in seven witnesses over two and a half days, laying out over ten long hours the most damaging testimony they would have presented at a dedicated immigration trial. My lawyers repeatedly objected as witness after witness was called, but they were overruled every time.

Thrust into the immigration case unprepared, we tried to mount a proper response—only to face objections from the other side that we were straying outside the scope of the trial.

Worse, the actual immigration charges in the indictment pertained to hiring and harboring illegals. A trial on those charges would have brought up every aspect of their presence, how they got there, and what, if anything, I was doing about it. I would have been able to clearly disprove all their claims, as I would eventually do at the state trial. The version they'd smuggled into the financial trial, by contrast, was much more limited and didn't allow me to get into efforts I made to screen, detect, and fire anyone not legal to work. By strictly enforcing the distinction through objections sustained by the judge, they prevented any effective response.

My lawyers were allowed to cross-examine the prosecution witnesses but they were limited to discussing the elements relevant to the prosecutors' legal angle. They couldn't flesh out the wider immigration issues with these witnesses, and certainly couldn't introduce new witnesses on those topics. Without bringing in other testimony to provide counterpoints and context, we couldn't effectively refute the prosecution's characterization and insinuations.

Their use of crippling legal maneuvers to avoid clarity made the civilized facade they put on the proceedings all the more ridiculous. One memorable example came about two weeks into the trial, on the date of my English birthday. I came into the "kill floor" that day to face off once again with my proposed executioners. In a bizarre, surreal moment, the court took a moment to note that it was my birthday, and even wished me a happy birthday, before proceeding to go on the record, back to the kill floor.

We presented as robust a defense as we could under the circumstances, starting from a very restrictive starting point and discovering new restrictions as we went. It was at the end of the trial, as the evidentiary portion drew to a close, that I was put on the stand. It had become clear that our case had been so severely undermined by these restrictions and manipulations, that there was no other way to make a real impact on the jury under the circumstances.

It was a risky move and something which many defendants avoid. Prosecutors are trained at courtroom interactions. The skilled ones use witnesses as raw material in creating precisely the impression they want—seizing on word choices, manipulating emotions, and blocking any explanations that might undermine their desired characterization. Testifying also means relinquishing the constitutional right to remain silent and the witness is compelled to answer any question posed.

Nonetheless, after agonizing over the decision, the legal team concluded that, in this case, it would be best if I testified. I was the only one with the firsthand knowledge and grasp of the details needed to address the false impressions the prosecutors had built based on omissions and ambiguities in the testimony of other witnesses. My father was asked by the defense to testify for similar reasons and he agreed.

I took the stand as a defense witness and answered all the questions the defense lawyers put to me. They didn't ask some of the accusatory questions they wanted me to address, confident that the prosecution would ask them during their cross-examination. After all, their accusations were directed at *me*. Who better to put under the microscope for a full examination of what, when, and why? There was no doubt that the prosecution would confront me when given the opportunity—except they didn't.

They lived up to their reputation, asking questions designed to get an answer they could frame as they pleased and then cutting off every attempt at context. They repeatedly ignored my answers and went on to ask follow-up questions that assumed I'd answered in a way that supported their narrative. In this way, they used the questions to tell the jury a ridiculous story while I sat there like a prop, my every correction entirely ignored.

They covered some contentious ground, but completely avoided the substantive issues I was best positioned to clarify if they wanted the truth. As a matter of fact, the day of my testimony, the prosecutors' boss came into the courtroom for the first time and physically took all the financial numbers off the prosecution table, so they wouldn't be accidentally used.

My lawyers were limited in their follow-up questions to issues raised by the prosecution, so I never got the opportunity to personally address the questions they'd avoided.

What had been underlined yet again was that the prosecution wanted certain things to remain vague and suggestive. They knew that by explaining in simple terms what I had done and why, I would dispel the cloud of confusion they'd so carefully created and they quickly rushed me off the stand without giving me the opportunity. My father, the actual owner of Agriprocessors and another witness who could contribute tremendously to clearing things up, had the same experience. When he got up to testify, the prosecutor didn't ask him a single question. Not *one*.

Before the case was formally closed and handed off to the jury for a verdict, each side was given an opportunity to sum up the case. These closing statements were not bound by the rules which governed the trial and the prosecution took full advantage of their freedom to draw conclusions, make assumptions and connections that were not supported by testimony, and use whatever rhetorical skill they had to persuade the jury.

On Monday, November 9, 2009, *chaf-beis* Cheshvan, the jury began their deliberations. The idea of a jury trial is that regular people, with real-world experience and common sense, will evaluate the truth of the matter. The reality falls far short of this.

For starters, the jury can only weigh what the judge agrees to put on the scale. They can only apply the legal standards that the judge presents to them—often without clarification, even when they request it, as I was about to see firsthand. Their decision is also made entirely blind of the consequences, as if condemning a man to a living death behind bars would not require more careful weighing and examining and a greater degree of certainty than imposing a monetary fine.

Whatever they were up to, we were no longer required to be in court all day, so we returned to the hotel a few blocks away to await and prepare for the verdict. Surrounded by the many *Yidden* who had made the trip to South Dakota to support me, I spent the day in the hotel conference room, learning Torah, *farbrenging*, and strengthening my *emunah* and *bitachon*.

The atmosphere was electric. We had all seen firsthand the absolute lack of integrity and truth in the courtroom. This left us leaning entirely on Hashem. We sincerely expected miracles, and the mood was a mix of anticipation and celebration.

One of our dear new friends, a Jew named Menachem Mendel, who lived in the spiritual vacuum of South Dakota, would stop by the courtroom throughout the trial whenever he had a free minute. Whenever he saw me or one of my family members, he would exclaim from the depths of his pure heart, with the last remnants of his schoolboy Hebrew, and with no basis other than unassailable *bitachon*: "*Zakai, zakai, zakai!*—Innocent, innocent, innocent!" During those days of jury deliberation, everyone felt like Menachem Mendel.

I spent the next morning at the large table we had set up in the hotel conference room, flanked by my father and my close friend Rabbi Manis Friedman. Around the table sat the many supporters who'd rallied at my side in my hour of need. We spent the day sharing stories of chassidim, insights into the purpose of *nisyonos*, and singing heartfelt *niggunim*.

In the early afternoon, we received a call from the court clerk. The jury wanted to ask a question and my presence was required for the judge to hear the question and respond. There was no need for supporters in the courtroom so I left them listening intently to Rabbi Friedman and went the few blocks to the courthouse.

I was dismayed to find that the conversation between the judge and lawyers had already begun without me. The question centered around intent, what they call *mens rea*, and whether it was critical for them to conclude that I'd acted with intent to return a guilty verdict on some of the charges. The court's guidance and wording were obviously not clear enough and the jury wanted clarity.

Imagine my shock when the judge's official response was to withhold any clarification and tell them to rely on the wording they were already provided. They were expected to base their decision, and potentially condemn a man to a terrible fate, on the strength of their untrained, best-guess answer to this critical question of law.

There was nothing I could do about it beyond internally dismissing this illegitimate charade and reaffirming my exclusive reliance on Hashem. When I got back to the hotel, my son Yossi asked what the jury's question had been, hoping to get a sense for which way they were leaning.

It brought to mind the teaching of the Rebbe Rayatz: When your direct involvement is complete and there are no longer natural efforts to be made, even grasping at straws is a lack of trust in Hashem. Our *hishtadlus* was now to rely on Hashem's salvation with pure *bitachon*. Instead of discussing the jury's question, I shared that thought with Yossi, threw an arm over his shoulder, and we walked, side-by-side, back into the conference room to rejoin the *farbrengen*, focusing on, *Whence our help will* [truly] *come*.

The Verdict

We continued our studying and *farbrengen* throughout the day on Wednesday, and Thursday began in much the same way. As we had since the trial began, our small congregation of family, friends, and staunch supporters from all over the US gathered in the conference room for Shacharis. After breakfast, we gathered around the tables to learn, talk, and strengthen each other.

My wife sat with the women who had come to support her. They shared thoughts and stories, upbeat in their strong *bitachon* that we would receive good news very soon and go home for Shabbos, leaving South Dakota and this whole tiresome ordeal behind us for good.

I went off on my own to say Tehillim, beseeching Hashem to save me from my predicament. When I finished, I took a walk to talk one-on-one with one of the *bachurim* from the yeshivah in Postville with whom I'd developed a particularly close relationship. We walked along the river near the hotel until it was time for Minchah.

After *davening* Minchah, we sat down to *farbreng* over an early supper. It was nearing the end of the court's workday, 5:00 p.m., and it seemed like the day would pass uneventfully. Then, my lawyer called. "Sholom, they have a verdict. We need to get down to the courthouse."

We headed back to the court, some by car and some jogging down the street, filled with giddy anticipation—the butterflies you feel right before something momentous happens. I went by car with my wife. A young woman who'd come to support and help us was driving. She called her parents to tell them that we were on our way to the court to hear the good news, that we won and we were going home. We were ready for our *nes*.

We filed through the metal detectors and into the courtroom and took our seats. The judge was already in the courtroom when we arrived. She looked up as we walked in, and when she saw me enter, she instructed that the jury be called. The jury entered the room and sat in the jury box. The judge asked them if they'd arrived at a verdict. "We have," the jury foreman replied. This was the moment.

He stood up and handed the judge a large envelope. She opened the envelope apprehensively, but the tension drained from her face and a calm satisfaction came over her as she silently skimmed the jury's decision. Over the course of the trial it had become quite clear that she was hoping for, and often steering toward, a certain outcome. From her face and body language it was clear to me before she even opened her mouth that she got what she was hoping for. Hashem's salvation would not come through this channel.

With a hint of satisfaction, the judge began reading out loud. "On count number one, such and such and such, we find the defendant…guilty," she read. "On count number two, such and such and such, we find the defendant… guilty." She continued reading, in full, all ninety-one charges and the verdict for each one. Just counting out loud to ninety-one takes quite a bit of time— this full reading of the verdict dragged on for an eternity.

I knew what was coming next.

In cases like mine, where there is no public safety concern and the court has measures in place to eliminate flight risk, the defendant would normally be allowed to post bail and return home until sentencing, but I was under no illusions. I'd had ample opportunity to see the nature and approach of the people prosecuting me (during and since the earlier bail denial) and I was sure they'd leap at the opportunity to return the Jew to prison.

The court had been working hand in glove with the prosecutors since the beginning and any "request" to detain me seemed to be entirely a formality, a matter of paperwork just awaiting a rubber stamp.

I felt my heart begin to sink but Rabbeinu Bacheye was there to catch me. His words in *Sha'ar Habitachon*, which I'd reviewed so often and so intently, sprang to my mind: "Nothing in creation can benefit or harm a person without the permission of the Creator, may He be exalted." I fixed my mind on those words, let them settle on my heart, and the fire of simple faith burned away the dread that had been welling up within me.

The words I was hearing, as painful as they were to hear, were not those of a powerful enemy, but of my loving Father. Instead of pulling back, I leaned into His decision with unqualified trust that "this, too, is for the good" and I would yet merit to be saved from the darkness that threatened to consume me.

I shook myself from my temporary paralysis and turned to look at my family and friends seated behind me. They looked exactly how I'd felt moments before—some were just frozen in place, mouths agape, processing this development; others were blinking back tears or gritting their teeth in anger and frustration.

I exchanged a glance with my wife, who'd stood by my side throughout this ordeal and who was a true source of calm and clarity, of strength and *bitachon*. She gave me a small, encouraging smile as if to say, "Don't worry—Hashem will help."

As I turned back to the table, the judge's voice filtered through the haze and snapped me back to the moment. It was taking her a long time, but she would eventually finish and then…the storm. They were going to take me away, separate me from my beloved family. My *emunah* and *bitachon* bolstering me, I felt strong enough to face it, but as a husband, a father, and a friend, I wanted to do my part to make sure that my family and friends were too.

They wouldn't allow me to speak to family, but if I acted fast, I could write them a note. There was no reason to listen to the judge's droning justification for the injustice they were bent on committing—my faith was strong that their plans would come to nothing anyway, with Hashem's help.

I grabbed a legal pad that lay on the table in front of me and quickly wrote a message:

> *Please stay strong through the ordeal. Tell the* bachurim *that I really loved learning with them and Hashem should save me even in this time, and who really knows.*
>
> *Just tell everybody I am unshaken in my faith of Hashem.*
>
> *A person goes through life and we are only the* avadim *of Hashem, so I am an* eved Hashem *and accept what comes.*
>
> *Sholom Mordechai Halevi*

I handed the paper to my wife, who read it and then passed it to my children. I thanked Hashem for giving me the presence of mind to write the note when I did. I had acted not a moment too soon. No sooner had I finished my note, than the judge completed her recitation. I had been declared guilty on eighty-six counts, all but five of the charges against me.[1]

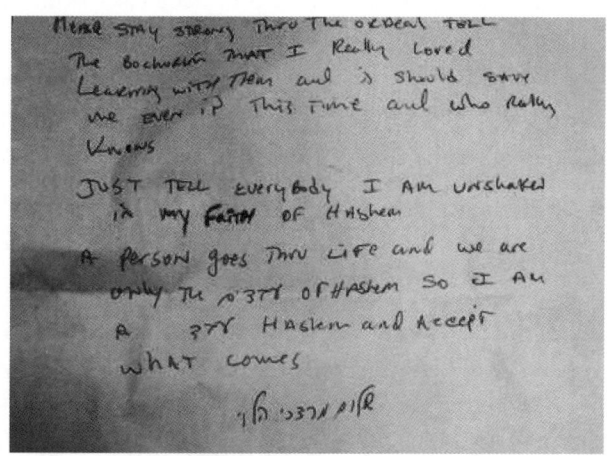

The note I wrote to my wife during the reading of the verdict.

---

1. Always seeking Hashem's fingerprints in what was happening to me, I noticed that 86 is the *gematria* of Hashem's name *Elokim*. That is the name of Hashem that is used when He conceals himself within the workings of nature—"*hateva*"—which also adds up to 86.

Sure enough, the Assistant US Attorney leapt out of his seat with a prepared motion, demanding that I be denied bail and be thrown into prison immediately, to be held while I awaited sentencing. In light of the barbaric and intolerable sentence I could expect—something the media had been gleefully calculating since the case went to the jury—I was to be considered a flight risk and immediately remanded into custody.

My lawyer, Guy Cook, challenged this request appealing to logic, legal principle, precedent, and basic human decency. He noted that there were no grounds to deny bail, since there was no suggestion that there was a danger to the community and I had carefully kept to the provisions of the hard-won and draconian pre-trial bail conditions.

Simply judging on the merits, the defense seemed to have the stronger argument, but instead of allowing me to go home with my family or even outright ruling on the spot to deny me bail, the judge delayed the decision, setting a hearing for later in the week. As the prosecutor wanted, I would languish in jail until the predictable decision to keep me there could be made with less of a public outcry. The shock of the verdict would have worn off by then, and some of the attention to the case would have faded. The decision to keep a man in jail would also be easier to swallow than the order to cuff him and carry him away.

An officer who'd been sitting in plain clothes in the gallery between my family and friends now joined his colleagues on my side of the barrier and ordered me to follow him into a back room.

The *Yidden* in the courtroom were in a state of shock. I smiled at them, trying to lift their spirits and reassure them. My son Getzel began singing, "*Utzu Eitzah V'sufar,*" Hashem's reassurance through Yeshayah Hanavi that although our enemies *hatch a plot [...] it will be foiled, they speak proclamations, but they will not stand because Hashem is with us.* I smiled at him and motioned my encouragement as I was whisked through the door into a different world.

As the door closed behind me, I twisted around for one last glimpse and a restrained goodbye wave to my wife and children. Who knew how much time it would be until I would be with them again?

The back room was essentially a tiny cell. I strained to hear what was happening in the courtroom with my family and friends, but it was no use. The room was soundproof and I'd been plunged into a very loud silence. I was left in the tiny cell for a long time. I had my pocket edition of the *Chovos Halevavos* with me and I spent the time learning from it, both out of opportunity and necessity, taking real strength from its words.

My study and reflection were interrupted by an officer entering the cell. He cuffed me hand and foot and walked me through deserted hallways to the back of the building. We'd almost reached the exit when he was suddenly instructed to return me to the cell. I naturally wondered what had caused the transfer to be canceled so abruptly, but I pushed the thought from my mind as idle curiosity and returned to the pages of my *sefer*.

I later learned that many *Yidden* had waited to see me off and encourage me. Apparently, the authorities had decided at the last second to deprive them and me of that encounter and they waited until everyone left before moving me again. My brother Yossi also told me later that the prosecutor had left the courthouse smiling and spitefully waved at them in a show of victory, a sight which added to the pain of my family, friends, and supporters.

Eventually, the officer returned and cuffed me again. I was bundled into the backseat of a police car and they drove me to a facility about twenty minutes away. Night had already fallen and it was dark outside. They parked the car and walked me into the facility. The metal cuffs around my ankles were overly tight and dug into my feet painfully with every step.

The verdict and the suddenness with which I'd been whisked away left my family stunned. My wife was the first to snap out of the haze of disbelief. Her first thought was to care for my needs. "We need to find out where they're holding him, arrange for kosher food, and get him his *tefillin*." She sent the children off to make the trip back to Iowa and stayed behind to make whatever arrangements she could.

CHAPTER SEVEN
Immediate Incarceration

South Dakota Jail

WE ARRIVED AT THE LOCAL JAIL. I ASKED FOR PERMISSION TO CALL MY lawyer, but my request was denied. I asked for kosher food. They gave me an open paper bag with food in it that they claimed was kosher but it was clearly not kosher, so I couldn't eat it. I repeated my request to speak to my lawyer but they claimed he could not be reached.

A guard instructed me to follow him into a room. There, he placed a large box on the floor at my feet, along with a set of prison clothes. "Change your clothes," he told me. I started removing my clothes, first my *kapote*, then my shoes and shirt. When I reached my *tzitzis*, I stopped. As a religious obligation, protected by the rightly celebrated American freedom of religion, I had, *baruch Hashem*, been allowed to wear my *tzitzis* during my first incarceration, before bail was granted.

Confirming the obvious, I said, "I can keep my *tzitzis*, right?"

The guard didn't hesitate and responded curtly, "Nope! Everything has to go in the box!"

Surprised and concerned, I tried to determine the extent of the problem. "What about my yarmulke?"

He just repeated himself. "Nope! Everything has to go in the box!"

This great country guarantees freedom of religion even for prisoners, which he surely knew. *Perhaps*, I thought, *because this is South Dakota, where there aren't many* Yidden, *this guard is simply unfamiliar with these garments and doesn't realize that they're religious articles and protected by law.*

As non-confrontationally as I could, I explained. "I'm Jewish. The Torah requires that I wear a yarmulke and *tzitzis* at all times. This isn't something

I'm inventing now that I'm here—it's explicitly and unequivocally stated in our holy books. It's so important, that a Jewish man is not allowed to walk four steps if he is not wearing his yarmulke and *tzitzis!*"

The guard looked at me with quiet menace and said words I will never forget—not so much for their intended effect, but for the message from Hashem they contained: "Listen, buddy. A lot of things are going to change for you tonight!"

As chilling as his words were in the moment, looking back, I'm eternally grateful for them. He was trying to intimidate me, but through Divine Providence he acted as Hashem's *shliach*, telling me exactly what I needed to hear at that moment.

The abrupt transition from freedom to incarceration is not merely a change of location or superficial circumstance. The cold and dark places called jail or prison overwhelm the person, by design.

From the moment he's taken into custody, the prisoner is made entirely dependent and helpless, relinquishing control over every aspect of his being. He's shackled hand and foot and led around by prison guards at whose command he walks and at whose command he stops. Marched through empty hallways of stark cinder block, with no decoration or hint of humanity, past heavy steel doors and tiny barred windows, the absolute authority of the prison personnel over the prisoners begins to sink in.

During the intake process, everything that reflects a person's humanity or identity is replaced or removed. His civilian clothes are confiscated and he is issued prison garb. Even his watch, if he has one, is taken away, leaving him dependent on others for something as simple as knowing the time. This psychologically enforces the feeling that he's been torn from his old world. It's a clean break—anything he had or used before has no place in this new world.

If all that doesn't make it clear enough, the inmate is given an orientation in which his name is superseded by his prison register number. He's informed in no uncertain terms that he's the property of the prison and that basic human needs are privileges that can be curtailed for any reason.

Having been stripped of the physical and emotional support structures of family and community, the prisoner faces this onslaught all on his own. His mind is barraged by thoughts of the past, straining to process the unfamiliar and painful present, and troubled by the uncertain, foreboding future. His heart ceases to be a tool of discernment and instead becomes a tangled mess of self-pity, apprehension, and sorrow.

Struggling with all of this, off-balance and in a fog, the guard's words suddenly put my situation in clear, stark terms. His phrasing could not have been more perfect. "Listen, buddy," he'd said, looming over me in his uniform as I stood in front of him half-undressed at his command.

This guy was definitely not my buddy. His words reminded me of someone else who likes to introduce himself as my buddy—my *yetzer hara*. My *yetzer hara*, too, tries to diminish my *Yiddishkeit*, disguising his attempts to pull me to the depths of *She'ol Tachtis*[1] as helpful, friendly advice, and the *yetzer hara*, too, has "a lot of things" he hopes to change. In his slyness, though, he tries to ensure that we don't realize that. It's always "just one small thing" and that's *it*, he'll stop bothering you.

Luckily, this guy, unlike the *yetzer hara*, had said the quiet part out loud— this was only the first of many changes they had in store for me. The thought of being forced to make changes to my *Yiddishkeit* hit me like a bolt of lightning, at once terrifying and illuminating. I was in extreme danger. Here, in a place called jail, they intended to force me to do things that would violate my connection with Hashem, the very essence of who I am.

My newfound clarity was quickly followed by balance, and then purpose. I was faced with an existential threat and the essence of my *neshamah* was awakened, imbuing me with iron resolve. I placed my trust in Hashem to help me in my time of need, and I made a firm commitment to Hashem to not allow "things to change for me." I would continue being the same Yid in the place called jail as I was in my home, come what may.

These thoughts and feelings take a long time to describe even partially, but they flashed through my mind and heart clear and quick as a flash. With firm resolve, I turned to the guard who was so intent on changing me and respectfully but firmly told him that, since Jewish law prohibits me from taking off my yarmulke and *tzitzis*, I wouldn't be able to take them off.

Angry, but uncertain how to proceed, the guard ordered me to follow him out of the room. I asked him if I could put my clothes back on, but he did not allow me to do so. He led me, half-dressed, into a nearby room and locked me into a large cage. There was a large cement block on one side of the cage, apparently intended for sitting, but it was very cold and uncomfortable, so I remained standing.

They'd taken my watch, so I couldn't tell precisely how long it took, but after

---

1. The nethermost depths of impurity.

what felt like twenty minutes, his superior came in. From his side of the bars, he demanded answers. "What's going on here?" I approached the bars and did my best to talk to him normally, as if there wasn't a cage wall between us.

I explained the situation as matter-of-factly as I could: The other officer had instructed me to take off my yarmulke and *tzitzis*, but I could not do that because I am a Jew. I repeated the explanations I'd given earlier about the importance of these garments and that, as a religious matter, I couldn't move from my place without them. This was a religious necessity and not a matter of personal comfort or preference.

He heard me out and said, "Okay, I'll check this with a rabbi." I wondered where he would find a rabbi in a prison in South Dakota at nine or ten o'clock at night, but it made no difference. Whoever he spoke to would surely inform him that a yarmulke and *tzitzis* are legitimate religious needs.

A long time passed. Eventually, he returned holding a printout. It was an email from someone calling himself a rabbi. It said, "You're in jail and they are the officers in charge. You need to obey them. Take off your yarmulke and *tzitzis*, and give it to them." To make his ignorance sound like an authentic rabbinic ruling, he threw in an (irrelevant) Aramaic phrase from the Talmud— "*Dina d'malchusa dina.*"

I was dumbfounded and hurt. Whoever this "rabbi" was, he could easily have quoted the clear sources which require every Jewish man to wear a yarmulke and *tzitzis*, knowing that the law of the United States affords prisoners their religious rights. I'm sure the officers would have complied if he would have supported me. Why was he sabotaging my legal right and religious duty by using his rabbinic status to give them a halachically invalid rubber stamp?!

The officer considered this a legitimate, binding decision by a credentialed rabbi. I had to show him it was not. I asked him if he knew what the Aramaic words meant.

"No," he said.

"I *do*," I told him. "The words mean, 'The law of the country is the law.' It's a principle by which the Torah gives religious standing to the secular regulatory and monetary laws of the land, which must be followed," I explained.

"It has absolutely nothing to do with matters of the soul and religious observance, over which the Torah retains exclusive and ultimate authority. Anyone applying this principle to the question at hand is a total ignoramus, ordained or not.

"Despite the appearances of my current predicament," I went on, "I've always obeyed the law of the land, as the Torah demands, and I will continue to do so, but I cannot, will not, and by law *am not required* to, cede control over my soul and its obligations to G-d."

Parenthetically, I was in places called jail and prison for nearly nine years, but when I left, my record was pristine, something which is extremely rare. I didn't have a single prison violation penalty, called a "shot," for violating any of the many rules that inmates must follow. *Dina d'malchusa dina.*

To bolster my statement, and also to benefit from the presence of the Rebbe Rayatz, who, like all tzaddikim, are present when their Torah is repeated in this world, I added:

"There was a great rabbi who was arrested and imprisoned in the Soviet Union in 1927, at a time when religious observance was under attack. On the steps of the train that was to take him from prison into exile in the frozen outlands of Russia, he declared that only our body was sent into exile, but not our soul.

"Applied to this situation, it is the proper role of a government to craft and impose laws and regulations to create a safe and productive society. Torah law *requires* us to follow those laws. However, if laws are made which infringe on our *souls*, outlawing the religious responsibilities which are the rightful domain of Torah, the Torah *requires* that we nonetheless continue to serve G-d exactly as He has commanded. No king or government has the authority to issue edicts which countermand those of G-d."

After paraphrasing the Rebbe's teaching, I got personal. "My parents immigrated here from the oppressive regime of Communist Russia which outlawed religion. Thank G-d, here in America we are guaranteed legal freedom of religion. If there seems to be any conflict between law and religion it *must* be a misunderstanding!"

I finished my long and passionate response by simply saying, "It's *impossible* that you are talking to a real rabbi. There's no rabbi in the world who would say that I need to remove my yarmulke and *tzitzis*, when the Torah demands that I wear them at all times!"

I got the feeling that the officer didn't quite get the nuances of my answer, but my sincerity and certainty and the talk about Aramaic and souls and exiles seemed to have created some doubt. "Okay," he decided, "I'm going to ask him again."

An officer reassessing a decision, particularly one already communicated to an inmate, is unusual in the extreme, a matter of both personal pride and institutional discipline. Seeing him reconsider strengthened my perception that if he was properly informed, he would allow me to fulfill my religious responsibilities.

He turned and left, leaving me locked in the cage, half-dressed on a chilly fall night with only a freezing cold cement block to sit on. Time passed slowly.

After what seemed like forever, the officer walked back into the room. I stood up and approached the bars. He informed me that he'd spoken to the "rabbi," who had agreed that I could keep one of the two—either the yarmulke or the *tzitzis*. All that remained was to decide: Which of the two would I be taking off and handing in?

I felt vindicated. Prevailing in an argument, even to this small degree, felt like an accomplishment. In a place called jail, it's rare to win *any* argument, no matter how unassailable your logical or legal argument is. My initial thought was to accept the compromise, but as I began weighing the two mitzvos in order to decide which to relinquish, I immediately caught myself, realizing my mistake.

When you get down to it, the details of each mitzvah had no bearing on why I was doing them. I was doing them both because they are the will of Hashem. It wasn't about what *I* wanted and which one *I* valued more; it was about what *Hashem* wants. To know that, we can only look in the Torah, where it says very clearly, as I'd been repeating all night, that I need to wear *both*, the yarmulke and the *tzitzis*! I couldn't surrender either one.

I said to the officer, "I'm not sure where this 'rabbi' is getting these arbitrary negotiating positions, but I *do* know that this is clearly decided in the Torah. I cannot negotiate over G-d's commandments or change His commandments to me. I need both."

Seeing that they wouldn't talk me out of either mitzvah, the officer changed tactics. "Listen, Rubashkin!" he threatened. "If you cooperate, we'll complete your processing and I'll let you out of here into the general population. If not, I'll throw you into the SHU!"

SHU (pronounced "shoe") is an acronym which stands for Special Housing Unit. It's a euphemism for solitary confinement, which is widely considered a form of torture. This great country values kindness and humanity, which is why it's not labeled honestly and is instead called "special housing," but that does not diminish its horror.

Despite the threat, I responded calmly, "I *want* to listen to you, but I need my yarmulke and *tzitzis*. It's a requirement of my religion."

He left the room and came back a short while later with five guards. The effect they were going for was "intimidating," but they only managed "ridiculous." They filed into the room in full riot gear; each officer wore a riot helmet and body armor and carried a large transparent body shield in one hand and a cudgel in the other.

Here I was, sitting in a cage, half-dressed and handcuffed, and they were advancing on me equipped for war. The contrast and the sheer disproportionality were so bizarre that I burst out in disbelieving laughter. They stood there, a wall of burly men projecting violence, but my reaction had defused some of the tension and somewhat de-escalated the situation. It reminded me of a chassidic interpretation of the *pasuk, Ki b'simchah seitzei'u*— "Joy will extricate you from all adversity!"

They entered the cage and forcibly removed my yarmulke and *tzitzis*. It was a devastating feeling to be stripped of my religious garments. I was handcuffed and in no position to resist, but when one of them then said, "Okay, now stand up and move!" I quietly reminded them that I could not move without my yarmulke and *tzitzis*. I was still hoping that, seeing my earnest commitment to my religion, they would allow me to continue to practice it, as is my right.

Instead, determined to get me to solitary, one of the officers left the cage and returned shortly with a wheelchair. They picked me up, placed me into the wheelchair, and wheeled me to the medical room for a perfunctory medical examination and then wheeled me to the building that housed the SHU.

They were using insanity as their pretext for throwing me into the SHU, so I was forced to wear an anti-suicide smock, which inmates call a "turtle suit." It's a thick, shapeless, sleeveless piece of material which covers the body from the shoulders to the thighs, fastened at the shoulders and sides with Velcro fasteners. The inmate's head, bare arms, and bare legs poke out of the "suit," like a turtle in a shell.

Many guards came to gawk at the spectacle, and I was forced to put on the clothes with the unnecessary, inappropriate, and humiliating audience of a handful of smirking guards. They sat me back in the wheelchair, placed a thin folded bedsheet on my lap, and wheeled me off to a cell in the special housing unit.

Solitary Confinement

The cell in the SHU was the kind of cell that comes to mind when you imagine a dungeon. It was small with a single tiny window at the top of the wall, too high to see through. A cement ledge jutting out of the wall, with a thin mat on top, served as a seat or bed.

In the center of the cell was an ominous-looking raised cement block, about six feet in length with two bolts at each end. I shuddered to imagine the poor fellow they deemed insane enough or for some other reason requiring restraint to the floor—for his own safety, of course. I hoped I would not be there long enough to confirm my suspicions about what the four bolts were for.

It may not sound like much, but the psychological toll of a stay in the SHU is enormous. Even seasoned inmates who have long made their peace with incarceration fear the SHU. A short anecdote from around a year later, in Otisville, demonstrates this very powerfully and is worth telling out of sequence:

It was a morning like any other in FCI Otisville. The barrack was fairly quiet. Most of the prisoners were out doing their mandatory prison jobs or following their own daily routine in the exercise room or prison yard.

I was walking up the stairs to the fourth level, where the computer room was situated, when I saw four officers come up the stairs from the other side and head over to a cell across from the computer room. They entered the cell and emerged a short time later with an inmate nicknamed "Fuzzy." Fuzzy was walking in front of the officers, his head lowered and his hands cuffed behind his back as they walked him down the stairs and out of the barracks.

His cellmate, "Bucky," was standing nearby. "Where are they taking him?" I asked.

"They're taking him to jail," he said.

I looked at him, leaning on the wall near his cell. "They are taking him to *jail?* Umm…where do you think *we* are?!"

He shook his head at my inexperience and naiveté. "They're taking him to the *SHU…*"

Even the difficult and painful confinement in a prison barrack feels like freedom relative to time in the SHU, and the inmate being taken there, to a lower level of gehinnom, feels the way a free man feels when he is first denied his liberty and incarcerated. The isolation and solitude strips the person of his humanity and his ability to express himself or connect to others, magnifying his pain to an unbearable degree. It was directly into this gehinnom that I was thrust as my introduction to this new world.

I wrapped myself in the single sheet they gave me, wearing it like a shawl. This enabled me to cover my head, which, since they stole my yarmulke, would otherwise have been uncovered, and also to cover my shoulders and upper arms, which were left bare by the turtle suit.

I sat down heavily on the cement ledge, in turmoil. I thought back over the last few hours. The trial that I should have won was lost. Instead of going home with my family to rebuild our lives, I was thrown into jail.

Most devastating of all, I fought hard for my right to wear my yarmulke and *tzitzis* and lost. Like everything in creation, my inability to keep these mitzvos was an outcome determined by Hashem and it felt like a repudiation, *chas v'shalom*. In Hashem's embrace, I could face any adversity, even being torn away from my loved ones, *Rachmana litzlan*, but in that moment, it felt like He was no longer embracing me. I was flying through a storm and it felt like I'd lost the wings keeping me aloft.

I sat there in solitary confinement, dressed like an insane person, feeling more alone than at any time since this had all began. This was the darkest moment of my *nisayon*. All the battles I'd fought until that moment had been against adversaries. Here, in the enforced solitude of the Special Housing Unit, physically suffering and mentally reeling, I faced every person's most real challenge—the internal struggle.

Exploiting my torment, the small, destructive voice of my *yetzer hara* echoed in my mind, slyly pushing me toward the abyss of depression and despair.

Born and bred in America, I now faced an entirely different form of *nisayon* than any I'd experienced in my life up to that point. In the past, the struggle was limited to *wanting* to do a mitzvah. Once that was achieved, actually *doing* the mitzvah was just a matter of implementation. Now, in an experience straight out of the most difficult chapters of Jewish history, I desperately *wanted* to do the mitzvah and I was being forcibly prevented from doing so by others.

"Look around," my *yetzer hara* whispered. "You've been forsaken, abandoned by G-d to rot in this terrible place. He doesn't hear your prayers and doesn't want your service. See? You fought to hold on to your yarmulke and *tzitzis* and not only did you fail, it brought you additional suffering. If you would've cooperated, you could have at least been in a better part of jail. You no longer have His protection and His love…"

I struggled desperately to stave off despair and depression, seeking answers to the questions racing through my mind and constricting my heart.

"Why?! How?! What next?!" My heart demanded answers, explanations, assurances—but my mind could offer none. My world had become incomprehensible. Waves of doubt and self-pity washed over me, my heart heavy with despair. It was the darkest, most difficult moment of my life.

My mind cast about for answers, knowing there were none. "Why is Hashem putting me and my loved ones through this?" Only Hashem knows. "What will happen next?" Only Hashem knows. "When will I see my family again?" Only Hashem knows.

As my mind flitted from unanswerable question to unanswerable question, in a fog of despair, one word stood out in its repetition: "…Hashem…Hashem…Hashem…" Slowly, it dawned on me. I was focusing on why, what, when— but I wasn't asking myself Who! It was the only question I could answer with certainty—the certainty of *emunah* in Hashem. This realization was a beacon of clarity, piercing the fog like a lighthouse promising safe harbor.

Eager to follow the thread of this thought, I explicitly asked the most important question I've ever asked, the most important question anyone can ever ask: "Who is doing all this?" With the clarity and simplicity that was the foundation of my *chinuch* in *cheder*, as it is for every Jewish child, I knew the answer: "…Hashem…Hashem…Hashem…"

There is no power but Him. No judge, no prosecutor, no prison guard. He works through them all, for appearance's sake, but it's all *Him*—and He is my Father Who loves me. His every action, even the act of creation, is for the sake of His beloved children. Like a little child, I couldn't understand Him or know His plans, but I trusted Him implicitly and absolutely.

The questions that had moments earlier threatened to consume me now held no threat. I still couldn't answer them—but I no longer needed to. My understanding was no longer necessary or relevant. I could see the facade for what it was and I could see Hashem behind it all.

Intellect and emotion, the natural guides of a person, were failing me here because they were the wrong tools for the job. The truth I needed to see was outside the reach of my heart and mind. To see this truth, Hashem gave me an even more powerful tool—*emunah*. I had found my bedrock, the foundation on which I could stand and face this *nisayon*.

On the strength of this *emunah*, I resolved, no matter how my story unfolded, to be the same Yid in *every* situation or place without self-interested calculation or prediction of the natural outcome. I trusted in Hashem that by clinging to Him without any calculations, He would respond in kind, *middah k'neged middah*, and protect and save me, miraculously if necessary, without calculations.

I had faced my *nisayon* and came out on the other side a new, stronger person. All I needed to do now was to hold on to *Hashem Yisbarach* through Torah and mitzvos and never let go.

The darkness of isolation now illuminated by the new-found clarity of *emunah*, I saw the earlier whispers of my heart for what they were—utter foolishness offered in a moment of weakness by the *yetzer hara*, contradicted by every tenet of *Yiddishkeit*. A Yid is *never* alone, Hashem is *always* with him. No matter where we are and what we face, Hashem is with us.

The difficulty or danger is created by Hashem just so we can overcome it by seeing through its lie with *emunah* and *bitachon*. He's always there. That is a principle of Jewish faith and it's the *truth*. Even when we can't feel it in our hearts or see it with our minds' eyes, our *emunah* reminds us and reassures us that Hashem is always with us, and our *bitachon* assures us that it will end well.

The *truth* is, as the Ba'al Shem Tov says, "Hashem loves every single Yid like a father loves his only child, born to him in his old age." This is a carefully chosen metaphor for an eternal, indescribable love, one that is certainly not conditional on behavior, accomplishments, or talents.

Nothing I had experienced belied the truth of Hashem's love. A father of ten, I knew that although not every action taken for the benefit of the child is pleasant or appreciated by the child in his childishness, everything a father subjects his child to is for his benefit and driven by love. This is particularly true of our infinitely kind, infinitely wise, and all-powerful Father in Heaven.

The *truth* is that Hashem always listens to our *tefillos*. Experiencing adversity is no proof to the contrary. Hashem tells us explicitly in His holy Torah that He tests us to know what is in our hearts and to reveal the innate love for Him which is rooted in our essence and is beyond limitations.

Hashem hears our cry when we call out to Him and we attest to that in our *tefillos* themselves. It is forbidden to take Hashem's name in vain or even make a *brachah* when we are uncertain it is required, so when our *chachamim* instruct us to say, *"Blessed are You Hashem Who hears our prayers,"* we know there is absolutely no doubt about it. He is listening.

We cannot understand our infinite Father's decisions, but we don't have to. The holy Torah tells us that sometimes painful experiences are because Hashem *desires* our prayers—not because He *ignores* them, *chas v'shalom*. This is one reason given for why our holy *Imahos* were naturally barren; because Hashem desired the *tefillos* they offered those many years until finally Hashem gave them the children they prayed for.

I don't know precisely why I was given my *nisayon*, but one thing is absolutely certain: My painful experience was definitely not because Hashem was not listening to my *tefillos* or didn't want my mitzvos.

Every aspect of the *yetzer hara's* approach was a malicious lie. The Torah assures me of quite the opposite of everything he was saying, and I latched on to that with perfect faith. Far from being a repudiation, my painful circumstance, including the theft of my yarmulke and *tzitzis*, was merely a *nisayon*, a trial designed to evoke my response: ironclad resolve that Hashem will save me from these tribulations—and Hashem Himself was giving me the strength to succeed.

I resolved in that moment to think and act the way Hashem teaches us to think and act, and to reject out of hand the natural way of thinking and acting—like the pilot in Iowa had taught me so long ago to trust the instrument, not my own senses, to guide the way.

In the ridiculous-looking garment they gave me, I *davened* Ma'ariv—a very emotional one after the struggle of the past few hours. I felt closer to Hashem than I'd ever felt before. My *neshamah* was on fire, overflowing with feelings I didn't know I had within me and a powerful, overwhelming desire to remain bonded with Hashem.

"You're doing a very good job of hiding Your presence," I said to Hashem, "but I know this is all from You. Although I don't see or understand, I know that everything You do is good. I'm holding on to You with all my might and all my soul and I will *never* let go!"

I knew with certainty, with complete *emunah* and *bitachon*, that Hashem would respond to my *tefillos* and help me, showing me that He is listening. The morning would bring good news. The turbulence in my heart and mind stilled, I felt strengthened and comforted. I lay down to try and get some rest.

I don't know how much I slept that night, but it wasn't much. Lying on the thin mat with no pillow and only a sheet to provide warmth and cover in the cold cell, I kept waking up. I awoke each time feeling exposed, groping around for my yarmulke, thinking it had fallen off, or puzzling over my missing *tzitzis*, only to remember they'd both been cruelly and unjustly taken.

Each time I awoke, I wondered what time it was. They had taken my watch and I had no idea if it was still the middle of the night or if it was almost daybreak. The small window near the ceiling was no help because a halogen light right outside lit up the night and made it impossible to detect the light of day.

I eventually decided to "wake up." Not long after, I heard the sound of someone opening the small slot in the door. It was a guard doing his regular morning rounds. He told me it was approximately 5:00 a.m.

There was an intercom in the cell for emergency use, so I buzzed the officer and asked if my lawyer had called during the night. I was told that he had not. I requested a phone call to talk to the lawyer and was told it would have to wait until a few hours later.

About 6:00 a.m., the small slot in the door opened again. Through the slot I could see a man peeking in. Clearly not a prison guard, he was dressed in a button-down dress shirt and wearing round, academic-looking glasses. He told me he was there to ask me some questions. I leaned closer to the door so he would hear me clearly. I could see that he was holding a clipboard which held many sheets of printed paper. He proceeded to ask me my name, where I lived, and so on.

At first, I couldn't understand why he was asking me for information he surely already had. Eventually, I realized that he hadn't been asking so that *he* would know, but to see if *I* knew, and also to observe my manner as I answered. He was a psychiatrist sent to determine if I was sane and competent, probably following a protocol triggered by whatever pretext they'd used to throw me into solitary confinement.

He patiently went through each question on his first page, turned to the second page, and then the third. As we went through his questionnaire, he abruptly stopped and asked me in bewilderment, "What are you doing here? You don't belong here!"

His honesty and sincerity took me by surprise and I quickly answered, "You're right! I *don't* belong here and I don't know what I'm doing here!" I related the sequence of events, triggered by my need for my yarmulke and *tzitzis*, which led to their decision to confine me to the SHU. Instead of getting back to his forms, he turned and left, leaving me wondering what was going to happen next.

A short while later, two guards opened the cell door and informed me that I was being released from the SHU.

Without prompting, they handed me back my yarmulke and *tzitzis*. I put them on immediately, a physical means of connecting to Hashem, like all mitzvos.[2] I was overjoyed.

It wasn't a feeling of triumph—I knew I hadn't prevailed by my efforts. An inmate cannot win in jail. The authorities can keep a prisoner in the SHU for weeks on end, day and night, without losing any sleep over it. They don't get bored, tire of the situation, and capitulate. It's invariably the *prisoner* who is sapped of his energy and will to resist, who goes through the mental and physical torture of solitude, who gives up. They don't muscle their way out, even metaphorically. They beg to be let out of the SHU at any cost, and then rejoice in their "freedom" when they're returned to the barracks and placed in a cell.

No, it wasn't a feeling of triumph—it was a feeling of vindication.

No one knew that I had been thrown in the SHU, the deepest dungeon of the place called prison, and stripped of my yarmulke and *tzitzis*—not my family, not my lawyers, and not any of the *askanim* who worked tirelessly to help their fellow Yid. No efforts or intercessions had been made at all. Yet there I was, the very next morning, released from the dreaded SHU and once again proudly wearing my yarmulke and *tzitzis*.

Hashem *Himself* had intervened. The sudden reversal of their decision and the return of my yarmulke and *tzitzis* was a reassuring message from Hashem. He was saying, clear as a bell, "Sholom Mordechai, I am with you! I love you, I hear your *tefillos*, and I want you to connect with Me. You did well. Here, take your yarmulke and *tzitzis* so you can connect to Me."

This put to rest all the nonsense about being alone and abandoned, unloved and ignored by Hashem. It confirmed the truth of the *emunah* and *bitachon* I'd fought so hard that night to maintain. It was very encouraging. Although my overall situation had not changed and I still found myself in a place called jail, separated from my family and cut off from the world, Hashem wanted me to know and *see* that He was with me and that I was not alone. This gave me the strength and energy I needed to face the challenges ahead.

---

2. The word mitzvah, in fact, is from the root "*tzavsa*," which means to connect.

CHAPTER EIGHT
Ejected from South Dakota

My Missing *Tefillin*

A NEW DAY HAD DAWNED. MY CIRCUMSTANCES HAD CHANGED dramatically, but my duties to Hashem remained the same. I needed to *daven* Shacharis.

I turned my attention to obtaining my *tallis* and *tefillin*. I renewed my requests for a call to my lawyer, which would have helped me get my *tefillin*, but they were denied, as they had been the night before. I was sure that personal calls wouldn't even be considered. Besides, my family didn't need prompting or reminding and were surely doing everything they could to get my *tallis* and *tefillin* to me.

A guard brought in food for breakfast. It wasn't kosher, but I didn't want to split my focus with a fight about kosher just then. I could go without food for a little while, but I'd never missed a day putting on *tefillin* in my life. "I'm sorry, sir," I told the guard, "but I can't eat any food before my morning prayers. I need my *tallis* and *tefillin* in order to pray."

He said that they'd inquired about the whereabouts of my *tallis* and *tefillin* when I'd last requested them, but they could not be located. "In that case I can't eat," I said.

"Are you refusing to eat?" he asked.

"Can't" or "won't" is not a trivial distinction. Engaging in a hunger strike in a place called prison has ramifications. Under certain circumstances, that would even give them the authority to force-feed an inmate. "I am explicitly *not* refusing to eat. I'm hungry and would very much like to eat, but for religious reasons I can't. I must first pray, wearing my *tallis* and *tefillin*."

Hearing this, he turned and left, taking the non-kosher food with him. I hadn't eaten in sixteen hours.

Two guards came in, cuffed my hands, and shackled my feet. They hustled me out of the facility and into the backseat of a police car. Two other guards sat up front and they pulled out of the parking lot.

I was hungry, tired, and a bit disoriented from the emotional whiplash. Twenty-four hours earlier, a terrible threat loomed, but I'd expected to win the fight for my life. The weight of the moment was also lightened by the support of the family and friends who'd surrounded me, some of whom had come from thousands of miles away. Now, less than a day later, the fight was over. I hadn't won. I was speeding across the expanse, the only presence my two silent jailers, and my friends and family didn't even know where I was or how I was faring.

The passing time weighed on me. I asked the guards if they'd heard anything about my *tallis* and *tefillin*. They had not. I asked them to call, which they did, but no further information was forthcoming.

The ride was physically painful. Sitting for so long in such a cramped space, unable to move, with the metal restraints digging into my hands and feet, the pain and discomfort increased with each passing minute. The pain would only be relieved when we reached our destination—and who knew where and when that would be.

In my years at the processing plant, I'd become well acquainted with the laws governing humane handling while transporting animals. It occurred to me, sitting in that car, that human beings subjected to incarceration would greatly benefit if those same standards (at a minimum) were applied to people as well.

The scenic Iowa landscape, fields and farms as far as the eye could see, once felt like an invitation—to plant and grow, to build and develop. Now I felt nothing. The locked door and shackles symbolized my complete removal from that world. Like a disembodied *neshamah*, aware of the physical world but unable to interact with it or influence it, I could no longer contribute.

This realization was more painful than I would have anticipated and would prove to be a big part of the ongoing pain of incarceration. I quickly turned my thoughts to the things I *was* still able to do, at least in theory, the most important one being serving Hashem. That brought me right back to the topic of my still-missing *tallis* and *tefillin*. I repeatedly asked if they'd been located and the guards repeatedly answered, "We haven't heard anything"—although, after the first time or two, they stopped calling to check and just repeated their response.

After a long two hours, we arrived at the Woodbury County Jail in Sioux City, Iowa. As we pulled into the parking lot, I was struck by a bizarre sight. A civilian was parking his car in the same parking lot and walking into an adjoining building to start his day. The thought of people going about their nine-to-five in such close proximity to people suffering behind bars was disturbing.

I was unloaded and led upstairs via elevator to the receiving room. We walked in and the guards bringing me in announced themselves in the same tone as a package delivery service dropping off the day's packages.

They were given a clipboard and signed over custody of their package—me. The officer at the new facility also had intake paperwork to complete. While those papers were being completed, I was finally allowed to make a call home. This was the first time I'd spoken with my family—or anyone other than prison staff—since they took me away the day before. It's hard to describe the joy a simple phone call can bring. I was very grateful to Hashem.

I fought to keep my overwhelming emotions in check, so as not to increase the pain of my loved ones. For the same reason, I didn't tell them that I hadn't been given food. They were understandably relieved to hear my voice and told me how difficult it had been for them to hear the unjust verdict and watch me being led away without any time to exchange some words or hugs.

I hadn't been the only one who'd had a spiritually and emotionally turbulent night. It was painful to hear about, but I was gratified that we had each come to the same conclusion, finding strength in Hashem. Our hours upon hours of studying and discussing the *Sha'ar Habitachon*, and *emunah* and *bitachon* in general, had stood us all in good stead.

I couldn't speak freely because the guards were listening to the phone call, but after informing them that I'd been transferred to Sioux City, I shared a sanitized version of the events of the previous night. I told them that my yarmulke and *tzitzis* had been taken away and how, without any earthly intervention, Hashem had miraculously returned them to me.

I emphasized this in order to show them that Hashem was with us. Seeing the Divine Providence in everything that occurred would strengthen their *emunah* and *bitachon* that Hashem would free me very soon as well as help us all be *b'simchah*, even under the circumstances, as Hashem wants us to be.

We were leaning on each other. Encouraging *them* to be strong and happy reassured them that my *own* spirits were good, which helped *them* be strong and happy, which helped *me* be strong and happy.

Having covered the key points and put their minds at ease, I turned to what was really on my mind: "Where are my *tallis* and *tefillin?*"

"What do you mean?" they asked, bewildered. "We gave them your *tallis* and *tefillin* last night, when you were still in South Dakota!" Shocked, I realized that the prison officials who kept responding that my *tefillin* were unaccounted for had been lying, plain and simple. What surprised me even more was that I was even surprised—after everything I had been through.

I was shaken by this disguised obstruction of my religious needs. Up to that point, I'd felt some degree of certainty that I would be able to obtain the things I needed to practice my religion and would be granted the time to use them. I was no longer so sure. This made me realize that I still based this expectation, at least to some extent, on the promises set out in the laws of the land, which I now learned are implemented by individuals who might subvert them.

Shifting my center of gravity, I leaned fully and completely on Hashem. *He* would help me fulfill His mitzvos. Any opposition shrank to irrelevance before Him, and my certainty returned. This is something *Sha'ar Habitachon* emphasizes; our *bitachon* that Hashem will provide our needs also applies to the needs of our *neshamah*. The will and commitment to do the mitzvah is *our* part, but we need Hashem to provide the means and we need to trust that He will do so.

Around noon, the intake forms were finally all filled out. The human transfer completed, I formally entered the local branch of gehinnom. Every facility issues their own prison clothes and I was issued a local set and instructed to change. *Baruch Hashem*, they didn't challenge my right to wear my yarmulke and *tzitzis* and the process was completed without incident.

I was led through a maze of hallways and doors until we reached a large room. Along one wall of this room was a series of arch-shaped cell doors. The walls were made of brick or stone and the cells were extremely small in height and size. Responding to my unspoken misgivings about these small closets, the guard assured me that this was only a temporary holding area. Incoming prisoners were usually held there for about a day, and I would be transferred out later. He opened one of the doors, prodded me inside, and slammed and locked the door behind me.

The cell was extremely cramped so I couldn't get comfortable, but, exhausted from my sleepless night in the SHU, I soon dozed off. Every now and then I awoke with a start, disturbed that I still hadn't put on *tefillin* and the day was passing.

The ability to fulfill the mitzvah was simply and entirely out of my control, a textbook case of *onnes*.[1] I would certainly not be faulted for failing to put on my *tallis* and *tefillin* that day, but a mitzvah is not just an obligation from which we might arguably be exempted by circumstances. It's an opportunity to connect with the infinite Creator.

At fault or not, if I missed that day's mitzvos, I would've missed out on that connection to Hashem and it could never be recovered. The words of Reb Yoel Kahan on the subject, which I'd heard often as a young man, echoed in my mind: "*A patch vestu nisht krigen, uber der panim vet bleibin shmutzig*—You won't get a smack for it, but your face will remain dirty."

I begged Hashem for the miracle I needed in order to serve Him that day by putting on my *tallis* and *tefillin*. I must have dozed off again, because I awoke with a start to the loud rasping sound of the steel door opening.

The guard instructed me to come out, mumbling something about being taken to another room. Somehow, I gathered that she was taking me to a rabbi who had come to see me. Worried that the day had passed, I asked her what time it was. It was just about 4:00 p.m., still some minutes before *shkiah*. I *davened* that this mysterious visit involved *tefillin* and that I would still manage to put on *tefillin* that day.

We passed the large heavy door separating the temporary holding area from the rest of the building, and walked through a series of hallways. Passing an open door, I peeked inside and saw a break room with a sink. I felt like a parched man in the desert stumbling on an oasis! This was a golden opportunity to wash my hands properly with *negel vasser*.

I asked the guard if I could possibly wash my hands in the sink, since while meeting the rabbi, I was going to do a religious ceremony. She seemed confused by the unusual and unexpected request, but she didn't object. Before she had a chance to reconsider, I bolted into the room and washed my hands with a cup from the countertop. The feeling of purity, readiness for the *kedushah* of the mitzvah, was indescribable.

---

1. When one is forced to transgress a halachah against his will and therefore not held accountable.

We finally reached the room where the rabbi was waiting. I entered and saw a Yid standing there with a *kippah* on his head. On the table next to him was my *tallis* bag! He greeted me with a warm smile and a handshake. "*Shalom aleichem,*" he said. "My name is Rabbi Greene. I'm the rabbi in this city."

A clean-shaven, middle-aged man, with a bushy white mustache and a jovial smile, he was clearly not a chassid. Before I could respond to his greeting, perhaps thinking I needed an icebreaker, he shared a little bit about his background, ending with, "Actually, years ago, I learned in Yeshivas Tiferes Bachurim."

I knew the yeshivah well. It's a Lubavitch yeshivah geared for *ba'alei teshuvah*, located in Morristown, New Jersey. It adjoined the main Lubavitch yeshivah in that city, where I had learned for three years. I spent quite a bit of time with the Tiferes Bachurim students while I was there, although it wasn't during the time that this Rabbi Greene was there.

Under other circumstances, it would've been a pleasure to reminisce about yeshivah days together, but this was not the time. The daylight was fading and time was running out. I needed to put on my *tallis* and *tefillin* before the sun set.

"*Aleichem shalom!*" I responded. "Thank you so much for bringing me my *tallis* and *tefillin*. If you'll excuse me, I need to hurry and put them on before sunset." He nodded in agreement as I opened the *tallis* bag. I reached in and took out my *tallis*. I checked the knots and the strings and made the *brachah* while wrapping myself in the *tallis*.

When we wear the *tallis*, we are physically encircled by Hashem's mitzvah, which is itself a reminder of all His mitzvos. I held the *tallis* tightly around myself for a long moment—reveling in Hashem's embrace and drawing strength in it when I needed it most—leaving go only because of the time constraint. I still needed to put on the *tefillin* before the sun set.

I quickly reached into the *tallis* bag where my Rashi *tefillin*[2] were supposed to be. They weren't there. I opened the bag more fully and looked inside. The Rabbeinu Tam *tefillin* were right where they belonged, but the Rashi set was definitely missing.

---

2. There are a number of opinions about the order in which the four *parshiyos* are to be arranged in the *tefillin*. The sequence universally accepted is known as "Rashi *tefillin*." Some have the custom to also put on a pair of *tefillin* with an alternative sequence, known as "Rabbeinu Tam *tefillin*," as stated in *Shulchan Aruch*.

I was baffled. I turned to the guard who was supervising the interaction and asked, "There were two smaller bags in here. Where's the other bag?"

She looked where I was pointing and said matter-of-factly, "They sent two of the same item. You had permission for one, so we took one out."

This was clearly ignorance, not malice, but what could I do about it? The prison staff is trained to mistrust anything a prisoner tells them. How could I convince her that the two sets were not duplicates, that they were different on the inside? Explain the opinions of Rashi and Rabbeinu Tam?! Yarmulke and *tzitzis* were relatively simple to understand and even there, I'd failed to persuade them. Even if I could eventually find the words, by the time I managed to give her even the basic outline, sunset would have long passed. Rabbi Greene didn't think to weigh in, so, considering the issue settled, she left the room to allow me to pray.

There was no time to waste. I grabbed the mitzvah in front of me, the Rabbeinu Tam *tefillin*. I opened the *tefillin* bag. Every aspect of this simple action washed over me. The feel of the velvet, the sound of the rickety zipper, the smell of the worn leather. My hands trembled as I removed the *tefillin* from their boxes and placed them on my arm and my head, wrapping myself in the leather straps and in Hashem's warm and holy embrace.

I said Shema, which asserts Hashem's oneness and describes that even the material blessings we enjoy are from Him. This got me thinking about *hashgachah pratis* and I was suddenly struck by a realization.

Rabbi Greene had made what I'd initially dismissed as small talk. I had gently discouraged it so that I could get to the mitzvah at hand, but I now realized that he'd said something very important about his background, something Hashem had provided to help me fully fulfill the mitzvah of *tefillin*. The open Divine Providence, that he would offer exactly that piece of personal information as a conversation starter, was astounding.

Hoping his initial failure to speak up was just an oversight, I turned to him and said, "Rabbi Greene, you said that you studied in Tiferes Bachurim. You must know that we put on two pairs of *tefillin* and they are not just duplicates. If *I* tell her that I need the second pair she won't believe me, but if you, the rabbi, tell her, she will surely give it back to me and I won't miss a day of putting on *tefillin*!"

Thankfully, my positive judgment of my fellow Yid was correct. When the guard returned a few moments later, Rabbi Greene told her that the two bags were actually not duplicates and I really needed both. *Baruch Hashem*, the guard accepted this and brought in my Rashi *tefillin*. I was fortunate and overjoyed to put on both sets of *tefillin*!

This was a real contrast to the night before, in South Dakota. There, a clergy-person had been a source of pain and obstruction to my religious needs. Now, the rabbi was a source of salvation and comfort, enabling me to fulfill my religious needs exactly as Hashem commanded me.

I marveled at the Divine Providence. Of all the people who could've been in the post of rabbi in a Conservative/Reform congregation in the remote Midwestern city where I was being denied my second pair of *tefillin*, Hashem ensured it was Rabbi Greene, an alumnus of Tiferes. Any of the typical clergy-people in this position, including the woman he had recently replaced, would more than likely not know or not care about the distinction between the two pairs of *tefillin*.

By sending a *shliach* to help me fulfill an important and irreplaceable mitzvah on that Friday, even in the darkness of a place called jail, Hashem was sending me a loud and clear message for the second time that day. I am not alone, He is with me, He loves me, and He wants me to connect with Him through His holy mitzvos!

Throughout my ordeal, remembering these embraces from Hashem helped me overcome the poisonous whispers of my *yetzer hara* and serve Hashem with *simchah* even in a place called prison. This connection to Hashem was a source of light and warmth in a place of darkness.

Another thing evident from these experiences was that Hashem's intervention comes in response to our own efforts. That morning, I'd focused my efforts on getting my *tallis* and *tefillin before* trying to address the food situation. Showing Hashem that His mitzvos are so important to me, more so than food or drink, and that I would serve Him without calculation, brought about, *middah k'neged middah*, a miraculous sequence of events which brought me my *tefillin*.

After I finished *davening*, I was allowed to spend some time with Rabbi Greene. I don't recall what we spoke about, but I do remember it as a very warm and *Yiddishe* discussion. I had the strong impression that I was sitting with a genuine Yid, with a caring Jewish heart, who truly cared about my plight and sought to ease the pain as much as he could. He was not judgmental and truly fulfilled the mitzvah of loving your fellow Jew as yourself.

He told me that he lived within walking distance of the county jail and, if I would like, he would be happy to visit on Shabbos. He would be granted access to me in his capacity as rabbi. Of course, I jumped at this generous offer. He also gave me a book that he had brought so I would have something to read.

The allotted time was up and he needed to leave. We parted warmly, wishing each other the Friday afternoon *brachah* of Jews everywhere: "Have a good Shabbos!" I fully intended to. I was determined to have a good Shabbos, even there.

The First Shabbos

My immediate religious needs met, I was returned to the closet-sized cell in the temporary holding area. I lay down to rest, but sleep doesn't come easily in those circumstances. Night fell, and with it, the holy Shabbos arrived.

After a while, the door opened and a guard came in with food. In response to my query, he claimed that the food came from a kosher place in Minnesota. I examined the tray. There was nothing to verify the kashrus. The fish "looked kosher" and the shape of the roll suggested it might have come from a kosher bakery, but any official seal of kosher certification, if there had ever been one, was gone.

To make matters worse, the food had been opened and warmed in their non-kosher kitchen. That settled it. I couldn't eat any of the food. By that point, it had been about twenty-six hours since I'd last eaten, with no reliably kosher food likely to appear soon. It looked like this Shabbos was going to be like Shabbos Yom Kippur.

Later that evening, they took me out of the holding area and brought me to a cellblock in the jail itself. The block was comprised of a number of cells on the ground floor, built around a central common area, with a staircase in the central area leading to more cells on a second level. During the day, the prisoners could leave the cells and sit at tables in the central area.

Under the steps, there was a shower stall with a thin plastic curtain. I was very happy to see it, and not just for reasons of basic hygiene. It was the closest I could get to a *mikvah*, something I used daily before this *nisayon* tore me from my home.

I was placed in one of the upper cells. It was intended for two people but, *baruch Hashem*, there was no one else assigned to it that day.

After my time with Rabbi Greene, they had allowed me to take the *tallis* bag with me, so I had my *tallis* to *daven* with on Shabbos and also a small siddur that was in the bag. It was Shabbos Mevarchim Kislev. I said the whole Tehillim, as is my *minhag*, and then began Shacharis, *davening* for miracles in the upcoming month of miracles. I *bentched* the *chodesh*, although there was no *gabbai* to announce the *molad*.[3]

Rabbi Greene did in fact come on Shabbos. Spending time with a fellow Yid was a ray of light, and his visit gave me strength and comfort.

Shabbos drew to a close. Fifty hours had already passed since a morsel of food had passed my lips. The individual guards had apparently failed to pass along my requests for kosher food, simply noting that I had not eaten. This hadn't caused any noticeable concern until now, but two days seemed to be where they drew the line on neglect.

An officer came sometime after Shabbos had ended to ask why I was not eating. I explained, as I had half a dozen times before, that as a Jew, I could only eat kosher food and that had not been provided. The officer asked me if there was anything I'm permitted to eat that they might find in a regular supermarket. I wasn't sure what kosher-certified products might be found in a supermarket in Sioux City, Iowa, so I suggested the ubiquitous classics: matzah and grape juice with the proper certification. Also, I could eat fruits or vegetables that hadn't been cut or cooked.

To my surprise, he returned sometime later with those items. I washed my hands and broke my fast. As I ate, I found myself humming the Motza'ei Shabbos song, "*Amar Hashem l'Yaakov*," and I realized something.

When I got married, some thirty years earlier, I made a resolution to always wash and have bread for the *seudah* of *melaveh malkah*. In all that time, I'd never missed a week. Most weeks I had a proper feast with family and friends, other weeks I made do with a little roll and some warm food, but not a week went by without a *melaveh malkah* of some sort.

Here I was, behind bars in a strange city, far from my loved ones, fasting for fifty hours for lack of access to kosher food, and yet, Hashem ensured that I could have a *melaveh malkah*. This was a personal connection to Hashem, one that was certainly not as critical as *tefillin*, and I found it very inspiring and encouraging that Hashem orchestrated events to clearly communicate that this very personal link was also precious to Him.

---

3. The exact time of the expected new moon.

I asked for and received permission to call my family using a phone in the common area near the cell. It was restricted in duration but compared to my quick call the day before, it felt luxurious. I wished my family a *gut voch* and sang with them the Motza'ei Shabbos songs we always sang. Before the call was cut off, I also managed to tell them how I was doing, mentioning the food and also that it was quite cold and I found the provided blanket insufficient.

Departure from Sioux City

On Sunday, I showered for *mikvah* and was again able to *daven* with my *tallis* and *tefillin*. I ate from the same food they'd brought the night before.

Later in the day, I was notified that I had visitors. I joined the prisoners lined up in the hallway where we waited to be allowed into the visiting room, about ten at a time.

A long divider split the room in half lengthwise, its top half made of transparent glass or plastic. Chairs were placed at regular intervals along the divider, with corresponding chairs on the other side of the glass. I sat down and looked across at two *bachurim* from the Postville yeshivah, five hours away, sitting there with warm smiles of encouragement.

The room was too small for the number of conversations going on, and the noise of overlapping conversations from all sides made it difficult to focus on my own discussion. I imagine this was extra painful for those trying to have a moment with their spouses or close loved ones.

The *bachurim* brought a dose of energy and life, and we strengthened each other in our *emunah*, *bitachon*, and *simchah*. Sharing a few laughs does wonders for people in difficult situations, but as you can imagine, laughter is a very rare sound in a jail visiting room.

They'd been told that I was cold so they brought along warm clothing, which the prison authorities allowed me to receive. This warmed me emotionally and, of course, physically, until I was transferred again and the clothing was taken away.

Monday morning, *chaf-tes* Cheshvan, dawned over the jail complex. I woke up, showered for *mikvah*, and *davened*. I was taken to the laundry area to eat, most likely because they didn't want the other prisoners to see that I was eating different food.

When I returned to the common area of the cellblock, I tried to call home but the phone was dead. Puzzled, I asked one of the others if he knew why the phone was not working. He'd been around long enough to understand what it meant. "Someone is being transferred," he said. "Whenever they move someone, they cut the phones for security reasons."

That someone turned out to be me. For the third time in five days, I was handcuffed, shackled, and stuffed into the backseat of a police car. They took along the leftover pieces of the matzah they'd bought for me.

Being put in a car and carted off, with no idea where they're being taken or how long it will take, is one of those things that really drives home a prisoner's situation. It's a stark reminder that they're not in control of their own movements and are entirely under the control of someone else. This is usually intimidating and disorienting, but not to me. I already *knew* control did not rest with me and instead rested with Someone else—but that Someone else was not the prison guard, as he no doubt thought. Control over my life rested, as it always had, with Hashem Himself.

The trip took close to five hours, made all the longer because they wouldn't tell me how long it would be. The shackles and cramped space were uncomfortable, and as the hours wore on, they became outright painful, but I reminded myself that I was being carried in Hashem's hands to a destination He intended, and this gave me peace of mind and heart.

It was such a long trip that the guards from Sioux City didn't make the whole trip. Guards from the receiving jail met them part-way and I was transferred to their car. They stopped for the exchange at a jail facility, and while we were there, they allowed me to use the restroom. One of the guards walked me inside and just stood there by the door. I asked him to close the door, but he refused, saying that I needed to be monitored at all times. Just the thought of this violation of *tznius* and basic human decency was sickening, and I asked again that he give me some privacy.

The guard was surprised at my request. "You'll have to get used to it—they all do," he said unsympathetically.

"Please, do me a kindness," I pressed. "For right now, I can't stomach the idea. Whatever will be later, will be later." Looking back with experience, I consider it nothing less than miraculous, but he actually did close the door from the outside and gave me a moment of privacy.

It may seem like just a small concession in a fleeting moment, but these moments when I was protected by Hashem and saved from efforts to dehumanize me gave me the strength I needed to make the next effort.

As for his claim that they all "get used to it," that was nothing more than a lie that the softer-hearted executioners tell themselves so they can sleep at night. It's something that no human being can get used to, even those barely worthy of the name. Later on, in Otisville, I met an inmate originally from Ireland who, before being caged, killed people for money. He told me that he got used to almost everything in prison. The one thing he could never get used to was the lack of privacy in those moments of personal hygiene.

CHAPTER NINE
Awaiting Sentencing

Back in Iowa

FINALLY, AFTER MANY HOURS OF SITTING SHACKLED HAND AND FOOT IN the backseat of a car, we arrived at Linn County Jail in Cedar Rapids, Iowa. I was taken first to intake and processing. My escorts formally handed over custody to the officer behind the desk, who processed the intake paperwork and gave me the items that are issued to all inmates. I took the opportunity to make some inquiries and requests.

I had already *davened*, so putting on *tallis* and *tefillin* wasn't an immediate concern, but there were other issues I wanted to take care of. I asked if there was a toilet in the cell. There was. "In that case," I asked, "could you please issue an extra sheet? I'll need it to hang a makeshift partition for religious reasons."

Unusually, by Divine Providence, the officer doing the intake processing was a lieutenant, with the authority to make decisions. Requests to those without authority could be passed up the chain but are more often simply denied. It's less work.

He looked at me inquisitively, trying to guess what religious reason might require a bedsheet.

I elaborated: "As a Jewish man, I need to pray frequently and invoke G-d's name in blessings and in study. It's obviously inappropriate to do those things in front of a toilet. The extra bedsheet will allow me to fashion a makeshift partition so I'm not in front of the toilet."

Hashem granted me favor in his eyes and he agreed, noting in the computer that he was issuing me the additional sheet. This small notation turned out to be extremely important. Throughout the time that I was in Cedar Rapids, various guards, and even lieutenants, confronted me about my extra sheet and about how I used it as a partition. Thanks to the note in my file, I was able to show them that the officer at intake had issued it to me and authorized its use.

Every aspect of the intake was very deliberate, every detail entered into the computer. One thing I found baffling—they issued a pillow case, but no pillow! I pointed out the oversight but he told me it wasn't an oversight. "We only issue the pillow case," he said, "no pillow."

Once the intake process was completed, I was taken to a small cell adjoining the shower room. It had four sleeping-shelves and a round table in the middle. If they ever actually placed four human beings in this little space, it would be terribly cramped and smelly. Again I saw that Hashem was with me because that specific cell was used mainly for prisoners with handicaps. Hashem ensured that during the time I was in Cedar Rapids there was rarely anyone in that category and the cell was never at capacity, which would have been torture.

The next morning, I was brought into a small interrogation room. Two large and brawny officers were already seated at the table, which made the room feel even smaller and more intimidating. The larger of the two did the speaking. The question they posed to me that morning was simple but important. "What are your religious requirements?"

He picked up his pen and hovered over the paper, ready to write. From his demeanor, I understood that this would be my only opportunity. Once he put the pen down, he wasn't going to pick it up again. If I didn't request it now, I wouldn't receive it.

I started listing the things I needed. Each one prompted a mocking facial expression or disbelieving grunt from the officer, but he noted them all in my file. I got the message. "Yes, you can ask for things, but remember who is in charge."

I reminded myself of the first halachah in *Shulchan Aruch*, discussing precisely this type of interaction: Do not be cowed or intimidated by those who mock you for doing the mitzvos. I set aside the pseudo-reality they were projecting, and instead focused on the truth. My words were spoken to them, but I consciously focused my mind and directed my request to the True Authority and asked Hashem for the things I needed to serve Him properly.

Divine Providence had allowed me to spend a night in the cell before this interview, which gave me added insight into what I needed to request and what I did not. I'd been successful in getting a partition to put around the toilet, for example, so I didn't need to ask for water from outside the cell. The showers, on the other hand, were not accessible, as they had been in Sioux City. Inmates were only taken every other day, and if I wanted to use the shower as a daily *mikvah*, I *did* need to ask for that. I also brought up *davening*, kosher food, and so on.

The request that got the biggest reaction was my request that I be taken to the shower every day. He sat back in his chair in surprise. "Why?" He simply couldn't detect anything religious or holy about this request. I explained that before praying, a Jew is supposed to purify and prepare himself by immersing in a *mikvah*. If one is not available, pouring water over his body is an alternative option, and a shower meets those requirements.

His facial expressions ran the gamut of disbelief, contempt, and mockery while I gave him my explanation, but he dutifully noted the request in my file. *Baruch Hashem*, his mockery notwithstanding, the request was granted and I was able to take a shower every morning before *davening*.

I was returned to the cell, but not for long. My lawyer arrived, and I was escorted out to see him. It was the first time we'd spoken since the conviction and surprise incarceration. It felt like a lifetime ago, although it had only been a few days.

My focus was on getting home to be with my family and also to help my lawyers prepare for the still-pending immigration trial. The hearing the judge had set on the question of bail was to be held the next morning, and now that my lawyer had arrived, I expected to discuss the strategy or arguments to be presented at the hearing.

Instead, to my dismay, he'd come with an unrelated offer by the prosecutors concerning the immigration charges. They were offering to drop the charges (without conceding they were wrong) if I would agree to hit pause on the clock and give them the right to bring the charges back at any time, essentially waiving the statute of limitations.

Even with my experience during the first trial, I was eager to face off with them in court, confident that I could decisively disprove the charges they'd leveled. I saw no sense in delaying the trial, and certainly not indefinitely. Nonetheless, I was willing to give them what they wanted if they would agree to my release on bail. From bitter experience, I knew they would do everything they could to deny me bail, and the judge would likely go along, regardless of any argument I made or assurances I offered. Perhaps a negotiation like this one would succeed in securing my release.

They refused my offer, intent on opposing any release, but they also proved that my confidence was not unfounded. After I rejected their ploy, they officially dropped the immigration charges.

They chose to dismiss "without prejudice," which means that they technically retained the right to pursue the charges at a later time, but this was just a hollow attempt to disguise the reality. They were just letting themselves off the hook for charges they couldn't prove.

Wednesday, the day of the bail hearing, finally arrived. I was brought into the courtroom in dehumanizing orange prison clothes. The room was filled with family and many friends, some of whom I'd never met but who had traveled from far and wide to show support.

My lawyers entered a formal request for bail and the government resisted.

Defense lawyers usually avoid putting the defendant on the stand. In this case, they decided it was necessary, in order to allow the judge to hear from my own mouth that I was not a flight risk and so I could make the personal case for my release to be with my family. On the stand, I detailed my careful adherence to all the restrictions and requirements of my pre-trial bail conditions.

Beyond personal assurances and past compliance, my family and supporters had put together a bond unlike any the world had ever seen.

Thanks to the tireless efforts of many, my plight was known far and wide in the Jewish world. Thousands of letters had been sent, pleading with the judge to grant bail. Friends and acquaintances testified to my character and their certainty that I would not flee. Some of them, homeowners, pledged equity in their homes as bond, and six *rabbanim* and *shluchim* even pledged holy *sifrei Torah* as collateral. At a total value of over eight million dollars, if accepted, it would have been among the highest bail amounts *ever set*, up to that date.

In addition to the monetary deterrent of the bail, we offered to hire a twenty-four-hour private armed security guard to monitor my home release, to be paid for by those who saw the importance of ensuring I could be home, both for my family's sake and to better formulate an appeal.

Quite aside from the financial and physical protections, the national display of trust in me made it clear that it was not necessary to keep me behind bars to ensure that I stayed to face what was to come.

Not only was there no reason to keep me in jail, there was a very strong reason to allow me to go home. Everyone has a family and should be allowed time to prepare them for such a traumatic event as incarceration, but in my case, there was an added dimension, one which the judge was legally obligated to consider.

My son Moishie is developmentally delayed and autistic. Years earlier, we had visited the well-known Autism Treatment Center of America to develop an individual treatment program. My close relationship to Moishie was noted by the experts, and was one of the linchpins around which his program was designed.

At that point, we'd been following this program for years and he had grown tremendously. At six years old, when we started, he was completely nonverbal and emotionally volatile, given to outbursts of frustrated violence. With years of loving guidance and with undivided attention, he had learned to communicate verbally (although still only in sentence fragments) and his emotional state had stabilized.

From the witness stand, I personally made the heartfelt case for my son. My absence would be more than just one piece of the program missing. For autistic people, any change is completely disruptive and would likely set him back years.[1] The temporary incarcerations I had so far endured had already had a marked negative effect, and any additional time I could spend with him would be of immeasurable value.

The prosecutors were unmoved. They did take the opportunity of my testifying to dig into miscellaneous issues upon cross-examination, but they maintained their firm opposition to granting bail. Despite their opposition, in cases like mine, where there's no danger to the community and any risk of flight has been adequately (and previously) addressed, basic human decency calls for bail to be granted and it's well within legal precedent to do so.

In all, we made a very strong case, both legally and morally. The feeling in the courtroom (of friends and family and even myself) was that we had made a

---

1. These were not empty words, and sadly came to pass. His verbal development stopped entirely and his emotional control deteriorated noticeably in my absence.

compelling case and that I would have bail. No one truly understood the level of personal hostility directed at me.

Thursday passed with no word. On Friday, my wife traveled the ninety miles to Cedar Rapids with the intention and expectation, based on pure *bitachon*, that a positive ruling would be issued and she would be able to bring me home for Shabbos.

I called her that morning to find out if she had news. She told me that she didn't, but that she was waiting outside so she would be where she needed to be when the good news came. She couldn't come in for a visit, but we came up with the next best thing. Across the room from where the payphone was, there was a small, sealed window overlooking the river and the street that ran along the opposite bank. If she crossed the river and stood across from the jail, we might be able to see each other from that window.

She went to the spot I had described, and when I called back, she told me she was there. I left the phone receiver hanging and went to the window. It was a lot further than I'd imagined. Squinting, I thought I could see her. I went back to the phone and told her. She was happy that I could see her, even though it was impossible for her to see me in the window from where she was. It was an odd mixture of connection and separation, so close, yet so far apart.

The day wore on, and Shabbos was drawing near. She had no choice but to head home, and she wrenched herself away from the spot across the river. Although she wouldn't bring me home that day, she still hoped to at least hear the good news before Shabbos. Sadly, it didn't turn out that way. When I called minutes before Shabbos, she told me that the lawyer had just called and informed her that bail had been denied. The timing wasn't accidental. Dumping news late on Friday is a classic technique used to minimize backlash, because the reporters won't get to it until after the weekend and by then it's already old news.

As always, she conveyed this difficult news with a strong sense of *emunah*, offering encouragement that *gam zu l'tovah*, and expressing firm *bitachon* that, at any moment, Hashem would save us from these *tzaros*.

Of course, we didn't simply accept this refusal to grant bail. We appealed the decision in the appellate court. The *askanim* also turned to the Washington DC Justice Department superiors of those who were fighting against my release in Iowa. Many of the nation's largest and most well-known Jewish organizations, including the National Council of Young Israel, Rabbinical Alliance of America, Aleph Institute, NCFJE, and Va'ad Harabbonim of Queens issued a joint appeal to the US Attorney General and held a press conference at the National Press Club. These efforts were ultimately unsuccessful, and I remained in Cedar Rapids pending sentencing.

When I had visitors in Cedar Rapids, they sat behind a transparent soundproof barrier and we spoke through a phone. If the next visiting booth over was not in use, I used its phone to speak to two of my loved ones simultaneously. The pain of separation was mixed with the encouragement and consolation we felt by being in each other's presence, albeit on opposite sides of a glass partition.

We dusted ourselves off and turned to the task before us—preparing to make our case on sentencing to a judge who'd already made up her mind, and simultaneously working to overturn the conviction she had presided over. It was going to be an uphill struggle fought at what we knew would be astronomical expense. Klal Yisrael didn't let us face it alone.

A thousand miles away, in Boro Park, 1,700 women gathered in the Young Israel of Boro Park, a large, historic shul not far from my parents' home. True *nashim tzidkaniyos*, they united in determination to help me in my misfortune. I managed to call my daughter while the event was in progress and listen in from afar. What I heard was a source of great encouragement and strength.

The event was chaired by Rabbi Lipa Brennan, a Lubavitcher chassid who was a *gabbai* to the Novominsker Rebbe and the director of Yeshivas Novominsk.

The event began by acknowledging the true Source of salvation with a *kapitel Tehillim*. Then, my daughter Roza Hindy appealed to the crowd. She poured out her heart to them, telling them about the tragedy that had struck her mother and her siblings and of the difficulties she faced scraping together the money that was needed to save her father. She told them how she was literally going house to house, knocking on doors and asking people to open their hearts and help. She thanked the women for coming and asked them to help in any way they could, which they did wholeheartedly.

Before the evening was over, they were also addressed by the *rav* of the shul, Rabbi Moshe Snow, and other rabbis and *askanim* who provided Torah clarity and guidance on how a Yid is to react to such a situation.

The rally was a success—a demonstration of true *achdus* with Torah, *tefillah*, and *tzedakah* that was sure to shake the Heavenly Throne. It also raised significant and critical funds. It was followed days later by a similar rally in Crown Heights. The financial support was not limited to those women who were well-off. These *nashim tzidkaniyos* were so moved by my plight, that some of them even sold their jewelry to be able to help and established a gold drive so others could do the same. This noble selflessness was very heartening and encouraging to myself and my family.

This outpouring of support was repeated many times in the months before the sentencing, with large gatherings taking place in Kiryas Yoel; Monsey; and Surfside, Florida. My ordeal stretched well beyond the sentencing and Klal Yisrael continued to be with me every step of the way, including many more large rallies. I will try to mention each of them at the appropriate point in the story.

Of course, this is not to minimize, in any way, the impact of the individual and smaller-scale undertakings, both in beseeching Hashem on my behalf and showing financial and moral support. In many ways, these were actually *more* important and will also be discussed in detail later.

Shakedowns, Bigots, and Self-Defense

The denial of bail pending sentencing resulted in a nine-month stretch of time in a place called jail that lasted until I was transferred to the federal system. My earlier stints were short by comparison and, despite some harrowing experiences, I hadn't yet experienced all the "wonderful" features of life in jail.

One feature of life in jail and prison is the "shakedown." Guards enter the cell and command the prisoner to leave. He is taken elsewhere and locked in, while the guards root around in his belongings and confiscate anything they deem contraband before he is allowed back in.

During one of these shakedowns, I was locked in the shower room. When I was escorted back to the cell, I saw that they'd stacked the *sefarim* on the table. They told me I could choose ten to keep, and the rest would be confiscated.

It's impossible for a Yid to have only ten *sefarim*. Just for *davening* and my daily study commitments I needed a siddur, Chumash, *Shlah* on the *parshah*, the *Alshich* on the *parshah*, mishnayos, Gemara, *Rambam*, a *Shulchan Aruch*, *Tanya*, and *Chovos Halevavos*. That's already ten. Keeping those would mean I couldn't keep the *Likutei Torah* to learn about that week's *parshah* on Shabbos, for example, or *sefarim* on the Megillah to prepare for the upcoming Yom Tov of Purim. It was an agonizing choice.

The *Chovos Halevavos* was my lifeline, so I wanted to make sure it was among the *sefarim* that stayed with me, but I couldn't find it in the pile. Discreetly glancing around the small, bare cell, I spotted the *sefer*. It was sitting in plain sight, on the supporting bar at the head end of the sleeping-shelf. It was readily visible, but Hashem had hidden it from their sight and they hadn't included it in their pile or in their *gezeirah*!

Of course, I didn't say anything and went back to choosing ten *sefarim* from the pile. I felt strengthened by Hashem's open help in ensuring that I would have the *sefer* I needed to keep my *bitachon* strong and not at the expense of my other learning. This was not the last time I had miraculous assistance in keeping this *sefer*, so important to my strong *bitachon*, available and at my side.

Another feature of life in jail and prison is the subset of guards who are not just there to do their jobs, but really enjoy their power over other human beings and take pleasure in making their lives more miserable than necessary. These guards were frequently also antisemitic.

One example of this in Cedar Rapids was a guard who showed her hatred for Jews quite openly. Unlike the standard non-kosher fare, the kosher food that I was given was packaged in disposable containers and included disposable utensils, none of which had to be collected and returned to the kitchen.

When the guards came to the other cells to take away the non-kosher food and dishes, which had to be returned to the kitchen, they would leave me to my meal, having no reason to disrupt it. If this guard was making the rounds, however, she made it a point to take away my food, for no reason other than that she could. I never gave her the pleasure of showing her that it bothered me.

She was also an active participant in unjustly punishing me for the crime of defending myself from physical assault.

The cell in which I'd been placed was used as an infirmary cell. I was the only one there for most of my stay, with two exceptions. The first cellmate they placed with me was a wheelchair-bound man who was charged with making violent threats to his spouse. He was only there for a few weeks before he was transferred out, and he was fairly calm and didn't bother me.

The next guy was a very different story. He was a one-legged man, a real nasty piece of work, jailed for some kind of domestic abuse or violence. Incarceration hadn't done much to sweeten his disposition and he was transferred into the cell I was in because of aggressive behavior toward other inmates. He was rude and aggressive to the guards as they brought him in, and he was fairly menacing to me as well. His threatening demeanor was so disturbing that, in a call to a friend, I told him about this new arrival and only half-jokingly said, "If something happens, you should know it's not suicide."

One morning, not long after he was transferred in, I was *davening* in a corner of the cell while he was watching the television. He suddenly became irked by my presence or behavior and, without warning, lunged at me. *Baruch Hashem*, I saw a blur in my peripheral vision and my reflexes kicked in. I threw up my arm to protect my face, deflecting his first punch. I rushed to the door of the cell and started banging on it to get the guards' attention. They quickly entered the cell, subdued him, and dragged him off to the SHU.

I finished *davening* and called home to tell them what had happened. Hours later, I was taken to the unmonitored phones to make a scheduled legal call, and when I returned to the cell, I was met by two guards. One of them was the hateful woman. She told me that because I'd been involved in a fight, I was to be placed in the SHU as well. I'd been *attacked* and had done nothing more than deflect the attack, but my protests were in vain. They transferred me to the SHU and also brought all my belongings from the cell. This was a kindness from Hashem, because it meant that at least I had my few *sefarim* with me and I was able to learn Torah.

Protocol dictates that participants in an altercation be confined to the SHU pending an investigation. They kept the first part to the letter, but they weren't so firm on the investigation part. Three officers are required to hear each person's side of the story but only one came to interview me—one of the two who'd thrown me in there to begin with. I ran through what had happened and pointed out that he could simply review the footage recorded by the camera in the cell. It would confirm my story and they could let me go in peace. He completed the interview, collected his notes, and left.

A few days passed in the SHU before I was notified that they had reached a conclusion: Due to my actions, I was to remain there for thirty days. This decision was based on the notes of the single officer who had interrogated me. They hadn't even bothered to watch the video.

I had been wronged but, *baruch Hashem*, I was not forsaken. Hashem was with me, and had already set in motion the means of my release. The very day after I'd been confined to the SHU, a rabbi from Chicago named Rabbi Gurevitch came for a clergy visit and was allowed to see me. He was surprised to hear my story and, as soon as he left, he got word to my family who had not known anything was amiss. They immediately reached out to the Aleph Institute for assistance.

In the meantime, the media got in on the story. The secular media presented it as a jailhouse fight, reflecting badly on me, as is customary. By contrast, the Jewish news website Matzav and Reb Pinchos Lipschutz's *Yated* presented the story accurately, and questioned why I was being punished, and punished harshly, for simply defending myself, speculating that antisemitism played a role.

After all, there was video evidence that I was the victim in the interaction, yet I was being punished and the investigators refused to review evidence that would clear me. What were people to think was driving that behavior?

While I awaited my release from this prison within a prison, Aleph contacted the warden directly and asked him to personally review the case, which he agreed to do.

With no natural means to change my situation, I threw myself with greater intensity and focus into *davening* and learning, doing whatever I could to rise above the even greater darkness of the circumstances into which I'd been placed. The tiny cell of the SHU did not offer a place to put my holy *sefarim*, so I moved the mat of the sleeping-shelf to the floor, where I slept, and I used the now-bare cement sleeping-shelf to hold the *sefarim* I had with me.

One of the extra hardships of incarceration in the SHU in that facility was that the mat was taken away every morning, leaving nowhere to lie down all day except the rock-hard, unyielding cement slab.

Although this SHU differed from the one at South Dakota in that it was not technically solitary confinement—the cell was often shared—this presented another hardship in its own way; I was confined to even closer quarters than usual with other inmates, and usually not the quiet, unassuming ones. There were some really low, rough characters, but they weren't all bad. The prisoner in the adjoining cell was a Jamaican with loud, hearty laugh. He laughed at everything. In this, he had the right idea—the Torah tells us that *simchah* helps us overcome even the most difficult circumstances.

People think that when you're happy, you sing. That's true, but so is the inverse: When you sing, especially happy songs, it can help you feel happy. This was a lesson I'd learned from my sister Gutel, who has gone through a lot of difficulties in her life. Sitting in solitary confinement, I sang the happiest *niggunim* I knew. It cheered me up, and the others seemed to appreciate it as well. "Hey, Rabbi!" came a sudden shout from my Jamaican neighbor. "Nice singing!"

He made a point of coming over during the daily thirty-minute reprieve when inmates in the SHU are allowed to leave the cell. The first time he came over, I thanked him for his loud laughter, which brightened the atmosphere somewhat.

During the time I was there, a lawyer came to see this fellow and told him that he would be leaving jail the next day. That evening, a particularly cruel guard was the one to bring the food and this Jamaican just let loose, yelling insults and verbal abuse. The guard was shocked to hear this from an inmate (as was I) and, sputtering, he said, "I didn't quite hear that… What did you say?!"

The Jamaican just continued the stream of abuse, interrupting only to explain himself. "I want to tell you what I really think of you!" The guard couldn't do anything to him. He was already in the SHU, so he couldn't be sent there, and he was leaving the next day, so his stay in the SHU couldn't be lengthened. The guard had nothing to threaten him with. He tried his best, threatening him with unspecified repercussions, but that only elicited another of the Jamaican's hearty laughs.

The guy in the adjoining cell on the other side kept banging on the wall because he wanted to speak to me, but I didn't respond. I'd been part of the captive audience—quite literally—to which he'd just finished giving a loud lecture on how to make a certain drug. I decided this was not someone with whom I wanted to converse.

Another "guest" in solitary was badgering me to buy him hand sanitizer from the commissary because he didn't have money and he couldn't buy it himself. At first, I took this at face value and wanted to help the impoverished fellow, but observing him for a couple of days I realized the real reason he couldn't buy it himself. Hand sanitizer has a small amount of alcohol in it. They wouldn't sell it to him because they suspected he would drink it and, after observing him, I suspected they were right. I didn't buy it for him.

On Friday, sometime after sunset, four days after the initial incident, the warden came to the SHU. He took me to a meeting room where he informed me that he'd seen the video and accepted that I should not have been sent to the SHU. He asked me if I would be satisfied with an immediate release. I told him that I would. Neither I nor my advocates were trying to pick a fight. I just wanted humane and fair treatment. He told me that I would be released from the SHU, though I was returned there pending implementation of his decision. It took much longer than it should have after he left, but I was eventually returned to the regular cell later that night. It was an eye-opening experience. The cell is a cage. It's an environment that is contrary to the needs of a human being, contrary to his very nature, but coming from the harsh experience of the SHU, it still felt like a relief.

The television had been turned on, but it was Shabbos and I didn't want to ask anyone to shut it off. This added to the discomfort but, mercifully, at a certain time it automatically shut off for the night, leaving me with a more appropriate Shabbos quiet.

The guy who had attacked me was gone, *baruch Hashem*, but he had taken one parting shot. Each morning, he'd seen me washing my hands into the cell's little plastic garbage bucket before getting out of bed. I'd also wash my hands for bread into this bucket. Out of spite, he had informed the authorities about this practice. They came to do a shakedown soon after I was returned to the cell and found that not only was it true, there was still a bit of water in the pail from when I'd washed for lunch!

The lieutenant reprimanded me very harshly about this. The plastic container was for garbage *only* and not to be used for any other purposes. Besides, the moisture in the cell could cause mold! As preposterous as this all sounds, they made the rules and I was no longer able to use the pail for washing.

Someone had sent me something in a large UPS envelope which was made out of some kind of waterproof material. I discovered that, by opening it wide and rolling down the top to form a rim, I could get it to hold an open shape and it would hold water. From then on, I washed my hands into that envelope.

The Yom Tov of Freedom…Behind Bars

The month of Adar came and with it, the Yom Tov of Purim. Feeling the spirit of Yom Tov was up to me, and I did my part, but to fulfill the mitzvos of Purim, specifically the mitzvah of Megillah, I had to rely on others. They also did their part and, *baruch Hashem*, I celebrated the *nes* of Purim as the Torah demands.

My reliance on others to provide those needs got me thinking about the upcoming Yom Tov of Pesach. The Pesach needs for which I would have to rely on others were a lot more complex than those for Purim. Would I have enough wine for the Seder? Would I have *shmurah matzah* and all the things I needed for the *ka'arah*? Would I receive *kosher l'Pesach* food?

I requested a furlough for Pesach, which would have resolved all these issues with one stroke, and also allowed me to fulfill the mitzvah of *v'higadita l'vincha*, but the request was denied.

Two of the dedicated *bachurim* in Postville offered to make the Seder with me, an offer that Aleph Institute's *askanim* put to the warden and which he accepted. The authorities told Aleph that they would make a special meeting with me to discuss what I needed, for Pesach in general and for the Sedarim in particular, and they would provide it.

I waited impatiently for them to call me for the meeting, but two weeks went by with no word. Finally, with less than two weeks to go, I was led from the cellblock to a small interrogation room. Two men were already there; one was the lieutenant who had threatened me over the *negel vasser* in the garbage pail, and the other was a man in a civilian suit. They asked me what I needed for Pesach.

My first concern was the schedule. I explained to them that it's a very holy service and I would need at least from nightfall until midnight. This is accommodated in other prisons in the US, which I made sure to mention, but they answered coldly: Impossible. The volunteer rabbis would have to leave the facility at 9:30 p.m.

I explained to them that the Seder could not begin before nightfall, which was at 8:00. There was simply not enough time to *daven* Ma'ariv with Hallel, make Kiddush, and follow the Haggadah—dipping the *karpas*, breaking the matzah, reciting the Haggadah and so on—all before 9:30!

They just repeated their decision: Out by 9:30. For all their promises to the *askanim* that they would provide my needs for the Seder, they were flat-out rejecting the most basic thing: a little bit of time. I couldn't compel them to honor their word, but I wasn't going to let them off the hook by endorsing their decision either. I just reiterated that it was impossible to make a Seder in the amount of time that they were discussing. They said they would get back to me with a final decision.

With a silent *tefillah*, I moved on to my other very simple needs. I needed about fourteen ounces of wine for the *dalet kosos*, something that is permitted to other religions when they require it. They noted the request.

I needed a new non-disposable plastic cup, since the one I was issued was used with my *chametzdig* meals and could not be used on Pesach. The officers glanced at each other. One of them was shaking his head, as if I'd made an especially difficult request. Over a silly plastic cup?! "We'll look into it," he said gravely.

I asked to be given a clean set of the garish orange clothing on Erev Pesach to be able to change from the *chametzdig* clothing to "Yom Tov clothing," I asked for a second shower on Erev Pesach in the afternoon, and I asked for permission to keep the *shmurah matzah* in the cell, to be sure it didn't get broken or wet.

These officers had the authority to sign off on these small requests even absent the warden's grand assurance that they would accommodate my Pesach needs. They chose not to do so. Instead, they dismissed me, saying they would let me know their decision.

I was eventually informed that I would be given until midnight to finish my Seder, but only alone—the volunteers would have to leave at 9:30 p.m. I would only be given one foam cup to use for the whole week. I would not be given wine and would have to make do with grape juice. They refused to give me a brand-new set of prison clothes, and only agreed to give me one from the laundry. They did agree to allow me to take a shower on Erev Yom Tov.

I had some experience by then, and knew that even these miserly concessions needed to be in writing or the guard on duty was liable to deny me any Seder at all. I asked for the decisions in writing, with no response.

Erev Pesach arrived and I still had not received formal written permission. I called Aleph to find out if they had news but they had also not heard anything. I called back every hour, but the response was always the same. In general, I hesitated to file official complaints, which often brought retaliation, but I felt that I had no choice this time and I wrote a "kite."

In a place called jail or prison, a kite is an official request or complaint by an inmate to an officer, and they are required to respond. I formally demanded to know what they would allow me to do in order to keep Pesach, a recognized religious activity. I called the Aleph Institute to let them know that I had filed formal paperwork and to check if they'd heard anything in the meantime, but they hadn't had any new contact with the jail. They promised to try to get to the bottom of it and we made up that I would call back soon.

Around 3:30 p.m., they brought me a fresh set of clothes, as they had agreed. A short time later, earlier than we had discussed, the lieutenant who'd been at the meeting came in and asked, with artificial kindness, if I'd like to go to the shower. I wondered why he came in person and why so early, but I wanted to be accommodating and agreed to go. He radioed for a guard to come take me to the shower and left.

The guard arrived twenty minutes later. I took the fresh clothes and followed him, turning the whole scene over in my mind. Why was the officer so personally interested that I go to the shower before the time we'd arranged? We arrived at the shower room. I entered and the guard closed the door, locking me in.

Suddenly it all clicked. I realized what the lieutenant was doing to me! He knew the official permission to make a Seder had not yet been given. All phone calls were monitored, so he also knew that I was in contact with Aleph to intervene and ensure that I got my Pesach needs.

In an attempt to prevent this from happening, he lured me away from the cell and had me locked in the shower, where I wouldn't have access to the telephone. By the time I returned from the shower, it would be after 4:30 p.m., and the phones are deactivated every day from 4:30 to 5:30. By the time they were reactivated, at 5:30, the officers would have already gone home without making the formal arrangements.

I began banging on the door as loudly as I could. The guard came to the door and asked me what I wanted. I told him that I didn't want to take a shower and I wanted to be returned to the cellblock. He couldn't understand what was going on—first I wanted the shower, now I wanted to skip it—but *baruch Hashem*, he agreed to move me back without consulting the officer.

I made it back around 4:20, only ten minutes before the phones would be deactivated. I called the Aleph coordinator and told him that the officers were misleading him and he should immediately call and arrange that I have a kosher Seder!

A few minutes later, the lieutenant stormed in, in a rage, demanding to know why I didn't want to take a shower. His irrational response to my decision was additional confirmation that his actions were a calculated ploy and not an innocent coincidence. I saw clearly how Hashem was protecting me.

I had only had time for one phone call and now the phones were off. No further *hishtadlus* was possible, and a total calm descended on me. I was in the hands of Hashem and I trusted that Hashem would ensure that I had a kosher Seder. I said Tehillim and *davened* Minchah.

Baruch Hashem, a little later I was taken to the designated room to make the Seder. I was overjoyed to see the two *bachurim* already there, along with a box of Seder supplies. As one of them took out the bottle of grape juice and placed it on the table, he remarked that it had taken a miracle to get it in. That same lieutenant had initially refused to allow it, insisting that they use the jail's non-kosher grape juice. It had a "K" on the label and the guard insisted that, as far as he was concerned, that was kosher enough.

The *bachur* tried to explain that "K" is nothing more than the company's assurance the product is kosher and doesn't necessarily represent a rabbinic certification, but to no avail. He tried to reach Aleph for guidance but by then, Pesach had already begun in New York.

He didn't have anyone to turn to for advice, but a Yid is never alone. Hashem gave him the solution directly. Having made no headway with the guard, he had carried the box back to the car, when it suddenly occurred to him that although the officer's bottle had a "K," it didn't say that it was kosher for Passover. They had agreed to provide my Passover needs, including kosher for Passover grape juice. He ran back and pointed that out to the lieutenant, who had no choice but to allow the kosher grape juice in and I was able to perform the mitzvah of drinking the *dalet kosos*.

The whole day had been a display of the *pasuk, Utzu eitzah v'sufar, dabru davar v'lo yakum ki imanu Keil!*—"They scheme and conspire and they are undone, they make proclamations that come to nothing, for Hashem is with us."

For my part, I had made every effort and then fulfilled the instruction, *Hashlech al Hashem yehavicha v'Hu yechalkilecha!*—"Throw your burden upon

Hashem and He will sustain you," or in an alternative interpretation of the word *yechalkilecha* as related to the word *keili*, "He will even make the *keili*."[2]

We *davened* Ma'ariv together as if we were together in shul, singing Hallel out loud with sincere gratitude to Hashem, and began the Seder with hearts full of joy to do the will of Hashem!

When we got to *Maggid*, we spoke about the miracles Hashem showed our forefathers, and also about the miracles Hashem had done for us that day, strengthening our trust in Him and our expectation of miracles to come.

It was very different from the Sedarim at home, sitting around a large overflowing table with my family and many guests. Here, there were only these two precious *bachurim* and a small table set with disposable utensils, no wine and less than the minimum of food, but it was the same taste of freedom of the *neshamah* that only a mitzvah can bring. It had none of the familiar trappings, but *baruch Hashem*, I was able to make a Seder. Sitting in Mitzrayim, I was able to experience the *Yetzias Mitzrayim*.

The time allotted ran out way too quickly. We had only really begun to immerse ourselves in the experience of *Maggid*, closer to the start than to the middle, when the *bachurim* were told to leave. They walked back to their motel and finished their Seder there, while I stayed in the small room to finish my own. There were no other people with me at the Seder, but I was not alone, *chas v'shalom*. A Yid is *never* alone! I continued the Seder with Hashem Himself, full of gratitude and praise to my holy Father in Heaven that I could make a Seder and do the mitzvos of Yom Tov.

---

2. The natural means through which His salvation comes, usually incumbent on the person to create.

CHAPTER TEN
The Sentencing Hearing

Pre-Hearing Drama

THE NEXT STEP IN THE LEGAL PROCESS WAS SENTENCING, AND THE first part of that was to be a hearing at which the sides would both present arguments and evidence.

It was at around this time that some of the most committed *askanim* got involved. There was a Yiddish-language magazine which was planning a feature article on the raid and the legal aftermath. They had already done an interview with my father about how the factory and the community had developed and they were among the few in the media who were telling the story truthfully.

Now they wanted to tackle the events surrounding the raid itself. In preparation for their feature story, they sent a writer, Shimon Rolnitzky, and photographer, Yoel Lefkowitz, to Iowa. They visited Postville and interviewed people, then they set out to meet with me in Cedar Rapids. They were granted permission by the jail authorities for the visit and I was taken to a conference room in the jail to meet them. We were able to speak for a few hours.

Before they left, they asked me about my appearance. Haircuts were only available in the jail on Shabbos, when I obviously couldn't go. My hair had grown pretty long in the six months since the verdict and my sudden incarceration.

The state of a person's appearance has an effect on their emotional state and it was wrong that I was denied the ability to keep myself neat and *menschlich*. Beyond that, I had court appearances coming up—the federal sentencing hearing, followed closely by the state trial—and my appearance would have an effect, one way or the other, on the judge and jury.

It disturbed them to think that I should have to stand in front of the court, not to mention my wife and children, looking unkempt and bedraggled as a result of my keeping Shabbos. Men of action, they took it up with the warden. Sure enough, permission was granted for a weekday haircut shortly thereafter.

I was touched by their care and concern. These were clearly people of great sympathy and sensitivity, rare among the general population and absolutely unheard of among journalists. They went well beyond a short, beneficial chat with the warden.

Our conversation, together with what they'd seen and heard in Postville, shook them to their cores, and the writer called some of his friends back in Kiryas Yoel, New York. It was after midnight on Motza'ei Shabbos and they were gathered for a *melaveh malkah*. He shared with them what he'd found on his visit to my home and my family, so vastly different from the lies that had shaped public opinion. He sent them pictures, including one of my large but simple home and the folding tables I used in my dining room, a far cry from what he had imagined based on the media coverage of a wealthy, greedy man. He shared his impressions of my family as *ehrliche Yidden* and explained to his friends the danger that loomed over our heads.

Those friends were moved to help a fellow Yid in need. These friends were all called Yoili—Schwartz, Sofer, Steinberger, and Reisman. Along with my son-in-law Yaakov Yoel Weiss, they became known affectionately as "The Five Yoilis." They formed a powerhouse group of *askanim* with limitless energy and *ahavas Yisrael*. Shimon Rolnitzky himself was an active part of this group of *askanim*, as were Yossi Weissman, Shlomo Leizer Meisel, Mordechai Wider, and others.[1] Their *middos tovos* and *mesiras nefesh* for their fellow Jew made them just the sort of messengers through which Hashem makes His miracles happen.

They worked tirelessly to galvanize their community and played a pivotal role in mobilizing the broader Jewish community as well. They got involved in bringing the injustice to the attention of government figures, and it was with their help that we raised the astronomical sums of money we needed in order to present our case in court. In fact, our funds had been depleted by that point and it was their efforts which enabled us to hire lawyers for the state case, an absolutely critical victory, as you will see.

They weren't just fundraisers. They were bright and talented men, and more

---

1. Including the name of everyone who was part of the many and varied efforts would be impossible, but in an attempt to show the proper gratitude, we have compiled a more comprehensive list at Rubashkinbook.com.

importantly, they cared deeply about helping me. They joined forces with Reb Pinchos Lipschutz and Yerachmiel Simmons and held weekly meetings to discuss the overall strategy and how to best direct their efforts. They helped to vet and hire the lawyers, and some even helped to formulate legal strategies and arguments. Yoili Schwartz, in particular, was credited by the lawyers as a brilliant mind who did much to help develop the legal arguments in the appeals.

That these fresh reinforcements were inspired to get involved over a *melaveh malkah*, a *minhag* which was so precious to me and which I always made sure to fulfill, was, to me, another wink and a smile from Hashem. It didn't make any practical difference that it happened that way but it was a reminder that there was an Author to this story and that He was with me, encouraging me to stand strong and He would pull me through.

The Yiddish magazine went to print with an in-depth, forty-page investigative piece for their Yiddish-speaking audience all about the raid and its aftermath. It was thorough and accurate, and it corrected a lot of assumptions and misperceptions that had crept into even the *frum* community. It did for the Yiddish-speaking readers what the *Yated* had been doing for English-speaking readers. There were positive articles in one or two other Jewish periodicals, but these had focused on informing readers of recent developments, whereas this piece covered the whole story, including the objectionable behavior by the prosecutors and the shortcomings and outright distortions of their case.

This is also a good place to mention the Kol Mevaser hotline, which kept the Yiddish-speaking public up-to-date on the case through frequent reports and interviews. They also broadcasted the many *tefillah* and *tzedakah* rallies that were held. Their efforts brought the truth of my case to a broad audience that mobilized in *tefillah* and *ma'asim tovim* and surely helped bring about my miraculous salvation.

The date for the sentencing hearing was set for April 28, 2010. The purpose of the hearing was for each side to present what they saw as a just sentence, and provide evidence that supported their request or that challenged the position of the other side. In preparation for the hearing, both sides submitted documents which outlined their position. This gave us, and the world, an early look at what the prosecution would be requesting. It was an absolute national disgrace, neatly justified in dry legal terms and calculations.

Their recommendation was based on something called the Sentencing Guidelines, created and mandated by law in 1984, a time when they were grappling with sentencing disparities. Different sentences were being issued to different people for the same offense, the difference in the cases often seeming to be about nothing more than race or class.

To ensure that this wouldn't happen, a system was created in which the various aspects of the case were to be reduced to simple numbers, called "levels" or "points." A simple chart would yield the length of the sentence corresponding with the number of points and the judge was required to issue that sentence. This was supposed to advance the cause of justice by ensuring uniform sentencing.

Many took issue with this formulaic approach to sentencing. They pointed out that reducing complex and nuanced events and behaviors down to a point system sacrificed justice for equality, but in the end it was something else that undermined the initial Guidelines system. Because the points in the Guidelines, and the prison sentences they produced, were influenced by facts and factors not presented to the jury, the US Supreme Court ruled it unconstitutional.[2]

Instead of scrapping them altogether, the Supreme Court "fixed" the Guidelines by removing the part of the law that made issuing Guidelines sentences mandatory. This resolved the technical constitutional issue but on the issue of just sentences, it actually made things worse.

Before the Guidelines, officials pursuing justice would assess the unique aspects of each case and advocate or impose sentences accordingly, while officials motivated by bigotry or unscrupulous ambition used their discretion to treat people differently and unfairly.

The Guidelines didn't stop that behavior—they just moved it from the sentencing stage to the stage where charges are formulated. With the Guidelines chart in hand like a map, the desired sentence in a given case could be engineered by being selective or creative, moderate or excessive with the charges and the underlying facts they alleged.

Not only could excessive or lenient prison sentences be achieved, the architects wouldn't even have to answer for them. Any criticism of a given sentence would be deflected by, "We're just following the Guidelines." The system also tied the hands of honest judges, who were relegated to rubber-stamping sentences they sometimes felt were unjust.

---

2. This was in 2005, more than twenty years after it had been instituted and after it had dictated the sentences in millions of cases.

The 2005 "fix" addressed the technical issues but gave any unscrupulous officials the best of both worlds. They have the discretion and authority to deviate from the now advisory Guidelines if desired, and, if challenged, they're still free to inflate or deflate the point counts and point to the Guidelines, which are still considered by the courts presumptively reasonable.

The prosecutors in my case had taken the second approach and done a very thorough job of inflating the point counts. It had taken them a staggering seven indictments and more than half a year, but they had inflated their charges to a whopping 163 counts, ninety-one of which they brought to trial.[3] Of those ninety-one, they had secured a conviction for eighty-six.

Among the mechanisms that the Guidelines provide for increasing (or inflating) the sentence, is the loss amount. The prosecutors in my case took more than full advantage of that. In their sentencing recommendation, they made the unsubstantiated claim that the bank had suffered a loss of $27 million and blamed it all squarely on me. This inflated the severity of the charges and brought the offense level, the points, up to forty-five. The chart ends at forty-three points—forty-five points was literally off the chart. Anything over forty-three calls for a Guidelines sentence of life in prison and that's what they wanted the judge to impose.

Maybe as an attempt to dodge the blame for a sentence that would (and did) outrage anyone not steeped in their distortion of the case, they never actually used the words "life sentence" in their recommendation. Instead they repeatedly said that I should be treated "the same as any other defendant brought to sentencing and given a Guidelines sentence."[4]

Even their most sinister telling of the story should not have been enough to support a life sentence to anyone interested in justice. A defendant charged with a similar calculated loss *to the same bank, in that same year,* was sentenced to a year and a day—yet I faced a life sentence. Not an "effective life sentence," longer than a person's life expectancy. An actual life sentence. Lock him up and throw away the key.

When their recommendation became known, it caused an uproar among

---

3. The other seventy-two were the immigration-related charges. Although they were ultimately dropped, their substance was allowed in the trial over defense objections and without allowing for a full defense. They also featured again in the sentencing arguments.

4. Federal statistics actually show that close to half of the sentences imposed that year were below the Guidelines, but their euphemism was abundantly clear.

honest and just people across the world. It was still only a recommendation, something for the judge to consider, and it was imperative that the judge recognize the outrage with which such a sentence would be met.

The Aleph Institute concerns itself with more than the spiritual wellbeing of Jewish inmates. They have an Advocacy Department, which does everything they can to ameliorate the suffering of men and women in prison and, if possible, help them win their freedom. The director of this department is a Yid named Zvi Boyarsky. People are sometimes described as a "force of nature," but that would be selling Zvi short. In his selfless, endless exertions on behalf of his fellow Jews, Zvi rises well *above* nature and is often Hashem's *shliach* for open miracles.

He is a real *ba'al bitachon* and he pairs his complete trust in Hashem with absolute devotion and dedication to doing everything he can with boundless energy and persistence. He's blessed with *chein*, grace in the eyes of those who meet him, and he was successful in recruiting the most prominent political and legal personalities to my cause and was involved in all aspects of the efforts to free me. He was a perfect *shliach* of Hashem to bring goodness and blessings and to bring about the eventual *nes* of my release.

When he found out that the prosecutors were recommending a life sentence, he was shaken to his core, as he felt every decent human being would be. Zvi felt that even former prosecutors, judges, and others dedicated to law and order would recoil at the mere thought of such a sentence. He decided to do everything he could to bring the case to their attention and solicit their thoughts on the matter.

Although the expert legal advisors were skeptical that anyone even formerly affiliated with the DOJ would weigh in on an active case in this way, Zvi succeeded beyond his wildest dreams. Along with other *askanim*, he reached out to the most prestigious names in American law enforcement. They reacted exactly as Zvi had expected.

Six former Attorneys General of the United States of America, the top law enforcement officers in the country, signed and sent a letter to the judge criticizing the government's recommendation.[5] The honorable Nicholas Katzenbach, Ramsey Clark, Edwin Meese, Richard Thornburgh, William

---

5. They, and the signatories of additional letters written on my behalf at later stages, all deserve individual recognition for their principled stand, but to list them all would turn this book into a catalogue of lawyers. A list of names can be found at Rubashkinbook.com.

Barr, and Janet Reno, representing both political parties and four presidential administrations, called the recommendation "troubling" and "disconcerting," and respectfully urged the judge to reject it.

They were joined in the letter by two former Deputy Attorneys General, Jamie Gorelick and Larry Thompson; a former Solicitor General, Seth Waxman; and fourteen former US Attorneys, among them James Reynolds, the former US Attorney for the Northern District of Iowa.

That men of the highest caliber and standing were willing to get involved on my behalf, speaking up about an active case and criticizing the prosecution's handling of it, was absolutely miraculous, a *nes* from Hashem.

A number of the prestigious signatories, and others like them, were so disturbed by the behavior of the prosecutors in the case that they got involved and helped the team *pro bono*!

Former US Attorney Brett Tolman wrote a separate letter along with Paul Cassell, a law professor who had been a federal judge, an Assistant US Attorney, and had clerked for a Chief Justice of the US Supreme Court. In their letter they made the mind-boggling point that the prosecution was recommending a sentence *longer* than would be given for second-degree murder, kidnapping, or providing weapons to terrorist organizations. They were calling for the same Guidelines sentence as that given for first-degree murder! They strongly urged the court to reject the prosecutors' recommendation and they were joined by more than six hundred lawyers from across the country who sent a letter supporting their request.

It wasn't just legal luminaries and former Justice officials who made themselves heard. Many religious leaders and civil rights organizations spoke up. Some sent their own letters to the judge and others wrote jointly, but all were outraged that this was even being considered.

This was before the broad public recognition of the fake news phenomenon and of the occasional co-opting of otherwise legitimate law enforcement apparatus. Many of my supporters conceded, whether out of misplaced conviction or for reasons of credibility, that, having been convicted, I must have committed a crime and deserved some degree of punishment. They only took public issue with the "overzealousness" and "overreach."

This was very painful to me. In the years since, very public cases involving public and private figures, going as high as the President of the United States, have opened the eyes of the public. Convictions and even confessions have been investigated and found to be without any shred of truth. I like to think that in this climate, those internal or external concessions would not have been made.

The eighty-eighth annual dinner of Agudas Yisrael took place during this period. Their focus was on demonstrating the *achdus*, strength, and determination of the Jewish People in a time of increasing danger to Eretz Yisrael from Iran and a time of increasing antisemitism in general. They drew particular attention to my case, going so far as to invite my lawyer, Guy Cook, to speak at the dinner. The sentencing recommendation of life in prison figured prominently as an example of the injustice that characterized my case.

Guy Cook speaking at the Agudas Yisrael dinner.

An online petition was created, denouncing the prosecutors' behavior in general and their recommended sentence in particular. It was signed by close to forty thousand people in the weeks between the notification of the requested sentence and the sentencing hearing itself.

Rabbi Sholom Ber Hecht of the Crown Heights Va'ad with Rabbi Chaim Dovid Zwiebel at the Agudas Yisrael dinner.

A spokesman for the US Attorney's office waved away all the criticism by these respected men and women, as well as the groundswell of public outrage at the proposed sentence, saying that all the opposition was based on misinformation.

The judge dealt with the input of experts just as dismissively. A former Attorney General called her about the case. He had actually been involved in writing the Sentencing Guidelines legislation and told her that they never intended for this sort of sentence in cases like these. Her response to him was, "I am the judge, I'm in charge, I can read."

Not content with leaving this to others, my daughter Roza Hindy was leaving no stone unturned. We are told that Hashem is *"makdim refuah l'makkah."* Before the blow falls, Hashem has already prepared the cure—and it was around this time, before the blow of the sentencing fell, that Roza Hindy made a connection that would prove vital, although its importance could not possibly have been known at the time. This was in 2010, half a decade before President Trump declared his long-shot candidacy which ended triumphantly in a miraculous victory.

One of the businessmen she contacted suggested that she meet with a young man named Jared Kushner. He was well-connected, had a brilliant strategic mind, and most importantly, a real *Yiddishe hartz*, a heart of gold.

Jared agreed to meet with her, and that first meeting turned into multiple meetings. Jared jumped right in, making introductions and offering advice. He contacted whoever he felt could help, sometimes in the middle of the meeting, and his advice was always on the mark and proved to be very valuable.

He introduced Roza Hindy to his family and they were just as supportive and kind-hearted. They were a true source of moral support to Roza Hindy and to my wife as well. Jared's parents, Charlie and Seryl Kushner, literally made Roza Hindy feel like a daughter. They were always there for her with advice, guidance, encouragement, and of course, practical assistance.

Charlie reached out to any and every connection he could on my behalf, going well beyond simple phone calls. When one of his efforts resulted in a well-placed Senator granting a meeting sometime in early 2015, Charlie took the day off, got a private plane, and along with Roza Hindy and his daughter, Dara, he flew to Washington, DC, to attend the meeting. This was clearly a family mission and Roza Hindy was part of the family. The relationship she formed with the Kushners is one she will treasure forever.

All of this was a great encouragement to me. When Roza Hindy came to visit, she would tell me about everything they were doing. She would be moved to tears as she described some of the meetings she attended with Charlie Kushner and his sincere and dedicated advocacy for someone he had never met. I knew the heavy burden she carried on her shoulders, and the way they stepped in to lighten it both with moral and practical support meant a lot to me.

Their extraordinary *ahavas Yisrael* and their willingness to act on it made them exactly the kind of people Hashem uses to bring about His salvation. There is, in fact, no greater endorsement of a human being than when Hashem makes them His *shliach.*

Against this backdrop, the lawyers developed and presented the legal arguments.

With no choice but to accept the premise of the conviction for the sake of arguing for a more reasonable sentence, my lawyers filed a motion countering the wild recommendation of the prosecution. It's not my purpose to re-litigate the case or even to provide a full account of the legal process, but as part of telling the story, I will try to summarize the points that were raised before the hearing, to the best of my understanding and in a way that a layperson can understand.

The key factor in inflating the point count and the length of the sentence was the loss to the bank. The court would use the amount of the intended or foreseeable loss or the actual loss, whichever was higher.

However, if Agriprocessors had been treated like anyone else, as any reasonable person would expect, the bank would have been repaid and no loss would have ensued at all.

It was not the disruption by immigration officials that caused the irreparable damage to the company. It was the ferocity with which they attacked and their subsequent behavior which destroyed the company and that was absolutely unprecedented and could not have been foreseen.

Even considering the possibility that the company would be forced into bankruptcy and sold, its market value, even in bankruptcy, was more than enough to cover its debts and avoid any loss to lenders. When the bankruptcy sale process started, offers were made that would have paid off the entire loan, with millions left over.

This outcome was prevented. The prosecutors, directly as well as through the bankruptcy trustee, threatened forfeiture if the purchaser employed any Rubashkins to help them learn and run the business. The condition was illegitimate and onerous, undermining the bidders' confidence that they could be successful, and even being on the other side of the table from a threatening US prosecutor was intimidating enough to change their calculus. As a result, bids were withdrawn or never finalized.

That the company was eventually sold for less than a tenth of even its depressed value—causing the bank a loss—was due to unforeseeable interference.

The defense filing presented an alternative loss amount, accepting that at this stage the jury findings on the financials were not contestable. My lawyers did as much recalculating as they could within the confines of the officially recognized, government-sponsored "facts" of the case, and came up with a Guidelines sentence of no longer than five years. (When more facts were known we could and did argue for a loss amount of zero and a corresponding sentence.) At the same time, they pointed out that others with similar convictions to mine were sentenced to as little as a year and a day—very far from the life sentence the prosecution wanted in my case.

The prosecution and defense had both made their written cases, but it's not just the two parties that prepare documents for sentencing. There's also a document prepared by an officer of the court, called the Pre-Sentence Investigation Report (PSIR). It compiles the history of the defendant, his criminal history (none, in my case), and information from the case which is relevant for sentencing. It concludes with a sentencing recommendation.

Unless and until prosecutors actively establish otherwise, an American citizen is innocent. Rumors, press reports, even assertions by prosecutors, are not enough to change that. The whole point of a trial is to test which allegations can be proven. Those are to be taken seriously and result in consequences and the rest are to be ignored.

Given all that, when you hear that they will be collecting "information from the case," for the purpose of determining a reasonable sentence, you might assume that they mean information relating to the charges on which the person was convicted. I know I did. Unbelievably, we're both wrong about that.

They actually prepare something they call the "total offense picture," which can include, *as a factor in sentencing,* anything that came up in the course of the case. After countless hours and countless dollars spent batting down baseless charges—successfully enough that they're rejected by the jury or not even brought to trial by the prosecution—they're all included in the sentence anyway, riding on the coattails of the few charges the prosecution did manage to push through!

They don't *have* to include rumors, insinuations, and disproven charges, but if you read my story until this point, you'll be able to guess what they did. Instead of a few pages describing the charges I was convicted on, the court officer compiled a huge report with every damaging accusation he could find, charged or otherwise. He threw in the thoroughly discredited claims of PETA, press claims of mistreating workers, and wickedly resisting unionization, among many others.

He even included the 9,311 state child labor charges, which were pending trial, as a mark against me! As you'll see in the next chapter, almost all were dropped before trial, and I was fully exonerated on those that weren't *before the official sentencing*. Even then, the judge refused our request to remove them and they stayed in the PSIR, with a small note that I'd been found "not guilty."

The computed "reasonable" sentence in this report was the same as the prosecutors' recommended sentence: life in prison.

They didn't need to paint this terrible picture in order to add to the actual sentence. They had already fully "justified" that based on the artificially inflated loss amount and the Sentencing Guidelines. These claims served another purpose. Decent people have always struggled with the age-old question, "Why do bad things happen to good people?"—but people don't lose much sleep over why bad things happen to *bad* people. By painting me as a monster, they were hoping to make people shrug their shoulders while they tried to crush me.

We filed a motion objecting to the report, but the judge dismissed our objections. Firstly, as we would hear so many times on appeal, the merits of our claim were irrelevant because the filing was late. Magnanimously commenting on the merits, she said that the law didn't require that the unsupported and contested claims be removed. It merely required that she not consider, for sentencing purposes, any of the material that was not supported by evidence at either the trial or sentencing.[6] Well, she assured us, she wouldn't—so there was no reason to remove it. Motion denied.

Even if it were humanly possible for her to be entirely unaffected by this poisonous "biography," the report is used for more than sentencing. It's used by the Bureau of Prisons, the BOP, to assess the prisoner in order to determine appropriate placement and treatment. It also introduces the person to the warden and staff. They wanted this libelous PSIR to accompany me to the destination they chose and poison the minds of the authorities there and they succeeded, as I will detail later.

The Hearing

The hearing took place in a temporary courthouse, the regular one being unusable due to severe flooding. Many friends and supporters took the time

---

6. Note that she is allowed to, and did, include things for which evidence was offered that did not convince the jury and even things that were blocked at trial for being hearsay or having other deficiencies but were allowed at the sentencing where the bar is lower.

and made the effort to be there, something which was encouraging to me and to my family. There were only about forty seats available, so many of the supporters had to watch the proceedings via live video feed in a nearby building.

The hearing itself was an opportunity to present additional evidence and present and cross-examine witnesses. It resulted in some important moments. Some seemed to go in our favor at the time, only increasing the sense of injustice when they made no difference. Others seemed terrible at the time, but by the kindness of Hashem were revealed, in time, to be critical to our cause.

Yidden drove in from Chicago, Illinois, and Minneapolis, Minnesota, to show support.

With the help of Hashem and the support of Klal Yisrael, an acclaimed nationally recognized expert on sentencing joined the team to argue against a life sentence. He prepared with the defense teams for weeks, but when the time came for him to make his case to the judge, drawing parallels and discussing precedent in similar cases, she didn't want to hear. She was abrupt and dismissive toward him.

In all our interactions he'd been the picture of polish and professionalism, confident in his expertise and his approach. Now, under her withering treatment, he seemed like a different man. Although he represented clients for more than forty years in countless courtrooms, he had clearly never encountered a judge who treated him this way and it was clearly flustering him.

She wouldn't even allow him to show a video he'd prepared of various character witness testimonies. "It's in the record, I'll watch it on my own," she said, waving him on to his next point, disrupting his flow and the momentum he was building. He couldn't get any traction and eventually just brought his presentation to a close and sat down in resignation.

The key issue in the sentencing debate was the loss. At issue was both the amount of the loss and who actually caused it. The main way the bank would have, and should have, been repaid was by the sale of their collateral—the sale of inventory could have chipped away at it and the sale of the company and its assets could have repaid the full amount all on its own, as collateral is designed to do. Both methods of repayment were severely undermined by others and then I was blamed for the loss.

Not only did the trustee sell the inventory at a far greater loss than even the thirty-to-forty percent loss expected in a bankruptcy, millions of dollars' worth of frozen inventory was brought back to the plant from cold storage and deliberately destroyed instead of being sold. This was attested to by a witness, who added that the meat was good and easily salable. Insurance payments for inventory lost in the great flood of 2008 should have been used to repay the bank, but no claim was filed, or, if it was, the money was not credited against the debt.

The prosecutors also took vindictive actions that bit into the company's coffers and diminished its ability to repay its debts. They forbade the company from using the vertically-integrated network of companies we had built over the years, such as the trucking company and chicken farms. A witness at the hearing testified that their ban on using our chicken farms cost the company hundreds of thousands of dollars—money that should have gone to pay the company's debts, reducing the loss.

That's a lot of money, but it's almost nothing next to the amount that selling the whole company should have brought in. Agriprocessors was a key player in the national kosher meat and poultry market, with annual sales of over $300 million. It had national name recognition and sales agreements with numerous national chains like Albertsons, Shop-Rite, and until the union's public relations offensive, Trader Joe's.

Potential buyers expressed serious interest as soon as the trustee announced it was seeking to sell. One of the largest meat packers in Israel made an early offer, one which would have repaid the bank with a lot of money left over. Many others were interested, and the resulting bidding war would have driven the sale price higher still. This is how this stage in a bankruptcy normally plays out—the collateral is sold on the open market and the creditor walks away with no loss at all.

This is where the prosecutors stepped in. Directly and through the trustee, they forbade any potential buyer from working with any Rubashkins in any way, including my father, under threat of forfeiture. This was like buying

Apple without the ability to employ Steve Jobs, or even consult with him on how to run the business.

In response, many potential bidders simply walked away. The prospects for a sale collapsed and the trustees and the prosecutors ultimately agreed to sell the company for only $8.5 million, far less than needed to repay the bank. It was an astounding *eighty percent* less than the initial offer they scared away, and who knows how high the final offer in a bidding process, free of interference, would have gone.

At the hearing, we brought affidavits and direct testimony from potential buyers, who explicitly blamed the actions of the prosecutors for discouraging them from making or pursuing their offers to buy Agriprocessors.

This so-called "No Rubashkin Edict" was common knowledge. The first witness the prosecution offered in order to deflect the blame for creating the loss tried to extricate them with some finesse. He tried to frame the restriction as focused only on whether the buyers were buying on behalf of Rubashkins in some way. He wouldn't admit to any decree excluding Rubashkins from helping the transition or being consulted on operations. He worded it carefully, misrepresenting what they'd done but in a way they could plausibly explain away.

What was new, and shocked our side of the courtroom into a stunned silence, was a witness who made a brazen denial of the whole thing. A local lawyer who represented the trustee was put on the stand by the prosecutors. During her testimony and cross-examination, she actually admitted that there was concern, first among the trustees and then among potential buyers, about the threats of the prosecutors.

But when she was asked the critical question—did this impact bidders?— she was unequivocal: "It did not." She then went on, at the prompting of the prosecutors themselves and at great length, to explicitly and repeatedly deny there'd ever been a prohibition at all! She claimed that involving Rubashkins was "not a deal-breaker." She said meetings had been arranged between any serious buyers and the prosecutors and at these meetings any fears of forfeiture, which she said were only based on rumors, were laid to rest. Involving Rubashkins was never an issue.

She was confronted with the sworn affidavit of a potential buyer who had been at one of these meetings, at which she was present. The affidavit testified that the man was told that if any member of the Rubashkin family had a management role, that would subject them to prosecution. She just flatly denied it. "No, I don't remember that being said, and I think I would."[7]

Hearing these brazen lies, I realized that there was someone in the room who could take the stand and disprove her—Steve Cohen! He was a food wholesaler with a long history of business with Agriprocessors and when it was put up for sale, he had explored buying it. He'd been on the receiving end of exactly the kind of threats and intimidation we were describing and she was denying. By *hashgachah pratis*, he had decided to attend the hearing that day and the lawyers went to see if he would testify.

He agreed and was rushed to the stand before the submission of evidence was closed. He testified that he'd been told by the trustee that there would be a problem if Rubashkins were involved—that it would be a "deal-breaker." He had explained to them that there wasn't any ownership aspect, but that the Rubashkins, who knew how to manage the plant and the business, were an important source of advice and instruction. He was told that he "would need to consider it differently." He testified that this was an important consideration for him, it reduced the value of the company by millions of dollars in his estimation, and, ultimately, he didn't make an offer.

The contradictory testimony was in. It was up to the judge to decide who to believe. She didn't have direct knowledge of the facts, but the prosecutors did. They knew the witness was lying when she said buyers were not told that Rubashkins' involvement was a deal-breaker. They knew because the lie was about their own behavior! Nonetheless, they solicited her testimony and let it go into the record as a trusted witness.

Of course, there was more discussed at the hearing, but I will leave a comprehensive description and analysis of the case to others and only highlight the aspects critical to understanding the *nisayon* I faced and the strength I found—and that every Yid has—to overcome and grow from such experiences.

Once the evidence had all been submitted and the lawyers had made their closing statements, I was offered an opportunity to speak. I took the opportunity, but it was excruciatingly difficult.

The whole hearing was for the purpose of discussing sentencing. It treated the jury's finding as established fact and punishment as inevitable, arguing only about the extent. Although I trusted wholeheartedly in Hashem's miracles, I

---

7. This topic is discussed in greater detail in Chapter Thirty-One.

prepared my words in the same vein. When it came time to speak them out loud, I was overcome with emotion.

The charges and the resulting conviction bore almost no resemblance to reality, but there were definitely things I'd done and decisions I'd made that, with the benefit of hindsight, I regretted. I had never denied making mistakes, and had said as much when I testified at the trial. In the time I was allotted, I again acknowledged my mistakes and applied to them the concept of *teshuvah*, both regret for past actions and resolve to change for the future. I spoke these words sincerely.

I apologized to my wife and children, whose pain was more painful to me than my own. "The sentence that's being requested is comparable to a death sentence and perhaps worse," I told the court, "because you only die once, and that's it. So I'm asking for mercy." I made this request sincerely as well, but the judge had given me no reason to believe she was capable of mercy, so I ended with the words a Jew says when he faces death—"*Shema Yisrael Hashem Elokeinu Hashem echad.*"

Anticlimactically, the judge followed up my impassioned plea by dryly noting that the hearing was now completed and a date would be set for the pronouncement of the sentence. The courtroom was cleared. I was led away, after a physically restrained farewell to my family, and returned to a place called jail to await the next ordeal—the state child labor case.

CHAPTER ELEVEN
State Case Preliminaries

Please, Plead!

AFTER THE FEDERAL TRIAL, THE STATE PROSECUTORS, WHO WERE charging me with the repugnant allegation of child labor violations, presented me with a choice, or as they put it, "offered a deal."

Conviction rates for state courts differ from state to state, but the general gist, as it is in the federal system, is that a conviction is a statistical certainty, or as close as makes any difference. What is essentially a hostile takeover of the defendant's legal team plays out the same way. A deal is offered that must be weighed against the relative certainty of conviction. This leverages the professional ethics obligations of the defendant's own lawyers, and forces them to counsel surrender as the best way forward for the defendant.

My case was no different. They made an offer which, from the lawyers' perspective, we almost couldn't refuse. If I would only agree to plead guilty to *one single charge*, accepting culpability and the consequences for that charge, they would drop the other nine-thousand-plus charges.

As the prosecutors knew they would have to, my lawyers urged me to accept. Their argument was bolstered by the "magnanimity" of the deal. I was facing 9,311 charges. They each carried a minor sentence, only thirty days, but collectively they added up to 776 years in prison if served consecutively. All that would go away if I would only admit to one charge.[1]

The mere thought of accepting this offer was abhorrent to me. I stood accused of knowingly exploiting non-Jewish children and placing them in

---

1. They constructed that charge to be multi-faceted and include one of each of the five underlying violations, but even that was a maximum of five months, weighed against 9,311 months.

danger for personal gain. This was as close to a blood libel as twenty-first-century America was likely to see. What they were asking me to do was to stand before the judge and before the world, Sholom Mordechai Rubashkin, a Yid and a chassid, and make a false confession.

I had never violated, and would never violate, the Torah's principles and exploit any person for any amount of personal gain. Ironically, I was now being urged to violate my principles (and cause a terrible *chillul Hashem*) by pretending that I *had*—and the main argument for that was my own personal gain, avoiding a difficult and dangerous trial.

Hearing of my objections and concerned as they were for my wellbeing, many friends and supporters added their voices and the weight of their opinions to the recommendation of my lawyers. I received many phone calls and even some personal visits by well-meaning people trying to protect me from myself. I needed to focus on appealing the federal case, they insisted. It was best for me to make this small concession, a trivial admission, and allow this whole child labor thing to blow over.

My experience with opponents, from local politicians to PETA and the Conservative movement, had taught me differently. I knew better. Going along with this would be an incalculable gift to my enemies and to the enemies of Hashem and *Yiddishkeit*, both foreign and domestic. They would portray this as a sincere admission of guilt and decry that I'd been allowed, by sly negotiation no doubt, to avoid facing justice for the other 9,300-plus crimes I had surely committed.

They would point to this "admitted" heartless and criminal exploitation to validate their negative portrayal of me, or of chassidic Jews, or of religious Jews, or of Jews in general, depending on their preferred target. The vast array of opportunistic vultures, who had no ax to grind with me or any of the communities to which I belong, but who saw opportunity in my troubles, would also endlessly trumpet the story as proof that we need to stop immigration or legalize immigrants or allow them to redefine kashrus or whatever their cause happened to be.

Unless I fought this and *won*, this would not blow over for a very, very long time to come. The vested interests would see to that. No, I had to fight all 9,311 charges and win. I also had the small advantage (and small it is, sadly) of being totally innocent.

I refused to be a party to a *chillul Hashem*. I stood my ground and insisted that we go to trial, firm in my conviction that this was the right thing to do and certain that my faith and trust in Hashem would be vindicated, as would I. My devoted wife and family, and my tireless and dutiful daughter Roza Hindy in particular, stood by me in that significant decision and her efforts were instrumental in gathering the funds needed to pay for proper representation.

Despite making every attempt, bail had not been granted and I had to help prepare for the state trial as best I could from a place called jail in the city of Cedar Rapids.

The charges against me had been filed in Allamakee County, where Postville is located. However, they quickly discovered that it would be impossible to find even the handful of unbiased and impartial people needed to fill a jury. They had no choice but to move the trial to Black Hawk County and its county seat of Waterloo.

The day before the trial was set to begin, a guard came into the cell in Cedar Rapids and told me that I would be transferred later that morning to Waterloo. I *davened*, ate the simple breakfast, and prepared my things for the transfer.

I had made every effort to avoid a repeat of the harrowing experiences of earlier transfers and intakes. When the trial was officially moved, I had tried, through my lawyers and through *askanim*, to ensure that the jail in Waterloo understood my legally protected religious rights and were prepared to accommodate them.

My lawyer confirmed that he had informed the jail in Black Hawk County that I needed my yarmulke, *tzitzis*, *tallis*, and *tefillin*, which they had agreed to accommodate, and that I could only eat kosher food, which they had agreed to provide. I had also been told that I would be permitted to take all the legal documents I needed for the trial. The record-breaking number of charges resulted in quite a large amount of paperwork, which I needed in order to be able to properly defend myself.

I prepared everything I would need and looked around the tiny cell in which I'd spent the last six months. I was a bit surprised to realize that the emotion I felt in that moment was satisfaction. My time there had been marked by an unexpected level of success in what matters most, living as a Yid. In this unlikely place, with effort and persistence, I had managed to fulfill the mitzvos incumbent on every Yid and even maintain the attitude of *emunah* and *bitachon* in Hashem that characterizes a *frum* Yid, marked by true inner calm and even joy.

From the depths of my heart, I thanked Hashem that He had given me the strength and clarity to avoid being dragged into the abyss of depression and repeatedly granted me success in my fight to serve Him as He commands. With a short but fervent *tefillah* to Hakadosh Baruch Hu for success in my trial, I walked out of the cell in Cedar Rapids.

After extensive bureaucratic out-processing, I was shackled hand and foot and loaded into a police car. Less than an hour later, we arrived at our destination. The county jail in Waterloo is a low, sprawling structure, linked by sky-walk to the courthouse. The car pulled through a large garage door into the prisoner unloading area. I was removed from the car and led into one of the holding cells lining the wall just inside the building.

Some time passed before a guard came in for the intake process. He ordered me to remove my clothing and change into their jail clothes. I obeyed, as I always did, until I reached the point at which I would be in violation of my religion principles, which are protected by law and had been pre-cleared by my lawyer for good measure.

When I got to my *tzitzis*, I explained to the officer that I'm required by my religion to wear my yarmulke and *tzitzis*. I added that I'd been told by my lawyer that this had been explained to and approved by the authorities at this jail.

He left, presumably to check with his superiors. To my surprise, when he returned, he told me that I actually *would* need to remove my yarmulke and *tzitzis*. I couldn't believe what I was hearing. I asked him to check again, repeating that my lawyer had told me that this had been prearranged and he'd been assured that there would be no problem. For good measure, I explained to him that my yarmulke and *tzitzis* were so critical a religious need that I could not move without them. He heard me out and left the cell without responding.

Here we go again, I thought. I had faced this test before, and done the right thing, but perhaps Hashem wanted to establish that it was a firm resolve, not just a temporary flash of inspiration that wouldn't survive a repeated challenge. My desire to be connected to Hashem had not wavered or weakened. In fact, it was stronger than before. I gathered my strength and braced myself with a *tefillah* for assistance in the impending confrontation.

A higher-ranking officer walked in, a man of very large build with an alarming potbelly. He informed me, in no uncertain terms and in a very condescending way, that I would not be allowed to wear my yarmulke and *tzitzis*. I would not be allowed to have my *tallis*, *tefillin*, or my "Hebrew books." I would not even be allowed to keep the legal papers I'd brought.

For my own protection, he went on to inform me with a straight face, they would also be putting me in solitary confinement. I don't know why asking for my religious needs meant I was suddenly in need of protection and he didn't offer an explanation.

I repeated what I'd told the guard: these were protected religious needs and the legal papers were critical for the trial for which I'd been transferred. He told me that his decision was final and would not be discussed.

He had shut down all avenues to an unaided resolution, so I asked to call my lawyer, which he permitted. I called and told the lawyer that nothing he'd prearranged was being allowed. The only thing they had not yet explicitly refused was kosher food, and that was presumably just a matter of time. The lawyer was puzzled by this and promised to do what he could from his end.

Having finished my phone call, I was brought back to the holding cell to await developments. Eventually, I was escorted to another room and given a set of orange prison clothes to put on. I complied, but did not remove my yarmulke and *tzitzis*. The guard stopped me. "Remove those items," he barked. I respectfully, but firmly, informed him that I could not do so, on religious grounds, holding out hope that he would follow the law and respect my religious rights.

As it had in South Dakota, my insistence on my religious rights resulted in a show of force. The door opened and five prison guards came in. They were not equipped with helmets, shields, and truncheons, as their counterparts had been, but they made up for it in sheer viciousness.

I was ordered to place my hands behind my back, which I did compliantly. They were roughly shackled. Once I was bound, my yarmulke and *tzitzis* were physically removed. "Move!" the ranking guard growled. I replied, in as calm and deferential a tone as I could muster, that I would like to comply, but simply could not move without my yarmulke and *tzitzis*.

In a dizzying flurry of violence, they unleashed their fury and hate. They grabbed me and beat me, then roughly dragged me across the floor toward the exit. The guard on my left side was particularly brutal, roughly yanking on my left arm in a way that would have dislocated it if the shackles on my hands hadn't held it firmly to my right arm. My wrists paid the price instead. The pain was excruciating. I didn't want to give them the satisfaction of seeing my agony, so I suffered in silence, suppressing my screams of pain.

We reached the elevator. It opened and they threw me in. I lay on the floor of the elevator, taking advantage of the reprieve to catch my breath and gather strength and endurance for the next stretch.

The time it took the elevator to travel the one or two floors was short, and before I could fully recover, I was again grabbed roughly and hoisted to my feet. They dragged me to the cell in the SHU, which was segregated from the rest of the jail. They threw me onto the cement slab and the cruel guard on my left side put his feet on my back, pinning me down. *"Don't move!"* he bellowed, as he released the cuffs.

"I can't move!" I pointed out.

Their job complete and their victim subdued, they filed out of the cell and locked me in. I lay there in considerable physical pain, bruises and scrapes all over my body, and in considerable spiritual pain, having been forcibly robbed of my yarmulke and *tzitzis*. The spiritual pain was tempered by deep gratitude to Hashem that He had given me the strength to withstand their torture and cling to Him and His mitzvos.

This was all so distressing and bewildering. Why were these people so dead set against accommodating the simplest requirements of my religion? They were not a harm or threat to anyone. Less than sixty miles to the northwest, in the jail in Cedar Rapids, they had no problem allowing (and had no problems *since* allowing) these small but important things.

Black Hawk County had advance notice and had assured my lawyers that they had made arrangements—yet they denied me everything I needed and beat me up for good measure, when it would have been just as easy to accommodate my rights and needs. Why?!

Talking to the Wall

My thoughts were interrupted by a tinny voice calling my name. "Hey! Rubashkin!" Startled, I looked around to determine where the voice was coming from. I spotted a small speaker on the wall just as the voice spoke again. "Your lawyer's here. Would you like to see him?"

"Yes!" I exclaimed. This was a gift from Hashem! I hadn't expected to speak to my lawyer until the next day, when we were to meet at the courthouse. In my hour of need, deprived of my rights and suffering a beating, Hashem had given him the thought to visit.

"Yes!" I repeated myself. "Of course I want to see my lawyer!"

"Step up to the door," came the response.

Protocol in prison requires that the prisoner come to the door and extend his hands to be shackled before the cell door is opened.

"I can't," I said.

"Why can't you go to the door?" the voice asked, perhaps expecting me to say I was too hurt.

"I can't walk without my yarmulke and *tzitzis*," I answered.

The voice burst out laughing.

"It's not a laughing matter. I want to, I *need* to, meet my lawyer, but I'm not able to do so unless my yarmulke and *tzitzis* are returned to me."

There was a pause. Then he said, "Does that mean you *don't* want to see your lawyer, then?"

I'd noticed this strategy a few times in these confrontations. If they were denying me something, whether it was kosher food or a religious object, they tried to shift the blame to me. If I couldn't eat the food they gave me because it wasn't kosher, they would try to get me to say I didn't want to eat, as if it was a preference. If I couldn't get to my lawyer, they wanted it on the record that I didn't want to see him. That way, it was my fault and they were in the clear.

"No," I insisted, "I *do* want to see my lawyer."

"Then step up to the door."

"I *can't*. I can't walk to the door without my yarmulke and *tzitzis*."

Another pause. "So you don't want to speak to your lawyer?"

He went around in this circular conversation for a remarkably long time, three or four minutes, perhaps hoping I would lose my cool and give him a different excuse to withhold the visit.

Hashem gave me the patience to play along and I repeated the same answers every time. Eventually, he tired of his game and the cell fell silent.

The silence dragged on and the small voice of my *yetzer hara* intruded on my thoughts. "Why am I doing this? He'll tell the lawyer I don't want to see him and the opportunity will be lost! Maybe I should have walked without a yarmulke so I could tell the lawyer about the denial of my rights and the physical abuse... Maybe he can help somehow."

Baruch Hashem, my *yetzer hara* had no more luck than the vicious prison guards. I was successful in standing my ground and clinging to Hashem without negotiating or compromising. I resolved to take all my cues only from Torah and not consider "alternative approaches" offered by others, whether they were inner doubts or uniformed thugs.

Ten minutes passed in silence before the intercom crackled back to life again. "Rubashkin! Your lawyer is here! Do you want to speak to him?"

It seemed he'd gotten a second wind. I replied, "Yes! I do!"

"Step up to the door!" I felt as if I'd heard this before.

"I can't."

"Why not?"

"I can't walk to the door without my yarmulke and *tzitzis*."

At this point I was tempted to offer to carry both sides of the conversation. There was no reason two people needed to be involved—I knew his lines by heart already. On cue, the next line came over the intercom. "So you *don't* want to speak to your lawyer?"

I could play this game all day, and it looked as if I might have to. We went around and around again, but he tired of his game quicker this time around. Eventually the intercom went quiet again.

A few minutes later, the door swung open with a clang and an officer walked in. His uniform told me that he was high up in the hierarchy. He told me to sit up, and said something about the need to see my lawyer. I couldn't focus on what he was saying, though, because I'd noticed that he was holding my precious yarmulke and *tzitzis*, his hands raised slightly in an unspoken offer.

I plucked them from his hands and put the *tzitzis* on with a heartfelt *brachah*. Finally able to move, I followed him to an upstairs visiting room where a lawyer named Mark Weinhardt was sitting behind a glass partition.

He had been hired to represent my father. My father was almost never in Iowa and wasn't involved in any way in hiring or firing line employees. No possible fault related to that process could be attributed to him, but the state prosecutors had charged him anyway. As the owner of Agriprocessors, charging him helped grab headlines and shape public perception and it also increased the pressure on me, their real target, to "play ball."

They never had any intention of taking these absurd and untenable charges before a jury. The moment for proving their charges had arrived, and the fiction could no longer be sustained, so they informed my father's lawyer that they intended to dismiss all the charges the next morning, before the trial began.

Now that he was available, he had been hired to represent me instead. Having been added to the team at the last minute, he was still unclear on a lot of the facts of the case as they related to me and the arguments that I wanted to make in my defense and he had come to prepare with me in person.

The painful events of the past few hours were front and center in my mind. As soon as I sat down, I told him everything that had happened. He was visibly disturbed by what he was hearing, and wrote it all down, promising to get to the bottom of it. He expressed his sorrow at what I'd endured and his satisfaction that they'd ultimately returned my religious items. Then he turned to the reason he'd come, which was to discuss the trial due to begin with preliminary hearings the next morning.

He had a very clear and incisive mind, and asked many good questions, which elicited information he felt was very useful for the case. We had a long and productive discussion. Satisfied with the results of our talk, he wished me a good night and left.

With my lawyer's visit over, I was locked in a small, empty holding cell while I waited to be transferred back to the SHU. The emotional whiplash of going from a stimulating and intelligent conversation with a bright, civilized, and good-natured individual to being prodded into a cage and degraded by ruffians is hard to describe.

No one came for me and there was no bell for room service, so I lay down on the floor to rest. It had been a long and hard day and I was exhausted. I kept reaching up to feel my yarmulke and running my fingers through the *tzitzis*, grateful they were with me and grateful for what their return represented—that Hashem was also with me, despite the turbulence I was experiencing.

I had been lying there for a while when an officer opened the door, muttering at me accusingly. Why hadn't I notified him that I was finished? I gestured at the empty box into which I'd been locked. "How did you expect me to do that?" He muttered something dismissively and prodded me back to the solitary confinement cell.

Sometime that evening, the small opening in the cell door slid open and a tray of food was pushed through with a grunt. "Food's here!"

I looked over at the tray and saw immediately that the open, heated tray of food was not kosher. Hoping to catch the guard before he was out of earshot, I jumped up and moved to the door, wincing through the pain.

"Come back!" I called out through the door. "I need kosher food!"

He hadn't gone far and walked back to the cell door. "It's kosher," he responded.

"There's no way this is kosher. Do you know what kosher is?" I asked, hurt that he would try to trick a man into violating his religion.

"Nope," he shrugged. "You hungry?"

"Yes, I'm hungry! I haven't eaten since early this morning!"

"Well, if you're hungry," he suggested flippantly, "eat."

"I am not a cow that grazes on whatever is in front of its nose," I protested. "I have religious needs and I was promised that I would have kosher food!"

At first, he seemed willing to discuss the issue, but after a minute or so, he just stopped mid-sentence and abruptly walked off, leaving me behind the cell door with no answers and no way to ask questions. Of course, I didn't touch the food, and the tray sat on the ledge of the door slot until they came to remove it.

It's absolutely unconscionable, particularly in the United States of America, that a person be denied food for over twenty-four hours because his religion limits him to certain food—which is readily available—simply because the authorities can't be bothered to provide it, even with two weeks' notice and after assurances that it would be arranged!

I was allowed a phone call later that evening. Like all calls from a place called jail, the calls were monitored. This usually makes people hesitant to speak freely about what they're going through, for fear of retribution. I was beyond worrying about that at this point.

I called home and told my wife everything that had happened, which was very distressing for her to hear. The call was cut short by a guard who started yelling that I needed to hang up and get back to my cell.

I asked the guard to allow me to make a call to my lawyer. My first call had been so short and I had something pressing to tell my lawyer. The guard's response was to threaten me with consequences if I didn't step away from the phone immediately. I dropped the issue, and the phone, and waited at the door to be led back to the cell, where I was locked in for the night.

I had to *daven* Ma'ariv and say *Krias Shema* without a siddur and I was thankful that Hashem had given me the foresight to carefully commit them to memory in case of a situation such as this.

On to the Courtroom

I awoke the next morning still aching from the mistreatment of the day before. I said *Modeh Ani* but had no pure water to wash *negel vasser*. The slot in the door again slid open and a tray was pushed through. As I had the day before, I jumped to the door and got the guard's attention before he vanished.

I told him that I couldn't eat because I only eat kosher food. I told him that it had ostensibly been arranged by my lawyer.

The guard the day before had been callous and flippant—this guard was just straight-out rude. "This is what I have and this is what you get. If you don't like it, you need to speak to someone else."

I gestured around the tiny box I was in. "How can I speak to someone else? I'm locked in this room. You're the only one here and you're already involved in the food." He simply shrugged, spun on his heel, and walked off.

My hunger pangs had intensified and I was still smarting from the abuse of the previous day, but I started to feel more angry than hurt. There was simply no justification for their treatment. This is the United States of America, not Soviet Russia. In keeping with the cherished right of freedom of religion, yarmulke and *tzitzis* are allowed in jails and prisons across the country and don't cost the authorities a penny. To deny them is indefensible and to do so with physical violence is an outright scandal!

The morning wore on. A guard unlocked the cell and instructed me to follow him. He led me to a room with a glass partition. To protect the presumption of innocence by the jury, I would be allowed to wear civilian clothes in court and I was in this room to receive them. I approached the partition. The guard behind the glass looked up and immediately noticed my angry demeanor. He apparently knew what had caused it, because he said to me, "I heard what happened yesterday. You need to know that I am not one of *them*."

This was unexpected, and a little suspicious. Why was he telling me this? Why would he side with an inmate against his brothers-in-arms? Not sure how to take this, I didn't respond. I silently took the clothes he slid through the window and went to the dressing area, where I could take a shower and dress properly for the trial which was about to begin.

During the next hour or so, over the course of the transfer, it became clear that this guard was actually exactly what he seemed like—a decent human being. He adjusted the shackles on my hands and feet so they didn't dig into my skin when I moved, and he also demonstrated sensitivity to my religious needs.

Entering the courtroom, I noticed a pitcher of water on the table alongside a stack of cups. I hadn't been able to wash my hands that morning, and I remembered a story about the Rebbe's father, Reb Levi Yitzchak Schneerson.

He was imprisoned and exiled by the Soviets. At one point during his ordeal, he was without water for an extended period of time. When he finally got some water, his first thought was to use it to wash his hands. Only once that was done did he permit himself to take a swallow to slake his intense thirst.

With this role model in mind and before anyone could react, I took the pitcher and confidently walked over to the plastic waste bin in the corner. Carefully, I poured the water over my right hand, then my left. By then, this guard noticed my unusual behavior and confronted me. "What are you doing?!" he asked, bewildered.

I explained to him that a religious Jew washes his hands of impurity first thing every morning and this had been my first opportunity. I can't say he understood the significance of what I was doing, but he had the decency to allow me to complete the mitzvah, in keeping with the best American traditions of freedom of religion.

My father was already sitting in the courtroom, so I said the *brachah* "*Al netilas yadayim*" loudly enough that he could hear it and answer amen. I went on to say all the morning *brachos* at the same volume, and he answered amen to them all. I took tremendous strength from that.

My fingers lightly traced my bruises as I said the *brachah* of "*Shelo asani goy*." I felt such sincere gratitude that I was not born into a nation which included such barbarians, that it brought tears of gratitude to my eyes.

In a flash of clarity, I saw the answer to a question that had often bothered me. Our slavery in Mitzrayim is referred to in Torah as a *kur habarzel*, a smelting furnace. This kind of furnace uses intense heat to burn away or separate worthless elements that are naturally mixed in with the ore of precious metals like gold or silver.

The intent of the *mashal* is clear—our experience in Mitzrayim was meant to refine us and separate us from undesirable influences and elements. What I'd never understood was *how*. How does excruciating physical and spiritual torment at the hand of an oppressor elevate and refine a person?

Painful personal experience had now provided the answer. The *Yidden* who had come to Mitzrayim were impressed by the great civilization and all its accomplishments. This appreciation led them to adapt and adopt various practices and beliefs from their neighbors. The terrible torture they endured at the hands of their "civilized" hosts cleansed them of this appreciation and the impure effects it had had on them.

Similarly, in a subtler sense, I had seen some wisdom and beauty in the culture and institutions of the nations around us. I had been, to some degree, impressed by them. This appreciation gave a small foothold to the values and principles they represented, introducing dross into true wisdom and beauty, which is only found in Torah.

The beating I had suffered, and their general treatment of me, both physically and legally, had burned away the dross. In that moment, I had lost any respect or appreciation I mistakenly held, and now saw them for what they truly were. Far better to be even a battered man than a triumphant beast.

That day's proceedings would not improve my opinion of my jailers.

The courtroom was fairly large. The judge sat on a raised dais at the front of the room, under the seal of the State of Iowa. Along the right wall in the front of the room were two rows of seats behind a waist-high wall, for use by the jury.

In front of the judge and jury was a large L-shaped table. The long part of the table was for the defendant and his lawyers, and faced the jury. I sat at this table, Monty Brown seated to my left and Mark Weinhardt to my right. The shorter part was for the prosecution and was angled to face the judge. At this table sat the highest-ranking officials in Iowa's Justice Department, the state's Attorney General and Assistant Attorneys General—an unusually prestigious representation.

Cutting across the room behind this table was a low wall, behind which were seats for the public to observe the proceedings. An aisle down the middle separated the gallery into two halves. Although there were no formal rules about who sat where, my family, friends, and supporters naturally gravitated to my side of the room and those who came to support the prosecution sat on the other side. Given the high profile of my case, many people were expected to attend on both sides.

Among the supporters were chassidim from Crown Heights. One of them had brought a white shirt that had been worn by the Rebbe. *Chassanim* under the *chuppah* are usually given the *zechus* of wearing this shirt as a *kittel*. I was to stand before a judge—the earthly courtroom reflecting the moment of judgment in Heaven where my fate was truly to be decided, and the Heavenly Judge before whom I stood. It was appropriate that I wear a *kittel*, as we do on Yom Kippur, and they had brought this holy garment for that purpose. I thanked them profusely and received permission to wear it for the duration of the trial.

Emotions ran high when my wife and children came in, but we greeted each other in a restrained manner, hoping the guard would not interfere. To his credit, he didn't prevent relatively close face-to-face interaction, a welcome experience after months of visits through a closed-circuit screen.

Physical contact, even from opposite sides of the low barrier fencing off the gallery, was absolutely forbidden. This was particularly hard for our special-needs son, Moishie. He couldn't understand why I wasn't showing him the usual signs of affection, why I wasn't hugging and kissing him as I normally would. Sixteen years old, he'd only just begun expressing himself verbally in one- or two-word bursts but, tragically, the trauma of this whole experience had caused him to regress.

We did our best to help him understand that I *wanted* to show him love and connection but the policeman wouldn't allow it. I prayed to Hashem that he would be able to make peace with this, and it would not negatively affect him.

This gut-wrenching inability to connect to him in ways he could understand was magnified at the end of each day, when we went our separate ways. He stood there behind the partition, holding his hand out to touch me and, although I was inches away, I could only raise my hand to him in a wave, trying to bridge the gap with a broad smile and the energy in my voice.

On one occasion, I couldn't restrain myself, and I touched his hand. It lasted for a brief moment

It was agonizing to deny my special needs son the physical contact he needed as he reached out to me from behind the divider.

but to both of us it was a precious moment of loving connection, a moment that gave us strength to carry on. *Baruch Hashem*, the guard who was right behind me, the one who had shown humanity and decency, decided not to notice and said nothing of it.

Although I wasn't allowed physical contact with the friends and family that had come to support me, there was a palpable spiritual bond I felt whenever we were together, rooted in the *achdus* which they expressed by their presence.

Throughout the trial, I would occasionally glance over at "my" side of the room, taking strength and encouragement from the many who had come to support me. I inevitably noticed those sitting on the other side. It was a hodge-podge of personal supporters of the individual prosecutors, family members of the various prosecution witnesses, and activists rooting for their cause at the expense of an innocent man.

After months of speaking through partitions or on the phone, the breaks in the trial gave me the opportunity to speak face to face with my family.

Among that last group were some priests and clergy from Postville. They had seen firsthand, time and again, my generosity and sympathy for those less fortunate, the very people they were claiming to champion. At my father's instruction, I had given financial assistance to individuals and also supported their communal charitable initiatives, such as the food pantry. How eagerly that was all ignored and forgotten, now that they had the opportunity to put themselves forward as the heroes of the downtrodden, fighting to see the Jewish villain punished.

The prosecutors took their seats, the public gallery slowly filled up, and the judge's entrance was announced. He took his seat with little ceremony and the pre-trial hearing began. There were a number of procedural issues to get through before we would have the opportunity to raise my mistreatment and hopefully resolve my somehow contentious religious needs.

Preliminary Business

The state was finally ready to come clean about their actual case. Since the day their charges were filed, the sheer number of charges had been a big talking point. In order to whip the media and the general public into a frenzy and overwhelm me into giving up, they had leveled a staggering 9,311 charges. "The numbers speak for themselves," the State Attorney General said in press interviews.

This mind-boggling number had been trumpeted for a year and a half by everyone from state officials to activists to commentators. It also put intense pressure on me to plead guilty—after all, the potential penalties of thirty days for each charge, served consecutively, added up to more than 775 years, functionally a life sentence.

Now, faced with the task of *proving* their allegations, they casually dismissed 9,228 of them, leaving me to face "only" eighty-three charges. They were perfectly content with painting me as a historic villain in the minds of the public and the media but they wouldn't back that up with evidence and argument when it mattered.

They blamed logistics for this decision, but that doesn't make it any better. If you don't intend on putting a charge to the test, it's not a criminal charge. It's nothing more than abusing the state's legal power to level charges to serve propaganda purposes. They knew when they made the charges that they had no intention of running a year-long trial to prove them all, and they made them anyway.

To me this was a stark demonstration of the true nature of a *nisayon*. It exists only to serve a purpose. Once the person overcomes it and that purpose is served, it ceases to exist. In a single moment, the terrible threat had shrunk to less than one percent of its original size, and I renewed my faith and trust in Hashem that it would dwindle away to nothing.

The prosecutors were ready to move forward to seating a jury, but my lawyers weren't. They had some issues to raise with the court before we could move forward.

First on their list was the pressing need to delay the trial in light of new evidence we'd only recently received. Days before the trial was set to begin, more than a year and a half since the charges had been filed, my lawyers received a notification from the prosecutor. He had evidence that had not been shared. A mere oversight, he assured them. *Oops.*

By way of background: Of all the potential witnesses, there was one in particular who caused the defense team the most concern. The head of human resources had given testimony at the federal trial that the prosecutors had successfully misconstrued and we expected the state prosecutors to try and replicate the trick. I'd been repeatedly told about these fears, including as an argument to pressure me into accepting the guilty plea, but I placed my faith and trust in Hashem that my innocence would be recognized.

Compelled to see the case through and anticipating this attack by the prosecution, the defense team spent a significant amount of time preparing ways to counter the expected distortions of this testimony. In the days before the trial, there were reports in the media that this witness had been transferred to Waterloo from the jail where she was sitting.[2] This transfer could only mean that we would indeed have to face her in court.

Imagine the elation of the defense team when they received the "new" evidence, days before the trial, and found that it was four hours of audio recordings of this potential witness which completely undermined the mischaracterization we feared. In the recordings, which documented interrogations of both her and one other potential witnesses, the witnesses insisted, despite repeated questioning, that they could not testify that I knew there were underage workers at the plant. Pressed by state investigators to say what they wanted to hear, one of them said outright, "If I said that, I would be lying."

Once the lawyers had digested the significance of these revelations, their joy gave way to anger and frustration. How could the state have withheld this information?! This wasn't something the state had just discovered or could possibly have overlooked—these were interrogations that they themselves had held, many months prior, with the employees closest to the central issue of the case and they related directly to the charges!

This was a practical grievance, not just a moral one. The lawyers had focused a large part of their preparations on defending against this set of misrepresentations, knowing that it was the only direct way for prosecutors to make their false case. Except it wasn't, as we now knew. Despite the charade of bringing her to town, they had no intention of bringing her as a witness—not with those admissions on tape.

In light of this unexpected and disruptive development, my lawyers made a formal request to delay the trial by thirty days. The judge saw fit to give us only a few days to investigate issues surrounding the recordings and adjust to them, and only once the jury was seated.

Another concern we raised in support of a delay was a potential scheduling conflict with the federal sentencing which was due to be issued three weeks later. In his determination to keep the two cases separate, the judge dismissed this argument entirely, but it was only a few short weeks later that this concern was shown to be very real and more serious than we even realized at the time.

The state trial ended up taking longer than expected. Days before the

---

2. The judge had sentenced her to a year and a day, less than prosecutors had requested, in recognition of the role her testimony had played in their narrative.

federal sentence was to be issued, with no resolution to the state charges, the federal judge suddenly announced that sentencing would be delayed. Her stated reason was that she needed more time to consider the matter. The new date she set was almost a month later, certain to be well beyond the end of the state case.

We didn't realize until years later the full weight and sinister purpose of this scheduling decision, and the extent of the Divine protection which had guided my refusal to plead guilty. If I had pled or been found guilty on even one of the 9,311 misdemeanor charges, I would, at the time of federal sentencing, have been classified as a repeat offender. This would have factored into the Sentencing Guidelines and helped legitimize the life sentence they had planned for me. I later met inmates, in jail for relatively petty crimes, who had been sentenced to life in prison because they were considered repeat offenders.

Next on my lawyer's list, although first on mine, was concern over my immediate predicament. He informed the judge that my religious needs were not being met, to the point that I hadn't eaten in over twenty-four hours. "I can't represent a man who's not eating!" he told the court. Other basic religious needs were being denied, including yarmulke and *tzitzis*.

The judge was unmoved by my plight. He casually dismissed my religion and its requirements as my "choice." An American state judge, he coldly said of my religion: "Mr. Rubashkin is incarcerated. One of the effects of incarceration is being deprived of things that are near and dear to your heart." If we were claiming that the jail was in violation of administrative codes, we would have to take it up with a district judge.

As a matter of form, he went on to request that my lawyer list my various needs, but he defended and supported the jail's behavior, equating my simple requests with a hypothetical American Indian requesting a sweat lodge be built (which, incidentally, *is* done, as I discovered in Otisville) or that hallucinogenic "plant matter" be provided.

As to the impossibility of carrying on a trial without providing for the basic needs of the defendant, he noted that, since the charges were technically misdemeanors, my presence in the courtroom was not actually required. They could decide my fate without my presence or participation.

During a break in the proceedings for lunch, I was transferred back to the jail building. An officer entered with a lunch tray for me to eat. "We're resolving the issue," he told me, "and you will have kosher food in two days' time. For now, here's a regular lunch." I reiterated that I could not eat non-kosher food under any circumstances and he left the holding cell disappointed. Two minutes later, he returned with kosher food. It took me some time to calm down enough to eat. Imagine the chutzpah of trying to convince a person to eat forbidden food when he had kosher food in the next room all along.

CREDIT: WATERLOO-CEDAR FALLS COURIER, RICK CHASE

With my father in the courtroom before they dismissed the charges against him. It broke my heart that they put my father through such torture and heartache for no reason at all.

I later learned that there had been efforts on my behalf by the local Jewish chaplain, but even his interventions with the jail authorities fell on deaf ears. He did get some concessions, but nothing approaching the bare minimum I required, and ultimately, they decided to kick me out of their jail. If I wanted my religious rights, they decided, I would have to be transferred back to Cedar Rapids, where my needs were somehow not a contradiction to order and security.

I was being returned to Cedar Rapids, but the trial would proceed in Waterloo. The Constitution guarantees a defendant the right to face his accusers and confront and cross-examine witnesses against him, but the only way I could exercise this important legal right was if the guard was willing to ferry me back and forth each day. He agreed, *baruch Hashem*, and until the end of the state trial he made the hour-long drive each way so I could be in court, for which I was very grateful.

As with every aspect of the case, those in opposition had the sympathetic ear of the media and the coverage of this episode reflected that. The sheriff in charge of this shameful operation claimed Cedar Rapids was "better equipped" to handle me—I assume because their guards were equipped with a modicum of restraint, humanity, and respect for human and religious rights.

To hear him tell it, they'd spent weeks preparing for my "stay," but he was unable to meet my excessive expectations. Instead of involving the Jewish chaplain in determining what qualifies as kosher food, he just had his food vendor call up a random synagogue or temple in Minnesota for advice and called it a day. He described my insistence on actual certified kosher food as petulantly turning up my nose at his food.

During the violence they'd inflicted on me, they created wounds which they then dragged through the dirt. Those wounds became infected and festered, landing me in the hospital. He had the chutzpah to describe that incident as follows: "He had to be carried everywhere he went, because he refused to walk without his sacred undergarments."

In closing, he did ultimately admit the truth about this unnecessary conflict. My religious needs (which he went out of his way to insist are not "needs" but "wants") were something that really "could have been met, we just weren't willing or ready to travel down that road" of "kowtowing" to an inmate. I was just trying to exercise my right to serve Hashem—he was playing power games. I was as happy to be rid of him as he was to be rid of me.

When I was brought back to Cedar Rapids, I was not returned to the cell I'd been assigned to before. The new cellblock was just a very small common area with two tiny cells connected to it. Each of these cells had two sleeping-shelves stacked one on top of the other. I was assigned the cell on the right side, without a cellmate. The other cell housed two older white prisoners.

The official daily schedule in this cellblock, besides for the days I was in court in Waterloo, began at 9:00 a.m. The guard would shout, "Lockout!" and the prisoners all had to exit their small cells, which were then locked. The common area had a small table, a telephone on the wall on one side, and a TV monitor hanging on the wall on the other side.

The audio from this TV was quite a nuisance. In His kindness, Hashem orchestrated a solution. The younger of the two took to escaping his troubles by constantly sleeping. When we were ejected from the cells, he would take the thin mat off of his sleeping-shelf and into the common area and go right back to sleep. The older inmate (quite an elderly fellow, in fact) didn't like watching much TV. When he realized that I was also ignoring it, he left it off during the lockout.

I thanked Hashem for arranging it all so neatly, and I spent the time learning from some *sefarim* I had in the cell, leaving that wretched place behind for the wonderful world of Torah.

One day, a particularly callous guard noticed this poor fellow lying on his mat in the common area, and coldly informed him that he was not allowed to move his mat out of the cell, mere feet away. The hapless prisoner still tried to escape into sleep, but sleeping on the floor was very difficult at his age. He felt very bitter that even this escape was denied to him, and for no real reason.

There was mutual respect between the three of us, *baruch Hashem*. We did spend some time talking together, although we steered clear of discussing our respective cases or situations.

For the duration of the state case, I had to start my day extra early in order to *daven* and say Tehillim before they came to begin the transfer. When it was time to go, a guard would come to the cellblock and escort me via elevator to the loading area. They would search me thoroughly to ensure I wasn't concealing anything under my clothes, and the guard would then shackle me hand and foot and put me in the backseat for the drive to Waterloo.

The streets and highways were familiar to me from years of living in the area, but now I was traveling as a handcuffed prisoner. It was a very degrading experience. Struggling with this overwhelming psychological effect, I turned to the teaching of the Ba'al Shem Tov, who says, "A man is where his thoughts are," also sometimes phrased as "A man is where his will is." My situation was established by my mind and by my heart, not by my environment.

My hands were bound, so I couldn't hold a *sefer*, but I could still leave the prison transport where my body was trapped by focusing on the parts of Torah I knew by heart. I transported myself to the world of Torah, to the reality described in the words of *Tehillim* and the *Chovos Halevavos*. The time I spent in that place of clarity and truth refreshed and strengthened my trust in Hashem and prepared me for that day's grueling grind in court. I used the same strategy for the drive back.

During one of these drives, the guard pulled into a gas station right behind a school bus. A gaggle of young students poured out, excitedly heading inside to buy snacks for their trip. Sitting in the back of a police car, shackled hand and foot, in front of these children, was particularly demeaning. This made it all the more meaningful when the guard returned and passed me a small bottle of soda he'd thought to buy for me. The expression of humanity, particularly in that moment of vulnerability, meant much more than the drink itself.

The state trial took over a month from start to verdict and I had to make this commute every day.

CHAPTER TWELVE
The State Trial

Jury Selection

THE CHILD LABOR CHARGES LEVELED AGAINST ME WERE MORALLY repugnant, but legally they were classified as lower level offenses; misdemeanors. Each charge carried a maximum penalty of "only" thirty days in jail. Since the stakes are lower for each charge, a six-person jury was considered sufficient, even though a conviction on even the remaining eighty-three charges meant a close to seven-year prison term if served consecutively.

CREDIT: AP PHOTO, CHRISTOPHER GANNON

An additional two jurors would be selected as potential substitutes called "alternates," for a total of eight. If one or two of the core six jurors was unable to participate in the deliberations for any reason, these substitutes could step in and we wouldn't have to repeat the whole trial.

The selection process involved questioning potential jurors to find eight people who were not bigoted or biased. Both the prosecution and defense asked each candidate a number of questions and the judge determined, based on the answers, if the juror was suitable. Each side also had a handful of vetoes they could use if they felt the juror would be prejudiced against them even though they had passed the court's test.

Learning Torah in the courtroom during breaks in the state trial.

We had relocated almost a hundred miles from Waukon, where finding a fair-minded jury was seen as an impossible task, but despite the distance, it was still proving difficult. So difficult, in fact, that after the first few had all been disqualified for bias, I overheard one of the prosecutors say, "Well, it looks like we'll be moving the trial again…"

They'd started with a pool of forty-five potential jurors but by the end of the day, they still hadn't filled the jury. They had to add another thirty people to the jury pool, and continue into a second day, before they could seat an eight-person jury.

The day that jury selection was completed, a rally had been scheduled in the Satmar community of Kiryas Yoel. Thousands gathered in a show of *achdus* and *ahavas Yisrael*. As they always did at these gatherings, they said a heartfelt *kapitel Tehillim* for me before they were addressed by *rabbanim* and *askanim*. Rav Menachem Meir Weissmandl, the *rav* who had overseen kashrus at the plant, addressed the crowd, among others. My son Getzel represented the family and shared some words with the crowd as well. The Torah, *tefillah*, and *tzedakah* were surely worthy advocates in Heaven and the funds that were raised helped buoy our efforts.

With the preliminary hearings and jury selection out of the way, the trial could begin in earnest. Monday, May 10, 2010, the prosecution opened the proceedings with their opening statement, the defense had an opportunity to present our opening statement, and the trial turned to the actual evidence and testimony.

One open issue that was hanging over the proceedings was the Yom Tov of Shavuos, which was only a week away. I obviously couldn't appear in court on Yom Tov. My lawyers brought this up during the preliminary hearings, and again, numerous times, as the date grew closer.

At first, the judge withheld a decision, pointing out that since the charges were misdemeanors, my presence was not actually necessary. As he'd noted in connection with the denial of kosher food, they could decide my fate in my absence, and he was therefore inclined to continue over Yom Tov without me.

This would have been a big blow for my defense. The team had been hobbled in their preparations by the denial of bail, and my ability to coach the lawyers in real-time, as testimony was given, was critical to their effective cross-examination of the witnesses.

By the end of the week, the judge had come to the compromise that the court would not adjourn for the two days of Yom Tov, but would also not hear new testimony on those days. Instead, they would deal with technical areas of contention that had to be hashed out between the lawyers.

This whole discussion soon became irrelevant anyway. The cuts I had suffered when they took my yarmulke and *tzitzis* and violently dragged me across the filthy floors had not been tended to and had become seriously infected. I was in quite a bit of pain, and although it wasn't easy, I eventually persuaded a nurse at the prison to look at my arm. She took one look and immediately made arrangements for me to be hospitalized.

At the hospital, I was treated like a dangerous prisoner and shackled to my bed at all times. Yet again, I had to defend my religious rights. When I asked to use my siddur, *tallis*, and *tefillin*, I was flatly denied. I pointed out that I was allowed to use them daily in the jail itself, and explained that until I prayed, I couldn't eat. One of the guards shrugged. "Starve, then." As if I had a choice. I did just that until late afternoon. By the end of the day, seeing that I wasn't budging, the guards yielded and brought me my siddur, *tallis*, and *tefillin* and I was able to *daven*.

It was a life-threatening infection. They hooked me up to an IV and began a regimen of strong antibiotics, but the infection was pretty persistent. It took over a week before I was released from the hospital.

I was not permitted to contact anyone and my family and my lawyers were not informed of what had happened or where I was. Concerned when they did not hear from me, my family asked the local hospital if I'd been admitted as a patient, but they denied that I was there.

As a matter of fact, the judge was in the dark too. Court resumed on Monday as scheduled, and, when I failed to appear, the judge had to scramble to determine where I was. He ended up canceling that day's proceedings and sending everyone home. Court was canceled again the next day, and formally adjourned until after Shavuos.

From the judge's statements, my family now knew that I was in the hospital, but they still didn't know why, or in what shape. Anxious that I be properly cared for, they tried to get permission for our local community doctor to be involved in my care, but the guards wouldn't allow it.

When it became clear that I would be in the hospital over Shavuos, food was arranged through a local *shliach*. My family also arranged that I be sent a *Tikun Leil Shavuos* by overnight mail so that I could properly observe the Yom Tov, but the hospital never gave it to me.

Throughout all of this, I focused on one thing—keeping my *emunah* and *bitachon* in *Hashem Yisbarach* strong and unaffected by all that was going on around me. It was critical that I process each new development through the Torah's explanation of reality, as a Yid should.

On Friday, I was released from the hospital and brought straight to the courthouse, where the trial resumed.

A Ludicrous Case

The case itself, as both defense and prosecution already knew and as the court and the world were about to find out, was entirely without merit and should never have been brought. As the lawyer, Mark Weinhardt, put it to my father: "The reason you're here [facing these ludicrous charges] is because of the way you look and what you believe."

Since they'd dismissed more than ninety-nine percent of the charges, the possible sentence in this case was far less than the one contemplated in the federal case, but the moral stakes were much higher. I stood accused of intentionally endangering children, working them long hours and in unsafe conditions in violation of both the laws protecting them and of basic human decency by any standard. The mere allegation was a monumental *chillul Hashem*, and various activists and organizations had already used it in their efforts to besmirch *frum* Jews and *shechitah*.

I was determined to counter the charges clearly and decisively and I was, *baruch Hashem*, successful. In fact, the State of Iowa agreed to expunge the case as soon as that became a legal option in 2016. The case was so decisively settled that it's as if it never happened at all. It's the closest our system gets to finding someone "innocent" as opposed to just "not guilty."

A proper analysis of the legal back-and-forth is beyond the scope of this book, but I accepted great risk in order to confront and undo this *chillul Hashem*, and I want to at least distill the sensational accusations and how they were discredited.

To start with, you would expect the presence of workers at the plant below a certain age to be an inescapable, clearly documented fact. Surely, at least that much was established. You would be wrong. In one of the greatest mockeries of justice that I experienced, in a case based entirely on age, the true ages of the workers in question were never properly established.

When they were hired, they'd all presented documents that established their work status and age, which turned out to be false. The state's claim was that not only had they been lying about their immigration status, they were also lying about their ages. Yet, they offered no proof that these people *were*, in fact, younger than stated in their documents. Even after the defense demanded that they do so, the judge did not require it—not original birth certificates, not passports,[1] not even parental testimony!

It was simply taken on faith as established fact that of the two inconsistent dates of birth they'd all given, the one which made hiring them illegal was the one that was true and the older age was the lie. This, despite the open incentive to lie about being too young in exchange for U-visas, which meant legal immigration for themselves and their families.

Even with the unproven assumption that these workers were too young to work, the state's case still had an insurmountable hurdle to clear. They accused me of *knowing* that these workers were too young and hiring them anyway.

Having been denied bail and the ability to properly prepare for the trial, I did my best to help with my defense during the trial itself.

The story they wanted the world, and now the jury, to believe, was beyond absurd. It was an uncontested fact that there was no lack of job applicants at the plant. Dozens were turned away every week for lack of positions to fill. There was also never any suggestion that these alleged minors were paid less for their work.

The state was asserting that instead of hiring any of the adults seeking those jobs, Agriprocessors had intentionally hired children to do difficult and dangerous labor. In doing so, it had accepted the significant additional costs in unthinkable risks—all for no financial gain whatsoever. In fact, the only ones who benefited from the employment of these alleged underage workers were

---

1. In order to testify, many of them had been flown back from Guatemala by the State of Iowa, so they definitely had passports.

the workers themselves, their families, and whomever they paid to supply their forged documents.

Beyond the obvious absurdity of the suggestion that Agri intentionally entered into such an arrangement, the testimony contradicted their story at every turn.

Every one of the workers and witnesses testified that the hiring department demanded documentation. A couple of prosecution witnesses even admitted under cross-examination that their documentation was considered insufficient and they were refused employment until they could provide additional documentation. One of them got this documentation by having his parents in Mexico buy a birth certificate on the black market there.

Witnesses testified that when someone had been discovered to have provided documents misrepresenting their age, they were fired immediately, and that I'd encouraged the office staff to investigate and fire anyone else who may have done the same.

These were not revelations to the prosecutors. This information was largely coming from *their* witnesses, people with whom they'd worked extensively in developing their charges and their case. Even if their depiction of the perils of the workplace was true (and it was not, as you'll soon see), there were absolutely no grounds to accuse me of knowingly including minors in the workforce!

One of the most direct testimonies to my refusal to hire minors also led to the most openly antisemitic statement to come out of this whole story. Two *bachurim* from the local yeshivah had no summer plans one year, and decided they'd like to work at the plant. When the HR department turned them away because they weren't yet eighteen years old, they approached me, hoping our close relationship would get them in.

Both of them, now adults, testified in court, under oath, how I'd responded. I explained to them that the law is the law, and as much as I wanted to help them find a productive use for their summer, this was not an option. One of them had gone as far as having his mother call me to try to convince me to overlook his age and she also came to testify. I had heard her out but would not even consider her request, telling her exactly what I'd told her son: It was illegal and out of the question.

There had been logistical difficulties in arranging for these witnesses to appear and the lawyers hadn't felt the testimony was critical enough to make the efforts required. Yaakov and Roza Hindy disagreed. They felt that the jury must hear this testimony and they did whatever it took to bring it to them. The powerful impression it made on the jury when it was presented in court drove home a truth that is often overlooked. Love and personal investment can often give a person wisdom and clarity that even expertise and experience cannot.

In an attempt to neutralize this indisputable testimony, the State Attorney General, in his closing arguments, said something that would not have been out of place in the show trials from the darkest moments in Jewish history.

He started by asserting to the jury that I was the most powerful man in Postville, who "knew exactly how he needed to go about making a profit." Sholom is not responsible for the poverty in Guatemala, he generously conceded, but he exploited that poverty.

Having hit the important buzzwords and laid down the broad strokes of the classic antisemitic stereotype, he said the following about the only witnesses who had testified to directly asking me to hire minors: "I don't challenge their testimony, but I do think it's less than coincidence that no one from the yeshivah was employed underage and yet the eighth and ninth grade classes of Postville [non-Jewish] schools were a feeder to the plant."

In other words (and entirely without basis): Sure, I accept that Sholom Rubashkin explicitly turned away minors because it's illegal, and the work is dangerous and they might get hurt, but he only cared about *Jewish* kids, you see. He was only too eager to exploit and endanger the *non-Jewish* kids.

This absolutely unfounded and unjustifiable claim was earnestly advanced by a State Attorney General, in the United States, in the twenty-first century.

With basic common sense on my side and the only

I couldn't believe the things I was hearing from the prosecutor during the state trial.

credible direct testimony about knowingly hiring minors being that I did *not*, the prosecutors were reduced to trying to prove that I'd seen these workers at the plant and could tell they were too young. They kept asking the workers that they had brought to testify if I'd ever happened to pass their stations while walking through the plant.

To make it seem like their age was obvious and I should have known, prosecutors showed the jury pictures of youthful-looking workers standing in their undershirts in their living rooms.

Firstly, that's nothing like the workplace appearance of a worker. They work in a refrigerated environment and are bundled up in hooded sweatshirts and wear butcher frocks, hair and beard nets, hard hats, and other safety gear—not to mention that workers are positioned facing the production line with their backs toward the area where people walked through each room.

All that aside, there's a reason documents are relied on to establish age, as opposed to appearance-based guesswork. To great effect, my lawyers put the state's lead investigator on the stand and let him make the point for us. In full view of the court and the jury, they showed him pictures of Hispanic teenagers, asking him to determine, based on their faces, whether they were above or below the legal age to work. Even given time to carefully study an unmoving, head-on picture, without any safety or work equipment obstructing their features, and with the weight of his decision obvious, he got it wrong *more often* than he got it right.

Two of the alleged minors even testified that during the raid, federal immigration agents, sitting across a table and carefully studying their faces, did not believe them when they claimed they were minors.

Not only are documents the only semi-reliable way to tell, the law doesn't even *allow* companies to treat people differently based on a youthful appearance. If their documents pass verification (and they all testified that documents were carefully examined by HR, not just rubber-stamped) job applicants cannot be forced to jump through additional hoops, no matter what they look like.

The hiring department did ask all applicants at the lower end of age-eligibility to bring additional records, but if they brought in a valid birth certificate, for example, that needed to be accepted. As the prosecution witnesses described, that's exactly what happened. They applied and were told that since they were close to the cutoff age, they needed to verify their age with supporting documents. It was only with great effort on their part, and in some cases on their *parents'* part, that they acquired false documentation sufficient to withstand scrutiny.

Their utter inability to establish that I'd knowingly hired, or even continued to employ, workers below the legal age should have been the end of it. As a matter of fact, now that their cards were fully on the table it had become clear to any observer what I'd known from day one—these charges should never have even been brought. That they had been was an outrage, at best motivated by opportunism and at worst by antisemitism and bigotry.

Without this foundation, the case became meaningless. Prosecutors focused on accusations that work at the plant was difficult and dangerous. That is a difficult reality of the industry, but it's certainly not a crime or even improper.

In fact, with great effort and at great cost, Agriprocessors went well above industry standards. We always paid above minimum wage, made extraordinary efforts to ensure a smooth and safe work environment, and offered medical insurance to every single employee, from the line worker up to the company controller. In fact, one of the state's witnesses, a line worker, told the court that he chose to stay at Agriprocessors because the company health insurance covered medical treatment he needed for a non-work-related health issue.

A former city councilman testified that Senator Tom Harkin had told him that he'd visited meatpacking plants across the country and "Agriprocessors is one of the cleanest and most well-run." An industrial refrigeration contractor, part of the team which designed and built the modern refrigerated extension to the building, had spent a lot of time in every area of the plant. In his sworn testimony, he described our plant as highly modern and in the same league as the top five companies in the field, giants with revenues measured in the billions. He specifically described the safety measures and workers' equipment as appropriate and comparable to other plants.

Workplace injuries at Agriprocessors were below the national average, so much so that Agriprocessors received refunds from its insurer!

Despite this, the alleged minors and other witnesses were trotted out to portray the terrible ordeal they endured. Time and again, the prosecutors built up a tear-jerking drama, only for the tears to turn into tears of laughter as soon as the defense had a chance to question the witness.

One alleged minor was asked to describe the superhuman task he was expected to perform. His job was hanging chickens from the chain moving by on overhead tracks as soon as the *shochet* finished his work. Chickens were being processed at a speed of sixty per minute, so you can imagine how demanding and exhausting this must have been for him, and how heartless the management must be to demand this!

The prosecutor had the witness step down and stand in front of the jury to mime this frenzied activity—grabbing the imaginary chicken by the legs, swiveling toward the imaginary line, reaching above his shoulders to hang the chicken, and swiveling back for the next one, all in the space of a single second, with no time to breathe before starting again. The day's testimony ended with this physical demonstration of injustice lingering in the minds of the jury.

The next day, the defense had a chance to cross-examine the worker. Under their questioning he admitted that, although the *line* was moving at sixty chickens per minute, there were actually up to seven teams working simultaneously, each comprised of one *shochet* and three workers. The actual pace of work for each individual worker, then, was an average of *eight* chickens per minute—a far cry from the superhuman sixty per minute he had not just implied but explicitly *acted out* for the jury.

To make it clear to the jury, and to undo the damage of the day before, Mark Weinhardt took a page from the prosecutor's playbook, and had the worker mime his work for the jury at the pace he'd *actually* worked at Agriprocessors. Mark counted out the seconds between chickens and indicated when he should mime the act of hanging the chicken. "One, two, three, four, five, six, seven, eight—chicken! One, two, three..." and so on. The worker followed instructions, clearly embarrassed that his dishonest performance of the day before was seen for what it was. This time around, it was plain to everyone in the room that he spent more time waiting for the next chicken than he spent working.

Witness after witness was prompted by the prosecution to talk about their work with dangerous chemicals and noxious substances—only to admit on cross-examination that the dangerous chemical they were referencing was refrigerant running in pipes behind the walls and the eye and nose irritants were spices mixed into deli products.

The "house of horrors" that the prosecution was trying to describe, and had described to the press for over a year, was revealed to be total fiction. The judge commented at one point that it all sounded like standard operations in a meatpacking plant.

Their strategy of getting a conviction by smearing me as a heartless exploiter, willing to see people hurt just to make a buck, was falling apart.

The defense couldn't always get the witnesses to answer questions. They didn't want to admit that they were misrepresenting things or outright lying.

Many fell back on, "I don't remember," as their lawyers had no doubt advised them. One worker testified that her sleeve got caught on a conveyor belt and she got hurt. When she was confronted on cross-examination with interviews with investigators in which she said she had never gotten hurt on the job, she suddenly couldn't remember that interview. These "amnesia" responses piled up, to the point that the judge himself commented, in discussion with the lawyers, on the "credibility problem" that was building up.

Seeing these workers willingly participate in this sham by testifying and evading corrective questioning was distressing to me, but not surprising. In exchange for their testimony, the prosecutors had offered them and their families citizenship under the U-Visa program. This would entitle them to stay in the US legally for four years, with the option to apply for a proper green card after three. With this visa, they could also get a legal work permit. They could have it all—for the low, low price of telling the authorities what they wanted to hear.

The media had reported that the former workers were thrilled at the offer. "Their spirits lifted [...] their families smiled and hugged," and they set out for the United States to take those smiles and hugs away from me and my family.

They only qualified for these visas if they'd suffered substantial mental or physical abuse, so they did their best to mislead the jury and win their prize at my expense. The prosecutors delivered on their promises. According to *New York Times* reporting, at the time of the federal sentencing, more than forty people and their families had been awarded these visas in exchange for their testimony or promise of testimony against me.

Obviously, bought-and-paid-for testimony violates every precept of justice and fairness and is a discredit to the legal system. A defendant who made similar arrangements with witnesses would be charged with witness bribery under 18 US Code § 201. The only concession to fairness was that they did allow our lawyers to question the witnesses on the stand about these arrangements, thereby at least alerting the jury.

One highlight of the trial, for me, was during one of its last days. The judge had excused the jury early and I got permission to *daven* Minchah in the courtroom together with those in the viewers' gallery. This was the first time I'd been able to *daven* with a *minyan* since the Minchah shortly before the verdict in Sioux Falls, over six months earlier.

Closing Arguments

Once the evidence portion of the trial had come to a close, my lawyers made a motion that the case not even be put to the jury. The evidence had been so weak that, even if it was considered in a light most favorable to the prosecution, it would not support the charges. Under those circumstances, the judge can and should dismiss the case himself. This motion was denied.

They also pointed out that sixteen of the charges had literally not been supported by a shred of evidence. The prosecutors had simply not brought *anything* to directly establish the facts they'd alleged. This was a statement of fact, not up for debate, and the judge dismissed those sixteen charges, leaving "only" sixty-seven to be considered by the jury.

With that out of the way, the trial moved to closing arguments. The prosecution made their argument to the jury first, an attempt to tie together all the testimony and persuade them that they'd proven what they had to, which they hadn't. My lawyers then had a chance to make their closing statement in response, to be followed by another speech from the prosecutors, who were given the last word to respond to things my lawyers had said.

These speeches are not governed by the strict rules of evidence. The prosecutors were free to say all kinds of unsupported and wild things, and they did—including the viciously antisemitic portrayal of my rejection of underage applicants as concern for Jewish children only, while exploiting and endangering non-Jewish children.

It was time to hand off the case to the jury, and we were about to witness as clear an instance of Hashem's direct intervention as a person can see this side of supernatural. My case required a unanimous decision by a six-person jury. During jury selection, an additional two "alternate" jurors had been added as backups in case any of the jurors didn't make it through the trial. As it turned out, we did need one of the substitute jurors. One of the jury members was no longer present because during the first week of the trial, drugs had been found in her car during a traffic stop. That still left us with one extraneous juror.

Now that the trial was over, the unneeded alternate was to be excused so deliberations could begin. The judge launched into a speech thanking the jury for their service and attention, working his way up to dismissing the extra alternate, when, suddenly, one of the jurors started frantically motioning toward his throat, indicating that he couldn't breathe.

A deputy noticed and hastily interrupted the speech, and the judge called a short break to allow the juror to get over his condition. The courtroom was cleared, and we waited a bit. Eventually, a court officer came in with information for the judge. The juror in question appreciated but dismissed the concern for his health, claiming it was just something he ate.

The judge instructed that the jury be returned to the courtroom and picked up where he'd left off, working up to dismissing the extra alternate. He didn't manage to get too far before the juror started choking again, motioning that he couldn't breathe and needed help. The courtroom was cleared once again, and again, after a short wait, the juror dismissed all concern, claiming this was a minor episode brought on by a bad lunch.

The judge was worried. He'd been scheduled to dismiss the alternate juror, which would leave them with the minimum required six-person jury. If this juror was ultimately unable to participate in the deliberations due to his health, only five jurors would remain, and the whole trial would need to be repeated.

One of the lawyers proposed that instead of dismissing him, the alternate could be formally seated as a full juror. This meant the jury's decision would need unanimity among a larger group, but on the other hand, if anyone dropped out, they would still have the minimum required six jurors. Both the prosecution and the defense agreed to the arrangement, and the alternate, a fellow named Quentin Hart, was seated as a full member of the jury.

The significance of that *hashgachah pratis* would become clear when the jury returned.

With that settled, the judge issued his final jury instructions, setting out for the jury the rules for their deliberations and what combination of facts were necessary to return a conviction.

The case had been tried over the past month or so around the question of whether I had knowingly employed minors. There had never been a case to be made for this accusation, and with Hashem's help, we had succeeded in making that clear. Imagine our dismay, then, when the judge decided to add some "nuance" to the jury instructions.

He told them that they should find me guilty if I had known or *should have known* that the employees were under the legal age for employment. If they were convinced that I didn't know, but felt that a reasonable man under those circumstances would have done more to find out, he wanted them to find me guilty!

My lawyers strenuously objected. It wasn't that we couldn't make that case just as conclusively if we had to, but the time for testimony, evidence, and summation had come and gone! Changing the question after the answers had been submitted was illogical, illegal, and immoral, and it undercut the legitimacy of the whole process. The jury should just consider the accusations that were laid out at the outset—whether I actually knew or not.

These objections were overruled, and on Friday, with these updated jury instructions, the seven-person jury went into deliberations.

An interesting thing happened that day. Throughout the trial, I'd been transferred back to Cedar Rapids each day after court as the only passenger in the back of a police car. That day, by *hashgachah pratis*, I was sent back with a van full of inmates en route to a different state jail. The van stopped at the state jail, and we were all unloaded while the state inmates were processed.

While I waited for the transfer protocols to be completed and the next part of the drive to Cedar Rapids to begin, I started thinking about where I was and why. The footsteps of man are prepared by Hashem. The Ba'al Shem Tov explains that we are always brought exactly where we're needed in order to do a mitzvah and elevate that place by including it in our service of Hashem.

Finding myself in an unexpected location and with that teaching in mind, I asked for a drink of water and made a *brachah* with *kavanah*, elevating the Iowa State Jail. I *davened* that this mitzvah accomplish all I needed to accomplish there, and that I never return to this jail.

Monday morning, I was returned to Waterloo. The jury was still in deliberation and I was not needed in the courtroom, but the judge wanted me close by, in case there were any questions that needed to be decided in my presence. For the day, I was kept in a cell in the Black Hawk County Jail right across the street.

The Verdict

The jury had no questions. The day wasn't even halfway over before the guard came into the cell and informed me that the jury had a verdict. I was led from the cell to the courtroom. My family was already assembled, and I smiled encouragingly in their direction as I took my seat between my lawyers.

The verdict had come back sooner than anyone had expected, and everyone was caught a little unprepared. Mark was jotting down numbers on his legal pad from one to sixty-seven, one for each of the counts. He was planning on writing the verdicts next to each charge as they were announced.

"With G-d's help you won't need sixty-seven numbers," I whispered to him, "just one—not guilty on all counts."

"You seem confident," he said with a smile.

I smiled back. "With G-d's help, it will be good news."

The jury was brought in and the foreman handed over a thick stack of papers, each containing the verdict on one of the counts. The foreman was none other than Quentin Hart, the alternate who had, by *hashgachah pratis*, been added to the jury at the last minute! The jury had chosen him to be their foreman and he had led the deliberations.

The judge verified that the papers had all been filled out correctly.

"Mr. Rubashkin, would you stand, please? I think I can make this brief. In the Iowa District Court, State of Iowa, Allamakee County, State of Iowa vs. Sholom M. Rubashkin, the jury verdict forms have each been signed by the foreperson. Each verdict has indicated 'not guilty.' You may be seated."

My heart was filled with gratitude to Hashem for this victory, happy for my family to get some openly good news, and overcome with relief that the *chillul Hashem* that these charges represented finally had a resounding, unqualified response, discrediting them for all time.

CREDIT: WATERLOO–CEDAR FALLS COURIER, MATTHEW PUTNEY

A moment of celebration as the house of cards on which they had built a terrible *chillul Hashem* officially collapsed.

Once the verdict had been officially entered into the record and the jury had left the room, the judge had something to say. His message? The costly prosecution "really was worth every penny" and sent an important message to others that if they have minors in occupations of this nature, something would be done about it.

I couldn't believe my ears. I, my family, and my community had been publicly maligned and put through a terrible ordeal on grounds that were so thoroughly debunked during the trial. The prosecution's thorough and well-deserved legal defeat, the result of leveling totally baseless accusations, revealed their spectacular moral failure. They deserved a harsh reprimand! Not only was *that* not forthcoming—the judge didn't even have the decency to wholeheartedly endorse the justness of the outcome, instead lauding the prosecution for bringing their baseless case and comforting them over their loss.

The prosecutor walked over to me and tried to shake my hand, but I refused. This wasn't a gentlemanly sporting match I'd just won through the protection of Hashem—it was a fight to defend my life and the reputations of myself, my family, and all Jews from an unscrupulous opponent who had fought dirty to triumph in a trumped-up case.

His civilized graciousness in defeat was so hollow that it only held up while we were in the same room. As soon as he got back to his office, he issued a statement repeating the allegations and downplaying the unequivocal verdict as a technicality—"the jury found reasonable doubt."

The media statements of the jury foreman, by contrast, were of an entirely different nature. To his eternal credit, despite being an ambitious public figure,[2] Mr. Hart did not try to grandstand like the judge or prosecutors by justifying baseless prosecution as a deterrent or, worse, insinuating that I had, on technicalities, evaded charges that had some merit.

In a very straightforward way and with crystal clarity he focused (and presumably had focused the jury) on the true heart of the case: there had been no credible evidence that I was aware that any workers were underage, applicants had repeatedly been rejected for being underage, in instances where minors had been discovered they'd immediately been fired, and on top of all of that, the alleged minors had all admitted to lying to law enforcement and were not trustworthy. The true heart of this case was that the case *had* no heart, much like those who had brought it.

Mark Weinhardt, reflecting on the trial, said that at times you "could feel the presence of G-d in the courtroom" and one of his examples was the way Hashem had put Quentin Hart on the jury—the inexplicable, repeated spells of choking by a juror who showed no health issues before those moments.

This victory should have had real repercussions. By declining to bring charges on the many incendiary allegations they'd been making in the press, like human trafficking or extortion, the prosecutors essentially announced

---

2. He was a city councilman at the time and he went on to run for and win the position of mayor of Waterloo, a position he still holds today, six years after his election in 2015.

that these charges had no basis or had nothing to do with me. Now that the trial had ended with a unanimous acquittal, even the charges that they *did* bring were shown to be groundless. The trial had been reported on in detail, and the whole world saw that the prosecutors had used everything they had and failed to support their terrible accusations.

Additionally, the accusation that I had knowingly hired minors was based on the same "evidence" and testimony as the accusation that I had knowingly hired undocumented immigrants. The jury's rejections of these charges were therefore essentially exoneration on those charges as well. The fundamental weakness on display in this case was at least a partial explanation for why the federal prosecutors had grasped at the thinnest excuse to avoid bringing those charges to trial.

Predictably and shamefully, those who had trumpeted these charges to promote themselves or their causes ignored these developments. They continued pushing these claims in the media and to their own audiences as if nothing had changed. The state prosecutors, as mentioned, went back to making these allegations and others the moment they were out of court and no longer had to back up their statements with tested evidence. The disproven charges were also still incorporated into the federal court officer's PSIR report recommending a life sentence in the upcoming sentencing. The verdict made no difference to them at all.

To my family and supporters and all people dedicated to justice, by contrast, the success in the state case was invigorating. This new energy was apparent in the rally that took place a few days later in Monsey. It was attended in person by three thousand *Yidden*—of all ages and from every community— and twelve thousand more participated via live teleconference arranged by the Chazak and Kol Mevaser phone lines.

Rav Weissmandl shared words of Torah and *chizuk*, followed by other rabbis and *askanim*. Mark Weinhardt, the lawyer who had played the central role in

A view of the tremendous crowd at the rally.

the state trial, presented the legal perspective. He recounted some of what had been established in the state case, explained the injustices that had been done in my case more generally, and described the steps which were, with Hashem's help and with the support of those assembled, being taken to remedy them.

My son Meir Simcha thanked them all, on behalf of myself and our entire family, for everything they had done and continued to do. There was palpable gratitude for the recent victory, but also recognition of the difficult road ahead.

My own celebration over the miraculous victory was particularly short. I hugged my lawyers and thanked them for the roles they each played in this miracle, then turned to my ecstatic family and friends in the viewers' gallery. I had only a few short moments to celebrate with them (without any physical contact, of course) before I was whisked out by guards to be returned in shackles to a prison cell in Cedar Rapids.

My son Meir Simcha addresses the crowd

With Hashem's help, I had emerged victorious, but it didn't improve my personal situation at all. Instead of leaving the court to go home with my family to a celebratory *seudas hoda'ah*, I found myself back behind bars. I comforted myself that I'd been fighting for the honor of Hashem, to undo the *chillul Hashem*, and that had been achieved. What would happen to me personally was in Hashem's hands, and I trusted in Him. It would all unfold according to His will, and I would do what He demanded until He sent me my salvation, which would surely not be long.

My son Mendel, then only twelve years old, led the assembled *Yidden* in saying Tehillim for my release.

Reb Pinchos Lipschutz presents Mark Weinhardt with a plaque in appreciation of his hard work in the state case.

CHAPTER THIRTEEN
Federal Sentencing

Sentenced by Memo

THE DATE THAT HAD BEEN SET FOR THE FEDERAL SENTENCING, JUNE 22, 2010, drew near and we fervently hoped and anticipated that the miracles would continue.

Federal rules of criminal procedure require that the defendant be present at sentencing. Adhering only to the letter of the law, but in strong violation of its spirit, the judge issued a fifty-two-page document the day before the sentencing hearing, in which she announced her intended sentence and "justified" it.

Unaware of these developments, I called home that day, as I did every day. My wife told me that the judge had announced the sentence.

I was surprised at the unexpected news. "What is it?" I asked.

"Twenty-seven..."

I did the math quickly. "Twenty-seven months... That's two years and three months." Feeling the need to comfort her, I added, "They'll subtract the time I've already been sitting. It will only be a matter of months, *im yirtzeh Hashem.*"

"No, not twenty-seven months," she corrected me. "Years."

It took a few moments for this to sink in. I asked her a few times to confirm that I'd heard correctly. It struck me how vicious it was for the court to make my wife the one to break this news, instead of doing their dirty work themselves. Perhaps the reason for the early announcement was to allow the shock and outrage at this monstrous sentence to come out early and expend itself a bit before the formal sentencing hearing, so there would be no "scene" in the courtroom when it was announced.

I was eventually given an opportunity to read this sentencing memo for myself. It felt like being transported to an alternate reality. Just reading the words was enough to make your head spin and your stomach turn, as much by its deceitful veneer of thorough, civilized authority as by the sheer ignorance and viciousness.

"When the sentencing reconvenes," she had written, "the court will impose a sentence of 324 months of imprisonment." This, she went on to say, was "sufficient, but not greater than necessary." She tacked on "five years of supervised release" after the twenty-seven years were over for good measure.

The memo addressed in writing the various issues raised in the sentencing filings and at the hearing. On the legal arguments, she accepted the arguments of the prosecution over ours, and in determining the facts, she accepted the testimony of their witnesses over ours. In the instance with the most impact, she accepted the testimony of the key witness who deflected responsibility for the loss away from the government, instead of the counter-testimony of numerous affidavits and two live witnesses.

Early in the document, she noted that the court is entitled to consider uncharged, dismissed, and even *acquitted* charges in sentencing,[1] and that for the purposes of sentencing she was, in fact, considering all "relevant conduct," including hearsay, as long as she finds (pay attention, now) "sufficient indications of reliability to support the conclusion that it is probably accurate." Unreal.

Under the heading of "facts," she included the immigration charges, which had never been directly presented to a federal jury and which rested on the same arguments that the jury in the state case had rejected in totally acquitting me of those charges. Apparently, she didn't consider the finding of the jury "sufficient indication of reliability to support the conclusion that those charges were probably" *inaccurate*.

During the pre-trial phase, my lawyer, Guy Cook, had tried to acquaint me with the harsh realities of the justice system and persuade me to plead guilty. He said at the time that "if the American people knew what was going on in courtrooms, there would be another revolution." He had pointed to this rule, that the judge could sentence based on unproven and even uncharged conduct, as an example. It's a very good example.

Working her way through the charges, she calculated an offense level of

---

1. Manifestly unjust, this is technically legal. Challenges to this immoral practice have been filed with the Supreme Court, but they have yet to agree to take them up.

forty-one, for which the Guidelines prescribe between twenty-seven and thirty-four years of imprisonment, *Hashem yiracbem*.

She declined to sentence below that range based on testimony to my character or in consideration for the special needs of my son Moishie, cruelly pointing to his "loving mother and [...] loving and wonderful community" as the reason such mercy was unnecessary.

Having come to a sentence two years *longer* than even the prosecutors had requested, she graciously declined to deviate *higher* than that range—although she spent a page and half insisting that she was really within her rights and had grounds to do so.

In closing, she threw in a chilling footnote, designed to dissuade us from challenging her calculations and appealing the sentence. I'll paraphrase it in English: "Even if I made a mistake in calculating the advisory Guidelines, I would still impose a twenty-seven-year sentence."

The actual sentencing was to take place in court the next day. They were on the verge of moving beyond *utzu eitzah*, the scheming and planning, to the stage of *dabru davar*, issuing formal decrees. I took comfort in knowing that *lo yakum*, they would not stand, *ki imanu Keil*, for Hashem is with us.

Klal Yisrael was with us as well, filled with righteous anger at the announced sentence, which exceeded even the prosecutors' request in its harshness. By *hashgachah pratis*, the dedicated core group of *askanim*, along with numerous *askanim* of local communities of every stripe, had already planned to gather at rallies scheduled to take place that night in Boro Park and in Los Angeles.

Provoked by this open antisemitism, they turned out in even greater numbers—to turn to Hashem together, to show the world their indignation and their solidarity, and to find out what they could do to help. Close to a thousand *Yidden* gathered in far-away Los Angeles and a staggering ten thousand *Yidden* showed up in Boro Park.

The crowd in New York grew so large that the police closed the streets outside the venue. Folding chairs were brought and arranged so that the masses who couldn't get inside could still participate, watching the speakers on large outdoor screens that the *askanim* rushed to set up. Tens of thousands more participated by phone using the Chazak and Kol Mevaser hotlines, and fourteen thousand more joined via live video broadcast set up by COLLive.

The crowd said Tehillim together and heard from *rabbanim* and *askanim*. My son Getzel spoke on behalf of the family, telling the crowd of the pain we were experiencing but insisting that they not mistake the pain for fear. We were strong in our belief that Hashem's salvation would come and that the ending of our story would be a happy one.

The crowd, moved by the threat to their fellow Jew and uplifted and inspired by the messages of *bitachon*, went above and beyond in their generosity. By the end of the evening, those present and those listening in from afar had donated over $500,000 for efforts to overturn the unjust sentence.

The *askanim* were greatly encouraged by the success of the rally and by calls from other communities which also wanted to participate in this mitzvah. In the following weeks, they organized rallies in two additional communities, Lakewood, New Jersey, and New Square, New York.

An estimated ten thousand *Yidden* came in person to show support and solidarity at two Lakewood events—one for men and one for women, held a week apart—and thousands more listened in remotely. The men's gathering was addressed by the Rosh Yeshivah of Beth Medrash Govoha, Rav Malkiel Kotler; by Reb Pinchos Lipschutz; and by Rav Ephraim Wachsman, who gave over the *psak* of Rav Chaim Kanievsky and Rav Aharon Leib Shteinman that my case was a true case of *pidyon shvuyim*.

The city and community of Lakewood actually deserves special acknowledgment for their *ahavas Yisrael* and *tzedakah* throughout the case,

The crowd at the men's rally in Lakewood.

which stood out even in the context of the unbelievable outpouring of support from Klal Yisrael in general.

A large rally also took place in New Square in the main shul, with the blessing and encouragement of the Skverer Rebbe.

The Actual Sentencing

The arguments had been presented and the outcome had even been announced, but protocol is protocol. The next day, I was dragged back to the courthouse one last time for the formal issuing of the sentence. My family and friends were on hand to give me moral support.

There was no jury involved and I was not allowed the dignity of wearing civilian clothes. I was led to the front of the courtroom flanked by two guards, shackled and wearing bright orange prison clothes. I shook my head at the wicked callousness of this policy. It would've been easy for them to give me my civilian clothes for this hearing and spare my family the heartache of seeing me in that state, but it wasn't even considered.

I looked up and noticed that my dear sister Gutel was crying. "*You* don't cry," I told her. "*They* should cry for what they're doing to us."

The judge read out the sentence and my lawyer made the obligatory request for bail pending appeal, knowing full well that the judge wouldn't give it a moment's thought. The request was promptly denied. He entered a formal request that I be transferred to New York, now that the proceedings that required my presence in Iowa were at an end. The judge took it under advisement and the hearing was over.

To my surprise, as soon as I was brought back to the place called jail, I was placed on suicide watch. For the twenty-four hours after an inmate is sentenced to a severe sentence, they're considered a suicide risk and are held under suicide watch. When this was explained to me, I laughed at the mindless absurdity of it.

The judge had announced her intent to sentence me to twenty-seven years in prison just about twenty-four hours earlier. If I was going to lose my mind over the sentence, I would have done it then, but no one had rushed to the cell where I was held out of concern for my wellbeing. Not that they had anything to worry about—I had remained calm in my conviction that Hashem is the only judge and I had nothing to fear.

Now, just because the judge had formally issued the sentence, they sprang into action! I was dressed in the scratchy, shapeless, sleeveless "turtle suit" smock and placed in isolation under constant supervision—all for my own protection, you understand.

Inmates used to comment, only half joking, that if someone wasn't thinking of suicide before, putting him under this protocol was enough to make him consider it.

Back at the courthouse, my family and my lawyers held a press conference outside the building to announce that the conviction and the sentence would be appealed. My wife also addressed the reporters, speaking emotionally about the way in which I'd been singled out and the suffering it had brought upon my family, specifically for my son Moishie, and vowing to continue to fight for my freedom.

The prosecutors held their own press conference in which they tried to justify the sentence that had horrified legal experts and the general public. These justifications notwithstanding, the imposition of the sentence was met by a new wave of outrage and concern from many.

Congressional Letters

Over the next few months and years, more than sixty Senators, Congressmen, and Congresswomen wrote to United States Attorney General Eric Holder regarding the extreme length of the sentence and allegations of prosecutorial and judicial misconduct on the part of the prosecutors and the judge.[2] My daughter Roza Hindy and her husband Yaakov led this effort and worked tirelessly to gather these unprecedented bipartisan individual letters by members of Congress. *Askanim*, community leaders, and dozens of Chabad *shluchim* throughout the country assisted in this effort by making meetings with members of Congress in their districts or with whom they had connections, to urge them to write letters.

Rabbi Moshe Kotlarsky, Vice Chairman of Merkos L'Inyonei Chinuch, encouraged *shluchim* to do whatever they could to help advocate for my case. Indeed, the majority of these letters came about from the efforts of the *shluchim*. I will be forever grateful to the many *shluchim* and *askanim*—too many to list here—who gave it their all to make these meetings and urge their Representatives to fulfill their oversight duty and try to correct this injustice.

Rabbi Moshe Vizel, a dedicated *askan* from Kiryas Yoel whom I had never previously met, selflessly traveled to Washington, DC, numerous times, and met with dozens of offices, garnering *six* letters from members of Congress! Others I must mention who made exceptional efforts on my behalf in order to get these Congressional letters include Simcha Eichenstein, Rabbi Menachem Genack, Rabbi Chaim Dovid Zwiebel, Rabbi Pesach Lerner, Rabbi Levi Shemtov, Willie Rapfogel, Howard Friedman, Gary Torgow, Avrohom Wolfson *a"h*, Moshe Wolfson, Abe Biederman, Rabbi Moshe Dovid

---

2. The many politicians who spoke up at critical points in my case deserve individual recognition but space constraints make that impossible. A full list of names can be found at Rubashkinbook. com.

Niederman, Rabbi Avrohom Korf, Chaskel Bennett, Doniel Ginsberg, Eli Slavin, Rabbi Marvin Heir, and so many more. The Klal Yisrael Va'ad led by Rabbi Pinchos Lipschutz and Reb Yoili Schwartz were a tremendous support as well for this particular effort.

The signatories of these Congressional letters represented remarkably diverse political viewpoints, but they all demanded the same thing: an investigation and explanation of this excessive sentence and how it came to be imposed. They were deeply troubled by the allegations of *ex-parte* communications between the judge and the prosecutors. They were also troubled that the Guidelines had been used to justify and pursue such a long sentence against the advice of past Justice Department officials, Attorneys General, and even framers of the Guidelines themselves. Roza Hindy and Yaakov were also able to get three members of the House Judiciary Committee to bring up my case at a Congressional hearing with Attorney General Holder.

The first phase of the process had ended.

I hadn't received my day in court—I'd been processed through a system. I'd been brought into a courtroom to make my case, but I was stymied and muzzled and never allowed to present the truth as I knew it. This wasn't the end, *chas v'shalom*, but it was the end of the beginning. My family would continue to fight to overturn this outcome with the help of the lawyers and the *askanim* and with the continued support of Klal Yisrael. Until those efforts bore fruit, I would continue the mission from Hashem that required me to be in Cedar Rapids and wherever He chose to send me next.

CHAPTER FOURTEEN
Transferred East

Leaving Iowa Forever

ONTHS WENT BY. ONE MORNING, OUT OF THE BLUE, A GUARD CAME
into the cell and coldly informed me to hurry up, pack, and be ready to
go. He felt no need to say more—after all, I was only an inmate, not entitled
to know what was happening to me. I hurried to pack my *tallis*, *tefillin*, the few
sefarim I had, and my legal notes and papers. I fit it all into the few plastic bags
they provided, and I was taken down to the waiting prison van.

One of the guards, seeing the bags I was carrying, informed me that I wasn't
actually allowed to take anything with me. I was supposed to leave everything
behind and my family would come and take it. With no choice, I put the
sefarim and legal papers down where he indicated, although this exposed my
legally protected confidential notes, but I wasn't letting go of my *tallis* and
tefillin.

"This is a religious item which I must have with me at all times," I told him,
showing him the *tallis* bag. I had seen inmates traveling with small medical
devices before and tried to draw a parallel. "You wouldn't take an insulin shot
from a diabetic, in case he needs it en route. This is like that. A *tallis* and *tefillin*
are critical to the life of a Jew."

Nodding his head in assent, the guard reached out for the bag. "Okay. It
can't travel with you, though. Give it here and I'll put it in the back of the van."
Relieved that this was so quickly and painlessly resolved, I gave him the bag
and got into the van.

The naive trust we place in the system is layered. Clearly, I had another layer
to work through. During one of the stops, I caught a glimpse of the back of
the van and saw, to my horror, that my *tallis* bag was not there. When I asked

the guard where he'd put it, he brazenly and matter-of-factly informed me that he'd lied in order to get his hands on my *tallis* and *tefillin* without a fuss. As soon as my back was turned, he had put my *tallis* and *tefillin* on the pile of other stuff that I'd so obediently left behind. There was nothing I could do with this information until we reached a phone, which left me in a state of concern and uncertainty.

I sat with hands cuffed and chained to my waist and my feet shackled for many painful hours. The van drove from jail to jail all day, picking up federal prisoners awaiting transfer. The van filled up as the hours wore on, and the poor prisoners passed the time sharing their personal stories. One man was a rap singer being returned to prison for violating his parole while shooting a music video. Another man spoke bitterly of his service to the country in Vietnam. A woman talked about her small children from whom she was to be separated for five long years.

By late afternoon, the van pulled up to an airport, where another bus full of prisoners was already waiting.

We all had "tickets" on an exclusive airline run by the BOP. Nicknamed ConAir, this "airline" transports 260,000 "passengers" a year—either bringing them into the federal prison system from the over five thousand state prisons and local jails or transferring them from one to another of the 110 federal prisons that dot the country.

We were prodded off the bus and lined up nearby to wait for the plane, which had not yet arrived. I recognized the airport as Rochester International Airport. I'd used it many times in my travels to and from our little *shtetl*. We were off to the side of the main terminal and we waited for about half an hour, watching as the commercial flights came and went. Eventually, a large white plane with no markings landed and taxied over to where we were standing. Boarding stairs were rolled up to the plane and eight or ten Federal Marshals came out and stood at the foot of the steps.

Their attire struck me as bizarre and incongruous. They were tasked with the grim job of tearing people from their loved ones and placing them in cages, at the direction of the courts and on the authority of the laws of the United States. You would expect their clothing to reflect the seriousness of their task and their official capacity. Yet, here they were, transferring human beings into gehinnom wearing light blue polo shirts and sport pants, as if they were there for a pleasant round of golf.

Uniforms serve an important purpose. Putting one human in a position of power over another can easily get to his head. He might begin to see himself as the master of his charge, entitled to mete out pain and misery on a whim. The uniform is a constant reminder that they're only empowered to administer the pain of punishment or incarceration as agents of the state, and only as dictated by the state—no more than that.

Later, in Otisville, I made the same disturbing observation. Most of the prison staff wore regular street clothes as they did their work, despite the nature of that work. Some wore dressy clothes like suits and ties, and a few even wore nice gold watches or jewelry as they exercised control over every aspect of the lives of people to whom these things were denied. They would openly discuss the various facets of their lives and personal relationships in front of the inmates, with no sensitivity or consideration to the inmates, who'd been forcibly torn from their own lives and personal relationships.

This may have made them feel better about their work, pretending as if it was just another day job, but it came at the expense of the inmates' added pain, seeing their punishment administered by casual civilians instead of solemn representatives of the state.

This reminded me of my *yetzer hara*, who also presents himself in civilian clothes, golf clothes, or dressy suits. He disguises his every action in a false and misleading facade to hide the fact that he is, in fact, my jailer.

One marshal noticed me standing there and walked over. He took out a cigarette, and started casually telling me about his last visit to Israel, pausing every few sentences to take a light drag. He chatted absent-mindedly, as I stood there in pain with both my hands and feet cuffed. For inmates who were smokers, suddenly denied this addiction, it would have been torture to have someone smoke in their face like that, something that either didn't occur to him or didn't bother him as he stood there enjoying his cigarette.

The marshals finished filling out the paperwork required to take custody of their "merchandise," and began moving prisoners to the plane. When they saw my yarmulke and *tzitzis* they insisted that I remove them, but to my grateful surprise, one of the guards from Cedar Rapids stepped in. She explained to the marshal in charge that I needed them and I couldn't walk anywhere without them, and, *baruch Hashem*, they allowed me to board the plane with my yarmulke and *tzitzis*.

The plane itself was a large flying prison. All of the "passengers" had their hands cuffed and chained to their waist and their feet shackled at all times. The windows were all shuttered—this was an involuntary transport, not a joyride.

As they made their final review before takeoff, I got the attention of one of the marshals. The metal handcuffs were digging into my wrists and growing increasingly painful. I politely showed him that the cuffs were too tight and asked him to loosen them just enough to ease the pain. He took my hands, examined the cuffs, and smirked. "I could make them tighter for you, if you'd like…" Of course, I didn't respond, but his sadism shook me.

The plane taxied to the runway and took off. I had left Iowa for the last time, G-d willing never to return.

After a two-hour flight, the plane touched down and taxied toward a large building with a single jetway extending outwards. I thought it was a small regional airport, but some of the other "passengers" had been there before and knew better. I overheard one of them telling his seatmate that this was actually the jail itself, a transit hub for the federal prison system. The jetway led right into the prison.

We had arrived at the Federal Transit Center in Oklahoma City—the BOP's transfer hub and holding facility, where inmates await long-term assignment. I *davened* that my stay there would be short. It was already Menachem-Av and I wanted to be closer to my family, if not home for good, before Rosh Hashanah and the festive month of Tishrei.

We were taken off the plane and walked down a long hallway which could have passed for an airport terminal. It was a surreal experience. Air travel embodies the spirit of freedom—escaping the grip of gravity and surpassing the limitations of terrain that slows or stops other forms of travel. Yet here I was, walking off this technological symbol of freedom through an airport designed to facilitate the imprisonment of human beings, enabling the authorities to strip them of their freedom, efficiently and effectively, at a scale unmatched around the globe and throughout human history.

The planeload of prisoners was herded into some semblance of a line to be processed. I was surrounded by people and conversations so far from anything I recognized as reality that it felt like a bad dream. At the end of the line was the first step of the intake process—the removal of the highly restrictive hand and foot shackles used for travel. The personnel were quite practiced and removed the hardware with a quick series of twists and clicks, almost without looking. They were so desensitized to their job that they were making small talk while facilitating my entry to gehinnom, chatting with me about the Land of Israel and whatever else they associated with religious Jews.

There was an added element of confusion and chaos because not all the prisoners were to be housed on-site. The "hotel" had been overbooked and some of the prisoners were to be taken by bus to a different facility nearby, while the rest would stay in this facility until their transfer to wherever they would be serving their sentences.

Next in the intake process, we were to be issued Oklahoma prison clothes. The various point-of-origin prisons had returned the inmates' civilian clothes so as not to lose their own inventory of prison clothes. A guard announced that those who wanted to relinquish their clothes and donate them to some organization would be processed first, and those who wanted their clothes sent home would be processed afterwards.

The majority of the prisoners opted to give away their clothes, possibly because they never expected to wear civilian clothes again. Others were reluctant to relinquish anything beyond what was already being taken from them. I opted to wait and send my clothes home. We changed into the prison clothes and our clothes were taken and boxed to be shipped. *Baruch Hashem*, no issue was made of my yarmulke and *tzitzis*.

We were then taken to a large holding cell and given forms to complete. Painful experience had taught me that it was important to make my religious needs crystal clear from the first possible moment. I spent time writing my answers, elaborating and clarifying as much as possible. The form was fairly thorough and also a little skeptical, asking not just if I keep kosher but, if so, why I keep kosher and similar questions about other aspects of religion.

While we were filling out the forms, a non-Jewish chaplain came in and asked if anyone had any questions. I told him that I'd been informed that my *tallis* and *tefillin* would be brought with me from Cedar Rapids. I would need them in the morning, and would appreciate if he could check up on that and facilitate it to the best of his ability.

He told me that I had been *mis*informed (lied to, in English) and my *tallis* and *tefillin* were not there. There was a *tallis* and *tefillin* in the chapel that I could use, and he would be happy to bring them to me in the morning, but he warned me that they were the property of the chapel, available to anybody, and they might not be in the best condition. I asked him to bring them anyway. They were my only option at this point, and I just hoped that they were kosher.

As part of the intake process, we were each assigned a federal inmate number. Mine was 10755-029. These numbers were used in place of names for formal identification within the prison system. My friends and family also had to use this number to identify me in visiting forms and mail, and they can all recite the number by heart even today, years after my miraculous release.

The prison authorities like to say that in the place called prison everyone is equal, often pointing to this number as an example of equality. This is, of course, complete nonsense. These numbers were not replacing titles or ranks which might indicate stature—they were replacing personal names, which have nothing to do with inequality. Personal names are simply a way to represent our distinct personal identity and they were replaced with numbers to better represent our new status, as inventory. This was just one of a set of intentional policies designed to degrade and belittle inmates for easier control.

Years later, during a Seder in Otisville, a guard entered to count those present as part of the frequent "count" procedure. Each inmate was required to recite their inmate number. There was a Yid there who was originally from Russia, and when it was his turn to recite his number he said, "My memory is terrible, I can't remember my number—only my name," and he announced his name for the count. Once the guard left, he told me that he found it too painful to identify himself as a number and this was how he ensured that he didn't have to. I noted that this was only accepted because they believed he couldn't remember his number. If he slipped and used his number, even once, he would no longer be able to use this excuse. This turned the conversation to the importance of being consistent in all our positive resolutions and we had a meaningful and productive *farbrengen* on the topic.

The intake in Oklahoma was a long and exhausting process, and it was after midnight by the time it was completed. When it was all done, we were divided into small groups and each assigned to a specific floor and unit of the multistory barracks. When I reached the cell in the unit to which I'd been assigned, I found that there was already a prisoner sleeping on the lower sleeping-shelf. I climbed to the top shelf as quickly and quietly as I could so as not to disturb him, and got some much-needed sleep. *Baruch Hashem*, this fellow was transferred out the very next night and I was able to move to the lower shelf, which made *negel vasser* a lot easier.

The morning came quickly and, despite the late night, I awoke early. I waited impatiently for the chaplain to bring the *tallis* and *tefillin* as he'd promised, but when he finally arrived, I was severely disappointed by what he brought.

The *tallis* was little more than a white scarf with frayed *tzitzis* strings and the *tefillin's* knots were jumbled and unrecognizable. The appearance of the *tefillin*, compounded by their dilapidated condition, gave me no reason to believe they were even remotely kosher.

I just stood there looking at these unusable *tefillin*, more than seven hundred miles from home and family and my own precious *tefillin*, contemplating the possibility of going the first day of my life without *tallis* and *tefillin*. It was too much for me to bear, and I broke down crying.

Suddenly, I heard a guard call my name. I put down the alleged *tallis* and *tefillin*, caught my breath, and wiped my face before going out of the cell and down the steps to see what the guard wanted. Without a word, he led me to a room on the bottom floor of the unit and motioned for me to enter. I walked in, and to my shock and surprise, I saw a Lubavitcher Yid standing there with a big smile, his hand resting lightly on a *tallis* bag lying on the table next to him.

We greeted each other with a warm hug and a hearty, "*Shalom aleichem!*" His name was Rabbi Goldman and he was the *shliach* in Oklahoma. When my family came to Cedar Rapids to collect my belongings, they were surprised to find my *tallis* and *tefillin*. They immediately realized that I would need help and phoned Aleph. Aleph reached out to the chaplain at Oklahoma and arranged that Rabbi Goldman be permitted to bring these precious mitzvos to me.

The deceitful act of cruelty by the prison guard was actually guided by *hashgachah pratis* to help me in an unexpected way. Rabbis are generally not allowed to visit prisoners in the Oklahoma Transfer Center, because they have a (non-Jewish) chaplain on staff. It was only because I'd been deprived of my *tefillin* that the rabbi was allowed to enter. Because of these events, I was not only able to *daven* with a kosher *tallis* and *tefillin*, I was also given the opportunity to spend time with a fellow Yid and take the strength and encouragement I sorely needed.

Noting Hashem's orchestration of events that I'd initially thought were a setback was an even greater encouragement in the face of my difficult *nisayon*. It reminded me that even what seemed to be painful and unnecessary acts of evil were from Hashem and for my good. It may take some time for things to play out, but Hashem was reminding me not to misjudge the painful moments. He had not abandoned me, *chas v'shalom*. He truly loves me, and allows me and wants me to do His holy mitzvos with which I connect with Him.

Rabbi Goldman continued coming every weekday until, with Aleph's help expediting things, my own *tallis* and *tefillin* were delivered, five days later.

When they arrived, I was called out of the unit to receive them. Before giving me the *tefillin* bag, the head chaplain opened the bag and removed a few *sefarim* that had been in there. Permission had been granted for the *tallis* and the *tefillin*, but anything else in the bag needed to be sent back. Among the *sefarim* that I watched him remove was my precious copy of the *Chovos Halevavos*, the one that had been miraculously spared in the shakedown back in Cedar Rapids. I asked him if I could possibly keep just that one book. He hesitated, considering my request, as I whispered a silent *tefillah* to Hashem. "Okay," he decided at last, "you can keep this one."

He placed it back in the *tallis* bag and handed the bag to me, dismissing me back to the cell. Once again, I had seen clear Divine intervention giving me the *sefer* I needed in order to keep a clear head while I went through this ordeal. Hashem was with me and reminding me that I only needed to be strong in my *emunah* and *bitachon* in Him and I would surely be saved from this *tzarah* with the *gimmel* of *geulah prati*.

Aside from the moral support I took from the *sefer* and the way in which I got it, the *sefer* was also precious because there were no other *sefarim* in Oklahoma with the exception of a siddur and an Artscroll Stone Edition Chumash that was kept in the chapel.

Food was a challenge in Oklahoma, since what they considered kosher was not kosher enough for a *frum* Yid to eat. When I asked the chaplain to arrange food with a proper kosher certification, he told me that the short amount of time I could expect to be there awaiting transfer was not enough time to make those arrangements. He did use money from the chaplain's fund to buy me matzah which I could eat, and I was grateful for that. For the few weeks that I was there, my diet consisted of that matzah and packets of margarine and a few other small items from the kosher meals which did have an acceptable *hechsher*.

Having arranged for the bare essentials as well as could be done under the conditions, I tried to settle into a routine while I awaited transfer.

Waiting in Oklahoma Transit Center

The *yetzer hara* often suggests that a person will be better liked if he compromises on his values and standards in order to fit in and get along.

Experience showed me, time and again, that the opposite is true. My commitment to my beliefs earned me the respect of the staff and the prisoners even over the short time that I was in Oklahoma.

As a transfer hub, Oklahoma was not as carefully segregated a prison population as the longer-term prisons, where the administration tries to separate people that might clash. This led to some unexpected and occasionally dangerous encounters.

I was sitting at a table on the first level one day, learning the *Sha'ar Hayichud* in *Chovos Halevavos*, when a large African American Muslim fellow walked over and started asking about Jews and the fictional country of Palestine. This was a very delicate situation. Failing to respond in some way would be seen as weakness, which is very dangerous in a place called prison, but responding the wrong way could trigger a confrontation then and there, with equally undesirable results.

I looked him in the eye and asked him if he'd ever read his "Book." He had. "Tell me," I asked him, "when G-d took the Jews out of Egypt, where did He take them?" He was quiet for a moment, trying to find an answer that wasn't a surrender.

"To the desert," he decided.

I pressed the issue. "Where did G-d take them then? Where were they going?"

"To Mount Sinai," he attempted.

"Yes, but en route to where?" I insisted.

He saw that I wasn't going to let him off the hook and stopped avoiding the question. "The Land of Israel," he admitted.

"Well, if G-d gave that land to the Jews, why are you trying to take it away from them?" I demanded. He abruptly tired of the conversation and just walked off.

The Friday after I arrived, I was sitting in the cell when there was suddenly a loud knock on the door and the chaplain walked in. He had some papers for me to sign—the federal visitation paperwork that would add my wife to the list of people cleared to visit.

As I looked over and signed the paper, the chaplain commented, "Boy, there must be some special people working for you. I've never seen these forms come through so quickly. It typically takes a few weeks." I silently thanked Hashem for His kindness, and for sending His messengers, the dedicated volunteers of the Aleph Institute.

The paperwork complete, my wife prepared to travel from New York, where she had moved with the children in anticipation of my transfer east. It was a long trip to Oklahoma and there was also no guarantee that I would even be there when she arrived, because transfers are done without notice, as a matter of security. Nonetheless, that Sunday she came to visit.

It was the first time since the night of the conviction, nine months earlier, that we were able to sit and talk face to face, not separated by a glass or video screen. I felt my burden ease and her words of encouragement full of *bitachon* in Hashem and her calm demeanor strengthened me. She's a true *eishes chayil*, her quiet resolve under fire fueled by her strong *emunah* and *bitachon*. I will be eternally grateful to *Hashem Yisbarach* for His everlasting kindness in giving me the gift of that visit.

I wanted to spare her the strain of another trip and assured her that she didn't have to come all the way to Oklahoma again. Seeing the strength and comfort I took from the visit, however, my wife nonetheless made the effort to visit once more while I was still there.

About three weeks after my arrival, sometime around one o'clock in the morning, loud banging on the cell door woke me up with a start. The guard unlocked the cell door, yelling that I only had a few minutes to be down in the main area. Obviously, I was being transferred out, which came as a relief. What I really wanted was a full transfer home to my family, but this was one step closer to that and I was eager to leave Oklahoma.

I was not allowed to take anything with me, with the exception of my *tallis* and *tefillin*. *Baruch Hashem*, the chaplain had succeeded in having them classified as items that must accompany the prisoner, like an inhaler or other critical medical devices.

I was led down to a holding cell together with other inmates who were being transferred to New York. We were forced to change clothes in view of the guards to ensure that we were leaving with nothing in our pockets or on our person.

The kind chaplain had given me a letter authorizing my yarmulke and *tzitzis* in transit. It met with some initial resistance by the guards but *baruch Hashem*, with effort, they ultimately agreed to respect the permission slip and I managed to keep my yarmulke and *tzitzis*.

When everyone had finished dressing, we were herded into another holding cell, where we waited for a few hours. There wasn't adequate seating, and those who hadn't managed to grab a seat either stood or sat on the floor. The room quickly filled with the hubbub of simultaneous conversation.

One prisoner sitting near me, a tattoo-covered American Indian, was loudly and dramatically recounting to his captive audience the story of how he'd been arrested. On the other side was a group of guys exchanging information and advice for drug-related adventures they hoped to have when they got out.

They'd woken us up in the middle of the night so we could hurry up and wait, stuffed into a too-small room. It took hours, but finally we were told that the plane was ready. We were lined up, shackled hand and foot, and led onto the plane. Some of the prisoners were restrained more than the rest, with their hands locked in rigid cuffs that didn't allow even the minimal motion that the chained cuffs did, which looked very painful. Word among the prisoners was that this concept was actually the idea of an inmate hoping to curry favor with the authorities.

The plane taxied to the runway and took off, but not long after reaching high altitude, the pilot announced that there were mechanical issues with the plane and we would be returning to the runway. This kind of announcement triggers anxiety even on commercial flights and doubly so on this flying prison. An emergency landing while shackled and helpless was a horrible scenario to contemplate.

This wasn't a baseless fear. During Hurricane Katrina, only a few years earlier, many prisoners had been abandoned for days to face rising floodwaters in locked cells without food or water while prison staff fled to safety.

Baruch Hashem, we landed without incident and were returned to the cells in Oklahoma. The whole boarding process repeated itself the next week. This time, I couldn't convince the guard to respect the chaplain's authorization and allow my *tzitzis*, though a higher-ranking officer directing movement "happened" to pass by, and signed off on the request and I again boarded a "ConAir" plane with my yarmulke and *tzitzis* safely on my person.

This time there were no flight disruptions and, after one stopover to transfer some prisoners, we reached New York, landing at a small regional airport upstate.

Arriving in New York

We disembarked, and I was again struck by the sight of the prison plane so close to a commercial airport terminal. Federal Marshals wearing casual attire and wielding military weapons stood along the length of the plane, monitoring the hundreds of inmates shackled hand and foot. Not too far away, regular people were scurrying around the airport, stopping for a bite to eat before going about their business, oblivious to the surreal scene taking place nearby.

There were two groups of inmates—those waiting to board lined up on one side, and those disembarking slowly shuffled along the other side toward buses that would cart them off.

We were marched from the plane to the buses and I was instructed to get on a specific bus. It was empty, save one other prisoner half asleep on a bench near the front.

A guard got on the bus and tossed some packaged food my way, but the *hechsher* was not a reliable one and I offered it instead to the other prisoner. He was astonished that I would just give him food without bartering for something in return, which simply doesn't happen in a place called prison, and he took it gratefully. A few more prisoners from ConAir boarded the bus, as did an armed guard who sat in a gated-off section in the back, and the bus pulled out of the airport. The constant presence of men with guns drove home that I was now lumped into a category with very dangerous people.

We were in a tranquil mountain region of upstate New York. The drive took us through sleepy towns and over mountain creeks and rivers. Some of the prisoners tried to make verbal contact with people in the cars or on the streets, desperate for some non-prison-related human contact, but I kept to myself.

At the outskirts of the small town of Otisville, New York, the bus turned up a narrow, twisting road labeled "Two Mile Drive." It snaked its way up a small mountain and ended at the entrance to a forty-acre prison compound surrounded by two rows of barbed-wire fence, the American flag proudly waving up front. The sign out front read "FCI Otisville." We drove past the main entrance and pulled into the compound through a side entrance. The driver opened the door and we got out of the bus.

The compound was deserted and eerily quiet. This was something of a relief to me, because I had been bracing myself to deal with a large or rowdy population. The calm and quiet gave me the impression that perhaps the prison population was smaller or quieter than I'd imagined. I later learned that they locked down the prison when receiving new arrivals to avoid dangerous situations.

The main entrance to FCI Otisville, through which
staff and visitors entered the compound.

A section of the fence around the Otisville compound.

We were hustled into a building and into a large cage where the intake process began. We were given a packet of forms to complete and papers to read and sign. Working through the paperwork, a shocking passage caught my eye and I stopped for a moment to process it fully. The inmate, explained this orientation package, is the property of the Bureau of Prisons. Not "a person with severely curtailed rights and freedoms." The full significance of incarceration boiled down to a single word: property.

It brings to mind slavery, but it's actually much worse in a way. A slave loses his self-determination and is forced to work for his master, but his role is one of constructive accomplishments. A prisoner is closer to an object, bound and restricted, his status defined precisely by his inability to do anything at all. This is why Yosef Hatzaddik, already a slave, was further (and unjustly) punished with incarceration. Even to a slave, imprisonment is a severe punishment, stripping him of all ability to act and reducing him to being kept in storage.

All the new arrivals completed their paperwork, but the intake process was still at a standstill. Hours passed and I began to worry. We had been roused long before dawn and we'd been traveling all day and I had not yet put on *tallis* and *tefillin*.

I asked one of the guards overseeing the intake process if it would take much longer. He claimed we'd be in the barracks before sunset. That was a relief, but clearly they were in no rush. Sunset was later than 8:00 p.m. that day. I gave thanks to Hashem for setting the date of my transfer during the summer, in a fulfillment of the *pasuk* in *Tehillim*, *Motzi asirim bakosharos*—"He takes out prisoners in fitting months." If I had been transferred in the winter, when the sun sets at four...

When more time passed with no change in our situation, I asked the same guard if I could just put on my *tallis* and *tefillin* and pray right there in the intake holding cell. He was initially willing to allow it, but a passing officer overheard and stepped in to prevent it.

They brought us food. It wasn't kosher, so I gave my portion to the others, which they appreciated.

Finally, the intake process continued. Each inmate had a one-on-one meeting with an intake officer where they would be assessed and placed in the facility. My turn came and I was called into the office. The officer sitting at the desk reading my file was the same woman who'd just prevented me from receiving permission to *daven*. She didn't acknowledge my entrance and just continued thumbing through my PSIR.

As I explained earlier, this is a report prepared by a court official. It summarizes the case to help the judge determine the sentence and it's reused by the BOP to assess the prisoner. Like every other aspect of the process in my case, it had been misused and weaponized and this "summary" was enormous.

In addition to the conviction, it included allegations that had never been made in court, allegations that had been thoroughly disproven in court, and even the state charges on which the jury had unanimously found me not guilty. It went so far as to include activity that happened in Postville, but that even the *prosecution* conceded I had nothing to do with. All of this was combined to paint a poisonous and wildly distorted picture of me.

This was the "report" that the intake officer was now reading in order to make decisions about my life in a place called prison. I sat quietly while she read, shaking her head and muttering to herself. At one point, she looked up and exclaimed, "I've been doing this job for over twenty years and I've never seen such a big report." She held her thumb and forefinger two inches apart, indicating the thickness of the report. "What did you *do?!*"

I should note that Otisville houses actual murderers and other violent and evil people but it was *my* report, in size and in substance, that shocked her. I started to respond, but she abruptly cut me off with a dismissive wave of her hand. "Shut up! I've heard all the excuses…"

The PSIR had exactly the effect intended by its authors, following me through the system and poisoning the minds of prison authorities who would not otherwise have had reason to be prejudiced against me.

She asked me a number of questions from a list, such as if I was part of any gang or if I knew anyone at Otisville, then dismissed me back to the cage.

When we'd all been interviewed, we were issued a sheet, a pillow and blanket, a towel, and a temporary set of khaki-colored prison clothing.

For the duration of their imprisonment, all prisoners are assigned and wear the same khaki-colored clothing. They referred to these bland and dehumanizing clothes as a uniform and insisted that they *remain* uniform, suppressing any expression of individuality. They each had the inmate's name and prison number stamped on the shirt pocket, but any attempts to personalize the clothing further, such as by adding pockets or a touch of color, was strictly forbidden.

Every other uniform that I know of is clothing which is not only distinctive to a specific group, but is also a source of pride. Think of uniforms for the military, police, sports players, even school children. Those khaki rags are the only uniforms that have the effect of shaming and belittling those who wear them. This contrasted very strongly with my uniform as a Yid, my yarmulke and *tzitzis*, and that helped me wear that uniform with added enthusiasm.

The sizes of the temporary set of clothing were limited to small, medium, or large. The pants had an elastic waistband to help somewhat with the overly-generalized sizes. We were also issued bright orange cloth shoes, like you might wear on Tishah B'Av. They called these "bus shoes" because, with the exception of those confined to the SHU, fresh arrivals off the bus were the only ones who wore them.

We were instructed to come to the laundry room the next day for a properly sized shirt and pants, underclothes, a towel, socks, and a pair of boots. The boots were so stiff that it was painful to wear them. The guard who issued them informed me, unprompted—just like a salesman, in fact—that sneakers could be purchased from the commissary. That was also where one could buy hygienic necessities like a toothbrush, toothpaste, and soap, as well as a number of food and grocery items.

The laundry room also measured my waist and issued me a fabric belt, which shocked me. Some wardens I'd encountered in the past had emphatically insisted that my *tefillin* needed to be confiscated because they were dangerous—their straps could be used by inmates to hang themselves. Here I was, in a secure federal prison, holding a belt that was issued to me by the prison authorities, as they are issued to every inmate.

There has never been an instance of someone hanging himself with *tefillin* straps. There *have* been cases of prisoners taking their own life using prison-issued items, like bedsheets or belts. While I was there, a non-Jewish inmate from Croatia, no friend of the Jews, couldn't take prison life and he was found dead in his cell, having used his bedsheet. Yet *Yidden* are often (and, as I'd experienced in Waterloo, sometimes gleefully) denied their *tefillin*, their religious right, using the catch-all defense of "security reasons," while other items which are proven dangerous are freely provided.

Finally, I was taken to a barrack and placed in a cell on the ground floor. The other inmate assigned to that cell was not there at the time and it was quiet. The first thing I did was put on my *tallis* and *tefillin* and *daven*. I was relieved and overjoyed that although there had been delays, I made it before *shkiah*. This was the fourth time I'd been at risk of being prevented from putting on *tallis* and *tefillin* and possibly missing a day, *chas v'shalom*. I was grateful to Hashem that every time, He had ensured that I could do the mitzvah after all. I never missed a day.

As I finished *davening*, I heard someone say *"Shalom!"* from the direction of the door. I looked up and saw a black inmate standing there, a huge smile on his face. He introduced himself by his prison nickname—"Panama," since he was originally from Panama—and said that he'd come to welcome me. He asked me if I'd eaten. When I told him that I hadn't, he said he'd go find something and left the cell. He later told me that his mother was Jewish and he wanted to learn more about his Judaism, which explained why he'd sought me out.

He returned twenty minutes later with the kosher shelf-stable meal which they were giving at the time. I thanked him for his trouble and had a bite to eat. It was already close to 7:00 p.m. and I hadn't eaten all day. Although shelf-stable food seems like a good idea in a place like that, the process which enables the food to last without refrigeration thoroughly destroys the quality of the food, giving it all the same bland, generic taste. It also gave me terrible heartburn.

Two other Jewish inmates came in to say hello. They were surprised to find that I'd arrived with my *tallis* and *tefillin*, something they knew was out of the ordinary and miraculous. This strengthened my gratitude to Hashem for this special *nes*.

They were housed in different barracks and would normally not be allowed to visit another barrack. They had received special permission to come over in order to greet me. There were only a handful of Jewish inmates in Otisville at the time, and the few Jews wanted to greet their brother on his arrival.

Having *davened* and eaten, I had just sat down to catch my breath when the other inmate assigned to that cell returned. This tall, muscular African American guy stopped when he saw me and looked around the cell, taking in the new arrangement. His eyes fell on the small plastic wastebasket in the corner, where I'd discarded a foam cup. He let out a totally unexpected, blood-curdling roar. "Why are you throwing trash in my garbage can?!"

Hearing the shouts, the guards rushed into the cell. To avoid a fight, they had me immediately transferred to one of the dormitory-style cells, where multiple inmates were kept in a single large room. Lying on the bunkbed in this new section, thinking about a grown man violently losing his temper because someone threw garbage in the garbage can, I shook my head at the insanity that prison breeds. Then I realized that he wasn't crazy, he was cleverly *acting* crazy. The whole thing was theater—a simple but effective strategy to avoid sharing his cell.

Welcome to Otisville.

NOTE TO READER:
We now take a break from Book One and begin Book Two, a description of my life in Otisville. The chronological sequence of events that comprises Book One will resume at the conclusion of Book Two, in Chapter Thirty.

BOOK TWO

A Jew in "A Place Called Prison"

CHAPTER FIFTEEN

A Place Called Prison

Life in Otisville

TIME STOPS IN PRISON, ESPECIALLY FOR THOSE WITH LONG SENTENCES. Plucked from a world of growth and progress, the days of an inmate fall into a monotonous pattern. Each day is just like the one before and all the ones to come, as far as the mind can see. Weeks, months, years—all lose their meaning.

Baruch Hashem, my experience was markedly different from that in many ways, but even for me, the chronological nature of my story has to take a little bit of a break. It would be more than seven years before I walked through those gates in the other direction. The mitzvos gave structure to my days, Shabbos gave structure to my weeks, and the Yamim Tovim gave structure to my years, so in telling the story of that time I will structure my story around them.

Before I turn to life in Otisville as a Jew, however, a guided tour of the facility and some related anecdotes will give you an idea of what life in Otisville is like in general.

FCI Otisville is a medium security facility. Medium sounds like it means moderate. It doesn't. Medium security is one small step below the highest security level, and is intended to house prisoners who have a history of violence or dangerous activity, including murder and arms possession, and those who have been sentenced to more than twenty years. At the time of my arrival, about eighty-five percent of the inmates were serving time for violent felonies.[1]

---

1. FCI Otisville, where I was, is not to be confused with the more famous *minimum* security facility, Otisville Federal Prison Camp, which is nearby. That facility houses non-violent inmates with short sentences and is far more lenient in almost every respect.

The Otisville compound sits on a scenic mountaintop in New York's Hudson Valley area, a jarring monument to human ugliness, pain, and punishment set in the picturesque natural beauty of Hashem's world.

It is surrounded by multiple tall fences topped with barbed razor wire, with additional large spools of razor wire on the ground between them for good measure. An armed guard constantly circles the perimeter in a security vehicle. At night, the glare of the headlights briefly but regularly illuminates the barred window of the cell in a mocking reminder of civilian traffic.

Eight barracks, also called units, form a large semi-circle, taking up the northern half of the compound. A web of footpaths links each barrack with the other buildings in the compound. At the time of my arrival, the barracks each housed approximately 120 inmates.

There was no attempt to group people by common characteristics like religion, age, education, or cultural background, although this would ease the lot of the inmates. As a matter of fact, inmates that might otherwise bond and support each other were intentionally divided so that there were no common interests and the population could be kept passive and docile.

Inmates were not allowed to enter a barrack other than the one to which they were assigned without express permission from a guard. The opportunities to meet were further carefully limited by restrictions on group sizes even in the barracks, and a careful mealtime rotation prevented different barracks from meeting in the chow hall.

An aerial view of the FCI Otisville compound. Throughout my time in Otisville I was assigned to the building to the right of the white arch-shaped greenhouse structure.

This was very hard on the *Yidden*. We rely on our unity and *ahavas Yisrael* to survive and thrive, especially in such foreign and hostile environments as a place called prison. Because of these restrictions, there were *Yidden* at Otisville that I only met during religious gatherings in the chapel.

One Friday, in the afternoon, I was in the chapel and saw a new face, a newly transferred Yid named Reuven. Under normal circumstances, seeing a new Jewish face is a cause for celebration—it's even a requirement in order to complete the joy of a *sheva brachos*—but in a place called prison, a place you wouldn't wish on anyone and least of all a brother, it's very much a bittersweet feeling.

I greeted him warmly and we got to talking. The first thing he said was that he normally wears a yarmulke but he hadn't been allowed to travel with it and he was waiting for it to arrive. It became clear from his explanation that all his things had been delayed, including his *tefillin*, which meant that he hadn't been able to put on *tefillin* that day either.

I immediately gave him my cap, so he could cover his head and, since he was not in my barrack, quickly found another Yid in his barrack who could lend him *tefillin*. There was still a little time until *shkiah* and he was able to go put on the *tefillin* immediately, *baruch Hashem*. Although we could have been a real support to each other, I wasn't able to see him on a regular basis without real effort and coordination, despite the physical proximity of the barracks to which we were assigned.

Simply entering the barracks often came at a price. A prison guard, more formally and euphemistically called a correctional officer or CO, stood at the entrance to the barrack and administered pat-downs. This is also a euphemism and it means a public, thorough, and invasive physical search of the inmate's body. The officer would firmly pass his hands over every part of the inmate, under his collar, and beneath his waistband. Sometimes he would even make the inmate remove his shoes and check beneath his socks and in his shoes. Some guards were selective about who they patted down, while others would pat-down every single prisoner entering the barracks.

This is not just a physical discomfort. It's a psychological blow, degrading the inmates by having them stand spread-eagled and submit to intensive, often baseless, searches. It was one of the things that I never got used to.

These pat-downs were not restricted to the entrance of the barracks. They occurred in various places around the facility, most frequently around the chow hall. In an attempt to maintain personal dignity, or at least avoid yet another indignity, many inmates avoided going to the chow hall for a meal whenever possible.

Inside the barracks, prison cells line all but one of the walls on each of the five stories, called "ranges," and overlook an open common area in the center of the barracks. The upper four ranges are reached by stairs and walkways which wrap around the inside of the building. Every few feet along these walkways is a heavy, solid steel door with a small window; the entrance to a small cell.

Throughout my ordeal, I never thought of or referred to the cell to which I was assigned as "my cell." Even though it was where I slept and kept the meager personal belongings I was allowed, it was certainly not mine. They could and did move inmates from one cell to another for the smallest reason and without consulting the inmate. The inmate had no special rights or control over the cell, even while he was there.

A non-Jewish inmate who occasionally came to me for advice once mentioned that he had a problem with his cellmate. The guy was a creep and he wanted him out. He'd demanded that the man leave or be transferred out of his cell, but his request was denied. He wasn't content to leave it alone. He was getting pushy about it and it was antagonizing the staff. "I need this guy out of my cell!" he insisted.

"It's not your cell," I pointed out, "it's *their* cell. They just keep you there." I knew he wanted to be in Otisville rather than a different facility and I advised him to drop it or he might be transferred. He felt it was his cell; he'd been there first, and he was entitled to have a cellmate he could tolerate. He was wrong, and he found out the hard way. Rather than deal with his not-unreasonable request, they just transferred him out.

Inmates were not permitted to congregate in the cells. When they were in the barracks, they gathered in the common area. There were eight or nine tables in this area, each of which was claimed by a gang or group and aggressively defended. The white supremacists, the Muslims, the Italians, the Latinos, and the Mexicans each had their own table and some groups had more than one. Sitting at a table where you were not welcome was a very bad idea. During my time there, I saw such transgressions result in violence, including, once, a stabbing.

There are two additional rooms in the barrack which were initially used as "day rooms." There, prisoners could read, play games, or look at a screen together. I imagine this space provided some sense of humanity, allowing the inmates a quiet place to sit and think, do something constructive, or just escape the stifling cell and the constant presence of a cellmate.

Due to overcrowding, these rooms were re-purposed long before I arrived into what they called "dormitory-style housing." A number of bunkbeds were placed in each room, accommodating in that one room many more prisoners than in the standard cells. After the antics of the inmate in the first cell to which I was assigned, I was moved to one such dorm for a few weeks and it was significantly more difficult than life in a standard cell.

The re-purposing of the day rooms was not just to the detriment of the inmates now housed in those specific rooms. The loss of a space which allowed the inmates some respite, a quieter place for private reflection on past behavior or constructive bonding with other inmates, negatively impacted every inmate in the facility.

The day rooms were one of many things, designed at a time when these facilities took their designation as "correctional facilities" seriously, which were later abandoned for logistical or financial reasons or even on an officer's whim. The sum of all these changes was that these facilities are, in large part, no longer correctional and are now simply punitive.

This was felt very strongly by the inmates. I once overheard someone complaining about some protocol or policy. The guy he was sitting with said, "Hey, man…this is the place where they correct you."

"What?!" spluttered the first guy. "This place is making me worse, not better." He paused, thinking how to illustrate this. "Hey, on the street I killed for a reason. Here?! I'd kill for no reason!"

The standard prison cells are each about six feet wide and eight and a half feet long. Initially, the cells had been designed for single occupancy, but long before I was brought there, they were converted to double occupancy. The bed which took up the six-foot width of the cell was replaced with two steel shelves, one above the other. This change didn't just over-pack the cells. The original beds had springs and a thin mattress, while the new bunkbed was an unforgiving steel plate covered with a few inches of flimsy mat.

Another detrimental effect of the change to double occupancy was that the upper shelf partially blocked the single, narrow, barred window and it no longer provided the same light and fresh air it had when there was only a single bed in the cell.

In the corner of each cell is a small sink and a toilet. There is no provision for privacy in the cell. This is degrading even when cells only held one prisoner, because the cell door has a small window which is not allowed to be covered. The change to two-person cells magnified this degradation and diminished the humanity and self-respect of the inmates. The people who most needed to rediscover some aspect of their humanity were forced to behave like animals on a daily basis, which could only increase or reinforce their disconnect from their humanity.

This diminished even those who had lost almost every shred of a claim to being called a human being. As I mentioned previously, an inmate serving a life sentence for murder-for-hire told me that he'd become accustomed to everything in prison. The one thing he could never get used to was being denied privacy in those moments.

This aspect of the cell caused me an additional hardship, too; the presence of a toilet in the room prevented me from engaging in any of the holy activities which may not be performed in a bathroom. This included *davening*, saying Tehillim, or even a simple *brachah* before or after food or drink.

As I had in Cedar Rapids, I asked for and received permission to hang a sheet around the toilet. This enabled me to say Hashem's holy name and learn Torah in the cell. This permission was often challenged by guards on duty and it was a daily miracle that it remained in force. Eventually, these frequent challenges by guards led to the chaplain making and issuing special *mechitzah* sheets under the religious allowances, which then became available to other Jewish inmates.

This was another instance where commitment to Hashem's mitzvos, without calculation or apology, resulted in Hashem's miraculous assistance. In this case, it helped not only me but all of the Jewish inmates. Not only did it enable us to serve Hashem better, but as with all the mitzvos that we do, it improved our lives in other ways. Thanks to this religious partition, the Jewish inmates had the added dignity of privacy when it was most needed.

Along the same wall as the sleeping-shelves are a few wall hooks, used to hang prison-issued clothes and dirty laundry bags, as well as two lockers, one for each inmate. This paltry storage space is all the prisoner is given for any clothes and belongings he might possess or acquire as he survives there for decades. Many inmates also needed the space to store legal paperwork for pending or ongoing appeals. At some point, they even reduced the inmates' personal storage space by replacing the lockers with ones that are shorter and narrower.

Much of the remaining floor space is taken up by a small table and two chairs. The space is so small that if one of the two occupants sat at the table, the other one would usually remain on his shelf.

Constructed of concrete, the cells are poorly insulated from the weather. In the summer, the cell gets terribly hot and humid. The only available relief from the sweltering heat comes from a small eight-inch stationary fan which inmates could purchase from the commissary if they have the money.

This is another example of unjustified and unwarranted deterioration of living conditions for inmates. The commissary used to sell larger fourteen- or sixteen-inch oscillating fans which were slightly better at relieving the discomfort and stress of living in a sweatbox. At some point, for some reason, an officer decided that the prisoners only needed the smaller, non-oscillating fans. The decision to pull this product, which posed no danger or security risk, caused the human beings incarcerated in Otisville to truly suffer every summer.

When the inmates were allowed out of their cells, they could find some relief from the heat with ice from the ice machines. When I arrived, there was only one solitary machine in each barrack. A few years later, they installed a second machine, bringing the number of ice machines serving the 100-120 inmates of the barrack to a grand total of two.

On really hot days, the demand for the ice was so great that prisoners would actually line up at the ice machine, hoping there would still be a cupful by the time they reached the front of the line. Waiting on a long line with hot, irritable, and often dangerous men is a dangerous proposition, and I avoided this option if the heat was at all bearable using some other means of relief.

During the cold winters in upstate New York, the inmates dealt with the opposite problem. The uninsulated cells are very cold, with only a small number of cells maintaining a tolerable level of warmth due to their placement within the facility. With no way to warm their cells, many inmates slept in their clothes and coats during the winter months. Eventually, some improvements were made to the heating and the winters became a little less intolerable.

There is a single shower stall provided for the inmates on each of the five floors (ranges) in the barrack. The shower is enclosed by an opaque plastic shower curtain, hanging a couple feet outside the edge of the stall to provide a small place for changing. At some point, they decided that the top half of the curtain needed to be semi-transparent, which, understandably, caused an uproar among the prisoners. Their feelings and opinions were not especially valued and the new shower curtain stayed.

The shower was available whenever the inmates were not confined to their cells. In theory, there was no time limit on the duration of the shower, but inmates would hurry each other along, often with the threat of violence. If a prisoner found the curtain closed, he would yell, "Shower!" to see if it was really occupied. Whoever was inside would yell back, "Five minutes!" or however long he hoped to take, or, "Someone's ahead of you!" if that was the case.

If the person was taking too much time, or the line was particularly long, those waiting would hound the person in the shower, yelling at him to hurry up. Frequently, the waiting inmate would shout, "If you don't come out yourself, I'm coming in to take you out." It wasn't an idle threat and the guy in the shower usually chose the former over the latter. If there was a disagreement about who was next, it was usually resolved very quickly in favor of the bigger and stronger inmate.

Shared showers present a heightened risk for infections. The commissary sold plastic shower shoes which offered some level of protection, but that was often insufficient. In fact, my frequent visits to the shower room resulted in a dangerous and painful skin infection known in Yiddish as a *"roiz"*—treatable with antibiotics, but quite painful.

Infection is not the only danger. The heightened vulnerability of the inmate in those moments made it a favored place for violence against the unsuspecting. Early in my time at Otisville, I was once headed to the shower room wearing the plastic shower shoes, when an inmate nicknamed "Flacko" stopped me.

"Rabbi! What are you *wearing*?!" he asked, gesturing at my feet and the plastic shoes. Pointing to his heavy black boots, he said, "Around here, always wear your boots, never those plastic things, even in the shower! Someone could attack you at any second, and then what are you going to do? You're gonna get hurt, is what you're gonna do, if you're wearing those slippers. Wear the *boots*, so you can kick the guy and run out without slipping and falling on your face!" I appreciated his concern and advice, but wearing boots to the shower was a step too far for me.

There were washing machines and dryers in each barrack and the inmates washed their own laundry. Giving them this responsibility allows them to take pride in their cleanliness, which struck me as a positive approach, beneficial to the inmates both psychologically and practically. In fact, one of the things that stood out to me when I was first transferred in were the clean, bright white T-shirts the prisoners wore, which gave the place a clean, sharp look.

Sadly, only about one year after I arrived, they removed the laundry machines and replaced them with communal washing machines, ostensibly in the name of ecology and the environment. They formed a laundry crew from their pool of prison labor to run the now-centralized laundry system.

These prisoners would make the rounds of the barracks once a week with large push-wagons. Every inmate was issued a numbered mesh bag in which to give in his laundry. The laundry was never removed from the bags. They were "washed" and "dried" and then returned a few hours later still closed—not the best way to wash clothes. The new machines also required a special soap which may have been "green" but wasn't too great at cleaning.

An inmate in the same barrack as me called me over once for a demonstration. He'd gotten his hands on a bucket, which he filled with water. He took the laundry that had just been returned and put it in the bucket. The water turned black and dirty almost immediately. This was visual confirmation of something anyone with a nose could tell—the clothes coming back were far from clean.

The poor results were very obvious on white garments, so they switched all the inmates to colored undergarments. This, in turn, meant that bleach could no longer be used, and the inmates were now exposed to all manner of disease and cross-contamination by ineffectively washing all their clothes together without proper disinfectant.

A similar inferior disinfectant was used to clean the showers, which led to many inmates, including myself, contracting serious infections.

Finding a Cellie

Prisoners are locked into their tiny cells for approximately ten and a half hours every weekday, and eleven and a half hours on holidays and weekends. Obviously, the nature of the person who is locked in that cell with him is very important, for the sake of his sanity and sometimes his safety.

All inmates recognize this, and most try to be accommodating to others in the hopes that others will be accommodating to them. The population is not exactly one that would score high in empathy and rule-following, but most did try and expected others to try as well.

For a Yid who wants to maintain his connection to Hashem and the purity of his senses, the nature of his cellmate is doubly important. A person's presence fills the space around him. The way a person dresses and speaks, the images and sounds with which he surrounds himself, his dignity and modesty in personal hygiene—or lack thereof—all leave a mark on the room and anyone else who's in the room. Living in a room with someone who is crass adds to the difficulty of surviving as a Yid.

A Yid also has many unique needs that not every non-Jewish inmate would be willing to accommodate. He has an extra need for privacy in his cell when *davening* or eating the Shabbos or Yom Tov *seudos*, the lights shouldn't be turned on or off on Shabbos, and *chametz* shouldn't be brought into the cell on Pesach, among other needs.

My personal efforts to strengthen myself only added to this list—I had begun waking up early to say the whole Tehillim every day and I needed a "cellie" who was okay with someone praying in the cell in the early morning hours.

After the turbulence of the first few weeks, Hashem blessed me with five consecutive cellmates that all accommodated my special needs as a Yid. I never took that for granted and never stopped thanking Hashem for this great kindness. As I struggled to overcome my *nisayon* and maintain and increase my connection to Hashem, seeing His assistance in this area was encouraging.

The story that best displayed this personal and detailed providence of Hashem actually involved my last cellmate. In 2016, a few weeks before Purim, my cellmate left. The authorities don't immediately fill the bed, leaving it instead to the remaining inmate to find someone that's willing to move and officially request the switch. If the bed remained empty for too long, the prison would place someone based on their own calculations, which often meant trouble.

In this instance, I couldn't find a cellmate right away. Being the only one in the cell was a big improvement. The ability to be alone with my own thoughts, without the pressure of someone else in my space, was a life-giving breath of fresh air, but it didn't last long. Only a few weeks went by, and an officer called me in and told me that I needed to find a cellmate or he would send me one of his own choosing.

I again considered every inmate that could potentially move to the cell I was assigned. There was only one who, from afar, seemed like he would be a good fit. I approached him, intending to suggest the new arrangement, but speaking to him up close, I realized that it would not end well.

I was now at a loss about what to do. I shared my problem with my friends. The experienced inmates said that the wisest course of action was to compromise and approach someone who would be "good enough." Even if they weren't the perfect candidate and they would be a detriment to me in my *Yiddishkeit*, it was preferable to letting the officer choose someone for me.

If I let the officer choose someone, they argued quite sensibly, who knows what type of person he'll send? He could send a murderer, drug dealer, or a criminal deviant. If *I* chose someone, I could at least decide what problems I would deal with, and try to negotiate and mitigate the effect of those problems as much as possible.

I saw the logic in their words and I ran through the candidates in my mind again. There was not a single one among them that would be willing or able to meet even the most basic conditions that I required to be able to continue living as a Yid in a place called prison.

On one hand, the Torah tells us that we must make an effort to the best of our abilities to obtain our needs. If I'm obligated to do something, I should choose the least bad of the bad options available. On the other hand, making that choice meant actively and knowingly diminishing my ability to serve Hashem properly—something I knew couldn't be right. Reviewing in my mind what I'd learned about *hishtadlus*, the right choice became clear.

There is a key point about *hishtadlus* that people often forget. Hashem wants our efforts and their "outcomes" to *look* like cause and effect, but our efforts are never really the cause of the outcomes. Hashem wants us to go to work to earn a living, but it's not really our work which results in the *parnassah*. Even when our efforts provide a plausible natural explanation for how we received our money, it's always and only from Him.

Since, in fact, our *hishtadlus* is not actually contributing to the outcome, we're not doing it to cause the result. We are only doing it at Hashem's instruction—and there are times when He doesn't demand it.

If there is no solution, or, as in this case, no *viable* solution because the available options will interfere with our connection to Hashem, there can be no clearer sign that this is one of the times that Hashem doesn't want us to be a part of solving the problem. Getting involved under those circumstances actually represents *confusion* about *hishtadlus*, the mistaken idea that your actions really control the outcome. Instead, we are told by Dovid Hamelech in *Tehillim, Hashlech al Hashem yehavicha v'Hu yechalkilecha!*—"Throw your burden upon Hashem and He will sustain you," or in a less literal (but no less practical) interpretation of the word *yechalkilecha*, as related to the word *keili*, "He Himself will even make the *keili*."[2]

This doesn't make a person's task easier; only different—he isn't faced with doing a difficult job but with the sometimes even more difficult task of letting go and wholeheartedly and completely throwing his burden upon Hashem, experiencing and expressing real *emunah* and *bitachon* in Him. When we do so, Hashem assures us that He Himself will not only ensure the success, He will also make the vessel—and it will result in a perfect and complete salvation.

My whole situation with finding a cellmate was a scenario that Hashem had teed off in order to see how I would proceed, whether with faith or with logic. I had no doubt that Hashem wanted me to choose the path of *emunah* and *bitachon* in Him. Recognizing that there was really no viable option, and therefore nothing for me to do, I chose to do nothing to resolve the situation on my own and instead put all my energy into achieving and maintaining iron faith and trust in Hashem that He would send me a respectful and accommodating cellmate.

A few days later, as I entered the barrack, one of the prisoners informed me that the officer had sent me a cellmate, adding that it was someone who had been charged with terrible crimes. I cautiously entered cell 307, and there he was, packing his things into his locker. As we often are in our service to Hashem, I was being tested with seemingly obvious failure. I didn't waver in my faith and trust in Hashem and the truth of the Torah. I was certain that whatever I was given would be to my benefit.

I said hello and introduced myself. I told him I was Jewish and explained a bit about what that meant—the times I prayed in the cell, the holidays, and so on. With Hashem's help, he decided on his own, the very next day, that this was too much for him. He moved to a different cell and I was spared an unpleasant and dangerous cellmate.

That sounds like a win, but I was still being tested. I was right back to where I had started, and now I even had personal experience pulling me in the wrong direction. I had just seen firsthand the dangers of doing nothing. Despite that experience and the misgivings it raised, I knew I was doing what the Torah teaches us to do when faced with this circumstance. I withstood the test,

---

2. The natural means through which His salvation comes, usually incumbent on the person to create.

strengthening my faith and trust that Hashem would send me someone who would not interfere with my connection to Him.

The officer warned me again to find someone on my own or he'd send whomever he sees fit. By now, Pesach was fast approaching and I still had no real candidates. As I cleaned the tiny cell for Pesach, I found myself thinking about the complications of the season. Would the new guy show up before Pesach, so I could explain the nature of the Yom Tov and ask him not to bring *chametz* into the cell? Would he come during Pesach? After Pesach?

Catching myself, I laughed at the foolish implicit acceptance of my current situation. "Where is my *emunah* and *bitachon*?" I asked myself. "If I'm thinking of the future, it should be in the anticipation that Hashem would certainly *free* me before Pesach and I'll be home with my family, not negotiating with a cellmate!"

Pesach arrived and I was still in FCI Otisville. *Baruch Hashem*, I merited to have everything I needed to fulfill the mitzvos of the Yom Tov. We made a Seder over a *ka'arah*, with just enough matzah and *maror* for all the inmates present. The Seder was uplifting and focused on Hashem's miraculous liberation of the *Yidden* so many years ago, and our firm faith and trust in His miraculous liberation in the here and now.

Although we were allowed to have the Seder, it came to an abrupt end at 11:30 p.m. when we were required to be back in our cells. The emotional whiplash of going from the taste of freedom at the Seder to the taste of slavery in the cramped cell was something I never got used to. As I did each year, I tried to continue my Seder in the cell. It was much easier that year, because there was no cellmate.

I awoke the next morning and left the barrack at the earliest possible time, ready to continue celebrating the Yom Tov of freedom by *davening* Shacharis with Hallel. As I walked out of the barrack, one of the laundry workers, a nice enough fellow with a mild stutter, called out, "Hey, Rabbi! You're getting a new cellie today!" The inmates who worked in the laundry area were the ones who prepared the clothes for new prisoners, so they were the most reliable sources for this kind of information.

The thought of an unknown person moving into the cell was always a little worrying and on Pesach it was doubly so. Who was he? What was his background? Would he bring *chametz* into the cell? These thoughts were disruptive to my *davening* and singing Hallel with true *simchas Yom Tov*, so I pushed the thoughts from my mind.

After *davening*, when I returned to the barracks, one of the prisoners informed me that the officer wanted to see me. It felt very strange to walk into his office on Yom Tov, a time when I'd internally disconnected from the mundane workings of the world around me to focus only on Hashem and freedom. He formally notified me that I'd been assigned a cellmate. He wouldn't tell me anything about the man or his background, only hinting that he would be an interesting cellie.

None of this required, or even allowed, for any involvement on my part, so I returned to the cell and sat down to learn. Around 2:00 p.m., the door opened and an inmate entered. He was a thin man with a white mustache and goatee. "Hi," he offered. "My name is Tom. They sent me to this cell." I returned the greeting. "I'll go get my stuff," he said and he left, returning a short time later with his few belongings and placing them in his assigned locker.

Officially moved in, he looked around the cell and noticed the piece of tape over the light switch. "Why is the light switch taped up?" he asked.

"I'm a Jew," I explained, "and today is a Jewish holiday. We're not allowed to open or shut the lights during the holiday, so I put a piece of tape on the switch."

"I see," he said. "Would you like me to turn it on and off for you?"

"That's very kind," I told him, "but for you to do these things for my benefit would also be a problem. Would it be okay with you if the light stays on until the holiday is over tomorrow night?"

He thought it over and gave a small shrug. "Sure, no problem."

I silently thanked Hashem, seeing my trust in Him affirmed right before my eyes. Here was a man I'd never met before in my life. He owed me nothing and hadn't negotiated any terms of human decency before arriving. He had as much claim to the cell as me, but he agreed to accommodate my religious needs, even if it meant he would have to sleep with the light on.

When he left the cell for his meal, I explained to him that the holiday I'd mentioned earlier was in fact Pesach, or Passover, and there are other laws I needed to follow. "I'm not allowed to eat, and would prefer to not even be around, any bread or cereal. Could you avoid bringing any open bread, cookies, or cereal into the cell until after the holiday, which is for one more week?"

Again, he simply said, "Sure, no problem. I'll just eat outside in the hall." I again thanked Hashem for sending an accommodating cellmate.

After the evening lock-in, as we were preparing to get to sleep for the night, I told him that I woke very early to recite Psalms. I would do so in an undertone, which I hoped would not bother him, but I wouldn't be able to respond during those times and I meant no rudeness or disrespect. There were also times when I would have to pray in the cell and I would greatly appreciate some privacy during those prayers. He took all this in stride. "Sure, that's all fine," he said again, adding a bit wistfully that his own life experiences had depleted any faith he'd had.

I saw his sincerity the very next morning. It was around 4:30 a.m. and I was saying Tehillim in a quiet whisper. I suddenly heard Tom's voice from the top shelf. "Hey, Rabbi! I can't hear you praying!"

"I'm whispering it quietly because I'm trying not to wake you up!" I responded.

"Don't worry, Rabbi, you're not waking me up—you're putting me to sleep!"

I thought he was joking, so I continued to say the Tehillim more quietly than usual. Again, he insisted, "Rabbi, I don't hear you praying!" I raised my voice slightly and said the Tehillim audibly, as I had done before, and he settled back into his bunk.

If I would have accepted the suggestions I was given, I would've negotiated with an unacceptable cellie and compromised on the only thing that really matters—my connection to Hashem. By recognizing that this situation *didn't* demand *hishtadlus*, and instead trusting completely in Hashem, throwing my burden on Him and letting Him make all the arrangements, not only did I not have to compromise, but I was blessed with a cellmate who was more respectful and accommodating than any other cellmate I had throughout my time in a place called prison.

The Special Housing Unit

As dismal as the cells are, they're downright comfortable relative to the dreaded special housing unit. As I'd first experienced in South Dakota, this bland name was a euphemism camouflaging one of the prison system's most painful tools of retribution and punishment. On paper, or even to the casual observer, it doesn't seem like much, but the experience is a dreaded torture for even the most hardened individuals, and it's often referred to as "the dungeon."

It's a common threat issued by the guards. When the threat alone doesn't cow the inmates, the guards have no qualms about following through and confining people to the SHU for extended periods of time until they succumb and comply with orders or are deemed sufficiently humbled by the experience. I once watched a lieutenant angrily throw a few inmates into the SHU because he disliked the tone of their response to a question.

The locker of an inmate sent to the SHU is immediately emptied and examined, and items are often confiscated, which is another reason inmates avoid that punishment as much as possible.

The discomfort brought on by seasonal weather is exacerbated in the SHU. Panama once described a stay in the SHU during the hot summer months. He told me that'd he lain flat on the floor so he could try to breathe cooler air from the crack beneath the door. The cold of the winter months is also felt more intensely in the SHU. Inmates in the SHU had to wear "special" clothes which offered less protection, and the cell itself was colder than the rest of the prison, sometimes downright freezing.

I always insisted on my religious needs, which was my right, but I was not a rule-breaker. I always made a point of following the rules and it's a source of pride that I had a spotless record after all the time I spent under their rules. Because of this, I had very limited personal experience with the SHU.

The first time was immediately after the conviction, when they took away my yarmulke and *tzitzis*. The second time was when I was isolated as a "participant" after being attacked by my cellmate in Cedar Rapids. The third and last time was in Otisville, and it's also quite a story.

It began unexpectedly during a routine afternoon count of the inmates. Everyone was locked into their cells and the noise level dropped from painfully loud to uncomfortably quiet. It was a good time to learn or say Tehillim.

That particular day, I was saying Tehillim when loud shouting broke the general stillness in the barrack. It was quick and indistinct, and I couldn't make out any words, but only a few minutes passed before it started up again, this time louder and clearer. I could now hear what was being said, but I wished that I couldn't—the stream of words bombarding my ears was offensive in the extreme.

Insulting a guard to his face was an invitation to be thrown into the SHU. No one dared, but some of the prisoners still wanted to tell the guards exactly what they thought of them. That day, one of them had the bright idea to insult the guards, publicly but anonymously, by shouting abuse during the lock-in. His words rang out from behind one of the locked cell doors and echoed off the hard, concrete walls. They were heard by everyone in the barrack, but the echo made it impossible to pinpoint exactly where they were coming from.

Oh, boy, I thought. *This won't end well...*

The guard who was the subject of the colorful tirade couldn't tolerate it for long and, infuriated, roared, "*What* did you say?!" at the top of his lungs. The prisoner, delighted at getting under the guard's skin, happily obliged the invitation to repeat himself. He started all over from the beginning, enunciating each syllable slowly and with relish. Incensed, but helpless to punish the unknown culprit, the guard struck on an idea. "I'll teach you *all* a lesson for this disrespect!" he thundered.

Oh, boy, I thought again. *This won't end well...*

He followed the threat with immediate action and "pulled the plug" on all the screens in the unit. This had an immediate effect. Many inmates would crowd near the small windows in their cell doors to watch the screens during the lock-in, and his revenge was immediately noted. The culprit zipped his mouth immediately, and even the rest of them swallowed their outrage for fear of prompting something even more drastic. The barrack fell silent.

When the lock-in was over, I left the cell, mainly to see what the general reaction would be. The inmates shuffled out of their cells looking sad and lost, like they were at a funeral. Their routine of sitting at the tables and watching screens was disrupted, and they didn't quite know what to do instead. Loss and confusion quickly turned to anger, and the barrack buzzed with angry complaints and empty threats. Some tried pressing buttons on screens, hoping to bring the darkened screens back to life, with no success.

Grateful that this revenge had not disrupted more substantive routines, I headed for the computer room to write an email of *chizuk* to my dear brother-in-law, Yossi Gourarie *a"h*, who was fighting a serious illness at the time.

I thought I had dodged the guard's revenge, but it turned out that I'd celebrated prematurely. Not much time passed before my cellie came in and whispered in my ear that there was a general shakedown going on in the whole barrack. In a targeted shakedown, the guards have a reason to suspect something unlawful in a specific cell or on a specific person. This time, they were just searching everywhere—looking for reasons to confiscate things and punish anyone they could.

The offended guard and one of his colleagues had taken a large garbage bag and were going from cell to cell. Prisoners were sprinting to their cells from all over the unit, and my cellie was offering a friendly heads-up. I thanked him for his consideration, but continued typing the email. I didn't have any contraband and therefore had nothing to worry about—or so I thought. I finished the email and returned to the cell to prepare for a 6:30 p.m. *shiur* with some fellow Jewish inmates.

In the middle of the *shiur*, a guard came in and told me to report to the lieutenant's office at once. This was a sign of trouble. I couldn't think of any reason I would be called, but I took my *Chitas*—a single *sefer* which bound together a Chumash, *Tehillim*, and *Tanya*—and dutifully reported to the office. I found my cellie already there.

On the desk were two small water bottles. One had a very small amount of grape juice and the other a small amount of water with a pink tinge.

"Are these your bottles?" the lieutenant asked sternly. They were, and I told him so. Hearing this, he dismissed my cellie and focused his attention on me. "These were discovered during a shakedown in your cell. They were tested for alcohol with results of .01 percent for one and .02 percent for the other."

The implications were severe. Making alcohol is one of the biggest violations in a place called prison and carries a hefty punishment. "Sir, the grape juice in these bottles was issued to me by the chapel for Shabbos a few days ago. If there was any alcohol detected in it, that's an issue with the official supply—I would not and did not do anything to cause them to become alcoholic."

Ignoring my words completely, the lieutenant informed me that I was being charged with making alcohol. I would be thrown into the SHU for the duration of the investigation, which could take thirty to forty-five days. He signaled that the "meeting" was over, and I was marched to the SHU.

The transparent absurdity of the charges and the injustice of the situation was obvious from every angle, and my mind was whirling with arguments and counterclaims. I was also concerned about my family, who were expecting a call and would be worried when they didn't hear from me. I hoped one of the Jewish inmates would think to get a message to them, and *baruch Hashem*, one of them did. Knowing what was happening with me was better than uncertainty, but hearing that I'd been thrown into solitary on trumped-up charges, possibly for a long time, was difficult news for them to hear.

They administered a drug and alcohol test—which was obviously negative—

and I was processed into the SHU. The rules in the SHU are designed to foil the most dangerous criminals and to be administered successfully by even the laziest, most dim-witted guard. This results in a lot of unnecessary pain for the prisoner.

Although the SHU is usually called solitary, it was overcrowded that day and I was placed in a small dark cell with another prisoner. There was a hole in the outer wall that was presumably a window, but it provided no light or air.

By Divine Providence, the email that I'd been writing a few hours earlier, in what seemed like a different world, held a message of encouragement I had intended for others but which I was able to lean on myself in my sudden *tzarah*.

Yaakov Avinu, when blessing his grandchildren, the sons of Yosef, made a point of switching the order. He *bentched* them that through the ages, *Yidden* would bless their children to be like Efraim and Menasheh and the Torah emphasizes this switch, saying, *And he put Efraim before Menasheh*.

Reb Levi Yitzchak Barditchever, the defender of *Yidden*, points out that Menasheh was named for the *tzarah* his father Yosef was in at the time, while Efraim was named for the salvation and the greatness Yosef would ultimately be granted by Hashem. Explicitly and emphatically placing Efraim before Menasheh shows that the salvation is prepared *before* the *tzarah*, and the only reason we go through the *tzarah* is to set the stage for the salvation and greatness that follows!

I took strength from this *dvar Torah*, which Hashem had sent me before my own *tzarah*, and looked forward to seeing this truth come to life before my eyes in my own situation. My *emunah* and *bitachon* bolstered, I looked around for any purpose I could find for my presence in the SHU.

I struck up a conversation with the other prisoner, a non-Jew, and turned the discussion to G-d and our purpose in life. We spoke for quite some time about Hashem's oneness and the seven mitzvos He gave to all mankind, starting from Adam and Noach.

When that conversation had run its course, I turned to my *Chitas*. By *hashgachah pratis*, I'd been carrying the *sefer* with me from the *shiur* and it was bound with a soft cover, so they allowed me to keep it when they processed me into the SHU. When a person is faced with adversity, *Chazal* say he should examine his actions and do *teshuvah*, so I decided to review the twelve chapters of the *Igeres Hateshuvah* of the Alter Rebbe, the Ba'al HaTanya, which is printed in the *sefer* along with the *Tanya*. I reviewed them carefully, trying to apply the Alter Rebbe's teachings in a real and practical way. When I finished, I turned to the *Tehillim* and poured my heart out to Hashem. It was in the wee hours of the morning when I finally finished the *Tehillim*. I felt that I'd done what I was there to do and lay my head down for a short rest.

Early the next morning, the assistant chaplain came by the SHU on her morning rounds. She was very surprised to find me there. In response to her questions, I explained that I was being blamed for a negligible level of alcohol content that they'd detected in grape juice that I was given by the chapel.

She promised to look into it and asked if there was anything I needed. "Yes," I replied, "I need my *tallis* and *tefillin* so I can pray." She assured me that she would take care of it. Sure enough, *baruch Hashem*, a short while later she brought them to me and I was able to *daven*.

As I was finishing up my *davening*, I was interrupted by a guard who'd come to take me to the investigating officers. I went along, hopeful for an opportunity to discuss the truth of the matter surrounding both the bottles of grape juice and the vengeful nature of the shakedown. Instead, they simply demanded that I affirm incriminating statements which were blatantly false. I refused to do so. This enraged them, and I was summarily dismissed.

I was taken back to the SHU, and, reassuring myself that the outcome was in Hashem's hands, I resumed my *davening* and learning. A short time later, the head chaplain came to see me and hear the story firsthand. *Baruch Hashem*, he accepted that what they'd found had been nothing more than what his department had given me. He reassured me that it would all be resolved quickly. He met with various authorities, and secured my release from the SHU pending the investigation—something which is very much out of the ordinary.

A few hours passed and I was notified that I was being released. I recognized that this was nothing short of a miracle and thanked Hashem with all my heart.

The guard behind the revenge shakedown, who had brought the phony accusation to the lieutenant, was on duty at the door when I returned to the barrack. He looked at me in shock. "You're back so soon?!"

His surprise was natural. It was unheard of to be released in under twenty-four hours after such charges were leveled. Typically, it took thirty to forty-five days just to get through the investigation phase. I got congratulations from many in the barrack who were just as surprised to see me back so soon. They felt it was only right—they knew me and were certain the charges were false—but it was still well out of the norm. I took the opportunity to make it clear that this was a miracle and give the credit to Hashem.

Hashem's salvation had come so quickly that I was released before visiting hours that day were over. I was able to see my family within twenty-four hours of the traumatic "arrest," which really helped calm my family and friends. My brother Heshy had made the 1,100-mile trip from Iowa, and I was able to see him at the visit.

Although I'd been so quickly released, the charges had not been dismissed and still hung over my head. The case would still go before an officer who would judge the case. This protocol was in place in recognition of the possibility that the guard who'd issued the violation might have done so unjustly, because he had a score to settle. An objective arbiter is expected to investigate and find the truth. In practice, however, the guard's word is trusted as that of an honest officer of the law, while the inmate's word is distrusted, so it's almost invariably just a bureaucratic rubber stamp. Procedural rules also tilt the outcome in favor of the accusing guard.

As soon as I was released, I informed Gary Apfel[3] of this latest development. He was very concerned, because their efforts to win my release could be complicated by a record of misbehavior. I insisted that there was nothing to fear. I was innocent. I had complete *bitachon* in Hashem that the charges would be fully dismissed and my record would remain untarnished.

He was still very worried. In an uncharacteristically harsh exchange, I told him that a weakening of complete trust in Hashem and a fear of nature makes a person subject to the very natural rules he fears. If anything bad happens, it will be because we faltered in our *bitachon*. My trust is as solid as a rock, I told him, and it was up to him to hold up his part.

When the day of the hearing arrived, the designated judge presented the case against me. They had thrown away the bottles and presented pictures of the bottles as their evidence. The alcohol levels they'd claimed to find could not be retested and were accepted as fact, based on their trusted word as law enforcement personnel. The pictures showed bottles which had been squeezed, making the water level appear much higher than the few ounces they'd actually held.

They had determined the alcohol content by squeezing the bottles and

---

3. My devoted lawyer; more about him in Chapter Thirty-One.

forcing the air in the bottle through an electronic alcohol-level detector, an oral breathalyzer. My son had done the homework and contacted the breathalyzer manufacturer directly. Based on what he learned, I pointed out that using these devices this way would not lead to accurate results. They are designed to mathematically extrapolate from very small amounts on the breath to show a larger number that must therefore be in the blood. Forcing vapor from the bottle directly into the machine would show a wildly inflated number.

Gary and the lawyers had also prepared a file which highlighted my clean record and included a very technical letter from a chemist at Kedem, the producer of the grape juice. The letter declared for the record that fermentation is a natural process that begins as soon as the package is opened. That this process has begun does not necessarily indicate that any action was taken to cause it.

I made the best case I could to meet my obligation to create a natural vessel for Hashem's salvation, but none of it really mattered. The letter from Kedem was dismissed out of hand as "untrustworthy," with the outrageous and offensive explanation that "you Jews help each other." The flaw in their method of testing for alcohol content was likewise rejected. This is how the BOP has always done, and will continue to do, this test.

Hashem's help comes in the blink of an eye. Now that the reasonable arguments had been dismissed, His help would be seen clearly for the miracle it was.

Seeing that they would not be persuaded, I made a simple and direct appeal. "Listen," I said, "this allegation is simply not true. I did nothing to make alcohol out of the grape juice I was given. If this false charge is allowed to stand, it will stain my record."

The judging officer thought for a moment and suddenly said, "Okay, let's say you're correct about the purple bottle, with the grape juice. What was in the bottle with the pink liquid?"

It seemed like a softball question to me. "There had been some drops of grape juice in the bottle and I refilled it with water. Water turns the grape juice pink." He looked skeptical, and even the Jewish chaplain who was in attendance seemed to think I was wrong. I had the benefit of knowing that it was true because that was exactly what had happened, so I encouraged the judge to try it out then and there. He and the chaplain went out to test it and saw it was true.

It seemed to me totally miraculous that he should seize on something so childishly simple. When he saw his objection so easily and conclusively explained, it changed how he felt about the whole allegation.

As the officer and the chaplain returned to the room, I heard the end of their discussion. The chaplain had found a way to bring up the significance of the day in the Jewish/chassidic calendar. It was *yud* Shevat, the *yahrtzeit* of the previous Lubavitcher Rebbe and the beginning of the era of leadership of the Rebbe. The date really had no bearing on the case and it seemed to me that the chaplain saw the injustice and was invoking the presence and help of the Rebbes by mentioning their names.

The judge sat down and gave his verdict. "I'm going to dismiss the charges. There will be no punishment." I was grateful to Hashem for this salvation, but the anxieties of my lawyer were fresh in my mind, so I pressed for more. I explained to the officer that having a stain on my record, even of dismissed charges and without punishment, would complicate my legal efforts going forward. He heard me out and thought for a long while. Finally, he said, "Okay. I'll also expunge the incident from your record. It will be as if it never happened." This was extremely rare and openly miraculous, but treating the charges as if they'd never happened seemed fitting—after all, everything they had claimed never *did* happen.

I left the room elated, focused more on the gift of Hashem's presence and love than on the narrowly avoided injustice. My assurances to the lawyer were borne out—*emunah* and *bitachon* bring *geulah*!

News of the miraculous outcome spread through the compound. One of the guards who was known for his antisemitic tendencies was overseeing the food distribution in the chow hall that evening and he made some strong negative comments about it. I looked him in the eye but said nothing. Anything I might respond would mean less than nothing to him, and I wasn't particularly interested in *his* opinion myself, so I said nothing in response. This was the attitude of the guards, even to non-Jewish inmates in these circumstances. The prisoner is always wrong, because the guard is always right—even when he's wrong.

Controlled Movement and Counts

Otisville is a "controlled movement prison," which means that all prisoners are confined to their location and can only move from place to place during specific windows of time called "moves." As part of the federal prison protocol, the inmates are also regularly locked down—confined to their specific cells—and counted to ensure they're all present and accounted for, something they called "counts."

The nightly lock-in ended at 8:30 a.m., when the barracks were unlocked and inmates had five minutes to move to other areas in the compound. At 9:30, there was another five-minute move. At 10:30, all inmates were recalled to the barracks and locked in, until they were released to the chow hall for lunch one barrack at a time. Further movement around the compound had to wait for the five-minute moves at 12:30, 1:30, and 2:30 p.m.

At 3:30, there was another recall, and all prisoners were locked into their cells for the 4:00 count. There were two more opportunities to move from area to area, during the five-minute moves at 6:00 and 7:30, and at 8:30 p.m., the prisoners were recalled to the barracks and locked in for the night. If needed, a special move would be scheduled as appropriate for those participating in periodic fitness, educational, or chapel programs.

The daily counts—supplemented by an additional 10:00 a.m. count on federal holidays—reminded me of the repeated counting of the *Yidden* by Hashem. Of course, those counts were motivated by Hashem's great love for the *Yidden* whereas the counts in Otisville were very much not motivated by love.

Every count was an ordeal that took at least about an hour and often longer. The inmates were locked into their stifling cells while they waited to be counted. They were not allowed to sleep during the count and were required to stand at attention when the guards doing the count reached their "range," their floor in the barracks.

Inmates passed the time speaking with their cellmate, straining to catch a glimpse of the screens in the common area through the cell door's window, listening to music, reading, or simply waiting around, some inevitably falling asleep despite the prohibition.

One afternoon, during the 4:00 p.m. count, I was sitting at the table learning. I heard the guards begin to make the rounds. They loudly called out the range numbers as they reached each floor. "Range One!" then "Range Two!" We were in cell 307, so when they called out "Range Three!" I stood up for the count.

Glancing over at my cellie, at the time a man named Jeff, I noticed that he was fast asleep on the top bed-shelf. My first thought was to wake him up, to spare him the punishment he would receive for being asleep during the count, but I hesitated. In a place called prison, an inmate was liable to get angry at someone "butting into his business," even in an effort to help him. Actually, that might make it worse by making them look or feel weak, as if they need your help.

I ultimately decided to risk his wrath and wake him. "Jeff, Jeff!" I called over to him. No reaction. I had been told about how long-term inmates become conditioned to prison life, what they called "institutionalized," and I decided to try something. Very softly, I used the prison phrase, instead of his name. "Count time...count time..." He jolted upright and jumped to the floor as if he'd been stung.

He was sleeping so deeply that he couldn't even hear me saying his name, something which famously reaches a person's core, but he was so conditioned to instinctively react to prison commands, that the words "count time" cut through his deep slumber. He was on his feet by the time the guards reached the cell.

Seeing the deep-rooted effects incarceration could have on a person, I resolved to not be incarcerated. My body wasn't going anywhere without Hashem making miracles, but my *neshamah* was *already* free. By focusing on my *neshamah* and remaining free internally, I would be spared these effects.

During the counts, the guards made their rounds in pairs. As they passed each cell, they peered through the door and noted the presence of the inmates on their papers. When they were done, they relayed the number to the supervising lieutenant. If the total number of inmates counted matched their "inventory," the doors of the cells were opened, allowing the prisoners to leave their confines and move around inside the noisy, crowded barracks until the next move.

If the count *didn't* match their "inventory," the prisoners were not allowed out of their cells until the mistake was identified and corrected, or the missing inmate was found. This could easily add an additional hour to the torturous lock-in.

Adverse Weather and Unscheduled Lock-ins

These scheduled "moves" and counts were all conditional on good weather. In bad weather, like rain or fog, there were different rules.

The "adverse weather" protocol was ostensibly put in place because reduced visibility and other aspects of inclement weather make it harder to secure the compound and guard the fences. In practice, however, declaring "adverse weather" was an arbitrary decision by the officer on duty. There were many times that the fog was as thick as pea soup but the lieutenant on duty didn't call it "adverse weather" for some reason, perhaps to avoid the hassle at the end of his shift. Other times, a hint of fog was enough to justify triggering an adverse weather lockdown, freeing the lieutenant and guards from having to deal with the inmates around the compound.

Whatever the true cause of the adverse weather lockdown, for however long it lasted, the entire prison population was locked into the barracks. They could gather in the common area during the daytime hours, but every two hours, they were locked into the tiny cells for an "adverse weather count." There was a time that these lockdowns also meant a total freeze on the visits which were so precious to the inmates and so important to their connection with their family.

"Adverse weather!" was a dreaded announcement for most, but not for all. One foggy morning, I was locked into cell 307 with my cellie for the count. I was sitting at the table learning, and the other guy was laying on his bed-shelf with closed eyes. "You know, Rabbi," he said, "I love adverse weather. I stay in bed all day… I feel like I cheated them out of a day."

I didn't see it that way. Every day is a gift from Hashem and a mission from Hashem, and the adverse weather impacted that mission. Being confined to the barracks meant no *minyan*, for example. No sukkah, if it was Sukkos. No volunteers to help with things we couldn't do on our own. I preferred if there was no lock-in so I could do all those things.

At these times, I reminded myself that my mission was given to me by Hashem and the lock-in was also from Hashem. Being locked in didn't mean I couldn't do what Hashem wanted, it just meant He wanted me to be doing something different. Mindful of that, I spent the time on whatever Hashem had left for me to do—*davening*, learning, and writing letters of *divrei Torah* and *chizuk*.

Sudden lock-ins were also sometimes called for breaches of security. If a fight broke out, or something potentially dangerous went missing, they would call a lock-in; the inmates would be confined to their cells until the issue was resolved.

In addition to the suffering of the inmates, these unexpected lock-ins caused uncertainty and anxiety for their loved ones by making communication impossible.

Each Motza'ei Shabbos, after Havdalah, I would call home to say *gut voch* to my wife and children and hear how their Shabbos had been. One week, an unexpected lock-in took place just as I was about to make the call. I knew they would wonder why I didn't call and worry that something bad had happened to me, which made me feel terrible.

There was nothing I could do, and no benefit to be had from these feelings, which is a sure sign that they come from the *yetzer hara*. I pushed those thoughts from my mind and those feelings from my heart and went back to the cell as instructed. I washed my hands and sat down to eat the matzah I'd prepared for *melaveh malkah*. As I ate, I pictured myself sitting with my family and friends, and I sang the *melaveh malkah* songs we always sang.

Eventually, two guards came to the cell door with a breathalyzer. My cellmate and I both obediently blew into the device and they turned and locked the door again with no hint as to when, or even if, the lock-in would be ended that night. The unknown duration of these lock-ins always magnified the anxiety and pain they brought.

Baruch Hashem, the lock-in actually did end that night—and with half an hour remaining until the regular end-of-day lock-in. I headed straight to the phones. After the long wait on line for my turn, I barely had enough time to wish my wife and children a *gut voch*, but it was enough to put their minds at ease and that was very important to me.

It was not at all unheard of for adverse weather or other unscheduled lock-ins to last long enough to run into a regularly scheduled count or even the next adverse weather count. I remember one such time. It was one of those mysterious "adverse weather" lock-ins when the sky was clear and blue. Everyone shuffled to their cells reluctantly, wondering why we were really being locked in and, more importantly, for how long?

The longest lock-in I had experienced to that point had lasted four days, the result of a fight in the chow hall. My cellie said he had been through a lock-in at a different facility that had lasted six weeks and his gut was telling him that this would be one of the long ones.

I shrugged. Decisions in a place called prison don't actually have to make sense, so it wasn't totally ridiculous to use the digestive tract instead of the brain to predict what came next, but whether it was one of the long ones or not, it was out of my hands. I said *gam zu l'tovah*—this too is for the good—and settled in with my *sefarim* and siddur to learn, *daven*, and say Tehillim.

We were counted immediately but were not released from the cells. The hours crawled by and at 4:00 p.m., the shout again came to stand for the count. This surprised me. We were still locked into the cells since the last count. It made no sense to count again, but it didn't matter. That was the protocol, these were their orders, so that's what they did.

As with everything we see and hear, it was a lesson in *avodas Hashem*—a powerful demonstration of *kabbalas ol*. We *Yidden* also have orders, mitzvos, some which we understand and some which we don't. As these guards were demonstrating, we have to fulfill our orders even when we don't understand them.

The comparison between our orders and theirs, *l'havdil*, between these pointless counts and Hashem's holy *chukim*, also highlighted to me an important distinction. Their orders aren't understood because they truly don't make sense. Orders like that can be followed, but without any real enthusiasm. By contrast, *our* orders are not understood because Hashem's will is beyond the limited understanding of a created being. Such orders can be, and ought to be, followed with the greatest energy and enthusiasm!

In fact, in a way, *chukim* are greater than mitzvos we understand, because they represent Hashem's will purely—not distorted or diminished by our understanding. Doing these mitzvos simply because they are His will allows us to connect with Him in a way that goes to our (and to His) very essence, beyond the rational.[4]

Finding and focusing on these lessons not only decreased the mental torture of the extended lock-in, it even gave those hours unique value and purpose in my service of Hashem.

Before moving on from the counts, there is one more aspect to highlight: the special provision for an "out-count." This was when inmates received permission

---

4. Common wisdom suggests that we should strive to fulfill the incomprehensible mitzvos as well as we fulfill those we understand. A Yid knows better. A Yid, who experiences the significance and the joy in the pure and un-rationalized connection to Hashem, will actually do those unexplained mitzvos with *greater* enthusiasm and energy. His aspiration will be to do the mitzvos he *does* understand with the same enthusiasm as the mitzvos which he does *not*, as the Rebbe Rayatz once famously said.

to be somewhere other than their cell for the count. It was mainly used for those in the visiting room during the time of the count or for inmates working around the compound, such as the food service crew who needed to be in the kitchen. Obviously, this exception was necessary so that the compound could function properly. For example, supper was served right after the afternoon count, so they needed inmates to be working in the kitchen at that time.

Superficial justification notwithstanding, we know that everything is created to serve Hashem. The out-count turned out to be a very important tool in doing mitzvos together in the chapel. Without it, we would often have had to cut short time in the chapel to get back for the count, and certain things would have been entirely out of the question, such as Shabbos and Yom Tov *minyanim*, candle-lighting during the winter, the Pesach Seder, and regular weekly *minyanim* during "adverse weather" lock-ins.

This brought to life the Torah's assurance that the world itself will help us do Hashem's will. We only need to do our part without fear or compromise and Hashem will arrange the rest.

CHAPTER SIXTEEN

Prison Food for Body and Soul

The Chow Hall

T HE MOST COMMON REASON TO LEAVE THE BARRACKS WAS FOR MEAL time. Meals in prison took place in a room officially called the dining hall, but which everyone referred to as the chow hall. It was a large room filled with tables, each with attached stools. Like the common areas of the barracks, many of the tables were claimed by one gang or the other. Any others who sat down at one of these tables were "politely" invited to leave. To decline was to accept a different invitation—to an unpleasant, possibly violent confrontation.

Although the chow hall may have been large enough when the prison population was smaller, it became far too small when they started doubling cell occupancy and added "dormitory-style" multiple occupancy cells. Their solution was to call each barrack to the chow hall separately. Each prisoner was expected to come to the chow hall during his barrack's slot, eat, and leave immediately, so the next barrack could be called in an orderly fashion.

In practice, this didn't play out quite as described. To get through the chore of running the meal shifts more quickly, officers would call more than one barrack at a time. Whoever arrived after the chow hall had reached capacity had to wait in line outside the building or miss that meal. The weather often made it a thoroughly uncomfortable experience, not to mention the humiliation of standing daily on line just for a few morsels of food. Confronted with the dehumanizing line, I often opted to forgo a meal and return to the barracks hungry, and I wasn't alone in that.

Another reason some people avoided the chow hall: it was a flashpoint for confrontation, and occasionally physical violence. Meeting with prisoners from another barrack sometimes prompted an inmate to settle a score or maybe he simply met someone he didn't like. An overheard expletive or insult was all it sometimes took for fists to fly.

When inmates came to blows, both prisoners were thrown into solitary, but those directly involved were not the only ones to suffer. All inmates were immediately rushed to the barracks and locked into their cells to avoid back-and-forth retaliatory attacks that were to be expected if the fight was gang-related. This lock-in would continue until the incident was fully investigated, and caused great difficulty to everyone.

One Erev Shabbos, the Shabbos after my grandson Shimi was born, there was a big commotion in the compound. Word spread quickly that a big fight had broken out in the chow hall. Sure enough, moments later the lock-in announcement blared from every speaker in the compound. I hurried to the cell, as did every other inmate in the barrack.

Shabbos was approaching and I couldn't call to wish my family good Shabbos. I didn't even have a way of letting them know what was going on in Otisville, so they'd know why I wasn't calling. The lock-in wasn't lifted that day, and Shabbos came without a change to the situation. There was no contact with my family, and no way to even share Shabbos with other *Yidden* in the place called prison, which reminded me of the isolation I experienced in the county jail.

Sunday brought no end to the lock-in either. Being cooped up in a tiny cell for over thirty hours with another human being is difficult on any day, but that day it was especially difficult. That morning, my son Shmuly was bringing his second son into the *bris* of Avraham Avinu and he was expecting me to participate, at least by phone.

I had prepared some Torah thoughts and stories to share by phone as my participation in the family *simchah*, and I hoped the lock-in would end in time. It didn't, and I was denied even a long-distance connection during those special moments for my son, grandson, and my entire family.

The lock-in ended up lasting four long days, from Friday through Monday evening. As with every extended lock-in, we weren't allowed out of our cells even for meals. Cold food, packed in brown paper bags, was brought by guards to the cells for four days.

During the intake process, each prisoner was issued a card with a magnetic strip and a PIN code. It was used for a number of purposes, but most regularly for meals. In the chow hall, inmates would line up at a food counter at the front of the room. Each would receive their tray of food only once they'd swiped their card to ensure they only received a single tray per meal.

According to the old-timers, the food in federal prisons was once sufficiently nutritious, edible, and in sufficient quantity that the BOP could justify its policy of denying inmates food packages from home.[1] Over time, the quantity and quality of the food was reduced in the interest of reducing costs. At the time of my arrival, the situation was already dismal and during my time there, I saw it deteriorate even further. It got to the point that many of the inmates who could afford the commissary products wouldn't show up at all, due to the low quality of the food. This left a lot of extra food, of course, but they absolutely refused to give any inmates the extra food, preferring to throw it all out. A disturbing amount of food ended up in the garbage on a regular basis.

When they served something the inmates *did* want to eat, the sticking point was the quantity. Once, a large prisoner complained about the very small burger he was given to eat. He was still hungry and demanded that he be given more food. The guard responded in a very dismissive and demeaning way, using the terms and tone normally reserved for speaking to an animal. This was too much for the prisoner to tolerate, and his reaction came as a quick punch to the guard's jaw.

When a prisoner assaulted a guard, all the guards would rush in to contain the prisoner and help their fellow officer. Once the prisoner was subdued, he was carted off to the SHU and from there, transferred to a different facility, unless he was one of the informers they found useful enough to tolerate the occasional outburst. This predictable scene played out here, with this large, hungry inmate, but this outburst did nothing to prompt change in the underlying cause; the inmates' hunger.

Over the time I was there, they eliminated choices of breakfast cereal and removed the coffee urn from the morning meal, replacing it with a single tiny packet of coffee in the breakfast tray, not strong enough for even one cup. They reduced the bread ration at each meal from three slices to two, replaced soft drinks with colored water, and removed the salt and pepper shakers from all the tables. These may seem like trivialities, but all of these reductions added

---

1. This policy is in contrast to many US state prisons and to the rest of the civilized world. Even in the Stalinist Russia of our grandparents, prisoners received food packages from their families which provided not only nutritional benefit but a taste of home—a comfort to the soul.

up to less nutrition reaching the prisoners and also increased the tension and stress unnecessarily, all in the name of cost reduction.[2]

The staff meals were not limited in quantity and were of respectable quality. Working on staff meal preparation was a coveted job, since it gave the inmate the opportunity to smuggle out good food, which was very valuable on the prisoners' black market.

Perhaps not coincidentally, inmates with some resources or family support turned to the commissary to buy food. This left many inmates out for lack of resources, but even for the more well-off inmates, who could afford to "eat out of their locker," as they called it, this source of healthy and nutritious products was short-lived.

The contract to supply the commissary, once awarded locally, was centralized. The result was shifting wealth to the central supplier and reduced offerings to the inmates, both in quantity and quality: No fresh fruits and vegetables and only precooked and sterilized foods, which are more easily warehoused and transported across the system, but which have very little nutritional value.

Even the paltry nutritional value on offer at the commissary for the general population was of little use to the Jewish inmates because it was mostly not kosher.

Further limiting the utility of the commissary as an alternative food source was the absence of any method of preserving food. Federal prisons don't provide, or even allow, any personal mini-fridges in which inmates might store food they buy or prepare from commissary-sourced ingredients.

As a weak substitute, they did at one point sell small ice coolers. This allowed inmates to use the ice from the ice machines to keep food cold imperfectly, for a short time, and with great effort—but even this primitive refrigeration disappeared when some officer made the decision for some reason to stop selling these ice coolers.

Of course, in implementing these changes, they kept to the letter of their policies, if not their spirit. For example, their policies require that fresh fruits be served with each meal for nutritional reasons. These types of policies are, rightfully, a source of pride for the department and those who established

2. A report that I found in preparing this book, dated 2012, put the average cost of food at Otisville at $2.45 per prisoner per *day*.

them. From before my arrival, this policy meant that inmates were receiving, depending on the day, fresh apples, oranges, bananas, or grapefruits.

Apparently, some officer or bean-counter realized that the policy insisted on fresh fruit, but didn't specify or enumerate the actual types of fruits to be served. In short order, all the fresh fruits were replaced with pears. And not just any pears, but plum-sized, rock-hard, canning pears which are difficult to eat and unhealthy to boot.

When apples did make an appearance in the chow hall, they were of similarly small size and poor quality and presumably offered the same cost savings. In this way, a policy instituted for the health of the inmates was fulfilled to the letter without the cost of fulfilling it in spirit, some bureaucrat or functionary earned his bonus, and life for the inmates became incrementally worse in yet another area.

All inmates have it tough, but those keeping kosher have it even tougher. There are two main groups within the category of religious diets—*Yidden* and, *l'havdil*, Muslims. Some calculating businessman came up with the concept of "common fare"—a meal that would be acceptable to, or at least usable by, both.

Kosher food is more expensive, having more stringent and costly requirements than halal. In order to produce a food tray at a price that was competitive with the less expensive halal-only offerings in use previously, the supplier had to skimp on portion sizes and quality. They succeeded, to their financial benefit and that of the BOP, but it resulted in a decrease in food quality and quantity for the Jewish prisoners, compounding their suffering in a place called prison.

Eggs are staples in institutional menus everywhere, because they're a source of protein that is both common and cheap. The menu for the general population at Otisville was no exception; the menu for the religious inmates was. The common fare offered to Jewish prisoners only included mass-produced scrambled eggs once a week. Fresh or leafy vegetables, even the small amount available to the general prison population, was entirely absent from the diet of the Jewish prisoners, replaced occasionally by a meager portion of frozen vegetables.

Breakfast was always a light meal, so inmates hoped for a substantive lunch or supper. This made the common fare meals feel even more inadequate. Once a week, the common fare meal would be a few ounces of peanut butter and two slices of bread for lunch and then a vegetarian meal consisting of a small tray of beans and rice for supper. Another miserable vegetarian meal was soy-stuffed cabbage which was so bad that you literally could not give it away—no one in the general population would even take it for free.

A meal based on chicken wings consisted of two chicken wings! In general, any meat and poultry was so overly processed (to maximize both shelf-life and profits) that it provided very little nutrition and very often, a large dose of heartburn to boot.

The meager elements of the meal were kosher but, when it comes to keeping kosher, the ingredients are only half the story. Even kosher food, if it's improperly prepared, can lose its kosher status. This can most easily happen when cooking or warming the food. In Otisville, the kitchen staff would heat the properly certified, plastic-wrapped common fare trays at the same time, in the same ovens, and on the same oven rack, as the non-kosher food trays.

This doesn't necessarily make the food *treif*. If the food is within a double wrapping, it would still be okay, which was why they were heated while still in their plastic wrap. The trouble was that the heat of the ovens would very frequently melt the plastic, reducing the number of wrappings to one or even melting all the way through to the food.

When I first encountered this issue, I showed the tray to an officer and explained the problem. Once he understood, he looked until he found a tray with the plastic wrap still intact so that I could eat. This became the backup plan whenever this situation came up, and I appreciated the effort, but too often, he was not able to find a replacement tray.

The first time he couldn't find one, he tried to give me back the problematic tray but I politely refused it. I could not eat kosher food heated in this way.

I tried speaking to the officers responsible for meals and food preparation. I also informed my family of this latest difficulty. I had done my part and, sporadically missing meals and going hungry, I awaited Hashem's help. When His help came, it was a general salvation in the whole area of meals, not just in the specific problem of properly warming the food.

Apparently, my family had reached out to the Aleph Institute, which had in turn reached out to the prison authorities through the proper channels. The head chaplain had also thrown his support behind their request that this issue be solved. The officer in charge had already been considering different solutions in response to my efforts on-site, but this support definitely helped speed up the process and find the right solution.

The solution they adopted was to wash their hands of the whole issue by authorizing me to take the tray of food, unheated, to the barracks. There, I could use the microwave in the common area to carefully heat it up without melting through the wrappers. This meant more work for me, but it was a real *brachah* from Hashem.

In general, prison regulations forbade removing meals from the chow hall—although (or perhaps because) every inmate would prefer to eat almost anywhere else, for the reasons described above.

In addition to the dehumanizing atmosphere and the violence, the chow hall was not conducive to eating as a Yid. At that time, there were no tables exclusively for those eating kosher. This meant that even if the Jewish inmate found a seat at one of the tables without being chased away by one gang or the other, he had to eat his meal surrounded by the foreign smells of non-kosher food, not to mention the usually very non-kosher conversation. *Netilas yadayim* was also difficult in the chow hall, because there was no sink available for inmates to wash their hands. I tried to wash at the drinking-water dispenser, and, when that was impossible, I just didn't eat the bread. I made it work, but it was far from an ideal situation, even for a place called prison.

This new arrangement, set up to solve the problem of properly heating the food, actually solved all of these things. They gave me an official letter to show the guards at the door and sent me to eat my meals in peace. Whenever I was stopped by a guard who didn't know of the special arrangement, I would show the letter and they would allow me to take the food out of the chow hall.

This was another example of how keeping Hashem's mitzvos as they were given, and not seeking to be absolved of the parts that were difficult, helped me not only spiritually but also physically. My insistence on maintaining the kashrus of the food I ate resulted in permission to take the food to the barracks—where I could wash my hands with ease and eat the meal quietly at a table without any disturbance, far from the sights, sounds, discomforts, and dangers of the chow hall.

It also helped others. When another Yid who felt the same way as me was transferred to Otisville, he was able to take advantage of this arrangement as well and reap the benefits both physically and spiritually. He thanked me for my part in making this happen. This was especially gratifying to me, since my ability to benefit others was severely limited in a place called prison. This was one of the few ways of doing *gemilas chessed* left to me in my situation.

There was one other reason to be in the chow hall, besides for the food—something inmates called "main line." The regulations required officer-level representatives of the various departments to be present at the midday meal. This was a direct avenue for inmates to raise issues or lodge complaints with authorities that were otherwise mostly inaccessible. It was a chance to speak directly with authorities ranging from the lower-ranking staff overseeing specific areas (like mail, medical, and the like), to the captain and lieutenants—even the assistant warden and the warden on many days. Some of them came just to blindly say "no" but others actually came to listen and help as appropriate.

The presence of these prestigious personages came with some negatives, though. The guards, who interacted with the prisoners on a regular basis, understood the need to make small concessions in the endless list of stringent regulations in order to facilitate peace. Officers, on the other hand, didn't interact regularly with the prisoners and often ignored the need to make these concessions and enforced things the guards would overlook, causing unnecessary tension and suffering.

For example, some prisoners were skilled in knitting and one Yid who had grown in his *Yiddishkeit* had knitted himself a white yarmulke. He wore it without incident for months until, one day, he walked too close to main line. An officer called him over and confiscated it, informing him that the white yarmulke was unacceptable and only black was allowed. The Yid, of course, complied, but he was very pained by this interference in something that he held dear and that wasn't hurting anybody.

The Chapel

The Supreme Court ruled that the constitutional right to freedom of religion applies not only to citizens in a place called freedom[3] but to those in a place called prison as well. To represent and to serve these needs, a chaplain is hired at all federal facilities to ensure that the religious needs of the prisoners are attended to. Space is also set aside as a chapel. In Otisville, three rooms were set aside for this purpose.

The primary chapel was a large room with a high ceiling and wooden wall

---

3. Just as being physically in-prisoned doesn't automatically mean one is imprisoned, *not* being in prison doesn't automatically mean one is free.

paneling. This gave it a more civilized, even impressive feel, and also gave it a warm feeling absent everywhere else in the cold, dark place called prison.

Along one wall, there were wooden cabinets, each designated for a religious group indicated on a label on the door. Despite (or because of) the long list of groups, there were no religious symbols hanging anywhere in the room. This was very significant halachically, because it means that the room was not identified with any specific religion and it was permissible for *Yidden* to enter and even *daven* there.

Since the chaplain's office has limited manpower, the BOP allows religious volunteers to visit and provide religious programs to teach and inspire the inmates. This provided limited opportunities for the small number of *Yidden* in Otisville to take strength and encouragement from other *Yidden* who came in person and spoke, learned, danced, and *davened* with us, each in the appropriate time.

These events and programs took place in the chapel and often made use of the speaker system there to play joyous music which lifted us out of our difficult circumstances. I will always be grateful to my many dear *Yiddishe* brothers who took the time and effort to travel all the way to Otisville, New York, to give help and support to *Yidden* they had never even met. I will go into more detail about those later.

The main chapel was the largest of the three rooms and allowed for the most people to sit together comfortably. This made it our first choice, but also the first choice of other groups. Because it was always in demand, we were constantly taking out and putting away the siddurim and other things we needed, instead of leaving them out and accessible. For that reason, we eventually leaned toward using one of the two smaller rooms, which saw less use by other groups.

The Torah is *chayeinu v'orech yameinu*, our life and longevity, and nowhere is this felt more clearly than in a place called prison. Our bodies were behind bars, but our *neshamos* were free and they lived and drew their strength in these rooms. One of the closets in the chapel had shelf space dedicated to the Jewish library which had been donated over the years—a complete set of Mishnayos, *Shas*, Rambam, *Shulchan Aruch*, *perushim* on the Chumash, and many more—each *sefer* a door to true freedom.

Because of the rule which limited the number of books a prisoner was allowed to have in the cell to no more than ten, I couldn't really have a proper collection of my own *sefarim*, but thanks to this library, I was often able to find the *sefer* I needed and study it there or take it to the cell temporarily.

Among the many *chassadim* and wonders which Hashem made for me, one that I treasured and from which I benefited constantly, was that I was actually not hassled by the guards when I occasionally went slightly over the ten-book limit.

I kept the clothes I had hanging in a laundry bag on the hook so that I could use the tiny locker shelf for my precious *sefarim*. My small collection expanded and contracted over time to match my study schedule, but, despite the many regular and unexpected shakedowns and inspections, a minimal overrun in my little library was generally not challenged.

The one time an officer did step in to limit the number of *sefarim* in my locker, the chaplain interceded and, with the help of Hashem, successfully persuaded the officer to allow it.

Each chapel also had a video machine so inmates could watch religious content, such as lectures or religious gatherings. Generous organizations had donated videos to the Otisville library, including a sizable number of videos of the Rebbe's *farbrengens*. These *farbrengens* transported me to a different time and place and were a real source of *kedushah* and strength in trying times.

The first time I entered the chapel and looked around, I noticed a rather large wooden box on wheels near one of the walls. I asked someone what it was, and found out that there was a large tub inside, which was used for a non-Jewish religious ceremony in which people are immersed in water.

I immediately thought of *mikvah*. If this tub was permitted, we should ask for permission for some kind of *mikvah* that the *Yidden* could use to immerse daily, or at least before Shabbos. How hard could it be?

Very hard, as it turns out, although there was no reason this should be the case. Significant accommodations were made for "minority religions." They had even built a dome-shaped hut as a sweat lodge for the Native Americans outdoors, near the yard. Inside, they would heat stones in a fire and pour water to create steam, in which they sat for extended periods of time. Compared to that, what's a request for a large tub, similar to one already authorized and in use? Yet, it was a request that met a lot of resistance from the beginning.

Another Yid at Otisville had requested a proper *mikvah* when he'd first been transferred there, years earlier. They held the request for a while and then formally denied it. This Yid and I learned *Rambam* together daily and one day, after learning, he told me all about his efforts. Years had passed since then, but he was still visibly upset by the unfairness of the refusal to accommodate Jewish needs while granting more onerous requests from other groups.

I suggested that he try again, this time explicitly requesting something similar to what was already approved and in use in the chapel. I explained to him, based on the *Rambam*, how it was possible to modify a tub to be a kosher *mikvah*. He discussed my idea with *rabbanim*, and when they told him it was halachically sound, he renewed his efforts to obtain a *mikvah* for the *Yidden* in Otisville.

Even this modified suggestion, so similar to the existing tub, was met with opposition at every level. What should have been a matter of paperwork and perhaps a month or two, turned into another years-long struggle. The wooden box in the corner of the chapel stood as a silent reminder that the Yid is always different.

My friend and the *askanim* he'd involved in this effort didn't relent, *baruch Hashem*. Eventually, their persistence was rewarded and the authorities finally agreed to hold practical discussions and negotiations on the issue. They ended up getting permission, but someone involved, eager for a "win" at almost any cost, made concessions that really hollowed out this victory.

The news that the *mikvah* had finally been approved caused great rejoicing in our group but, when we heard the conditions, that was quickly replaced by the sinking feeling of disappointment. The agreement that had been reached not only didn't allow for daily use, it didn't even allow for *weekly* use on Erev Shabbos! We would only be able to use this hard-won *mikvah* before certain special days throughout the year.

We finally had a *mikvah* but were all but forbidden from using it. We sincerely appreciated the few times a year we were able to use the *mikvah*, but it also increased our pain and bitterness at the injustice each Erev Shabbos, knowing that the *mikvah* was so close but out of our reach.

Even this small achievement was constantly under attack. One of the guards made it her mission to stop us from using the *mikvah* at all.

A guard is never just a lone voice. He or she usually has relatives and close friends working in the same facility and this particular guard recruited all her allies in her fight against the *mikvah*. She even got the prison guards' union involved.

The union riled up even more guards to oppose the *mikvah* and directly pressured the chaplain to stop its use. They used their tremendous clout and the same battle-tested pressure and scare tactics that I had myself faced so long ago.

For example, they argued that the Jewish tub was near an electric outlet and posed a danger to their members. These anti-Semites, using the same tactics as their counterparts had in Iowa, pretended that their opposition was about honest and legitimate safety concerns, but this was clearly the thinnest of facades. To start with, they raised no such issue about the non-Jewish tub. Even more telling, the outlet in question was one of those designed to be used safely near water, as you find on any kitchen countertop or laundry room in America—there was no legitimate safety concern whatsoever.

Baruch Hashem, their efforts were unsuccessful at preventing use of the *mikvah*, but they did infect many guards with their poisonous message. Once, when I was leaving the visiting room, a guard asked me about the "Jewish pool." The wording and tone of his question made it clear that he believed it represented some sort of special treatment the Jews received, overriding many and various safety concerns. He told me he'd heard all about it from his union.

I generally did not converse with the guards. For one thing, they often looked down at the prisoners, which is a bad starting point for any substantive conversation. Their role and position also made every conversation a minefield, with real consequences for the most trivial misstep.

Faced with this *chillul Hashem*, however, I asked the guard if he knew about the non-Jewish "pool" which was a prominent fixture in the chapel. He admitted that he did, and I made the obvious point. "Do you consider it special treatment to give Jewish inmates an equivalent level of accommodation as that given to the other religious inmates?" To his credit, he was willing to admit that it was only fair that the *Yidden* have a *mikvah*, and he'd been wrong to suggest that there was special treatment.

It's worth noting that I had said nothing about the safety concerns. Once I reminded him about the non-Jewish tub, which did not concern the union, he realized himself that the safety concerns were just a nonsense cover for their real motivation.

CHAPTER SEVENTEEN

The Daytime Hours

Working Hours

WORK IS NOT FOOD FOR THE SOUL LIKE THE CHAPEL OR THE *MIKVAH*, but it is certainly food for the spirit. Or, it would be.

With some medical and security exceptions, federal inmates are all required to work. Many facilities "employ" their inmates at a government corporation specifically established to manage prison labor, called UNICOR. It generates close to half a billion dollars in sales and sometimes substantially more, clocking in at over $800 million in 2009. It operates close to seventy factories at federal prisons, and produces and provides a hundred different products and services.

As property of the BOP, inmates are not covered by minimum wage laws. This may surprise you, but they aren't even covered by the constitutional ban on slavery. It explicitly excludes prisoners, saying, "Neither slavery nor involuntary servitude, except as a punishment for crime [...] shall exist within the United States." With that as an alternative, I guess any pay at all is outright generosity, but inmates had a hard time feeling grateful for wages of $0.23 to $1.15 an hour for UNICOR jobs and $0.20 to $0.40 per hour for non-UNICOR jobs.

Otisville had a UNICOR solar panel factory at one point, but it was shut down. Even paying such pitiful wages, I guess they couldn't compete with factories in China. This was a big loss for many penniless prisoners. They were already barely earning enough to purchase basic hygiene products from the commissary, and now had to make do with the even smaller non-UNICOR wages.

There was a small number of inmates who worked in their specialty—there were a few electricians, for example—but most inmates were not able to do work that utilized their individual talents or abilities and the work they were assigned was mostly menial tasks and chores.

Of course, any work is better for the spirit than doing nothing, but the sense of accomplishment and contribution that proper work would have brought was lost in this arrangement. Many didn't even feel like their work meant anything at all. Referencing this and the shockingly low wages, I once overheard an inmate summarize it like this: "They make believe they're paying and we make believe we're working."

Instead of providing the inmates with the energy and motivation that might drive them to grow and improve themselves, the work became just one more thing that sapped their dignity and self-respect.

For me, this sad state of affairs injected extra meaning into the *brachos* we make thanking Hashem for giving us His Torah and mitzvos. No matter what our daily occupation might be, we always have the privilege and benefit of our full-time work for Hashem. By learning His Torah and doing His mitzvos, we are both creating benefit and receiving benefit—a job which fills our hearts with joy and gratitude to our Creator.

Another *chessed* from Hashem in the area of work, one from which I benefited on a daily basis, was that my work assignment was actually to care for the (air-conditioned) chapel. This meant that during work hours, I could quickly complete my assigned tasks and spend the remainder of the time with the *sefarim*.

If the inmates were lucky, their meager earnings were placed into their account at the end of the month. If they weren't lucky, the payment was delayed. It was heartbreaking to see people checking their account on payday, only to see that the thirty or fifty dollars they'd earned for a full month's work was not actually paid. The curses and obscenities that poured out of their mouths in frustration would have made truck drivers blush and made me thank Hashem they sold ear plugs in the commissary.

A quick tour of the commissary, since I've brought it up a few times without describing it:

The inmate is dependent on the prison to provide everything he needs, and the prison is obligated to provide them—but that's defined a lot more narrowly by the prison than it is by the inmate. Reasonably comfortable footwear, toiletries, and thermal clothing for the winter cold are only some of the things an inmate can't really live without but that are not provided by the prison. Instead, these items are offered for a price at the commissary.

Commissary purchases could only be made one time per week. The specific "commissary day" for each inmate was determined by their prison number. The inmate would fill out a form detailing what he wanted to buy and bring the form to the commissary in the main building. The guard on duty would charge the inmate's account using his card and the prisoners working behind the window would then put the order together.

The commissary room could hold forty at a time, but only the fifteen or so inmates that could be served more or less simultaneously were allowed in. The others had to wait in a long line outside, sometimes in conditions of extreme heat or cold.

Although the inmate is paying for the products, access to the commissary is a privilege, not a right. Prisoners can lose that privilege on various grounds, and even those who are granted that privilege are limited to a maximum spending limit of a few hundred dollars a month. The limit is raised from time to time, but so are the prices—the net outcome being an increased cost to the prisoner with no increased buying power.

Certain items were also restricted in quantity. For example, an inmate could only buy one ice cream each week. Buying items through a friend is a common way around the commissary restrictions but there were penalties and consequences for that kind of behavior. Seasonal or holiday items—macaroons on Pesach, to give a Jewish example—were also restricted and frequently out of stock.

"Leisure" Hours

The work hours took up a large part of the day. The rest of the day, the inmates were left to their own devices. Obviously, having over eight hundred people cooped up in a confined space with nothing to do is a recipe for disaster, so there were a number of facilities to preoccupy and pacify the prisoners.

One of the more popular areas, at least during the warm months, was the yard. Walking from building to building in the compound was only allowed during specific five-minute windows of time, as I described earlier, and stopping and standing around outdoors in transit was not allowed. This made the yard the only place an inmate could be outdoors for any length of time.

For new arrivals fresh off the bus from county jails or urban detention facilities, simply being outside under the wide blue sky felt like freedom. Of course, to really mistake that place for freedom, they'd have to ignore the two rows of high razor-topped fences surrounding them and the tall guard tower overlooking the area, but it was closer than they could get any other way.

The yard offered a view of the densely wooded area around the Otisville compound. Although they were out of reach behind the tall fences, the sight of the trees had a positive effect on the atmosphere. The first time I went out to the yard, my mind flooded with happy memories—Lag B'Omer, family outings, even my childhood summer camp experiences.

I often said Tehillim in the fresh air of the yard. One winter day, maybe four years after my arrival, I went out to the yard with my *Tehillim*, but something felt different. I couldn't put my finger on it, but I couldn't shake the feeling that something had changed. It took me a while to realize what it was—or rather, what it wasn't. What was different was the absence of all emotional reaction to the sight of the world beyond the yard. It triggered no memories and no increased feeling of warmth, peace, or freedom, as it had in the past.

I was experiencing the damaging effects that long years in a place called prison have on a person—slowly disconnecting him from his past until it fades away completely, leaving him no more than a prisoner.

Whenever I noticed the effects the place had on me, I made every effort to overcome and counteract them by strengthening my *neshamah* through learning Torah and doing mitzvos, the true essence of who I was before and of who I continued to be.

In truth, every Yid faces this challenge. His *neshamah* is a part of Hashem, not subject to the limitations of nature. When it enters his body, its true nature is concealed. He learns from infancy to think of himself as subject to the limitations of nature, a prisoner to the "reality" of this world. It's our task—through Torah and mitzvos and our connection to Hashem, which never changes despite changes in our environment—to rediscover and reconnect with who we really are, stronger than any obstacle in this world.

The clarity that I found in the reflections that these low moments triggered was an important part of how I survived in that place, spiritually and physically.

The more jaded inmates, the ones who had already internalized the reality of prison, also preferred the yards to the walls of their cell or barrack, not for the reminders of freedom but because it offered fresh air and room to stretch and exercise.

In addition to the open space and a few tables where people could just sit and talk, basic facilities and equipment were provided to give the inmates an outlet for their pent-up energy, redirecting it away from any destructive behavior.

There was a long looping track on which many inmates walked or jogged, weights and other bodybuilding equipment, and a variety of game courts— baseball, handball, tennis, basketball, and others. There were also a couple of indoor areas for use in inclement weather, including a basketball court, handball courts, and some weight-lifting equipment as well.

For less strenuous recreation, there were options besides the yard. The common area in the center of each barrack had a number of screens on the wall, the accompanying audio streaming to the inmates via a small radio device available for purchase in the commissary.

There was also a "leisure room," a fairly large room with a number of screens on the walls, a pool table, and regular tables where other indoor games could be played.

The atmosphere in the leisure room was quite jarring. The raucous sounds of inmates laughing and howling, taunting each other, and competing for respect by being crass and crude were all good incentives to stay away at all costs.

Despite that, when more *Yidden* were brought to Otisville and we would gather to learn together, we often had no choice but to meet in the leisure room because the chapel rooms were locked or occupied. It was quite a scene, and one I think gave the Eibeshter much *nachas*—a group of *Yidden* huddled together around a table over *sefarim* of the holy Torah, leaning in to hear and be heard over the loud and rowdy sounds of empty revelry and rivalry.

Reading these last few paragraphs might leave you with the impression that this was some kind of resort. This is a perception that was actually utilized by the facility. They pointed to or described these facilities as if the inmates lacked nothing and were even "living it up."

It's true that on paper it sounds a bit impressive, but even the most deluxe versions of these facilities—and these were very far from deluxe—are nothing more than the "body" of the experience. The true experience depends entirely on the spirit. Even all the pleasures of a resort are like ashes if the person is experiencing depression or anxiety or physical or spiritual pain of one kind or another.

Every person there was torn away from their families and their lives, locked into a cage, and subjected to the many and varied humiliations and indignities of prison for decades, or even for life. What is a basketball court or a pool table next to that?

There was also a leisure library, for those inmates inclined to read for pleasure, and a legal library, for those inmates who still believed they could discover a way to extract a measure of justice through the system but who had no money to pay a qualified professional.

During my time there, the legal library went digital. The bookshelves were replaced by computers with digitized legal references and a printer. This printer could only be used to print prison notices or forms, existing documents from the collection on the legal computers, or emails the inmate had received.

This printer could have been a great help to the inmates, and at one point, it had been. If an inmate needed to write his own legal documents or type up a formal complaint to the officer, he was able to benefit from the ease and efficiency of modern computers to easily correct mistakes, copy and paste, spellcheck, and so on. He could then simply print out his work and submit it to the court or the prison authorities.

This "perk" was withdrawn some time before I was transferred. In its place, inmates who wanted to type something up were reduced to using a couple of daisywheel typewriters, a technology that became obsolete in the eighties.

Though powered by electricity, these typewriters work on the same principle as the old mechanical kind. The alphabet letters are plastic stamps on the end of long thin sticks arranged so that they poke out of a center wheel like the petals of a flower—the daisywheel. As the person types, the letters strike the paper through an ink ribbon, making an indelible mark on the paper. Inmates who wanted to use these typewriters needed to each buy and use their own daisywheel and ink ribbon.

It was quite a sight to see men hunched over these typewriters in the twenty-first century—not by choice, but because this was the only option they had. Their typing produced a drumbeat of clicks and clacks and the occasional whirring when the paper was shifted down to the next line or backwards to strike through a typo.

In the wrong hands, these machines created more frustration than printouts, and most inmates didn't use them, simply accepting the diminished ability to create legal documents and formal complaints. Others didn't have the luxury of avoiding these typewriters. Inmates who had no money for legal representation but were not quite ready to give up and spend their lives in prison had no choice but to represent themselves, which is referred to in court as *"pro se,"* and it was almost always an exercise in futility. There were exceptions. More than one of these inmates found the right legal detail or error in their case and successfully won their freedom, returning home to their overjoyed families.

Taking on the system is a formidable task for an untrained citizen, even on the outside. When he finds himself on the inside, unjustly incarcerated, that task gets dangerously close to impossible. Denying him access to the simplest modern tools with which to create the mountain of paperwork the courts demand is an unforgivable, unconscionable handicapping of these people by professed representatives of justice.

The Prison Economy

Time not spent working at assigned jobs was not only spent on recreation. For some, it was also spent "hustling"—working unassigned and unsanctioned jobs in exchange for prison currency or "shopping" for goods and services from those who did. Enterprising inmates had a full underground economy going.

Allowing prisoners to hold cash is pretty obviously a bad idea. Many of the men in Otisville had been put there for harming other people in order to get their hands on money; even among those who did not have such a history, many were not above trying their hand at it.

During the intake process, any money the prisoner had in his possession was taken away and placed in an account. His meager earnings from prison work or outside support from family or friends was also placed into this account, which functioned as a restricted bank account of sorts.

After money was deducted for any restitution, fines, or fees, the inmate was allowed to use the remaining money, if there was any, but only to make purchases from the commissary and to pay for phone and computer use. To send any of the money to a third party, such as to help pay family expenses with the pennies he earned in prison, the inmate needed to fill out a formal request to the prison counselor for approval. If the counselor signed off on the request, the BOP would issue and send a check to the intended recipient.

These policies kept the prison free of legal tender, but not free of currency altogether. Money is a basic part of human interaction and its value is primarily by social consensus. In theory, anything which is limited and can't be forged would make usable currency. Denied access to dollars, the inmates simply agreed on alternative currency and used that in all their dealings.

Postage stamps are sold in the prison commissary, and, by consensus among the inmates, that became the informal and illegal currency of prison. There was a thriving stamp-based economy, with inmates buying all kinds of items, paying for others to do their laundry, paying for valuable legal expertise, and betting on televised sports. This was all strictly forbidden, but the authorities knew all about it. Unless it was too overt to ignore or they were otherwise motivated, they turned a blind eye.

Everyone needed something at one point or another, and they could get it all with stamps. An inmate nicknamed "Hustler" claimed he could get you *anything*—besides the key to go home—if you had enough stamps. That was his reputation, at any rate. His competition in the barrack, "Bozo," used to walk around screaming, "On deck! On deck!" hawking used shoes, sweatshirts, even food items smuggled out of the kitchen.

The kitchen detail worked with knives. As you might expect, they were closely monitored during their work and very carefully checked at the door on their way out to ensure no one had kept any sharpened steel. How did food get out of the kitchen? Simple. The guards allowed it, turning a blind eye to the smuggling.

This may have been driven more by pragmatism than by pity. There were a relatively few inmates preparing the three daily meals for the whole compound. For their pains, they were not paid very generously—something like $50 a *month* for the workers and $80 for the inmate that served as the manager. Responsible for ensuring results, the guards on duty found that the best way to keep morale high enough to be productive was by looking the other way while the kitchen workers supplemented their income.

Not unlike their counterparts in broader society, the prison authorities were willing to let certain things slide, but they kept the rules and punishments on the books so they could go after specific inmates as the need arose—utilizing "prosecutorial discretion," of course. They also didn't want things to get too far out of hand, so commissary sales of stamps were limited to one book of stamps a week and an inmate was not permitted to have more than three books of stamps at any one time.

To be fair, someone did try at one point to nip this whole stamp thing in the bud by removing them from the commissary and moving to postage-paid envelopes instead of stamps. This only lasted a short time because it was totally ineffective. The inmates just switched the currency to tuna fish and mackerel pouches and carried on as if nothing happened. Once the stamps were reinstated, the economy switched right back to stamps.

The value of a single stamp, like the value of any currency, fluctuated—a sort of stamp exchange rate. Unlike most currencies, though, the value was also affected by the condition of the physical stamp. Stamps in good condition, referred to as "mailing stamps," were of higher value, only in part due to their actual usefulness for mailing. Stamps that had become worn and tattered were referred to as "compound stamps" because they were only of value on the prison compound, and they traded for less.

When I arrived, compound stamps were being traded at three stamps to a dollar and mailing stamps were closer to the face value, the price they cost in the commissary.

Buying stamps at the commissary was one way to get stamps. The industrious alternative was to offer a product or service in exchange for stamps, but the more creative inmates were always looking for easier ways.

When mail is processed in the postal system, a cancellation mark, also called a "killer," is ink-stamped onto both the envelope and the stamp to indicate that it's been used and can't be reused. This mark is often improperly applied or too small to cover all the stamps needed for postage. Once they noticed this, inmates began carefully peeling off any used but unblemished stamps on the incoming mail they received, creating prison money from nothing.

To counter this, the mail room decided to rip or cut the used stamps off of all incoming envelopes, but their motivation didn't overpower their laziness for long. The practice petered out and inmates went back to peeling off the unmarked stamps.

One of the truly talented inmates even discovered a method of dissolving or erasing the cancellation marks, essentially finding a prison goldmine. I learned of this accidentally.

It was well-known in the barrack that I received a large volume of mail from my dear brothers and sisters throughout the world who cared for me and *davened* for my release. One day, I was approached by an inmate and asked for my discarded envelopes. When I pointed out that the stamps were all inked and useless, he dismissed the problem with a wave of his hand. "We can take care of that," he said. I politely declined to give him the envelopes, unwilling to participate in illegal activities.

Most transactions used compound stamps. Occasionally, an argument would break out when a seller would demand more stamps than agreed upon because the buyer offered compound stamps instead of the crisp mailing stamps.

One day, I was in cell 307 when my cellmate came in looking agitated. He threw open his locker and rifled through it. As I watched, he took out his pocket radio, fresh batteries, and some coffee, and stuffed them all into various pockets.

"What's happening?" I asked him, curious and a bit concerned for his wellbeing. "Is everything okay?"

"I'm going to the SHU," he grunted.

This was a bizarre response. When an inmate was condemned to solitary confinement, he wasn't given notice—the officer or guard who decided to impose this punishment just hauled the hapless prisoner off then and there. Caught off-guard by the unexpected answer, all I could manage was, "What? Why?!"

Without stopping his preparations, he explained himself. He'd made a forty-stamp sports bet a few weeks earlier and had won. The loser wasn't paying up and kept pushing him off. He'd finally had enough. He wasn't going to be "taken" for forty stamps and he was on his way to "knock the guy's head off."

Fighting is a "high severity prohibited act" and a guaranteed trip to the SHU. This wasn't deterring him from "knocking the guy's head off," but he did want to be prepared for his stint in the SHU to the best of his ability. An inmate was permitted to take to the SHU any non-restricted things that were on his person at the time of his "arrest," so he was placing into his pockets anything that he wanted to have for the duration of his punishment.

Thankfully, this episode ended better than anticipated when the other fellow saw the wisdom of repaying his debt without further drama, but this exchange stayed with me for a long time.

It was absolutely astonishing. This man was ready and willing to voluntarily endure the torment of the SHU over forty compound stamps—less than twelve dollars!

The Ba'al Shem Tov says that everything a Yid sees or hears is a lesson in his *avodas Hashem*. This is a teaching I tried to put into practice throughout my ordeal, which took me to many strange places and showed me many strange things.

The importance this man placed on the stamps got me thinking. They have no real value in the wider world. The faded and tattered compound stamps, which were the majority of them, couldn't even be used to send mail. Nonetheless, prisoners expended a lot of energy to earn them and protect them, carefully accumulating them over years and some, sadly, over decades.

Among the inmates were some who'd acquired a truly large number of stamps, enough to buy anything on offer with ease. They were considered— and considered themselves—wealthy in the place called prison.

I imagined the day one of these "stamp-wealthy" prisoners would be granted his freedom. Packing his belongings, he would certainly include his most valuable asset—his stockpile of stamps, the hard-earned product of so many years of difficult work and savvy negotiating.

In my mind's eye, I saw him making his first visit to Starbucks, an experience which he'd been looking forward to for twenty years. Having selected his Frappuccino, he pulls twenty stamps out of his bursting wallet, magnanimously telling the barista, "Keep the change!"

Obviously, he would be helpfully reminded that in the "real" world, those tattered bits of paper have zero value. Even if he empties all of his "millions" onto the counter, he can't walk out with even a simple black coffee.

This is not a reflection on the worthlessness of compound stamps—the totally different (green!) bits of tattered paper that they *do* accept in exchange for a Frappuccino are no more inherently valuable.

Compound stamps, like every paper currency, only have value because, as a population, we've decided we will value them and willingly exchange goods and services for them. That value judgment is limited to the context in which it's made and won't transfer to another context.

As a Yid, this observation was a great reminder to focus on true, eternal value instead of on value that's merely by agreement and limited to one narrow context. The Torah and mitzvos that Hashem gave us provide that real value— the opportunity to serve the eternal Creator and connect to Him.

Best of all, the artificially and temporarily valuable bits of paper (*both* postage stamps and the revered dollar) can actually be exchanged for *real* value by using them for mitzvos.

Of course, I couldn't have cash, but I could buy stamps in the commissary. The mailing stamps had a legitimate face value, which meant they could halachically stand in as money for mitzvos that require money, the most obvious being *tzedakah*. Before each *tefillah*, I would give *tzedakah* using stamps. Every so often, I would calculate the value of the stamps that had accumulated and ask my family to give the equivalent in dollars to a worthy recipient.

An empty plastic peanut butter jar served as a makeshift *pushke*. I taped a piece of paper around the jar, labeling it as charity, and kept it in the locker in front of my *sefarim*. One day, during a sudden shakedown of the cell, a guard came across the jar of stamps in my locker. Puzzled by its purpose, he confiscated it and left.

I was in the visiting room at the time and knew nothing about the shakedown, so it was unexpected when I was called to the lieutenant's office, something which only happened when there was a problem. The lieutenant in charge had the jar on his desk and asked me to explain what it was for. I explained to him that charity is a very important part of life for a religious Jew and that I had purchased the stamps properly so that I could fulfill this mitzvah daily.

One by one, he began counting out how many stamps were in the jar to establish that I had gone over the three-book limit, but then he seemed to change his mind. He abruptly stopped his counting and handed me the jar. "You're fine," he said, motioning for me to leave. "Don't leave it so exposed in the locker next time!"

This was another instance where staff recognized from my general behavior that I was an upstanding individual and not a threat to law and order. These moments were indications of the *kiddush Hashem* I was making and they meant a lot to me.

These mailing stamps also enabled me to fulfill the *minhag* of *kapparos* on Erev Yom Kippur, as I will describe at the appropriate point.

CHAPTER EIGHTEEN
Health Services

Medical Care

MEDICAL CARE IN OTISVILLE WAS PROVIDED AT THE HEALTH SERVICES unit, a cluster of rooms located in the main building. It was primarily administered by medical assistants, overseen by a single doctor. If an inmate had a health issue, he needed to present himself during the short triage/sick call in the morning or suffer for another day.

One morning, not long after I arrived in Otisville, I woke up with a sore throat. The pain intensified when I tried to swallow, and I realized that I needed medical attention. I hadn't yet learned all the ins-and-outs, but I knew that the medical unit opened at 7:00 a.m. to provide medical care, for which inmates were allowed to leave the barracks, so I made my way there at the appropriate time. To my dismay, I learned that "open" meant they would treat those on their roster, but they wouldn't help anyone who hadn't been at the 6:45 a.m. sick call.

I was still experiencing sharp pain every time I swallowed, so I went to the lieutenant in charge. He agreed to inquire for me and see what he could do, but returned with an apology. They would only see me the next day, and only if I came to the sick call the next morning. They would leave me in pain for twenty-four hours because my symptoms didn't take into account their fifteen-minute early-morning scheduling window.

It reminded me of the story of a man suffering from an illness for which doctors offered no cure. He came to the Maggid of Mezritch for guidance and the Maggid told him to go see the specialist in Anipoli. When he got to the hamlet and asked around for the address of the specialist, the townspeople just looked at him without comprehension. "A specialist?! We don't even have a doctor here," they told him.

"Well, what do you do when you're sick?" he asked.

"We *daven* to Hashem," was their simple reply. The man got the Maggid's message. He placed his trust in Hashem and *davened* for good health and he recovered fully.

Clearly, I was in a place like Anipoli. Like the good people of Anipoli, I turned to the only doctor a person can really rely on, the *Rofei kol basar—Hashem Yisbarach*. I returned to the barracks and placed my trust in Hashem to heal me even without medical intervention and, *baruch Hashem*, the symptoms eased later that day without their help.

Prisoners are viewed with suspicion even in matters of health. Their complaints are too often taken with a grain of salt or dismissed outright. Even once medical treatment has begun, there is a high bar before the medical staff will accept that they can't handle the problem on-site and agree to take the inmate elsewhere.

One Friday, I noticed an African American inmate being wheeled into the visiting room on a wheelchair to meet his family. He was a robust young man I'd often seen exercising in the yard or gym, easily keeping up with the others. Now he looked surprisingly frail.

He apparently had a serious medical issue. The medical staff had attempted to treat it themselves, but their treatment was not helping and he was deteriorating from day to day. It reached the point that the BOP finally agreed to transfer him to their dedicated medical facility, and he'd asked his family to visit before he was transferred out. They posed for a picture against the cheery, painted backdrop and parted with a final hug and a kiss. It was the last time they saw him alive.

The next morning, during the 10:00 a.m. count, he was found dead in his cell. A sign was posted in the chapel announcing a vigil in his memory, and within a short time, he was all but forgotten by everyone but his family, who were sadly no longer counting down the days until his release.

No one knew if he passed away in his sleep or if he'd tried to call for help. He had been alone in his cell, with no one to help him, and there's no emergency buzzer in the cells. Facing imminent danger and failing to get the attention of a guard, no matter how hard they bang on the bars or how loudly they yell, is a nightmare of many inmates, and the nightmarish reality of more than a few.

I had my own experience urgently calling for help when I was attacked in Cedar Rapids, but *baruch Hashem*, I never needed urgent medical attention myself. I did have to call for help for a cellmate, though. One night, after lock-in, my cellmate suddenly took ill. He was in bad shape, and couldn't even get to the door to bang on the bars himself. When I noticed something was off, I offered assistance. At first, he refused. Asking for help is a violation of the macho code many inmates followed. Eventually, he realized that it was too serious for silly games and accepted my repeated offer. I shouted for help and banged on the door, doing everything I could to get the guard's attention. It took a while, but eventually they showed up and brought the doctor to the cell.

As with every aspect of a place called prison, the person implementing the regulations and procedures had as big an impact on the experience of the inmates as the details of the rules themselves.

One particularly malicious staff member was a woman assigned to the medical unit. She was callous, and treated inmates with open contempt and disrespect, earning her the reciprocated hatred of all the prisoners. I made every effort to avoid direct contact with her.

I was once waiting on line at the medical unit and watched from a distance as an African American inmate had enough of her personal disrespect and her weaponizing of the rules, and failed to show her the proper deference. Astonished and outraged, she threatened to send him to the lieutenant's office and have him thrown into the SHU. He just shrugged and said, "I don't care. Do it."

That pushed her over the edge. She lost her cool entirely and angrily marched him off across the yard to the lieutenant's office. I saw him an hour later, obviously not in the SHU. It seems the lieutenant knew of her tendency to provoke the inmates and didn't punish him as harshly as she had threatened.

My own run-in with her happened when I contracted a serious infection in my leg. The antibiotics weren't working and the doctor had told me to return for a follow-up. I set out from the barracks in good time but due to the pain in my leg, I couldn't walk fast enough. I arrived a few seconds late and she refused to allow me in. I tried to explain that the infection was worsening and the doctor wanted to see me, but she just brusquely ordered me to leave.

I went to the lieutenant's office and reported that I needed the doctor and the doctor wanted to see me, but this guard was not allowing it. The lieutenant agreed to look into it and I returned to the barracks. *Baruch Hashem*, a short while later, the doctor called for me and I was allowed to go from the barracks to the medical unit.

To help the prisoners deal with the mental strain of incarceration and the increased strain of negative legal or personal news, there was also a psych unit.

There were five or more psychiatrists in Otisville—which is at least as many as the medical professionals treating all physical ailments *combined*. The ratio in the US civilian population at that time was one psychiatrist for every seven or so general practitioners, and that tells you all you need to know about the mental and emotional toll of prison.

The deep inner traumas and their side effects were frequently treated by prescribing pills. The need was so frequent and widespread that these pills were referred to in Otisville as "Skittles."

Pill Line

Baruch Hashem, with the exception of two times over a serious infection and a couple of times for minor issues, I managed to avoid the medical unit. Some didn't have that luxury and needed to go regularly to pick up pills they needed for a mental or physical condition. Those people could come three times a day for the "pill line," a literal line which formed at the appointed times in one of the rooms in the medical unit where guards would give them their pills.

The line was frequently longer than the room could hold and snaked out into the yard. The prisoners needed their pills and had no choice but to wait in the heat of summer or frigid temperatures of winter. On those days, the arguments over who was where in line were more frequent and more intense. A guard was posted specifically to keep the peace in this stressful environment, but due to his "charming" personality, he often had the opposite effect.

When they reached the front of the line, the medical staff would check the inmate's ID card, find his prescription, and give it to him. To prevent medication from reaching the black market, the guard on duty would ensure that the inmate swallowed his pills then and there. The procedure for confirming they had actually done so was as thorough as it was degrading.

After the inmate swallowed the pill with a gulp of water to wash it down, he was required to open his mouth wide and present it for visual inspection by the guard. While the guard was examining his mouth, the inmate needed to move his tongue up and down and side to side to prove that the pill wasn't being concealed anywhere.

It's a particularly demeaning experience, often made worse by guards who overdo it, either out of zeal or spite. My cellmate at one time needed medication regularly and he would often come back to the cell fuming and humiliated. The guard on duty often made him feel more degraded by demanding that he repeatedly stick out his tongue and move it around on command.

At some point, they came up with an additional method of preventing the medication from being smuggled out. They crushed the pills and had the inmates swallow the powder. This stripped the pill of any outer coating, giving the inmate a bitter pill to swallow, literally and metaphorically. This also undid any time-release characteristics of the pills, at best an inconvenience, and in some cases rendering the pills ineffective or even harmful.

Initially, there were three pill lines scheduled: 7:00 a.m., 4:30 p.m., and 8:40 p.m. A few years after I arrived, this became another area which suffered deterioration because of prioritizing money over human beings. In a freely-admitted effort to save money, the 8:40 pill line was eliminated. The limited opportunities to take medication, until then an inconvenience, were now a real problem.

Many prisoners suffered from anxiety which affected their ability to fall asleep. For this, they were prescribed medication by the doctor or shrink. The 8:40 pill line was right before the nightly lock-in and they were able to take these sleeping pills right before they went to sleep. Now that this late distribution was eliminated, the latest they could get their sleeping pill was the 4:30 pill line—and remember, they weren't allowed to pick up the pills. They had to ingest them on the spot.

One inmate I knew, who had trouble sleeping, couldn't make this adjustment. He had things that he needed or wanted to do in the evenings, and taking the pills made him too drowsy to do anything. He couldn't give up the hours from 4:30 p.m. and on, so he decided to stop taking the pills altogether. I knew that the sleep deprivation he would suffer if he couldn't sleep was a real threat to his fragile mental state. I tried to talk him out of this decision, but he insisted that he would be able to calm his anxiety without the pharmaceutical assistance. After all, what choice did he have?

As it turned out, he found another choice, one which had a lasting effect on his life. A few months later, they did a shakedown in his cell and accused him of making alcohol. It seems he couldn't make it work unaided after all, and, being denied the pills at a reasonable time, turned to the other choice—highly illegal prison-concocted alcohol. This carried severe penalties and had a lasting impact on his file. Sometime later, he was again disciplined severely—they had found illicit pills in his cell, which he'd somehow acquired to fill the need they had created by functionally withholding the pills he needed in order to sleep. He was one of many in similar straits.

The prison saved a little money by eliminating a necessary pill line, and the staff member who suggested it might have even gotten a bonus for the suggestion, but it was this guy and people like him that ended up paying the price.

Dental Care

The dental care department had its own unit with a few small rooms, each outfitted with a standard dental chair, a small sink, and cabinets to hold supplies and equipment. It was perhaps a bit spare, but it looked more or less like what you'd expect from a modern dentist's office.

Watching the patients come and go, however, gave a more accurate and entirely different impression. A disproportionate number left with a bloody gauze filling the gaping hole left by their missing tooth. For many reasons, modern dentists only consider extraction as a last resort, but in a place called prison, it is one of the most common methods of dealing with a toothache—no tooth, no ache. One of the prisoners in my barrack told me that they extracted one tooth, they extracted another tooth, but he couldn't go back to the dental unit or he wouldn't be able to eat properly.

An unsettling psychological aspect of this procedure is that the extracted tooth is the property of the BOP. A Jewish inmate told me that when he had a tooth pulled, he asked for the tooth, only to be told, "The tooth doesn't belong to you, it belongs to us!"

It may seem odd that he asked for the tooth, but this was a man from whom everything had been taken, including his freedom. It's understandable that he instinctively held on to whatever he had left, as illogical as it might be out of context. The fact that they laid claim even to his teeth really substantiated what he was told (and was required to acknowledge with a signature) upon his arrival. As far as they were concerned, he was the property of the BOP.

This Yid was so traumatized by this exchange and experience that he avoided the dentist from that day on. When he began to feel pain in one of his molars, he chose to regularly swish with salt water as a feeble substitute for medical attention rather than relive that painful moment.

One day, I discovered that I couldn't eat on one side of my mouth without terrible pain. A visit to the dental unit revealed that one of my molars had cracked, which is normally handled with a dental crown, or cap. They don't do caps, I was told, but they would be happy to remove my tooth. When I firmly refused their generous offer, they insisted that I sign a paper that they were not to be held responsible for any infection and pain that might result, and sent me on my way.

I didn't suffer the pain and discomfort of the damaged molar for long. *Baruch Hashem*, I was miraculously freed not long thereafter and regained access to proper dental care. One of the first things I did, after the intense celebrations quieted a bit, was to visit a dentist who set up a lengthy schedule of visits to address all the neglected or mishandled aspects of my dental health.

CHAPTER NINETEEN
Staying Connected

Visits from Family and Friends

Some prefer to ignore or "forget" this, but every prison number represents an actual human being; someone's child, parent, spouse, or friend. They each have loved ones, and these relationships, although they've been so thoroughly disrupted, are very precious to the inmate and to their families. They are also critical to their mental and emotional wellbeing.

In fact, the forcible separation from loved ones is the most painful part of incarceration. Even Yosef Hatzaddik, who practically ruled Mitzrayim, wielding great power and living in the lap of luxury, was only complete when he was finally reunited with his father and his family.

The inmates feel, constantly and acutely, the pain of their loss in being separated from their family. Simple everyday interactions like seeing one's kids off to school in the morning, eating a meal together, or doing homework in the evenings, may feel ordinary or even sometimes difficult when they're a daily blessing, but the deep power and beauty in those moments is felt very strongly by those to whom they are denied.

Even more painful to the inmates is the pain that their loved ones suffer by their absence. The heaviest weight falls on their wives, who've lost their husbands and partners and carry the simultaneous burdens of fighting to restore them to freedom and of continuing a normal life for themselves and their children.

The burden of the children is not as heavy but, absorbing this blow during sensitive, formative years, they often suffer worst of all. Young children, in particular, need a strong relationship with their fathers as they grow and develop. A father is a source of guidance, of strength and stability, of wisdom and experience. He's always ready to catch them if they fall and help them learn from their experiences so they grow to face their mission in life with the ability to succeed.

Being denied the presence of a father is detrimental to children in ways they often don't even realize at the time, and the pain the father feels for this damage done to his innocent children far outweighs his pain and sorrow over his own suffering.

Baruch Hashem, this forcible separation was not a total separation. Even the BOP officially recognizes the importance of strong family and social ties and they have a number of policies and protocols created specifically to promote family connections. They often tout their efforts to keep families connected, on grounds of basic humanity and their positive effect on reform and rehabilitation.

A visiting room picture with my father *a"h*.

There were a few methods for interacting or connecting with family and friends, none of which were a real substitute for actual and ongoing presence, of course, and all of which were severely and often arbitrarily restricted.

The most precious form of interaction with loved ones is an actual visit. It's also the most difficult: It's difficult for the family to see the inmate in his sad state and environment, it's difficult for the inmate when his family sees him that way, and it's difficult for both when the visit ends and they must bid each other goodbye and go back to life on opposite sides of the barbed-wire fence.

With my loved ones in the visiting room.

A special moment in the visiting room with my youngest son, Uziel. He was only four years old when I was torn away from my family.

Although the parting is painful even for the adults and older children, they are at least able to look forward to the next visit to soften the blow. The smaller children are not. They simply don't understand why their father refuses to join them as they head back to the car for the drive home.

Some of the most difficult moments for me came when my youngest son would tug on my hand at the end of the visits. "Come, Tatty. Come!" he would plead. I tried to gently explain that I couldn't, pointing to the guards. "I don't care!" he would say. "Come!" I had no choice but to stay in my seat and watch my wife carry him, crying, to the door.

Painful as these moments were for all of us, the few hours of respite that sitting with my family brought were too precious to forgo. As *Yidden*, we were able to comfort ourselves with the knowledge that Hashem would surely reunite us and we eagerly awaited that day.

Before they could even face these emotional difficulties, they had to overcome the logistical difficulties involved in even making the visit.

Remotely located as it is, traveling to Otisville is quite an undertaking in and of itself and many simply couldn't make the trip. Those who could first had to deal with the bureaucracy. To be eligible to visit, the potential visitor had to fill out and submit a visitor information form, used by the BOP to conduct security and background checks. It could take weeks to receive the go-ahead.

Next, assuming the potential visitor was cleared to visit, the inmate had to have them added to his list of approved visitors before they were granted access. This list was arbitrarily limited to twenty-five people, no more than ten of whom may be friends or associates who are not related to the inmate.

This small allowance of cleared visitors was a big hassle for me at first. Like many Jewish inmates, I'm blessed with a large family and a twenty-five-people allowance wasn't nearly enough. The only way to enable them all to visit at some time was by cycling names off or on the visitor list as needed. It was a combination tightrope walk and juggling act to ensure that my loved ones could all get some time to visit. If my brother was on the East Coast and wanted to visit, I might have to take my son off the list temporarily so my brother could be added. Once he left, I would want to return my son's name to the list, so that he could continue coming with his family. All of this had to be done with the utmost delicacy so as not to irritate the counselor through whom all changes to the lists were made.

Over time, the inadequacy of my visitor allotment became clear and the officer in charge agreed to increase the size of my list to fifty. This made it a lot easier, but it didn't entirely eliminate the need to occasionally make temporary adjustments. That officer eventually left and his replacement informed me that this regulation never included immediate family to begin with!

This was an example of the disservice to the inmates caused by the general failure to introduce and properly explain the policies under which they live. Many of these policies were formulated to meet a recognized need or avoid undue strain or difficulty, but because they are not properly explained, the inmates often suffer more than they have to.

This new understanding of the regulation finally laid the entire hassle to rest and gave my whole family the ability to visit, which gave me much needed strength and support.

The list was a limit on the number of potential visitors. The number of actual visitors during each visit was also limited. At first, they only limited the number of adults, which they defined as anyone over sixteen, allowing only four adults at a time. The number of children was not limited, which was a *brachah* because it meant my family could come visit without making special arrangements.

A group picture in the visiting room with two of my sons and some *bachurim*.

Later, the number of children was also restricted to four, a targeted policy that only affected me and one other inmate. We were the only ones at Otisville who had more than four children at their visits. The change caused us great difficulty. Before this new rule, either or both parents could come with all their children, without making extra arrangements. This new restriction meant that some of the children had to stay behind, and that made it impossible for their parents to come without making arrangements for them. Either one parent needed to take off work and stay with the children who couldn't come, or they had to find and pay for a babysitter.

I brought this to the attention of the assistant warden at the next opportunity, during main line in the chow hall. Instead of rescinding the onerous rule, his solution was that I request special permission from the captain for additional children visitors whenever needed. If it was granted, I needed to take this permission to the counselor to enter it into the system and the children would be allowed in.

Baruch Hashem, they granted this waiver whenever it was requested, but this new process still reduced the visits I could receive. I didn't always know about a visit long enough in advance to catch the captain when he was available. There were times I couldn't get the waiver in time for the visit to happen at all. Even when I did, I could tell it was an annoying intrusion to both the captain and the counselor, who often openly grumbled about it and presumably held it against me.

Even with all the paperwork, clearances, lists, and group size restrictions worked out and the potentially hours-long drive factored in, a visit could still be impossible: Even an authorized visitor would only be allowed into the compound if the inmate they'd come to visit had sufficient "points."

Inmates were allotted twelve visiting points per month. Weekday visits cost the inmate a single point and weekend or holiday visits cost two. (Official legal or religious visits weren't deducted from the points.) When the inmate was out of points, visitors were turned away unless special permission was granted by the supervising officer on duty.

This system was occasionally abused. Not infrequently, a visitor would take time from their other responsibilities and make the long trip up to Otisville only to be told, incorrectly, that I had no more visiting points and they could not visit. When these instances were raised with the lieutenant in charge, they were invariably explained away as accidents or misunderstandings— innocent mistakes. I always let it go at that, but I'm convinced that it was often intentional, either to punish me for some imagined slight or out of sheer bigotry.

One Friday, my son Yossi came to visit and was told that he couldn't visit because I had insufficient points. Yossi knew that this was impossible—the amount of visiting days that had passed that month (excluding Shabbos) simply *could not* add up to twelve points. He showed the guard his calculation. To the guard's credit, he accepted that there was something wrong and reached out to his superior.

Yossi overheard the phone call and it became a point of discussion for weeks to come. "Regarding Rubashkin," he heard the guard say. "I know someone inside made a mistake and double charged him, but the system says that he's over the limit on his points. Should I go by what the system is saying and deny the visit or should I let him in?"

Baruch Hashem, the decision was made to allow the visit, but just contemplate that question! He was seriously considering making a decision on information he *knew* to be wrong, simply because that is what is in the "system." It sounds ridiculous, but, as the Ba'al Shem Tov instructs, we need to turn every observation inward and apply it to our *avodas Hashem*:

We all know the truth about the world—it's not really hard work or clever strategies that bring success, it's not really indulging our appetites that make us happy, and so on—but we keep looking at what the "system" says. We consider information that we *know* is wrong and we struggle to make the right decision. Should I take this meeting and miss Minchah with a *minyan*? Should I pursue forbidden fruit in order to be happy? These are not legitimate alternatives to be weighed—they are temptations based on known falsehoods! We need to grab hold of ourselves and remind ourselves that we know the system is wrong and we shouldn't even be considering its arguments!

Not every story ended well and there were many occasions when my family or friends made the long trip only to be turned away with the mistaken or dishonest claim that I didn't have the points. I wasn't unique in this respect and the visitors of other Jewish inmates had similar experiences. I'm not suggesting that the non-Jewish inmates did not, but I heard much fewer complaints about this from them.

Visitors were also turned away for other reasons, such as if their clothing violated Otisville policies. These included many reasonable restrictions but also unexpectedly forbade innocuous things like slippers, and my family often witnessed others being turned away for their attire. More than once, these visitors would drive to the nearest store to buy new shoes or clothes so they would be allowed to visit their loved one.

Visitors also needed to be able to pass through the sensitive metal detector, which frequently went off because of something as small as the clips sewn into a *sheitel*, for example. My mother actually didn't come for a few years because once, when she came, her *sheitel* set off the machine and they had harassed and intimidated her over it, leaving her frightened and reluctant to return.

When I was first transferred there, visiting days were scheduled for Sunday, Monday, Thursday, Friday, and Shabbos, as well as on legal holidays, from

8:00 a.m. until 2:45 p.m., more than six hours. Give or take, I should say—the clock in the visiting room was often set five minutes fast so the guards could end their visiting room duty a little earlier, at the expense of the inmates and their visitors.

Every hour spent with family or friends in the visiting room, apart from the value of being together, is also one hour less in a place called prison. Knowing this, they made every effort to visit and to be there from the moment the doors opened until the visiting hours were over.

Sometime in 2012, the new warden made an abrupt and extreme reduction in visitation. Under the new schedule, Monday and Thursday were no longer visiting days, leaving only Sunday, Friday, and Shabbos—a reduction of forty percent of the visiting time.[1]

For *Yidden* this was actually more than a fifty-percent reduction, since Shabbos is never an option and Friday wasn't a full visiting day during the winter months, when visitors have to leave with enough time to make it home before sunset.

Eliminating some of the visiting days had the predictable effect of overcrowding the visiting room on the remaining days, which resulted in the occasional unpleasantness. The officers had taken to turning visitors away without a visit if the room was at capacity or ejecting visitors already in the room in order to make space for new arrivals.

Once, the visiting room was at capacity and I had a visit ended abruptly in order to allow another inmate to receive visitors. I was told that my visit was chosen because the other visit they might have ended early involved visitors who'd traveled from out of state. It was painful and it was only necessary because of the reductions in visiting hours, but under the rules as they stood, I saw the justice in his visit being given priority. Unfortunately, when that same logic and fairness ought to have been applied to me, it wasn't.

Not three weeks later, I had two visitors from out of state—my sister Guttel flew in from Florida and my brother Heshy from Iowa. My sister arrived first, followed shortly thereafter by my wife. My brother Heshy was expected within a couple of hours, as were my son with some of his children.

You can imagine my dismay when we were approached by a guard and told that the room was too full to allow in waiting visitors and my visit was being

---

1. When this warden was replaced, Monday visits were restored.

terminated. I was far from the first in the visiting room that day, but they'd chosen to cancel my visit. As I always did, I first said "Okay," but I immediately followed that up by informing him that my sister had traveled from Florida to visit me, and my brother, who'd made the trip from Iowa, was waiting at the security checkpoint and hadn't even been in to see me yet. My understanding of protocol, based on direct personal experience, was that they considered those factors, and I asked him to double-check with the officer on duty.

A few minutes later, the guard returned and told us that the duty officer had instructed that my visit be terminated. He wouldn't even bring the lieutenant in to adjudicate the issue, which is the usual procedure when there is a dispute about visits. Through the large windows which gave a glimpse of the parking lot, my wife had seen our grandchildren arrive and that had opened up a new possibility: If the children were allowed in, we'd be entitled to use the "children's room." This would allow them to deduct my visitors from the visiting room capacity without wronging me or my loved ones who'd both traveled over a thousand miles.

Although the guard saw the merits of the idea, the duty officer didn't want to see it happen. My visitors were officially entitled to special consideration because they'd come from far away, but I hadn't and I wasn't. He simply had me removed from the room. Without an inmate with whom to visit, my visitors no longer had grounds to be there and were sent out. With nothing more to be done, my wife and my sister left. My grandchildren, who'd been waiting at security, also left disappointed, without even seeing me.

Ejected from the visiting room, I went to the chaplain to share my pain about what had happened and he brought the story to the lieutenant. Upon review, the lieutenant decided that the wrong decision had been made and notified my family that they would be allowed entry.

That only takes two sentences to describe but it took hours to accomplish and my wife, sister, and the children had already gone far enough away that they could not return in time. *Baruch Hashem*, Heshy was still in the area, and we managed to spend some time together, less than an hour, before he had to travel back to the Midwest.

The visiting room itself was a large L-shaped room. Along one side of the room were a few small rooms in which an inmate could have legally protected private discussions with his lawyers. There was also a small room with books and toys, the aforementioned children's room, where a single inmate could sit with his visitors if they included small children. The shared wall between each of these rooms and the main visiting room was made of glass, so they could be visually monitored by the guards at all times.

To be allowed access to the quieter, slightly-more-private room with the kids, an inmate was required to pass a special "parenting course." This course was "taught" by two inmates, a fellow nicknamed "Gifted" and his co-teacher— long-time residents of Otisville courtesy of armored car robbery.

I sat through this class for the benefit of my children and endured many hours ostensibly on the topic of parenting. Very little was actually said about parenting. Instead, the participants spent the time complaining bitterly about their relationships and the impossibilities prison added to the mix. More than one shared that they had only the slimmest hope that their children would even come to visit. The women accused them of abandoning their family by going to prison, and showed their anger by not allowing visits. What little discussion there was about parenting focused on dealing with an ex-spouse, which, in their lives, was sadly a large part of the task of parenting.

I felt bad for them—their lives and situations were truly tragic—but I didn't see how these sessions were helping anyone parent better, least of all me, for whom parenting was still only about helping a child grow to be a true *eved Hashem*, with the right *middos* and *hashkafos*. I stuck it out, thinking of the small bit of additional privacy my children would surely enjoy when we were allowed to use the children's room.

A facilitator occasionally sat in on these "classes." On one such occasion, one of the inmates was saying that his "baby's mother" was accusing him of not taking an interest in the boy's education. "But how can I help him with his homework or talk to his teacher," he complained, correctly, "if I'm only allowed three hundred phone minutes a month?!" (That was the maximum amount of phone minutes an inmate could buy each month.) The cost per minute was also prohibitive, but he didn't even bring that up because, even for those who could afford it, the amount of minutes is nowhere near enough.

The facilitator apparently only had a limited number of pre-programmed responses and the inmate's mention of her trigger words "education" and "homework," set one of them off. She launched into a speech on the importance of our children's education and of our involvement with both the child and their teachers to ensure they grow up properly. Her prepared speech made no mention of the very real obstacles the man had brought up which made achieving those goals impossible, and I couldn't resist pressing the issue. "But how?!" I asked, gently but firmly. "How can we do these things without any real amount of phone time?"

"Write a letter!" was her glib response. Clearly, she was just there for the paycheck or to feel like she was helping but wasn't offering any real guidance or support. No one dignified her suggestion of "parenting by post" with a reaction.

Eventually, I received my "diploma" from this course and I was able to put the whole thing behind me. They built a whole ceremony around the graduation, public evidence of their commitment to family ties and rehabilitation. The prisoners' wives and children were invited to an event where the importance of family interaction was emphasized and some games were played.

When it was all over, the only thing that changed for those who participated was the small perk in the visiting room when the children could make a visit, a rare occurrence for most. The prison's commitment to family interaction didn't extend to any substantive changes that might allow a father to be a greater presence in his child's life on a regular basis, such as easing up on phone restrictions or even reverting to the old system, which did not restrict the minutes of the phone calls.

The visiting room looked out at the barbed-wire-topped fence at the edge of the compound. A small yard stood between the visiting room and the fence, and half of that yard, paved and fenced in, was accessible from the visiting room. It served as a patio, and allowed inmates and their visitors to sit outside around circular picnic tables during the warmer months. They even allowed us to walk around that area together and enjoy the sunshine and the breeze. This was a much more pleasant setting for a visit, despite the shadow cast by the tall fences and coils of barbed wire, and I made use of it whenever possible.

Spreading the inmates over a larger area meant adding an extra guard, and a few years after I arrived, they decided to save that extra expense by no longer allowing inmates to have visits outdoors.

Near the visitors' entrance, there was a relatively small nook, strictly off limits to the inmates themselves, which held five vending machines. These machines sold drinks, snacks, and packaged meals for the visitors, inmates, and guards who spent hours in the visiting room.

Outside of the vending machine nook, a bit further along the wall of the visiting room, there was a special vending machine which sold frozen treats, and it played a role in a very special story. My son Uziel, eight years old at the time, was visiting. It was a summer day, and the visiting room was stiflingly hot.

Mr. Klein, of Klein's Ice Cream, would often come to visit a different Jewish inmate at Otisville. Not long before this story, he'd promised Uziel that he would arrange for *chalav Yisrael* ice cream to be added to the machine. Since then, Uziel had been impatiently waiting for this exciting new development. The unusual heat that day was an added reminder.

He noticed one of the other Jewish visitors buy an ice cream bar to cool off, and he tugged on my sleeve. "Tatty, look! There's kosher ice cream in the machine. Can we buy one?" I looked over and saw that the ice cream in question was a *chalav stam* product, not Klein's.

"Sorry, Uziel," I said. "I don't think Mr. Klein got his ice cream in the machine yet. That's *chalav stam* ice cream."

"I want ice cream!" he kept insisting. "Why can't I have ice cream?! I don't care!" We reminded him that our family eats only *chalav Yisrael* and it just wasn't an option, but he couldn't drop it.

I tried to reason with him. "After you leave, on your way home, Mommy will stop in Monroe and buy you an ice cream," I promised, but he refused. He wanted an ice cream *"now!"*

He was digging in and working himself up, and more than once he got up to walk around the room in frustration. The guard called me over and threatened to terminate the visit if Uziel wouldn't calm down, so I tried bribing my son. "Mommy will buy you *two* ice creams!" Nothing doing. *"Five* ice creams!" He wouldn't back down. *"Ten* ice creams!!" I was getting nowhere with bribes, and his agitated behavior earned me another warning from the guard.

I couldn't reason with him and I clearly couldn't bribe him—I was out of ideas. Then I said to myself, "Why don't I try speaking to him the same way I speak to *myself*, when *I* have a *nisayon*? Why don't I speak to his *neshamah*?"

"Listen, Uziel," I said. "You're hot and you want an ice cream. I understand. You have two options: You can go over to that machine and buy an ice cream that's not up to our kashrus standards, and *you'll* be happy but Hashem will *not* be happy. Or, option two, you can wait an hour and buy a properly kosher ice cream in Monroe—then you'll be happy *and* Hashem will be happy! In fact, Hashem will be *very* happy!"

He took a minute to digest this thought and then I saw him visibly relax. He just totally switched gears, and let go of his frustrated insistence. He abruptly brought up a totally unrelated topic of conversation, as kids do, and the words "ice cream" didn't come up again that day.

This incident was a tremendous lesson to me. Although we're all aware of our *neshamah*, we usually see things from the distinct perspective of our body, the perspective of the world. We often tackle our problems from that perspective, and it's only when we fail or flounder that we reach for the perspective of Torah, the perspective of our *neshamah*.

We need to remember that, at our very foundations, we are *neshamos*. Our children are *neshamos*. We should learn to see the world around us and the *nisyonos* we face from *that* perspective, the true perspective. Ten ice creams couldn't buy Uziel's cooperation, and he wasn't persuaded by any explanations, but when he considered that Hashem would be unhappy with one option and would be very happy with the other, he chose to do the thing that would make Hashem happy. This is an important lesson in general, and it's also an important key to *emunah* and *bitachon*. Our *neshamah* sees clearly and already has *emunah* and *bitachon*. Any shortcoming in those areas are the result of seeing things from the natural perspective, the perspective of the world. By realizing that we are truly a *neshamah*, and accepting the truth that it sees, we claim the strong *emunah* and *bitachon* which is our *neshamah's* inheritance, its true nature.

Back to the visiting room. Visitors were allowed to bring money for use at these vending machines, but nothing larger than a five-dollar bill. Inmates were, of course, prohibited from handling the money.

The food was of the quality you might expect from a vending machine, which meant it was considerably better than the food I was eating from the chow hall. Using one of the two microwaves located nearby, the food could be properly heated, which was also a treat for me during the time before I received permission to take my meals to the barrack.

Naturally, only a limited amount of space was designated for kosher food. The kosher food was of marginally better quality than the non-kosher offerings and many non-Jewish visitors chose to buy the kosher food. This caused the kosher slots to empty quicker than anticipated and there was often nothing at all for the *Yidden* to eat.

There was obviously no microwave dedicated for kosher food, which made warming up the food a little tricky. The food packages were always shrink-wrapped, but the heat could cause the plastic to melt and expose it to the non-kosher microwave. My family's solution was to place the package inside a gallon-size Ziploc bag and protect the Ziploc from fusing to the shrink wrap and melting by wrapping the food package itself in a layer of paper towels. To their credit, the guards allowed them to bring in these empty plastic bags, although visitors were generally permitted to bring in only money for the machines.

Along the back wall of the visiting room, two or three guards sat on a raised platform behind a desk, monitoring the room directly and using screens fed by monitoring devices on the ceiling at strategic spots around the room. Occasionally one of them would stand up and walk around the room looking for violations of the visiting room rules.

I received a personal introduction to these rules and their application during one of my family's first visits to Otisville. My son Moishie came along to visit, possibly his first face-to-face visit since my incarceration. Moishie is autistic and speaks mostly in single-word statements. Forcibly separated from me for so long, he craved the affection and connection that he wasn't capable of expressing or understanding in words. I showered him with hugs and kisses, and communicated with him in the unique vocabulary we'd developed over the years.

Abruptly, I was summoned to the guard desk. The guard on duty reprimanded me for excessively kissing and hugging Moishie, and insisted that I limit myself to "a single restrained kiss" at the beginning and at the end of the visit.

Upset, I went to the captain and described to him the damage this would do to my son. In his condition, he wouldn't be able to understand why I'm withholding the affection that he needed and was asking for. Although the reflex of officers was usually to support the guards in order to maintain discipline and respect for authority, in this case, *baruch Hashem*, the captain understood and stepped in to resolve the situation. The *Chovos Halevavos* writes that Hashem sends His salvation through good people, and this upstanding captain was Hashem's messenger many times and in many areas.

There were a number of other restrictions on visiting room behavior. Like all the prison's restrictions, these were enforced selectively, and occasionally conspicuously so.

During one visit, one of my children, then around ten years old, was reclining on my lap as we chatted. The officer in charge at the monitoring station beckoned to me and warned me that this was not allowed, ordering me to ensure that it did not happen again. He even made a note of this "violation" in his book. I returned to my seat, explained to my puzzled family why I'd been summoned, and tried to brush it off, picking up our conversation where we'd been interrupted.

As *hashgachah pratis* would have it, a non-Jewish inmate was sitting with his visiting wife and son not far from where we were. His son had curled up and fallen asleep across both their laps. It was not unusual to see children and occasionally even adults nodding off in the visiting room. Many visitors woke up very early to make the long drive to the remote village of Otisville in order to make the most of the visit, and it was a tiring trip.

My daughter noticed that they were sitting exactly as we'd been sitting, without comment by the guards, and she wondered out loud why we were being treated differently.

I didn't confront the guards right away, certain that they would just claim they hadn't noticed. Instead, I waited to see what would happen. A full hour passed with no interference on the part of the guards, when suddenly, Hashem made it much easier to make my case. The officer who'd reprimanded me walked over to the microwave to warm his lunch, a spot from which he had a clear view of this family. As he waited for the food to warm, he turned around, scanning the room. Returning to his station, he even walked past their chairs.

Some more time passed, still with no comment to this family. It was undeniable. He wasn't just strictly but consistently applying these callous regulations. He had singled me out. Still, I held my peace.

Then he summoned me again to the guard station. A visitor to another Jewish inmate, who'd been sitting not far from us, had been using a Chumash and left it on the table near me—a lapse in order and cleanliness which they were going to hold against me. At this point, they'd gone too far. They were looking for reasons to write me up and I needed to point it out and put a stop to it.

"I'm not looking to make trouble," I told him, "but what do you have against me?"

"Nothing," he claimed.

Moving out of his line of sight, I silently pointed to where the non-Jewish family was sitting, still cradling their sleeping son on their laps. He understood immediately.

Of course, his first response was, "Oh, I didn't notice that. I would have said something to him, too!"

I told him that they'd been sitting like that for over an hour, during which time he'd surely seen them, especially when he'd walked right by them going to and from the microwave and during the five minutes he'd stood right in front of them while his food warmed.

I assured him that I didn't want to escalate the situation or formally complain by writing him up, but I'd noticed that I was being singled out. I only wanted to be left alone to connect with my family and to serve Hashem without discrimination or nastiness.

He got the message. *Baruch Hashem*, that was the last time I had to deal with this kind of behavior from this particular guard.

Among the prison jobs assigned to inmates was the job of authorized photographer. This inmate was issued a pocket-sized digital camera during work hours, and he would take pictures of inmates upon request. He was paid by the inmates with "picture tickets," which they purchased from the commissary for a dollar a picture. The photographer was a regular presence in the visiting room, where inmates often paid him to take pictures of them posing with their loved ones against a painted backdrop that was placed in the visiting room for this purpose.

The guy assigned to this job was fairly accommodating. He was usually willing to take a few snaps until he captured one that was satisfactory, deleting the unused ones and keeping only one to be used in exchange for the picture ticket.

The digital images were carefully reviewed by security before they were approved for release. One of the things I know they looked for in the photos was any hint of the security elements of the compound. The photographer occasionally asked us to move slightly so that the barbed-wire fence would not be included in the picture and result in it getting rejected.

The security benefits of this censorship were small. Pictures of the fence are readily available online and it's even partially included in the official picture on their website—but there were other benefits. Censoring these pictures helped them maintain their image. The pictures he took looked almost ordinary, with no hint of the suffering and hardships that the subjects endured. If not for the khaki uniform, they could have been taken anywhere.

The visiting room pictures were treasured by the inmates because they were mementos not only of their loved ones, but of those precious few moments they could still spend together. These pictures, as well as those taken outside the visiting room, were often sent home. They were the only way families could have an up-to-date visual memento of their husband, father, son, or brother.

With the help of loving and caring fellow Jews, my family moved to the East Coast not long after I was transferred to Otisville. With the exception of one son and his family in Florida, this meant that my whole family was now within a two-and-a-half-hour drive. My parents also lived in Brooklyn, as did many of my relatives and friends. Although the trip was difficult, I was blessed by Hashem in that I never lacked for visitors and the points restricting visits were the only thing preventing more visits.

Generally, the visits were a source of strength and inspiration and I appreciated them greatly. There were, however, some people who came to offer their sympathy and condolences, a *nichum aveilim* kind of visit. They would sit and commiserate with my terrible plight, expressing their pain that I was so unjustly imprisoned and had been sentenced to sit for so many years. I valued the *ahavas Yisrael* that prompted them to visit, but this was exactly the opposite of the truth and the reality that I worked so hard to inhabit. The clarity we reach through *emunah* and *bitachon* needs to be constantly defended, and these visits made me work a little harder to hold on to my own clarity as well as to try to share it with them.

Inmates whose families lived very far away, or who were physically close but were not on close terms—and this was unfortunately a large majority of the inmates—received visits only very rarely. Some received none at all. It always warmed my heart to see people step up and step in for the missing family and friends, volunteering to make the difficult trip to offer emotional support to these isolated or forgotten people.

There were official clergymen from various groups who came to visit the non-Jewish inmates, as there were for, *l'havdil*, the Jewish inmates. There were also an incredible number of regular *Yidden*, not with any organization or volunteer group, that came as visitors. They came simply to raise the spirits of a fellow Jew they'd never met, who the wider society had rejected and isolated.

The number of Jewish inmates receiving visits was totally out of proportion with their percentage of the Otisville population.

One of these distinguished visitors was the Sadigura Rebbe *zt"l*, who came to Otisville to offer *chizuk* to the *Yidden* there. After spending time in the camp, he was allowed to visit us in the prison and we were able to *daven* Minchah together. I made my way to the chapel and prepared for *davening*. I grabbed my *gartel* and stood by the door awaiting his arrival. It meant so much to me that such a person was coming to breathe oxygen into my *neshamah*, that when I saw him I broke out in a wide smile. We sat and spoke for a while on *inyanei bitachon* and when it was time for him to leave, we danced a little as we sang.

With Hashem's help he took a liking to me and he phoned his relative, the well-known *askan* Rabbi Yitzchok Shapira of London and Tel Aviv, and asked him to get involved in helping me win my freedom. The next time he was in America, Rabbi Shapira reached out to Rabbi Pinchos Lipschutz and they met to explore how he could help get me out of the place called prison. He agreed to reach out to noted attorney Alan Dershowitz, and two days later they met in his home and convinced him to take on the case. Rabbi Shapira covered all the associated costs. I am eternally grateful to him, and when I was in Israel I ate a celebratory reception in his home with my wife.

I maintained a relationship with the Sadigura Rebbe until his untimely passing, visiting him in Brooklyn, Bnei Brak, and in California, where he was undergoing treatment. The last time we met, he spoke of the critical importance of teaching *emunah* and *bitachon* in yeshivos and he encouraged my efforts in this area. His friendship and support was overwhelming, and his loss pains me until this day.

In addition to these precious volunteers, the chaplain, in partnership with *askanim* and organizations, occasionally organized visits by spiritual leaders to uplift the *Yidden* of Otisville. Very respected people came under these programs, including a number of *rabbanim* and *admorim*, and they had a profound impact even on those who had not come from *frum* or chassidic communities and didn't consider themselves observant.

Occasionally, prestigious and holy people also came for personal one-on-one visits. I merited visits from the *rav* and *rosh kollel* of the central Lubavitch *kollel*, Rabbi Heller, and from the *rosh yeshivah* of Beth Medrash Govoha, Rav Yerucham Olshin. I was also visited by the executive vice president of Agudas Yisrael of America, Reb Chaim Dovid Zwiebel, and the rabbinic administrator of the OU, Rabbi Menachem Genack, among others.

Reb Yosef Ostreicher was instrumental in arranging the visit by the *rosh yeshivah*, Rav Yerucham Olshin. I awaited this visit with great anticipation,

The precious picture with Rav Olshin which displays his tremendous *ahavas Yisrael* and the lengths he went to, to give *chizuk* to me and my family.

and I was sure it would be a source of real *chizuk*. Upon his arrival, the *rosh yeshivah* apologized to me that he would only be able to stay for twenty minutes. He had to return to Lakewood to attend a sudden *levayah* of a relative, *lo aleinu*. I was very touched that he had even come— Lakewood is a solid three-hour drive from Otisville, and he undertook the tiring six-hour round-trip for a twenty-minute visit, just to offer *chizuk* to a fellow Jew he'd never met. Not only that, but he ended up coming back for a second time to make up for this abbreviated visit. What *gaonus* in *chessed*!

Something happened during the second visit which was a true example of *ahavas Yisrael*. At the security entrance, the guards insisted that the *rosh yeshivah* remove his hat and leave it with them while in the visiting room. This was a real affront to his dignity and that of those he represents, but he felt that the benefit I would derive from his visit was more important. Instead of engaging in a futile debate, he acquiesced so he could get to the visit.

He shared words of encouragement and *divrei Torah* on *emunah* and *bitachon* which inspire me until today. My son Yossi was there and I wanted him to have the memory of the *rosh yeshivah* visiting me. I asked the *rosh yeshivah* to take a picture with us, not realizing that he was not wearing his hat. He instinctively put his hand to his head and I quickly realized my mistake. It was unbecoming for the *rosh yeshivah* to be pictured without his hat. I apologized and withdrew my request, but the *rosh yeshivah* insisted that we go ahead and take a picture together. To him, the *chizuk* this would give me and my family outweighed every other consideration.[2]

---

2. Upon my release, the first place I visited outside of New York was Lakewood, New Jersey. It was a huge source of *chizuk* and support to me and I wanted to thank them. I visited Rav

Connecting by Phone

After an in-person visit, the phone provides the next best form of connection with loved ones. You miss out on their physical presence, their body language, the sight of their smile, and the feeling in their eyes, but at least you can hear their voice, which communicates more heart and connection than the written word ever could.

The phone was actually *superior* to physical visits in one important way: It allowed the inmate, in a very limited sense, to go "visit" their loved ones. Family or community celebrations of special life events, like a birthday, wedding, or graduation, couldn't come to Otisville but, using the phone, it was still possible for the inmate to take part, in a small way, in the larger celebration.

During the time I was in a place called prison, my immediate family celebrated two bar mitzvos, a wedding, the birth of a number of grandchildren, and even a few *brissim*. We tried—and failed—to arrange furloughs for some of them, as I will describe later, and at each of these *simchos*, my only possible participation was via the phone. The calls were severely limited in duration, cutting off after fifteen minutes. If that wasn't enough, twice or three times during each phone call, a recording would interrupt the call, announcing, "This is a call from a federal prison." This was a painful reminder even during a regular call, and it was absolutely heartbreaking during a family *simchah*. Nonetheless, I was grateful to Hashem for giving me the ability to participate in this small way, when I would otherwise have none.

Each barrack had only four phones, which could be used whenever the cell doors were open. To use the phone, the inmate would first enter the personal PIN number linked to his prison ID, enter a phone number from his list of thirty cleared numbers, and then speak his name so the voice recognition system could confirm his identity. This was to prevent inmates from using someone else's account to get more than his allotted phone time or to avoid or confuse the officials monitoring his calls.

For a time, I was assigned to cell 217, which was very close to the phones. Some inmates had trouble remembering to use their indoor voices and I was subjected to many of the louder conversations. One rainy day, I heard someone

Yerucham Olshin and Rav Malkiel Kotler in their homes and was overwhelmed by the warmth with which they treated me. The *achdus* my case generated was a major source of *chizuk* to me while I was away and still today. I had never been to Lakewood before and was treated like a brother by all I met.

saying "rainy" loudly and repetitively, his voice sounding increasingly agitated with each repetition. I couldn't imagine why the rain was bothering him so much, being inside, but I chalked it up to the effects of incarceration and didn't think much of it.

The next day was a nice sunny day, so you can imagine my surprise when I again heard the frustrated voice wafting through the cell door, repeatedly saying "rainy!" I got up to see who was talking and realized it was a guy named Rainey. My curiosity was now replaced by commiseration. The poor fellow was being tortured by the voice recognition system which would not recognize his name and allow the call to go through.

This was a problem I unfortunately experienced myself. For some reason, the name "Sholom Rubashkin" gave this system trouble. At first, almost every time I called, an electronic woman's voice kept apologetically informing me that she didn't recognize my name and insisting that I repeat it. She wasn't the most patient type, and after the third time she would just disconnect, forcing me to repeat the whole process of entering the PIN code and phone number so I could try my name again.

The recording to which they matched the name was made as part of the intake process, during the days immediately after the inmate's arrival. As you can imagine, the tone and emotion in their voice was often heightened or strained. Whatever the cause, persuading the machine that I was Sholom Rubashkin was a struggle until I accidentally discovered that taking a gulp of water immediately before saying my name somehow made it match. I started bringing a cup of water with me to the phone, and things went a little smoother from then on.

As soon as the call connected, the clock would begin ticking. Quite a few inmates would bring a literal clock, a wristwatch or stopwatch if they had one, so they could see it tick and keep track of the time. This was important for a number of reasons.

Firstly, inmates are limited to only three hundred minutes of phone usage a month and unused minutes are not carried over to the next month. That works out to just under ten minutes a day on average. This is obviously not enough to maintain the critical relationships with family, especially for inmates with larger families or children in school.

If an inmate took the time to properly participate in a family discussion or deliberation, he would possibly find himself without any minutes left to call and participate in equally important discussions later in the month. If he allowed himself the luxury of spending a few more minutes talking to his wife, he might run out of minutes he needs to call his child or sibling.

The inmate can't even use functionality like conference calling or three-way calling to speak to his family as a group, because this is strictly prohibited and would result in the loss of phone privileges for a few months.

Keeping the time was also important in order to anticipate when the call would be cut off, so the inmate could end the call gracefully instead of being caught mid-sentence. Regardless of how many monthly minutes remained, each phone call was limited to fifteen minutes, at which point it would abruptly end to allow others to use the phone. To ensure that, in fact, someone *else* got the phone, that inmate's PIN code would not even work again for another half hour. This made it impossible to call back and finish your thought, even if no one else was waiting for the phone.

But perhaps the most important reason for most inmates to carefully count the minutes and seconds spent on the phone was the inexcusably high cost of phone calls, another example of the outsized role money plays in so many parts of the prison system. Inmates (most of whom, remember, are paid twenty to forty cents an *hour*) are charged twenty-one cents a *minute* to call anyone out of the local area of the prison, and a whopping one dollar per minute to call international. If an inmate went even one second into a minute, it was charged as a full minute—hence the stopwatches.

One prisoner actually broke down crying, describing to me the huge personal cost he paid for his phone calls to his elderly mother, who lived outside of the US. Every minute he spent on the phone meant a whole dollar less that he could use on the food, toiletries, and random items that might make his life a bit more bearable. Knowing what it meant to his mother, he made the calls anyway. The cost that was extracted from him for expressing his dedication to his mother in such a small but meaningful way—in the United States, in the twenty-first century—was a personal tragedy and a national disgrace.

Connecting by Post

Mail provides the next best form of connection with loved ones. You may not be in each other's presence or even hear the emotion in each other's voice, but you can at least read each other's words.

Mail was not as difficult as a visit and not as restricted as the phone. It was actually the only way of staying in touch with any real frequency and at any real length. It was also the only method of communication that was not restricted to a small list of family and friends and it enabled me to interact with the many precious *Yidden* around the country and around the world who wrote either to give me encouragement or because they faced their own challenges and wanted some encouragement from me.

This contact meant a lot to me for many reasons, not least among them the ability that it gave me to have a positive impact on the lives of others, something a place called prison usually denies a person.

All mail was processed in the mail room. Each envelope or package was opened and carefully scrutinized to make sure it didn't contain any contraband. If they found anything they didn't like, they would confiscate it or return the mail to the sender. The ever-changing list of what would and would not be allowed kept everyone guessing. At one point, they decided that crayon markings in a drawing by a toddler were henceforth to be considered a menace to the institution and the precious children's heartfelt artwork was returned.

The inmates assigned to the mail room would then divide the mail by barrack, and the guard assigned to that barrack would be given a canvas sack of mail to distribute. The guard would bring the mailbag to the common area of the barrack and announce, "Mail call!" This announcement always brought the inmates in a hurry. They would gather around the guard as he picked out envelopes one at a time and called out the name of the recipient, each hoping that their name would be called and they would receive word from someone who cared about them enough to write.

I received an unusually large amount of mail, sent by *Yidden* all over the country and occasionally from abroad. The letters were written by individuals of all ages and from all communities, and were full of love, concern, and encouragement. They told me how they were *davening* for my freedom and doing mitzvos in my *zechus*. Many teachers sent envelopes which included letters from each of their classes.

Some Torah and Jewish periodicals and newspapers also arrived in the mail, sent by their publishers or by people who felt I would benefit from their contents. I was never a man for newspapers, but I made sure to read the *Yated*, published by my dear friend Reb Pinchos Lipschutz, when it arrived.

The letters meant so much to me that I never threw one out. I kept every single letter. When I had too many to keep in the cell, I would put them in a box and mail them home.

Touched by these precious *Yidden*, I made every effort to respond to each one, but it quickly became clear that it would be impossible to keep up with the volume of letters. I decided to prioritize the letters from schoolchildren and began ongoing correspondence with a few classes. Once I had responded to those, I tried to answer the people I felt most needed to hear back immediately or who were due special consideration for one reason or the other.

It was very gratifying and encouraging to receive so much mail from friends and supporters. In the dark pit that is a place called prison, a letter from someone who cares enough to write is an emotional lifeline which helps an inmate lift himself up. It almost doesn't matter what's written in the letter. I had the added benefit that the letters that I received were full of *ahavas Yisrael, divrei Torah*, and words of encouragement rooted in Torah, *emunah*, and *bitachon*.

My good fortune didn't go unnoticed. When the guard distributing the mail called out the names of the happy recipients, my name came up again and again, often many times in a row. Other inmates were lucky to get even one letter—many walked away disappointed that their name was not called at all, and a greater number of inmates didn't even bother gathering around for mail distribution, so certain were they that no one had sent them anything.

Some of them began to resent me for receiving so much mail. One inmate started calling out, "Rubashkin!" before the guard even got his hand all the way out of the bag with an envelope. Once, when the guard read my name on a number of successive envelopes, another inmate spat out in disgust, "Why don't you just give him the whole bag?!"

One inmate came out and challenged me about this directly. "Hey, man!" he called to me one day in the common area after a mail call. "Why you taking all the mail, man?"

I wasn't sure what to say to that. "If I get less letters, is anyone else going to get any more? Am I stealing letters written to someone else?"

In a flash of inspiration, I held out a letter I'd just opened, spreading it out so he could see the whole page. "Look at this—it's written in Hebrew! If you got my mail, you wouldn't even be able to *read* it! Besides, even someone who *does* speak the language wouldn't get anything out of taking my mail. Whatever feelings are written in the letter are directed at *me*. They would be totally meaningless and wouldn't apply to anyone else!"

He shrugged and muttered something inaudibly as he wandered off, but clearly there were hard feelings going around. Hard feelings can quickly turn into harsh actions and I felt it would be safer to avoid the mail distribution. *Baruch Hashem*, my cellmate agreed to pick up my mail for me, and my absence from the "ceremony" somehow made it easier for the others to tolerate the volume of my mail.

The danger had subsided, and I learned a valuable lesson which stayed with me and provided clarity and consolation in the most difficult moments. We sometimes look at the lives of other people and contrast them with the details of our own lives. Why do I have to struggle financially? we might ask ourselves. Why can't I be well off like So-and-so? Why do I have to go through the hardships of legal proceedings or even incarceration? Why can't I be left alone like others around me?

Such complaints are common; I'm sure you don't need me to provide more examples.

My exchange with this inmate gave me the clarity to decisively address all these complaints in one stroke: My life and everything I experience is like my mail, written specifically for me and sent to me by Hashem. The life of the person next to me is *his* mail, written specifically for *him* and sent to him by Hashem. Trading something in your life, even a difficulty, for something in someone else's life, even something that looks like an advantage, makes as much sense as reading heartfelt professions of love and friendship directed at someone else.

Hashem's letter to me, the experiences of my life, are the missions He assigns to me. At one point, He put me in the position of a businessman and a community leader. That might sound prestigious or glamorous, but believe me when I tell you that it wasn't easy. I don't only mean the time and energy required to fill those roles; I mean the challenge of never losing sight, in the midst of all that activity, of what Hashem wanted me to do, and never forgetting that everything was His doing. It was hard work. *Baruch Hashem*, I was successful, and in my beliefs and choices I brought Hashem's presence and His will into the company and the community.

When I'd found the strength and clarity to overcome those difficulties, growing in my connection to Hashem and filling that corner of the world with His presence, my mission changed. I was now tasked with seeing Hashem's hand in the loss of the things I'd built, and in the painful separation from my family and community—which, according to the natural order, would likely continue for decades. I needed to hold on to my connection to Him in very challenging circumstances and in the face of very plausible arguments from my *yetzer hara.* I needed to find and show Hashem's presence in this new corner of the world, a corner that seemed to deny His presence emphatically.

In other words, every challenge and difficulty I faced was written specifically for me, so I could accomplish the things that Hashem created me to accomplish. My incarceration wasn't just an arbitrary occurrence that could be swapped out of my life without effect. Without that experience, I wouldn't face the difficult darkness I was facing and, as a result, I wouldn't find the overpowering light, clarity, and connection to Hashem that helped me survive and that showed that He is present even in a place called prison.

Trading that experience for the life of someone else, who did not face this experience, would deprive me—and the many who were inspired by my experiences—of that *kedushah* and of that strengthening of *emunah* and *bitachon.* I would have lost my own precious mail from Hashem. In exchange, I would have received someone else's mail—experiences that have no relevance to my mission in life and that grant me no opportunity to serve my Creator and reveal the capabilities He has hidden within my *neshamah.*

(Of course, we *daven* that our difficulties be resolved and replaced with abundant *brachah,* but that's not a request for someone else's mail. What we are requesting is a *brachah* that can be written into our own mail—a *brachah* that doesn't avoid our mission, but that facilitates it and eases its completion.)

Another aspect of our individual lives that is similar to personal mail: Just like my Hebrew letter would have been incomprehensible to any of those envious inmates, if I would receive benefits designed for someone else, they would be "incomprehensible" to me. I would not find happiness in having their wealth or comforts, since those things would have no role in my *neshamah's* mission, which is the real source of true and lasting happiness.

This insight was not just a comfort in the face of adversity. It was a source of confidence and tremendous joy. Realizing that everything in my life was personal mail from Hashem gave me the certainty that I had the strength to overcome every challenge. After all, Hashem would certainly not give me a mission without also giving me everything I needed to accomplish it. Knowing that every success brought *nachas* to Hashem also infused every aspect of my life with *simchas hachaim,* even and *especially* the parts that were difficult.

Legal Correspondence

Even after conviction, a person is entitled to confidential communication with his lawyer, so that legal strategy and information can be discussed without it ending up in the wrong hands. Instead of being opened and processed like all the other mail, inmates were informed when legal mail arrived. They needed to go to the mail room, show their ID, and sign that they had received the mail.

I was first transferred to Otisville not long before Tishrei, the month of Yamim Tovim. Rosh Hashanah and Yom Kippur came and went and the joyous Yom Tov of Sukkos arrived. Celebrating *Zman Simchaseinu* in a prison cell doesn't come naturally, but with Hashem's help, I was able to overcome the feelings that the cell and the prison were designed to evoke and *daven* and sing Hallel with sincere feelings of joy and gratitude to Hashem.

One of the days of Sukkos, while I was *davening*, I was notified that I'd received legal mail. As a matter of halachah, I wasn't allowed to pick up mail on Yom Tov. I didn't even want to think about mail on Yom Tov, especially not *legal* mail. The legal fight was a struggle conducted on the world's terms. It was only done to comply with Hashem's instructions to act within nature but, even so, it was an intrusion on Yom Tov and a contradiction to the hard-won tranquility and joy I'd achieved by rising *above* the world's terms. I removed the whole existence of this mail from my mind and continued *davening*.

Suddenly, the door to the cell burst open, and the mail room officer barged inside, shouting my name. "Rubashkin! I found you!" he exclaimed. "You can't hide from me!" It was his responsibility to ensure that inmates received their legal mail. Some inmates had once avoided picking up their legal mail and later claimed they hadn't received it, blaming him and his office. To counter these people, he took to personally making certain that everyone picked up their legal mail promptly.

I was in the middle of Hallel when he burst in, so I couldn't even respond. Instead, I motioned to him that I was praying and would be with him shortly. In a miraculous reversal of prison roles, he willingly stood and waited for me, muttering under his breath about inmates and their mail.

I finished Hallel and respectfully explained that I couldn't sign for the mail because it was a Jewish holiday. He could confirm this by looking at the official calendar which showed religious holidays. I assured him that I wasn't one of those inmates who wouldn't show and then claim I never got my mail—I would come in the next day and sign for the mail and write and sign a note that the delay was due to my holiday and not any failing on his part.

He accepted my explanation and assurances and calmed down. With an agreeable, "I'll see you tomorrow," he turned and left the cell. Of course, I kept my word and went to him the next day. I also made sure, from then on, to give notice to him and to the lieutenant whenever there was a holiday coming up and I couldn't sign for mail. He took this as a general rule which applied to all Jews and didn't bother any of the *Yidden* on Yom Tov from then on.

One day, during the mail call in the barrack, when personal mail was distributed, I was handed an envelope which had been sent to me by my lawyers. It had been treated as personal mail and opened. There was nothing confidential about this particular letter, but it was very concerning that they'd opened legal mail, which was supposed to be sacrosanct. If I did nothing, they might do it again, perhaps when something confidential actually *was* being communicated.

I went to the mail room and showed the officer that the envelope was clearly marked "legal and confidential." Why had it been opened and sent through the regular mail channels? As is customary, the first response was that it was actually *my* fault and that there was some previously undisclosed hoop to jump through. If I'd only done something differently, my rights would not have been violated.

Apparently, the return address of my lawyer's firm and the clearly marked "legal and confidential" were not enough to clearly establish that the contents of the envelope were actually both legal in nature and confidential, to be opened only in the presence of the inmate.

The law firm's name needed to be followed by the name of the lawyer, with the title "esquire" or "lawyer"—the officer claimed—and the words "legal and confidential" needed to be paired with an explicit "open in front of inmate" in large letters.

I looked at him in disbelief. Was he suggesting that it had been unclear that this was protected mail? No, they'd known what it was, they'd opened it anyway, and now they were hiding behind this fig-leaf of an excuse to justify violating the privacy of my legal correspondence. I said none of this out loud and sufficed with a quiet "Ah…"

I turned to leave, judging further elaboration to be fruitless, but on second thought, I turned just as I reached the door. He had trusted my sincerity when I'd promised to come after Yom Tov and I reciprocated the trust. "Just tell me. Did you read what was inside or not?"

"Look, Rubashkin," he shrugged, "I don't care about you or why you're here.

I didn't read it. We know who we have to watch out for and it's not you." This was a strong statement and a telling admission, and I considered it a real *kiddush Hashem*.

Now that he'd said it, I started paying attention and began noticing that he really meant it. Among the mail I received was a lot of mail from *kinderlach* in *cheder*. This mail officer allowed me to receive letters from some of the younger children even when they contained drawings done in crayon and were decorated with glitter or scraps of colored paper. His interactions with *Yidden* had made a *kiddush Hashem* to the point that it was obvious to him that *Yiddishe kinderlach* were only sending heartfelt words, and he didn't have to worry that there was contraband mixed into the glue.

A few years later, he retired. He was replaced by an officer who was less understanding, and introduced a much stricter interpretation of the rules and regulations. These changes were implemented without warning or notice, something which caused a lot of grief and complaints amongst the inmates.

One day, soon after the new officer came, I received an envelope from a class of children. It seemed unusually light and flat. Looking inside, I found only a single scrap of paper, put there by the mail room staff. It said that the contents of the envelope had been rejected and returned to sender because it had been written in an unknown substance, which I later learned was Crayola crayons.

The class tried to send their creations a few more times, but their letters were repeatedly returned and they eventually gave up. Far from elevating the stature of the law and law enforcement in the eyes of these impressionable children, I expect that this experience left them with a lasting impression of unreasonable restrictions imposed by uncaring authorities.

Connecting by Email

Physical mail had two main drawbacks. Firstly, writing at any length using pen and paper, or even those frustrating daisywheel typewriters, especially with any frequency, is slow and difficult. The second drawback was the slow transit time. It took days for letters to reach their recipients and days more for their response to come back.

The prison email system, called CorrLinks, offered a communication option that solved these problems. Emails could be written with the benefit of at least basic digital word processing, so they were easier to write than letters, and they went back and forth more quickly.

Of course, even emails were restricted by the authorities. They used a closed email system, which meant that recipients had to log on to CorrLinks to retrieve anything I'd sent them instead of using their regular email addresses. This allowed the authorities to control and restrict who could receive the emails and they limited the number of recipients to twenty people.

Emails could also only be written in English characters (which was more of an issue for *Yidden* than for their average user) and, for security reasons, they put a one- to two-hour delay on all messages, which meant a single exchange still took three to four hours to complete.

Each barrack had a computer room which contained six computers for use by the over one hundred prisoners in that barrack. This was where the inmates accessed the email system, among other things. The room was accessible whenever the prisoners were not locked into the cells and the computers shut off automatically at 10:00 p.m.

The cost to use the computer was five cents per minute for up to an hour. After an hour, the session automatically ended. If no one else took the computer, the inmate could start another session after fifteen minutes.

It was from here that I was able to be "present" at my family's Shabbos and Yom Tov meals, *melaveh malkahs*, and special occasions. I spent countless hours typing letters to my family. They were mostly filled with *divrei Torah* and insights filtered through the unique prism provided by my *nisayon*. I drew my strength to persevere from the Torah and tried to share it with them. I also included anecdotes and experiences, mostly those in which I saw a lesson in *avodas Hashem* or which illustrated how Hashem was caring for me and protecting me even as we waited for His complete salvation.

These emails were a source of strength for them. The twenty people who were able to receive them directly shared them with others. Those others often shared them in turn, and they were eventually prepared and shared in print form in various schools and shuls, another way in which I merited to help others despite my isolation.

Among these Torah emails were long-running correspondences with Reb Elchonon Jacobovitz's class in Detroit, in English, and with Reb Leibish Lish's class in the Stoliner yeshivah in Boro Park, which I wrote in transliterated Yiddish. The precious children would respond each week and I looked forward to those emails eagerly. They were a highlight of my week and gave me great strength.

Reb Leibish would retype the emails in Hebrew characters and, under the title *Kol Sholom Mordechai*, they were distributed each week in many shuls, a *zechus* which should stand them in good stead.

The visiting room pictures with Reb Elchonon Jacobovitz (L) and Reb Leibish Lish (R), when we were finally able to meet in person.

Both sets of correspondence were later compiled into books, the English letters in a number of books called *Inside Out* and the Yiddish letters in two volumes called *Kol Sholom Mordechai*.

The number and length of these emails grew over time until I was sending five or six emails every week, each one running four or more printed pages long. One was a general email on the *parshah* of the week, usually containing a thought from the Rebbe and any interesting happenings in FCI Otisville from which I could derive and teach a lesson. The others were each dedicated to the *parshah* as explained by one of the *mefarshim* I was learning at the time; the *Shlah, Alshich, Ohr Hachaim, Kedushas Levi*, and more.

The sheer volume of these *divrei Torah* made an impression on my dear son Uziel. One day, when he was still very young, Uziel proudly told his *rebbi*, "My *tatty* loves to learn." When I heard about this comment, my heart swelled with gratitude to Hashem.

It's a father's responsibility to be a role model for his children and show them by example what is truly important in life. Uziel had been four years old when I was forcibly taken away from him and I never had that chance, certainly not in the usual ways. He didn't grow up sharing a Shabbos table with me and we never had the opportunity to review his homework each night when he came home from *cheder*.

Yet, despite my absence from his daily life, he still recognized that his *tatty* loved to learn and absorbed that priority into his own life. How? Of course, he overheard the conversations between the adults during the visits, conversations which always revolved around Torah, but he also saw five or six emails, a total of twenty or thirty pages, printed out every week to be read by the Shabbos *seudos* and *melaveh malkah* and he got the message loud and clear.

My constant preoccupation with these emails didn't escape the notice of the other inmates either. One day in the computer room, a non-Jewish inmate sat down while I was hard at work on a weekly *dvar Torah*. As he logged on to the computer, he leaned over and said, "Hey, Rubashkin. I see what you're doing. I'm following your lead—I'm gonna type my way out of here, just like you."

His words were music to my ears. I truly *was* typing my way out of there, each keystroke a strong connection of love both to my family and to Hashem, an act of defiance against the perspective of nature that insisted I was a prisoner and a victim. As these activities showed, I was a *shliach* of Hashem doing my best to fulfill my mission, certain that Hashem would free me. My job was just to hold on to Him and follow His will. That *emunah* and *bitachon* were not just the keys to my survival. They were also the keys to my release, as Hashem promises they will directly result in a *geulah*.

(This other fellow kept his resolution and he became a regular fixture in the computer room. While I typed *divrei Torah*, he typed content for a webpage dedicated to advocacy and publicity for his case, which he emailed to the friend who managed it. *Anu ameilim, v'heim ameilim…*)

There were other uses for the computers as well. They could be used to read postings by the prison staff, file complaints (for those not afraid of retaliation), and to notify medical staff electronically of any issues—although they officially had twenty-one days to respond so it was of limited use, medically speaking. It was also the preferred communication of inmate informants, allowing them to "drop a dime" without being seen talking to the guards directly.

About four years after I was brought there, they expanded the computers to something beyond reading and writing. They announced an exciting new product for sale to the inmates—an MP3 player. They had a—literally—captive market, so they were able to charge twice as much as a similar gadget would cost on the outside. The inmates who bought the devices would be able to buy music using the computers.

Up to that point, the prisoners had been limited to buying a handheld radio and listening to whatever was broadcast. Despite the cost, they were very excited at the prospect of choosing their own music. Once these devices became available, the computer rooms saw a lot more visitors, as inmates spent their time and money adding to and managing their music collections.

One day, while I was drafting an email, I overheard a conversation between two prisoners. One of them was using the computer to buy or manage his music and the other was waiting his turn. They were talking about their musical tastes, new releases, and the like, when the one who was waiting asked, "How much more time do you have?"

Without thinking, the other responded, "Two years," referring to the years remaining in his sentence.

The first guy did a double take and then burst out laughing. "I meant how much time until you're done with the computer!"

This was an insight into the mind of an inmate and, as the Ba'al Shem Tov teaches us, a powerful lesson in our *avodas Hashem*.

This prisoner was managing his song collection, very aware of the limited time he was granted to do so. They were also talking about the music. The context could not have made the meaning of the question more obvious. Yet, when he was asked how much time he had, his automatic, spontaneous reply was two years.

What was really on his mind and in his heart, when the subject of time came up, was the remaining time he would have to suffer the torture of prison and how long until he would taste the sweet air of freedom. So it should be with us in our torturous prison of *galus*, in which we are separated from our Father and besieged by our *yetzer hara*. Our yearning for Mashiach should never be far from our hearts or minds.

It happened that some inmates decided that the computer room was a good place to stash contraband. An informer caught wind of this and the staff searched the room thoroughly, discovering a knife and other contraband hidden in an air duct. This resulted in the whole barrack being deprived of the computer room for days, but eventually even this blew over and the room was reopened.

CHAPTER TWENTY
Painful Absence during Joyous Moments

Family *Simchos*

THE FORCED ABSENCE OF A MAN FROM THE DAILY LIVES OF HIS WIFE AND children is a source of constant pain for them all, but his forced absence during life's many important milestones is even more painful.

Some of those milestones come regularly, like birthdays and anniversaries, and others are rare life events: the birth of a child or grandchild, a *bris*, a bar mitzvah, an engagement, wedding, or, *lo aleinu*, a funeral. During my long ordeal I, of course, missed many birthdays and anniversaries, but I also missed the bar mitzvos of two of my sons, Mendel and Uziel, the engagement and marriage of my daughter Chaya Mushka, and the births and *brissim* of many grandchildren. Compounding the pain of missing these events was the fact that, in many of the cases, my inability to attend was not warranted.

A wonderful protocol that appears in the BOP policies is the furlough—a temporary release from custody, with appropriate safeguards, to be granted when circumstances warrant.

At the state level, the authorities made sure to fully inform each inmate arriving at their facility. They laid out the mechanisms and conditions for making complaints and the various requests that a prisoner might be entitled to make in order to alleviate one issue or the other. This was not done at Otisville. The policies and all their details were in writing and in force, but the inmate was left in the dark as to what they were, how to utilize them, and what conditions might entitle him or disqualify his request.

The inmates who learned about furloughs from more experienced inmates or from a charitable guard and actually requested one quickly found that this was mostly an "on-paper" kind of policy. Though provisions for furlough were written into prison regulations by predecessors who understood the need for such considerations, the current staff chose to ignore the options their regulations provided and "just say no."

One inmate, who'd already been imprisoned for over twenty-five years, requested a furlough for just a few hours in order to attend the wedding of his youngest child. His request was quickly denied. "If we allow you to go, we'll have to let everyone go," he was told in explanation.

I heard this "explanation" time and again in response to my own requests and I never understood the problem. If a request fails to meet your requirements, decline and point to a valid reason. If the request *meets* the criteria that your policies set out, why not let them go?! Unfortunately, this never seemed a persuasive point to the authorities, and practically every request for furlough that I knew about was denied.

If a furlough *was* granted, it was under onerous conditions that almost took the joy or heart out of whatever special moment warranted humanitarian reprieve. Imagine an inmate attending the wedding of a beloved child or the funeral of a cherished parent—shackled, wearing the degrading prison uniform, and under close watch by two guards always standing at his elbows.

Even so, prisoners desperately wished to receive permission to be present at important milestones, even just for a few hours, and almost every single one of them was flatly denied.

The first of these milestones I reached during my time in Otisville was the bar mitzvah of my son Mendel, which took place about two months after my transfer. I knew that my presence was very important for my son's wellbeing, and, hoping they would live up to their talk about the importance of family ties, I requested a furlough to attend the bar mitzvah. It was denied. "You just got here," they said, as if I'd asked for a perk or privilege I hadn't earned.

The bar mitzvah was celebrated without me.[1] Many *Yidden* took the time to celebrate with my family, and they gave Mendel a bar mitzvah celebration filled with *simchah*—something for which I am deeply and eternally grateful.

I was very happy about the beautiful *simchah*, but it was still important for him and for me that we find a way to celebrate together. *Askanim*, supported by the chaplain, tried to find a solution, and, with the help of Hashem, their

---

1. Although I was able to call in.

efforts bore fruit. We were given permission to use the visiting room during a time when it was otherwise vacant. Mendel was able to come along with a few other family members for a special visit.

We made a makeshift *seudah* from the vending machine in celebration of this important milestone, and I was relieved to see that Mendel was happy. He didn't complain that I'd been prevented from attending his official bar mitzvah celebration. Instead, he recited, by heart, the *ma'amar*[2] traditionally said by bar mitzvah boys and shared a *dvar Torah*. We even danced a little bit before our precious time together was all too quickly ended by the guards.

Two years later, the family was celebrating another extraordinary *simchah*— the engagement of my daughter Chaya Mushka. It was in the visiting room, weeks later, that I first met my future son-in-law.

Tremendous efforts were made—by family, *askanim*, and *rabbanim*—to arrange a furlough that met the demands of the warden so I could attend the wedding itself, all to no avail.

They even rejected a request to allow me to participate in the wedding via video call, using the system already in place to facilitate court appearances by video. My only option was to call in, and their generous "concession" to a father marrying off his daughter and to a daughter walking to the *chuppah*, was to allow that call to be in addition to my three hundred monthly minutes and to grant an extension of the call duration—they would allow me to have a phone call lasting a whole thirty minutes!

When the assistant chaplain, who would be supervising the call, spoke to me about it, the first thing she said was that her superiors had warned her that the call was to be *only* thirty minutes and she should not give me any more time. The callous cruelty of this arbitrary restriction, and the pain it caused, stands out even now, looking back with the context of all the many injustices I endured.

The day of the wedding arrived with no last-minute changes to their position on a furlough. When the amount of time it would take to travel to the *chuppah* became longer than the amount of time remaining until it was to begin, I accepted that I would not be physically present at the wedding of my dear daughter. I would participate from afar like the previous generations, *l'havdil*

---

2. A formal discourse of chassidic teachings delivered by a rebbe. It is a chassidic practice to recite specific *ma'amarim* at significant life events, like a wedding, bar mitzvah, *bris*, and the like.

bein chaim l'chaim, whose *neshamos* are present in those holy and precious moments. I *davened* that my *brachos* for the young couple would be accepted as are those of our holy grandparents.

The scheduled phone call, my single avenue of participation, actually afforded me a moment of crystal clarity. It allowed me to witness Hashem's careful and loving orchestration of everything I experience, even if I fail to immediately recognize it for what it is. It happened like this:

The miserly thirty-minute phone call was to take place in the chapel office. It had been scheduled to coincide with the start of the *chuppah*, the true heart of the wedding. We hoped that the thirty minutes would suffice to allow me to participate, in this very small way, in the whole *chuppah*, listening as my daughter began her new life *k'das Moshe v'Yisrael*. I would be able to hear and answer amen as my father and other righteous men recited the seven special *brachos*, and listen as my new son-in-law broke a glass underfoot, commemorating the pain of *galus* present even in the moments of our greatest joys.

I came to the chapel at the appointed time and was met by the assistant chaplain. She ushered me into the office, showed me to a phone, and stood off to the side while I tried to make the call.

I lifted the receiver and, when prompted, raised my hand to enter my PIN number—and then I froze. For the life of me, I could not remember my PIN. I had used that number multiple times every day, for more days than I cared to count, for all the various purposes it served. Now, with the moment of my daughter's *chuppah* inexorably approaching, I simply couldn't remember what it was.

The officer saw me standing like a deer in headlights and asked me what happened. "My PIN code… I can't remember it!" My mind barely registered the exchange, I was so focused on trying to remember that number. I kept trying different combinations for about five minutes before I noticed that I was trying the same numbers again and again. The chaplain tried to calm me down, reassuring me that it was probably just nerves and as soon as I calmed down, it would surely come back to me.

The scheduled time of the *chuppah* came and went and I was standing there, still stumped. Try as I might, the number would not come to me, and the precious moments were slipping away. Why was Hashem doing this to me?!

As I did whenever that question occurred to me, I focused my mind on the second half of the question, which totally disarmed the first half—Hashem is doing this to me. Anchored to that truth, the *yetzer hara's* "why"—the rhetorical expression of complaint implying that there can be no possible justification for your discomfort—loses all its steam. You might still wonder why—but it's a very different why, rooted in the certainty that there's a good answer, and expressed with a willingness to trust that it's from Hashem and therefore for our best, even if we never find out why.

Sometimes, in His infinite compassion, He *does* let us find out why, and this was about to be one of those times.

I decided to stop trying essentially random numbers and instead take a walk around the chapel. Maybe distraction would help. I paced the room for almost ten minutes, trying and failing to relax. In some corner of my heart, I started to feel resigned to not even have the *zechus* to participate in my daughter's wedding from afar, when, like a bolt of lightning out of a cloudless blue sky, it hit me. The number. I remembered it! I quickly picked up the receiver and punched in the numbers, hoping to catch something, anything, of this precious moment in my daughter's life.

The phone rang once and my wife picked up. It took a few seconds for the automated message to identify the source of the call and then to get her approval before I was put through. "Where are they up to?!" I blurted out.

She answered calmly and I could hear the smile in her voice. "We're running late. Chaya Mushka is just walking out to the *chuppah*. I was hoping you wouldn't call 'on time' and have the phone call cut off before we even started."

Tears of surprise, joy, and gratitude welled up in my eyes when I realized the *chessed* that Hashem had performed for me. He had plucked the number from my mind and withheld it until the precise moment that would allow me to participate in the *chuppah* to the greatest extent possible for me in my circumstances.

My wife handed the phone to my daughter, whose tears of joy at her wedding mingled with tears of pain at my absence. I *bentched* her with all the *brachos* a father gives his daughter at her wedding and tried to share with her some of the strength I had found for myself.

She was very emotional and couldn't bring herself to walk to the *chuppah* without me. She wept for a few minutes, until she mustered the strength to tear herself away from the phone. As I listened from afar, she walked to the *chuppah* to the strains of the holy *niggun* of the Alter Rebbe.

Roza Hindy took the phone and tried to describe the scene to me as it unfolded, so I could feel like I was there. There was not a dry eye among the assembled guests. She painted the picture for me as the *chassan* walked to the *chuppah* led by his father and mine, as Rabbi Groner read the Rebbe's letter, the *kesubah* was read, and the *sheva brachos* were recited. I then had an opportunity to give my daughter and her new husband another *brachah* over the phone as they stood under the *chuppah*.

I only realized the full extent of Hashem's kindness when the phone call was unceremoniously terminated—mere moments after I heard the *chuppah* draw to a close with the sound of shattering glass and the cries of "mazel tov!!" Hashem's timing had allowed the call to begin at the perfect moment and run through all the way to the end. If I'd remembered the PIN code even one moment earlier, I would have been cut off in the middle.

The call had happened precisely on schedule—His schedule—and I was grateful both for His intervention in the call and the glimpse of the Divine Providence it provided. It gave me immeasurable strength to withstand the physical and emotional stress of my ordeal.

After the phone shut off, I was returned to the barracks. I wanted to call in from there to continue my long-distance participation, but they hadn't waived the restriction which required me to wait half an hour before I could call again.

By then, the participants were already back at the wedding hall. Holding the phone tightly against one ear and putting my finger over the other, I was able to block out the deafening noise of the barrack enough to hear the joyous music. The phone on the other end was passed around to various family members and guests. Hearing the familiar voices so full of joy and receiving their *brachos* for the young couple helped to lift me out of the pit and feel a bit more as if I was there with them.

The tears of joy mixed with tears of pain and longing on both sides of the phone call. I turned to Hashem with a broken heart and *davened* that He reunite me with my family, reminding myself that He would surely do so if I put my trust in Him.

In no time at all, the fifteen-minute limit had been reached and the call was terminated. I couldn't call again for thirty minutes but I wanted to continue the celebration. I went to the computer and spent the time with the *Yidden* from all over the world who had sent me their heartfelt *brachos* for the *chassan* and *kallah* along with additional *brachos* for the reunification of our family. The feeling that we are all one big *mishpachah* was very uplifting, and I responded to as many as I could. I shared my appreciation and a *brachah* that we should experience *"simchah goreres simchah"* with the joy of our national *Geulah* with Mashiach Tzidkeinu.

When the half hour had passed, I called back in to the *chasunah*. The first dance was over and the *seudah* was being served. They connected the phone to the speaker system, enabling me to share a few words with the celebrants in honor of the *simchah*.

Lock-in was at 9:30 p.m., and at that point I wasn't able to participate even by phone or email. I returned to the cell and thanked Hashem for the kindness He had shown me in allowing me to participate to the extent that I had. Taking a *sefer*, I sat down at the small table and immersed myself in the holy words of Torah, soothing water to a weary soul, lifting me above the limitations of my circumstances.

During the week of *sheva brachos*, the *chassan* and *kallah* made the journey to Otisville so that I could celebrate with them in person in the visiting room. Still smarting from the pain of my absence at her wedding, my daughter decided to come to this visit in her wedding dress. *Baruch Hashem*, she was not denied entry.

The sight of a *kallah* in a prison visiting room was bizarre, but it wasn't *she* who was intruding on the *prison* reality—it was the *prison* which was intruding on *her simchah*. We put our external environment from our minds and celebrated the great milestone in the lives of the young couple. We were even able to buy sandwiches from the vending machines and, since there were enough *Yidden* within earshot to make a *minyan*, we made *sheva brachos* in the visiting room of FCI Otisville. I, the father of the *kallah*, was the *panim chadashos*.

Approximately five years after the wedding, seven years since my transfer to Otisville, we again prepared to celebrate a *simchah*; the bar mitzvah of my youngest child, Uziel, who had been a preschooler, only four years old, when I'd been torn from his life.

As is the Chabad *minhag*, Uziel was to begin putting on *tefillin* without a *brachah* two months before his thirteenth birthday, training for the day he would finally be obligated in mitzvos as an adult. I was bit more familiar with the procedures by then, with years of experience behind me. I requested permission for *tefillin* to be allowed in the visiting room during his visit so that

I could show him how to put them on myself, as my father had taught me and as I had taught his older brothers before my ordeal.

My request was denied. First, the excuse was that no religious activities are allowed in that room. That was demonstrably false. Quite aside from the numerous religious books in the visiting room, which inmates and visitors or volunteers often used to study and meditate together, I pointed out that the room had even been used by the chaplain to officiate religious weddings. As valid as my arguments were, they didn't address the real reason for the denial—which was that they simply didn't want to authorize my request—and as such, they were dismissed.

I persisted and approached the officers in the chow hall at main line. The captain was not there that day and I was instead directed to his substitute, the acting captain. I handed him my written request and explained the issue. He looked over my request and simply responded, "No."

I repeated my observations that the room was readily made available for other religious family moments, like weddings. All I was asking was for *tefillin*, an item already authorized on the compound, to be allowed into the room. There were no possible security concerns. "And what if someone asks me for permission to bring in a Muslim prayer rug?" he asked rhetorically, as if I was dimwittedly overlooking the obvious.

"If it's a religious need and there are no security concerns that should be allowed too!" I answered. He refused to discuss the matter further and just repeated his denial of my request.

With enough time before the date of the bar mitzvah itself, I made an official request for a furlough, noting the important role of the father in this milestone from a religious standpoint and also urging that it be granted as a matter of basic humanity. Uziel had endured a trauma at a very young age, when I was plucked from his day-to-day life where a father belongs.

From afar, I'd done my best to be there for him and help him grow into the Yid I knew he could be, but it was very hard on him. Allowing me to participate in his bar mitzvah was the least they could do for a hurting child and, again, protocols designed specifically for this purpose and for these reasons were already on the books.

Only three days after I made the request, I received the response. This was very quick, by prison standards, and certainly not enough time to think about this decision and consider ways in which it might be met without compromising

My son Uziel grew from a preschooler to a bar mitzvah
boy while I was in a place called prison.

their interests. The request was curtly denied. Undaunted, I took the request
to the warden herself. One particular officer, notorious for his efforts to make
life a little extra miserable for the Jewish inmates, did everything he could to
convince the warden to deny my request, and she did.

With that option off the table, I requested a special visit for the occasion
similar to what they'd allowed for Mendel's bar mitzvah seven years earlier.
The warden hadn't heard of that visit because she had arrived after that
period, but she looked into the details and authorized a similar visit for Uziel.
She assigned the task of overseeing both the arrangements and the visit itself
to none other than the officer who had personally and successfully lobbied
against my request for a furlough.

The bar mitzvah was on a Monday, which was by then reinstated as a general
visiting day. To allow for this private visit, the room was opened a bit earlier,
before the other inmates and visitors arrived, and I was allowed a few more
visitors than were normally allowed. The Jewish chaplain agreed to participate
and that brought our number to ten adults, enabling us to *daven* together as a
minyan. I was able to watch with true *nachas* as Uziel *davened* as the *chazzan*
for the first time.

Incidentally, we were all allowed to bring in *tallis* and *tefillin* for this *minyan*.
I was very grateful for this, but it underlined how baseless and capricious they
had been in their refusal to allow me to teach my son to put on *tefillin* two
months earlier.

I'd asked the inmate photographer to come to the visiting room to capture
the special moments this visit afforded. Despite the early hour, he agreed. Early
that morning, he went to the lieutenant's office and picked up his camera and

made his way to the visiting room as usual. When he arrived, he was met with a classic example of the power that individual guards hold to hurt prisoners by selectively or creatively using the rules. The bigoted officer who'd undermined a possible furlough and had been tasked with overseeing this visit turned the photographer away, informing him that this was not a regular visit, which the photographer had standing authorization to attend, and since he didn't have special permission, he was summarily dismissed.

My last attempt to use the visiting room to participate in a family *simchah* took place in 2018. As I mentioned earlier, a number of grandchildren were born during the time I was in Otisville. Generally, I would call to wish mazel tov to the new parents and also write an email focusing on the *simchah*. In it I would share my *brachos* as well as *divrei Torah* either on the *parshah* or upcoming Yom Tov, or from my own experiences that connected to the *simchah*. In the case of a boy, I would always call in to participate in the *bris* while it was taking place.

Getzel's son Levi Yitzchak was born almost eight years after my transfer to Otisville. By that point, I'd been reinforcing and acting on my *emunah* and *bitachon* in the context of my ordeal for close to a decade. Throughout that time, I had emphatically rejected the power of the natural world and recognized only the power of Hashem. I had seen time and again the hollowness of the obstacles with which I was confronted and it emboldened me.

In the excitement over the news of the new baby boy, I decided that I would try to attend the *bris*. I put in a request for a furlough, which was promptly denied, but I didn't stop there. I requested permission for the *mohel* to come to Otisville and perform the *bris* in the visiting room so I could be part of this great mitzvah and family milestone. They were flabbergasted at the request and dismissed it out of hand, but it would be the last time they interfered with my ability to celebrate with my family.

The next *simchah* was not only celebrated together with my immediate family or my extended family but with the whole family of Klal Yisrael, who joined me to celebrate my miraculous release less than two short months later.

CHAPTER TWENTY-ONE
The Prison Population

The Personnel

BUREAUCRACY IS A GEHINNOM, SO IT SHOULD COME AS NO SURPRISE THAT gehinnom is a bureaucracy, and one with a strict hierarchy. Before I get into the details of the setup in Otisville, I want to note that a hierarchy in the administration of punishment is the subject of a very important passage in *Sha'ar Habitachon*.

The *Chovos Halevavos* points out that a person subjected to a king's justice would be a fool to appeal to the whip for mercy, less of a fool—but still a fool—to appeal to the one who wields the whip, and so on, up the chain through sergeant, officer, commander, and deputy. Ultimately, each of these links in the chain are only *implementing* the king's justice, and mercy can only be elicited from the king himself.

The rigid hierarchy in a place called prison was a constant reminder to me not to appeal to anyone in that chain for mercy. Instead, I turned to the King Himself, *Hashem Yisbarach*, and only interacted with the deputy, commander, officer, and so on, to the degree that the King instructed.

Every inmate is familiarized with the hierarchy of authority during the intake process. At the very bottom of the staff hierarchy in Otisville, starting from those who are in direct contact with the inmates, are the guards, formally and euphemistically called correctional officers. It's their job to monitor and control the inmates. They're the ones who enforce the rules and regulations and conduct counts, shakedowns, and "random" body searches.

They are authorized to use physical force against inmates, including deadly force if they deem it necessary. They have the power to throw a prisoner into the SHU for almost any reason, including perceived disrespect.

Moving up the chain of command, the guards report to a lieutenant, whose job it is to supervise them and make decisions that they are either not authorized or not willing to make. The lieutenant is the one who investigates violations by the inmates, such as fights or discovered contraband, and decides on a punishment. He's also supposed to investigate violations by the guards under his command.

The lieutenants report to the captain, who is the department head responsible for everything to do with the staff and inmates.

Parallel in the hierarchy to the lieutenant, each inmate is assigned to a counselor. Despite the name, the counselor doesn't actually counsel the inmate in any way. Instead, they're the ones who assign "housing" and jobs, oversee visitation forms and permissions, mail privileges, and similar control and oversight. They're also the ones who decide how to punish prisoners who receive a violation notice, called a "shot." The counselor reports to the unit manager, another department head.

At the top of all this bureaucracy sits the warden, the final authority in the prison. The warden has a number of assistant wardens, each responsible for different aspects and departments of the prison. This is the executive staff and under normal circumstances, they don't have much direct contact with the inmates, with the exception of the "main line."

Regardless of their role or their place in the hierarchy, inmates will judge and classify the personnel on their single most important attribute: their attitude toward their job and the people over whom they have so much power.

Having experienced prison in Soviet Russia, the Rebbe Rayatz identified two types of prison guards. For those in the first group, it was just a job. Everyone needs to make a living and this was the work they'd found. They came in each day, did whatever the job required, and went home. They approached their job professionally without seeking to inflict additional, unnecessary pain on the wretches under their control.

The second group took enjoyment and satisfaction in causing pain to the prisoners—whether out of sheer innate viciousness or because they saw the inmates as subhuman criminals to be punished as much as possible. This abuse of authority unnecessarily increased the suffering of the prisoners.

One example of this happened during a count one day. The guards reached the cell to which I was assigned and, peering through the aperture in the door, saw my cellmate still lying in bed. Wordlessly, the guard kicked the iron door with his heavy boot, which made a painfully loud noise in the small cell and left our ears ringing.

Through the locked door, I told the guard that my cellmate was very sick. This was not just an "inmate's excuse." He'd been officially diagnosed by the doctors and was being treated. I explained that, due to his condition, it was very difficult for him to come down from the top shelf and, since he was clearly visible from the door, I asked the guard to just count him while he lay in bed.

The protocols do require inmates to stand during the count, but the guards have a lot of leeway in implementing the regulations. A guard of the first group might have had the basic humanity to let a sick man stay in bed.

I had seen this guard interact with other inmates before, and I knew him to be firmly in the second group, so I wasn't the least bit surprised when he ignored my reasonable humanitarian request on behalf of my cellmate. Even a direct plea by the invalid himself, who very clearly looked and sounded ill, made no impression on the guard. He just stood there and demanded the inmate come down onto the floor for the count.

The distressed and hurting prisoner had no choice. He very slowly and very painfully climbed down from the shelf. Only then was the guard satisfied. He made the necessary notation on his clipboard and left. My cellmate climbed back up to his shelf, now hurting not only physically, but emotionally as well.

Clearly, there was no need to point to antisemitism to explain the occasional abuse of power, but that was definitely present too. One day, on my way out of the chow hall, I encountered a guard who I generally tried my best to avoid. His dislike for Jews was common knowledge. He was standing right outside the building with a field sobriety test, a breathalyzer, and he was spot-checking the inmates.

He called me over and commanded me to blow into his device. Not satisfied with the first reading, he fiddled with the gadget and had me blow again. When the second reading cleared me as well, he dismissed me with a wave of his hand. I walked away quickly, eager to be out of his immediate vicinity. Once I was clear, I glanced back and saw that he was administering his test to another Yid he'd stopped.

Arriving back at the barrack, I met a third Jewish inmate. He'd *also* been randomly selected by this same officer to blow into his device and the guard had been very nasty to him while doing so. This made three *Yidden* that I knew of. Something seemed off. I asked around, and discovered that most of the *Yidden* in that barrack had been "randomly" selected to be tested.

The next day, I inquired of those in other barracks and discovered that out of the sixteen or so *Yidden* who had gone to the chow hall that night, twelve had been "randomly" stopped and tested. There was clearly nothing random about it. He was intentionally targeting and harassing Jewish inmates.

We got word to the advocates at Aleph and gave them all the information they needed to persuade the warden that this officer's behavior was antisemitic. Presumably as a result of their efforts, this officer was taken off any duty involving direct contact with inmates for a long time.

Another time, I experienced an inexplicable delay in my legal mail. It was withheld with no word or explanation. After a couple of days, I went to the mail room looking for my mail and for some answers. I got both.

As I quietly waited my turn, I overheard the two guards in the mail room chatting. The word "annex" caught my ear. "They want to annex 504 acres from Monroe..." one guard was saying. "It's unlawful! It's criminal what they're doing, but they'll get away with it..." I realized to my shock that the "they" under discussion were "the Jews."

The other guard jumped in. "Yeah! And it's being funded with state money! Do you see what they're doing around *here*? Coming up here and taking over, buying houses all over the place, knocking on doors and buying houses in cash..." He turned around and, noticing me on the line, he trailed off. When my turn came, I inquired after and received my mail, but I didn't ask why it had been held up. I already had my answer.

Inmates

When I was first brought to Otisville, there were a handful of inmates incarcerated for white-collar crimes with extended sentences, but the population was mostly comprised of violent offenders.

These men, some of them quite dangerous, often had colorful, playful-sounding nicknames which were based on their crimes, antics, place of origin, or personal attributes. Blue, Gifted, Ice, Flacko, Panama, Poochy, Ghost, Fuzzy, Bucky, Crime, X-bot, Bozo, Hustler, and Butchy were just a few of the characters I encountered. These nicknames gave them a feeling of individuality and also helped obscure their true names from other inmates who might do some research to discover information they could use against them. I was also given the "honor" of a nickname; "Rabbi," for obvious reasons.

Many of the inmates were affiliated with one gang or another. Even those who hadn't been gang members before incarceration would often join a gang in prison. In that lonely and dangerous world, friends or associates gave an inmate a feeling of fellowship and camaraderie. The gang also afforded its members some degree of protection and security, but it's debatable whether it actually accomplished more good than harm. Their new gang affiliation occasionally earned inmates enemies who had nothing against them personally, but who were enemies of their newly adopted gang.

A few years after I was brought there, they made an attempt to get rid of the real gangs and troublemakers. They locked all the inmates in their cells and instructed them to take off all outer clothing and their undershirts. Cell by cell, they called the inmates, who were to go to the counselor's office shirtless, where they were visually inspected by a civilian who specialized in gangs and gang tattoos. If he saw a gang tattoo, they added that inmate to the transfer list.

When I was called, I followed their instructions with the exception of removing my *tzitzis*. One of the guards demanded that I leave my *tzitzis* in the cell or he would send me straight to the SHU. I respectfully reminded him that I couldn't walk to the office without them and I would remove them for a moment when needed. *Baruch Hashem*, he relented. They took one look at me in the office and waved me back to the cell. They knew who they were looking for and who they weren't.

About three hundred gang-affiliated inmates were transferred out. They were replaced with a different class of inmates, whose offenses were less violent but more repulsive. I didn't consider it an improvement.

Those who didn't join a gang sometimes sought allies by means of flattery and bribery. Every Sunday, one prisoner would hold a "feast" to which he would invite all his friends. He would purchase and prepare a number of pizza kits from the commissary. These kits were basically small pizza crusts, a handful of shredded cheese, and assorted *treifus* to scatter on top. When combined and heated in the microwaves, these kits would fill the barrack with a truly nauseating smell.

I thought it was simply a nice display of camaraderie, sharing something he enjoyed with his friends, until one day, I bumped into him in the computer room and realized I hadn't smelled his feast in quite a while. "It seems like you stopped making those pizzas," I commented.

His answer surprised me. "Yeah… I'm leaving in three months. I'm not eating that garbage!" Disappointed, I realized that his feasts weren't about sharing something he enjoyed—they were nothing more than a display of wealth meant to win friends and influence people, an effort to impress others with his good fortune and success, in sharp contrast to the functional poverty all around him.

Of course, I didn't join any gangs, and, while I did try to help people when I could, it wasn't in the hopes of gathering useful "friends." Hashem was my protection and I was truly secure, even in situations where friends or allies would be of no use.

Once, on my way to make a phone call during Elul, I passed a few inmates huddled over a game of cards. It was a hot day and they were using a large fan to keep cool. They had plugged it into the wall and left the wire dangling across the walkway. In order to protect my *neshamah*, I generally avoided looking around as much as possible and I was also a bit lost in thought that day. My mind elsewhere, I tripped over the plug of the fan, disconnecting it.

The leader of their group, a husky Mexican of unusual height, angrily sprang to his feet and began berating me. I had encountered him on the bus to Otisville and shown him kindness, so this "grateful" attitude was to be expected in return. He had diamonds affixed to his front teeth which glinted in the light of the fixture overhead as he screamed at me. I assume they were either permanent and unremovable or worthless fakes.

I was surprised at this unexpected rage over something so trivial. His anger made a response pointless, and under the circumstances, an apology would be a dangerous sign of weakness on my part anyway. Instead of speaking, I silently and without emotion turned and replaced the plug. With the fan working again, I tersely told him that it had been unintentional. "Drop it," I said, and turned to walk off.

He had not, in fact, dropped it. He followed me at a dangerously close distance, berating and threatening me as he walked. "You *disrespected* us! I'm gonna knock your head off!"

Hashem sent His salvation in the form of Butchy. Butchy was a large inmate, a Bronx boy originally from Puerto Rico. He respected me for my principled and religious behavior and had stepped in to defend me in the past. Seeing the threatening posture of this goon, he hurried over and they exchanged words in Spanish.

I would have liked to hear exactly what combination of mouth-noises could possibly convey the severity of my crime and justify his aggressive behavior, but I couldn't follow the rapid Spanish. When they'd each had a turn to talk, there was a tense face-off for a few moments before the Mexican abruptly turned and left. Butchy turned to me with a self-satisfied smile. "I took care of it, Rabbi, but that dude's a gang leader. Stay away from him!"

This was sound advice. I made a mental note to remember to stay away from violent gang leaders in the future, but he apparently hadn't given the Mexican the same advice about me. Over the next few days, I noticed this fellow and his crew glancing at me and talking amongst themselves, a sure sign that they had plans for me.

In a place called prison there are too many isolated corners and quiet moments for even five Butchys to watch my back, but I was under Hashem's protection. I reached for my *Tehillim* and asked Hashem to save me from their evil scheming. His salvation came swiftly.

A week or two later was Erev Rosh Hashanah. I was in the cell preparing for the holy day, when I suddenly heard the guards shout, "Lock-in! Lock-in!" It was not time for a scheduled lock-in and the frantic, urgent tone told me right away that there had been some sort of fight and this was a security lock-in to prevent a riot from breaking out.

My thoughts immediately went to Yom Tov. The selfless volunteers who were scheduled to complete our *minyan* would certainly not be allowed in during a lockdown, which meant there would be no *minyan* for Rosh Hashanah. It was possible that we would not be allowed to gather in the chapel to *daven* together at all, even without a *minyan*. I realized with relief that, if it came to that, I at least had the shofar with me in the cell and would be able to fulfill the mitzvah.

I'd been allowed to take the shofar to the cell to fulfill the *minhag* of blowing it every weekday in Elul. I was the only one in Otisville at the time with that *minhag*. It looked like having kept the *minhag* would now enable me to keep the mitzvah, but I still worried for the others.

My thoughts were interrupted when Panama walked into the cell for the lock-in. He had seen the fight and was eager to share his information. A new prisoner had just been transferred in and was being escorted by a guard into the barrack. Two of the Mexicans who were stalking me were in the common area and they recognized him immediately as someone from a gang with which they were at war.

They walked over to him and casually asked if he wasn't So-and-so. When he replied that he was, they unexpectedly attacked him, viciously beating him right in front of the guard. The guard panicked and called for immediate lock-in.

I went over to look out the small window in the cell door which overlooked the common area of the barrack. Sure enough, the gang leader who had threatened me was being cuffed and taken to the SHU together with his second-in-command. From there, they were moved to a different prison, and I never saw them again.

I clearly saw the hand of my Protector. No inmate in his right mind would make a premeditated attack, even on a hated rival, right in front of a guard. They would bide their time and wait to strike until they were alone and could get away with it. Hashem had riled up these seasoned prisoners and caused them to act without thinking, resulting in consequences which saved me from harm. I again reached for my *Tehillim*, this time with words of gratitude and appreciation.

Baruch Hashem, the lock-in was lifted only a few hours later and the volunteers were allowed to join us for Rosh Hashanah as scheduled, completing our *minyan* and our Yom Tov.

The danger of violence from other inmates was very real and I thank Hashem that, despite a few assaults over the years, I was never seriously harmed. That always makes me think of a certain Jewish inmate, who deserves credit as Hashem's *shliach*. He was a real *macher* and was very well liked and respected by inmates of all groups and religions. I don't know his financial status before, but he was definitely "prison rich." He was able to obtain a huge number of stamps and was always willing to give some to someone who needed help, as I personally observed a number of times.

We developed a very warm friendship. We even had a deal in which he would agree to put on *tefillin* if I would exercise with him. It was only after he was transferred away from Otisville, however, that I learned just how sincere a friend he was. In the months after he left, I was approached a number of times by inmates who asked about my wellbeing and if I was being harassed by anyone. I appreciated the concern, but I couldn't figure out why these relative strangers had suddenly taken an interest in my safety. I found out later that this fellow was behind it. He had made arrangements with some of his acquaintances to watch over me after he left and jump in to help if needed.

The proud *Yidden* in Otisville were certainly not a "gang," and we relied on Hashem to sustain and protect us, but we did stick together, recognizing the importance and the power of *achdus* and *ahavas Yisrael*. Our success wasn't automatic and it often didn't come easy—petty infighting can occur in any community and our little community faced bigger challenges than most. We were obviously all contending with very difficult circumstances and there were also subtle but effective efforts by authorities to undermine cohesion between inmates.

If I saw a personal spat starting to take root and threaten to become something more, I always did what I could to smooth things over. In one such case, I was walking with a Yid who had a grievance against another Jewish inmate and he spent our walk laying it all out, in an attempt to persuade me to "be on his side" which meant, necessarily, being "against" the other Yid.

"We're all *Yidden!*" I reminded him. "We have to ignore these personal slights and stick together, like real brothers, with *ahavas Yisrael*."

He didn't appreciate my response, perhaps thinking that I wasn't taking his pain seriously and was just mouthing empty slogans. "Is that how you would treat the people who put you in this place?!" he demanded.

This was obviously something I had grappled with for a long time. I had given that question a lot of thought and learned in *Tanya* and in *Sha'ar Habitachon* the Torah's instructions on how to react to such people, so I had an actual answer to his rhetorical question.

"For choosing to do evil," I answered firmly, "they will have to answer to Hashem, but in no sense did they put me here. Hashem is the One who put me here and Hashem is the One who will take me out!"

I could see that my words didn't satisfy him. He didn't see it that way and I understood him. Taken superficially, our experiences seem to show that people are often the cause of our pain. Being able to blame and hate someone for your troubles is also much easier. It's far more difficult to peel back the facade and recognize that nothing and no one on earth can cause you pain or give you relief, and that unpleasant experiences come from Hashem for a constructive purpose.

Even if you've learned Torah and know the truth intellectually—obviously a necessary first step—it still takes real effort to absorb the truth and change the way you react emotionally, changing the way you actually see the world and interpret events in your own life. At the start it isn't your first reaction, but it can be your conscious second thought. With time it eventually becomes more instinctual.

I had said all there was to say in the moment, so I dropped the matter with one final word. "My dear brother, it's time to stop thinking the way the street taught you to think. It's a lie. It's not real. Hashem is the only cause of anything and everything, in the world and in your life. Learn to see that. You will be better off for it. You'll start to see the good in everything and stop being aggravated by other people or by difficulties in your life."

He accepted my words graciously and we turned the conversation to other topics.

In my efforts to keep the peace between my brothers, I also appealed to their more practical sides. A fellow Jew once told me about a "beef" that was heating up. Someone had obtained some extra food and brought it to the barrack. It was clearly intended for him, but another Jewish inmate insisted that it was for him!

This relatively trivial argument escalated quickly, as they so often do. The exchange of words became heated, and hurtful things were said. As the shouting match went back and forth, each one tried to outdo the other, responding in increasingly harsh terms. What had begun as a silly disagreement had turned into a real fight and if allowed to fester, it would become an ongoing *machlokes* in our midst.

One of the two came over and filled me in. He said he was just keeping me in the loop but he wasn't really the type to gossip. It seemed to me that he really came over to talk because things had gotten out of control and he was hoping I could find a way to untangle the mess, a way for him to walk away without losing face. A cynic would say he was just trying to recruit me to his side of the feud, but I chose to judge him favorably.

With a silent *tefillah* to Hashem to give me the right words, I gave it my best. "I once heard you say that 'the only thing I'm busy with are things that'll help me get out the door,'" I said. "Tell me. Will *machlokes* help you get out the door or will this be a distraction that takes your time, energy, and focus off your real goal?"

The answer was obvious and he didn't bother responding, so I answered my own question. "*Machlokes* will *not* help you get out the door. It will only distract you from your legal work and any other things you are doing. Take my advice. Go back and give that man what you think is yours, and he thinks is his. Tell him you won't allow such things to get between the two of you and you will focus instead only on what will get you out the door, and the most important thing that will do that is *shalom*."

How rare is it for a man to concede without receiving anything in return, when he is right and the other guy is wrong! In this instance, I was pleased to see that judging him favorably had been judging him correctly. He had clearly been looking for a reason and a way to squash the *machlokes*. He reaffirmed his own words—the only thing that matters is getting out the door—and assured me that he would take my advice.

The next time I saw him, he told me that he'd tried to make peace but had been rejected. I reassured him that the other man was probably still hurt by the things that were said and wasn't ready to let go, but if he stayed committed to peace and friendship, it was only a matter of time. Sure enough, a short time later, the other man also put it behind him and today they are friends again.

We need to take a lesson from this Yid and apply it to our lives in a place called *galus*; we need to always ask ourselves what will get us out the door. When the destructive fire of *machlokes* begins to burn, we have to remember that no matter what rationalization our *yetzer hara* offers, it will not get us out the door—it will only take us further away from it. We need to make the simple—although sometimes difficult—decision to refuse to fight and put our focus, together, where it truly belongs.

Gangs notwithstanding, there really is no unity between the prisoners. Reduced to a struggle for survival, they turn bitter, ugly, and selfish very quickly. "You do you, I'll do me," is the motto of many prisoners. As I heard one short African American fellow shouting one day, "I didn't come to prison to make friends!" They may sit near each other, but they don't sit together. The hierarchy is determined by strength and machismo, and everyone else is placed either above or below them in a constantly evolving pecking order.

Although it's a very confined space and people are constantly and repeatedly passing each other in close proximity, many don't bother with a friendly greeting. Nonetheless, I made an effort to greet people pleasantly, even strangers, which is how the Torah tells us to greet every person. This seemed bizarre to some, but most responded positively.

One new arrival, an older Native American fellow, ignored my greetings at first. One day, he approached me and asked if I had some time to talk, saying that he wants to know what Jews believe. Really, the mitzvos Hashem gave

Yidden are not relevant to non-Jews—Hashem gave them their own mitzvos and that's where they need to put their energy. But, since the Rambam says that it's part of *our* obligation to teach those mitzvos to the world, I agreed to have a chat with the guy about what the Torah says.

When we sat down to talk, the first thing he said was that my strange appearance and frequent mumbling out of a book had given him the idea that I was crazy and that's why he'd ignored and avoided me. "What changed your mind?" I asked with a grin.

He laughed. "I'd never seen a Jew before," he said. "Once I figured out it was a religious thing, I really wanted to talk to you. I like to learn about other religions."

I told him that Jews don't try to convert others, because each person has their own part in the Creator's plan and they don't need to become someone else. It's also important to realize that it's not up to us to decide, on our own, how we want to serve G-d. We need to do what *He* wants from us, not what makes us feel spiritual. I explained to him that all of humanity were instructed to follow the *sheva mitzvos Bnei Noach* and I explained them to him. He listened politely, and, although he wasn't yet ready to accept what I was saying, he showed me great respect going forward.

The "experts" said it would be better to learn the rules of my new environment and adapt, but instead, I earned the respect and even trust of the general population, not by playing their games, but by being who I am supposed to be without compromise.

There was once a young man standing in front of me on line at the commissary when I was waiting to pick up pictures from a family visit. I'd met him before and we'd had a few conversations about Hashem and fulfilling our purpose in life. I had taught him about the *sheva mitzvos Bnei Noach* as well and we were on friendly terms.

He was also picking up pictures. When it was his turn and he received his pictures, he flipped through them with obvious enjoyment. "Hey, Sholom!" he called out. "Look at these!" I assumed he wanted to show me a family member, maybe his child or his spouse, but they were all pictures of him posing alone for the camera in front of the beige cinder-block wall. He cut an impressive figure, over six feet tall, with well-developed muscles. His eyes covered by dark sunglasses, he was striking a dramatic, aggressive pose in every picture.

I politely flipped through his collection. "That's a real 'tough guy' look you have in these pictures…" I said.

He nodded, smiling proudly. "That's right!"

"Tough guy" was his aspiration and it was exactly the compliment he had hoped for.

Later that week, I met this aspiring tough guy while leaving the unit. I was heading to the yard to walk around the track and get some fresh air while I said Tehillim. I greeted him with a smile and we made small talk as we walked to the yard. Once we had passed the heavy metal doors and were out in the open area, I politely explained that I'd brought along my *Tehillim* because I would be praying as I walked, and I would be happy to continue our chat some other time.

"Sure, Rabbi," he said with a smile, but he didn't peel off and head to the gym or to a different part of the yard. Instead, he kept walking alongside me. I hesitated for a moment, wondering how to handle the situation. I decided that I had done all that politeness demanded. I'd told him I'd be busy with something else, and had no further obligation to engage with him. I opened my *sefer'l* as we walked, and began saying Tehillim.

From the corner of my eye, I watched my unsolicited companion. I was walking at a very slow pace as I concentrated on my Tehillim, and he was clearly staying at my side on purpose. I thought he had something else to say and was waiting for a good time to interrupt, so when I reached the end of the *kapitel*, I apologized and said again that I needed to read Tehillim and couldn't talk.

He nodded as I spoke and said, "I know, Rabbi. I got it..." but he continued walking quietly alongside. It seemed like he just wanted to hear my Tehillim for some reason. We walked for a while in full view of the general population, which included many of the people this guy hoped to impress—the bearded chassid with his *Tehillim* and the tough guy inexplicably walking along and listening quietly. He interrupted me only to warn me if I was about to step into a puddle or to say "Heads up!" if someone was about to bump into me.

This wasn't the only time a non-Jewish inmate stepped in to ensure I wasn't disturbed while I served Hashem. It happened from time to time that I had to *daven* in a common area. Trying to remove myself from my surroundings as much as possible, I would pull my *tallis* over my head and stand in the corner facing the wall. One inmate made a point of standing behind me, between me and the rest of the inmates. If anyone approached, he would stop them. "You can't bother Rabbi now," he would tell them, "he's praying." I saw in this both the respect that serving Hashem had earned me in the eyes of the other inmates and, of course, Hashem's miraculous protection as I tried to stay close to Him.

One night, when they were celebrating their new year, I stood off to the side in the common area and watched them celebrating. This same inmate came over and, with a big smile, forcefully blew a lungful of air in my face. I didn't know what to make of this bizarre behavior and didn't respond immediately. He looked at me expectantly and, seeing my confusion, he tried again, blowing another lungful of air in my face.

His breath smelled like alcohol and it suddenly hit me what he was doing. Alcohol was strictly forbidden in prison and was very difficult to procure, but he had somehow done it. He was drunk, or at least a little tipsy. He wanted to let someone in on his joyous secret, sharing his good fortune and implicitly bragging about his skill or connections, but he couldn't share it verbally from fear of being overheard and reported.

This was a real mark of respect and trust. He had other friends, people he played cards with or exercised with, but he worried they'd sell him out to a guard for a pack of stamps. Of all the inmates he knew, he trusted the religious Jew from Brooklyn with his secret. I smiled back at him and wished him a happy new year, a year of freedom from the place called prison.

This wasn't an isolated instance of *kiddush Hashem*. I was sitting and learning with another Yid when "Blue" walked over to say something. "I apologize for interrupting you guys, but I have to tell you something. I've been in here more than twenty years and I've never met people as good as you."

Two nights before my miraculous release, another inmate, a real tough guy, said to me, "Sholom, before I was sent here, if we would pass each other on the street, I would have barely noticed you. Now that I've met you, I thank G-d that I was able to get to know you."

Not all inmates sought safety in numbers and in friendships of varying degrees of sincerity. Some took a different approach, watching out for themselves at the *expense* of others, trying to curry favor with the guards by informing on their fellow inmates. The inmates called these prisoners "guards in khaki uniforms," or, somewhat less flatteringly, "rats."

These prisoners were sometimes rewarded with prison currency; stamps that had been confiscated from other inmates during a shakedown. They were also often given a pass on violations of rules and regulations.

One such prisoner was Otisville's unofficial tattoo artist, a guy responsible for almost all of the fresh tattoos in the barrack. Giving tattoos is strictly forbidden in the place called prison, but apparently his "reporting" was so important to the counselor that he allowed him to continue his illegal work. I once heard the counselor scolding him and actually hinting that if he didn't cooperate, he would stop him from making tattoos, but no action was ever taken to stop him, and he continued his work unimpeded.

His work wasn't subtle either. I remember a new arrival who made a striking first impression because his clean-shaven head had two large tattooed horns. Within a few months of his arrival, his whole head was covered with tattoos, courtesy of this tattoo artist rat.

The desecration of the human body shocked my eyes and turned my stomach, but not as much as this sadly familiar pattern. Officers charged with enforcing the law pick the target that they're interested in pursuing and ignore crimes committed by those they've chosen to ally themselves with. In the place called prison, it was tattoo artist rats. Civilians in cities across the country see it play out with petty criminals who are allowed to sell drugs or avoid arrest for other things, if they only inform on whoever happens to be law enforcement's preferred target of the day.

In their zeal to curry favor or get out of a tight spot, these informers would occasionally fabricate accusations if they had nothing to report. True or false, these accusations often resulted in major inconvenience and disruptions for the other inmates. I remember one morning, while I was preparing to *daven* in the cell, I heard a loud call. "Everyone out!" An officer ran by the cell, pausing just long enough to bellow, "Leave *now!*"

I followed the stream of inmates out of the barracks and we all waited out in the yard to be let back in. Guards kept streaming into the barrack, hurrying the inmates out before they had a chance to hide any contraband they may have had, either in their cell or on their person—all on the word of an informant.

This was not the only such incident. There were times that the guards did not do a full barrack search, but even when they were given very precise information, they would search many cells besides the one they were targeting, just to make it difficult to figure out the identity of their informant. These flash shakedowns occasionally resulted in the discovery of contraband, but far more frequently, they came up with nothing. It got so bad that the guards began to generally distrust information they were receiving from the rats.

The inmates also didn't take the activities of the rats quietly. One of the first prisoners I met in the general population was a Latino fellow who became a Muslim and joined the group of other Muslim inmates. His commitment seemed sincere. At the time, we were both assigned to the dormitory cell, and I would see him wake early to say his prayers.

One day, he was attacked by the other Muslims. The guards broke up the fight and he was subsequently transferred out of Otisville. Apparently, a new arrival had read his name on his shirt and recognized him as an informant in another time and place. This information caused his new friends to see his conversion in a new light and they decided it warranted a beating.

Perhaps this showed the authorities the drawbacks of having an inmate's identity displayed on their shirt, or perhaps it was completely unrelated, but shortly after this story, they discontinued the policy of stamping the shirt pocket with the inmate's information. To myself and others, no longer walking around with the dehumanizing prison number prominently displayed was a welcome change.

Prison of the Mind

The inmates were, generally speaking, obedient—at least when they were being monitored and under threat of punishment, which was almost all the time. They accepted the hierarchy and power dynamics, and did what they could to survive within it. They internalized the schedule and regulations until they were practically instinct, and began to think of themselves in a new light— as prisoners, there to stay. They call this state of mind "institutionalized."

Walking back from the chapel one day, not long after I had arrived, I heard a guard tell a Jewish prisoner, "Go to your house!" Out of context and to my inexperienced ear, it sounded almost like he was telling the inmate that he should report to the office for release. I was very happy for him and instinctively said a silent *tefillah* to Hashem that I also merit to return home to my family and friends very soon.

To my astonishment, instead of heading to the administrative offices to be released, the prisoner turned down the path heading to the barracks. It took me a second to realize that I'd misunderstood what the guard said. This prisoner understood immediately that "your house" referred to his cell in the barracks.

I cringed at the use of the word "house," a place where a person is in his own domain and can fully express himself without external restraint, to refer to the prison cell where he is held captive. The next time I saw this fellow, I commented to him, "Isn't it terrible that the guards call the prison cell your house?!"

He shrugged. "I get my mail here, don't I?"

Walking out of the cell one day, I passed Bucky, who was sitting in the common area looking at the screens overhead. "Hey, Rabbi!" he called out to me. "Look at the dog in the show up there… It's so ugly, it's cute!" Saying it out loud, he must have realized how idiotic it sounded, so he gave me a long, drawn-out explanation of the concept. He was watching a dog competition which showcased the ugliest-looking dogs, and they were so ugly, it made them cute to look at. I thanked him for this "explanation" and his invitation, which I politely turned down.

This was so typical of that place. The isolation from reality and mental deterioration that brought people to find ugliness charming was the same distortion that warped a person to accept and adapt to the ugliness of prison as a "new normal."

More relevant to us all and in keeping with the teaching of the Ba'al Shem Tov, it is the same distortion that leads us to find charm in a life distant from Hashem, feeling at home in *galus* and in a life centered around our bodies and their whims. Seeing an *aveirah*—something that is truly ugly—as appealing or "cute" is a loud wake-up call, a red flag warning us that we're becoming institutionalized by our *yetzer hara*. We need to see the ugliness for what it truly is and reject it or, if possible, transform it by using it in the service to Hashem. Then it becomes *truly* beautiful, an expression of *kedushah*, the fulfillment of Hashem's intention in creating the world.

The passage of time is a major factor in institutionalization. At first, incarceration is a source of tremendous pain. Those who have not experienced it often trivialize it. After all, in first-world prisons inmates are not shackled to the wall, not flogged, not forced to do hard labor in sub-zero temperatures. How bad can it be? I put the question to those around me in Otisville: Given the choice between their average twenty to twenty-five years in a modern medium security facility on the one hand, and ten years of hard labor on the other, which would they choose? Every last one of them chose hard labor.

Think about that. "Civilized" society shrinks from imposing hard labor and prefers to sentence people to "more merciful" extended prison sentences instead. It may be easier on *them* to bury the problem, but hard labor was unanimously voted a greater mercy by the ones who are being buried.

And they *are* being buried. The emotional and psychological sensation caused by incarceration feels like suffocation, like sinking beneath the water. The loss of freedom hits a person just like the loss of air, something so elementary that the person almost doesn't know he has it until he loses it—and his entire being reflexively focuses on the loss and is consumed by it. As the seconds tick by endlessly, the person sinks deeper beneath the surface, further and further from anyone who might see their pain and further beyond their reach to help.

Like a person drowning, a prisoner first goes through a stage of intense pain and distress but with time simply "loses consciousness" and goes numb. The many years that have passed and the seemingly endless years to go make freedom seem like a distant dream. He's been here forever and he'll stay here forever—this is who he is now.

That's not to say the pain is gone. The inmates call death in prison a "back door parole" because, in dying, the inmate has at least and at last escaped the pain of prison. But after a while, the inmates accept their painful situation and try to adapt as best they can, which leads to becoming institutionalized.

Sitting in the chow hall one evening, I overheard an inmate at the next table listing for another inmate the various educational programs available in Otisville, their schedules, and how the various courses or degrees would benefit a person in life. The other inmate listened politely for somewhere between three and four seconds, the average twenty-first-century attention span, before interrupting this "advertisement." "They put me in here two decades ago and I've still got one and a half decades to go. What do I care for all of that?"

I refused to allow this place called prison to change who I am. I would *not* become institutionalized. One of the moments that I cherish from my time there relates to institutionalization—specifically, my success at avoiding it. It came on a hot Thursday afternoon. I had a lot to get done that day. In addition to the weekly emails, which were my participation in my family's Shabbos meals, I had been corresponding with a number of *Yidden*, and I really needed to spend some time writing.

The heat was unbearable that day and the noisy oversized fan in the corner was not helping at all. The only available relief was a cup of ice from the lone ice machine in the barrack. I left the computer room, hoping no one would take the computer while I was away, and hurried down the flights of stairs to where the machine was located.

To my dismay, there was a long line formed at the ice machine. It would take a lot of time to reach the front, time I didn't have. Looking around, I noticed that someone I knew was already on the line. He seemed to be a generally unassuming, agreeable fellow and I'd done him favors in the past. We weren't friends, but we'd smile and wish each other a good day when we passed each other around the barrack.

I motioned to him that I wanted to ask him something. Once I got his attention, I asked, "Hey, would you do me a favor? Take my cup and grab some ice for me too? I'm really tied up at the computer and I need to get back. It'll shut off soon."

His face turned slightly hostile. "No," he said curtly, and turned away.

I had obviously said something to anger him. I didn't know what exactly, but I did know enough not to press the issue. Forced to choose between the ice and the emails, I went back upstairs to the stifling heat of the computer room to write the rest of the *dvar Torah*.

The next time I saw this inmate, later that day, he cornered me in a quiet spot. Fists clenched, he said, "Rubashkin! You disrespected me today."

Stripped of the possessions and positions which had previously determined their place in society, the inmates put a lot of emphasis on respect. The whole hierarchy in prison was determined by respect, usually mixed with a dose of fear. Disrespecting someone in prison is a mortal sin and the "victim" would look for ways to balance the scales.

This particular person was no one to laugh at, literally. His sentence in prison was a result of his earlier career as a hitman, a murderer for hire, and laughing at him would not end well.

"What did I do to disrespect you?" I asked, sincerely puzzled.

"In front of my guys, you ask me to get you a cup of ice? What am I—your messenger boy?" he barked angrily. "In front of my guys?! There are rules in prison!"

Now I understood what I had done wrong. It was lunacy, but I understood. By asking him for a favor, I had given the impression that I was superior to him and could send him on errands. It was demeaning and offensive, and if he let that stand, it would endanger his place in the hierarchy.

He launched into an angry lecture on prison etiquette and hierarchies while I warily kept an eye on his hands. At some point he stopped to breathe, and I jumped in with an apology. "Listen. I'm sorry about offending you. It was an honest mistake. I didn't realize how things work here and, now that I know, I'll be sure never to ask you for anything again…"

He must have noticed that throughout his lecture I'd been alert and attentive but with an entirely uncomprehending expression, so he took my words at face value. He threw up his hands and said, "Rubashkin, you're not even here! I see you going up and down with your nose in those books you're always carrying! You're not even here! Never mind!" and he stomped off.

To my relief, the danger had been averted, *baruch Hashem*. What contributed more to my happiness, though, was his observation. Becoming institutionalized was like sinking to the bottom and here he was, inadvertently confirming that I was successfully raising myself *above* the place, enough so that it was obvious to the people around me.

The psychological effects of incarceration are devastating, first and foremost because inmates lose the things by which they define themselves. Being a spouse, a parent, or a member of a family or community is a big part of many people's identity. Being torn away from that leaves the inmate with a real crisis. The lucky few have a small taste of what they lost in the occasional visit by family or friends, but those precious moments with loved ones are insufficient to replace what they lost.

These relationships, such a big part of who they were, are often gone forever, especially for inmates with long sentences. I was sitting with a few others one day when an inmate nicknamed DeeDee mentioned that he was being freed very soon. Although most inmates feel a powerful envy when someone else receives this news, we were very happy for him and offered him a hearty congratulations.

"Na, guys," he dismissed our warm wishes, "I'll be back. Soon as I'm out, I'mma do something that gets me back here." He explained to us that he no longer has any family or friends because he has been "down" for so long. "For me," he concluded sadly, "this is home."

Another source of identity and self-worth is found in working and contributing to the world. This is something the Torah tells us is fundamental to our nature. *Adam l'amal yulad*—"Man is born to toil." We are tasked with building and transforming Hashem's world and we only feel complete when we are able to pursue that mission.

Incarceration steals that from a person as well, stripping him of the ability to toil and produce. Whatever jobs inmates are assigned don't come close to utilizing their abilities and you might find an accomplished physician mopping floors.

Unable to really contribute to the world, some inmates bitterly joked that they were on vacation. It was tongue in cheek, obviously, but the comparison was interesting. People don't seek help from mental health professionals when they get back to the office after a month-long cruise, but many do need help reentering society after time in prison.

A real vacation, a healthy vacation, is when we rest to restore our strength and to prepare ourselves to continue our task. Permanent or aimless "vacation," on the other hand, is contrary to our nature and our identity and it quickly erodes the spirit, making the person feel useless and worthless and giving rise to distress and despair. This is particularly painful for those whom the system has vowed to continually incarcerate for decades or even until death.

This also explains why I myself did not need help readjusting when I was finally freed with Hashem's help. The toil that gives my life purpose is not found in my job or even in my personal relationships, but in my duty and service to Hashem, which was not interrupted by my ordeal even for one moment.

The judicial system, in the form of various types of appeals, holds out a glimmer of hope that some inmates might regain their freedom. Many of the prison personnel were very supportive of these efforts. Of course, not in any helpful way, such as by providing the access to tools they would need to be effective, but through verbal encouragement.

They readily suggested to the inmate that he was sure to benefit from some recent change in the law or some new legal argument they'd developed, when in fact, the systemic imbalance of the justice system meant that most appellants were on a roller coaster which took them to the heights of hope only to plunge them at dizzying speed to the depths of despair.

I'm sure some of those encouraging staff members were well-meaning, but the consensus among experienced prisoners was that they were just using false hope to pacify their charges and make their own jobs easier. One inmate felt, more cynically, that it was the emotional destruction of the inevitable denials they were after, whether out of sheer viciousness or because it broke the inmate so thoroughly that they often slumped into easy-to-manage despondent inactivity.

Over the years, I had occasion to see a number of inmates notified that their legal efforts had failed. The news would bring many of them to the brink. Some would retreat to their cells to sulk and brood, drowning in the hopelessness of their situation. Others would break down, sobbing and wailing.

There was one Jewish inmate, a Yid who came closer to Torah and mitzvos in Otisville, who was told at some point that he was eligible for early release as part of a law that had been passed. As described, a number of prison staff were very encouraging and offered him false hope.

Sure enough, after building his hopes for early release, his application was summarily denied, which was devastating to him. Sadly, sometime later, he fell down and hurt himself so severely that he needed to be transferred to a facility with better medical care and we lost contact with him.

A note about false hope. You might wonder how I, of all people, could possibly call hope "false." You might even suspect, and rightly so, that I tried to give this man hope myself. I certainly did. I encouraged him to look at his situation as I looked at my own—as under the sole authority of Hashem—and to dismiss out of hand any proclamations by the earthly court that they could hold him at all, much less indefinitely. Given the statistical near-certainty that his appeal would be denied, wasn't I also giving him false hope?

Of course not. Where you put your hope is not only about where you think your salvation will come—it's about where you believe true power lies. Pinning your hopes on the laws of nature is implicit acceptance that those laws will decide the outcome. Doing so, when those laws offer only disappointment, is not only wrong but foolish, and when the denial comes, it's experienced as what it appears to be—a negative, devastating outcome.

Placing our hope in Hashem is different. Firstly, by doing so, we are asserting that true power lies only with Hashem. Secondly, and most importantly, if our hope does not materialize, *chas v'shalom*, it is experienced totally differently. Instead of a binding resolution by a final authority, it is correctly seen as merely another step in the journey Hashem has prepared for us, Divine indication that there's more work to be done. Although there may be the very human disappointment, it is not a devastating repudiation of our hope. Our salvation will still certainly come and our hope and our trust will ultimately be rewarded.

Legal efforts and lost relationships aside, even the simple daily realities of prison are psychologically crippling, and many inmates turned to the shrinks simply in order to cope. With or without the help of the shrinks, I observed four distinct coping mechanisms. Interestingly, these approaches correspond to the categorization of the world into the four classical categories of creation; *domem, tzome'ach, chai,* and *medaber*—the inanimate, vegetation, animal, and human.

One approach sees the prisoner surrender to the grim and hopeless forecast for his life and simply stay in bed like a clump of earth, sadly or bitterly pining for the life he lost.

Another approach has him escape into a vegetative state, spending every possible moment with his earphones in his ears and his eyes glued to the pacifying screens above while his hands mechanically bring some morsels of food to his mouth—a couch potato without the couch.

In the third approach, the prisoner embraces the animal pleasures and activities of the body as his method of escape. Trying to find a measure of freedom, he paces back and forth in his enclosure, trying to live (as he defines it) as much as possible under the limits imposed upon him.

He engages in the prison economy, trying to acquire somewhat better food or other contraband items. He spends his days in the yard, building his physique, lifting heavy objects only to place them down again, and running in endless circles alongside the razor-wire enclosure, finding some solace or distraction in physical expression.

This was the most common and also the most visible approach. One morning, I was startled to notice a prisoner drinking from a coffee mug with the Starbucks logo that he'd somehow obtained. Ripped away from his life, he was attempting to recreate it in some small way. He used to start his mornings with a real coffee, at Starbucks or at the office, so there he sat, trying to imagine the taste of a proper coffee in the watery dregs he was drinking in prison.

There was another inmate who somehow got his hands on a tray, around which he constructed his morning breakfast ritual. He would carefully place a paper towel on the tray, arrange his bagel or hot cereal and a cup of coffee just so, and eat his breakfast prim and proper, as if he was being served in a hotel or cafe.

In another example of this approach, I was once sitting next to a prisoner who was eating a shelf-stable meal from its small plastic container and he bragged that he has every type of spice for his food. You or I might be puzzled as to why he thought that worthy of a boast, but for many in prison, this was a worthy aspiration and a real accomplishment.

Even if these men had gotten closer in their attempts to simulate freedom, if they had real Starbucks coffee, a real meal properly presented, or the same food as "on the outside," they would not satisfy the basic human need for actual, not simulated, freedom. Whatever you're eating in prison, you're still eating it in prison.

Obviously, I didn't begrudge them the attempt, but in my experience, this approach not only failed to help, it actually *exacerbated* the problem. The more a person attempts to improve their material standing, the more strongly they cement in their own minds and hearts the idea that their material standing is important and valuable. Inevitably, this intensifies their misery due to the inescapable, largely unimprovable, and objectively miserable state of their material standing.

The only real way to avoid being pulled down by our material standing is by subordinating it to our *neshamah* and the duty and privilege of serving and connecting to Hashem, which is what is truly important and valuable. This is as true "on the outside," in a place called freedom, as it was in a place called prison.

There was one exercise in the yard that encapsulated, in a single clear visual, the irony of these efforts to be free which were indelibly marked with the reality of subjugation. The first time I saw it, I couldn't believe my eyes. I watched from a bench in the yard as a younger inmate, as part of his body-building regimen, strapped a yoke to his shoulders. Attached to the yoke by a sturdy rope was a heavy disc-shaped weight. He planted his feet firmly in the ground, strained against the rope for a moment, and managed to move, first walking, then running, dragging the heavy weight behind him.

I shook my head in amazement. A ball and chain is the classic image of imprisonment and here this guy was, in an effort to feel free, voluntarily putting one on. He was really putting himself into it, trying to find freedom in a yoke and a weight.

The fourth approach is adopted by the inmate who realizes that he cannot escape his suffering in his bed or in a video monitor, and also finds the body's exertions poor replacements for freedom. Instead, he focuses on his human intellect, attempting to escape into the world of knowledge using the extremely sparse resources available. Abandoning his body to its cage, he finds freedom in his mind. He spends as much of his time as he can there, but the pains, needs, and wants of his body always insist themselves upon him, dragging him back to the reality of his incarceration.

Clearly, none of these four approaches really provides true freedom. There is a *fifth* approach, the Torah approach, which does. It's available to and adopted by the Jewish inmates. Simply put, the Jewish inmate finds his freedom in his purpose, in connecting to Hashem through learning His Torah and doing His mitzvos.

The pain of imprisonment is primarily that it prevents a person from expressing his nature and identity, but the nature and identity of a Yid—and his true purpose, wherever he might be—is to express with both body and mind the will of Hashem. His limiting circumstances are *also* part of the will of Hashem, so when he serves Hashem through Torah and mitzvos to the fullest degree that Hashem allows him to in the moment, he's fully expressing himself. He is truly free.

Where the other approaches surrender either the mind, the body, or both, the Yid recognizes that neither his mind *nor* his body are truly in prison and neither are prevented from expressing themselves in the things that really matter.

A Yid has two *nefashos*, one which identifies with the world and one which identifies with Hashem. The first is a source of imprisonment, and the second, a source of freedom. In a place called prison this is magnified, but even in a place called freedom the part of ourselves that relates to the world is the origin of our ego, our appetites, our inhibitions, and our fears—every one of them a prison. Freedom in every context is found in the *nefesh Elokis*, our G-dly *nefesh*.

This is counterintuitive to us because our intuition is shaped by the world, but through studying the Torah and carefully observing the truth in our lives and that of those around us, it becomes clear.

This is a good place for a "Ghost" story. The story demonstrates that a Yid that acts like a Yid experiences a freedom he can feel, even if he doesn't necessarily understand it and even if he is not yet acting like a Yid and rising above his incarceration in every way.

I was passing by a line of new arrivals when one of them made what sounded like a snide remark about the "strings" hanging out of my pants. I turned around to confront the mockery and, seeing my reaction, he hurried to smooth things over. "I know what those are!" he called out. "They're *tzitzit*!" Clearly, I was talking to a fellow Jew and he hadn't meant to offend.

We struck up a conversation, and he told me a bit about himself. He grew up in Florida and had even learned in a Talmud Torah as a child. He was a wild kid, always looking for adventure in the streets, and he ended up in a Mexican street gang. Over time, he became their leader.

As part of that life, he did something violent. He was arrested and sentenced to twelve years in high security federal prison. This was the last year of his sentence and, as part of easing him into his eventual release into society, he was transferred to Otisville, a medium security facility. He never explained why, but he went by the nickname "Ghost."

We had been brought together by *hashgachah pratis*, and I resolved to do my part in helping him grow closer to Hashem. I would invite him to cell 217 and we would talk about his Jewish heritage. Whenever we met, I would offer to help him put on *tefillin* and he would often take me up on it. On occasion, I would even proactively go up to the fifth level, where his cell was, to check if he would make time for this mitzvah. He would usually take me up on the offer, and sometimes he would even come find me a little later if the timing wasn't great.

Although he grew more comfortable with his Jewish identity, enough to come to the chapel for the Jewish services on occasion, he was still Ghost, the wild kid who was drawn to the streets.

One day, there was a knock on the door of cell 217. It was Ghost. I invited him in and immediately noticed his agitation. "Rabbi, good morning," he said. "Do you have time to put on *tefillin* with me?"

I was happy to oblige and didn't want to say anything that might discourage him, so I helped him put on the *tefillin* without probing further, but I thought

I helped many of my Jewish brothers in
Otisville fulfill the mitzvah of *tefillin*.

something was up. He seemed a bit on edge and he'd never taken the initiative and come to me to ask for the *tefillin* before.

When we had finished, as I was wrapping and putting the *tefillin* away, I asked him about it. "You look very nervous, my friend. What's going on?"

"I'm really uneasy, Rabbi," he confessed. "I'm being released in a few weeks and it's got me feeling really anxious. I can't sleep at night, worrying about how I'll be able to reintegrate into society, find a job, and build a new life. I can't calm myself, so I thought I'd come here and do a mitzvah."

We spoke a while about his future. I reassured him and reminded him that Hashem would care for his needs and his role was only to make appropriate efforts and trust in Hashem.

After he left, I thought about what had just happened. Here was a guy experiencing debilitating anxiety. He had, unfortunately, eleven years of experience. He knew his way around and could have gone to the psych unit and picked up the drugs they prescribe for exactly these conditions—but he didn't.

He didn't run for the pills, because he had experience with something better. He knew that a mitzvah soothed his soul, satisfying its discomfort—like food relieves hunger—in a way that pills simply could not. When he had put *tefillin* on in the past, it had given him a real sense of calm and security by connecting to Hashem. Now, when he was so desperately in need of these things, he came to do a mitzvah.

CHAPTER TWENTY-TWO

Jewish Life in Otisville

Holy Foundations

THERE ARE MANY SPECIAL TIMES AND SPECIFIC OBLIGATIONS WHICH fill the life of a Yid, but Jewish life rests on the bedrock of the *mitzvos timidios*, our constant, continuous duties. We are instructed to be aware of and believe in Hashem and His oneness, not to believe in any power other than Him, to love Hashem, to stand in awe of Hashem, and not to pursue the passions of our heart or stray after the temptations before our eyes. There are also *middos*, such as *simchah*, that are supposed to be a constant presence in the life of a Yid and form a foundation of his life and his *avodas Hashem*.

These beliefs and these good character traits are embedded in our *neshamah* from birth, but they blossom into the specific feelings and attitudes through action and through studying the holy *sefarim*.

It's difficult to break through the natural perspectives that we develop just by living in a world that seems to be independent of its Creator and to resist the external challenges, obstacles, and temptations that are thrown our way. It takes conscious and almost continuous effort, even in the most conducive environment.

In a place called prison, these difficulties are intensified. The Yid finds himself under near constant spiritual attack. Some of those attacks are direct and open assaults on beliefs we hold, and others are more subtle, drawing the Yid into seemingly unrelated thoughts or actions which actually undermine our very foundations.

An inmate's physical suffering is felt with all five of his senses but the attack on his *neshamah* is waged mainly through two; his sight and his hearing.

See No Evil

Wherever an inmate looks, whether indoors or outside, he is confronted by the instruments of his imprisonment: the two rows of high fencing topped with barbed wire encircling the compound; the cold, spare, cinder-block walls, broken only by small and thickly barred windows and doors; the ubiquitous roving prison guards, always watching and occasionally accosting someone.

All of these sights are a constant pull to the pit of sadness and self-pity. Giving in to that pull, *chas v'shalom*, would be to diminish the certainty that Hashem is the only power, and that He orchestrates the life of a Yid for the Yid's benefit. This inevitably weakens one's love of Hashem, and his joy in serving Him.

Another angle of attack through the eyes are the unholy sights which surround the Yid, stemming from the behavior of those around him or from their media, whether printed or broadcast on the screens overhead.

The only real counter to these visual attacks is a clear Torah perspective, but this defense is only needed when the sights are unavoidable. Very often these sights are *not* unavoidable and the attack only begins when the Yid looks around more than necessary and invites it on himself. Those are fights we can win without fighting, by simply avoiding the fight!

When I would walk through the barrack or the compound, I would look straight ahead or shift my eyes downward, as if engrossed in thought, completely avoiding the barrage of foreign and harmful sights. (As an added benefit, this often enabled me to escape into my thoughts.) This was not just a fleeting victory. We tend to remember the things that we see for a long time to come. Echoes of these unwanted scenes can resurface for years, and at the worst possible times. By not seeing these things, I avoided not only the immediate challenge, but also those recurring struggles.

One evening, I was returning to the cell from the computer room. As usual, I didn't look around as I walked. I could easily find my way to the right cell without looking up by counting the doors as I passed them.

That day, there was a group of Hispanic prisoners sitting in a semi-circle in the corridor near the cell, playing cards. Still thinking about the correspondence I'd been reading and formulating my response, I didn't notice that they fell suspiciously silent as I approached. I excused myself as I squeezed past them and pulled the heavy door open.

Looking around the cell, I instantly and instinctively recoiled. My reflexes had me out of the cell and slamming the door almost before my mind processed what I had seen. I stood outside the door with my hand on the handle, dazed and confused. Extremely inappropriate magazines had been strewn all over the floor of the cell.

I looked up to see if I'd miscounted and entered the wrong cell by accident, but no—the door number showed that it was cell 217. Suddenly, my mind registered that my hasty exit had triggered uproarious laughter. I turned to look at the suddenly boisterous group of inmates and one of them pushed by me into the cell, scooped up the magazines, and came back out, to the merriment of his friends.

I'm not sure if it was just a prank on "Rabbi" or some sort of bet about what my response would be, but seeing the sincerity with which I lived my beliefs and standards, that group was noticeably more respectful in the future.

The phrase "*shemiras einayim*" is a familiar one to *Yidden*, more so in this generation than ever before, but it's worth noting that in addition to physical eyes, "*einayim*" symbolize our perspective, our mental clarity. *Shemiras einayim* is a call to defend the eyes of our mind and of our *neshamah* and that only begins, but certainly doesn't end, with taking care and control of our physical eyes.

As if the live "performances" were not enough, the authorities piped in additional sights through screens overhead. The word "screen" also means partition, and these overhead screens were definitely overhead partitions. By distraction and preoccupation, they separated the prisoners from any aspiration to rise above their situation, a pacifying effect that was surely the primary reason they were installed. The actual content goes a step further and doesn't just prevent a person from going higher—it actively drags him down to the lowest state a human being can inhabit.

As a Yid, my *whole life* is an aspiration to go higher. I would have nothing to do with any screens over my head and I certainly didn't want to allow a handhold to anything that would drag me down.

You might be thinking, "Well, what's the harm in looking?" The Arizal writes that Adam Harishon and Chava were so far removed from evil, that no amount of persuasion by the *Nachash* could have led them to sin. Instead, the *Nachash* first persuaded them to "just" look, to become aware of what exists in the realms of evil. This created a connection, a bridge to the other side. It opened up the possibility of sinning, and, as we know, ultimately led to the actual sin and the consequences we all bear.

Of course, like the arguments of the original *Nachash*, the bilge these screens pipe to the eyes and ears is presented in the friendliest, most attractive way. "It's entertainment—a way to unwind and relieve the stress!" This was the go-to rationalization, and I heard it more times than I can count. I knew the pain and stress of daily life under those circumstances, and I understood the problem—but I also knew, with equal clarity, that this was not the solution!

Adopting the perspectives espoused on these "shows," whether in the category of news, opinion, drama, comedy, or any of the other wrappers they wrap around the same core content, only "blurs a Yid's eyesight," making him view the world from their perspective rather than the perspective of the truth of Torah. This is an indirect attack on our foundations.

To use the tragic circumstance of incarceration as an example, in their reality a person in a place called prison is an irredeemable "bad guy" rightly and eternally under the power of the authorities. Entering that world, even superficially or temporarily, the Yid relinquishes the truth—that he is a *neshamah*, created by Hashem and given a unique mission in life. He was brought to his current situation by his loving Father so that he could grow from the experience and find a closer connection with Hashem, and perhaps also to bring some G-dliness to other people or to use an object or a place for a Divine purpose.

My experiences had inoculated me against the slick, deceptive charm of the snake. I could see the venomous fangs beneath the smiling facade of these "shows," and resolutely avoided the screens. I wouldn't even look at them to know the time.

There was another issue with the screens, which I only realized during a discussion with another inmate who questioned my behavior. A fellow Jew, unaware of my stance on the screens, invited me to join him in watching a certain show. I declined, explaining that I don't watch TV. "Oh, I understand," he assured me, "but this is a *family* show…for relaxation!"

"I'm not picky," I told him. "I don't watch any TV at all."

"But why not?"

I wanted to give some thought to which of my reasons would most resonate with this person, so I suggested that we meet the next day in the yard for a walk and we could talk it over then. Thinking it over that night, a new angle occurred to me, one I thought he would appreciate.

We met as planned the next day, and took our walk around the yard. We discussed truth and how one ascertains it. Of all our senses, the most certain is sight: We may still be in doubt after having heard something, but if we see it with our own eyes, no doubts remain.

This is why Hashem brought us to the mountain and gave us the Torah as we stood and witnessed, as Moshe Rabbeinu later said, *"With your own eyes you saw Hashem give you the Torah."*

"One issue with these shows," I explained to my friend, "is that you learn to no longer trust your own eyes. Special effects convincingly show you people flying through the air or doing things no man can possibly do. Animals that never existed and can't possibly exist seem to live and breathe on those screens.

"Your eyes can't distinguish these sights from reality, but your mind knows that they're fake. The natural conclusion is that seeing is not believing. By exposing yourself to undetectable fakery, you lose confidence in the very tool that Hashem gave you to see reality."[1]

I was able to illustrate this from protocols right there in Otisville. "Even the guards, who set up the screens, only trust their eyes when it really matters. They continually drive and walk around to inspect the fence even though they surely have sensors and screens that tell them if there is a breach.

"They also continuously count us to be sure no one escaped. Even though it's the twenty-first century and the technology exists, they don't give us high-tech gadgets, like tracking chips, that they can monitor electronically. They're still doing what prison guards have been doing for millennia. They physically walk around every barrack and peer into every cell to see with their own eyes that everyone is there."

Now that I'd put my finger on this phenomenon, I realized that I had seen its effects for years before Otisville. As an adult, I noticed that the glimpses of holiness afforded by going to shul or the *beis midrash* and observing a holy or learned person like an *admor* or *rosh yeshivah* didn't seem to ignite and inspire people to the extent they had when I was a child. I'm sure there are many reasons for this, but I'm certain that exposure to screens, and the resulting disconnect from the truth of what we see, plays a very significant part.

This was not my main objection to the screens and their content, but my

---

1. Earlier I noted that you have to trust your flight instruments—the Torah—and mistrust your eyes, your instinctive perceptions. In that case, the subject is not perception but interpretation. For that you must turn to the Torah. What the screens threaten, in addition to interpretation, is perception itself. That is so fundamental that without it we cannot proceed at all, similar to the fake news and mistrust which is now paralyzing society.

new friend appreciated the thought. For myself, I was very happy to have discovered a new insight which bolstered my commitment to protect my eyes. My circumstances made it extra important to be able to differentiate between reality and fiction, between what truly is and what is merely claimed. If I lost sight of that, I would start to forget that I am exclusively in Hashem's power and start to accept that I was in *their* power, *chas v'shalom*. I recommitted myself to protecting my physical eyes and the eyes of my *neshamah* and the confidence I have in what is real.

There was a total solar eclipse in 2017 which had the whole compound buzzing. There were constant reminders of the danger of gazing directly at the sun, especially during the eclipse, when to all appearances, the danger from the intensity of the sun's light is diminished. This reminded me of these discussions about the dangers that could be inherent in "just looking," even when to all appearances, the danger has been diminished or removed, like from a "family show."

Hear No Evil

It may be difficult at times to avoid simply looking around, especially when something is doing its best to get your attention, but at least you have the equipment you need in order to do so. Pointing your head in a different direction or closing your eyelids will usually do the trick, once you muster the strength to assert the will of Hashem over your *yetzer hara*. The ears are physically a lot harder to protect.

Walking around the barrack or compound, or even just sitting in the cell, waves of noise were constantly washing over me, tsunamis of sound unrestrained in every respect. My head would ache from the sheer volume, amplified as it bounces off metal and stone, and my heart would ache from the substance, crass and vulgar.

Like every aspect of incarceration, this physical and emotional discomfort could easily lead a person to sadness and self-pity. Beyond that, the frivolous, flippant, and outright disrespectful attitudes toward everything serious and holy, peppered with obscenities, clouded the mind and made it difficult to think. If the words seeped in and registered, they could also desensitize a person and cloud his heart.

This abhorrent soundscape was physically inescapable and it required great effort to focus on other things to the point where the sounds around me faded.

Of course, there were some places that were worse than others. Leaving those places wasn't always an option—sometimes I needed to be there to use the phone, for example, or I was literally locked into the situation—but when it *was* an option, you can be sure I went to a quieter place.

Once, miraculously, it happened the other way around. I was sitting in the computer room, making every effort to finish a lengthy email on the *parshah* before Shabbos. Two inmates sat down by another computer and started chatting about the contents of their email, which reflected the contents of their lives and ideals, such as they were. Their conversation would have made a truck driver blush. I reflexively put my fingers in my ears, but I quickly realized I couldn't continue typing without taking them out again. I really needed to finish the email and, because of the time, coming back when they were gone wasn't an option.

I did something then that I very rarely did, and imposed on other inmates. Anticipating a harsh response, but with no alternative, I spoke up. "Excuse me," I said. They looked up, surprised at the interruption. In an inquisitive, non-confrontational tone of voice I continued, "Would you mind continuing that conversation somewhere else? I'm really not old enough to hear this conversation."

Instead of the barrage of curses and threats, or even violence, that normally resulted from interruption by another inmate, they just looked at me, almost embarrassed. "Oh! Sorry, Rabbi! We didn't realize we were bothering you!" They shut the computer and went off to continue their conversation elsewhere.

I discovered an interesting phenomenon in which my defense of my sight helped in my defense of my hearing. The four phones that served the barrack were placed in a common area far from the cells. One year, the warden moved one of the phones, relocating it right outside the cell to which I'd been assigned. The noise level in the common area afforded some degree of privacy by masking the phone conversations, but here, where it was quieter, there was no privacy at all. Every word of those phone calls echoed off the walls, and could be heard clearly in quite a few cells.

Of course, I tried to ignore these private conversations. I couldn't help hearing them, but by focusing on other things, I tried to ensure that they wouldn't really register. One afternoon, there was a lull in whatever I was doing, and I registered the words floating through the slot in the door. The words were so repulsive, and the substance so ugly, that I was thunderstruck.

I couldn't imagine a human being saying what was being said and using the words being used. I jumped up to see what kind of animal was talking that way.

Mid-leap, I remembered my commitment to not make any hasty moves in a place called prison. This was a totally foreign and hostile environment, one which I had no prior experience understanding and navigating. It was no time or place to be reacting without thinking, and I had resolved to always take a beat to think over what was truly happening and how I should react.

I stopped. "Why do I want to see who's speaking like that?" I asked myself. My initial justification was that it's important to know which people are of such low character, so that I can avoid them. Spelling it out like that, I had to admit that it was pretty flimsy—a sure sign it was just an excuse by my *yetzer hara* and somehow would come back to bite me.

I thought about it a bit, and realized that if I put a face and a name to those words, they would echo in my head every time I saw that face or heard that name. I very much wanted to wipe the memory of those phrases from my mind, which argued against looking, but I still struggled with what I now realized was cheap curiosity. I stood for a few moments, grappling with the urge. Ultimately, remembering my own discussions about the danger of screens and the power of sight tipped the scales to the right side. If I didn't look, I wouldn't know who said it, and the memory, resting only on sound, would fade. If I looked, those ugly words and thoughts would come and live with me in my world. No, thank you.

Thanking Hashem for His gift of clarity just in the nick of time, I sat down and continued learning. I will always remember my visceral reaction and that inner conflict, but I quickly forgot what was actually said. Seeing the success of this strategy, I included it in my "survival kit." Over time, I heard many things there that I wished I hadn't, and I always made sure not to turn and look at the person who'd spoken. Happily, my memory does not include those words and many like them, thanks to that decision to avoid thoughtless reaction, and thanks to Hashem's timely gift of clarity.

As if the existing noise wasn't enough, the authorities kindly offered devices which could pour additional sounds straight down the ear canal. They sold small radios with earphones that could be used to voluntarily subject yourself to a number of radio channels. On some channels, they also transmitted the audio that matched the visual garbage that radiated out of the screens overhead.

As I described earlier, this was later supplemented by MP3 players which the more fortunate inmates could buy and load with their own selection of songs available for purchase. Declining to contribute to the attack on my own *neshamah* through my ears, I never obtained either of these devices. This was another fight I could win simply by avoiding it.

One inmate, trying to explain his excitement about the new devices, exulted that now he can listen to gangster rap—"music" celebrating the life and "culture" of gangsters—all day, every day, all week long. This seemed to me to be more of an argument against the device than a reason to be excited.

Using one of the *yetzer hara's* familiar strategies, they eventually baited the MP3 player hook with Jewish songs. Even this nod to the Jewish inmates took many requests, by them and by others on their behalf, and took a very long time to deliver. I still chose not to get a device, although it did work for other *Yidden* there.

Not long after these new MP3 devices were made available, I was approached in the computer room by the inmate considered the leader of the Otisville Muslims. "You have a minute?" he asked. "I heard you're not buying the MP3 player. Is that true?"

He was not a violent fellow, and he didn't incite his followers against *Yidden*. We had a civil, cordial relationship and I didn't want to be disrespectful by brushing him off. Although he was technically prying in a way that was strongly discouraged by the local culture, I answered his question.

"That's correct, I won't be buying one," I responded, hoping he would leave it at that and let me get back to my work. He didn't.

"Why not?!" he demanded.

I wasn't really interested in *farbrenging* with an Imam about this topic, but the question was asked and I answered it.

"They may have a hold on my body, but they have no hold on my soul and I refuse to give them one."

"What do you mean?" he pressed. "They're just songs…"

This is a classic tactic of the *yetzer hara*, a real giveaway that you're dealing with him. He always says "*just*," minimizing the impact of whatever he's offering, as if it's no big deal. If that was true, saying "no" shouldn't be a big deal either, but if you refuse, you'll see what kind of big deal he considers it after all. I tried to explain why they're not "just" songs.

"These songs express—in lyrics, melody, and musical style—attitudes and values, aspirations and ambitions, likes and dislikes that are absolutely antithetical to everything I am. They want to inspire me to feel what they feel and want what they want. The music is very moving, but to places that I don't want to move. That's why I'm not getting an MP3."

The sheikh appreciated the thought. "You know what?" he said, smiling. "I'm not going to buy an MP3 either!"

Some weeks later, I noticed him in the common area, looking up at a screen, listening through one of the new MP3 players. I felt the urge to ask him what had happened to his decision, but on second thought, I realized it was not only condescending, but actually unfair of me.

Raw willpower can carry you through the rough patches in life, but every person still needs to find joy and pleasure in his life. I am a Yid with a *neshamah*, with Torah and mitzvos which connect me to Hashem—the Source of all life, joy, and pleasure. I didn't need to search for those things in empty amusements, but how could I begrudge those things to those who don't have that same connection?

It didn't take long before the MP3s were ubiquitous. Even at a price that was equivalent to two months of work for many inmates, it seemed like everyone who wasn't generating noise was consuming it through the earphones.

Of course, the initial decision to plug in and tune out was voluntary, but the "peace" that came from drowning out every inner thought, many of which were painful, was very enticing, even addictive. What started as background music in the common area quickly became a soundtrack that accompanied the inmate everywhere on the compound, drowning out every thought, observation, or introspection the person might have had and that might have contributed to the "correction" that was ostensibly the goal of this "institution."

The Profound Effect of Outer Appearances

Some find this surprising, but another important foundation for a healthy and holy inner life, which impacts every aspect of our day and everything we do to some degree, is our outer appearance. Some aspects of our appearance are not connected with a specific mitzvah—staying clean and neat and making refined choices in our clothing, headwear, footwear, and hair styles. Other aspects are dictated by halachah—yarmulke and *tzitzis*, full coverage as *tznius* demands, *peyos* and beard, etc.

Making the right choices, and insisting on those things that are really not our choice, help a person feel that they are truly standing in Hashem's presence throughout the day. This helps them feel the appropriate love and awe which connects them to Hashem, and gives them an allergy to anything that might mean distance from Hashem.

Initially, I avoided taking a haircut entirely, for fear that they would cut my *peyos* or beard. Your local barber knows that the customer is always right, but the inmate given barber duties isn't overly worried about positive reviews and customer retention, and might disregard a request.

After a few months, they agreed to allow me to cut my own hair. Because of the difficulty in doing any precision barbering on myself and the possibility of *chas v'shalom* cutting the *peyos* too short or even slipping and cutting beard hairs near the *peyos*, I avoided cutting the hair on that whole part of my head.

I also took extra precautions with the length. Although the *minhag* of Chabad, based on the *minhag* of the Arizal, is to cut the *peyos* at the cheekbone when possible, I held my *peyos* far away from my beard hair to cut them, resulting in much longer *peyos*. To satisfy the *minhag* of the Arizal, I tucked the *peyos* behind my ears as is done when hair can't be cut, such as during the year of *aveilus*, R"l.

Living between non-Jews, where many suggest blending in, my new, highly-visible *peyos* made it clear from quite a distance that I'm a Yid who is *shomer Torah u'mitzvos*. This expression of Jewish pride helped anchor me and ensure that I made choices permeated with proud *Yiddishkeit*. I had to live up to my *peyos*!

I also tried to help others who struggled with these things. One of the *Yidden* there was a man of Sephardic descent. He embodied the strong, uncomplicated faith and pureness of character that marks his community, even those with no formal education in Torah and mitzvos and who may not be fully observant.

He had a strong commitment to *davening*, and we *davened* together every day. One day, I left the barrack at the appointed time and headed to the chapel. I met up with him along the way, as usual, and we continued the walk together. Something seemed different about him, but I couldn't figure out what it was. I slowed my walk and gave him a quick once-over. It took me a moment to realize that he'd had a shave and a haircut. Then I realized that his *peyos* were gone.

In a mild, friendly tone I asked, "Hey… What happened to your *peyos?*"

He seemed surprised at the question. "Sholom, look around!" he said, gesturing at the compound and the heavily-tattooed inmates walking by. "Do you know where you are?"

"Yes, I know where I am," I said. "You think Hashem is not here, *chas v'shalom?* Hashem is everywhere, including in Otisville!"

He was lost in thought as we walked toward the chapel. "Listen," I said, breaking the silence. "You're on your way to *daven.* You'll stand there and say to Hashem, 'It's me, I'm here. I have a request, please grant it to me.' But with your new look, you're unrecognizable!"

He smiled at the thought and nodded his head. "Next time, I'll leave the *peyos,*" he said, still grinning—and he did! We may sometimes need a loving reminder or word of encouragement, but the *neshamah* of a Yid is always ready to do what Hashem wants.

The Chaplaincy

As *Yidden*, every facet of our lives is imbued with our purpose, which is to serve Hashem. Whether we're eating and sleeping to gather the strength we need, working to have the resources we need, or taking a break to restore ourselves, everything we do can, and should, be in service of Hashem—holy and G-dly.

It took some time, but even the guards eventually understood this. Once, I went to the law library to print mailing labels. It was a five-minute task, but due to the controlled movements, I couldn't just leave when I was done. I had to wait for the next move. It was going to be a bit of a wait, so I sat down and opened my *Tehillim.* It was almost time for the move when a guard came in. This particular guard was infamous for interfering with what he deemed religious activities around the compound, Jewish or otherwise.

He looked at me sitting with a *sefer* and inaudibly saying the words. "Hey!" he interrupted me gruffly. "This is not the chapel! Are you doing something religious here?"

I looked up from my *Tehillim* with mild surprise. "I'm Jewish," I told him, as I stood up and prepared to leave with the move, still saying Tehillim. "*Everything* I do is religious." He deemed this a sufficient response and moved on.

Those needs that are formally religious, which are protected in the United States by the constitutional right to freedom of religion, are facilitated by the chaplains' office. The office is staffed by a head chaplain and two assistant chaplains. To their credit, religious needs were definitely better handled at the federal level than they had been in the county jail.

The day after I arrived, I found out that a new assistant chaplain had been hired. His name was Rabbi Avraham Richter, a fellow Jew and a Lubavitcher. His hiring, underscored by the timing of it, was one of the most impactful and clear examples of *hashgachah pratis* during my time there.

I didn't expect preferential treatment for Jewish inmates, nor did we get any. Still, his presence enabled us to serve Hashem properly, to a degree we otherwise would not have, simply because he understood our needs. We had all experienced difficulties obtaining our religious needs from officials who didn't understand or respect them, and we were all grateful to Hashem for sending Rabbi Richter.

He did his job fairly and conscientiously, doing everything he could so that each of the religious groups had what they needed to practice their faith, whether they were Jewish, Christian, Muslim, or any of the other of the seven religious groups there. His efforts could be credited for the absence of tension between the groups, as each felt that their needs were adequately addressed without favoritism.

He was one of two assistants under the direction of the head chaplain and his commitment to his job reflected that of his superior. The head chaplain took his job seriously. He made proactive efforts to provide for the inmates' spiritual needs. For example, he allocated funds for screens in the chapels which inmates could use for religious videos—services, lectures, and the like.

Sometime after I arrived, the head chaplain began feeling that his efforts were being undercut by some in the administration and he decided not to stick around. He was replaced by a new head chaplain who was less than enthusiastic about providing for the inmates under his care. His lackadaisical attitude trickled down to one assistant chaplain, who was remarkably unhelpful during his tenure. Rabbi Richter, by contrast, maintained his dedication to serving the inmates as best he could.

The new guy also had the bizarre habit of standing in the chow hall by the food line and greeting each prisoner with a great big smile and telling them that he was having a "great day!" In most contexts, this would be considered mildly eccentric, but in prison, where the people on the other end of that announcement are most assuredly *not* having a great day, or a great decade for that matter, it was terribly insensitive and hurtful. I think he had the idea that this would tempt people to join his religion so they could have a great day like he was having.

He showed very little empathy and didn't do anything that he wasn't strictly required to do. In one instance, inmates who practiced a minority religion had received permission for grape juice for their service, to be issued by the chaplain. When they came to get it, he insisted that the permission stated only that they receive "juice," not "grape juice," and they would therefore be given apple juice instead.

The inmates involved, whose religious rights had been arbitrarily denied, filed a formal complaint against him, which was really all they could do. One or two complaints would likely not even be noticed, but this guy was on a roll and the complaints had been piling up. Shortly after this one was filed, the prison administration finally had enough and he was shuffled off to a different prison facility to become other people's problem. This was a standard solution to problematic staff in the prison system.

This was, at least, an improvement for Otisville, but it did come at a price, paid by the prisoner who'd filed the complaint. The chaplain had friends in the facility who were upset that he'd been transferred. They took their revenge by having this prisoner transferred to a distant facility to finish his sentence far away from his family and friends.

With the job now open, Rabbi Richter was promoted to head chaplain. He brought energy and devotion to the job. His dedication was mirrored by his assistants, and the overall services of the chaplaincy took a real turn for the better. The assistant chaplain who'd emulated her previous boss, and had been reluctant to help inmates more than strictly necessary, now emulated her new boss and became much more willing and energetic in providing the services that the government hired her to provide.

CHAPTER TWENTY-THREE
Daily *Avodas Hashem*

Consciously Working

IN OUR GENERATION, THE MAIN CHALLENGE TO *AVODAS HASHEM* IS usually not the *means* to serve Hashem, but the motivation and structure. In my situation, the means were occasionally also an issue, but the main challenge was still motivation and structure. In fact, when I arrived, there was really no structure to speak of—no regular *minyan*, no *shiur* to run to, and no community of brothers and friends to encourage or support my personal efforts.

I realized that I would have to create a structure for myself if I hoped to succeed. At the earliest opportunity, I acquired a notebook from the commissary. At the start of each week, I would write a list of what I wanted to accomplish that week. I divided my list into three areas: Torah, *avodah (tefillah)*, and *gemilas chassadim*, the pillars on which the world (and each person is a world) stands. Every day I would mark off the goals that I had met.

This habit had numerous practical benefits. Knowing what I wanted to accomplish before the day even began kept me focused and motivated, and checking items off the list gave me a real boost. Having clearly defined goals, and accounting for them daily, also helped me quickly recognize what areas were more difficult for me, where I needed to improve.

The Rebbe taught, based on the *ma'amar Chazal, One who has one hundred desires two hundred, and one who has two hundred desires four hundred*, that the same should be true of spiritual riches, our connection to Hashem through Torah and mitzvos.

In that spirit, I used this list not as a way to check off my obligations so I could relax once I'd "done my duty," but as something to keep me always stretching, reaching for more than what came easily. If I found that I was able to finish my list with time to spare, I would add something to the list going forward. This helped me grow in my *avodas Hashem* even in a place called prison.

Communal *Tefillos*

Tefillah is the heart of a Jew. The Torah helps us see the truth and gives us clarity, but it's during *davening* that we make it personal. When a Yid directs all his requests to Hashem, trusting that He is the only true Provider, his connection with Hashem becomes very real in his life and his *emunah* and *bitachon* are strengthened.

The structure and wording of *tefillah* were chosen very carefully by the *Anshei Knesses Hagedolah*, and this structure serves as a map to the path of connection to Hashem. *Davening*, though, is not about reading the siddur, perusing the map, as it were; it is about *walking* the path, opening our hearts, and seeing and feeling and living the truth that the words are presenting. None of that is possible without first understanding the words of the *tefillah*, and actually focusing on the words as you say them. At the beginning of each week, I would decide on a specific part of *davening* that I wanted to work on, as the Rebbe suggests. I would try to improve it by first studying the meaning of that part (and there is always a deeper or different way to understand each part) and then by being particularly careful to concentrate during that part of *davening*.

This is obviously a very personal thing, something which no one else can do for you. Nonetheless, *davening* is also a communal activity. Not just because a *minyan* is how Hashem wants us to *daven*, but also on a practical level. Joined together as a group, we strengthen each other in breaking through the natural perspective, asserting that our physical requests are properly directed to Hashem and that we need to trust and rely only on Him. From the day I was transferred in, I made every effort to get together with other *Yidden* to *daven*.

Generally, I awoke at 4:30 a.m., when the doors to the cell were still locked. I began my preparations for *davening* with my daily Tehillim, which I will describe later. Once the doors to the cell were unlocked, at 6:00 a.m., I would use the shower in place of a *mikvah*. Then I was ready to *daven* Shacharis, in the chapel if it was a *minyan* day or right there in the barrack if it was not. *Davening* was a highlight of my day—the ability to connect with Hashem, to thank Him for the past and the present, and to request from Him everything I needed for the future.

When I first arrived, I inquired about gathering a *minyan* each morning and discovered that it just wasn't possible. Only three or four other *Yidden* were interested in joining. There were more than ten *Yidden* overall, enough to form a *minyan*, but I couldn't persuade them to overcome the reluctance all inmates have to associate with anyone outside their trusted circle, Jewish or not.

I myself took tremendous strength and comfort from my fellow Jews and I didn't understand this reluctance until someone explained it to me. They were afraid of the "guards in khaki," inmates who informed on their fellow inmates for infractions, real or fabricated, in exchange for some trivial benefit. No matter how hard I tried, I couldn't allay this fear, and I had to *daven* without a *minyan* for a while.

It didn't take long before I saw that there were real grounds for their concern. Tishrei was approaching, and I renewed my efforts to convince my Jewish brothers to *daven* together. The *neshamah* of every Yid is stirred during the holy months of Elul and Tishrei, and a number of those who turned down my earlier efforts agreed to gather on Rosh Hashanah. (Sadly, though, not enough of them agreed in order to form a *minyan* that first year.)

One of those who initially had misgivings about attending was not *frum* himself, but had grown up near a *frum* community and had very warm feelings toward *Yiddishkeit*. He had tremendous respect for those who learn Torah, and, once we got to know each other, he would even join me once a week for a walk around the yard during which I would share a *dvar Torah* with him.

He was a savvy fellow with well-placed connections around the compound. That year, he used one of those connections, and surprised me with honey cake, "*lekach*," that he'd procured from the stockroom so I could fulfill the custom of giving *lekach* on Erev Yom Kippur. Someone who attended the chapel that day reported this to the authorities, and it resulted in punishment for his connection in the stockroom. As a result, he stopped coming to *davening*.

We didn't have a *minyan*, but that didn't mean we couldn't *daven* together. I gathered as many *Yidden* as I could to come together and *daven* as a group. Among them was a Yid who was not otherwise noticeably observant, but who nonetheless woke up very early in the morning to *daven* with us. He took tremendous strength from those moments of connection with Hashem.

Our little group met each morning in the chapel with the help of then-Assistant Chaplain Richter. He could not be on-site so early in the morning himself, but he arranged for a member of the prison staff to facilitate the *tefillos*.

When the helpful head chaplain retired and was replaced by someone more adversarial toward the inmates, this guard was instructed to stop facilitating the *davening*, on the grounds that she was not part of the chaplaincy team. With the chapel no longer available, our small group took to *davening* in the barracks.

We couldn't *daven* as a *minyan*, but that is where our brothers, Klal Yisrael outside Otisville, came in—quite literally.

The doors to a place called prison are closed and locked not only to those wishing to exit, but also to those wishing to enter. There were two exceptions; heavily restricted visits by family and friends, and organized (though also restricted) programs by volunteers.

The BOP's efforts to provide for the religious rights and emotional needs of those they incarcerate are directed and implemented by the chaplaincy but even they recognize that they can't meet all the various rights and needs on their own. To make up the shortfall, the BOP allows volunteer organizations to visit and provide religious and emotional support as well.

This arrangement made it possible for Jewish volunteers to enter the compound. Their visits were a tremendous encouragement and support to all of us, but their physical presence did much more than boost our morale. Whenever ten *Yidden* are together, the *Shechinah* itself is present—we were finally able to *daven* with a *minyan*, hear, "Yisgadal v'yiskadash Shmei rabah!" and answer together, "Amen! Yehei Shmei rabah..."

I'll always remember the first time the volunteers came to complete our *minyan*. It was my first opportunity to *daven* Shacharis with a *minyan* since Shacharis on the morning of the conviction, five long years earlier in far-away South Dakota.

This wasn't just a couple of altruistic people stopping by in the afternoon every now and then to give encouragement to those less fortunate. This was a group of six people who woke up early and made the trip up to Otisville, week in and week out, to be there for their brothers and help them serve Hashem. *Mi k'amcha Yisrael!*

The volunteers were only allowed to come for *davening* one day a week. Monday morning was chosen, because it includes a Torah reading. The *minyan* became a high point of my week. All week long, I looked forward to the next *minyan* with anticipation, and I looked back to the previous *minyan* for the inspiration, clarity, and strength I needed to face each moment as a Yid should.

I will forever be grateful to those special volunteers who made the effort to come and gave of their time to make it possible.

Of course, the Jewish inmates themselves were also needed for the *minyan*, and that itself is a priceless gift in a place called prison where the message that reverberates in the minds of those plucked from their productive lives and now restricted in so many ways is, "You are not needed. The world can function just fine without you."

Obviously, that message is wrong. We don't need to look further than our continued existence for incontrovertible proof from Hashem Himself that it is wrong. The world needs us in it, and we have to do our part by fulfilling the mission Hashem has given us. For many Jewish inmates who had not had the benefit of a *frum* upbringing, being told that the *minyan* could not happen without them was their first concrete demonstration of this truth.

Although they needed a bit of prodding at first, over time, they also began looking forward to the Monday morning *minyan* and also became interested in learning Torah and doing other mitzvos. *Mitzvah goreres mitzvah!*

Eventually we had enough "locals" willing to come together for an additional day to have a *minyan* without the volunteers. We would've liked to pick Thursday, another Torah reading day, but other groups had reserved the chapel for Thursday mornings, so we requested Wednesdays instead. Our request was granted, and we had another weekly opportunity to *daven* in the ideal way—with a *minyan*.

The dedicated chaplain deserves special recognition here. As mentioned earlier, the smallest hint of fog would result in a lockdown of the entire compound. During these adverse weather lockdowns, inmates could not move from building to building, including from the barracks to the chapel. If a lockdown was in place when it was time for the *minyan*, Rabbi Richter would make the rounds of the compound and personally escort each inmate from their barrack to the chapel so that the *minyan* could take place. This wasn't special treatment—he displayed the same selfless dedication for all—but it was appreciated immensely.

Beyond the time and effort, taking part in the morning *minyan* occasionally required another sacrifice. The *minyan* would begin at 8:30 a.m. and, with *Krias HaTorah*, would only end around 9:30 a.m. Since visits can begin at 8:30 a.m., being at the *minyan* meant giving up a full hour of precious visiting time. If there was a lawyer coming to visit, it meant giving up a full hour of the practical efforts which seem to be the only way an inmate can change his situation. Choosing between the *minyan* and a visit, particularly a lawyer visit, was a precious moment when a person could put his *bitachon* into practice in his life.

One interesting instance of this happened when my lawyers were working on the final appeal. They were nearly ready to file and they wanted to sit with me and go over the appeal together in person. Gary Apfel called to tell me that he'd be flying in from California and Steve Locher would be flying in from Iowa. (They both deserve a proper introduction, which I will save for when I turn to discussing the legal efforts.)

They had arranged to arrive early in order to get the most out of their trip, but when Gary told me the date, I had to interrupt him. As *hashgachah pratis* would have it, they were coming on a Monday, when I was busy *davening* and I couldn't be in the visiting room until an hour after it opened. "What about *hishtadlus?*" he objected.

"The *Chovos Halevavos* makes it clear that *hishtadlus* cannot conflict with our duties to Hashem," I reminded him. "Choosing a meeting over a *minyan* would be treating the meeting as if it had some benefit besides for its role as a vessel for Hashem's *brachah*. The right thing to do is to prioritize the connection with Hashem, and only make the vessel second and secondarily."

He agreed, and we made up to meet that Monday at 9:30 a.m., as soon as the *minyan* was over. As agreed, I waited to be called immediately after the *minyan*, but time passed with no summons to the visiting room. It was 9:45 a.m. before he finally arrived and I was called.

I hurried to the visiting room. Gary was there, but there was no sign of Steve. It turned out that there had been bad weather that day which impacted many flights and Steve's flight had been canceled. Creative and persistent, he booked another flight to a different destination in upstate New York. He'd rented a car and was expected to reach Otisville around 10:15 a.m.

Giving up our connection with Hashem in exchange for "real world" efforts is always trading something for nothing, but in this case, Hashem made that immediately obvious. We couldn't accomplish anything without the other lawyer and if I had chosen to sacrifice the *minyan* it would have literally been for nothing. I thanked Hashem for the clarity and strength to make the right choice and not skip the *minyan* and reaffirmed my commitment to making decisions guided by Torah and *emunah*.

I pointed this all out to Gary and reassured him that Hashem could, and would, grant us success in using the diminished time productively and we'd accomplish more in the time we had than would be naturally expected even in the full visiting time. This was in fact the case—we got through everything we needed to review and Hashem granted me clarity to make some important notes. The appeal was completed to their satisfaction and it was filed on time without deviating from the approach a Yid should take as described by the Torah in *Sha'ar Habitachon*.

Chazal tell us that Minchah is especially precious to Hashem, because it requires stopping in the middle of our day and taking the time to *daven*, affirming that turning to Hashem for all our needs comes before whatever natural efforts we're pursuing to improve our situation. For the same reason, Minchah was precious to *me*, especially in my situation.

Stopping everything to *daven* Minchah with a *minyan* is something people often find difficult even under the best circumstances. In a place called prison, the difficulty is magnified by "controlled movement." As explained earlier, this means that inmates can only move from building to building during five-minute increments which were at least an hour apart.

As a result of this policy, coming to the chapel for Minchah wasn't a matter of taking ten or fifteen minutes and getting back to what we were doing. It meant waiting a full hour until the next opportunity to move elsewhere on the compound. Because of this, we didn't have a *minyan* for Minchah until five or six years after I was brought there. By then, there were enough *Yidden* willing to make this sacrifice, and *baruch Hashem* we had a *minyan* for Minchah on most days.

Even then, we couldn't gather again for Ma'ariv. The only exception was when there was a volunteer program during the months when nightfall was early. We took advantage of those opportunities to *daven* Ma'ariv with a *minyan* as well.

Friday nights, we managed to gather for *Kabbalas Shabbos*, and most Yamim Tovim we also managed to gather a *minyan* for Ma'ariv, at first with help of the volunteers and later from within the compound.

Personal *Tefillos*

At its core, *davening* is very personal. Even during a *minyan*, we're supposed to be experiencing a personal connection with Hashem within the group context.

At other times, we can always turn to Hashem with an impromptu *tefillah* of our own. As a matter of fact, the scheduled *tefillos* are *mitzvos d'Rabbanan*, but turning to Hashem when you are in need is a *mitzvah d'Oraisa*.

I had a long-standing practice of saying the whole Tehillim every day. I first started this in the early days of my work in Postville, helping to build the company and the precious Jewish community in the face of constant difficulty and opposition. I kept this *minhag*, with increased intensity and concentration, in the period after the raid, during the trial, and throughout my time in a place called prison, waking at 4:30 each morning to complete the Tehillim.

One year, just before Tishrei, my brother-in-law Yossi Gourarie *a"h* was diagnosed with a serious medical condition. That Chol Hamoed Sukkos, I was in the sukkah with my *lulav* and *esrog* and his troubles were on my mind. On the spur of the moment, I decided to say the entire Tehillim with *kavanah* and without interruption, beseeching Hashem for this specific salvation. This is a special *segulah* for meriting miracles, attributed to holy men. I had my *Tehillim* with me and immediately acted on my resolution, opening it up and starting to *daven* for a *refuah sheleimah* for Yosef Yitzchak ben Vichna.

Suddenly and unexpectedly, a "recall" was announced over the loudspeakers. That meant that all inmates had to return to the barracks immediately. I left the sukkah and headed back to the barracks, holding my *lulav* and *esrog* in one hand and my open *Tehillim* in the other, hoping that I could make it back without interruption.

It was not meant to be. The path back to the barracks took me past the lieutenant's office. As I walked by, an assistant warden and another officer walked out of the office. Pointing to the *lulav*, the assistant warden called out in a tone of friendly curiosity, "Hey, Rubashkin! What are you holding?"

Friendly tone or not, interactions with an officer are not something to take lightly. Speech (or lack of speech) that a guard or officer deems disrespectful could easily mean a stint in the SHU. Despite that, fresh off of my resolution and without thinking, I gestured to my open *Tehillim* and then to my mouth. "Nu," I explained, "nu-uh."

The officer wanted clarification. "What?" he asked.

"Nu. Uh-nu," I offered, pointing again to the *Tehillim*.

He seemed to want to further explore the issue but, miraculously, the other officer grabbed him by the arm. "Leave him alone," he said. "Let's get out of here."

Thanking Hashem for allowing me to keep my resolution without consequence, I continued to the barracks without further incident. Back in the cell, I completed the Tehillim without interruption.

Later on, I thought it over and decided that I should go to the assistant warden and explain myself. I went to his office and gave him the background, but he waved away my explanations as unnecessary. "Believe me," he said, "I had *no idea* what you were saying, but I knew that it was one of your 'things'— and that's good enough for me."

I left his office, thanking and praising Hashem for His miracles. This officer was known as a strict disciplinarian. In his willingness to casually overlook something which could easily be interpreted as disrespect, I saw an open miracle from Hashem as well as confirmation that my behavior was making a *kiddush Hashem*.

Learning Torah

Learning Torah is a mitzvah. It's also our means of surviving and even thriving. Torah is the *chachmah* of Hashem Himself which He has shared with us and through which we can connect to Him. Torah is our life and the truth through which we perceive everything else.

Each week, alongside the *davening* goals in my small notebook, I would list the various things I planned to learn that week. I had an ongoing study session in the *Sha'ar Hayichud V'ha'emunah* of *Tanya*, in order to internalize my *emunah*, and I also made time to learn from *Sha'ar Habitachon* each day in order to keep my *bitachon* strong.

An important part of learning Torah is setting a consistent schedule. I had a few topics already built in, three of them known as *Chitas*,[1] an acronym for Chumash (the weekly *parshah* with *Rashi*), *Tehillim*,[2] and *Tanya*, a daily schedule of learning followed by Chabad chassidim universally.

In 1984, the Rebbe instituted another universal learning program, the study

---

1. *Chitas* is also a word from the *pasuk* that describes Hashem's protection of the family of Yaakov Avinu—*And the fear of Hashem was upon the cities that were around them, so that they did not pursue Yaakov's sons (Bereishis 35:5)*. In the merit of this study, may Hashem protect each one of us from our enemies.

2. During the harrowing days between the World Wars, during the terrible Soviet oppression of *Yidden*, the Rebbe Rayatz requested that all Jews recite, each day after *davening*, the portion of Tehillim as it is divided for monthly completion. Although those dark days have passed,

of the Rambam's *Mishnah Torah*. Since it covers the entirety of the Torah, it's the most basic way to fulfill our obligation to study the whole Torah. Learning it according to the same schedule as other *Yidden* also achieves a powerful *achdus*, and through the most fitting medium—the Torah, to which we are all equally connected.

I followed a learning cycle that completed the entire *Mishnah Torah* each year. This schedule, which allowed me to review every aspect of Torah and crown it with an annual *siyum*, had a very powerful sustaining effect.

I also joined the *Daf Yomi* schedule, another beautiful example of *achdus* through Torah.

These universal learning programs were firmly entrenched in my schedule. Barring circumstances beyond my control, I made sure I did not go to sleep before completing that day's learning.

One day, the three chapters of *Mishnah Torah* spanned two volumes. Two chapters were at the end of one volume and the last one was at the beginning of the next. After we were locked into the barrack for the night, I realized that I didn't have the second volume and there was no way to get to the chapel to fetch it.

I was very bothered by the prospect of failing to complete the day's learning quota. It seemed out of my control, but I wasn't willing to just give up on my commitment. I racked my brains for some solution to this problem. Suddenly, I had an idea. I ran to the barrack phone and thanked Hashem that it was available. I called my son-in-law and asked him to read the missing *perek* over the phone. He managed to complete it before the call got cut off.

It came at a heavy price. Each inmate is only allowed three hundred minutes of phone time a month to speak to family or friends. Every minute I'd spent learning over the phone was one minute less for personal use, but I went to sleep that night happy, feeling that those minutes had been well spent.

Beyond those fixed, universal learning schedules, I had my own personal learning schedule, which included *Shulchan Aruch* as well as the Rebbe's *sichos* on the weekly *parshah* and on the many special dates in the calendar.

In order to really live with the *parshah* of the week, I wanted to add another

---

baruch Hashem, the need for Tehillim did not diminish and the Rebbe Rayatz instructed that the practice continue.

perush to the *Rashi* I was already learning. I chose the Shlah Hakadosh; as his direct descendant, I'd always wanted to learn his *perush* on Chumash.

One day, I received a letter from a *yungerman* in Lakewood. He wrote that he was *davening* for my release and had, as a *segulah* for me, begun learning the *Ohr Hachaim* on the *parshah* every week. I was touched by his concern for a fellow Yid, and I thought that if *he* was learning the Ohr Hachaim Hakadosh in my *zechus*, I should certainly be doing the same for myself, so it was added to my weekly roster.

Since I was already learning two *perushim* of tzaddikim our *mesorah* calls "kadosh"—the Shlah and the Ohr Hachaim—I decided to add the *perush* of the Alshich Hakadosh. The insights of these great men opened a whole new world for me into parts of Torah I always thought I knew.

The Torah I studied was what I was living with each day, so when I responded to letters or emails, it was only natural that it formed the core of my correspondence, in addition to the bits about life in a place called prison and the lessons I learned from my experiences.

I also had regular scheduled "correspondence *shiurim*" drawing from these studies. I already described the family emails and those to the classes of Rabbi Jacobovitz, Rabbi Lish, and others, but there is one particularly precious *shiur* that deserves to be mentioned here.

Of all the things I'd built in Postville, the most precious to me was, and still is, the yeshivah. It blossomed into a place of *chinuch* and Torah on par with yeshivos in the large Jewish centers in America. Despite the heavy responsibilities I'd had at work, I made every effort to connect to the *bachurim* on a personal level, learning with them, hosting them at my home for a weekly *melaveh malkah*, and in general, spending time with them at every opportunity.

One of the *bachurim* with whom I had a particularly strong connection, Dovid, flew in from Florida to visit me. We reminisced about old times and he filled me in on what had happened in his life since we'd been together. By *hashgachah pratis*, it was snowing that day and the visiting room was quite empty. It was *yud* Shevat, the day on which the leadership of the Lubavitcher Rebbe began. We started softly singing some *niggunim*, which made it feel like a *farbrengen*.

He asked me if I exercised daily. I explained that I was focused on the health of my *neshamah*, which was of paramount importance. "That's all very good," he insisted, "but you *must* exercise."

With some of my beloved *yeshivah bachurim* and *rebbeim*.

We went back and forth on the topic for a few minutes when I had an idea. "I'll make a deal with you," I said. "I'll commit to exercising ten minutes a day, if you commit to adding to your learning."

"Deal!" he said. "But you have to be a part of the learning."

From then on, I would send him a *dvar Torah* each week, built around a *sichah* or *perush* I'd learned that week and found particularly interesting or inspiring. I never missed a week, *baruch Hashem*. He also took his commitment seriously and invited another Postville yeshivah alumnus, Eli, to join him. They made it into a small weekly *shiur*, which consisted in part of learning the *dvar Torah* I'd sent that week, after which they would *farbreng* a bit. Over time, other local *bachurim* and *yungerleit* joined, some of whom had known me back in Iowa and others whom I'd never met. It turned into a small group of ten *Yidden* or so learning the *parshah* together each week, plus, of course, myself, from afar.

Learning with Others

In a place called prison, Torah also comprised a large portion of the *gemilas chassadim* that was possible to do. Exchanging anything of value was strictly forbidden and, while occasionally an opportunity to do someone a favor presented itself, on a regular and consistent basis, learning Torah with someone or helping them to perform a mitzvah was the primary way to do a *chessed*.

In some ways, learning with others isn't a conscious decision to make—it just happens. When the Torah you're learning is real to you, it sets you in a new reality, one that's different, better, and more truthful than the one which surrounds you. It's not just an intellectual experience. It surrounds you and infuses you with light and life, mind, heart, and soul. How can you keep something like that to yourself?!

I've always had a habit of sharing a new (or newly appreciated) statement of Torah with anyone who would listen. In my excitement, I'll often reflexively grab the person by the forearm to ensure their full attention and forestall any interruption.

In a place called prison, sudden and unexpected physical contact or even a sudden movement, no matter how innocuous, is treated almost as a declaration of war. Before an inmate will stand up from a shared table, he will rap on the table once or twice to alert the others that he's about to stand, so his movement is not misinterpreted. This is so deeply ingrained, that "institutionalized" prisoners are said to continue this habit long after they're released. Despite that, it was widely recognized that I was not a part of that life and, incredibly, no one ever responded badly to my reflex—"Rubashkin's wrist grab," as they called it.

My sincere excitement and desire to share led many individuals—even those who would otherwise be disinterested—to join me and study Torah. Sometimes these were one-session affairs, but sometimes they turned into longer-term scheduled *chavrusos* or even *shiurim* with a number of participants. Many of the people developed an appreciation for Torah study, and would linger over a mealtime or Shabbos or Yom Tov *seudah* discussing *divrei Torah*.

Group picture with some of my Torah study partners.

There were also some study sessions established for a specific purpose. The Torah was my guiding light through the darkness and the *Chovos Halevavos* in particular was a great source of clarity. It was only natural that I wanted to share its lessons with my brothers who were living through the same challenges as I was, and we started learning it as a group.

We learned *Sha'ar Habitachon* a few times, spending part of the time on the text and then shifting to long discussions about how it applied to our lives and situation. In the course of these discussions, I noticed that some of the group were confusing having trust in Hashem with "positive thinking," which is actually very different than *bitachon*. To address this, I took my cue from Rabbeinu Bacheye himself.

In the last chapter of *Sha'ar Habitachon*, after defining *bitachon* and explaining how it can be acquired, Rabbeinu Bacheye lists things which undermine or prevent *bitachon*. One of the items on that list is an insufficient understanding of the oneness of Hashem, which he explains in the first section, *Sha'ar Hayichud*.

This topic is only directly explained in a small number of *sefarim* and those who haven't studied any of them either have gaps in their understanding or, worse, they fill those gaps with their own guesses, assumptions, or ideas that they absorb from the society around them. I explained to the group that we were missing an important ingredient, and suggested that we learn *Sha'ar Hayichud* together. They agreed.

We were a very diverse group. Some of us had had the *zechus* to learn in yeshivah and others had not, but all were able to follow Rabbeinu Bacheye as he went through three steps, proving in ways that even the rational mind could understand that there must be a Creator, that there can only be one Creator, and explaining the absolute nature of that oneness. This put the contrast between Creator and creation in focus, and helped the group understand the underpinning of *bitachon* in its proper light and distinguish it from the shallow positive thinking with which it was being confused.

Yud-tes Kislev is a very special and powerful day. In Czarist Russia in the year 5559 (1798), the Alter Rebbe, the Ba'al HaTanya, was slandered by his enemies and accused of treason for his teachings. He was incarcerated in a fortress prison and tried for his "crimes." The Alter Rebbe and the future of the *chassidus* itself were in grave danger. On the day of *yud-tes* Kislev, he was cleared of all charges and released from prison.

Since then, it has been a day of great celebration and a day of recommitment to his teachings and his guidance. To those of us in a place called prison, this Yom Tov of freedom and deliverance held even greater significance than it does to the general public, and we gathered in the chapel for a *farbrengen*.

The first time we did this, I shared the history of the day and how it had become a holiday celebrated through the ages, which gave us all great strength and inspiration. In speaking of how the day is celebrated, I told the group about a letter to chassidim in which the Alter Rebbe instituted a division of *Shas* in each community. Each person commits to completing one *masechta* in the coming year, and between them, *Shas* is completed each year. This is done until this day in communities around the world.

Telling them about this, I felt a strong desire to participate in this special custom. "Let's commit to finishing a *masechta* together!" I suggested to the group. "We all need a miracle to be freed from this place called prison, and in the *zechus* of Torah which 'shields and saves' we will certainly merit the *brachos* of *Hashem Yisbarach!*"

I recommended *Maseches Megillah,* in which we could learn about Hashem's miracles in the time of Mordechai and Esther while we *davened* for and awaited our own miracles. It's one of the shorter and easier *masechtos,* and it's full of interesting stories and interpretations of the Megillah.

On the technical side, I reminded everyone that we had the perfect time to learn together. As I mentioned earlier, when we gathered for Minchah each day at 2:30 p.m., we were locked into the chapel until the next move. That gave us a good thirty or forty minutes after we'd finished *davening* which we could use to learn together.

As to the difficulty of the learning itself, I assured them that for such a good cause, a kind donor could surely be found who was willing to donate Gemaras with translation and explanation, which make even the most difficult *sugya* accessible to beginners. I finished my "pitch" by describing the great satisfaction and joy we would experience when we made a *siyum* together.

We were a group of thirteen *Yidden* at the time. Some had prior experience learning Gemara and some never had the *zechus,* but the response was unanimous—we all committed to finishing *Maseches Megillah* that year. As I'd expected, sufficient Gemaras soon arrived, donated by our kind and generous brothers to allow us to learn together.

From then on, every day after Minchah, we sat down to hear our daily *shiur* in Gemara, given by the elder *talmid chacham* in our group. Some were skeptical that our *shiur* would last more than a few days, but they all felt good to be learning, and everyone took *chizuk* from the first day.

My feelings that first time as I looked out over the table and saw a *minyan* of *Yidden* gathered together over their holy *sefarim* are very difficult to put into words. The *Shechinah* itself is present when ten *Yidden* gather, *Chazal* tell us, and in that heartwarming, soul-soothing moment, I felt it firsthand.

The gloomy and claustrophobic feeling that always hung over the compound vanished entirely. We were transported in that moment to a place of warmth and holiness, of light and life. Closing my eyes to the physical structure around us, it felt as if we were in a warm, *heilige shtiebel*, sitting together as brothers connecting to our loving Father through His holy Torah.

It was a sensation that didn't diminish with repetition.

We completed *Maseches Megillah* before Pesach. We made our *siyum* on Erev Pesach, a day when *siyumim* are made in many Jewish communities—our first communal *siyum* in a place called prison and it was even more joyous than I had promised when we started. We thanked Hashem for giving us the strength and the *zechus* to complete a *masechta* and immediately began our next *masechta* together. We chose *Brachos*, *davening* that Hashem bring His *brachos* into our lives and take us out of a place called prison. We went on to finish that as well, and many more *masechtos* followed.

It's worth recording here that, as of this writing, six people from that *chaburah* ended up miraculously released from prison before their scheduled release date.

Learning together with others was complicated by the question of location. The obvious place to learn would be in the chapel, but it was shared by many groups and was often not available. The rules in FCI Otisville forbade more than two people from being in a cell at one time which meant that that couldn't even be used for a *chavrusa*, much less a *shiur*.

When the weather was good, we were able to meet in the yard and learn at one of the tables, but on rainy or foggy days and throughout the winter months that wasn't an option. If the chapel was unavailable at those times, the next best place was the reading room. If that was *also* closed, which did happen, we would have to try to learn in the gym or the leisure room, both of which were filled with people entertaining themselves in one way or another—not the most conducive place to study Torah.

The learning had a powerful effect on the participants. One Yid was raised so far removed from his heritage, that he didn't even know that Jews don't eat pork. It was one of the things he learned in our "yeshivah" in Otisville, along with the general responsibility of a Yid to steadily improve himself and serve Hashem.

One day, not long after we'd started learning together, they served pork in the chow hall. He made his way over to me and proudly said, "You told me to add things I do for Hashem, so I am. I'm not going to eat the pork!"

This action, which was a real sacrifice to this Yid, represented an enormous leap forward. I'm sure it gave Hashem great *nachas*, and the power of this mitzvah propelled him to more mitzvos, closer and closer to Hashem. I myself saw him continue to grow in Shabbos observance and other mitzvos.

CHAPTER TWENTY-FOUR
Shabbos in Otisville

Preparing for Shabbos

SHABBOS IS A PRECIOUS ISLAND OF *KEDUSHAH* AT THE END OF THE physically and spiritually difficult week of work. It is a day of perfect *emunah*. It reminds us that Hashem creates the world in every moment, and that everything that exists and that happens comes from Him. It's also a day of *bitachon*, best symbolized by the *lechem mishnah*, the two challos that commemorate the double portion of *mann*. That miraculous sustenance came down from Heaven every single day in a desolate desert, without effort on our part, and we ate from it even on the day when we were prohibited from having any part in collecting it.

Shabbos comes, ready or not, but that doesn't mean that we experience Shabbos properly whether or not we prepare. The *chachamim* tell us that only those who prepare for Shabbos eat on Shabbos. This is true literally, when it comes to food, and it's also true about the *neshamah's* experience of Shabbos, which is also dependent on our preparations.

There are, of course, spiritual preparations, but because our *neshamah* is one with our body, there are also many physical preparations to be made before Shabbos and things to do and to avoid doing on Shabbos itself, which are critical to the *neshamah* experiencing Shabbos fully.

This is all the more true in a place called prison. Even apart from the obstacles created by rules and regulations, the rowdy atmosphere created by the inmates' behavior in general, and their recreation in particular, intensified on Shabbos when they were not required to work. Going out to the common areas, or even just passing through in order to go to the chow hall or out to the yard, shattered the spirit of holiness and tranquility that Shabbos bestows.

For that reason, I stayed in the cell on Shabbos as much as I could, *davening* longer and learning more, bringing the feeling of *kedushah* into my reality and rising above the *tumah* of a place called prison.

On weeks when I was particularly successful, I would have the same feeling leaving the cell as a person feels Motza'ei Yom Kippur leaving shul after an entire day spent *davening*. That feeling—that the world around you, with all its hollow certainty and bluster, is a bit surreal and unfamiliar, that it has no claim or hold on you—is a great gift in a place called prison, which tries so hard to thoroughly own those in its power.

The clarity I was granted during my *avodah* on Shabbos gave me the strength to navigate the days of the week as a Yid should. In a very real way, this embodied what the Torah says; the days of the week are all blessed by Shabbos.

Cleaning our house for Shabbos isn't just a nice thing we do because we're expecting guests—it's a halachah, part of honoring Shabbos. The same is true for showering for Shabbos, wearing Shabbos clothes, and eating special foods.

Even in a place called prison, I did my best to honor Shabbos in these ways. Each Friday, I would tidy up the cell and cover the small table with a makeshift tablecloth—the spare white bedsheet that they provided.

Among the prisoners, there were some who had developed respectable knitting skills. One of them figured out how to knit roses in beautiful red yarn, which he attached to a long, green, knitted stem. One of these flowers quickly became part of my "Shabbos table." This gave me one more way to honor Shabbos and gave the cell a special Shabbos feeling.

In another effort to make the little table look more like a Shabbos table, I poured the grape juice I received for Kiddush from its paper carton into a plastic bottle and put it on the table as if it were a bottle of special wine *lichvod Shabbos*. It felt like an improvement, but when my cellmate noticed it, he shook his head. "Bad idea," he said. "Don't do that."

He had the "benefit" of years of experience, and he warned me that putting the juice in a new container could result in the guards accusing me of making "hooch"—prison alcohol. I took his advice and dropped the idea.[1]

Only prison clothes were permitted in Otisville and no other clothing was available. This made Shabbos clothes a challenge, until I remembered the white *kittel* I wore on Yom Kippur. It was considered a religious garment,

---

1. Years later, I forgot his warning and did indeed suffer the consequences he warned about.

exempt from the prohibition on non-prison-issued clothing. I took to wearing it on Shabbos while I was in the cell. To go along with my *kittel*, I bought a pair of shoes from the commissary that were very different from the shoes I wore all week and kept those as my "Shabbos shoes." As my Shabbos hat, I wore a knitted black cap crafted by one of the knitters, shaped like a *kutchmeh*.[2]

These small things that I was able to do in order to fulfill the *halachos* of honoring Shabbos made Shabbos look and feel different than the other days of the week. Each one was small on its own but, added together, they really helped me experience a *Shabbosdig* feeling.

This precious feeling of *kedushah* needed to be protected—*Shamor es Yom haShabbos*. We were expected to obey orders from the staff, so it was very important that they be informed about what a Yid can and cannot do on Shabbos. We did our best to inform them and—as is proper, not to mention constitutionally required—they assured us that they would not force us to be *mechallel Shabbos*.

On the institutional level, this policy was uniformly and consistently upheld. For example, Jewish inmates were not assigned any work duties on Shabbos and Yom Tov. When it came to interactions with individual guards, however, things were less predictable.

This played out most often in the random alcohol screenings. Guards would frequently accost inmates walking from building to building in the compound and demand that they blow into a breathalyzer. Many guards respected the Shabbos rules and didn't randomly test *Yidden* on Shabbos. Others were either ignorant of their own rules or outright ignored them and did confront *Yidden*, demanding that they violate Shabbos by using their gadget or suffer the consequences.

Those consequences were not insignificant. Refusing a breathalyzer test is treated as an admission of guilt and is in the highest-level offense category, subject to the same set of punishments as killing, rioting, taking hostages, or using drugs. Consequences could include loss or delay of parole date or other sentence reduction options—meaning more time in prison, incarceration in the SHU for up to a *year*, monetary fines, loss of privileges such as visiting, phone, and commissary, and more. For many, the temptation to just blow into the device and avoid the threat of punishment was intense.

---

2. An old-fashioned fur hat with ear tabs worn for warmth.

One Shabbos, we were finishing *Mussaf* in the chapel when the PA system sounded a recall. Inmates began streaming to the barracks from all over the compound, and those in the chapel rushed to join them. As was my habit, in an effort to resist becoming institutionalized, I didn't rush to be the first one out. This put me toward the back of the swarm of people heading to the barracks. As I walked, I noticed a guard up ahead randomly calling inmates out of the pack and administering the breathalyzer test.

This didn't immediately worry me. I had every expectation that the guard would respect the policy and not administer the test to me or any of the other Jewish inmates, absent a real cause for suspicion. It looked like I was wrong. As I watched, the guard called over a Yid who had only arrived a few days earlier. I saw him recoil and say something to the guard, who continued insisting emphatically, imperiously holding out the device.

I wasn't close enough to politely interject and the number of people between us made it impossible to close the distance in time, even at a run. Under normal circumstances, an inmate would never shout out to a guard on pain of consequences for insubordination but I had to take the risk. "Hey!" I yelled out. "It's Shabbos! He's not allowed to do that!"

The guard looked up, astonished and unsure of how to respond. His hesitation bought me the few seconds I needed to get close enough to talk properly. "I'm sorry for yelling like that," I said, "but today is Shabbos and this fellow is Jewish. He isn't allowed to do that."

The guard was actually one of the decent ones and had just made a mistake. He took a closer look at the man he'd stopped. "Oh, I hadn't noticed the yarmulke," he said, and he waved us both along.

When we reached the barracks, the Yid thanked me for saving him from *chillul Shabbos*. He hadn't been certain that using the breathalyzer was actually strictly forbidden and he'd considering doing it when I called out. We wished each other a good Shabbos and each went our own way.

As I walked, I thought about the *hashgachah pratis* of the encounter and the lessons to be learned. The guard hadn't intentionally singled out the Yid, but Hashem had orchestrated his "random" selection to teach us both a few important lessons.

First, we had both seen that we can help our brother even in a situation where we seem powerless. By rejecting the popular slogan "mind your own business" and doing what we can with sincerity, we can really have a positive effect. I didn't have any influence or connections—I hadn't even spoken fully in English. I was so hurried to get my point out that I had said "Shabbos," instead of something closer to the guard's vocabulary like "Sabbath" or "a holy day." Yet, I had spoken from the heart and with Hashem's help, my words had the desired effect.

This episode also demonstrated to us the true nature of the challenges we face. What had seemed at first to be a real obstacle carrying a real threat was nothing more than a test. When we weren't embarrassed by Hashem's mitzvah and stood our ground, the danger dissipated completely.

Not every incident had such a happy ending. One Shavuos, after Shacharis, everyone headed off to the chow hall to pick up their Yom Tov meal. I avoided the common areas on Shabbos or Yom Tov in an effort to preserve the feeling of the holiness of the day, so I stayed in the chapel and settled down with a *sefer*.

Not ten minutes had gone by when three *Yidden* came back into the chapel looking devastated. As they had reached the chow hall, they'd been accosted by a guard with a breathalyzer who demanded that they blow into the device. "It's a Jewish holiday today!" they had protested. "It's forbidden!"

The guard wasn't willing to leave it at that. "What do I do with these guys?" he yelled to a lieutenant who was standing nearby.

"If they refuse to blow in the thing, throw 'em in the SHU!" came the reply.

The *Yidden* panicked and succumbed to the pressure. Afterwards, they retrieved their food from the chow hall and hurried back to the chapel, completely distraught. One of them felt so hurt and violated, that he decided to risk retaliation and lodge a formal complaint that he'd been forced to violate his religion.

It soon became clear that this hadn't been an innocent mistake. Word began to spread that there had been other incidents over Shavuos. Even in the lower security compound, a few *Yidden* had been forced to blow into the breathalyzers. Jewish inmates were afraid to leave the barracks and warily watched the doors in case guards came in to administer the breathalyzer in the barracks, which was uncommon but not unheard of. The violation of religious rights that were thought to be sacrosanct left everyone feeling vulnerable and distressed even after Yom Tov was over.

When our families and the caring *askanim* found out about what was going on, they contacted every official they could reach, insisting that the BOP comply with their own regulations. These efforts bore fruit, *baruch Hashem.* The warden held a retraining session with all the guards on duty to review the policies on religious rights. Many of the guards welcomed the clarification of the policy and did their best to abide by it, to their credit, but there was also some hostile grumbling from some guards around the compound.

After the retraining, the lieutenant who was the subject of the formal complaint called the Yid who'd complained into his office and asked him to retract the complaint, which would otherwise go into his file. Still hurt, the Yid declined and demanded an apology. The officer apologized and assured him that it would never happen again, and the Yid agreed to drop his complaint.

Discussing Shabbos needs with personnel was critical, but it was also important to discuss them with my cellmates. For example, even on Shabbos, I would wake up very early, while it was still dark, and say Tehillim or learn. The cellmate might notice that I was sitting in the dark, and thoughtfully turn on the light so I could read more easily. That would be a problem, since I could not benefit from his doing a *melachah* on Shabbos on my behalf. I ensured that every cellmate understood that I didn't want them to do that and it would actually violate my religion.

On the other hand, I really did need the light on in those pre-dawn hours. Since neither I nor they were permitted to turn it on (for my needs) the only way that could happen was if the light was left on all night. I never *demanded* this of my cellmates but I did explain it and ask for their cooperation. This made it more difficult to sleep but, with Hashem's *brachah*, each successive cellmate, most of whom were not Jewish and could not be expected to be sensitive to these matters, nonetheless agreed to this arrangement.

The Holy Shabbos

Since the days of Sarah Imeinu, Shabbos has been ushered in by lighting Shabbos candles. This mitzvah is normally fulfilled by the woman of the household, one of three mitzvos especially associated with Jewish women, but we had been forcibly separated from our families and it fell to us to do this mitzvah for ourselves.

Lighting any sort of fire in the cells was entirely out of the question, but I was sure that we could come to some other arrangement. I discussed it with the head chaplain and he managed to arrange for me to light the candles in the guard's office in the barracks to which I was assigned.

I encouraged the few other *Yidden* in the barrack to join me. Each Friday, we would hurry to the guard's office at the appointed time and light the candles. Standing in the light of the candles, we would *daven* for Hashem's salvation so we could rejoin our families and bask in the glow of the Shabbos candles together with them. We were only allowed in the office for a few minutes before being ushered out, but I would linger outside the door as long as possible, looking through the small window at the dancing flames and thinking of my family so far away.

This arrangement didn't last long. The officer assigned to our barrack was reassigned sometime later. While his replacement was willing to allow the candle-lighting to continue, he insisted on extinguishing the candles shortly after they were lit, well before night fell. Obviously, we needed a new solution. We went back to the chaplain and he did his best to help, experimenting with different arrangements. Eventually, he landed on the obvious solution and we were granted permission to light the candles in the chapel.

The authorities actually went to unusual lengths to accommodate this mitzvah, something for which I credit our united insistence that this was an important religious need. Not only did we receive permission to use the chapel each week, but they made sure we could get to the chapel even during the short winter Fridays when candle-lighting time was during the 3:30 to 4:30 p.m. count. This count in particular is sacrosanct to the BOP, yet they allowed us to remain in the chapel and escorted us back to the cells when we finished performing the mitzvah.

What had seemed to be a setback actually ended up bringing us a great benefit. Because the candles were burning in the chapel, we would reconvene there after the count and sit in their light. We ended up receiving permission to be in the chapel from 4:30 to 6:30 p.m. and the mitzvah of candle-lighting blossomed into a whole set of mitzvos. We used the extra time in the chapel to start a new *shiur*, eventually working our way up to *davening Kabbalas Shabbos* with a *minyan*, and we even had a makeshift *seudas Shabbos* together after *davening*.

Lichtigkeit tzit tzu—"people are drawn to light," and to warmth—and the Shabbos candles provided both in large measure. The number of inmates who took the time to gather in the chapel for *licht tzindin* grew. One Jew who joined us jumped at the opportunity to help prepare the candles. He had few Jewish memories, but he fondly remembered that in early childhood, he would help his mother prepare the Shabbos candles and watch her light them as night fell. He made sure to be there every week, and never missed a Friday night candle-lighting.

Reliving those childhood moments helped him feel closer to Hashem and to his Jewish brothers, and became a source of strength and inner tranquility that he treasured and looked forward to all week. Over time, this had a marked effect on his *Yiddishkeit* and he began keeping Shabbos more as time went on, avoiding checking his emails, not turning lights on or off, and so on.

Even before our candle-lighting was moved to the chapel and brought about all those other mitzvos, there had been a regular "service" scheduled for Friday night in the chapel. Attendance was very high, even among those who were not really interested in the service, because each attendee received a small carton of grape juice and two challah rolls for Kiddush and *lechem mishneh*.

My first Friday in Otisville, I met six fellow Jews in the chapel. I introduced myself and offered them a heartfelt "Good Shabbos!" Once we'd all made each other's acquaintance, I launched into a relevant and topical *dvar Torah* on the *parshah* of the week. I kept it to five minutes, and they enjoyed the insight.

This became a weekly tradition and to my great satisfaction, their interest and attention spans grew until they were able to engage in an interesting *dvar Torah* for twenty minutes at a time.

Initially, I *davened Kabbalas Shabbos* alone. As interest grew among those already there and our population was augmented by new arrivals, we began *davening* as a group. It took years, but eventually we had a full *minyan*.

In the early days, those who had gathered for the Friday night service would leave at the first opportunity, as soon as the next move was called. I couldn't understand why people would rush to abandon the Shabbos atmosphere and the camaraderie of the chapel for the crowded and raucous barracks. It was nice to see that as time went on, people grew to appreciate the Shabbos experience enough to stick around past that first possible move.

After *davening*, we would sit down together around a table, make Kiddush on the grape juice, and wash on the challah. The rest of the meal was served in the chow hall—depending on the season, either before or after the Friday night service—and consisted of meatballs and spaghetti, not quite your traditional Shabbos food. As a more *Shabbosdig* alternative, we held our own makeshift *seudah* in the chapel. We would bring whatever food we'd managed to buy from the commissary—tuna fish packets, crackers, and whatever else caught someone's eye.

Everyone did what they could to enhance our Shabbos meal. One guy had a knack for food preparation, and he would prepare a fresh salad with vegetables he'd managed to procure from the kitchen. Sometimes, he would even prepare a handful of instant ramen-noodle soups as a stand-in for the traditional Shabbos chicken soup.

There were periods of time when there was shelf-stable gefilte fish for sale in the commissary. It didn't taste great but we bought it anyway so that our *seudah* would have some food traditionally associated with Shabbos.

When it was time to head back to the barracks, we would walk together as far as we could. When the paths to the different barracks diverged, we'd part with warm wishes for a good Shabbos.

One Friday night, I returned to the barracks with a fellow Jew assigned to a different barrack. We had just parted ways with the customary "Good Shabbos" when a guard called me over. He had seen our interaction and he found it suspicious. "Rubashkin, what's that code you're calling out?" he asked me. "You guys up to something?"

I burst out laughing. "You're kidding! You've heard of the Sabbath, right? In Hebrew, it's pronounced Shabbos. G-d rested on the seventh day, and so do all Jews. You've seen the light in 307 stays on every Saturday. I was just wishing him a good Sabbath day!"

Since that interaction, this guard always greeted me with a "Good Shabbos!" and from then on, I referred to him as "Good Shabbos."

The chapel time scheduled for *davening* on Shabbos morning was from 8:30 to 9:30 a.m. As with the Friday night services, they gave attendees grape juice and challah, so attendance was higher than it would otherwise be. On Shabbos day, they also gave out some cake. It was a way to honor Shabbos, but it also provided a sad reminder of the poverty which inmates suffered when the occasional argument broke out over unequally sliced pieces of cake.

The extra food may have been what brought people who otherwise wouldn't have come to *daven*, but they all had *Yiddishe neshamos*. They readily agreed to *daven* a few parts of *brachos*, say *Krias Shema* with some help, and stick around for a few minutes for a thought on the *parshah* or some other Torah topic.

We used our one hour in the chapel as best we could and were happy for it, but once we had enough people for a *minyan*, we had a dilemma. One hour is simply not enough time to *daven* Shacharis, *Mussaf*, and read the Torah portion of the week.

As much as we tried, we couldn't convince the authorities to give us more time. After much discussion and deliberation, and after consulting with *rabbanim*, we settled on each person *davening* Shacharis alone and doing *Krias HaTorah* and *davening Mussaf* with the *minyan*. After *davening*, someone made Kiddush for all the assembled to hear, which is also a mitzvah, and then everyone went their separate ways.

One week, the 8:30 a.m. move was delayed for some reason and it was already after 9:00 before we got to the chapel. Our time would still end at the 9:30 move, which meant that we had less than half an hour—not even enough time for *Krias HaTorah*. Instead, the grape juice and rolls were distributed and we made Kiddush. Hoping to still hear the Torah reading that Shabbos, I asked each of the people who had come if they would be willing to come back at the 12:30 p.m. move. They agreed.

I hurried back to the chapel as soon as the 12:30 move was called. I was a bit nervous that one or two wouldn't make it, so I stood in front of the chapel, where I could spot people passing by and call over additional *Yidden* who could help complete the *minyan*. I was surprised to find someone already standing there, a Yid from Russia, trying to persuade his friend who was passing by to come in for the *minyan*.

His friend was a recent arrival. He had stayed away from the chapel until that point, but after some persuasion, *baruch Hashem*, he agreed to come in. As I'd feared, two of the ten who had agreed to come back failed to show up, and we ended up needing both this new fellow and one other unexpected attendee, also a newcomer.

We began reading the Torah as soon as we had a full *minyan* and finished with some time to spare until the next move was called. While we waited, we sat together and I started singing, "*Nyet, nyet, nikavah*," a song in Russian which proclaims that there is none like Hashem and we should fear nothing but Him. It's a lively song, and I started dancing with one of the *Yidden* while the others watched and sang along.

When I finished that song, one of the others took my example and haltingly began to sing a song which he only half-remembered. A few notes into the song I recognized the melody. It was a well-known Jewish children's song, and I joined in enthusiastically: "Hashem is here, Hashem is there, Hashem is truly everywhere! Up, up, down, down, right, left, and all around! Here, there, and everywhere—that's where He can be found!"

The faces of the two newcomers lit up with delight hearing this song, which clearly brought back fond memories. It was nice to find out later that one of them, our tenth man that day, had participated in the "Released Time" program as a child.

Under this program, public school students could opt into a weekly one-hour program of religious study. Soon after his arrival in America, the Rebbe Rayatz charged Rabbi JJ Hecht and the newly founded NCFJE[3] with utilizing this Released Time to bring the basics of *Yiddishkeit* to Jewish public school students. This was done with the help of many dedicated volunteers who taught the classes. I had merited to be among the volunteers.

Now, years later, I had the pleasure of seeing the enduring impact that program had on its "graduates." The songs he'd learned there helped awaken the pure and simple connection to Hashem which would turn out to be a source of strength to him in this difficult place.

I marveled at the complex chain of *hashgachah pratis* at work. Something had happened on the compound which led to a delay of the 8:30 a.m. move. The late move then led to the abbreviated chapel time, which led to the second, less reliably attended gathering. That, in turn, led to our standing outside the chapel, anxiously recruiting new guys for the *minyan*—all culminating in the encounter which brought this young fellow back in touch with his fellow Jews and his Jewish roots.

The Shabbos day meal was, superficially, even less *Shabbosdig* than the night meal. Throughout the Jewish world and through the generations, *Yidden* have always served a hot dish on Shabbos day. Cholent is not just another "cultural food," it's a *minhag* which reaffirms the truth of *Torah sheb'al peh*. As a point of principle, *Yidden* have been serving it for over a thousand years.

Despite its importance, we had no way of fulfilling this *minhag*. Any hot food served by the kitchen would have been heated on Shabbos, a problem even when done by a non-Jew. The authorities refused to allow a crock pot which we could have used to keep food warm. We had to content ourselves with the official lunch from the kitchen, which was a four-ounce package of cold chicken bologna slices, or we could eat tuna packets from the commissary.

Of course, a Shabbos meal needs a Shabbos guest. I always invited one or another of the Jewish inmates to the cell for *seudas Shabbos*, where we made Kiddush together and "feasted" on challah rolls with mayonnaise, or whatever

---

3. National Committee for the Furtherance of Jewish Education.

other food I managed to prepare. One of these guests, a Yid from Russia, really enjoyed singing songs together, especially those that had lyrics in Russian, and we spent many *Shabbosim* bonding and singing over these *seudos*.

Once we had a core group studying during the week, we decided to also get together on the long Shabbos afternoons in the summer. I tried to make those gatherings more inspirational and practical than academic, more like a *farbrengen* than a *shiur*. I brought some kosher nosh that was sold in the commissary and we reviewed some of the stories from the *parshah* and the lessons we could take from them. It was always a very warm and heartfelt gathering, and I developed some very strong friendships during those *farbrengens*. We kept the *farbrengens* going until we had enough people and we were able to make a *minyan* for Minchah during that time instead.

Motza'ei Shabbos

Shabbos is a haven of *kedushah*, but inevitably, the time comes to leave that haven. It is our mission from Hashem to reveal the light and the holiness hidden within the darkness of the world. When night falls on Motza'ei Shabbos, we return to the weekday world, using the strength and clarity of Shabbos to fulfill our important task. We mark the transition with Havdalah, which describes the important distinction and separation between the holy and the mundane, between light and darkness.

In Otisville, grape juice for Havdalah was provided to us through the chaplain, but the authorities were so worried about the possible production of hooch, that they only gave one juice-box to one of the inmates in each barrack.

I was the designated person in my barrack, which I saw as both a *zechus* and a responsibility. I made sure to invite to Havdalah even those Jews in the barrack who would otherwise have been content to miss it. I taught them its significance and translated the words for them. They appreciated the general gist of it and especially the words, *LaYehudim haysah orah*—"For the Jews there was light and joy, gladness and honor." Once they got the hang of it, they would call out those words of Havdalah with the same enthusiasm as *Yidden* all over the world, culminating in the exclamation: *Kein tihiyeh lanu!*—"So may it be for us!"

For *besamim*, I would pass around the leaves of the *hadassim* that I'd saved from the *dalet minim*. The sense of smell is especially close to the *neshamah* and its calming effect helps console us over the ending of Shabbos and the inevitable exertions of the new week.

I taught them the *minhag* of dipping our fingers into the wine and passing them over our eyes, which symbolizes the preciousness of Hashem's mitzvos and their role in giving us clarity, and then placing them in our pockets, as a *segulah* for *parnassah*. We would then wish each other a heartfelt *gut voch* and all go our separate ways.

Initially, our Havdalah group consisted of just two people, but it soon grew to include six *Yidden* who gathered to start the week together in the right way. It was a treasured moment in our week.

One Motza'ei Shabbos, we were gathered for Havdalah and I had already raised the cup to begin, when I noticed someone looking into the cell through the small window in the door. It was a lieutenant with a history of negative dealings with the Jewish inmates. He was wagging his finger from side to side. His meaning was very clear.

I put down the cup and asked someone to open the door. Everyone turned toward the unwanted guest, who coldly informed us that only two prisoners are allowed in a cell at a time. The Yid who'd opened the door told him, respectfully, that we only needed three minutes for a religious prayer and then they would all leave. He wouldn't hear of it and insisted that everyone leave immediately.

It wasn't that this man was simply a stickler for the rules. To get to cell 307, this officer had passed through the common area, where more than a few tables were openly and illegally gambling, and there were two full floors on his rounds before he got to us, each floor full of cells where more than two inmates had congregated. He hadn't interfered with any of them. It was only when faced with a handful of *Yiddelach* gathering together for five minutes to do a mitzvah that he reached for the rulebook.

We obeyed the order and dispersed after making up to meet a bit later in the ironing room for Havdalah. Looking to the future, it became clear that we had a problem. We were only issued one cup of grape juice, so we needed to do Havdalah together, but it was now clear that we would not be allowed to gather.

There were a few ways the authorities could solve this issue, granting us the religious freedom we were entitled to. The easiest and most obvious one was to continue the status quo and allow us to gather informally for the few minutes we needed each week. It hadn't caused any problems before, and there was really no reason to create an issue by singling us out for strict enforcement of this rule.

The other two options were to open the chapel so we could gather for Havdalah there, which would mean paying more hours for the chaplain, or to give each Yid his own grape juice to use in his cell.

The question was in the hands of the bureaucracy, which meant that it wouldn't be resolved quickly. We would have to come up with a creative interim solution until the decision was made, because none of the available options was legal.

When the next Motza'ei Shabbos came with no official solution, we hit on a way to fulfill the mitzvah without breaking any rules. I prepared the Havdalah in the cell, as we had done in earlier weeks, but this time, the other *Yidden* didn't come into the cell and just stood in the corridor right outside.

We propped the door open and I made Havdalah as loud as I could. My voice reverberated in the cinder-block barracks and the constant background hubbub quieted down as everyone in the barracks stopped for a moment to hear what was going on. The whole barracks heard Havdalah that week, whether or not they'd signed up for it. At the appropriate point, the *Yidden* came in one at a time to smell the *besamim* without violating the two-person rule.

It took the decision makers quite a number of weeks to make their decision, but ultimately, more competent officers overruled the lieutenant and allowed us to resume making our Havdalah quietly in the cell as we had done until this unnecessary and spiteful disruption.

After Havdalah, during those weeks when Motza'ei Shabbos was early, I used some of my phone time to call home and say *V'yiten Lecha* with my wife and wish the whole family a *"gutte un a freiliche voch!"*—a good and happy week, and we would *bentch* each other that this would be the week when Hashem would free me and reunite us.

This brings us to *melaveh malkah*, the meal we hold as the proper send-off to *Shabbos Kodesh*. *Melaveh malkah* helps us bring the spiritual high and strength of Shabbos into the week, something which is even more important in a place called prison.

This special *minhag* had always been important to me. I hadn't missed a single *melaveh malkah* since I got married—including, miraculously, the traumatic week of the conviction in South Dakota. When my ordeal had begun, I'd resolved to keep up this personal commitment, and *baruch Hashem* I managed to keep that resolution even in the county jails, where keeping leftover food for later was forbidden.

Our *melaveh malkah* had always been a family gathering, and even under these circumstances, I very much wanted to be part of my family's *melaveh malkah*. There were months in the summer when I was locked in for the night before Shabbos was even over and there was no way to bridge the distance between us. During the other months, I used Hashem's gift of modern communication technology to have a presence at the family *melaveh malkah* through email.

I would write a story for them to read at the table, usually a story of miraculous salvation sent by Hashem through the Ba'al Shem Tov or other tzaddikim. Besides for adding my voice to their meal, these stories reminded us that Hashem makes miracles for His people in their time of need and they helped strengthen our belief in the miracle that He would surely make for us.

The email system had a built-in delay of two hours, so I tried to get to this as early as possible. Although I could have typed a story on Friday and sent it immediately or saved it as a draft to send on Motza'ei Shabbos, I felt that this fell short. I wanted to "tell" the story on Motza'ei Shabbos itself, even if only through typing.

After I sent the email, I turned to my own *melaveh malkah*. It was a far cry from the full meal I would share with family and friends in better times, but, *baruch Hashem*, I always managed to wash for bread and have something to eat. I would sing the songs we always sang at home; an old Chabad *niggun* to the words, "*Al tira avdi Yaakov,*" and "*A Gutte Voch*" and "*A Tatteh Bistu,*" both by Avraham Fried. I would also read a story of a *nes* of the Ba'al Shem Tov or of other tzaddikim.

In later years, I was asked by the chaplain to teach a class and they allowed me to have a CD player in the cell so I could prepare. This lasted for a couple of months. A generous Yid had stocked the Otisville library with a number of Jewish CDs, including many of the Rebbe's *farbrengens.*

During that period, I spent many Motza'ei Shabbos hours with those recordings. They transported me to a different time and place. The bars around me would fade, and I again felt myself pressed between my fellow chassidim, awash in the warmth and light of *kedushah*, listening with every fiber of my being and drawing holiness, insight, and inspiration from the holy words of the Rebbe.

Some of the recordings I had were actually of *farbrengens* I'd attended in person, and I was able to immerse myself in memory instead of imagination. The Rebbe's voice was a beacon of *kedushah* in the darkness of the place called prison and further strengthened my resolve to fulfill the task Hashem had set for me, the task that He sets for all of us, to discover in our surroundings—however lowly they may be—the expression of His holy will and to fill them with *kedushah*.

Once a month, the moon shrinks down to nothing and then is reborn, slowly returning to its full glory. The *Yidden* are compared to the moon. Even in the darkest times, when we seem to have diminished to the point of almost vanishing, we are assured by Hashem's promise that we will be redeemed and fully restored.

Each month, we make a *brachah* on the new moon once it is large enough to see easily but while it is still in the process of growing, between the third and fifteenth day of the month. If possible, it's customary to recite *Kiddush Levanah* on Motza'ei Shabbos.

In the winter months, when night fell early, this didn't present a problem, but during the summer months, it was still light when we were locked into the barracks for the night. I requested a special release from the barracks after nightfall in order to perform this monthly mitzvah. To their credit, they granted my request and I excitedly informed the other *Yidden* in the barrack that we would be able to fulfill this mitzvah.

The lunar calendar can't be predicted based on the standard calendar so they would check with me each month to know when we would need to make *Kiddush Levanah*. On the appointed night, a guard would open the barrack and escort us out under the open sky where we had five minutes or so to say the *tefillah*.

It must have seemed bizarre to anyone watching. The guard I called "Good Shabbos" referred to it as "the moonwalk," but it was really more of a dance than a walk. Together, we said the special *tefillah*, exchanged *brachos* of "*Shalom aleichem!*" and "*Aleichem shalom!*" and wished each other and all of Klal Yisrael good *mazel*. When everyone had finished, we would dance together, overjoyed at the opportunity to fulfill the mitzvah and eagerly anticipating our own restoration to freedom by Hashem, which was symbolized by the moon's rebirth.

Standing outside in our little bubble of life and holy excitement gave me a greater degree of distance and a better view of the barrack's other inhabitants, visible through the barred windows. The general mood was clearly more subdued now that they'd been locked in for the night. They congregated around the tables in the common area, some meager snacks strewn in front of them. Some were exchanging tales of another day in prison while others were trying to lose themselves in the screens overhead.

For all the movement and interaction, the scene looked flat, dispirited, and aimless, each person alone in the crowd, just trying to survive as best he could. I felt a strong sense of pity for these people, along with an intense gratitude to Hashem for the gift of His mitzvos.

Baruch Hashem, we were able to do *Kiddush Levanah* every month that the moon was visible for the duration of my time in Otisville.

CHAPTER TWENTY-FIVE

Yamim Nora'im in Otisville

The Month of Elul

A YID IS A YID IN EVERY PLACE AND AT EVERY TIME, BUT EACH PLACE presents unique challenges and each time brings with it different obligations. I was determined to rise to every occasion, and, with Hashem's help, fulfill the mission He put before me throughout the year.

My arrival in Otisville actually coincided with the beginning of the year, just as Elul was about to begin. Technically, the year begins with Rosh Hashanah, when we accept Hashem as our King, but everything really starts with its preparation—Tishrei actually starts in Elul.

The day after my arrival, a meeting was arranged with the Jewish chaplain and I was asked what I would need. After I listed my ongoing needs, I brought up periodic holiday needs, specifically the upcoming month of Elul and the daily need for a shofar to fulfill the *minhag* of hearing its call. His first suggestion was that I meet him each day at the chapel where he would provide the shofar. In discussing how that might work, we realized that if he wasn't there every day (and he wasn't sure that he would be) I would not be able to blow the shofar that day.

We discussed alternatives and, *baruch Hashem*, he agreed to let me keep the shofar in the cell so that I would be sure not to miss a day. At the end of the meeting, he gave me a formal authorization memo which I could show any guard who challenged me over the shofar.

Rabbeinu Bacheye puts our obligations to Hashem in a similar category as our material needs when it comes to *bitachon*. We're expected to do our utmost to live up to those obligations but then we must ask and rely on Hashem for a successful outcome. Heading back to the cell, I thanked Hashem for His constant help which allowed me to fulfill all His mitzvos and even *minhagim* in a place called prison.

This shofar arrangement which enabled me to blow and hear the shofar every day of Elul remained in effect throughout my years in Otisville. I always invited other Jews to hear the shofar as well, and throughout Elul, the sound of the shofar echoed through the barracks and in our hearts, moving us to shake ourselves out of the passivity and sleep into which our *yetzer hara* lulls us.

Each day, as we drew nearer to the awesome days of Rosh Hashanah, we intensified our introspection. We took stock of where we stood in fulfilling Hashem's will so that we could truly crown Him as our King by accepting and embracing our obligations—in our thought, speech and actions—to Him. As part of that commitment, we also did our best to evaluate and correct our shortcomings in the year that had passed.

The Motza'ei Shabbos before Rosh Hashanah, the first night of *Selichos*, Jews around the world gather in shul at 1:00 in the morning, awash in awe and trepidation.

The *chazzan* takes to the *amud* wrapped in his *tallis* and begins to chant the familiar melody, "*As the day of rest departs, we precede You in prayer...*"

I couldn't join a *minyan* that year by Divine decree, so I timed my own *davening* to coincide with the *tefillah* of the *tzibbur*, as per the *Shulchan Aruch*.

When the inmates were confined to their cells each night, the unbearable and incessant ruckus in the barracks abruptly died down and the place fell silent as a tomb. That night, at 1:00 a.m., I sat at the small table in the cell, projecting myself far away to my fellow chassidim who were gathering around their own tables and preparing together for the holy moment.

I didn't need much imagination or a rousing *farbrengen* to evoke a yearning to escape my current state and be closer to Hashem. The time for *Selichos* finally came and I stood up from the table to join my fellow Jews, who were physically so far away and yet right beside me.

I could hear the *chazzan's* thunderous voice in my mind as I whispered along with him the powerful opening words, mindful not to disrupt the sleep of my cellmate. *Ashrei yoshvei veisecha*—"Happy are those who dwell in Your house!" Even in Otisville, I dwelt in Hashem's house, and considered myself lucky, full of gratitude and praise for my connection to Him. When I finished *Ashrei*, I paused, allowing time to hear the *chazzan's* Kaddish in my mind before continuing on.

I was still physically in Otisville, but I felt transported to the packed shul, where I could see the *aron kodesh* opened, along with the Gates of Heaven. "*Shema koleinu*," the *chazzan* cried out with emotion, followed by the whole congregation. "Hear our voice, Hashem our G-d! Have mercy on us and accept our *tefillah* with compassion and willingness!" I whispered along with the *chazzan*, making up with intensity what I lacked in volume.

We *daven* aloud because "the voice stimulates *kavanah*." I couldn't use the voice of my body beyond a whisper, but this inability itself brought out the voice of my soul, the inaudible inner voice which reaches Hashem Himself.

That was the first *Selichos* in a place called prison and it was repeated every year more or less the same way. The repetition and the years that passed between them didn't dull the jarring incongruity of *Selichos* in a cell. Although I did my best to fulfill the task Hashem put before me, I never stopped beseeching Hashem and doing whatever it was my obligation to do to rejoin my family and community where I could serve Hashem properly.

Erev Rosh Hashanah

Erev Rosh Hashanah was a busy day with a tight schedule. There are a lot of personal preparations for the holy day and it's also an important day for parents to connect with their children, guiding them in their own approach to this special moment and *bentching* them for the coming year.

Initially, the evening *davening* started a bit early so we could do *Hataras Nedarim*, because there was no regular morning *minyan*. The extra time also enabled us to get into the spirit of the day before Ma'ariv started.

One year, as we settled down to get ready for *davening*, I noticed that one of the *Yidden* was keeping to himself but seemed to be very agitated. When an opportunity presented itself, I privately and gently asked him what was bothering him.

He answered quietly but with an intensity of emotion that would be hard to describe. It had been eleven years since he'd been torn from his family. His children had grown and had lived through entire phases of their lives while he'd been absent.

Every letter or phone call, inestimably precious though they were, was another reminder of his absence from their lives. Like me, he'd called his family to wish them a sweet new year. He managed to speak to everyone in his family, but it had taken a heavy toll on him. The sensation of absence and loss had been crushing. Describing his feelings, he literally jumped out of his chair in pain. "I can't take it anymore!"

I felt his pain and wanted very much to alleviate it in some way. I couldn't change his situation any more than I could change my own, but I hoped to share with him the thoughts that helped me when I felt those feelings myself.

Torah and *tefillah* are full of examples and I was able to point to the *machzorim* right there on the tables in front of us to ease his pain. Chanah Haneviah, whose story is the *haftorah* of the first day of Rosh Hashanah, faced a situation similar to our own. Her problem was infertility, not incarceration, but she had also been told by the "experts" that what she needed was impossible.

Chanah dismissed these pronouncements—not because the experts were wrong, but because they were irrelevant to the outcome. She knew that the natural order which dictates what is possible is not the final word. The world and everything in it is subject to the will of Hashem, and He is willing to suspend the natural order for His children. She *davened* to Hashem and the impossible happened. She gave birth to the boy who grew to be Shmuel Hanavi, a great leader in Klal Yisrael and Hashem's messenger to anoint Shaul Hamelech and Dovid Hamelech, whose eternal dynasty will culminate in Melech HaMashiach.

This story is part of Torah, which means it is a message for us in our lives. One of the obvious messages in the story is that we too can ask for the impossible and Hashem, in His love and mercy for us, can make it happen. "*Yehi ratzon,*" we often say in our *tefillos.* "Let it *become* Your will…" Even if it was Hashem's will that we endure unpleasant things, we can implore Hashem to adopt a *new* will and give us a new reality.

(It's important to note that, sure enough, this Yid went on to receive his *nes*. He'd been sentenced to many decades of incarceration, functionally a life sentence, but in 2020, he was miraculously released when our dear President Donald Trump issued an order of clemency.)

My voice had risen as I shifted from speaking about his personal and private woes to speaking about our relationship with Hashem and His continuous and complete power over His creation. The people sitting around had taken notice and leaned in to hear the discussion from that point—it was the perfect way to begin the day of Hashem's coronation by His beloved people.

This impromptu *farbrengen* was not unusual. In fact, just about every year after *Hataras Nedarim* and Minchah, while we waited for Ma'ariv time, the conversation would turn to a thought on some part of *davening* or on the idea— and practical implications—of crowning Hashem as King. As an expression of our inspiration, many of us would resolve to strengthen or increase our fulfillment of a specific mitzvah. Sharing this resolution with others was always a great help in sticking with it throughout the year.

Rosh Hashanah

That first year, Rosh Hashanah was too soon after I arrived for the dedicated advocacy organizations to arrange volunteers for the *minyan* on Rosh Hashanah. Instead, we had to rely on participation of Jewish inmates. There were enough Jewish men to form a *minyan* but, to my dismay, not enough of them were willing to take the time to *daven*, even on the High Holidays. *Davening* had to proceed without a *minyan*.

Davening is a personal connection, a matter of the heart, but as a *minyan*, we help each other in that connection. This is true in the spiritual sense, but it's also true in the most practical sense.

Imagine a Rosh Hashanah *tefillah* without a *chazzan*, whose emotional recitation of the *nusach* brings the words to life and sweeps the whole shul along with him as they stand before Hashem Himself. Imagine calling out the words, "*V'Atah Hu Melech Keil chai v'kayam!*" proclaiming Hashem's reign in a single solitary voice, without hearing the proclamation thundering from the throats of your brothers alongside you. Words cannot describe the loss I felt.

In later years, with enough time to make the necessary arrangements, the Aleph Institute would send volunteers to complete the *minyan*, bringing encouragement and a Yom Tov atmosphere to those in a place called prison. Obviously unable to return home after *davening*, and with no hotels close enough to FCI Otisville, they would rent an RV which they parked within walking distance and they would stay there over Yom Tov.

I had felt the anguish of spending Rosh Hashanah alone, so I want to highlight an instance when one of the volunteers suffered the same experience. He had come to join us for Rosh Hashanah, leaving his community, his wife, and his children, and came with *mesiras nefesh* to help his unfortunate brethren. He was not unknown to the authorities—he had been in Otisville before—yet to our great dismay (and to his, I'm sure) he was not allowed in.

By the time all efforts to reverse the decision proved fruitless, there wasn't enough time for him to return home. He spent Yom Tov outside the compound, *davening* alone on the most holy of days. I knew what he sacrificed and what he experienced, and I felt deep gratitude and appreciation to him.

One of the guards had what they call a "higher education." By virtue of his college degree, he carried himself a little differently and spoke with a slightly more professional tone than his colleagues. It happened that he was the guard on duty in the chapel during one of these volunteer Yom Tov *minyanim*. I can't recall the reason, but an unscheduled recall was announced on the loudspeaker. This meant that we all had to return to the barracks, and the volunteers had to be escorted out of the prison compound.

The dehumanization of inmates was never so clear as in the way he managed that recall. "Inmates to the left!" he barked as soon as he heard the announcement. Then he turned to the volunteers, suddenly the embodiment of polite professionalism in manner and speech. "If I can ask you gentlemen to stand on the right side here? Someone will be with you shortly to escort you off the premises."

So sudden and drastic was the change in his manner, that under different circumstances, I would have thought that he suffered a split personality, but I unfortunately knew better. Both interactions came from a single personality—it was his audience that was so starkly split in two. The volunteers were part of society and to be treated with respect. The prisoners were not—they were subjects, to be driven as necessary with no accommodation for their dignity or self-respect.

The refreshing arrival of these volunteers for Yom Tov stopped once there were enough willing Jewish inmates to gather a full *minyan* among the "locals." Although we were able to replace their number, there was no replacing the breath of fresh air and the joy the volunteers brought with their arrival. They were sorely missed. Also, even though we had enough people on paper, it was at times a real struggle to start the *minyan* and keep the required number of people in the chapel for the whole *davening*.

With or without the volunteers, our *minyan* was always a beautiful rainbow of *Yiddishkeit*. *Yidden* of all countries of origin, religious backgrounds and customs, and even different degrees of knowledge and commitment, all united to serve Hashem. I always appreciated seeing this unity in *avodas Hashem* and it struck me as a wonderful parallel to the community we had built in Postville.

After Ma'ariv, we wished each other a heartfelt, "*L'shanah tovah tikasev v'sechasem*—May you be inscribed and sealed [in Hashem's book] for a good year." We gathered around the table, made Kiddush, and sat down right there for a *seudas Yom Tov* over the food each person had brought to the chapel.

One year, after Ma'ariv on Rosh Hashanah, one of the *Yidden* quietly pointed out to me that, whether in innocent ignorance or disregard, one of the others had brought the standard, non-kosher meal for his *seudah*.

The next day, when everyone gathered in the chapel for the first day of Rosh Hashanah *davening*, I made this fellow an offer. If he agreed to forgo the standard meal from the cafeteria, I would give him my kosher meal. He agreed, excited to eat kosher in honor of the holy day. In order to keep my end of the bargain, I broke my custom of avoiding the chow hall, and went to retrieve the kosher meal designated for me. Walking into the chow hall, I felt the disruptive clash between the atmosphere there and the feeling of holiness and sensitivity I'd been working so hard to feel on Rosh Hashanah, but it was worth it. *Baruch Hashem*, at that lunchtime *seudah*, everyone ate kosher. I offered him the same deal on the second day of Yom Tov, and he took me up on that as well.

Yom Tov *Mussaf* brought with it another special mitzvah—*Birkas Kohanim*. There were a few *kohanim* in our group, and they had enough familiarity with the *brachah* to do their part with some assistance. After one or two Yamim Tovim, one of the other *frum* Jews asked me if I would spend some time with them and teach them the relevant *halachos*, proper pronunciation, and the customary tune before the next Yom Tov came around. I was happy to oblige.

We gathered twice a week in cell 307 and over the course of a month or so, we learned the necessary *halachos*, practiced pronouncing the words until they came easily and smoothly, and then we moved to practicing the tune. At first, they were a little self-conscious, but they quickly overcame that feeling and before long, full-throated renditions of, "Ay-ay-ay-ay-ay-ay... Yivarechicha!" could be heard in the barracks.

The next Yom Tov, I served as the *chazzan* for *Mussaf*. At the appropriate part of *davening*, the *kohanim* gathered near me and sang the words of the *brachah* as we had learned. They sang the words of Hashem's eternal *brachah* to the *Yidden* so naturally, with such warmth and energy, that almost before they finished, the overjoyed *Yidden* gave them an excited, "Yasher koach, Kohen!" One of the *Yidden* told them that if he closed his eyes, he could have been in any *shtiebel* in Brooklyn. They beamed with pride.

Chazal say that doing one mitzvah brings a person to do another. I saw time and again the impact that doing a mitzvah had on even hardened individuals. Celebrating Yamim Tovim had a particularly strong and speedy effect, and Yamim Nora'im stronger and faster still.

One incident which made a particularly strong impression on me happened one year right after *davening* on Rosh Hashanah. Sitting not far from me was a Yid who had not had the benefit of a *frum* upbringing. He'd only recently begun to take his first slow steps toward living his life according to Hashem's mitzvos, and as part of that, he joined the Rosh Hashanah *minyan*.

We'd just finished *davening* when the door swung open and the mail room officer walked into the chapel and called out his name, announcing that there was legal mail waiting for him in the mail room.

Legal mail is either part of the inmate's efforts to win his freedom or it's bringing news about the outcome of those efforts. In this case, it was the latter. It was common knowledge that this man was in the final stages of a legal effort and was anxiously awaiting news.

Usually, when an inmate is notified that he has legal mail, he quickly runs to the mail room, his heart pounding, hoping that there's some positive news that will bring him one step closer to home and to his loved ones. To my pleasant surprise, this Yid didn't run off at hearing the news. He took the few short steps over to where I was sitting and leaned over to consult with me. "I shouldn't pick up the mail on the holiday, should I?" he asked. "I'd have to sign for it…"

I could have kissed him. His innocent sincerity must have caused tremendous *nachas* to Hashem. I confirmed his assumption. "We're not allowed to sign on Yom Tov." The officer had already left, having delivered his message, and this precious *neshamah* left to track him down. He met him at the mail room, and informed him that he would not be able to pick up the mail until Wednesday. It was a Jewish two-day holiday and, as a Yid, he couldn't sign, even for this long-awaited notification.

Here was a Yid relinquishing the illusion of control, which drives a person to scramble for scraps of information he can use to make decisions and forecast the future. He understood that his fate is in Hashem's hands and that any efforts he made could only be successful if they are in keeping with Hashem's will.

I marveled at seeing his *neshamah* blossom. Only a few years earlier, this Yid had to be persuaded to come to the chapel to help us with the *minyan*—now here he was, unwilling to compromise on Hashem's mitzvah even to put his mind at ease over his pending appeal.

The shofar is a very profound expression of our connection to Hashem. The Ba'al Shem Tov famously compares it to a son in distress who cries out, "Father! Save me!" The Rebbe Rayatz clarifies that the central point of the *mashal* is not the specific wording of the cry, but the deep bond between son and father that results in that cry and which the cry expresses.

In this, we are all equal. The specific expression and wording of this connection may differ from Jew to Jew, but the bond of son to Father that we each have with Hashem is identical. The shofar gives voice to that connection to Hashem which is the fundamental nature of the *neshamah*.

This connection is so strong that it wasn't only expressed by those who cared enough to come to the chapel. There was one Jewish inmate, originally from Russia, who never wanted to participate in any of the Jewish services or events. One Rosh Hashanah, we crossed paths as I was leaving the chapel carrying the shofar. The *hashgachah pratis* could not have been more obvious, so I caught up with him and told him that it was Rosh Hashanah and we have a mitzvah to hear the shofar. "Do you want to hear the shofar?" I asked.

"Okay," he said, "but only if you blow it right now." He even resumed walking, leaving me to keep up or let go.

Despite the public setting, I wasn't about to let the opportunity slip by. I walked alongside him through the compound with the shofar to my lips, blowing *tekios* and *shevarim* and *teruos* at full volume. We received more than a few puzzled looks, but no interruptions, and that year, this Yid fulfilled the mitzvah of shofar.

The power of a mitzvah was again on display in this Yid—by the time Pesach arrived, his earlier refusal to join us softened, and he came to the chapel for the Pesach Seder. Years later, after his release, he met some *bachurim* who asked him to put on *tefillin*. He did the mitzvah, and then took to chatting with the boys. Among other things they spoke about, he told them, "My *neshamah* opened up in Otisville."

The Jewish spark was not limited to the inmates. One of the officers on staff in my early years there was Jewish. At that time, we were using chapel A, the larger of the rooms, which was nearer to the entrance of the building. Leaving the chapel after *davening*, I encountered this officer in the hallway.

"Happy New Year," I said. The officer nodded, returned the greeting, and kept on going. Before I could offer the opportunity to hear the shofar, the officer had already passed through a security door, but I decided to make an effort anyway. I ran over to the door and, through the bars, I asked, "Do you want to hear the shofar?"

The officer came back through the security door and walked with me into the chapel. There were still a few inmates there and they watched in amazement as the officer listened intently to the *brachos* and to the sounds of the shofar.

When we were done, the officer thanked me profusely and left, leaving me to marvel at what had just happened.

The guards and officers generally avoided fraternizing with the inmates in any way, doubly so if the activity put them in a subordinate position. Listening to the shofar involved standing silently as I did something for them that they couldn't do for themselves. Yet, when the *Yiddishe neshamah* was given the opportunity to do a mitzvah, the officer set aside all the unwritten rules and conventions and came to hear the shofar.

Even the non-Jewish officers, with no commitment to Torah and mitzvos, respected that commitment in the Jewish inmates. One year, there was a frantic recall during *davening* on Rosh Hashanah. There was a suspected escape and the staff were frantically rushing to lock everything down and get a handle on the situation. The inmates realized this was no ordinary recall and there was an added urgency in the rush back to the barracks.

I headed back with the others but, only a few steps outside the chapel, I realized that I should have taken the shofar. There was a very real chance that the lock-in would last all day, and without it, I would miss *tekias shofar*. I turned to head back, against the flow of the crowd, the advice of my friend, and protocol.

The guard in the chapel was surprised to see someone walking in, when everyone was moving in the other direction under orders. "What are you doing here?!" he challenged.

"I just came back to grab the shofar. It's a religious thing." He knew about my general permission to take the shofar and his respect for my commitment to my religion outweighed his need to see everyone out of the room.

"Okay. Grab it and go," he allowed, and I did.

I also did my best to proactively bring the shofar to *Yidden* who didn't or couldn't make it to the chapel for *tekios*. One year, two of the Jewish inmates participated in Rosh Hashanah Ma'ariv but didn't come for Shacharis and *Mussaf*. One of them came after we'd finished and managed to hear the shofar then, but the other didn't show up at all. I sought him out and invited him to come to the cell to which I was assigned to hear shofar, which he willingly did.

On the next visiting day, one of those two inmates was visited by his father, a Russian Jew originally from Bobruisk. I was in the visiting room not far away and I was able to see the father beaming with joy at his son's account of his Rosh Hashanah. More than once, he leaned over from a few seats away and wished me, "*A gut gebentcht yahr.*"[1]

Hashem orchestrates everything that happens in the world for some purpose related to the service of Hashem and to help those who serve Him. So much so, that *Chazal* say that a castle and all its attendant buildings may be built and stand for many years and then fall to ruins, just so a traveling Jew can find shelter in a rainstorm. The spot that we used for Tashlich seemed to me to be one such spot.

Years before there were any *frum* Jews at Otisville, a talented inmate persuaded the authorities to build a small greenhouse—right next to the barracks to which I was assigned—to be used for an agriculture program to be taught by him.

Other inmates were able to work in the greenhouse, planting and tending to vegetables. Gaining knowledge and experience in landscaping and light agriculture helped their morale, and it was a marketable skill they could use if they were ever released. The program was ultimately abandoned, but the greenhouse was never dismantled.

The greenhouse included an artificial fish pond and waterfall which had been part of the irrigation system and added a touch of beauty, and it was this feature that made this whole spot so precious to the Jews at Otisville. It enabled us to fulfill the *minhag* of Tashlich properly.

We would stand at the water in the afternoon of the first day of Rosh Hashanah and invoke Hashem's Thirteen Attributes of Mercy. The *tefillah* of Tashlich speaks of Hashem's protection, overturning all harsh Heavenly decrees and the schemes of our enemies, and asks for forgiveness from our *aveiros* and a sweet new year filled with *brachos*.

Throughout the year, passing this small spot and reflecting on its preparation years in advance in order to facilitate a mitzvah served as a constant reminder of Hashem's providence.

Yom Kippur

Creating and preserving the special feeling of Shabbos and Yom Tov was always a challenge, and the unique feeling of Yom Kippur took even greater effort. I wore the *kittel* every Shabbos in order to distinguish my Shabbos

---

1. A good, blessed year.

clothing from the weekday, which had the desired effect all year round, but diminished the power of the *kittel* to add a special feeling to Yom Kippur.

To compensate for the absence of some of the more superficial or environmental influences, I would spend extra time during the Aseres Yemei Teshuvah learning the relevant *sefarim* and delving into the inner meaning of Yom Kippur.

When Erev Yom Kippur arrived, I would wake in the pre-dawn hours to do *kapparos*. The proper way to perform this *minhag* is with a live animal—a rooster or, if that's not available, a fish. This is especially true in our times, when activists in open opposition to Torah try to prey on the compassion and naiveté of the general public to undermine our holy *minhagim*.

I asked multiple times for permission to use a live chicken or fish. All but once, these requests were denied. I was prohibited from having legal tender, so I reluctantly used the mailing stamps, which have some face value. I whirled the stamps above my head at the appropriate part of the *tefillah* and then placed them in my *pushke*. My family redeemed them by giving a corresponding amount of money to the poor. On years that Erev Yom Kippur was a visiting day, my family helped me do the *minhag* with actual currency in the visiting room.

Another Erev Yom Kippur *minhag* mentioned in *Shulchan Aruch* is for a father to *bentch* his children. It's supposed to be done after the *seudas hamafsekes* before leaving to shul for *Kol Nidrei*, but in my situation, the closest I could get was earlier in the day during visiting hours, and even that, only on years when Erev Yom Kippur was a visiting day. In other years, I would give the *brachah* on the visiting day prior to Erev Yom Kippur.

It was a very emotional moment when the children would stand up (one at a time, so as not to antagonize the guards) and stand in front of me with their heads bowed to receive their *brachah*. The heartache was mixed with *nachas* to see how precious and significant the *brachah* was to them.

I would put both hands on the child's head, as my father had done, and give the *brachah* of *Yivarechicha*, always adding a *brachah* for that child's specific needs in the year ahead. I ended with the *brachah* that we as a family all needed so urgently, that this would be the year that I would return home to them. I lingered over those entreaties and embraced and kissed each child before continuing on to the next one.

Some years, my father was able to come before Yom Kippur. On those occasions, I had the *zechus* of receiving my own *Birkas Habanim* from him, right there in the visiting room.

Another *minhag* we were able to fulfill in years when there were visiting hours on Erev Yom Kippur was asking for *lekach*. We would buy a sweet cake or pastry from the machine—one year there was actual honey cake—and my children would ask for *lekach*. I would put it in their hands with a kiss and *bentch* them that they would not have to ask for anything else in the coming year.

I called my family on Erev Yom Kippur. If it was a year when I'd given my children the *brachah* early, and hadn't seen them on Erev Yom Kippur itself, I made the extra effort to get through to all of them. It wasn't easy to make so many calls on the same day.

A remarkable story happened around these phone calls which was a powerful demonstration of the role of *bitachon* in *avodas Hashem*. It also helped me and my family properly react to a big setback that happened shortly thereafter in the legal case.

That year, a special "move" was organized for the Jewish inmates to go to the chapel at 5:10 p.m., to better prepare for the holy day. This gave us twenty minutes more than we would have had by waiting for the scheduled move at 5:30.

I wanted to call each of my ten children to give them their *brachah*, but I was working against the clock. Even if I kept each phone call short, say two or three minutes, the system locks the inmate out for a full half-hour after a successful call before allowing him to make another. Because of this, I got started on my list as soon possible that Erev Yom Kippur morning.

The phone calls were like cold water to a parched soul. The crass tumult around me faded as I spoke to each child, hearing the hustle and bustle of home behind their cherished voices. I wished them the traditional *Birkas Habanim* and a year full of *brachos* with all the love that fills the heart of a father and reluctantly said goodbye so I could eventually make the next call.

At 3:30 p.m., when the phones were deactivated for an hour due to the count, I had only three more calls to make—but I realized that, despite my efforts, it would be impossible to call all the children.

My next call had to wait until 4:30 when the phones turned back on. Allowing a few minutes for the call and then the thirty-minute waiting period, I would only be able to make the second call at around 5:10. Choosing to make the second call meant missing the special move. Adding in the *third* call, which couldn't take place before 5:45, meant missing the 5:30 scheduled move and the chance to go to the chapel entirely.

I obviously couldn't give up on the *davening*, so I couldn't make the third call, but I decided to forgo the extra twenty minutes for my own personal *avodah* in order to at least make the second call.

I made the call at 5:10 and then prepared to head to the chapel for *Kol Nidrei* and Ma'ariv during the 5:30 move. The time came and went with no "move" announcement. Slight delays to the schedule were not unheard of, but I had an uneasy feeling this time. I went to the guard's office to inquire and was told that the yard and gym were closed and there would be no afternoon moves that day. "You're stuck in here until tomorrow."

This was a blow to all the inmates. Their lock-in would now be extended until the next morning, without the usual opportunities to stretch, get some air, and take care of any tasks around the compound during the late afternoon. For me, the news was infinitely worse. I wasn't being kept from the exercise equipment—I was being denied the ability to *daven* with a *minyan* on Yom Kippur!

I tried to communicate the seriousness of the situation and implored the guard to help me find a way to get to the chapel. He initially declined to get involved, but my heartfelt words softened him a bit and he called the lieutenant's office for permission to release me to the chapel with an escort.

This is not an unusual request. It's routine for a guard to be authorized to move an individual inmate if he's needed somewhere on the compound between moves. This time, however, the request was denied. The guard put down the phone with a puzzled expression and shrugged. "I tried," he said, semi-apologetically.

I left his office with a heavy heart. I passed through the common area. With the doors locked, the deprived inmates had gathered around the tables, snacking, chatting, watching the screens overhead. Snippets of their conversation intruded on my thoughts, some of them so repulsive, I physically recoiled. This was the place where I would stand before Hashem on the holiest of days?

I slowly walked by the heavy metal doors that stood between me and my fellow Jews in the chapel. The orange light of the setting sun streamed through the barred windows. Yom Kippur was about to begin.

Cell 307 offered some welcome relief from the noise. I sat down at the table, which I'd covered with a white sheet in honor of Yom Tov, and thought about my situation. The first order of business was to get my emotions in check. The Ba'al HaTanya teaches us that the heart will, and should, follow the mind and not the other way around. My heart was pulling me toward sorrow, but I didn't have to follow.

I considered the cause of my feelings. I very strongly wanted to *daven* with a *minyan*. To *daven* alone would fall very short of fulfilling this mitzvah properly and, seeing no way to avoid this, I was feeling dejected. Clarifying and recognizing the cause of my sadness immediately brought to mind something from *Sha'ar Habitachon*.

Rabbeinu Bacheye notes that it's not only for our own needs that we must trust in Hashem. Even our Torah and mitzvos require *bitachon*. The choice to do the mitzvah and the resolve to act is *our* responsibility, but we have to remember that the implementation of our decision is not really up to us. Factors beyond our control can prevent us from doing what we otherwise would. We need to ask Hashem to help us and allow us that final step into the realm of action, and trust in Him that He will do so.

Realizing that my situation was exactly what Rabbeinu Bacheye was describing, I affirmed my strong desire to *daven* with a *minyan* and explicitly recognized that whether I would be able to do so was solely in Hashem's hands. I turned to Hashem and asked that He grant me my desire. Having done everything I could, I let go of the destructive emotions and placed my trust in Hashem.

Once again calm and happy, I opened the *Sha'ar Habitachon* to *perek dalet*, where this is discussed, to refresh my memory and strengthen my resolve while I awaited Hashem's salvation.

I sat absorbed in the *sefer* for a while when I realized that enough time had passed for my phone access to be reactivated. I was now able to make the call I'd been resigned to missing. I made my way to the phone and called my son Meir Simcha, a Chabad *shliach* on the college campus in Oneonta, New York.

I could hear in his voice that he was surprised but happy to receive the phone call. I shared his gratitude to Hashem for this *hashgachah pratis*, which I trusted would ultimately not come at the expense of a proper *minyan*. Meir Simcha gave me a lot of *nachas* with his report on his Yom Tov preparations. He was expecting two hundred Jewish students, many of whom would otherwise not have observed Yom Kippur. I wished him continued success and we *bentched* each other with a *chasimah tovah*.

After I hung up, I went back to my *sefer*, still relying on Hashem to help me take my sincere desire to fulfill His mitzvah that one last step that was out of my control. It was quite some time, after 6:00 p.m., when my help finally came. "Rubashkin!" It was the guard on duty in the barrack summoning me to his office. I knew it must be good news, so I grabbed my *machzor* and ran to his office. He looked up with a smile when I knocked on his door. "Be ready—they're making a move for you."

My joy was indescribable. I was overwhelmed with a powerful feeling of gratitude to Hashem for His kindness, and it was all I could do to stop myself from breaking out into a dance right there in his office. It wasn't bashfulness which held me back—I was simply running very late. It was only fifteen minutes to *shkiah* and I had to get to the chapel, put on my *tallis*, and prepare for *Kol Nidrei*. There would be time for dancing later.

I was escorted to the chapel right away. As we approached, I saw my good friend Moishe peering out the small window in the door. When he saw me, his face lit up, and he half-ran, half-danced to get the chaplain to unlock the door. As soon as the door was open, he hugged me and we danced with joy. "I knew it!" he kept saying. "I knew it! I knew Hashem would help you! I told them you would be coming to *daven* with us!"

Once we had *davened*, they filled me in. After the special move was over, the assistant chaplain had noticed my absence and commented on it. Moishe had assured her, "Rubashkin is coming."

"No way," the chaplain had insisted. "The compound is locked down and they denied his request for a personal move. It's impossible."

Moishe wasn't persuaded. "It might be impossible, but believe me—he's coming. Hashem is going to help him."

Seeing my *tzarah*, the other *Yidden* also approached her and asked her to do something about my problem and enable me to come. She couldn't override the lieutenant's denial of an escorted release, but, seeing the concern of so many of my dear brothers, she understood how important this was for all of us. She put some thought into it and found a way out. The Muslim inmates also needed to pray and had also been trapped by the cancellation of the 5:30 move. She requested a special move for them, and when permission was granted and the doors were opened, I was allowed to go to the chapel as well.

The sincere and powerful *ahavas Yisrael* clearly played a key role in this salvation, transforming the denial of my request into permission to open the locked doors of the barracks. I was certain that the *ahavas Yisrael* that so many *Yidden* around the world were displaying in fighting for my *full* release would similarly bear fruit.

Shortly after Yom Kippur that year, an important appeal was denied. It was this experience that helped me take that setback in stride, sure that this denial would also be reversed and the doors would ultimately swing open for my full release.

Initially, I ate the *seudah* on Erev Yom Kippur in the cell, using whatever I managed to put aside or buy from the commissary, as did the handful of other *Yidden* there. In later years, when more *Yidden* were brought to Otisville, we would come together in the chapel to eat the *seudah* together. This was a bit of a sacrifice, because while the barracks each had a number of microwaves, the chapel had only one microwave for all of us. We didn't have enough time in the chapel to warm everyone's meals one at a time, and some of us had to eat our food cold. Nonetheless, sitting together was such a comfort and a help in getting into the Yom Kippur spirit that we considered it worth the sacrifice.

Before Minchah, there's a *minhag* to receive *malkos*, which stirs our hearts to *teshuvah* and helps us feel the appropriate awe and trepidation as we prepare to serve Hashem. The *malkos* are supposed to be given with a leather strap. People usually use a belt, but there are no leather belts in a place called prison. I set my mind to finding a way to fulfill this *minhag*. *Baruch Hashem*, I remembered the prison workshop where prisoners worked making leather goods. One of the prisoners was able to obtain a long leather strap from the scrap leather and I used that from then on.

The regular shoes and boots had leather in them and could not be worn on Yom Kippur so, as night approached, we put on "bus shoes." These were provided to us by the laundry room at our request through the chaplain.

Unsupervised fire was out of the question and they wouldn't allow fire in the cells, but they allowed us to light a candle that can last through the twenty-five hours to use for Havdalah, in the lieutenant's office. Every year, but one, this precious candle was mysteriously extinguished sometime over Yom Kippur.

The *minyan* gathered for *Kol Nidrei*. As the Day of Atonement began, I often noted the contrast between the earthly courts, who had placed us in this place of punishment and pain, and the Heavenly Court of Hashem, Who is eager to forgive us and bless us with a sweet future, if we only ask sincerely.

After *davening*, we had to return to the barracks and the cells, but I would stay up in the cell and say the whole Tehillim, as is the *minhag* Yom Kippur night.

In honor of Yom Kippur, we were allowed to stay in the chapel for an unusually long amount of time during the day. We spent the day *davening*, as *Yidden* do all over the world. I was often the *chazzan* and I immersed myself in the entreaties in the *machzor*, calling out to Hashem to raise me, and those who were with me, out of the depths.

One year, it was foggy on Yom Kippur and, due to the low visibility, they didn't allow any movement on the compound. The only way to move from place to place was with an escort. The non-Jewish chaplain on duty was supposed to come get us for the scheduled time of *davening* but the time came and went with no sign of him. When he finally came, he apologized for his lateness. To make up for it, he arranged for an "out-count" that day, which would allow us to remain in the chapel uninterrupted, without returning to the barracks for the 4:00 p.m. count.

I always felt an elevated spirit by the end of Yom Kippur, but the uninterrupted stretch that year gave me an extra boost. Spending an extended period of time immersed in the reality of Hashem, of *emunah* and *bitachon*, my clarity and certainty that I was in Hashem's hands was refreshed and I felt sure that this would be the year of my *nes*.

I tried to hold on to that feeling as long as I could, even walking back to the barrack wearing my *kittel*. Time marches on, and any special sensitivity connected to special days goes with it. We can only hope to hang on to a remnant and bring it into the mundane weekday life. The bulk of those feelings fade quickly just by returning to the world. I always felt a sense of whiplash going from *kodesh* to *chol*, most intensely on Motza'ei Yom Kippur going from the intense heights of Ne'ilah back to the barrack and its population.

After Havdalah, I would call my family to tell them about my Yom Kippur and wish them a good Yom Tov—Motza'ei Yom Kippur is a Yom Tov on which we celebrate the forgiveness and the sweet new year that Hashem has undoubtedly granted us.

We would also make a point of talking about building the sukkah, my only way of beginning the process that night, as is the custom.

CHAPTER TWENTY-SIX
Sukkos and Simchas Torah

Sukkos

AFTER THE SOLEMN DAYS OF ROSH HASHANAH AND YOM KIPPUR, WE celebrate Sukkos, a Yom Tov of intense joy. Days before the first Sukkos that I was in Otisville, I was instructed to go to the supply room, along with a number of other Jewish inmates, to pick up the wooden panels for the sukkah. We were to bring them to the yard, where we would put them together under the supervision of a guard. They were simple painted wooden panels, a bit old and weather-beaten, but that sukkah looked nicer to me than the most majestic palace.

The Maggid of Mezritch taught in the name of the Ba'al Shem Tov, "The cloud of the *Ketores* [which is the height of the *avodah* of Yom Kippur] becomes the *schach* of the sukkah." When we sit in the sukkah, we're immersing ourselves in the connection to Hashem expressed in those most sublime moments of Yom Kippur, this time from a place of great joy. The mitzvah of *lulav* and *esrog* is preferably performed in the sukkah and their movements as we shake them—outward in each direction and then back toward our hearts—represent internalizing this connection and including it in every aspect of our lives.

That year in Otisville, I saw the connection between Yom Kippur and Sukkos play out right in front of me.

There was one Yid, who considered himself traditional, who had not participated in the Rosh Hashanah or Yom Kippur *davening* that year. It's not our place to judge him; his absence was surely not a sign of apathy or, *chas v'shalom*, rejection or rebellion. People in prison are living under circumstances successfully designed to be crushing to the human spirit. The inmate experiences denial of his most basic needs—to be free, to be constructive, to connect with loved ones—which are critical to a human being, punctuated by instances of real or perceived insult and injustice, and aggravated by the seeming hopelessness of the situation. Pushing through all of that, even just to function and not to give in to despair and depression, is a tremendous effort.

Whatever the cause or justification, this Yid couldn't participate in the *avodah* of Rosh Hashanah and Yom Kippur but he was back on his feet and wanted to help build the sukkah. He joined us and reported to the storage area to carry the panels to the spot where the sukkah was to stand, but he was informed that he would not be allowed to participate. Why not? He was wearing his sneakers and not the heavier boots required when engaged in this kind of work.

Enforcement of such rules is so sporadic and unpredictable that when they *were* enforced it meant something, both in the mundane reality of navigating life in a place called prison and, more importantly, in the reality of *avodas Hashem*. The teaching of the Ba'al Shem Tov, that in everything a person sees or hears he can find guidance in *avodas Hashem*, was a guiding principle for me and one I constantly repeated to others in person and in correspondence.

In this case, the denial that this Yid unfortunately suffered brought to life the connection between these two Yamim Tovim. Sukkos flows from Rosh Hashanah and Yom Kippur and missing out on one negatively impacted the other. It also reminded me of the *Sha'ar Habitachon's* message that while we control our desire and intent to do the mitzvah, the ability to successfully carry it out is a gift from Hashem. I firmly resolved to help strengthen this Yid and any other in their moments of weakness so that they would have Hashem's *brachah* to fulfill other mitzvos in their time of strength.

Building the sukkah was the backdrop to one of the most shocking and vicious displays of open antisemitism that I experienced in my time in Otisville. A couple of years after I'd been transferred to Otisville, I left the barracks in early Tishrei only to find, to my surprise, that the sukkah had already been built.

It had clearly been built without the involvement of the Jewish inmates. The panels had been placed with their eye-pleasing, painted side facing outward, and the crude, unfinished side facing inward. I peeked inside and saw that the environment inside was as unpleasant as you would expect. It might have looked prettier to those looking from the outside, which is of paramount importance in certain circles, but it was at the expense of those actually sitting inside and using it. It was certainly no way to fulfill and show respect for the mitzvah of sukkah.

Just then, another Yid passed by and made the same observation. We discussed the issue, and decided to inquire of the lieutenant about how we could arrange to have the sukkah taken apart and reassembled properly.

We walked together toward the chow hall and found the lieutenant standing with another officer just outside. They were there as part of the "main line" policy to make officers available to inmates for complaints or inquiries. I walked over to the lieutenant, explained our problem, and asked him how we could go about fixing it. When I mentioned the sukkah and gestured toward it standing in the distance, he turned around to look at it.

"That?!" he said. "They should burn it down!"

I was horrified, stunned into silence. While I was searching for the right response to this outburst, he continued, "And they should put all the Jews in there first!"

I looked over at the other Yid in total shock. The look on his face said, "Let's get out of here!"—which was a good idea. We quickly went into the chow hall. After I'd collected myself somewhat, I returned to the barracks, still in shock.

News of the exchange had spread quickly and the barracks were roiling. One prisoner, a killer-for-hire in his past life, was beside himself over this malicious behavior and insisted that I file an official complaint. Another prisoner, no wimp himself, disagreed, and called me to the side when he had a chance. "Listen," he said. "I'm not here to educate you or tell you what to do, but I like you. Listen to me. You're in *their* house. Do *not* file a complaint because they *will* retaliate!"

When I told the chaplain about the incident, he demanded that I report it. I wanted something done on the matter, but I also wanted to avoid retaliation. As the *Sha'ar Habitachon* writes, a person is not supposed to intentionally put himself in danger, and I told the chaplain that I'd rather not. Neither I, nor anyone affiliated with me, made a formal complaint, but the story had spread amongst the inmates and the assistant warden eventually found out. When he heard the story, the assistant warden demanded an explanation from the lieutenant—and the predicted retaliation was not long in coming.

Three days before Sukkos was a Friday, a visiting day, and my family came to visit. They filled out the sign-in forms and brought them to the desk, as they did every time, but they were told by those on duty that the visit was denied because I didn't have enough visiting points.

I was expecting the visit, but time was passing and I wasn't being called to come to the visiting room. Confused and a little concerned, I called my wife to make sure everything was okay and to find out the reason for the delay. It took a number of tries, but I finally got through and was told that they'd been turned away for lack of points. We always scheduled and rationed visits very carefully to ensure that we didn't run out of points. I was sure that we hadn't.

The antisemitic incident hadn't been reported, as far as I knew, but it was still fresh on my mind, as was the warning of that inmate about retaliation. A few inquiries quickly clarified that the story *had* somehow been informally reported and that it had been this officer who had interfered with my visit.

The assistant warden was, *baruch Hashem*, the approachable sort, and I went straight to him. I told him that my family had been turned away in what was clearly retaliation. The excuse about the points was obviously a false pretense, as a quick review of the visiting record for that month would show. He checked the record and agreed.

He authorized the visit for that day and insisted that I go to the visiting room area to see if they were still around. They weren't. They had wanted to wait until this was resolved, but the front office had told them that they couldn't "loiter" and that they had to leave. I could imagine the heartache of my wife and young children who came to visit me before Yom Tov only to be unjustly denied, and it added to my own heartache.

I headed toward the office to report back to the assistant warden and discuss the matter further. As I walked, lost in thought, I heard my name being called. I turned around to see this lieutenant. I had no interest in interacting with him, but the rules dictated that if he called, I had to answer. I stopped and waited for him to reach me. He apologized for the incident, an almost unimaginable thing from a lieutenant, and assured me that I would get a visit after all.

The day was too short and the drive was too long for them to return that day and get back to Monsey in time for Shabbos. Instead, the assistant warden gave permission for a visit on Sunday, Erev Yom Tov, although I didn't have enough points for the more "expensive" weekend visits. Because it was Erev Yom Tov, they could only stay for an hour before they had to head back, but it was a very meaningful visit. My father was also able to join on Sunday and I had the benefit of his presence which I would not have had otherwise.

The story showed me that although the place called prison naturally works the way the "experts" predicted and there *was* retaliation, I was protected by Hashem and the result was not only an otherwise impossible visit on Erev Yom Tov, but the disciplining of this hateful individual, who *baruch Hashem* never bothered me again.

About four years after I was transferred there, they bought a new sukkah. It wasn't much bigger than the old one, but it was so much nicer! The fresh wood panels brought back memories of home, but even for those without the benefit of nostalgia, anything not made of metal or painted a drab gray is a soothing sight in a place called prison. It was also gratifying to our *neshamos* to have a touch of *hiddur mitzvah* in the beauty of the new sukkah.

One year, we were sitting inside the sukkah when a curious guard wandered over. He stood in the doorway chatting with one of the other *Yidden* about the sukkah. "Tonight it's going to be thirty degrees," I heard him say. "Wouldn't it make more sense to do this in the summer?"

He was paraphrasing the exact question the *Tur* suggests the nations of the world would ask! It felt like we were acting out the halachah. He did his part and asked the question, and I was excited to play my part and present the answer—which says so much about how and why a Yid should do a mitzvah.

"That's *exactly* why G-d gave us Sukkos in the fall!" I exclaimed. "If it made sense to be outdoors because of the weather, it wouldn't be clear that we're doing it because of G-d's commandment. This way it's crystal clear to everyone, and especially ourselves, that we sit in the sukkah to remember for all generations that G-d protected us when He took us out of Egypt, and will continue to protect us as we make our way through the dangerous Desert of the Nations!"

It also reminded me of the Rebbe's explanation of a Gemara describing uncomfortable conditions in the sukkah and the Yid's reaction to them. The Gemara is describing the objections of the idolatrous nations, after Mashiach comes, to the rewards Hashem gives the *Yidden* for keeping the mitzvos. They claim that they would have earned those rewards, if only they would have been given the chance.

Hashem will offer them a chance to demonstrate by sitting in the sukkah, but will make it uncomfortably hot. At this point, they will abandon the sukkah, kicking it on the way out.

The Rebbe explains that because the discomfort exempts us (and them, in that instance) from the obligation to stay in the sukkah, it also means there is no reward. The reaction to the suddenly not profitable mitzvah is the key difference. Although a Yid can *also* halachically leave the sukkah under those conditions, he would not kick the sukkah. A Yid does the mitzvah because it's the will of Hashem. Profitable or not, the sukkah is a precious expression of our connection to Hashem, not a worthless waste of time to be kicked with frustration or kicked aside with indifference.

The mitzvah of sukkah requires that we reside in the sukkah. They weren't about to transfer us from the cells full time, but the chaplain did submit for their approval a schedule of permitted times that would allow us to "reside" there as much as possible. The proposed schedule would make the sukkah accessible not just during meal times, but throughout the day as well, whenever we were allowed out of the barracks.

There really was no substantive reason to quarrel with this arrangement and certainly no call for an officer, untrained in religious matters, to contradict a chaplain, but there was opposition nonetheless, something I can only attribute to antisemitism. The captain at the time was a good person, *baruch Hashem*, one of those through whom Hashem does kindness, and he was not swayed by the opposition. The chaplain's recommendation was accepted and it became the official policy.

The barracks were opened each day between 6:45 and 7:00 a.m. From then until the end-of-day recall at 8:30 p.m., with the exception of counts and adverse weather lock-ins, we were officially allowed in the sukkah. On the evenings of Yom Tov itself, we were granted more time, usually an additional fifteen minutes, so that we could make Kiddush and eat our "*seudah*" after nightfall.

Like other policies, particularly religious policies, the mileage varied based on the guard we were dealing with at a given moment. Once, in my third year there, a guard ordered me out of the sukkah while I was *davening*, on the grounds that it was not a meal time. Of course, he was wrong as a matter of official policy, but my protests and explanations fell on deaf ears and I had to leave. (To avoid a repeat of this in the future, the chaplain scotch-taped a copy of the policy memo to the wall of the sukkah so no guard could claim ignorance.)

Throughout my ordeal, I forcefully resisted the argument that my circumstances or location made things "different" and I could (or should) compromise on *halachos* or even *hiddurim*. I made every effort to fulfill the mitzvos and *minhagim* in a place called prison no differently than I did before. I had always kept the *hiddur* to abstain from eating even a *Shehakol*, or even taking a drink of water, outside of the sukkah. I didn't compromise on that in Otisville, even though it meant fasting during the hours that we were locked into the barracks.

I did my best to spend all my time in the sukkah. In addition to helping me feel the *kedushah* of Yom Tov and giving me the pleasure of doing a mitzvah and connecting to Hashem, the sukkah was also an escape from the environment and atmosphere of the place called prison. Within its walls, the sights of prison disappeared, and even the sounds faded somewhat, bringing our surroundings more in line with the inner freedom we struggled to maintain.

It was a refuge we occasionally needed to rebuild at the start of the day. Not infrequently, we would come into the sukkah and find the tidy state in which we had left it completely overturned, the aftermath of a thorough search. The sukkah was an empty wooden structure with tables and chairs, but it was still considered suspicious enough to warrant numerous disruptive searches—once while we were actually sitting there. As with many procedures in a place called prison, these invasions left us feeling violated and dehumanized.

There were other ways that the place called prison intruded on our sukkah. One year, our sukkah had all the required components; four walls with a small door, sufficient *schach*, four narrow tables, and eighteen chairs. It was only missing one critical, but intangible thing—light! The light fixture was hanging in its spot and it was plugged in, but the electricity was turned off.

Without electrical power, the only light in the sukkah came through the narrow doorway, supplemented when evening fell by the light of the few candles we lit *lichvod Yom Tov*. It was not even enough light to learn from a *sefer* or *daven* from a siddur, and it was definitely not conducive to a feeling of *simchah*. Sitting in the feeble light, we turned up the inner light of our *neshamos*. We told stories, sang happy *niggunim*, shared words of Torah and *hisorerus*, and lifted ourselves out of the darkness.

Some in our group were inexperienced enough to assume that it was accidental and that if they brought it to the attention of the guards, it would be corrected. They did their best to correct this "mistake," to no avail. The lights stayed off throughout the first day of Yom Tov, despite their continued efforts to inform personnel of the mistake. Finally, they had to concede that it was a decision, not an oversight.

Their decision would have stood and the sukkah would have remained unusable in the dark, if Hashem had not sent the chaplain, who happened to pass by and peek into the sukkah. She was puzzled and asked us why we were sitting in the dark. We explained the situation, and she promised to look into it. Unwilling to leave us in the dark even temporarily, she wedged her flashlight between the door and the door frame and left. Within a few hours, the light was restored and the light of the sukkah shone bright and uninterrupted for the rest of Yom Tov.

Living in a place called prison is like living in outer space, especially for a Yid. Everything needs to be piped in from the outside, down to the smallest thing. Things like the non-leather shoes we needed for Yom Kippur and Tishah B'Av were often available without being specially imported, but things like a *lulav* and *esrog* were obviously not. *Baruch Hashem*, the chaplain took religious rights seriously and made sure we had a proper set of *dalet minim* for Sukkos.

Initially, one set was provided for all the inmates to use. The *minim* are delicate and liable to get damaged, even when handled with care, and the only set we had was passed around to many people who had no experience in handling them. Having only one set increased the risk that we could be left without a kosher *lulav* and *esrog*, so I requested that I be allowed my own set.

My request was granted, *baruch Hashem*, and the permission was extended to others who wanted the same. From then on, whoever requested a set would receive one from the chaplain. I observed with satisfaction that *kinas sofrim tarbeh chachmah*—wholesome envy and competition, applied to learning and good deeds, can be very constructive and results in an increase in wisdom and righteousness. While in the beginning, there was very little demand for personal sets of *dalet minim*, eventually every Yid wanted to fulfill the mitzvah in the best possible way, with their own set.

Each morning, as soon as we were released from the cells, I would make a beeline for the sukkah with my precious *lulav* and *esrog* to do the mitzvah at the earliest opportunity.

Throughout the day, I would seek out Jewish inmates who might not do the mitzvah without encouragement and assistance, and offer to help them shake the *lulav* and *esrog*. This met with quite a bit of success. I would also try to find out if any staff members were Jewish and help them with the mitzvah as well. There were two that I managed to identify, and they agreed to let me help them.

There's an old Yiddish expression to describe something that is totally out of place; *azoi vee a Yevani in sukkah*—"like a Greek in the sukkah." For a few years in Otisville, we experienced this almost literally.

The authorities allow prisoners to identify their own religion and religious needs, and officially provide for those needs, within certain limitations. As a result, there were some in a place called prison who would stretch their beliefs to include as many benefits as they could.

One of the religious groups in Otisville practiced a strange mixture of religions, including, *l'havdil*, elements they took from *Yiddishkeit*. On these grounds, they requested and received some of the benefits that the *Yidden* receive; grape juice and challah on Shabbos and Yom Tov and the additional food for Pesach Sedarim, for example.

When Sukkos came, they said that they also needed to be in the sukkah. Why not? It was an open-air clubhouse that offered a pleasant alternative to sitting cooped up in the barracks. They could even use it for their meals, which could otherwise not be taken out of the chow hall. Their request was granted.

They were often in the sukkah at the same time as us, which was an intrusion and interference in our ability to serve Hashem. Their presence made some of the more self-conscious Jewish inmates reluctant to properly *daven*, to sing and dance, even to open up and talk with their fellow Jews.

They clustered around their own table in the sukkah and laid out their *treife* food, which filled the sukkah with a physically and spiritually repulsive stench. They watched what we did, occasionally asking questions, and requested and received their own *lulav* and *esrog*. They did their best to imitate our *avodah*, often to humorous effect.

The one thing they never tried to mimic was our joyous singing and dancing. It made them uncomfortable—so uncomfortable, in fact, that one year, the sustained dancing on Simchas Torah drove them from the sukkah, as I will detail shortly. The year after that, they asked for and received their own separate "sukkah."

The first improvement they made to their clubhouse was to replace the *schach* with a much more practical solid roof, so the rain and the cold wouldn't bother them. They were very happy with their upgrade and so were we. Now that they were satisfied elsewhere, we were able to sit in the sukkah and immerse ourselves in the *kedushah* and *simchah*, without the intrusion of incompatible sights, smells, and sounds, and this greatly enhanced our Yom Tov.

Stepping outside the sukkah during the *seudos*, you could hear the joy and life streaming out on the soundwaves and feel the presence of Hashem there with us in FCI Otisville. By contrast, although sounds of discussion or prayer were sometimes audible from the clubhouse "sukkah" with the sturdy roof nearby, there were never any sounds of singing or joy.

This didn't particularly surprise me—how could you expect to hear joy from imprisoned men? Their response was the normal and rational response to being incarcerated. It was *our* response that was unnatural and inexplicable.

They had fled the shared sukkah because our joy befuddled and irritated them; a feeling the guards shared. One time, we were sitting in the sukkah after dark and someone was repeating a *shmuess* he remembered from yeshivah. It was meaningful, but also had very humorous parts, and the sukkah kept breaking out in hearty laughter. Suddenly, a guard appeared in the narrow doorway, obviously irritated by our joy. "Do you want me to pull out the plug?!" he asked angrily, gesturing at the light fixtures.

If he disconnected the light, we would obviously have to leave. The speaker respectfully explained the cause of the laughter, but in doing so reminded the group of what he'd said before—prompting another wave of laughter.

An interaction with an irritated guard was no laughing matter and would often result in real and unpleasant consequences. This time, however, the power of *simchah* was on display and the merriment seemed to disarm him. He abruptly turned on his heel and disappeared. We thanked Hashem for His protection and continued to celebrate *Zman Simchaseinu* with hearts full of joy.

Sukkos has a greater emphasis on joy than even other Yamim Tovim, and one expression of that is the celebration of *simchas beis hasho'evah*. In the times of the Beis Hamikdash this was a jubilant celebration of a special *avodah*, pouring the water, that was unique to Sukkos. In our times, we celebrate this special aspect of Sukkos by gathering to sing and dance with musical accompaniment, often in a public place.

We were able to dance together despite our situation, but the added merriment of music was not available to us. *Baruch Hashem*, the devoted volunteers made efforts to come at least once over Chol Hamoed and bring this aspect of Yom Tov with them as well.

They would bring singers and musicians along, including many who were very much in demand. These singers could have been elsewhere working

Dancing with volunteers who came to lift the spirits of the *Yidden* in Otisville.

for their *parnassah*, but came instead to bring *simchas Yom Tov* to their less fortunate brothers in a place called prison.

One such *simchas beis hasho'evah* provided a valuable lesson in making Jewish decisions. A few weeks before Sukkos that year, the volunteer who was organizing the Sukkos celebration presented us with a choice. We could have our musical night on Chol Hamoed with less skilled and in-demand performers, or we could choose to schedule it for after Yom Tov, when the top singers would be able to come.

The way he presented the alternatives, it was clear that he felt the second option was better. His intention was to bring some joy to suffering people and it seemed obvious to him that the better the music, the greater the positive effect.

We, however, had been practicing a different way of evaluating our choices. We had recognized that our freedom depended on centering ourselves on the reality of our *neshamos* over that of the world around us, and in fact, we'd made a resolution that Rosh Hashanah that we would approach decisions in our situation from that perspective.

It was the fulfillment of the mitzvah that would elevate our *neshamah*, not the quality of the vocals and musical arrangements. A strengthened, invigorated *neshamah* would also mean positive emotions and state of mind. The mitzvah was to rejoice on Yom Tov and, while that would be enhanced by the musical accompaniment, a "superstar" wasn't critical. Our choice was clear. We asked for the performers to come on Yom Tov.

Today, most people live with a constant soundtrack, and the power and effect of music, although superficially acknowledged, is rarely appreciated. The reality is that music has tremendous power. Few need music's elevating and rejuvenating effects more than those in a place called prison and yet, we chose to forgo aesthetic excellence in order to use the opportunity to connect to Hashem.

Imagine our pleasant surprise, when the day of the event came and we were greeted in the chapel by the volunteers who'd brought with them Avraham Fried and Lipa Schmeltzer, who are in the top tier of Jewish singers. They greeted us warmly, and, after we took advantage of the *minyan* for a *Krias HaTorah* and Minchah, they played song after song of energetic and uplifting music. We danced with all our hearts, twirling and tumbling around a room that no longer seemed to be surrounded by bars and barbed wire.

At the request of some of the *Yidden*, they settled down at some point to sing slower, more emotional and heartfelt songs. I leaned over to the organizer and pointed out that we'd risen to the challenge and made the Jewish decision and Hashem had ensured that the finest singers would come and the *simchah* would not be diminished. Of course, he was happy and so were we, and we thanked Hashem for His kindness.

When the time came for the event to end, we *davened* Ma'ariv with a *minyan*, thanked them all from the bottom of our hearts for coming, and went back to the barracks, bracing ourselves for the inevitable shock of transitioning from the vivid experience of freedom that *kedushah* brings to the struggle of life in the barracks.

Hoshana Rabbah

Returning to the cell, I began the customary reading of *Chumash Devarim*, infused with the *simchah* of the evening's celebration. By 9:30 p.m., the inmates were locked into their cells and by 9:40, it was as silent as a graveyard.

The silence was soon shattered by the shouting and snarling of the guards as they did their rounds for the count, yelling at the inmates who weren't standing for the count, and kicking cell doors as they went. Anyone who'd fallen asleep was jolted awake and anyone who'd had some measure of success at achieving a feeling of inner peace or calm had his progress wiped out.

The holiness of the night gave me a needed boost to remain emotionally oblivious to the disturbance. In my mind and my heart, I was with my children in shul, surrounded by the murmur of Chumash and Tehillim. I managed to finish *Devarim* and some learning I had yet to complete, and then moved on to saying the Tehillim. I must again thank Hashem for ensuring that I shared a cell with people who were accommodating of my needs, even at odd hours, although it was well within their rights to demand that the light be turned off. Of course, I also expressed appropriate gratitude to them for their choice.

There's a *tefillah* that is said after each *sefer* of *Tehillim*. On Hoshana Rabbah, there's a different *tefillah*, one which asks Hashem to open the gates of Heaven for the specific *brachos* we need in the coming year. I said those *Yehi Ratzons* with care and concentration and asked to be freed and reunited with my family.

By then, it was in the early hours of the morning. I lay down to rest for a few hours and woke up at six. I felt excited from the moment I opened my eyes and said *Modeh Ani*, because it was a Yom Tov and volunteers were coming to make a *minyan*. I quickly made my way to the sukkah to *bentch lulav* and *esrog* as soon as the barracks were opened, and then headed to the chapel for *davening*.

I walked into the chapel with one of the other Jewish inmates, and when we saw the volunteers, fellow *Yidden* wearing *shtreimelach* and *bigdei Yom Tov* and holding *hoshanos* for the day, we spontaneously grabbed each other's hands and began dancing. We danced and sang, "*V'samachta b'chagecha*," overflowing with *simchas Yom Tov*. We could have danced like that for hours, but someone suggested we start *davening*. "We need to leave by ten thirty," he urged.

"We need to leave NOW!" I said with a smile and, with that wish for our physical freedom, we turned to our eternal inner freedom in serving Hashem.

"*Hodu laHashem*," we began. "Thankfully acknowledge Hashem, proclaim His Name; make His deeds known among the nations." We sang Hallel joyfully and gratefully performed the special *minhag* of *hoshanos*, circling our "*bimah*" seven times and beating our bundles of *aravos* on the floor, symbolizing the sweetening of all stern or harsh decrees. After *Mussaf* we had one last dance before we let the dear volunteers go and went back to the barracks in elevated spirits, ready to celebrate Shemini Atzeres and Simchas Torah.

Shemini Atzeres/Simchas Torah

After supper and the afternoon count, we returned to the chapel. Once we were all gathered, we took candles for *licht bentching*, the *sefer Torah* for *hakafos*, and food for our Yom Tov *seudah*, and made our way to the sukkah where we were going to *daven* Ma'ariv and have the *hakafos*.

We were a diverse group of *Yidden* with a wide array of *minhagim*, but we joined together as one to serve Hashem. Experiencing other *minhagim* and seeing the sincerity with which our brothers fulfilled them actually added to the *simchah* for each of us, and the *achdus* of celebrating together brought a special *kedushah* to our Yom Tov.

We always got into the spirit of Yom Tov even before Ma'ariv. This was the time we taught each other our favorite Yom Tov *niggunim*. One year, I taught the group *"Atah Bechartanu,"* a song which celebrates Hashem's love for us, how He chose us and lifted us up. It quickly became a favorite and for quite some time after, whenever something good happened to one of the *Yidden*, they would burst out into a rendition of *"Atah Bechartanu"* in celebration and gratitude to Hashem.

Another year, I taught them *"Hup Cossack,"* starting with the story behind the song: Around three hundred years ago, a tzaddik called the Shpoler Zeide secretly took the place of an incarcerated Yid the night before this Yid was to be dressed in a large bearskin and forced to dance for his life before the evil *poritz* and his guests. The grateful Yid returned to his family, while the tzaddik, now imprisoned in his place, was taught how to dance by Eliyahu Hanavi. When the travesty of a competition was held the next day, he handily out-danced the drunk Cossack, winning his freedom.

The song connected to this story is a rousing tune that starts slow and reflective, but gets more and more lively until it's a frenzy of joy and energy. It's easy to learn and became an instant hit that we sang over and over all Yom Tov. We sang and danced to this song with such enthusiasm, that when we returned to the barracks, more than one of us was asked, "What were you guys *drinking?"*

For Shemini Atzeres, we were allotted only fifty minutes for *hakafos*. We used those minutes to their fullest and danced with pure joy, transcending time until we had to leave. The feeling of joy strengthened and multiplied, as did the time we were allotted: On the night of Simchas Torah, our time allotment was doubled, and then, on Simchas Torah day, our *hakafos* took place in the chapel and we were able to dance with Hashem and His Torah for three hours.

As described earlier, there was a group of non-Jewish inmates which intruded into our religious programs and became a thorn in our side. It was the joy of Simchas Torah that finally shook them off. It happened one year on the night of Shemini Atzeres.

As Yom Tov began, we lit the candles and prepared to *daven* Ma'ariv. There wasn't yet a reliable *minyan* at Otisville, and we were without one that night. Nonetheless, in order to strengthen the Yom Tov atmosphere, I *davened* as a *chazzan* for our little group. I said all the appropriate parts out loud, and we sang together, although of course, we could not say Kaddish or *Barchu*.

Suddenly, from the corner of the sukkah, foreign chanting intruded on our *tefillos*. I turned around and saw one member of this group with a "*tallis*" wrapped around his shoulders, leading their service. In an attempt to embellish the ceremony, he was even holding a *lulav* and *esrog*, brandishing it to all sides while he aped our Ma'ariv.

Davening is about focus and concentration. They were making it harder, but by intensifying our focus, we could still block them out. *Hakafos*, on the other hand, are about dancing and rejoicing, something which doesn't lend itself as well to screening out aggressive nuisances. There was nothing to be done about it and we could only leave it to Hashem, trusting that He would take care of it without our efforts. For our part, we resolved not to allow anything to distract us and we soldiered on.

We began with saying the *pesukim* of *Atah Hareisa*. One at a time, those who could read Hebrew were honored with saying a *pasuk* which we then all repeated. Those who could only read English repeated after one of the others, while following the translation in their English siddur. At first, they were just repeating the sounds, but after a few *pesukim*, they began to pay attention to the words they were saying. Their *neshamos* awakened by the holy words, they found them to be very meaningful, and their recitation took on emotion and energy. Once we had finished, we "opened the *aron*" by unwrapping the Torah from the *tallis* in which it was bundled.

The *gabbai* gave me the Torah and the *zechus* to lead the first *hakafah*. We stood together, preparing to circle our "*bimah*" (the table) and I called out to Hashem from the depth of my heart: "*Ana Hashem, hoshiah na*—Please Hashem, save us!"

Our small group cried out their repetition together, some in Hebrew and some in English. "*Ana Hashem, hatzlichah na*—Please Hashem, grant us success!"

After we finished the words of the first *hakafah*, we broke out in a joyous dance. Everyone knew the main songs by now—we had been singing them all Sukkos—"*V'samachta, b'chagecha…ay, ay, ay-ay-ay-ay…*"

Some of them had humorously commented on Rosh Hashanah that we could probably *daven* a bit faster if we cut back on the number of somber "*ay-ay-ay's*," but these "*ay-ay-ay's*" were full of joy and no one was complaining. (In fact, I think I may have even heard a few extra "*ay-ay-ay's*" thrown in.) They all joined in with the enthusiasm of the *Yiddishe neshamah* celebrating its connection to Hashem.

The *gabbai* suddenly cut in and announced the end of the first *hakafah*.

This time we sang "*Atah Bechartanu*," singing our appreciation to Hashem and our happiness that He chose us to be *Yidden*, even in a place called prison, something we had spent a lot of time discussing together over the past few Yamim Tovim. The shining faces and the energetic dancing of every person there showed that each one truly felt this way with heartfelt sincerity.

The sukkah itself seemed to be dancing as we spun and whirled around the table. The words filled the small space, and we felt them come to life: *You chose us from all the nations, You loved us and wanted us. You elevated us over all tongues and sanctified us with Your mitzvos, and Your great and holy Name You proclaimed over us!*"

I had entirely forgotten the "Greeks" who were with us in the sukkah, but some noise from their direction caught my attention and I threw a glance their way. They were frozen in place, staring slack-jawed at the whole scene. The noise I'd heard was one of them leaving the sukkah and, as I watched, the rest of them turned and hurried silently after him.

We were overjoyed by this development, and many finally felt free to fully express themselves. It injected fresh energy into the dancing, and the singing rose even higher than before. The reminder that we were still in *galus* came from the *gabbai*, who apologetically announced the end of the second *hakafah*. He pointed to his watch, explaining that the Torah needed to be returned to the chapel by 8:30 p.m.

For the seventh and final *hakafah*, we sang, "*Ki MiTzion Teitzei Torah*." The Torah goes out from Tzion and the word of Hashem goes out from Yerushalayim. With Hashem's mercy and compassion, Hashem's people would go out from Otisville! The knowledge that this was the last *hakafah* reinvigorated us, and the dancing intensified until the *gabbai* announced that it was 8:30.

When the *hakafos* ended, the *sefer Torah* was returned to the chapel with a full procession. We half-walked, half-danced alongside it, singing the joyous Simchas Torah tune that was sung at the Rebbe's *hakafos*, known as "Reb Levik's Niggun," because it was favored by the Rebbe's father, Reb Levi Yitzchak.

It was time for the evening lock-in and we had to return to the barracks. After they were locked into the barracks, inmates had some time before they were locked into the cells. Taking advantage of this time, I joined another Yid in his cell and we continued dancing there until the guards began shouting for everyone to return to their assigned cell.

Locked into the cell, thinking back to those beautiful *hakafos*, I began to wonder why the "Greeks" had suddenly fled the sukkah. They usually stuck around to take notes, so they could incorporate our *avodah* into their "*treife* cholent." A simple explanation occurred to me.

In their efforts to imitate us, they obtained everything that could be bought. They had prayer books, they had prayer shawls, they had grape juice and Kaiser rolls, they had access to a sukkah, they even had a citron and a palm branch. Having all of the things a Yid would ask for, they claimed to be Jews. But being a Jew is not about what you *have*, it's who you *are*. It's your *neshamah* and its connection to Hashem.

When they saw us shaking *lulav* and *esrog*, it didn't spook them—because they could also shake a palm branch and a citron. But then they saw us dancing, overcome with ecstatic joy with Hashem and His mitzvos—even in a place called prison—and it was something they didn't feel and couldn't counterfeit. It forced them to confront the fact that their claim was a lie, and who they were and what they were doing was very far from authentic *Yiddishkeit*, no matter how much paraphernalia they got their hands on. This made them so uncomfortable that they fled.

One final anecdote connected with *hakafos*. One year, during *hakafos* in the chapel on Simchas Torah night, a guard interrupted to notify us that an unscheduled total recall had been announced. When that happens, every prisoner must report back to their barrack. This was not unprecedented, but the guard's demeanor gave us the impression that it was something very much out of the ordinary. He spoke with an urgency that had the slightest hint of panic. No one was tempted to test his patience or restraint under the circumstances, and the inmates were even more compliant than they would normally be.

Everyone immediately turned and headed to the door, but I couldn't bring myself to put away the Torah without finishing the *hakafos*. I knew we would not be able to return that night to finish, and there was a very real possibility that the lock-in could last for days, preventing us from doing the *hakafos* of the next day.

In theory, recalls require immediate reaction. In practice, though, it took time for the more than nine hundred inmates to get from the ends of the compound to the barracks. Taking a little extra time wouldn't be a major issue, as long as I got back in less time than it took to get back from furthest part of the compound.

Inmates who become institutionalized would not dare negotiate in a moment like this, but I made constant and conscious efforts to not be one of them. I held on to my identity as a Yid, put in my situation by Hashem in order to react as He wants, and I boldly but respectfully approached the guard with a request.

Still holding the *sefer Torah*, I asked him if I could complete the required prayers. To my relief, he agreed. I thanked him and quickly went back to our makeshift *bimah*, my heart full of gratitude to Hashem for this gift. I completed the remaining *hakafos*, circling the *bimah* and saying—with great concentration, but without delay—the *pesukim* which tell of Hashem's might and greatness, and beseeching Hashem to rescue me and to grant me success.

Once I had finished, I again thanked the guard and joined the throngs of inmates still streaming toward the barracks. I walked with *simchah*, feeling not only the glow of the connection to Hashem that a mitzvah can always provide, but an extra feeling of closeness because I had *fought* for the *zechus* to do the mitzvah and succeeded.

We later found out that the unscheduled lockdown had been triggered by the disappearance of a cutting tool of some sort from the maintenance area. These things are carefully inventoried in a place called prison and they don't just go missing. If one was missing it was because an inmate had taken it. Worried about an escape or attack, the authorities immediately locked down the compound and searched it very thoroughly.

This is exactly the sort of lockdown that could last for days, but *baruch*

Hashem, the tool was quickly found in a deep drain hole. The person who had taken it had seemingly panicked upon seeing the intense reaction, and had thrown it down the nearest hole. The lockdown was concluded and we were able to go to the chapel the next day for the scheduled Simchas Torah *hakafos*.

Before moving on from the Yamim Tovim of Tishrei, I want to note their powerful impact. These special days always brought in people who ordinarily didn't come to the Jewish services or affiliate with the Jewish group throughout the year. Many were very taken by the energy and joy they experienced over Yom Tov, and grew in their Torah, mitzvos, and their connection with their fellow Jews as a result.

One of these *Yidden* first came on Sukkos one year and I got to know him a little. He had non-Jewish father but a Jewish mother. Some of the *Yidden* were skeptical that he was actually Jewish, but I had exchanged a few words with his mother when she had come to visit him and she'd confirmed it. She had sent him to a Hebrew school as a child, but he had only the vaguest memories of that time, remembering only a handful of letters and very little about the substance of *Yiddishkeit*.

I offered to help him put on *tefillin* and he accepted. He'd never put on *tefillin* before, so after he finished saying Shema, I told him, "This is like your bar mitzvah!" and we made an impromptu celebration. I grabbed his hands and danced with him, singing the classic song of celebration, *Siman Tov U'mazel Tov*. Words cannot describe the joy radiating from this Yid even after he went off to continue his day.

This sweet Jew actually had a condition which made smiling painful, and he rarely smiled. He needed a medical procedure to open his esophagus, he lost his teeth, and his health was very poor, but that day, the joy of his *neshamah* would not be contained. He was smiling so wide as he went about his day around the compound that people were stopping him to ask what happened.

CHAPTER TWENTY-SEVEN

Holidays of Miracles

Happy Chanukah

IMAGINE A WARM *YIDDISHE* HOME ON CHANUKAH. THE WALLS ARE LINED with bookshelves full of *sefarim*, pictures of tzaddikim or *roshei yeshivah* adorn the walls, the smell of frying latkes fills the air. There's an atmosphere of *kedushah*, of peace, happiness, and excitement, as night falls and the family gathers around the small table near the doorway with lovingly prepared *menoros*.

The father lights the *shamash* and closes his eyes in concentration. He opens his mouth to begin the *brachah* when there is a loud "crash" and the door bursts open. A parade of drunks and ruffians march through the pristine home, whooping and hollering, cursing and laughing. Their wild appearance is a disturbing contrast to the holiness of the moment, but it pales in comparison to the disgusting and indecent conversation, the sounds of their vulgar music, and the smells of their forbidden food.

Imagine the feelings of that family at that moment—that's what Chanukah felt like in a place called prison.

On Chanukah, we emphasize that Hashem and His mitzvos are not limited to small pockets of holiness, to our homes and our neighborhoods, but that all the world is His. We do this by taking our Yom Tov and the light of the menorah outside, to the domain of everything that is wild and uncivilized. In Otisville, the outside was inside, and even indoors, we were *yotzei* that aspect *l'mehadrin min hamehadrin*.

Importantly, Chanukah is about the *triumph* of light over darkness and holiness over impurity. We're not visiting the streets—we're transforming them. That part needed a little more effort in a place called prison than on your average street, but by the light of our menorah, we banished the influence of the impurity around us and any fear or anxiety brought on by our situation.

The Chanukah candles bring a light and warmth into our lives that's even more welcome to those in the cold, dark place called prison. The reminder that with the help of Hashem the few can triumph over the many, and the weak over the strong, is a powerful encouragement, and it brought an extra enthusiasm into our Torah and mitzvos.

The first year in Otisville, I'd only been there a few months and I didn't know what to expect. As Chanukah drew closer, I made the rounds and spoke to as many *Yidden* as I could find, inviting and encouraging them to come to the menorah lighting that had been arranged. At the set time, I went to the chapel and was happy to find fifteen people or so. It was the largest gathering of Jewish inmates I had seen up to that point.

I lit my own menorah. Closing my eyes, I imagined myself home, standing with my family in front of our *menoros*. I said the *brachos* slowly and clearly, in the singsong we all know so well. Opening my eyes, I touched the *shamash* to the wick and as the flame first struggled and then calmly danced on the wick, I softly sang "*Haneiros Halalu.*"

Composed by chassidim of the Rebbe Maharash, it begins with a long wordless melody and, once the words are added in, phrases are repeated numerous times. The forty-seven-word *tefillah* can take as long as seven or eight minutes to sing. This overextended length was originally intended to give the chassidim more time with the Rebbe Maharash, who famously prized every minute and returned to his study as soon as the menorah was lit and "*Haneiros Halalu*" was sung.

In my circumstances, elongating and extending the time I spent immersed in the mitzvah was equally appreciated. Focusing on Hashem's miracles and our gratitude to Him is a lifeline to someone very much in need of Hashem's miracles. As the song reaches its end and its peak, it transforms into a joyous song of celebration, culminating in the words, "*Al nisecha...v'al yeshu'asecha,*" offering thanks and praise to Hashem for His miracles, wonders, and salvations.

The song ends with an endless loop of joyous repetition at which point, at home, I would always grab my children's hands and we would dance to these words until we couldn't dance anymore. That first year I danced alone, but as our group grew both in size and in warmth and connection to Hashem, this became the "*minhag*" in FCI Otisville as well.

When I finished, I helped those who needed assistance saying the *brachos* and they lit their *menoros*. I had imagined that after lighting the candles, we would sit around and talk about Chanukah, maybe reminiscing about happier days. It was not to be. Many of them sadly had no memories of Chanukah to speak of, and the others hadn't yet warmed up to the idea of connecting with their fellow Jewish inmates over Torah and mitzvos.

It was almost a "blink and you'll miss it" moment. Everyone made the *brachos*, lit a single candle, and they were gone. The chaplain told me that on the second night there would be potato latkes and I hoped that might hold their attention a bit longer. Even if not, they would have to stay at least the few additional moments it would take to light the additional candle.

At this point in the night, I would normally give my children Chanukah *gelt*. The best I was able to do under the circumstances was to ask for a check to be issued from my BOP account and mailed to my children. I sent one-dollar checks, because the account had strict limits on the amount of money I could spend a month on everything from commissary to computer time, and these checks counted toward those limits.

I sat down and watched the single candle burning in my menorah. Memories of Chanukah at home flooded my mind. I focused on the one flame I had lit at the command of the One Eibeshter, by Whose will I found myself in my current situation and by Whose will I would hopefully soon be restored to my family. That single candle was the embodiment of the well-known teaching that even the smallest amount of light can dispel much darkness.

In later years, I sat around the menorah with *Yidden* who did have memories of happier Chanukahs. It was bittersweet to picture ourselves surrounded by our smiling children, dancing and rejoicing in the warm glow of the menorah.

So much of Yom Tov had been stripped away by our circumstances and we missed those things terribly, but by their absence, we were forced to recognize and focus on the true essence of the Yom Tov, which goes beyond all of those things—our connection to Hashem by fulfilling the mitzvah of *hadlakas neiros*.

In Dubuque, in a place called jail, getting permission to light the menorah had been a battle. In Otisville, a federal prison, religious accommodations were more readily made and *menoros* were issued to all Jewish inmates, but there were still some aspects that needed improvement.

The standard-issue *menoros* were the familiar tin kind with thin colored candles. Fulfilling the mitzvah with those candles is very difficult, because

Chanukah candles have to burn for a minimum of half an hour and those candles will only last that long if the wicks are carefully trimmed before lighting. Besides, I'd always followed the *hiddur* of using olive oil and I wanted to continue. I made a request for an oil menorah and it was *baruch Hashem* granted.

It took a few years, but the other *Yidden* developed a taste for lingering over the warmth and light of the mitzvah as well. Noticing that the oil burned longer, they all gradually switched to oil *menoros* too.

Scheduling was the other aspect of the mitzvah that required initiative. Ideally, we're supposed to light the candles right after *shkiah* and I was very grateful that the chaplain scheduled the candle-lighting to accommodate that. The problem arose when the 4:00 p.m. count was prolonged for one of the seemingly endless list of reasons, delaying us past the scheduled start time.

One year, the count finished without incident, but a fog had rolled in during the count and the compound went into adverse weather lockdown. No movement was allowed, with the exception of an abbreviated forty-minute meal-time release to the chow hall.

As soon as we were released for supper, I ran to the chow hall. I had an idea that, if we asked, we might be allowed to make a detour to the chapel during those forty minutes. It would mean skipping a meal, but that seemed an insignificant sacrifice. As I walked toward the chow hall, I scanned the grounds for someone with the authority to make a decision and noticed a senior officer standing near the entrance to the chow hall. I started explaining our predicament and my proposed solution, but his facial expression and body language made it plain that he was hearing me out only because protocol demanded it.

Just at that moment, by clear *hashgachah pratis*, a chaplain walked by. I signaled to her that we would benefit from her participation and she joined the discussion. I quickly recapped the situation and explained that I was requesting permission for the Jewish inmates to go to the chapel to light the menorah and watch them for thirty minutes.

Recognizing its religious importance, she added her weight to the request. After considering it for a moment, the officer relented and gave us permission to go to the chapel for the amount of time we needed. I thanked them both and hurried off, thanking Hashem for enabling me to fulfill His precious mitzvah.

I lit the menorah, and was soon joined by other Jewish inmates, whom the chaplain had informed of the arrangement. We decided to *daven* Ma'ariv first, after which we each lit our menorah. We sat together near the candles, savoring our own little Chanukah miracle, when the chaplain stepped into the chapel with new orders. We were to return to the barracks immediately, although only twenty minutes or so had passed.

Without objection or request for clarification, a number of those present stood up and walked out. I wasn't willing to give up so easily. I knew that the moment we left the chapel, the candles would be extinguished as a fire hazard, but the candles hadn't burned for the minimum of thirty minutes necessary to fulfill the mitzvah.

The officer had given permission for the time required for the menorah, so I asked the chaplain if she could check with him if that permission exempted us from the recall. Even if the answer was negative, I hoped that the delay in getting a response would carry us over the thirty-minute mark.

Of course, communication was suddenly and remarkably efficient, and she returned after only three minutes with word that we were not exempted and needed to leave immediately. We were so close! I couldn't just give up. I explained to her that we only needed seven more minutes to do our duty to G-d, and asked her if she could make our case to the officer. She was uncomfortable pushing it, but reluctantly agreed to make the call from the chapel phone. She told the officer we only needed five or ten more minutes and listened to his response with a look of surprise. She was happy to inform us that we'd been granted permission to stay the necessary minutes. Our Chanukah miracle was complete!

We walked back to the barracks through the deserted compound, looking back at the events of the evening. We expressed gratitude to Hashem for His kindness, delivered through the good chaplain and the officer. Granting us success in our efforts was a clear sign that Hashem had *nachas* from our *avodah*, and was only throwing obstacles in our way so we would rise to the occasion and grow from the experience.

I pointed out that we'd only merited to fulfill the mitzvah because we resisted the "institutionalized" reaction of simply accepting and adjusting to our circumstances. We felt bad that the others had left so fast, and resolved to encourage them to make the extra effort the next time it came up. Beyond the immediate benefit of doing the mitzvah, every opportunity to establish the sovereignty of the *neshamah* helped us rise above our circumstances in a place called prison.

This episode was a really close call and clearly, formal arrangements were needed. Pointing to this and other close shaves, we requested an out-count during Chanukah. Requests such as this had a very low probability of success, but we made it anyway, following the example of the Chashmona'im who didn't allow logical calculations to prevent them from doing whatever was necessary to serve Hashem in the best possible way.

Miraculously, permission was granted, and from then on, anyone participating in lighting the menorah was allowed to be in the chapel during the 4:00 p.m. count and was counted there. This turned out to be my last Chanukah in Otisville, and my gratitude to Hashem for allowing us to fulfill this mitzvah in the most ideal way is actually the subject of one of my last emails from Otisville, written on the day of my salvation itself, Zos Chanukah 5779.

In a place called prison, there are no Chanukah parties to run to, no public gatherings, no streets full of the sights and sounds that put us in the Chanukah mood. For the first five years or so, we couldn't even *daven* Shacharis and say Hallel with a *minyan*. Most days of Chanukah, the celebration was limited to the time we spent with the candles, watching their holy light, singing songs, and telling stories.

Thanks to the dedicated volunteers, one night of Chanukah was different. Each year, they organized a festive celebration on one of the nights. They would bring live music, and usually also a singer. One year, they even brought a *badchan*. We were able to *daven* with a *minyan*, light the menorah with the full pomp and ceremony, and then dance to the lively music until they had to leave.

The heartfelt and joyous singing of the singers pierced the shell of even the most apathetic or disheartened *Yidden* and revealed the pure, unsullied essence of their *neshamah*, the *pach shemen tahor*.[1] It was a sight to see, the small flames dancing in the *menoros* and the Jewish *neshamos* dancing alongside them, their flames ignited as their spirits and their feet were lifted by the festive music.

The dancing was vigorous and lasted for quite a long time. It occurred to me that many of us, myself more than most, would not be able to reproduce that level of exertion if we were doing exercises in the gym or the yard. We simply didn't have the strength or endurance. Yet, as I danced, I noticed that my energy was not diminishing at all and neither was that of the others who were dancing.

---

1. Lit. a pure jug of oil.

I puzzled over this for a moment when it occurred to me that we were able to dance beyond our natural threshold because our *neshamos* were dancing. The joy and energy of the *neshamah* suffused the body and carried it along, which made the dancing almost effortless for our bodies.

The final day of Chanukah is not just one more day of Chanukah. The special name that this day is given by *minhag Yisrael* is Zos Chanukah—literally, "This is Chanukah." Chanukah is about bringing the light of Hashem and of Torah into the world, and on the eighth and final day, we have fully illuminated every potential candle so that it is an *actual* source of light in the world.

I always marked this special day with as close to a *seudah* as I could get in Otisville, usually with some matzah and a packet of tuna fish. I would make this *seudah* on the evening of Zos Chanukah, as the sun was setting and Chanukah was ending. In this way, I bridged the Yom Tov—which expresses gratitude to Hashem for past miracles—and the regular day which follows—expressing my preemptive gratitude for the miracle I was expecting at any moment.

In fact, it was during one of these *seudos* that I was ushered out of the cell and informed of my miraculous release, as I will detail at the appropriate point in the story.

Yaakov Shwekey and other volunteers after bringing
so much joy to the *Yidden* at Otisville.

A *Freilichen* Purim

As each Yom Tov approached, we prepared by learning the relevant *halachos* and the background of the Yom Tov. One of the *halachos* of Purim is that if someone reads the Megillah out of sequence, he has not fulfilled the mitzvah.

In the context of our *avodas Hashem*, the Ba'al Shem Tov interprets this to mean that if someone reads the Megillah with the idea that it is not relevant in the present—that it's nothing more than a story from another time, out of sequence with his life—he's not fulfilling his obligation.

Reviewing the Megillah in preparation for Purim, reading about Esther's plight, it struck me how superficially different but how fundamentally similar our situations were.

She had been taken by force to a place surrounded by walls and guards, and sentenced to remain there for life, surrounded by people with whom she had nothing in common, and bombarded daily by sights, sounds, and smells that were totally repulsive and counter to everything she was and aspired to be. She was required to wear clothing that not only didn't reflect who she was, a *bas Yisrael*, but actively presented an entirely different image and threatened to influence her profoundly, as our clothes always do.

She fully recognized the danger to her *neshamah*. As our *chachamim* describe, she took steps to ensure that she remembered who she truly was and that she could nourish her *neshamah* as much as possible, even in a place called a palace.

To start with, she only participated in palace life to the degree that she was forced to. She ensured that she could keep Shabbos by using a clever work schedule for her handmaidens, the *kedushah* of Shabbos strengthening her *neshamah* for the week ahead. She arranged periodic visits from Mordechai Hatzaddik and consulted with him before she did anything.

As Purim approached, I discussed with my fellow Jews how we could follow Esther's example in our daily lives.

Mordechai and Esther were also examples to us in our efforts to overturn the harsh decrees issued against us. The Rebbe notes that their primary efforts were *teshuvah*, fasting, and *davening* to Hashem. Esther showed this most clearly in her preparations to approach the king. Although it would diminish her beauty and her grace, which under the natural order were critical to her success, she undertook three days of fasting and prayer. Esther recognized that salvation would come from Hashem and prioritized her appeal to Him.

Like Esther and Mordechai, we resolved to put our trust in Hashem and to see our legal efforts as merely channels Hashem expects us to create, channels through which His *brachah* will be fulfilled. We also took great encouragement in the Megillah's description of a decree which was legally *irreversible* and yet, with Hashem's help, it was fully reversed.

Usually, volunteers were allowed on the compound to read the Megillah. If Purim began on Motza'ei Shabbos, and they couldn't make it in time, I stood in for them and read the Megillah for our group. When we reached the words, *LaYehudim haysah orah*—"And for the Jews there was light and joy, gladness and honor"—which is a phrase we quote in Havdalah, the next words of Havdalah always resounded in my mind. I had to make a conscious effort to stop myself from verbalizing them. Instead, I directed them as a silent, heartfelt request to Hashem and simultaneously, a statement of confident expectation: *Kein tihiyeh lanu*—"So should it be, and so *will* it be, for us!"

When Purim came out on a Sunday or Monday, which were visiting days, it was possible to spend some part of Purim with the family. You can imagine the effect on myself and everyone else in the visiting room when they marched into the room one year in full Purim regalia! They were each wearing something outlandish and flashy. Moishie was wearing a bright blue Hawaiian shirt, Uziel was wearing a lion costume, and even my wife joined in with a large, frizzy Purim *sheitel* and oversized glasses.

They had originally dismissed the idea of even trying to get through the prison security wearing such costumes, when one of them asked a good question: "How will they be able to tell the difference between our Purim clothes and the average daily clothes of some of the other visitors?" They laughed at the thought, but it gave them the audacity to try. To their pleasant surprise, the guards waved them in.

With this escapade, they really brought the joy of Purim into the darkness of a place called prison. We spent the day immersed in the *simchah*, whether it was through sharing the snacks from the machine, hearing about their *mishloach manos*, sharing thoughts on the Megillah, or just sharing a laugh.

One of the things that weighs the most heavily on a husband or father in a place called prison is the impact on his loved ones. The next year, I remembered how happy it had made me to see my family celebrating, and I really wanted my friends to have the same experience. I approached the captain and explained, as best I could, the Yom Tov of Purim and the way we celebrate. I asked him, in honor of the holiday, to officially allow visitors to come dressed in Purim costumes. He considered my request and consulted with the chaplain. In the end, *baruch Hashem*, he decided to grant permission for Purim costumes, with the exception of masks that would cover the face.

One year, Purim was on a Thursday and I had to wait for a visit until the next day, which was Shushan Purim. To my surprise, my family *still* came in Purim costumes. Once they were seated, they explained very matter-of-factly that Otisville is *mukefes chomah*—surrounded by a wall—and it's only appropriate that we celebrate Shushan Purim. Who could argue with that? They brought real *simchah* not just to me, but to all the *Yidden* who saw them, and even to the non-Jewish inmates and visitors who noticed the festive clothing and atmosphere.

We gathered in the chapel on Purim afternoon for a makeshift *seudah*. We would each bring whatever we had managed to buy or save for the occasion. The chaplain would issue us some grape juice, which we drank in place of wine, and we used the chapel CD player to play some music.

Even when volunteers were granted entry for the Megillah reading, they had to leave soon after, so we were always on our own for the *seudah*, but we made the most of it. Some of the inmates came wearing some sort of costume, which always took real ingenuity. For my part, I felt that the prison-issue clothes were costume enough. I focused on other ways to feel and express the unique *simchah* of the day—mainly through dancing and *farbrenging*.

Without any alcohol to help things along, the *simchah* needed to be generated straight from the *neshamah*. Fermented grains will get the job done in a pinch, but rising above the limitations of your circumstances and doing the mitzvos with *mesiras nefesh* will give a person a much more intense and real "high"!

As the years passed and the population grew, our small group's festivities were augmented by various talents including a talent for making real delicacies out of the ingredients on hand and a talent for real Jewish entertainment. Our Purim *seudah* was graced by real *Yiddishe grammen* and we sang and danced and asked Hashem to give us our own miracle for Purim and reverse our situation, turning darkness into light and sadness into joy by freeing us and reuniting us with our families.

There were few things as inspiring as watching the *frum Yidden* at Otisville fulfill the mitzvah of *mishloach manos*. Even those who had very limited finances managed to buy two food items from the commissary—the more fortunate usually bought a little more—and everyone exchanged these gifts when we gathered in the chapel.

The feeling of *ahavas Yisrael* and solidarity in that moment was palpable. Every person there was living through a gehinnom of his own. Naturally, people turn inward and conserve whatever resources they might have for their own survival. It's a real gesture of love when someone takes some of the extremely limited funds he would otherwise use to ease his *own* plight, and instead buys something he thinks will do the same for someone *else*—and gives it away wholeheartedly.

This was not lost on the recipients, who were usually visibly touched by these gifts. Although the contents of the gifts were humble—they were limited to cookies, nuts, tuna fish, matzah, candies, or soda—the gesture of friendship and good will was, for some of these Jewish inmates, absolutely unique in their experience.

One such person was an inmate I discovered a few weeks before Purim one year. We had gotten very close to forming a *minyan* and I was on the lookout for more *Yidden*. Someone told me there was a Yid in the barrack who didn't want anyone to know he was Jewish. He pointed him out to me the next time we were all in the same area, but I couldn't make a direct approach.

One morning, not long thereafter, I was saying Tehillim in a side room when this fellow came in, by *hashgachah pratis*, to do some ironing. I took the opportunity to strike up a conversation and first made friendly small talk. As first conversations usually do, this one centered on light background information. When he mentioned where he was from, I casually asked if there was a Jewish community there, and followed it up with, "How about you? Are you Jewish?"

He admitted he was. He told me that his mother had wanted him to go to Hebrew School, but he'd been a rowdy child and preferred to fool around with his friends. By that point in the conversation, he'd finished his ironing, so we left it at that. I wished him a good day and he left.

I had no further opportunity to make a connection with him until Purim came, a few weeks later. I took the opportunity and prepared a nice *mishloach manos* package and brought it to his cell. He was surprised to see me, but I explained about Purim and the mitzvah of sharing gifts of food with our fellow Jews, and he accepted the gift.

"Okay," I said, "now you can do the mitzvah if you gift it back to me." He was puzzled and a little amused at this unexpected twist, but he good-naturedly passed the gift back. "Mazel tov!" I wished him. "You've done the mitzvah. Now take the package back and enjoy it." I gave him a warm handshake and left him in his cell, smiling and shaking his head while he opened the unexpected gift.

Later that day, I poked my head into his cell to ask him if he wanted to join us in the chapel for the Purim *seudah*. Apparently, he thought the *mishloach manos* had strings attached, and he didn't like that at all. He jumped up and said that he shouldn't have taken the *mishloach manos* and if I wanted it back, I was welcome to take it. Of course, I said not at all—the two were not connected. I was just inviting him to join us in celebrating the Yom Tov and if he didn't wish to do so, I wouldn't bother him any further. I wished him a good day and a happy Purim and left.

I saw that he was sensitive on the subject, so I treaded carefully, but I did try again at Pesach time. I told him that there was a festive *seudah* with good food that would be served in the chapel to which he was invited. He declined, saying that he didn't want to go to the chapel.

Months went by, almost a full year, and it was Purim again. My *yetzer hara* was suggesting that I leave him alone, but I overcame the impulse and went to give him *mishloach manos* again. I found him sitting in the common area. I told him that it was Purim again, and reminded him of the mitzvah we had done the previous year. "Happy Purim!" I concluded. "Here's a *mishloach manos* gift for you."

He accepted the gift with a warm smile and thanked me very much. Then he told me to follow him. He took me to his cell and showed me the calendar hanging on the wall. In pen, he had repeatedly drawn a large circle around March 22nd and next to it was scrawled, in large capital letters, "IT'S OVER." That was the day he was scheduled to be released from prison.

I felt that the moment was right to encourage him to do another mitzvah. "Let's put on *tefillin* and make your bar mitzvah!" I urged.

He thought for a moment and then asked, "Would we have to go to the chapel?" I assured him that we could put *tefillin* on right there in the barrack, and, after thinking it over a second time, he decided that he would put on *tefillin*.

That morning, Erev Shabbos *Parshas Ki Sisa*, in the cell assigned to me in FCI Otisville, he put on *tefillin* for the first time in his life. He got very emotional, and he mentioned a few times that he was sure his mother could see him at that moment and was very proud of him. He told me to call him Michoel.

This experience changed him and he was a different person from that point on. He even "forgot" to take off the large black yarmulke I lent him and he walked out of the cell wearing it. I was thrilled to see this, and I was certainly not going to ask for it back. Eventually, he returned it.

Now that I knew of the tremendous *brachah* of his imminent release, I realized that he needed clothing to wear when he left. At the next opportunity, I brought him a sweatshirt and a pair of sweatpants that I bought from the commissary. He became very emotional. "You're the only person in this block," he said, "that has ever shown me love and kindness." We became friends for the short time until his release, and he repeated this sentiment more than once.

On the day of his release, I gave him a yarmulke to remember me by. He put it on and kept it on as he walked out of the cell and into the block. He waved to me as he left. I waved back, marveling at his transformation, from someone who didn't want anyone to know he was Jewish and who stayed away from the chapel, to someone walking through the barracks to freedom proudly wearing a yarmulke. Set into motion by a small package of *mishloach manos*, given with love and kindness…

The one Purim mitzvah that I couldn't fulfill properly was giving money to the poor because money is strictly forbidden to inmates. Instead, my family gave money on my behalf to poor people in Eretz Yisrael and in America. Many, if not all, inmates qualify for the status of an *"evyon"* so I also tried to fulfill the mitzvah by giving food as *matanos l'evyonim*.

CHAPTER TWENTY-EIGHT
The Holiday of Freedom

Precious Preparations

MY MOTHER, *ZOL ZEIN GEZUNT*, WOULD ALWAYS START CLEANING FOR Pesach right after Chanukah. Not everyone gets that early a start, but by the time Purim is over, everyone's in Pesach mode.

There are those who think that the cleaning and scrubbing is only a technicality, a chore that needs to be done because there's *chametz* around. They think Yom Tov would be a better experience if we could somehow escape the need to clean. Lately, this mindset has become very prevalent.

It seems to me that this is a mistake. Those difficult preparations are a critical part of what makes our Pesach. The physical efforts mirror and bring into focus the inner reality of Pesach—the efforts to cleanse our *neshamos* from any *chametz* and discover the pure connection to Hashem which leads us to Har Sinai and *Mattan Torah*. The time that we spend scrubbing floors and vacuuming the car slowly helps the reality of Pesach and its impact on our lives sink in. After all that hard work, we can welcome the Pesach feeling that we've done everything we could to scrub away any past *shmutz* and are ready to celebrate our newfound cleanliness and freedom.

Contrast that with a month of Nissan devoid of any preparation, a situation in which we don't exert ourselves and don't learn to shudder at the sight of *chametz*. Life goes on as always, and one day, it's just Erev Pesach. Candle-lighting time comes and, with the strike of a match, it's Pesach!

That's not the kind of Pesach I would ever choose, but it's the reality in a place called prison. There is no hustle and bustle, no scrubbing or scraping, no weeks of exertion to prepare for Pesach. I found this to be a terrible disadvantage in my efforts to go to the Seder with a Yom Tov feeling and a sense of freedom.

There's no real cleaning, no shopping or cooking to be done, but there's one preparation that's, *baruch Hashem*, mandated in halachah, and which we were therefore able to do: *bedikas chametz*.

The first Pesach, I inquired about the arrangements for *bedikas chametz* and I was told that the search could be done with a flashlight and that the *chametz* could be flushed down the toilet to fulfill the mitzvah of *biur chametz*.

I wasn't satisfied with that, and I made every effort to do the mitzvah as closely as possible to how it's described in *Shulchan Aruch*. I wanted to search by the light of a candle, scoop the pieces of bread into a spoon with a feather, and set them aside to burn in an actual fire the next morning. I couldn't get permission to light a candle in the cell but we did manage to get permission for a carefully controlled fire in the yard for *biur chametz*.

I started with the widespread and beloved *minhag* of preparing ten pieces of bread to be hidden—in my case, throughout a six- by eight-and-a-half-foot cell. I tore a piece of bread into ten small pieces and carefully wrapped each one in scraps of paper, memories of home flooding my mind.

As in every Jewish home, my children would come to life over this *minhag*, huddling together to discuss the best hiding places, carefully writing down where each piece was hidden, and making sure Tatty wasn't peeking, all with infectious energy and joy-filled laughter. As I made my way around the house in the dark, searching by the glow of the candle, the giddy tension in the room would get higher and higher, exploding into laughter when I finally found the elusive piece of *chametz*. If I found any real crumbs they'd missed in the Pesach cleaning, they would run off to get the vacuum, whooping and hollering, and quickly fix their oversight. When we finished our tour of the house and put the bag on a high shelf for the night, we all felt finally ready for Pesach.

I shook myself out of my nostalgia and tried to do my children proud with my hiding places. The cramped cell offered only one small barred window, two steel shelves they called beds, one smaller steel shelf they called a desk or a table, one locker assigned to me, a sink, and a toilet. My options were very limited, but I did my best under the circumstances.

Now I was ready to begin. I opened my siddur to the correct page and tried to filter the loud, *chametzdig* background noise out of my conscious hearing. It struck me that I was about to search carefully for small crumbs of physical *chametz*, while surrounded on all sides with spiritual *chametz* of every description. I was grateful that that mountain of spiritual *chametz* didn't belong to me, and I silently thanked Hashem for teaching us how to uproot any *chametz* that finds its way into our character.

I finished the *brachah* and set out on my search. There would be no grand tour here—I was able to do a thorough search practically without moving from where I stood. I had wrapped a paper towel around a pen to simulate a feather, and I carefully swept each of my ten pieces into a plastic spoon I'd kept for this purpose. As I found each piece, I carefully deposited it into a small paper bag. When I was done, I said the *nusach* nullifying any *chametz* and relinquishing ownership over it, and my search for physical *chametz* was complete.

The next morning, we met at the chapel and proceeded to the spot where *biur chametz* was to take place. It was a small outdoor area near the chapel building that was used by Native Americans for something called a sweat lodge, which involved fire in some way. In that spot, they allowed us to light a fire in a large steel drum and throw the *chametz* inside.

As it burned, we again nullified any *chametz* we hadn't found and fully relinquished ownership over it. Then, with great focus and concentration we said the *Yehi Ratzon*, beseeching Hashem to isolate and destroy all that is wicked and evil in our hearts and in the world just as we had sought and destroyed *our chametz*.

We lingered over the flames, taking strength from the mitzvah and *davening* that our own personal *gezeiros* be cast into the fire and consumed.

On years that Erev Pesach was a visiting day, the visitors knew to come a bit later to allow time for properly burning the *chametz* before the visit.

My regular roster of visitors was always supplemented in the week or two before Pesach by family and friends who were visiting New York for Yom Tov. It took some juggling to enable them to visit, but they really added to the feeling that a new and special time had arrived. Among the regular pre-Pesach visitors was my dear nephew Rabbi Eli Nosson Silverberg, the *rosh yeshivah* of the Chabad yeshivah in Chicago.

We had an ongoing correspondence throughout the year which was full of deep *divrei Torah* as well as stories and practical insights that gave me real support and encouragement. But, as the Ba'al HaTanya notes in the introduction to *Tanya, Eino domeh re'iyah l'shmiyah*—"Seeing and reading [a person's words] cannot compare with hearing them in person."

I very much looked forward to his in-person visits before Pesach, when we would delve into the subtle nuances of the Haggadah, and then discuss its practical application, finding the freedom in our *neshamah* irrespective of the situation of our physical bodies. He would also bring his family along, and I had great *nachas* from watching them grow. I kept a direct correspondence with a few of them throughout the year as well.

Of course, these visits were in addition to the precious visits from my wife and children. They always came on the visiting day closest to Pesach and they would even make the time to come on Erev Pesach itself if it was a visiting day, setting aside the many preparations for the Seder in order to have some time together.

Once *biur chametz*—and the visits, if it was a visiting day—ended, I would begin the practical Erev Pesach preparations. They were the same as those for a regular Shabbos or Yom Tov, with the added effort of obtaining "Pesach clothes." Some years, the best we could do was use clothes fresh from the laundry. Other years, the inmates working in the laundry room were able to obtain clothes that had never been worn before, which felt a bit more *Pesachdig*.

There was nothing to distinguish these clothes from other prison-issued clothes, but something seemed to catch the eye of the other inmates, and I heard comments or compliments more than once. It seemed to me that it wasn't the clothes that were giving a better impression than usual, but the ones wearing them. On the Yom Tov of Pesach, the other Jewish inmates and I were actively feeling the freedom of the *neshamah*, more so than usual, and it must have had some outward effect on the way we appeared to others.

When the signal was given that the afternoon count was complete and the cells were unlocked, I left the cell, physically and spiritually prepared for Yom Tov, the clash between my inner reality and my surroundings hitting me harder than usual. My mind and heart were unfettered, preoccupied with the greatness of Hashem, His closeness to us, and the joy of His Yom Tov. My physical senses, as I stepped through the iron door, were bombarded by the sights and sounds of people in various states of undress making crude conversation, the waning light of the day streaming through and highlighting the bars on the windows and doors.

My heart and my eyes yearned to see the holy sights of Pesach but I had to make do with a phone call. I headed to the telephone, endured the torture of the voice-recognition system, and called first my parents to wish them *gut Yom Tov* and then my wife and children. I managed to snatch a few words with each of the *kinderlach* and give and receive *brachos* that we merit to fulfill *v'higadita l'vincha* that night in person, around the Seder table. We ended our call by singing together, *"MiMitzrayim gei'altanu, mibeis avadim pidisanu!"*

asking Hashem to grant us our very own *Yetzias Mitzrayim* from a place called prison.

Official permission was granted for the Jews to gather in the chapel for the Seder, but the time was limited. We needed to be out by 10:00 p.m. Obviously, every minute was precious, so during the early afternoon move, I went with a friend to the chapel to see the preparations and ensure there would be no delay once we all gathered.

The room they allocated was typical of a room in a place called prison, very much unsuited for a Seder. It was a bare, windowless room with four cold, blank, cinder-block walls illuminated by a single light fixture. A tall pedestal fan stood in the corner, circulating the stale, warm air. Arranged in the center was a folding table and enough plastic chairs to seat all the expected attendees.

I imagined sitting in this room in only a few hours with a heart full of thanks and praise to Hashem, reliving the exhilarating moments of *Yetzias Mitzrayim* with the matzah, the *maror*, and the four cups, feeling the freedom of kings… It was hard to imagine. Everything about the room quietly but firmly expressed incarceration and slavery.

I would need to find and sustain the feeling of *cheirus* from within, and help those with me to do the same. The key to our success would be in realizing that only the physical actions of the Seder would be taking place in that room—the true Seder, the celebration of our freedom from Pharaoh and our feeling of connection to Hashem, happens in our hearts and in our minds. I couldn't make the room a place fit for a Seder, but I would do everything I could to make sure that the inner Seder permeated our hearts and allowed our *neshamos* to lift us up and out of that dismal room.

I thanked Hashem for the Torah, in which a person can always find light and warmth. Like every *nisayon*, the room would disappear around us as soon as we proved equal to its challenge. This would also serve as a perfect guide to all the participants on how to rise above the effects of the facility in general and find the true freedom of being a Yid.

We returned to the barracks, and I took to my *sefarim* one more time before the Seder, preparing to experience a true Pesach even in Otisville and to take along whoever wanted to come.

The Seder

Eventually, the move was announced over the loudspeaker. The outer doors were opened, and hundreds of people streamed out of the overcrowded common area into the wider compound, heading out to some errand or activity or just in search of some fresh air. For the *Yidden*, this night was not like all other nights: It was time to head to the chapel for *davening* and a Pesach Seder.

This Yom Tov, which is celebrated even in communities that have drifted from other aspects of their heritage, always brought new faces to the chapel. Because of this, Pesach was one of the first times we had our very own *minyan* from within the Otisville population, though it did take a few years for that to happen. In the years before that, our small group gathered to *daven* and say Hallel without a *minyan* before sitting down to celebrate Pesach.

It might seem odd to celebrate a holiday of freedom behind bars but, as a matter of fact, the focus of Yom Tov was more accurate under those circumstances. The freedom we celebrate on Pesach is not about independence or self-determination, something that waxes and wanes over time. When we were freed from Mitzrayim, we became servants of Hashem, never to be enslaved again. *That* is the freedom we celebrate, and it's permanent and unchanging. Bars and walls do not constrain or diminish our true nature. We are *Yidden* and, wherever we find ourselves, we are not victims, but emissaries on a mission for Hashem.

This was the annual topic of discussion when we gathered in the chapel, waiting for nightfall so we could *daven*.

More than once, I told a story that my father often repeated about a Kotzker chassid, Reb Yisrael, who once traveled to a distant city. On his return to Kotzk, his friends asked him about his trip. He looked at them with a twinkle in his eye and said, "I went to the theater."

This was clearly a joke of some sort—Reb Yisrael would never walk into an actual theater. He didn't leave them puzzling over his comment for long, and after a few moments, he continued.

"When I arrived, the local chassidim took me around to see their community. Whenever they showed me something, whether it was a Yid *davening*, a communal building, or something else, it was always with the same comment: 'See! Just like in Kotzk.' I concluded that I must be in some immense theater, where nothing is what it *is*, but is instead only an imitation of something *else*."

Understanding the difference between aping the superficialities of life elsewhere on one hand, and zeroing in on the essence of life and actually living, on the other, is the difference between living *behind* bars and living *above* them.

It was easy to fall into the habit of comparing our activities with what they ought to be and playing "pretend." We *lived* in a place of imitation and parody. Every aspect of our daily lives was full of mocking euphemisms and comparisons; time spent rotting in a cage is "time served," a metal shelf is a "bed," solitary confinement is "protective custody," and degrading garments are "uniforms," just to name a few examples.

Our spiritual lives followed the same pattern. A fresh set of prison clothes is "Yom Tov clothes," saying the Haggadah around a folding table in the chapel is "*v'higadita l'vincha*," grape juice is "wine," and opening the chapel door out to the locked compound is "opening the door for Eliyahu Hanavi."

Nothing we could do would bridge the gap between our superficial reality and the ideal, but that gap is only an issue if we are trying to compare things to "how it is in Kotzk." Our true nature lies in serving Hashem in *our* circumstances. A sincere *davening* offered without a *minyan* when none can be had—it may not be like in Kotzk, but it is *davening* and it's precious to Hashem. A Seder shared by a handful of *Yidden* of differing levels of interest, miles away from one's precious *kinderlach*—it's not like in Kotzk, but it is a Seder, in the fullest sense of the word.

It's what Hashem wants from us in each moment that expresses our true nature and purpose, and no chains or bars can prevent us from doing His will. We are eternally free to be who we are. The Otisville *Yidden* found this thought and similar discussions intriguing, and there was always a robust conversation until Ma'ariv.

In those early years, it was left to me to explain and demonstrate to those who had not had the *zechus* of a full Jewish education how to properly perform the mitzvos of the night. I had no official role and everyone was free to take the officially issued supplies and run their own Seder, but I welcomed those who wanted to join me and most of the attendees took me up on the invitation.

Together with them, I began Ma'ariv. Closing my eyes, I let my imagination transport me to shul, surrounded by my sweet children, singing praise and thanks to Hashem. Although they didn't know the words or the melodies, the *Yidden* with me were swept away by the emotion and energy. They clapped along or bounced their feet, getting into the Yom Tov spirit.

On the second night, I would announce that we had an additional mitzvah to do: counting the Omer.

Many of them had heard of Moshe Rabbeinu's demand to Pharaoh, in the name of Hashem, "*Let My people go!*" Of course, that's only half the sentence, the half quoted by people who think freedom is a lack of restrictions. The part of that demand that is the true foundation of freedom, and which was the purpose of *Yetzias Mitzrayim*, was the second half of the sentence; "*So that they may serve Me.*"

I explained to them that the purpose of *Yetzias Mitzrayim* was to receive the Torah at Sinai, and that the *Yidden* had so eagerly anticipated that moment that they had counted each day that passed as they prepared themselves to stand before Hashem and receive the Torah.

This prompted a discussion of the preciousness of time, which, unlike physical possessions, once lost can never be retrieved. They had never considered the cruel irony in the phrasing that they and their loved ones had adopted from their jailers. When referring to their sentences, they would say, "I got ten years," "I received twenty years," and so on. We were not men to whom time was *given*, but men from whom time had been *taken*, a situation which threatened to continue for years to come! This was time we would never get back.

The harshness and severity of taking a day from a person, not to mention decades, was a bitter reality, but important to recognize. I gently turned the discussion from what had been taken from them to what was truly given to them. Every morning when we open our eyes, even behind bars, Hashem has actually given us another day, and along with it, He has given us a mission and a purpose for that day. Like the *Yidden* in the desert, we must count each day and ensure that we use it to do that mission and also improve ourselves and prepare ourselves as we draw ever closer to Hashem.

When we had finished *davening*, we turned to the folding table that had been prepared. Near it lay a box with our Pesach provisions. We started, as I always did at home, by laying out the *ka'arah*.

As we placed each item, I explained the significance and symbolism of not only the item, but the quantities, placement, and sequence in which it is added to the *ka'arah*. Every small detail of the Seder is full of rich meaning, and I tried to use each item to bring some aspect of Yom Tov to life.

Everyone followed along and we finally had a table full of *ka'aros*. We were ready to start the Seder engulfed in a sense of *ahavas Yisrael* and camaraderie. Regardless of background, each participant fulfilled every mitzvah together, seriously and conscientiously.

It was quite a sight to see a table full of *Yidden* wearing prison clothes, reclining like kings while they ate and drank. The Seder proceeded at a slightly accelerated pace. I struggled between the need to actually have a meaningful Seder, which required slowing down, and ensuring that we managed to finish before we were expelled from the chapel. We found a reasonable balance, and managed to spend a bit more time during *Maggid* to discuss the parallels between our situation and that of the *Yidden* in Mitzrayim, gleaning relevant lessons.

We unfortunately related only too well to the Haggadah's description of Pharaoh's cruelty in separating men from their families. We truly celebrated our forefathers' redemption from those circumstances, and *davened* that we too would merit to reunite with our own beloved families. We shook our heads in knowing disgust as the Haggadah told of the *perach*, the terrible ordeal that was foisted on the *Yidden* with a *peh rach*—seemingly soft, reasonable, even kind words. Our own suffering was always couched in reasonable, technical, legal words, which only served to satisfy the consciences of those on the outside, without diminishing the harshness in our own lives.

I pointed out that our *yetzer hara* operates the same way, always disguising his traps and enslavements in soft, appealing words until the trap is sprung. I urged my brothers to learn to see through these tricks and not to be lured into the trap—to stand firm and fight for their freedom from the *yetzer hara*.

We got into the discussion of our history, and its lessons in the current day really came to life. It made me think of years past when I would experience this feeling with my wife and children, fulfilling the mitzvah of *v'higadita l'vincha*.

At the end of *Maggid*, the Haggadah shifts from talking about what happened to simply thanking and praising Hashem. Everyone lifted their cups and repeated the words after me, out loud. At that first Seder, it was all still new and strange to some of them and they were a bit stiff, but by the second night, they felt more comfortable and had warmed up a bit and they put real energy and gusto into the words.

We tried to time our completion of *Maggid* for 10:00 p.m., when the guards were scheduled to come and count us. We didn't want this symbol of our incarceration to intrude on our celebration of our freedom. The kindness of Hashem and the *hashgachah pratis* over our affairs didn't escape our notice; even when we were running slightly behind schedule, the guards were always somehow delayed and we were not interrupted until (sometimes only moments after) we finished.

A notable exception was one year when a guard barged in unexpectedly early, just as I'd begun the final *brachah* of *Maggid* in which we express our gratitude for our freedom. Fully immersed in the feeling of freedom, I decided that I would complete the *brachah* fully and properly, without rushing to finish. To the surprise of those assembled, the guard respected that he was interrupting a religious moment and left the room, returning a few minutes later to conduct the count.

As we said the *brachah*, the energy in the room intensified and, after we all drank the cup (leaning, of course), I jumped up and started singing "*MiMitzrayim Gei'altanu!*" while everyone went to the sink to wash for matzah. I was very happy when some of the others joined in my song and dance. It may not seem remarkable, but allowing yourself to be moved to dance and sing in front of other people without any music is a rare occurrence outside of the *frum* community and it said a lot that these men, from such a different background, were moved to do so.

It's worth noting here that Pesach was the one time of year that the Jewish prisoners were able to eat normally. The *kosher l'Pesach* food was generally made with less additives and fillers and, because it was a religious meal, the quantity was also less restricted, which meant people could actually eat their fill.

At the appropriate time, I explained that we would now open the door for Eliyahu Hanavi. The bearer of the news of *Geulah*, he would grace our Seder in Otisville as he does Sedarim all around the world. We all stood up, and two of the participants took some of the candles we had lit for Yom Tov and opened the door leading out of the chapel into the compound. A feeling of awe and reverence came over us. We felt that we were standing in the presence of Eliyahu Hanavi, and we all whispered a personal *tefillah* to hear the good news of our personal redemption along with the news of the Final Redemption.

We sang Hallel and ended off with a heartfelt cry of "*L'shanah haba'ah b'Yerushalayim.*"

Walking back to the barracks one year, I was surprised by the consensus that the best part of the Seder had been sitting and watching me eat the matzah. In response to my surprise, one of them described what they had seen. "You were leaning over in your seat—looked like you were about to fall off. You were holding your matzah in both hands, your face was red like a beet, and you were motoring through it at top speed. Your eyes were closed and your forehead was wrinkled in concentration, and every few seconds you looked at the clock. I've never seen anyone eat like that in my life!" I explained that we're supposed to eat two *kezeisim* within a few short minutes. Casual munching just won't get the job done. Chuckling, we parted ways at the barracks.

I couldn't fulfill the *minhag Yisrael* of leaving the door unlocked on this special night and, after I'd said *Krias Shema*, I turned to Hashem and said that it was up to Him to unlock the door and usher all the *Yidden* in Otisville out with an outstretched arm.

The Sedarim didn't always go this smoothly. A few years after I was transferred to Otisville, we gathered at the chapel on the evening of Erev Pesach, matzos and *Haggados* in hand, only to find the doors locked. It's not that they didn't know Pesach was coming: It's printed on even secular calendars, the chaplain had worked hard to prepare a detailed schedule of the religious services, and various staff had spent time preparing and coordinating the food, security issues, and so on.

What's more, the Seder was actually on a Friday night that year and we anyway had a regularly scheduled Friday night use of chapel A. The chaplain had even arranged that we would have the use of the room Shabbos morning, and again the next day on Yom Tov morning, in the hopes that we could gather a *minyan* and *daven* together and read the Torah.

All that is to say that there wasn't any reason we should be standing in front of a locked door, the precious minutes allotted to us slowly ticking away—yet there we were. To make matters worse, we hadn't lit the candles yet and *shkiah* was fast approaching.

It turned out that someone had decided this was a good time to close down chapel A for two weeks to have the vinyl flooring torn up and replaced. It was difficult to avoid the conclusion that this was more than an innocent mistake. As I said, it was common knowledge that this was the busiest time of year for us, and extensive preparation had been made across multiple departments for the Jews to use this room, yet work which could easily have been delayed was specifically undertaken over Pesach.

We had no choice but to wait for one of the other rooms to become available, which took about an hour. Around 7:30 p.m., minutes before *shkiah*, chapel B became available. We quickly set up and lit our Shabbos and Yom Tov candles and *davened* Ma'ariv without a *minyan* because our tenth man had been put in the SHU a few days before Yom Tov.

After we had sung Hallel, we gathered around our hastily set-up table to start our Seder, determined to clear our hearts of any frustration or sadness stemming from our own situation, and fully and sincerely celebrate *Yetzias Mitzrayim*.

As I mentioned earlier, our Pesach preparations were limited to cleaning the cell and *bedikas chametz*. All the food preparation was handled by others. The box of items we needed for the Seder, for example, was packed by Jewish inmates in the Otisville minimum security facility.

One Pesach, we gathered in the chapel, as we had every year. By then, more *frum* people had been placed in Otisville and they chose to make their own Sedarim. Instead of a single table, three had been set up. Of course, I didn't begrudge them that choice, but I felt the loss of our *achdusdig* single Seder.

I was looking through the Seder box as we waited for Ma'ariv, when I got a terrible shock. The *zeroa*, the roasted chicken neck, was missing. I carefully took everything out of the box and spread it all out on the table to see if I'd somehow missed it, but no matter how many times or how carefully I looked, there was no *zeroa* to be found.

I immediately alerted the others of the problem but it didn't seem to trouble them overmuch. "We don't actually use it during the Seder, it's only a reminder of something. We'll just use something else in its place—maybe a second hard-boiled egg..." I couldn't believe what I was hearing! Even if we don't always understand it, every small detail and custom during the Seder has great significance, as the Maharil points out, and one out of the six items on the *ka'arah* itself is far from a small detail. I was determined to get a *zeroa*.

The chaplain on duty was a large, friendly, African American fellow. I approached him about this problem, but I was worried. If the Jewish people couldn't see the problem, how could I expect the non-Jew to understand? How could I make him see the tremendous importance of the *zeroa* to my Seder?

They say a picture speaks more than a thousand words, and Hashem gave me the idea to just show the man the "Seder manual." I turned the pages of the Haggadah to one which showed a picture of the *ka'arah*, and showed it to the chaplain. "We're missing one of the items that go on the Seder plate, the roasted chicken neck, here," I pointed. "Without it, we can't start the Seder. Whoever packed the boxes in the camp must have forgotten to put it in."

He looked at the picture silently, thinking. "Rubashkin," he said after a few moments, "prison means you've got to make do sometimes. Five out of six ain't too bad!"

Hashem put the right response into my mouth. I smiled and said, "Sometimes it's all or nothing. Imagine you go out to the parking lot at the end of your shift and find that someone took off one of your car's wheels. Three out of four 'ain't too bad,' but not for the wheels of a car. Five out of six is a nice percentage, but it takes six items for the Seder to run!"

He laughed at the picture I'd painted, but more importantly, he was persuaded. An honorable man, seeing there was a problem in an area for which he was responsible, he set out to fix it. He tried calling over to the camp, but no one answered. He then called in to the lieutenant's office and requested that someone run over to minimum security for the missing religious items, but they declined to take care of it. Unfazed, he decided to handle it himself and left the room, an unusual exertion to take on behalf of an inmate, for which I thanked Hashem.

I will never forget the scene of his triumphant return. He walked into the chapel beaming and holding the two packages of chicken necks up in the air victoriously. I was overjoyed. I jumped out of my seat and ran over to him, thanking him profusely. Overcome with excitement, I grasped his hands holding the precious mitzvah and broke into a happy dance. Proud of his accomplishment and seeing how much it meant to me, he danced along for a few moments. I went off to make a Seder with a full *ka'arah* and a full heart. It was only a few years later that I merited to be miraculously released from prison with a *zeroa netuyah*—Hashem's outstretched, mighty hand.

Seder *Goreres* Mitzvah

The Seder always had a tremendous impact on all of us, and it sparked one of the most inspiring displays of Jewish dedication to Hashem that I witnessed in all my time in Otisville. One year, there were approximately fifteen *Yidden* in the compound at that time (that we knew of) and every one of them came to participate in the Seder. The holiday program started with Minchah, and then we needed to wait until nightfall before we could *daven* Ma'ariv and start the Seder.

Rather than wasting the time, we sat together to review some of the *halachos* and *minhagim* of the Seder. I began with discussing the *Korban Pesach*—an expanded recounting of the one that all *Yidden* were reading at that moment in shuls everywhere.

There's a very strong connection between *Korban Pesach* and the mitzvah of *bris milah* and it came up in the discussion. I mentioned it in passing and I was about to move on, but by *hashgachah pratis*, I chose that moment to glance up at the *Yidden* around the table. I noticed a couple of inmates that I knew were born in Russia. Estimating their ages and making a quick mental calculation, I realized that they were probably born during the most repressive period of the Communist regime, and it was more than likely that their parents were prevented from fulfilling the mitzvah of *bris milah*.

Instead of moving on, I decided to shift the conversation to the importance of *bris milah*. I recounted, as vividly as I could, the midrash which tells of Moshe Rabbeinu's *Korban Pesach*. It was roasted whole, per Hashem's instructions, which meant it was roasted outdoors, and the delicious smell of roasting lamb—mingled with the scent of Gan Eden which Hashem sent—spread on the breeze throughout the Jewish quarter.

Yidden flocked to Moshe's home for a portion of the Heavenly-smelling meat, but Moshe told them that only someone with a *bris* could participate in this mitzvah. Due to the difficult and lengthy *galus* and Pharaoh's vicious decrees, the majority had not been circumcised. They all made a *bris* immediately, and they merited to join Moshe in the special mitzvah of *Korban Pesach* as well.

I spoke quite extensively about the spiritual significance of a *bris*. These *Yidden* didn't have the background and knowledge to fully appreciate all of the concepts, nor did they have the personal history to draw on in relating to the emotional aspect, but I spoke from my heart, trusting that "words spoken from the heart, enter the heart" and that it would resonate with their *neshamos*, which understands fully. The auspicious moment and its link to *bris milah* would certainly also have an effect.

We went on to celebrate Pesach with happiness and holiness without the topic coming up again. The Friday after Pesach, one of the *Yidden* said he had something important to tell me. My words before the Seder about the importance of a *bris milah* had made a big impression on him and his friend and they had decided together to request permission to have a *bris* right away.

They met with the Jewish chaplain to make an official request, and he took their request to the top officials. They granted the request and made all the arrangements. It was to be the first time in the history of the US Bureau of Prisons that an inmate would be allowed to make a *bris*. All previous requests had been denied, under the claim that it was an elective procedure, which has to wait until the prisoner is released.

The plan was to take them under guard to the city of Kiryas Yoel, which is forty-five minutes away from Otisville. The *bris* would be performed there, and they would be immediately returned to Otisville. For security reasons, they would receive their *brissim* on separate days, and they would not be informed what day it would be ahead of time.

The *zechus* of a mitzvah is inestimable and the full reward is reserved for a world beyond our own, but Hashem showed His pleasure with their tremendous mitzvah in our world as well. Both saw a clear and miraculous salvation in the weeks following their *brissim*.

Everything went off without a hitch for the first Yid, Ephraim. His convalescence was slow and difficult, but he was proud of his decision to do this great mitzvah. A few weeks later, he was suddenly notified that he was approved for transfer from the medium security compound to the low security satellite camp. The camp is two security levels below the compound, which is an improvement in living conditions that would be difficult to overstate.

He was a native Russian, and that had always counted against him in determining his security level. Suddenly, a few weeks after his *bris*, they decided that it wasn't a barrier after all. He saw it as a gift from Hashem in the merit of his *bris*.

The only catch was that instead of leapfrogging him two security levels down, they wanted to transfer him first to a prison in New Jersey, one step down on the security scale, and only later to transfer him to the camp. This would have entailed significant hardship, and he asked me if any of the people working on my case could possibly intercede to have the BOP forgo that step.

I agreed to ask, but before I even had an opportunity to do so, he got his second miracle. He was notified that they'd dropped that requirement and he would be transferred to the camp immediately. He was transferred out without warning, so quickly that I didn't even have a chance to say goodbye.

The *bris* of the second Yid, Yitzchak, was mysteriously delayed. He was actually scheduled for release a few months later, and this delay started giving him ideas about delaying the *bris* until he was home. The rationalization was that it would be more hygienic, but I pushed him to act immediately. Every moment a Yid hasn't yet fulfilled this mitzvah is a moment lost in this unique connection to Hashem, a missed opportunity that can never be regained.

The imposed delay by the authorities continued, by *hashgachah pratis*, until the week of *Parshas Lech Lecha*, which describes the original *bris* performed by

Avraham Avinu. I urged him to follow Avraham's example and do the mitzvah with *zerizus*.

To make it easier, I offered to be his nurse. I bought a few meals from the commissary and told him that I would bring him food and anything else he may need from around the compound and in every way help him through his convalescence. *Baruch Hashem*, he agreed to do the *bris* without delay and took the added name "Baruch." He had a strong constitution, and with Hashem's *brachah* he healed very quickly. He was standing on his own two feet the very next day.

Yitzchak Baruch *a"h*, the hero who became one of the first two federal inmates to undergo a *bris milah* while incarcerated.

He also saw a miraculous salvation shortly thereafter. He was often my Shabbos guest for a makeshift *seudah* in the cell to which I'd been assigned. One Shabbos, he told me of his anxiety surrounding his upcoming release. He had emigrated as a young man from Soviet Russia during the time when it was falling apart, and he hadn't been issued a passport. This resulted in a complicated immigration status, and he was very worried that he would be released from Otisville to his family, only to be picked up and detained by immigration while his status was worked out.

He was hopeful that he would be allowed to stay in the US, because he was officially considered a "person without a country," but that could take months or even years. He missed his wife and daughter terribly and couldn't bear the thought of coming home to them on the long-awaited date, only to be torn away again for an extended period.

I urged him to write to the Rebbe for a *brachah*, which he did. When I suggested that he mention his recent *bris* (in merit of which I was sure he would be helped) he shook his head, smiling. "Sholom," he said, as if explaining something obvious to a young child, "I have to *tell* him? The Rebbe *knows*."

A few weeks after his *bris*, he walked into the cell just as I was finishing *davening*, with a huge smile on his face, the kind of smile that says, "I just won the lottery" or "I was just freed from prison." He wasn't scheduled for release, but Hashem's salvation comes in the blink of an eye. "What's going on?" I asked. "Are you going home early?"

No, there hadn't been a change in his release date, he told me, but he'd just been called in to speak with his case manager. She informed him that she'd received notification from Immigration Enforcement that they have no interest in his case and they would not be detaining him after his release. He would be free to go home!

I jumped up and danced with him a dance of celebration and gratitude to Hashem for this great *nes*. Sure enough, a few weeks later, he was freed and went straight home to his family.

The commitment to Hashem, which he had so heroically shown by having a *bris*, extended to his home life. He *kashered* his home and arranged for his daughter to be sent to a Jewish day school.

Sadly, a few months after he was freed he was diagnosed with the dreaded illness and some months later, he returned his body and soul to his Maker— his body perfect with the *bris* of Avraham Avinu, and his soul coming with the *zechus* of the unique circumstances he had overcome in order to enter into that holy *bris. Yehi zichro "Baruch"*!

For a grown man to decide to have a *bris* is *mesiras nefesh* even under the best of circumstances. In a place called prison, that's magnified by the difficulty of his situation. These men were heroes showing true selfless dedication to Hashem's will, as well as strength and fortitude to overcome the many obstacles, including the whispers of their own *yetzer hara*.

They were an inspiration to everyone around them and they blazed a trail that others followed. After these two established the precedent and showed others the way, there were a number of *brissim* in the satellite camp—six or seven by the time I was miraculously freed.

The Second Days

Chol Hamoed Pesach was usually uneventful. There were no special volunteer programs in Otisville, but there was another volunteer program that needs to be mentioned here. An organization called Dror, which was created during the years I was in Otisville, arranged special Chol Hamoed trips for the families of incarcerated *Yidden*. On Chol Hamoed, families usually spend time together, and these sensitive *Yidden* did everything they could to ensure that the families of inmates didn't miss out. Of course, nothing can replace the presence of a father, but the children really enjoyed the trips and that meant a lot to the inmates too.

My family also tried visiting at least once during Chol Hamoed, which added to the *simchas Yom Tov.*

The second days of Pesach are very special days. Shevi'i shel Pesach is the night we crossed the Yam Suf, and Acharon shel Pesach is a day especially associated with Mashiach and the coming *Geulah*, but they were treated like a regular Shabbos at Otisville and no special *seudah* or program was organized. In the first years, we didn't have enough people for a *minyan* and if there was no volunteer program, things would be fairly quiet and personal.

One year, I sat in the cell on Shevi'i shel Pesach and asked Hashem to splinter every obstacle to my personal freedom and to our national freedom with Mashiach Tzidkeinu, just as He split the Yam Suf for our forefathers.

Sitting alone, I thought of the many miracles that happened at that moment; the sea splitting with a roar into individual tunnels that formed for each *shevet*, the undersea paths blossoming with fruit trees, birds flitting around chirping and singing praises to Hashem. It was quite a contrast with the stark, barred cement cave in which I found myself.

It occurred to me that I should gather the other two *Yidden* of my barrack and tell them the story of *Krias Yam Suf.* I approached them one at a time and suggested that we commemorate the great miracle. The first one was busy, but the next one said he would be willing to hear the story if I came by at 9:00 p.m. I returned at that time and was surprised to see him sitting and waiting to hear about the Yom Tov together with, *l'havdil*, a Christian and a Yemenite Muslim!

I was taken aback at this unexpected audience and for a few seconds I stood, dumbstruck, while they just sat there looking at me expectantly. Apparently, they had heard good things about the Seder and were intrigued. I decided that if this was the audience Hashem had prepared for me, then this was who I'd talk to.

I sat with them for a long time, recounting in detail the miracles of *Krias Yam Suf.* Then I moved to the significance of that moment for the world. The world and its natural order was created in Tishrei. Although there's nothing more wondrous than creation, the regularity of nature hides Hashem. When that regularity is broken by a miracle, everyone can clearly see the Creator. This is the power of *Krias Yam Suf*, which showed the presence and power of Hashem to the whole world.

Frequently, Hashem's miracles have an additional purpose. His beloved people, the Jewish Nation, is the smallest among the nations and their eternal survival is only ensured by Hashem's miraculous intervention. As He did with *Krias Yam Suf*, Hashem intervenes to save the *Yidden* and punish those who have wronged them.

The third reason for this *nes* was to take the *Yidden* to the Land of Canaan and give it to them as an eternal inheritance, as Hashem had promised their Forefathers, Avraham, Yitzchak, and Yaakov.

At this point, I noticed the Muslim fellow squirming. He obviously had some thoughts on the "controversy" over Israel. I don't believe in shying away unnecessarily, and I thought a simple explanation would settle the issue. "We both accept the books of Moshe as the truth, don't we?" I asked him.

"Well, yes," he admitted.

"Okay. When G-d took the Jews out of Egypt, where did He take them?" He thought about that for a moment and had to concede that it was G-d who took the Jews to Israel and made it theirs. For people who believe in G-d, there really is nothing more to discuss at that point and we moved on.

At Har Sinai, Hashem instructed the *Yidden* through Moshe Rabbeinu to teach the rest of the world their role in fulfilling the seven universal mitzvos of Hashem. Our conversation now shifted to that and we discussed those mitzvos and mankind's obligation to fulfill them until the guards announced that everyone was to return to their cell to be locked in for the night.

I returned to the cell, but I stayed up all that night learning Torah, as is customary on Shevi'i shel Pesach. I managed to study until five in the morning. I had prepared my cellmate in advance. I told him that Hashem had split the sea for the Jews on this night and that I would need to stay up all night. At dawn, I told him, I would relive this great miracle and Hashem would part the prison walls and free me as He had freed my ancestors. He grinned at the idea. "Count me in!" he said. When he woke up in the morning, he looked at me bleary-eyed and said, "Hey, what are you still doing here?" I have to say—I didn't really know, but I trusted in Hashem that He would free me very soon.

In later years, there were more *Yidden* and we were able to have *minyanim* even on the second days of Yom Tov, both in the evenings and in the mornings.

This enabled us to read from the Torah and we even had a proper *Birkas Kohanim*, which uplifted all of us tremendously.

During those years there were always a few *Yidden* interested in joining me for the *seudah* in the evening of Acharon shel Pesach, known as *seudas Mashiach*. We always told stories of the Ba'al Shem Tov at this *seudah*, since it was he who revealed the significance of this time and this *seudah*. It was a time to focus not just on the miracles of the past, but on our *emunah* and *bitachon* in the miracles of the future—most important among them the coming of Mashiach.

We never voluntarily wrapped up this *seudah*, always continuing until we were forcibly interrupted by the announcement of "Recall!" Then we would *bentch* and wish each other that this year we would all be recalled from Otisville and from *galus* in general.

We were in *galus*, but that could all change in a moment. Hashem once helped me visualize this concept during the *seudas Mashiach*.

It was the second year I was in Otisville. There weren't yet any guests to invite, so I laid out a meager meal of matzah and a grape juice box in the cell and washed. I had just sat down at the table, when a large contingent of guards burst suddenly into the barracks and hurried everyone out into the compound. A total shakedown was in progress. I took my meal with me and made my way to the law library, where I continued where I'd left off. I'd sat down thinking I would eat in the cell, and suddenly and unexpectedly, I found myself somewhere else. That's exactly how it will happen when Mashiach comes.

CHAPTER TWENTY-NINE
A Jewish Summer

Lag B'Omer and Shavuos

Pesach marks the change of the seasons and the beginning of the summer. We counted down the days from Pesach until the great Yom Tov of Shavuos. On the thirty-third day of the Omer, of course, we celebrated Lag B'Omer, which Rabbi Shimon bar Yochai describes as a day of great celebration.

Some years, this celebration was limited to a small gathering in the chapel with a few other *Yidden*, where we would wash and eat. The good people at JEM Media had donated to the chapel many audio and video tapes of various events with the Rebbe, including the famous Lag B'Omer parades. While we had our small *seudah* in the chapel, we were able to watch these parades, which gave the gathering a very festive feeling. Hearing the rousing music, watching the beautiful floats and the classes of sweet *Yiddishe kinderlach* march by so full of *chein* and pride, and most importantly, hearing the Rebbe's words, brought us a true feeling of Yom Tov.

Another year, we sat out in the yard together, which was as close as we could get to the custom of going out to the fields, and we learned the Torah of Rashbi as well as *divrei Torah* about the importance of the day. When we finished, we stood in a circle, held hands, and broke into a lively song and dance. A prison yard is a place of physical exercise and activity, but singing and dancing was very much out of the ordinary and we had a large, if furtive, audience.

In the early years, Shavuos was a quiet, almost personal Yom Tov. There was not enough interest to warrant a special *seudah* in the chapel, and I was given a cup of grape juice to make Kiddush in the cell. The unrelenting tumult of the barracks echoed off the walls—the card playing, filthy language, and repulsive humor. Ironically, it helped me concentrate that night.

Shavuos is the day that Hashem set us apart from all the nations and that distinction was (too) loudly and clearly being demonstrated from every side of the barrack. The louder the tones and the more uncivilized the substance, the more gratitude I felt as I said the words of Kiddush, that so poignantly express this idea: *U'vanu vacharta*—"You chose us," *v'osanu kidashta*—"and You sanctified us from among all the nations."

Since the Shavuos that I'd been hospitalized with a severe infection and recovered, that Yom Tov held an added layer of personal gratitude.

I sat down quietly to eat my Yom Tov *seudah*. There were no family or friends with whom to share a *dvar Torah* or sing a rousing Yom Tov *niggun*. Before long, "Lock in!" was called, and everyone returned to their cell. Quickly, the silence of a tomb descended on the barrack, broken periodically by the jingling key rings of the guards making their rounds. As they passed the cells, they occasionally shined their flashlight through the window in the door, illuminating the cell for a brief moment.

That night, the jingling and flashing lights were welcome—the periodic disruption kept me from dozing off as I said *Tikun Leil Shavuos*. Before Yom Tov, I had prepared my cellmate for another all-nighter. "Today is the day that G-d came down onto Mount Sinai and gave the Jewish People the Torah," I told him. "Tonight I will be preparing so that I, too, am ready to stand at the mountain and receive the Torah."

"Rabbi!" he said. "I want to be with you at Mount Sinai!"

I smiled. "Really? I'll be staying up all night tonight reading Torah in preparation."

"On second thought," he said, "you go to Mount Sinai—I'll sleep tight on the top shelf. You're welcome to leave the light on." This was very generous of him, because that year, Shavuos was on Motza'ei Shabbos and that meant the light was on for two nights in a row. I thanked him and wished him a good night. He gave me a good-natured grin and wished me good luck before climbing onto the shelf and closing his eyes for the night.

I consider it one of the great *nissim*, a gift from Hashem that I benefited from daily and which strengthened my *emunah* and *bitachon*, that Hashem always sent me a cellie who accommodated my needs in keeping mitzvos as I always had in the past.

A Yom Tov is more than a commemoration of a special moment or event. On each Yom Tov, the moments which make that day special are truly repeated. When we read the *Aseres Hadibros* on Shavuos, we are again standing before

Hashem, accepting the Torah with perfect obedience and affirming and experiencing the eternal bond with Hashem that He first made with us as a nation over three thousand years ago.

Obviously, it was very important to me to be able to hear the *Aseres Hadibros*, which I could only do with a *minyan*. For the first few years, my efforts were unsuccessful, but eventually there were enough people at Otisville that we were able to *daven* together and stand at Har Sinai together, even in a place called prison.

One year, the second day of Shavuos coincided with a legal holiday, which meant there was an additional scheduled lock-in and count at 9:30 a.m. and we would have to return to the barracks for the count right in the middle of *davening*. The only way around this was to arrange an "out-count," which would allow authorized inmates to be counted someplace other than the cell.

We asked the chaplain if one could be arranged for us and he agreed—on the condition that we actually had a full *minyan*. We had already been soliciting commitments for the *minyan*, but many people had been noncommittal—I'll see, I'll try, and so on. Now we had a good reason to push for commitments, and *baruch Hashem* we managed to get a full list of ten people who were to be included in the out-count.

The first day of Shavuos came and went without incident. Our *minyan* came together and we were able to *daven* and read the Torah. Those who came also received an extra *milchig* dish in honor of Shavuos, which was in itself a good incentive for attendance. Despite that added incentive, the next day at the appointed time of 8:30 a.m., some of our number didn't arrive.

Some of the *Yidden* were worried, but I had a hunch that our help would come from an unexpected source. Sure enough, shortly before 9:30, when the holiday lock-in was called and inmates began streaming toward the barracks, two inmates could be seen walking in the opposite direction—from the barracks to the chapel.

They hadn't felt like getting out of bed so early and had decided to stay in bed. Suddenly, at 9:00 or so, a guard entered their cells and woke them up, reminding them that they were supposed to be in the chapel for the out-count. They tried to persuade the guard to let them sleep but the guard refused to hear it. "Go to the chapel or else…"

With no other option, they dragged themselves out of bed, and *baruch*

Hashem we had a *minyan* for *davening* and *Krias HaTorah* both days of Yom Tov.

It was a reenactment of the very first Shavuos playing out right in front of me. We're told that Hashem held the mountain over the heads of the *Yidden*, in a sense coercing them to accept the Torah—but why was this necessary? After all, the *Yidden* had enthusiastically counted down the days to *Mattan Torah* and had willingly accepted the Torah, famously saying, "*Na'aseh v'nishma!*"

One answer given is that, although the *Yidden* accepted the Torah willingly, some of the more overwhelming aspects of *Mattan Torah* might have caused them to panic and back off. For this reason, Hashem took measures to ensure a constant and unwavering commitment.

These two *Yidden* had signed up for the *minyan* willingly before Shavuos, but then, faced with the reality of getting out of bed for an 8:30 a.m. *davening*, they became overwhelmed and wanted to retract. Hashem ensured that they would fulfill their commitment, involuntarily if necessary. Of course, once their *yetzer hara* was out of the way, and they were out of bed and in shul with their brethren, the true interest of their *neshamah* could be expressed and they fully enjoyed the *davening* and the *divrei Torah*. And, of course, the special *milchigs*.

Tishah B'Av

Like *Yidden* across the world and through the generations, for three weeks before Tishah B'Av, I was steeped in the mourning over the destruction of the Beis Hamikdash and the presence of the *Shechinah* in *galus* alongside us.

The day before Tishah B'Av, I set aside some extra food to eat for a *seudas hamafsekes*, and went to pick up the bus shoes from the laundry room, as we did for Yom Kippur. These shoes were very fitting for Tishah B'Av, because they were also used for those sentenced to the SHU, which is usually a personal Tishah B'Av.

After *davening* Minchah, I took off my leather shoes and put on the bus shoes, turned the chair upside down so it formed a lower and less comfortable seat, and sat down for my *seudah*. The chaplain had arranged for a hard-boiled egg, which is customarily eaten at this meal as a sign of mourning. The contrast between my thoughts and the hubbub in the barrack, punctuated every now and then by outbursts of laughter or shouting, was stark.

As described earlier, the cells did not afford any privacy between cellmates and if one or the other needed a moment of privacy, it meant that the other cellmate had to leave the cell. One year, as I was about to begin the *seudas hamafsekes* in the cell, I noticed that my cellie could use a private moment. To give him his space, I took a cup with which to wash my hands, the bread, the egg, and the shoes, and left the cell. I found a relatively quiet spot in the corner of the common area, and sat on the floor to eat my meal. I sat and ate the bread and the egg and tried to dwell on the loss of the presence of the *Shechinah* and the physical structure of the Beis Hamikdash while the environment around me felt like a train station.

There was no evening gathering in the chapel. Night fell after the final lock-in of the day and I would have to read *Eichah* alone in the cell. As usual, it quickly fell dead silent as the inmates turned in for a night's sleep. After *davening* Ma'ariv, I moved the chair to one side and sat near the sleeping-shelf, my feet just about touching the facing wall of the cell.

I read *Eichah* in an undertone, considering each word as I sang it softly. My heart filled with pain for the tragedy of the *Churban*. I had wondered if I would even feel the pain of Tishah B'Av through my own pain. Clearly, I would. I was. I thought about why.

My personal suffering in Otisville had begun almost a year earlier and my incarceration and the earlier troubles had started long before that. In all that time, I had never sat on the floor to mourn my forced separation from my family, the destruction of my life's work, or the injustice which promised to keep me imprisoned for close to three decades. Yet there I was, sitting on the floor mourning the exile.

Our personal lives may include difficulties, but our lives are much bigger than ourselves—which make our personal problems much, much smaller. We are fortunate to be servants of Hashem, created to fulfill His purpose in creation by bringing G-dliness into the world through Torah and mitzvos. As painful as our personal troubles may be, they affect only our circumstances, but not our essence. They don't go to the heart of who we are, and certainly don't overshadow the true tragedy of the *galus*, when Hashem's presence is not felt in the world and even worse, not felt in our hearts without tremendous effort.

If you can internalize, even for a moment, the unfathomable greatness of Hashem and His will for the world to be one with Him, you can truly feel a sense of horror and mourning when you think of the destruction of the Beis

Hamikdash and the time when this was a reality. You can feel a yearning for the full and permanent expression of that oneness with the coming of Mashiach. This is normally the domain of tzaddikim, but once a year, on Tishah B'Av, even simple people are given a day to see and feel that.

Sitting on the floor in the cramped cell, I was face to face with the plumbing under the sink. It reminded me of the last time I'd been down there—the night of *bedikas chametz*. It occurred to me that the two nights are linked. In fact, Tishah B'Av is always on the same day of the week as the first day of Pesach.

If you think about it, the two are really about the same thing. Our mourning is rooted in the realization that we are not private people but servants of Hashem, and that same realization is the secret of our eternal freedom, which we celebrate on Pesach. It is our duty to recognize this truth in the darkest days of our *galus*, both national and personal, and to live that truth to the best of our abilities even on a regular weekday—that is the heart of Tishah B'Av. In this merit, we will see how the truth of Hashem's presence destroys the walls of *galus* which keep us from Him—that is the heart of Pesach.

On this more cheerful, uplifting note, I sang out the repeated *pasuk* at the end of *Eichah*: *Return us to You, Hashem, and we will return. Renew our days as of old.*

The link to Pesach and the expectation of *Geulah* lingering, I thought to myself that if the 210 years in Mitzrayim gave the *Yidden* the Yom Tov of Pesach, imagine the great Yom Tov we will have after two thousand years of this bitter *galus*. It will certainly be an infinitely greater rejoicing, prompted not only by the darkness of the *galus* night, but by the brightness of the day that follows, the ultimate *Geulah*.

We were fortunate to have volunteers come on Tishah B'Av so that we had a *minyan* and *Krias HaTorah*. That breath of fresh air only lasted fifty minutes and then it was back to the cell for the *Kinos* of the day. These are longer than the *Kinos* of the night, and more specific. The background commotion was also at daytime levels, both in terms of volume and substance.

Imagine reading the heartbreaking story of the children of Rav Yishmael Kohen Gadol, or the recounting of the brutal murders of the *Asarah Harugei Malchus*, punctuated by the occasional roar of wild laughter and pounding on the tables.

It brought to mind the story of Rabbi Akiva, who was traveling with other

Tanna'im near a Roman city in the time following the *Churban*. From afar, they could hear the happy sounds of life and, faced with the stark contrast between the fates of the *Yidden* and of the nation which oppressed them, they wept. All except Rabbi Akiva, whose reaction was to laugh. Hearing their good fortune made him think, *If this is the good Hashem gives those who violate His will [for the little good that they do] how much more good is in store for those who fulfill His will?*

This story often came to mind when I watched other inmates being released early over a legal technicality, a change in the law, or during President Obama's clemency for drug offenses. This sight drove many inmates to tears or anger, seeing good fortune come to others but seemingly passing them by, although they felt more deserving. I always turned to Rabbi Akiva's words and had the opposite reaction. I felt *encouraged* by the sight. "If this is the good Hashem gives those who violate His will, how much more good is in store for those who fulfill His will?"

As the years went by and more *Yidden* were there and interested, the time we were allowed to spend in the chapel for *davening*, *Eichah*, and *Kinos* was extended. The additional two hours were appreciated, but still not enough time to finish *Kinos* and I would always finish in the cell.

One year, I was walking back to the barrack to finish *Kinos*, already a bit weak from the fast, when a guard shouted at me, "Hey! Stop dragging your feet!" I turned, wondering what rule I was breaking, but all he said was, "Dragging your feet could hurt your shins." I looked at him for a moment in disbelief. As if this guy had any real concern for my wellbeing and was worried about my posture or my shins! He turned away and I continued on.

At 2:30 p.m., I took my *tallis* and *tefillin* and headed back to the chapel to *daven* Minchah, walking slowly. Another Jew, also heading to the chapel, passed in front of me. Hashem was setting me up to be exactly where I needed to be for the scene that followed.

A guard assigned to the chow hall suddenly barked at the Yid, "Hey! You! Why are you wearing those shoes?!" The Yid either didn't hear him or didn't think he was talking to him and continued walking. The guard called out to the lieutenant standing up ahead to stop the Yid.

The lieutenant stepped out in front of the Yid and stopped him. "Why are you wearing those shoes?" he demanded.

"It's a religious thing," the Yid answered.

The lieutenant obviously had an issue with *Yidden*, or with religion in general, and this just set him off. "You can't just *say* that!" he screamed, red in the face. "With that attitude, I'll throw you straight in the SHU!" The Yid was taken aback and tried to explain himself.

I half-ran the distance between us and interjected in his support. "Excuse me for interrupting. Today is a Jewish fast day and we are forbidden from wearing shoes. You probably got a memo about it…"

The guard who had been worried about my shins only a few hours earlier was standing nearby, and decided to weigh in at just that moment. "I've been here for years," he said. "First time *I'm* seeing this." I couldn't believe it. He had been giving me passive-aggressive grief over how I was walking just that morning. He had obviously seen my shoes and hadn't brought them up because he knew they were authorized. Now he was claiming he'd never seen people wearing bus shoes for religious reasons. Thankfully, I didn't have to bring it up, because the lieutenant just gave up the fight and waved us on.

I thought about the guard's behavior in light of my own mission in life. I had seen this play out on countless occasions—a guard or officer knows something, but when it's convenient, such as when his superior says the opposite, he suddenly "forgets" what he knows.

If we're not careful, we can fall into the same trap. In fact, we had been warned about this exact thing in the Torah reading that very morning. We had all been shown through His wondrous miracles and His loving gift of *Mattan Torah* that *Hashem Hu ha'Elokim, ein od milvado*—"Hashem alone is G-d, there is nothing but Him."

Yet, like this guard, we are tempted at times to "forget" what we know so clearly and replace it with what we imagine is to our own advantage. In the Torah reading of Tishah B'Av, it describes how, in our bitter *galus*, *Yidden* might, *chas v'shalom*, worship the idols of the nations amongst whom they live. We need to abandon what we know to be false, and reconnect with the truth—*Hashem Hu ha'Elokim, ein od milvado*.

CHAPTER THIRTY
The Long Road Home

Sibos and *Hishtadlus*

O   UR TOUR OF OTISVILLE COMPLETE, LET'S NOW RETURN TO THE
chronological story where we left off, at my arrival to Otisville. As you've
read, I didn't allow the need to escape my difficult circumstances to consume
me and distract me from the mission for which Hashem placed me there
to begin with. I did everything I could to serve Hashem in every way, while
simultaneously, my family and I, and the many who came to our aid, worked
to reverse the *gezeirah* and win my freedom.

The strenuous battle was fought by many people on many fronts, each with
his own expertise and perspective, and each would highlight different aspects
in telling the story. There is the story as a lawyer would tell it, the story as a
grassroots *askan* would tell it, and the story as a political *askan* would tell it.
I will strive to include the important activities of all of these, but, above all, I
want to tell the story as a Yid would tell it.

To do that, we need to first discuss *hishtadlus*.

Emunah and *bitachon* mean that we believe that Hashem provides us with
everything that we need and we trust in Him completely. Whenever anyone
speaks about this, either the speaker or someone listening immediately adds,
"But, of course—*hishtadlus*!" By that, they mean that we can't just sit back and
expect things to happen miraculously. Hashem wants us to do our part.

They're absolutely right. This is clearly laid out by Rabbeinu Bacheye in
Sha'ar Habitachon. But, in my careful study of the topic, I noticed something
very important that's often missed.

The word "*hishtadlus*," which means efforts or exertions, is commonly used
to describe the things we need to do to obtain our needs as dictated by the

natural order. People will describe their nine-to-five job as their *hishtadlus* in receiving their *parnassah*, visits to the doctor as their *hishtadlus* in receiving a *refuah*, and working with a lawyer as their *hishtadlus* in receiving a *yeshuah*.

In learning and relearning *Sha'ar Habitachon*, I noticed that Rabbeinu Bacheye does not actually refer to those things as *hishtadlus*. Instead, he calls them *sibos*, which can be translated as "means." He reserves the word *hishtadlus* primarily for Torah and mitzvos.

This is a very important distinction. *Hishtadlus*, efforts, are something that you do to effect the outcome. Whether you do it and how you do it will make a difference. This is not true of a *sibah*, which is simply something Hashem uses as a means of getting His *brachah* to you. It's something that you set up so there's a natural explanation for how you get what Hashem is giving you, but it's a facade. The details won't determine the outcome.

It's critical to recognize this difference, because it guides our efforts and determines our practical and emotional investment. If our job, our doctor, or our lawyer is only the *means* through which Hashem's decision is implemented, it would be foolish to try to change that decision by working through *them*.

Trying to change a Heavenly decree by speaking to a doctor is like trying to settle your invoice by negotiating with the mailman who delivered it.

The outcome is decided and effected only by Hashem—so the actual *hishtadlus*, the attempt to intercede and change it, must be directed to *Him*, by strengthening our *emunah* and *bitachon* and by growing in Torah, in *tefillah*, and in *ma'asim tovim*. That's our *hishtadlus*, not going to a lawyer or a doctor. We go to the lawyer and we go to the doctor and we do so sincerely, but only as obedient servants of Hashem, not as efforts to change the outcome.

I took this distinction to heart and constantly reminded myself and those around me that the efforts we were making in the legal and political arenas were only a facade for Hashem's blessings. This helped us keep our focus where it really belonged, on strengthening our connection—and directing our pleas—to our Father, our King.

This attitude and approach rippled out to everyone involved in the case, and the response from every side to the unfolding drama, both on a personal level and on a communal level, was a serious increase in Torah, *tefillah*, and *avodas Hashem*.

Hashem often allowed us a glimpse of the power of these efforts. Milestone successes in both legal and political efforts very often coincided with public *tefillah* rallies or noteworthy undertakings in Torah and *avodas Hashem*. This pattern was so obvious that my wife and my daughter Roza Hindy always made sure appropriate *hishtadlus* was made whenever there was a critical effort being made in the category of *sibos*.

What follows is a recounting both of our continuous *hishtadlus* and *sibos*. As you read it, I encourage you to hold the distinction clear in your mind and to never confuse the two.

Family and *askanim* at a *siyum sefer Torah*, completing a Torah written in my merit.

United They Stood

I can't jump back into the chronological story without first mentioning the efforts that were not specific to any one point in time, but were a constant throughout my ordeal. I'm referring to the ongoing *hishtadlus*, the constant efforts of Klal Yisrael in the realm of Torah and mitzvos.

Throughout my ordeal, I received a steady stream of letters from fellow Jews all over the world. In addition to their warm words of encouragement, the overwhelming majority of them went on to share the ways in which they were strengthening their connection to Hashem in my merit.

One wrote from rural Wisconsin to tell me of his family's tear-filled *tefillos* on my behalf. Another wrote from Lakewood, New Jersey, that my public ordeal had inspired him and those around him to strengthen their *emunah* and *bitachon* in various practical ways. A third started supplying his local *beis midrash* with coffee and milk for those learning Torah, in my merit. This is just a small, random sampling of an endless stream of inspiring love and devotion to helping a fellow Jew in the ways that really count.

Sometimes, these individual efforts were encouraged or coordinated for greater impact. I often received letters from a class or school in which the students each wrote a few words of encouragement and a personal resolution they'd taken. One extraordinary letter came from a small Monsey yeshivah of eighty high school-age boys. As *bachurim*, they wrote, they couldn't donate money to help with my defense, but they'd committed to collectively completing *ten thousand blatt of Gemara* in my merit, three thousand of which they had already completed.

These letters were very precious to me. I would read and reread them and they filled my heart with gratitude and encouragement, each word cementing my belief that Hashem would turn to the *tefillos* and mitzvos of the entire Jewish People, particularly those of the pure children, and send me home.

A coordinated effort was launched by the Chafetz Chaim Heritage Foundation in which people were encouraged to join what they call a "*machsom l'fi.*" It meant committing for a set period of time to take extra care to avoid hearing or speaking *lashon hara*. Many joined the effort, adding their fulfillment of the mitzvah of *shemiras halashon* as a *zechus* to prompt my miraculous release.

Another beautiful effort was called "Fill an Empty Chair for Sholom," encouraging people to add a chair to their Seder table and to fill that seat with a guest who might otherwise not have a Seder or might be alone. This, too, was met with enthusiasm by many who hoped the *zechus* would help tip the scales and I would also be able to sit at the Seder with my family.

There were also public gatherings of Torah, *tefillah*, and *tzedakah*. At one or two of them, I was able to call a family member who was attending and listen in, and I always heard the reports afterwards about the tremendous participation—the sheer numbers of attendees, the unprecedented uniting of communities, and the overflowing generosity.

Underlying all these beautiful resolutions and actions was the most noteworthy *hishtadlus* of all—the *achdus* and *ahavas Yisrael* displayed by everyone who heard about my situation, at every level. From the moment the troops first stormed our factory and our story hit the headlines, when it came to "Rubashkin," the usual boundaries—between individuals and between communities—vanished.

United, my Jewish brothers and sisters undertook powerful efforts on my behalf—in storming the Heavens and, *l'havdil*, in the courts and in the halls of power—but in a very real way, the *achdus* underlying it all was more precious and powerful than the specific efforts themselves.

This wasn't only expressed in efforts to help me in my plight. These precious *Yidden* truly rejoiced in our personal *simchos* as well, whether it was a *bris*, bar mitzvah, or a wedding. It truly felt like we were not just a nation composed of families, but one extended family, large enough to call a nation—which is truly what we are. I made sure to send public invitations before each family *simchah* encouraging everyone to come, and many actually did. I marveled at this beautiful *achdus*, and it was a constant source of *chizuk* to me, since I know that the best vessel for Hashem's *brachah* is peace and unity.

When it came to my situation, the feeling of *achdus* went beyond emotions and into the realm of action. *Yidden* of every group and station in life did what they could to help, some giving their time and volunteering with the various initiatives, others with their money, and many, I'm sure, with both.

All the efforts by the lawyers and *askanim* were only possible due to the generosity of the precious *Yidden* who donated funds. Men and women of means donated large sums, while those of more modest means donated more modest sums, which often meant more to them than the largest donation meant to the biggest *gvir*.

Part fundraising effort, part publicity drive, part celebration of the unprecedented *achdus*, a New York filmmaker named Danny Finkelman brought together more than two dozen well-known Jewish singers and released a music video entitled "Unity for Justice."

Many gave with true self-sacrifice. I remember one letter from a *kollel yungerman* and his family which I treasure to this day. They wrote that they were sending the money they'd put aside for their vacation, because they couldn't possibly go off and enjoy themselves knowing the pain that my family and I were suffering. As I mentioned earlier, many *nashim tzidkaniyos*, without the resources to send large monetary donations but inspired to do what they could, actually sold or sent in personal jewelry so the fundraisers could exchange them for the money that was needed.

I also occasionally received letters, and sometimes even pictures, of small children who'd set up lemonade stands or the like to raise funds to help me in my *tzarah*.

The generosity of all my fellow Jews was so much more than a way to pay the bills. The selfless *ahavas Yisrael* represented by each and every penny donated was a most powerful *hishtadlus* before Hashem.

The *achdus* on display when it came to my case was the kind of *achdus* that so many Jews, weary of division and *machlokes*, fervently wish to see become the norm. Seeing it even in one specific area was refreshing and reinvigorating, a reminder that it *is* possible. It was also a tremendous *brachah* in its own right.

I'm often asked for my thoughts on why I merited to be the catalyst for such *achdus*. Hashem's kindness is infinite and needs no justification. Even to the extent that this might be more than *chessed chinam*, it's a question that's certainly beyond any specific answer or explanation I can come up with. Nonetheless, I feel that there *is* one thing to gain from speculating. Associating the *brachos* we receive—even tentatively—with aspects of our *avodas Hashem* increases the energy and enthusiasm we feel for those activities, both for ourselves and for others.

With that in mind, and based on the concept of *middah k'neged middah*, I would suggest that perhaps my strong commitment to *achdus* in building and running a united Jewish community in Iowa was the *zechus* which rallied a united Jewish nation around me when I needed their help. It also seems to me that the risks and costs I accepted in order to defend *shechitah* and kashrus on behalf of the *klal* stood me in good stead, and Hashem inspired the *klal* to rise to my defense in turn.

We can't truly know why Hashem gives us the personal experiences and the impact on others that He does, but we can certainly strengthen our commitment to ensuring our surroundings are permeated and characterized by *achdus* and face all challenges to our *Yiddishkeit* proudly and firmly, whatever the price.

Appealing in Iowa

Now we can turn to the *sibos*, the things that were done to create a means through which Hashem's salvation could be expressed. What follows is a description of the various legal and political efforts to appeal and overturn the decree against me. Bear in mind that I'm not a legal or political analyst. It's not my purpose or goal to lay out the defense's case in all its intricacies, or to describe the ways in which legal experts or politicians decide when and how to intervene in a case.

My intention here is simply to tell the story of what happened to me, the strength I drew upon to persevere, and the miraculous salvation of Hashem. I will try to stick to the basic information of what happened, which is necessary in order to follow the story, and I'll include additional details that help dispel the presumption of merit that society affords prosecutors and the charges they make, or details which contribute to the appreciation of the miracle that occurred.

Within the legal system, a person only has the power that is granted to them. They can only make the arguments the system allows them to make, and only for as long as the system allows them to be made. Even then, the system can dismiss the most compelling arguments and shocking evidence and, unless they say so, there's nothing you can do about it.

You can be one hundred percent provably right and the charges can be demonstrably false—and it means nothing at all. It's only when you truly understand this, that you begin to appreciate the true powerlessness of a man ensnared in their net and the crushing helplessness he feels.

If I can give a sense of this seemingly insurmountable misfortune, you will better understand the task I faced—to counter this "reality" with the truth revealed in our *emunah* and *bitachon*—and you will see the true power we all possess if we stubbornly hold on to Hashem and to the truth.

This overview will also give you a greater appreciation for the miraculous outcome that came specifically when all legal avenues were cut off and all natural hope was lost.

To that end, I will do my best to share, from a layman's perspective, the extraordinary efforts, powerful arguments, and shocking discoveries we made—and the dismissive reactions of the courts at every level.

Like in the Megillah, it's hard to get a sense for the passage of time when only the milestones are described, but bear in mind that it was more than eight years, just shy of three thousand days, from the verdict until my miraculous release. Also like in the Megillah, there are no dramatic, supernatural interventions in this story. It is up to the observer to recognize the astronomic improbability of many of those events and to realize just how many of those far-fetched events happened in sequence to lead to the outcome. Like in the Megillah, it is clear as day that this was nothing but *yad Hashem*. *Emunah* and *bitachon* brings *geulah*.

As soon as the unjust verdict was returned, even before the sentencing, the lawyers began the appeals process. Their effort took the form of a motion to the district judge to unilaterally set aside the jury's verdict as "unsupported by the evidence." Failing that, they requested a declaration of a mistrial and a new trial on grounds including the improper exclusion of certain defenses and witnesses, and also improper inclusion of immigration testimony and other information.

The motion was denied by the judge, who had, after all, made all the decisions they were challenging. This was not unexpected, but the request still had to be made at the lower level before the case could be appealed.

The lawyers now shifted their efforts to the Court of Appeals—more specifically, to the Eighth Circuit, the Appeals Court that covers Iowa. Nat Lewin, a well-known lawyer who specializes in appeals, joined the team, and took the first step by officially filing a request that the Eighth Circuit hear our arguments.

The team was preparing to expand and present those same initial arguments to the Eighth Circuit, until, by Divine Providence, something new and shocking fell into their laps—something which the prosecutors had successfully hidden for close to a year and a half.

Around eighteen months earlier, as part of routine preparation for the trial, the lawyers had looked into the circumstances surrounding the raid and the development of the charges against me. To that end, they had requested certain information from the prosecutors. I was legally entitled to that information and the prosecutors' office assured the lawyers that it would be provided.

Time was passing and the trial was looming, but the documents still hadn't arrived. Repeated reminders to the prosecutors were, for a time, answered with reassurances, and it was only after stringing the defense team along for a number of months, that the prosecutors informed the defense that they would, in fact, *not* give us the information willingly. If we wanted it, we would have to file a lawsuit to compel them to provide it.

Timing is everything in a court case. We were reminded of that time and again in judicial rejections which swept aside strong legal and moral arguments by pointing to the calendar. This delaying tactic of theirs had bought the prosecutors quite a lot of time, and by the time the lawsuit to compel them to follow the law was filed, processed, granted, and begrudgingly complied with, the trial was long over and the verdict had been returned.

The documents arrived in three separate mailings. Poring through the heavily redacted stack of paperwork, Nat Lewin—one of the appellate lawyers—was stunned to discover that the judge who'd presided over my trial had been heavily involved in the preparations for the raid.

She had numerous off-the-record meetings about the raid with the prosecutors, including meetings which covered "charging strategies" and other matters exclusively within the realm of law enforcement and prosecution and well outside the appropriate role of a judge. She had expressed a willingness to "support the operation in any way possible" and had made repeated requests for a "final game plan" and a "briefing on how the operation would be conducted." ICE had referred to her in emails as a "stakeholder" in the raid and had seemingly timed the raid around her vacation schedule, which she helpfully provided.

None of this extensive cooperation had been revealed to the defense. If this information had not been hidden from us, we would have certainly demanded that she remove herself from the case, and the trial lawyers wrote and signed affidavits to that effect.

The lawyers maintained that they'd only known of very limited involvement by the judge, little more than signing off on the raid.[1] Now, a year and a half later, we knew better. The new documents proved that she had been involved much earlier and to a much greater degree than could be waved away as merely the "logistical cooperation" she had claimed it was.

This put a whole new light on the legitimacy—or rather the illegitimacy—of the trial and offered a real prospect of overturning it on appeal.[2]

The defense team immediately asked the Appeals Court to grant a delay to

---

1. When other defendants charged after the raid had demanded that she recuse herself on those grounds, she had indignantly refused, asserting that her involvement had been limited to "logistical cooperation" and her impartiality was not in question. Working from the same set of incomplete facts, my lawyers felt it was pointless and dangerous to antagonize the trial judge by making the same demand only to get the same answer.

2. Even if she had only looked bad but was actually innocent, the law demands not only that

the already scheduled appeal so they could file an emergency motion for a new trial under "Rule 33," which allows for a new trial (within three years of the verdict) if new evidence is discovered.

This motion would have to begin back at the lowest level, at the district court—which meant making these arguments to the trial judge herself before we could take it up to the appellate level. The delay to the appellate level proceedings was granted and the lawyers went back to the district court.

They penned a new motion to the judge in which the explosive new revelations and their legal ramifications were clearly laid out. In legal terms, the judge had engaged in what they call "*ex-parte* communications"—dealings with one party in a case outside the presence of the other party—since she hadn't disclosed the meetings to the defense, and she had failed to recuse herself when the case came to her to judge. This disqualified the initial trial and the defense demanded a new trial.[3]

The defense was supported by leading authorities on legal ethics, Professor Gillers and Professor Harrison, who actually helped write the Model Code of Judicial Conduct. They each focused on one party and concluded that both the judge and prosecution had violated their specific codes of conduct and the applicable laws. They both strongly dismissed the prosecution's arguments in defense of their actions, which Professor Gillers called, in part, a "tortured interpretation of an ethics rule."[4]

The motion for a new trial on those grounds was filed with the district court,

judges *be* impartial but that they protect the *appearance* of impartiality, and the judge should have stepped aside and allowed a different judge to handle the case.

3. Even if the court would rule that the documents weren't conclusive, at the very least, they raised serious questions that justified further investigation and the defense asked, in that case, for hearings and discovery so the full facts could become known and a just decision could be reached.

4. Professor Harrison pointed out that their claim that the meetings were necessitated by difficult logistics was totally irrelevant. Not only doesn't that negate the prohibition on *ex-parte* communications, it *certainly* doesn't explain or excuse the failure to keep a record of those interactions so others can determine whether they were prejudicial and to disclose the meetings to the defense at the earliest possible time.

Remember—in our case, the substance of the meetings was not recorded and even the fact that these interactions occurred had not been disclosed *at all* and, in fact, were only discovered in documents we forced them to provide under the Freedom of Information Act. Denied this information before the trial, I wasn't able to defend my constitutional right to an impartial judge.

along with a request that this question should be transferred to a different judge, so it would not be left to the judge to rule on whether her own behavior crossed ethical lines and warranted a new trial.

Close to three months after the motion was entered, the judge filed her decision. In it, she played the roles of both key factual witness and evaluating judge. She laid out her version of the events in question, some of which were outright contradicted by the documents, and characterized them differently than had the defense and legal ethics experts.

Then, she put on her "judge hat," evaluating the two versions and issuing her ruling. On the strength of her own testimony, she decided that the motion was "totally devoid of merit" and that not even further hearings or discovery were warranted. Any more time spent on this would be a "useless waste of time," she wrote.

Besides, the newly discovered evidence did not directly relate to the charges. They were "only" about the fact that the judge was not, or at minimum did not appear to be, impartial. As such, she ruled, they did not justify a new trial in the interest of justice.

Motion denied.

The Eighth Circuit Appeal

We were disappointed by the judge's decision—which is not to say that we were terribly surprised by it. Focused on the next step, the lawyers turned their attention back to the Eighth Circuit appeal, which had to be filed within the next two months.

The road had lengthened. Our struggle for justice and freedom would take more time and effort, which meant we would need more money. Klal Yisrael continued to be there for me in my time of need, and bundles of envelopes containing small donations arrived daily to the offices of the askanim at the pidyon shvuyim fund and elsewhere.

Yidden also continued to gather together to rally in my defense. In the last week of 2010, over a thousand Yidden packed into "The White Shul" in Far Rockaway to show solidarity and hear what they could do to help. They heard from the Novominsker Rebbe zt"l and Reb Pinchos Lipschutz, who represented the Torah perspective and what was being done by the askanim. Former US Attorney for Utah Brett Tolman explained the injustice from a legal perspective. Hearing from a former prosecutor—who was so disturbed that he was helping pro bono—made a deep impact on those assembled.

The Novominsker Rebbe speaking at the rally in Far Rockaway.

The massive crowd in the White Shul.

The crowd at the event and the many who were watching and listening from afar were moved by the plight of their fellow Jew, and collectively contributed around $160,000, a much-needed injection of lifeblood into our legal fight.

With Hashem's help and the financial support of Klal Yisrael, the appeal was filed with the Eighth Circuit Court of Appeals. It included numerous grounds relating to issues with trial and the excessive sentence, but the revelations of misconduct by the district judge and prosecution were front and center. In addition to raising the issues presented by these revelations, the appeal addressed the defective legal arguments the judge had made in refusing to act on them. The ruling that new information that uncovers bias and breaches of ethics by the presiding judge doesn't invalidate the trial was of particular interest because it contradicted established precedent in numerous circuit courts.

The lawyers asked the Eighth Circuit judges to overturn the district judge's ruling and grant a new trial in light of these and other arguments, many of which were supported by rulings of the Eighth Circuit itself. At minimum, the court should authorize a different judge at the district court level to hold hearings and decide if a new trial was warranted.

Independently of the ruling on the trial, the lawyers also requested that the sentencing be invalidated and a new sentencing hearing be held with a different judge. In fact, *any* further proceedings needed to be assigned to a different judge because the judge had announced that if I bothered to appeal and managed to get sent back to her for re-sentencing, she would issue the same sentence, and even held out the possibility of giving a longer sentence.

The case had been high-profile since the dramatic raid that had launched it. The inexplicable behavior of the prosecutors from the very beginning, especially in light of this new discovery of their extensive meetings with the judge, made this a case that many prestigious individuals and organizations wanted to weigh in on in court.

The way they do this is by filing what is called an *Amicus Curiae Brief*. Latin for "friend of the court," the purpose of these documents is for those uninvolved in a case to point out aspects of the law or of the case that might not occur to the judges in the case.

In our case, a total of six such briefs were filed in support of our appeal, including one signed by eighty-six former senior DOJ officials, and another signed by twenty-seven former judges who had sat on the Federal District Court or the Appeals Court. Three prestigious organizations—the ACLU, Washington Legal Foundation, and National Association of Criminal Defense Lawyers—each filed one as well.

Amicus Briefs are not uncommon, and it's mostly as a formality that the consent of the opposing party is requested when filing. To their surprise, instead of the expected go-ahead, these legal experts and organizations were met with a denial of consent by the prosecutors. The US Attorney went further than passively withholding consent, and actually submitted a written motion demanding that the court refuse to accept the filings, which it may do even without the prosecutor's consent.

The response to this move by the national legal community as a whole was immediate and very critical. Respected publications including the *National Law Journal* and *Bloomberg Law Reports* ran articles calling it "unusual," "bizarre," and "heavy-handed." They saw it as most likely a "mean-spirited response to public criticism of the government's conduct" and totally out of the norm, with worrying ramifications for the broader legal system.

The ACLU went on the record saying they had never before had a case where the government opposed their brief and neither they nor other experts could find a precedent for the DOJ to oppose an *Amicus* filed by a respected legal organization.

After a few weeks of heavy criticism, the prosecutors withdrew their motion in opposition and granted their consent to the filings.

The *askanim* recognized that there were other ways to reach their objective, beyond persuading the judges. Generally speaking, a judge's role is to decide between positions taken by the two sides. That means that if the prosecutors don't object to a motion, under normal circumstances it will be accepted. This is the principle behind the negotiations and plea deals the prosecution offers, and the *askanim* wanted to make it work for us. Perhaps, in light of the shocking misconduct and the possibility of a judgment against them, they could get the prosecution to stand down and agree to our requests.

Though the local prosecutors had repeatedly proven themselves to be unreasonable, the Iowa US Attorney works for the central Justice Department in Washington and the *askanim* involved hoped that the new information about misconduct in my case would persuade them to intervene with the local office.

They brought the new developments to the attention of the many prestigious former DOJ officials and law professors interested in my case, a group which grew significantly due to the new revelations and the hard work of my son-in-law Yaakov Weiss and other dedicated *askanim*.

They were all deeply troubled by what they heard, and reached out to the Attorney General of the United States, Eric Holder. They sent him a letter urging a "full and prompt investigation" in order to "remove the cloud that is growing publicly and in judicial circles."

The signatories to this letter were a veritable "Who's Who," esteemed national figures in the world of law and law enforcement. Notable even in this distinguished company were Philip Heymann, former Deputy Attorney General of the US and law professor at Harvard; Charles Renfrew, former federal judge and former Deputy General of the US; and Larry Thompson, former Deputy Attorney General of the US, law professor, and Senior Vice President and General Counsel at the mega-corporation PepsiCo. These were brilliant men of wisdom and experience, whose services were not on offer in the marketplace, but they were so disturbed about what had been done to me that they became active participants in the effort to free me, *pro bono*.

They reviewed and refined legal arguments and lent their names and their support, something which opened many doors—and they went even further. Although they were distinguished men in their seventies and eighties, they flew across the country more than once to meet DOJ officials together with *askanim* from our team. At each meeting, they forcefully made the case to DOJ officials that the misconduct in my case—which we would discover was much, much worse than we knew at this point—was a stain on the DOJ's record and must be rectified.

In addition to these men, who had been leaders in the nation's justice system, the *askanim* also rallied support in the political world, continuing their work of bringing the case to the attention of sitting Congressmen and other politicians.

Disturbed by the prosecutorial misconduct and spurred by the resulting public outcry, they also wrote letters to the Attorney General calling on him to look into the misconduct. This ratcheted up the Congressional pressure on the DOJ, which had already been going on in less direct ways. In one example of this, Congressman Ted Poe had brought up my case in a Congressional hearing about half a year earlier, criticizing the prosecution's charges and the extreme sentence they had sought and obtained.

The fight was dragging on and the cost of fighting the case weighed heavily on my family and on the *askanim* who had dedicated themselves to helping with the financial burden. My son Meir Simcha rose to the challenge with a new initiative. It wasn't a revolutionary idea—he was simply going to organize volunteers to go door-to-door asking for support—but he approached it with tremendous energy and creativity.

He came up with a catchy name, "Sholom Across America," and had a logo made up. He created a website where people could donate and printed shopping bags with the logo and website for local supermarkets to use instead of their usual bags. He printed small posters with the logo and the words "Proud Supporter" for stores of all kinds to display in their windows.

Once he'd caught everyone's attention and he had people talking, he recruited volunteers to stand outside supermarkets and go door-to-door. They distributed a DVD with an hour-long video overview of the facts of the case and reactions from legal experts and public figures, and asked people for financial support.

Sholom Across America had its first run in Crown Heights and they raised a very impressive $80,000 while also sharing the informational DVDs and raising awareness of the injustice. The campaign also helped show the world that I had the support of the community.

After this initial success, he was asked to come to Australia by local community leaders there. They also wanted to show their support and allow their community to be part of this great effort to help a brother in need. His visit, which he billed as "Sholom Across Australia," was also a success and he came back to the US refreshed and invigorated.

By then, the summer season was about to begin, and the various communities he'd intended to visit were all about to empty out as people went to the mountains for the summer. Adapting to this challenge, Meir Simcha found a small, used, van-sized motor home and had it covered with a Sholom Across America design. He was hitting the road. He planned to visit all the vacation towns, bungalow colonies, and summer camps in the Catskills.

As everything fell into place, Meir Simcha realized that what had at first seemed to be a problem—so many people leaving the city, where he had hoped to find them—was actually a gift from Hashem. This large and diverse collection of *Yidden* from so many different communities had all

Askan Shimon Rolnitzky standing next to the "Sholom Across America" RV at a bungalow colony in the Catskills.

relocated within miles of each other, and he was able, with minimal effort, to reach them all. In addition to his fundraising efforts, he spoke about *emunah* and *bitachon* at various summer camps, and helped organize a large women's rally in the area.

Meir Simcha was energetic and tireless in his efforts and he was seeing *hatzlachah* in his work. Around this time, I found out that a *shlichus* opportunity had become available for him at a SUNY college campus in upstate New York. He'd always aspired to become a *shliach*, and he wanted to pursue this opportunity. On the other hand, doing so would necessarily diminish his ability to continue his efforts to help me by raising money for the defense costs. He quietly decided to make the sacrifice and stay focused on my needs—he didn't even feel like he could mention it to me.

Although I was relatively isolated and out of the loop in Otisville, I found out about it from someone else. I called Meir Simcha as soon as I heard. Reminding him of the implications of our *emunah* and *bitachon*, I strongly encouraged him to pursue this opportunity. He must not allow the Sholom Across America campaign or any of his other current efforts to discourage him. The real *hishtadlus*, the efforts that actually would affect the outcome, were precisely the things he would be doing as a *shliach*, by strengthening the connection of *Yidden* to Hashem and helping them do more mitzvos. The money, the lawyers, the activists—all those were *sibos*, *means* through which Hashem could send the *yeshuah*, not the *cause* of it.

He accepted my guidance and applied for the posting. Before long, he moved to Oneonta, New York, and joined the global family of *shluchim* dedicated to bringing Torah and mitzvos to every corner of the world. It meant the end of the Sholom Across America campaign, but he went on to establish a Chabad House which met with tremendous success. His success continues to this day, *baruch Hashem*, and he continues to be a source of great *nachas* as he strengthens the *Yiddishkeit* of hundreds of students and their families each year.

Our appeal had been filed with the Eighth Circuit and the prosecutors had filed a response urging the court to reject it. As they often do, the court granted an oral hearing where both sides would make their case in person and respond to any questions the judges might have. While preparing for the hearing, the lawyers discovered something almost too absurd to be true, something an author might exclude from a work of fiction because it sounds too fantastical:

Also making an appearance at the Eighth Circuit's St. Louis courthouse on the very day of our hearing, scheduled to sit on a case together with the Appeals Court judges as a temporary "fill-in" for the first time in five years, was none other than the district judge herself. She wasn't just going to sit as a judge in the same courthouse and on the same day—she was actually going to sit in judgment, as a colleague, with two of the very same judges who were supposed to decide on formal complaints about her behavior as a judge.

This was reported in the media and caused much disbelief and consternation.

Many among the family and *askanim* wanted to make an issue of this, but the lawyers, always afraid to offend the judges who could end up judging the case, dismissed the idea out of hand. I could only shake my head at the news and remind myself and my family that it wasn't really the legal system to whom we looked for justice, but to Hashem Himself. We were petitioning this court only because Hashem wants us to do so.

On June 15, 2011, my lawyers traveled to St. Louis, Missouri, to address the panel of three judges who would be ruling on my appeal. My father traveled from New York along with some of the family, a number of *askanim* flew in, and some of the local *Yidden* came to the courthouse to show support as well.

Nat Lewin did the talking and laid out the arguments, focusing on the extensive un-transcribed and undisclosed interactions between the judge and prosecution and the judge's failure to recuse herself. He pointed out that one of three appellate judges on the panel had himself ruled that this kind of flaw, even if it's discovered after the trial, could still be raised as potentially invalidating.

The claim that a biased judge doesn't influence the verdict is absurd on its face. Obviously, the control that judges have in shaping a case by scheduling related trials, gate-keeping evidence, and issuing rulings all contribute to the verdict, and a biased judge can shape the outcome of a trial without ever overstepping his or her official authority. Public confidence in the courts demands that judges be beyond reproach.

To address our appeal, the circuit court didn't even need to criticize the judge or even conclude there was actual bias. They could simply invalidate the trial and return the case to an impartial judge for retrial—or at least re-sentencing—on the grounds of maintaining the appearance of impartiality.

The prosecution's presentation mainly rehashed the written arguments without addressing the points the defense had just presented at the hearing. When the judge put some of the defense arguments to the prosecutors, the answers were hesitant and unconvincing, and in one instance, even took a few sentences from a Supreme Court ruling out of context—something our lawyer was quick to point out the next time he spoke.

At the end of the hearing, and in light of what they felt was a very strong appeal, the defense team notified the court that they would be submitting a request for bail pending the decision on the appeal.

The lawyers were very encouraged by the hearing. The judges seemed to be asking the right questions and our answers were well grounded, in fact and in law, whereas the prosecutors offered only fumbling, unsatisfactory answers. This led to some optimism among friends and family.

I shared their optimism that the *yeshuah* was close, but I warned them not to attribute it to what they imagined the judges were thinking or what they might do. Justice would come from Hashem *alone*, and not necessarily the way they expected it. Bitter experience had taught me that being right was not strictly relevant to judicial outcomes.

Three months later, almost to the day, my skepticism was unfortunately validated. The three-judge panel of the Eighth Circuit Court of Appeals published their opinion. It endorsed, wholesale, all of the district judge's behavior and rulings in the most dismissive way possible. They accepted her characterization of her work with the prosecutors, dismissed all the other legal challenges, and declared the outrageous sentence to be reasonable.

The defense team was stunned by the complete one-sidedness of the response, but the biggest shock of all was that they dismissed the judge's involvement with the prosecution as entirely irrelevant, even if it was true. Although they acknowledged that doubts about the jury's neutrality entitled the defendant to a new trial, they denied me a new trial because, for some unstated reason, the bias of the judge can't be assumed to have played a role in a guilty verdict.

Not only is that obviously ridiculous to anyone with any common sense, it's actually contrary to the way three other circuit courts interpret the law.

Around this time, the White House unveiled a new way for the general public to petition the administration—a page on the official White House website called "We the People." It promised a response to any petition that garners over five thousand signatures in thirty days.

The day this platform was launched, a petition was created calling for an investigation into the judicial and prosecutorial misconduct in my case. Word spread, and the petition reached the number of signatures required for a response very quickly. There was a feeling amongst the general public that this would have a positive effect, and people encouraged everyone they knew to sign the petition.

Although they tried to temper people's expectations that this would have a direct result, the *askanim* felt that it was an important statement of public support and enlisted Lipa Schmeltzer and other popular figures to promote it. They even brought devices that could be used to sign the petition to communities where internet-capable devices were not generally used.

By the time the thirty days were over, almost 53,000 people had signed the petition. It was actually the *second largest* petition in the nation at the time. The promised response was not long in coming. A week after the deadline to sign the petition, an official email from the White House went out to all signatories thanking them for their participation, and, despite the purpose and promise of their petition platform, they declined to comment.

Chassidim cluster around a laptop to sign the petition to the President.

Supreme Court of the United States of America

With the astounding ruling by the Eighth Circuit, the only earthly court left to petition was the Supreme Court of the United States. It's not simply a matter of filing an appeal. First, a request has to be made in which arguments are laid out as to why the lower court's decision needs to be reviewed. If the judges are persuaded to hear the case, they issue an order, called a *"Writ of Certiorari,"* instructing the lower court to deliver the record of the case to them for review. Only then can the full arguments in the case be made to the Supreme Court, in writing and in person.

Although they only agree to hear two or three percent of the cases which seek their ruling, our case had a real shot at being among them because it was on an important issue of law which was interpreted differently by different circuit courts. When regional courts disagree, only the Supreme Court can restore uniformity in the law, which is important to a functioning society.

The legal hurdles are not the only obstacles to a Supreme Court hearing. Even many cases with strong legal merits can't get to the Supreme Court because of the heavy costs involved, and that was the position in which we found ourselves. The *va'ad* overseeing the financial support told us that they didn't have the money needed to take this step. Fundraising efforts were redoubled, and, *baruch Hashem*, between the grass-roots support that continued arriving daily, the occasional larger donation from more well-off supporters, and continued rallies, the necessary funds were raised.

One such event took place in Montreal, Canada, toward the end of 2011. Over two thousand people attended the men's event and many more participated via live video. Reb Pinchos Lipschutz and the *askan* Reb Shlomo Leizer Meisels traveled there to speak, as did Mark Weinhardt, one of the lawyers on the team. My son, Meir Simcha, made the trip to represent the family. The event was praised for its tremendous *achdus*—the different communities in Montreal all joined together in a show of real *ahavas Yisrael*, which was the real *hishtadlus*.

My wife also traveled to Montreal to speak at a women's Bikur Cholim event that took place a day earlier. At that event, over 1,500 women heard her words of inspiration, as well as her words of gratitude for everything Klal Yisrael had done and continued to do on our behalf.

As the legal arguments were being formulated and fleshed out, the defense team added Paul Clement, a universally respected lawyer and former US Solicitor General—the lawyer who represents the federal government at the Supreme Court. His involvement sent a strong signal about the merits of our case and he became the lead attorney for the Supreme Court appeal. A delay of a few months was granted for his sake and to allow a number of interested parties time to weigh in with *Amicus Briefs*. On April 2, 2012, we officially filed our motion asking the Supreme Court to intervene and overrule the lower courts' rulings.

Six *Amicus Briefs* were filed in support of our appeal by eighty-six former Attorneys General, senior Department of Justice officials, US Attorneys, and federal judges; thirty criminal law scholars and professors; and the Washington Legal Foundation, the Justice Fellowship, and the Association of Professional Responsibility Lawyers.

These respected individuals and organizations put their weight behind our appeal and further fleshed out the arguments: The law was being interpreted differently in different circuits, the sentencing was legally unreasonable and unsupported, and the judge's *ex-parte* meeting and her rulings and sentencing met the threshold for reasonable people to question her impartiality. Each made the case that these were issues that needed to be settled decisively by the Supreme Court.

Once the government had filed their opposition to our appeal, and we filed our counter-response, we were told that the matter would be considered by the justices and voted upon. The lawyers settled in to wait for their decision. I took the opportunity of the lull in legal efforts and the natural anticipation of a positive result to write to those who had helped us reach this point. Here are some excerpts of the open letter I wrote:

> Rosh Chodesh Elul is a fitting time to say, "Thank you!" to all of my brothers and the families who have the heart to think of me and the time to write me letters and emails… You should all have a kesivah v'chasimah tovah.

> Although Hashem requires us to engage in this sibah, we are not allowed to attach any importance to it. We make a sibah—a vessel for the salvation within nature—only because we are commanded to. We work at it as best we can, and appreciate those who give of themselves and their talent to help us, knowing all the while that we look only to Hashem for our yeshuah, not to human efforts.

> We do not preoccupy ourselves with what this one or that one said. We only preoccupy ourselves with learning Torah and doing mitzvos with bitachon in Hashem.

> May Hashem reveal His unlimited rachamim and koach and quickly bring the geulah prati we are all davening for, to every single Yid and their families, and the Geulah Klali that we are awaiting for so many years, with the coming of Mashiach Tzidkeinu.

Like every legal effort we made at this point, the appeal to the Supreme Court ended in disappointment. We got the news on the happiest of Yamim Tovim; Sukkos—Zman Simchaseinu: They would not take up our case.

The decision itself was issued on the second day of Yom Tov, but obviously we didn't find out until nightfall. Hearing the news, I worried that it would make a "Tishah B'Av" out of the joyous Yom Tov. I immediately called my son Getzel and asked him to arrange a public simchas beis hasho'evah with great joy and celebration and make every effort that this news not sadden everyone's Yom Tov. I suggested that he call every entertainer he could get hold of, and ask them to participate in a grand public celebration.

There was already a public simchas beis hasho'evah scheduled to take place that night in Boro Park. Getzel called the organizer, Rabbi Ginsberg, and joined forces with him. Next, he called world-renowned singers Avraham Fried and Benny Friedman, both of whom agreed to participate, despite the last-minute notice. My request that the joy of Yom Tov not be disturbed by this news was publicized, and the response was very strong.

One week later, on Shemini Atzeres, still processing this latest development, I had an experience which was an almost perfect representation of the way a Yid grapples with and overcomes adversity.

That year, all the various rooms of the chapel had been reserved by other groups and we had to meet in the sukkah for Ma'ariv and *hakafos*. As *hashgachah pratis* would have it, it started to rain shortly after we'd gathered. My companions decided to leave the sukkah, but I chose to stay. It was cold and wet, but it was still the sukkah—infinitely better than any warm and dry spot in a place called prison.

As I sat alone in the sukkah, I started thinking about my family, sitting in their own sukkah far away at a *pre-hakafos farbrengen*, intensifying their joy in preparation for *hakafos*. Or perhaps they'd already gone back into the shul and joined the community—dressed in their Yom Tov best, spirits soaring, joyously and lovingly embracing the Torah scrolls as they sang and danced the holy *hakafos*.

Perhaps still reeling emotionally from the great blow to our legal efforts, I felt a wave of melancholy wash over me, as I contrasted my surroundings with the ones I could so vividly imagine.

As I dwelled on my low spirits, the thought drifted across my mind that perhaps this was my fulfillment of *simchas Yom Tov*—if the joy itself was denied me, maybe the right thing to do was to mourn its loss. With a jolt, I took control of my own thoughts and noted their absurdity. *Simchas Yom Tov* through mourning?! I couldn't imagine a more bizarre idea.

But where did that leave me? *That* was certainly not the way to celebrate Yom Tov, but what *was* the way? I was alone, with no family or friends to join me in my celebration, I had no *minyan*, no shul, not even a Torah to dance with on my own. Suddenly, I remembered a story of the Rebbe that had happened during *hakafos*.

During the rejoicing, the Rebbe pulled someone into the joyous dancing. Afterwards, the Rebbe asked the man's pardon, to which the man responded, "Quite the opposite—it's a tremendous honor for me to dance with the Rebbe!"

The Rebbe gently corrected the man: "*Simchas Torah tantzt men mit der*

Oibershter—When we dance on Simchas Torah, we are dancing with Hashem Himself!"

The message was clear. When we're dancing with Hashem Himself, all other considerations and details of any kind fade to total insignificance. This man experienced something he felt ought to contribute to his celebration, while I felt that I was missing something from my celebration, but we were both getting it wrong.

I had none of the trappings of Yom Tov—not even a Torah to hold in my arms—but, as important as those are to celebrating Yom Tov, they are not the *essence* of the Yom Tov. The core of Simchas Torah is our unbreakable bond with Hashem and the deep and enduring joy it evokes. "*Simchas Torah tantzt men mit der Oibershter!*"

With my clarity restored, I stood up from my seat to dance with Hashem. I began a joyous *hakafos* song and started to dance around the tables. I danced slowly at first, a bit reluctantly. My mind had reached its conclusion and it was driving my body forward, but my heart still hadn't caught up. As I danced, however, I felt my spirits begin to lift. Before long, I was whirling and spinning as I circled the small space faster and faster, my voice lifting and my heart soaring. In those moments, nothing else existed. It was just me and my beloved Father, in an infinite sea of love and joy, dancing the seven *hakafos*.

Eventually, I heard the voice of the guard, as if from a million miles away. It was time to return to the barrack. As I entered the cell, I called out to my cellmate, "Panama, you missed the most *amazing hakafos!*" He had been actively exploring his possible Jewish roots and he knew what *hakafos* are, but he looked at me so strangely that I glanced down at myself to see what he was looking at. My shoes and shins were caked with mud and some spatters from the more energetic stomping had even reached close to my waist.

I laughed and sat down on one of the chairs. Those were the most special *hakafos* I had ever experienced and I very much wanted to continue them. I had an idea. "Panama, let me tell you what *hakafos* look like in a real shul.

"Try to picture a large, well-lit room. It's filled with hundreds of *Yidden* in their Yom Tov best, all in high spirits. Happy children are running here and there, waving small holiday flags. The leader of the community stands up front near the ark. The Torahs, bedecked in vibrantly colored mantles and crowns of silver or gold, are distributed to members of the community. At the signal of the community leader, the whole room bursts out in song and they begin dancing in a large circle. Like this."

I leapt to my feet and began full-throated singing, "*V'samachta B'chagecha!*" as I made small, lively circles around the chair. I waved my hands, hopped, skipped—in short, I danced *hakafos*. After some time, I stopped suddenly and continued my descriptions.

"Then," I told Panama, "the leader bangs on the table and calls out, 'Ad kan hakafah aleph!!' and the dancing stops. The Torahs are given to other community members, they say a few verses together, and then, the dancing starts up all over again, this time with a different song. Like this."

I resumed my dancing as abruptly as I'd stopped, to the lively *niggun*, "*Sisu V'simchu B'Simchas Torah!*" I danced all seven *hakafos* again, ostensibly demonstrating for Panama, but really just holding on to my special *hakafos* with Hashem.

I'd never had such extraordinary *hakafos* and, until Mashiach comes, I don't think I will again. I didn't even want to wash the mud spatters off of the pants I'd worn that night. I left those pants hanging on the hook in the cell and drew strength and holiness from the reminder of that special night until the mud dried so thoroughly that it fell off on its own.

That night, my escape from the depths of sadness to the height of joy followed the path which leads us safely through all the difficulties in our lives. I had begun, as we all do, in a state of darkness and confusion. My problems seemed real and there seemed no way out. Of course, there *was*—as there always is—and the first step out was the mental clarity provided by the Torah and our holy *chachamim*. In this case, it was a story of the Rebbe, but other times, it's something you learn in a *sefer* or a Torah perspective you hear from a friend.

The next step out was *acting* on that clarity. In the words of our *chachamim*, *Acharei hama'asim nimshachim halevavos*—"The heart is drawn after our actions." Don't wait until you feel happy. Once you know that you ought to be happy, just do happy things and let the feeling come. It will come, and that's the last step, the step to freedom—when the truth, and the life and joy that come with it, permeates your heart and transforms your world.

Find the mental clarity, act on it, and experience emotional clarity. The only thing missing from this roadmap for dealing with adversity as a Yid is our defense. In order to be able to find the mental clarity and for our heart to be receptive and sensitive to the truth, we need to protect ourselves from those things which coarsen and desensitize us or which cloud our hearts and minds with ideas and beliefs that conflict with the truth. I went into some detail about this in the beginning of the section on Jewish life in Otisville.

Once Yom Tov was over, we returned to battle. The public was outraged at this latest refusal to put things right and the lawyers and *askanim* vowed that they would fight on. There was still a legal path forward and Nat Lewin quoted the *pasuk, Tzedek tzedek tirdof.* Justice is something that doesn't always come easily, and must be pursued.

CHAPTER THIRTY-ONE

The Constitutional Challenge

2255 Motion

THE LAST REMAINING LEGAL AVENUE WAS SOMETHING CALLED A "2255 Motion." Section 2255 of the laws governing judicial procedure covers the right of someone in custody to challenge his incarceration if it violates the Constitution or laws of the United States. I learned that this law is a version of something called "*Habeas Corpus*." That's Latin for "have the body [brought to us]," the summons that a court issues to a jailer so the judges can decide if the imprisonment is legal.

I found this abbreviated title very fitting, because although they might "*habeas*" my "*corpus*," they can never imprison or enslave my *neshamah*. We were all fighting for my release from imprisonment so I could be restored and reunited with my family and community, but even before Hashem granted us success, the problem was limited to my body. My *neshamah* always remained free to serve Hashem.

By the time they reach this point in their case, most defendants have been cleaned out of all their money. They can't afford the lawyers needed to challenge any injustices that may have shaped their case and resulted in illegal imprisonment. The more determined ones in this situation file the appeal on their own behalf, without a lawyer, which is called "*pro se*." Going up against trained professional prosecutors, who also have systemic advantages, is obviously tremendously difficult. The prosecutors very often don't even bother responding to these *pro se* filings because they are dead on arrival.

Financially speaking, I myself had been carefully and methodically disarmed by the prosecutors very early on and would have been helpless to defend myself in court if not for the selfless devotion of Klal Yisrael. Their support continued even at this stage, and I was grateful to Hashem and to His messengers that my family was able to hire lawyers to continue the fight.

A 2255 Motion is often based on the claim that the defendant had "ineffective counsel." The Constitution guarantees the right to a lawyer, and many argue in their motion that for all intents and purposes they didn't have one, which invalidates the whole process. This was usually on the grounds that the lawyer they hired or were assigned made critical mistakes at the trial, refused to listen to them, or even pressured them to plead guilty, despite their innocence, when they had better alternatives.

Many of those in Otisville who filed 2255 Motions made this argument. It was sad to see people whose lawyers had totally failed them, and who had been sentenced to decades in prison as a result, try to get a new trial on these grounds. Their one-time lawyers fought viciously, tooth and nail, to avoid taking any blame for the disastrous outcomes. They made strenuous efforts to block this exit, rather than admitting to making a mistake which might impact their career but would save the life of their client.

Another route for a section 2255 Motion is to show the court that the defendant did not get a fair trial either because the prosecutors hid favorable information, knowingly used false or misleading information, or because of issues of justice or objectivity with the judge, jury, or witnesses.

Unbelievably, the motion is first filed with the trial judge (here we go again…) and can only be taken to the Court of Appeals if it's rejected. It's filed in two parts; first the motion itself—a general filing which enumerates the claims, and then a later filing that fully fleshes out the merits of the arguments, called a "Merits Brief."

It was at this point that Hashem sent Chaim Yosef Apfel. Known at work as Gary, he's a senior partner at the prestigious law firm of Pepper Hamilton and the managing partner at their Los Angeles office. My plight had struck a chord with him from the very beginning and he had wanted to help in whatever way he could, but there didn't seem to be a role for him at the time.[1]

One Thursday evening, not long after the Supreme Court had declined to hear our appeal, Gary received a phone call from Zvi Boyarsky. Zvi was

---

1. He specialized in corporate work—mergers, acquisitions, bankruptcies, and the like—and although he's a very skilled and well-respected lawyer, trusted with huge cases like restructuring General Motors, his expertise and experience didn't really translate into anything that might be of service in my case.

Chaim Yosef "Gary" Apfel—my lawyer, my friend, my brother.

moving heaven and earth on my behalf, but that didn't mean he wasn't also helping others. A Yid in LA was struggling financially and couldn't pay his rent and Zvi was calling Gary for financial assistance, which Gary immediately promised to give.

This was not unusual. Gary proudly upholds the tradition of selfless *chessed* for which his father was so well known. His father was so synonymous with *chessed*, that someone once saw him at work and said in surprise, "Willie! I didn't know you work!"

A busy lawyer, Gary was scheduled to leave Monday to Philadelphia to work on a project for the Federal Reserve Bank. His father had taught him not to leave *tzedakah* commitments outstanding, so he went to Zvi's house to deliver his pledge in person before he left. When he arrived, he found Zvi working on my case.

"Oh! You're involved in the Rubashkin case?" he asked. Always on the lookout for allies, Zvi was happy to fill him in on his efforts. At that time, as part of building support in legal and political circles, the team was trying to get a hold of Louis Freeh, a former federal judge and former director of the FBI, without success.

"What *hashgachah pratis*!" Gary exclaimed. "He's actually the chair of my law firm! I will be meeting with him and I'd be happy to introduce him to the case." Not satisfied with this assistance, Gary offered further help. Grateful for the offer, Zvi gave him the latest legal filings to read and arranged for him to meet with Roza Hindy in the airport in Philadelphia where he could hear more and provide some legal advice and guidance.

Gary had always been distressed by my situation, and reading the legal filings only distressed him further. There was no logical reason that the Supreme Court didn't take the case. The facts of the case and the legal issues it presented were tailor-made for Supreme Court involvement.[2]

The Supreme Court's refusal to take up the case made it immediately clear

---

2. In fact, he later learned that former Solicitors General of the United States have an informal group in which they discuss pending cases, and my case was one of six cases they were certain would be addressed by the court.

to Gary that Hashem's salvation would not come through the legal system alone, and he told Roza Hindy as much when they met.

The way he saw it, a sincere effort had to be made to pursue a legal remedy, but the legal efforts would also serve other goals. The information that was discovered and the arguments formulated and presented—not to mention the prosecution's responses and the judicial dismissiveness—would clearly establish the moral and legal outrage that had been perpetrated and would help make our case to the public and to public officials. Strong public and political support might induce or compel the prosecution to accept a negotiated resolution, and would also be important to any pursuit of presidential clemency.

This integrated approach he was describing required much more than his legal guidance and advice, and Gary—without being asked and without being paid—stepped up in every respect. His approach was very much in line with that of the *askanim*, and Gary's formidable leadership and organizational skills and methodical approach took everything they were doing to new heights. More importantly, his *ahavas Yisrael* and *mesiras nefesh* made him a worthy *shliach* for Hashem's miracles.

He became an integral part of the legal team, crafting court documents and coordinating legal efforts, and he put in considerable time, effort, and countless miles of travel into marshaling the support of legal luminaries and political leaders. He even went out with Roza Hindy to collect the money they needed to fund the effort—all without taking a penny himself! He always kept his eye on the next step and expertly wove the various efforts together so that each action supported the others in advancing the goal.

As a first step, when he got back to Los Angeles, he discussed the case with his partners at the law firm. Although this case wasn't within their area of expertise, he succeeded in persuading them to allow him to take on the case *pro bono*, which means he was free to donate his time instead of billing hours for the firm's paying clients, as he was otherwise obligated to do.

They wouldn't have any complaints, but this still meant he would be giving up *parnassah*—and Gary didn't do this part-time. He put everything to the side, passing up on opportunities for personal enrichment and career advancement just to help a fellow Jew he never met—something for which my family and I can never fully express our gratitude and appreciation.

In the early days of his involvement, he met my father for the first time, at the Boro Park butcher shop. He was surprised to find, among the many other pictures and paintings in the office, a large oil painting of the Kopyczynitzer Rebbe, Harav Avraham Yehoshua Heschel, displayed prominently on the wall in front of my father's desk. "I'm a Kopyczynitzer chassid!" Gary told him proudly. Gary merited a close and personal relationship with the Kopyczynitzer Rebbe and his family, and he began telling my father about it.

"You don't have to tell me about the Kopyczynitzer Rebbe," my father told him. When my father had first opened his butcher store, he had been denied access to the available supply of meat from the *shochtim*. The kosher meat market was closed and very tightly controlled by the existing butchers and they refused to allow him in. It was due to the Kopyczynitzer Rebbe's intervention that they changed their tune and he was able to get his new business off the ground, for which my father felt true *hakaras hatov*.

"When I heard that you're a Kopyczynitzer chassid," my father told Gary, "I knew that your rebbe[3] had sent you as a *shliach* to help my son!"

Gary came to meet me at the first opportunity and we connected not just as lawyer and client, but as fellow Jews and as brothers. It was not just his *ahavas Yisrael* that made him a perfect vessel for Hashem's *brachah*. He was also strongly grounded in *emunah* and *bitachon*. With Hashem's help, the Otisville staff agreed to weekly legal calls during our preparation of the 2255. We started every call by saying six *kapitlach Tehillim* together, then I would share a thought on *bitachon* with him, he would share a thought on *bitachon* with me, and only *then* would we get to the legal business we had to discuss.

Any other lawyer would decry the "waste of time," but Gary knew "from where my help would come," and his *bitachon* made him worthy of being Hashem's *shliach*.

He was also full of joy and good humor. More than once, he made me laugh out loud and I had to admonish him. "Gary! You'll get me in trouble. No one laughs on legal calls. They'll think I'm up to something!"

The Judge Decapitates the Defense Team

The first hurdle the team faced in preparing the 2255 Motion was finding the right lawyers. Because the case was complex and—given the past rulings of the trial judge—was expected to end up in the Court of Appeals, they hired an accomplished lawyer from Kansas City, Jim Wyrsch, as the lead lawyer.

---

3. Who had passed away in 1967.

He was a very capable lawyer with decades of experience in complex cases and had a good track record with the Eighth Circuit. They also hired an expert on sentencing, Doug Berman, and an expert on legal ethics and recusal, Richard Flamm.

To fill the role of local counsel, they interviewed a few promising candidates and hired a lawyer from Des Moines named Paul Rosenberg. They had been impressed by a lawyer named Steve Locher, but he turned out to be ineligible because a partner in his firm had worked on the appeal. If we decided to argue that I wasn't represented properly at the appeal, we would be attacking the firm that employed him, which would be a conflict of interest.

The new legal team got to work and crafted a strong initial motion outlining the arguments, but something happened less than three weeks before the deadline that threw the whole effort into disarray.

It began with a routine investigation. One important difference between a direct appeal and a 2255 Motion is that an appeal has to be based on evidence that's already in the record and arguments that have been carefully preserved, but a 2255 Motion can introduce new arguments and even new evidence.

Although we felt that the arguments we'd been making all along were solid—an opinion shared by so many legal scholars and authorities—we had so far been unable to convince any of the judges. We needed some new angle to convince the judges that I'd been denied a fair trial.

We had made some shocking discoveries since the trial and we knew a lot of what had transpired out of the public eye. We also knew that there were enormous gaps in our information and there was far more that we didn't know that would certainly help our case. This was the time to challenge the proceedings on the basis of new evidence, and the Klal Yisrael Fund hired private investigators to look for something we could use, some concrete evidence that the trial had been flawed and biased.

Since the jury plays such a large role in the trial, it's common practice to check with them when investigating the integrity of a trial. If there's some indication that they were improperly swayed or had shown pre-existing bias, that would go a long way. There's also a chance the jury may have seen or overheard something useful pertaining to the impartiality of others involved in the trial from their perspective behind the scenes.

For these reasons, the investigators wanted to interview the jurors. They ran this idea by the appellate lawyers, who ran it by the local trial lawyers.

The legal consensus was that this would be permissible. My daughter Roza Hindy was asked to accompany an investigator to provide the benefit of her knowledge and experience with the case. Before she went, she visited me in Otisville to ask for any thoughts I had, any areas of concern that I thought might be worth exploring.

On the question of jury bias, there were exchanges during jury selection that had disturbed me. As mentioned previously, too often, jury candidates had admitted that they knew about the case and had strong negative feelings about it. As a matter of fact, the juror who wound up being chosen as jury foreman initially said that he couldn't be impartial because he read about the raid and specifically about the plight of the immigrants after the raid, which really bothered and angered him. This wasn't just a ploy to get out of jury duty—his posture and body language were broadcasting his antipathy and agitation for all to see.

Instead of dismissing him, the judge waved away any concerns on the basis of his—decidedly reluctant—agreement to "set aside" his bias. My feelings aside, this wasn't actual proof of bias, but it made me wonder. Perhaps there had been indications to others on the jury that some of them hadn't lived up to their aspirations of objectivity.

Another incident that had unsettled me happened during the trial. One morning, early in the trial, the judge informed us that she'd been notified by the jury that my Jewish supporters had defaced the courthouse steps, marking them with cryptic letters. This shocking claim had been investigated and it turned out to be a normal mark made by architects or construction workers which had been there for more than nine years. The judge had assured us that they would inform the jury of the innocent nature of the marks.

However she handled it, this episode suggested to me that at least some of the jury's minds were poisoned against me. These kinds of markings are fairly common, and even if they saw something unusual, a neutral person wouldn't jump to the assumption that this was vandalism by people supporting me.

I shared these and other ideas with my daughter and she flew west to join the investigator. Out of twelve jurors and four alternates, only three jurors and one alternate juror were willing to speak to them. Among the things they discovered was that, although they remembered the incident with the marking on the courthouse steps, none of them recalled receiving a message explaining it away. The court officer who was supposed to have told them also didn't remember passing the message along.

A short time later in Otisville, days before Sukkos, I was notified that I had a legal call. Gary Apfel was on the line. One of the jurors who'd been visited by my daughter and the investigator had called the prosecutors to complain about the visit. Instead of reaching out to the defense lawyers and discussing the matter, the prosecutors had gone straight to the judge. They filed a motion that the defense had broken the rules by reaching out to the jurors and demanded the judge intervene to prevent further contact and take whatever other measures she felt would be appropriate.

Surprised, I asked how they could claim this was a violation of the law. Hadn't the lawyers deliberated and concluded it was legal? Gary explained that the lawyers had a number of reasons for their conclusion. Among them was the fact that there's no universal prohibition on discussing a case with the jury after the trial's over. Some states have rules which prohibit contact to protect jurors from harassment, but South Dakota, where the trial had taken place and where the jury was from, is not one of them.

Iowa does have rules prohibiting contact without permission, and the prosecutors were asserting that these rules applied, but even under those rules, there was room for debate. At the end of the trial, the judge had explicitly told the jury that they were now free to speak to whomever they choose, and the defense lawyers took that to mean that contact was now permitted.

They had made a good-faith judgment, but if the judge disagreed and ruled that the contact had not been permissible, the ramifications for the lawyers could be quite serious. The only way to avoid the issue was to try to negotiate an agreement with the prosecutors in which they would retract their complaint and we would agree not to use any information from the jury interviews.

The revelation that the jury went into their deliberations thinking that we'd vandalized court property was important, something concrete to which we could point as an indication that they weren't neutral. I was reluctant to relinquish any grounds to argue that the jury was biased. The 2255 Motion was the last avenue to make my case in the courts and I couldn't afford to voluntarily disarm myself of helpful arguments or evidence.

Gary understood my position, but on balance he felt that the appropriate course of action was to offer some sort of compromise with the prosecutors. After grappling with the decision, I agreed to make the offer. The deciding factor for me was that these motions were merely the means through which Hashem's *brachah* would be implemented, and if it would hurt someone else, it could not be a fitting vessel for Hashem's *brachah*.

However, after all that, the prosecutors refused to negotiate and preferred to drag it in front of the judge. The judge was furious and demanded that a number of the defense lawyers appear at a hearing to face charges of contempt of court—a very serious charge that can destroy a lawyer's career.

On the second day of Sukkos, Friday afternoon, I was sitting in the sukkah eating my meal, when the counselor poked his head inside. "You need to go to the office and call in to a hearing," he said.

"Now?!" I asked, surprised. "It's a holiday today and a Jew is not allowed to use the phone!" Although the topic was a hearing called by a federal judge, this wasn't the first time he had heard of the religious restrictions on Shabbos and Yom Tov.

He said, "Okay," and left.

As it turned out, the hearing wasn't even that day. It had been rescheduled because of Yom Tov and apparently the Otisville authorities had not been notified. Nonetheless, it says a lot about the religious freedom we enjoy in this great country, that, even in a place called prison, religious obligations can take precedence over a federal court appearance.

This interruption of my Yom Tov meal brought up the whole precarious situation of my lawyers and my final appeal. I made the effort to take my mind and heart off of these things again, and, *baruch Hashem*, I succeeded. I celebrated the rest of Yom Tov with joy and tranquility.

The hearing was held after Yom Tov. Some of the lawyers who had worked on earlier stages of the case were still officially on the team. Hoping to escape the judge's wrath, they had requested to be formally removed from my team, a request the judge had declined to fulfill before the hearing.

At the start of the hearing, the judge officially accepted the requests of the lawyers to resign, and turning her attention to the remaining lawyers, she let loose. She treated my lead trial lawyer, Guy Cook, with great disrespect. He's a distinguished and respected lawyer, the president of the Iowa State Bar Association and a former Assistant US Attorney, but she treated him like a misbehaving child.

She even chastised Mr. Wyrsch—the lead lawyer of the new legal team—for relying on Mr. Cook's interpretation of her words and very disparagingly brought up the incident at the trial when Mr. Cook was forced to mention my son's condition to counter a mischaracterization by the prosecutors. She quoted chapter and verse from the trial transcript in what was clearly a prepared, researched insult, not an off-the-cuff outburst.

The lawyers each repeatedly tried to clarify and justify their limited part in the jury interviews, all worried about the very real consequences she held over their heads. They apologized for any inadvertent violations and rushed to assure her that the information discovered would not be used.

After everyone had said their piece, the judge ruled that two of the lawyers and one associate were in violation of the rules, but withheld a final ruling on whether they would be held formally in contempt of court and what the consequences would be.

The deciding factor on that question was to be whether or not our discoveries would be used. She wanted a formal statement from me that they would not be and she scheduled a follow-up hearing on the day after the 2255 was due, by which time she would know for certain whether we used the information. She would then decide the consequences for the lawyers.

The lawyers were effectively hostages. If I decided to use the information to try to obtain my freedom, my lawyers would be harmed as a result. I had already decided to allow the information to be taken off the board, as frustrating and unjust as that was, so I signed the necessary document and it was presented to the judge at the follow-up hearing.

Although she made a comment that she expected this information to be off the board not only in court proceedings but also in pursuit of presidential clemency, she accepted the document and closed the hearing without formally finding the lawyers in contempt of court. The hostages, having served their purpose, were off the hook.

The fallout from this episode was immediate and enormous. The very real possibility of being held in contempt of court had not only rattled Mr. Wyrsch, it presented him with a problem of legal ethics. Just by making the threat, the judge had embedded personal consequences to the lawyer into decisions that should only be about the best interests of his client—me. Faced with this conflict of interest, he felt compelled to resign from the team after the first hearing, with only a week to go before the filing deadline.

We were left, at this critical juncture, without our lead lawyer. It was like losing the pilot of a giant airliner minutes before landing. The important work of crafting the 2255 Motion had been done, but if we couldn't find someone to stick the landing, it would all go up in flames.

Time was very short. It was literally impossible to replace Mr. Wyrsch in time. Even if we could find a qualified lawyer to join the team on such short notice, no respectable lawyer could submit someone else's work without first familiarizing himself with the case. That was particularly true in this instance, because the motion was expected to end up before the Court of Appeals, and the claims would need to be presented and defended against both the prosecution and whatever arguments the district judge would make in her almost inevitable denial.

It was natural, under the circumstances, to feel a sense of panic, but it was our job to see *through* nature. I reminded myself, my family, and my team that this was all orchestrated by Hashem for our benefit and our enemies could not possibly hurt us. I urged them to have *emunah* and *bitachon*.

We overcame the *nisayon*, renewing our *bitachon* and calming ourselves, and Hashem provided a solution. Although our motion was a direct attack on the prosecutors, with whom he would have to work for a long time to come, Paul Rosenberg, already on the team as our local counsel, courageously agreed to put his name to the filing. *Baruch Hashem*, despite the drama and the uncertainty, the 2255 Motion was filed on time. It included no less than three "grounds for relief"—three ways in which my conviction and sentence, and therefore my very presence in a place called prison, were in violation of the Constitution.

I'm convinced that this episode was an intentional, strategic attempt to undermine the last legal opportunity to challenge the unjust sentence. The shocking and underhanded maneuver drove home, yet again, the injustice which so easily subverts human courts and drew me closer to the one True Judge, the Source of justice, kindness, and mercy. I placed my trust in Him and awaited my salvation.

The courageous local lawyer's willingness to file the motion solved the immediate problem and got us through the deadline for the motion itself, but it only *neutralized* the damage that was done when Mr. Wyrsch was forced to resign. The Torah tells us that any adversity that we experience ultimately results in something *better* than what came before, something which could not have been obtained in any other way, and we waited for Hashem's kindness to unfold.

Before long, we merited to see the true *brachah* that Hashem had hidden in this unjust "dismissal" of the lawyers. Back at square one, Gary and my son-in-law Yaakov Weiss threw themselves into the task of finding the right lawyer to flesh out and present the arguments in support of the 2255 Motion. They interviewed as many as twenty qualified and respected lawyers from across the nation to find the right man for the job.

This time, they were able to include Steve Locher, an Iowa lawyer whom they'd originally wanted to hire but who had been disqualified as local counsel for conflict of interest. At this point, the conflict of interest was no longer relevant and nothing was preventing him from joining the team.

Steve was approached, and, after reviewing our 2255 Motion, he agreed to represent me as counsel and dove into the case with his characteristic energy. He wanted to start by meeting me in person, and he made the long trip from Iowa to Otisville. We were able to discuss the case for a whole hour and Steve made a very good impression on me.

The judge, in executing the maneuver to eliminate my legal team, had tried to deprive me of proper representation at a critical time. As Yosef Hatzaddik said, "[They] intended to do me evil, but Hashem intended it for good." We now had an even better lawyer than we had before, a lawyer who was a tremendous asset in our efforts and proved himself again and again.[4]

He'd only been on the case for about a month when he unexpectedly notified us that he wouldn't be able to work for a bit. Something had come up, and he needed time to figure out if he could stay on our team. Surprised and troubled by this unexpected and cryptic message, we leaned once again on our *bitachon* and trusted in Hashem that it would be resolved for the best.

It turned out to have been yet another underhanded attempt by the prosecutors to derail my fight for justice, instead of just facing us in court. Steve had received a call from the prosecutor, who said that in his opinion, Steve could not legally represent me, for various technical reasons. They were clearly not satisfied with prompting the resignation of our first lead lawyer using the jury interviews—now they were going after the lawyer I had found to replace him.

Steve had obviously considered this question before taking on the case, like every responsible lawyer does, but the unsolicited phone call from the government concerned him, as I believe it was intended to. He lost a few precious days of preparation making a careful review of the facts and legalities, but in the end concluded that there was no merit to the prosecutor's position and he fully and wholeheartedly rejoined the team.

Around this time, the top spot in Iowa's US Attorney's office opened up. Unlike his predecessors, the new US Attorney was not promoted from within

---

4. In 2020, his high caliber was recognized by the Judicial Nominating Commission and he was elevated to a federal judgeship.

the office and had had no involvement in the misconduct in my case. There was a chance he would be willing to correct it. Guy Cook, who had been the master of ceremonies at his investiture, reached out to him and arranged a meeting.

A distinguished delegation of three former Deputy Attorneys General of the United States flew out to Iowa to attend the meeting. Larry Thompson flew in from New York, Charles Renfrew flew in from San Francisco, and Philip Heymann flew in from Boston. Gary Apfel joined them from Los Angeles. Louis Freeh, former director of the FBI, also wanted to participate, but couldn't make it for family reasons.

At the meeting, these prominent men explained their involvement. "Why am I here?" one former Deputy Attorney General asked rhetorically. "Because I care about the Department of Justice. What this office did put an indelible stain on this office and on the entire DOJ. Someone in this office decided that they wanted to punish Aaron Rubashkin. For whatever reason, they couldn't do it in court, so they did it by destroying his business of sixty years—without due process—and as a result, his son is sitting in jail with a twenty-seven-year sentence."

He then turned to a methodical and thorough analysis of the case and the inappropriate actions of the prosecutors. He contrasted the testimony they had presented with the growing mountain of affidavits that plainly contradicted it. At one point, Judge Renfrew couldn't contain himself. *"Perjury!"* he burst out, enraged. "Your prosecutors knowingly presented the court with perjured testimony!"

The ramifications of taking this to court were clear and they implored the new US Attorney, for the sake of the DOJ, not to do so. Not only would such a course lead to the misconduct becoming widely known, an evidentiary hearing would also mean that the prosecutors and the government's witness would have to explain themselves under oath, something which would significantly increase the DOJ's shame in the eyes of all who value justice and integrity.

They offered him a dignified solution that had been utilized by the DOJ before—he could simply choose not to oppose our 2255 Motion and settle for time served, allowing me to return home to my family.

The US Attorney was cordial throughout. He was surprised by some of the information they shared with him, and he said as much at the end of the meeting. "I must tell you that I met with my team to prepare for this meeting and they didn't tell me a lot of what you shared today."

He also seemed willing to consider their proposal. In parting, he asked, "So all you're asking is that we agree to settle for time served?" His phrasing encouraged them, but as is often the case, it was an empty reassurance. They corresponded for a while about aspects of the proposal, but Hashem had decided that the time had not yet come. The new US Attorney ultimately decided to defend the actions of his predecessors and his current underlings and the 2255 Motion moved forward.

This roller coaster of encouragement followed by disappointment was another reminder to take to heart the words of Dovid Hamelech, *Al tivtichu b'nidivim*—"Do not trust in great men." Regardless of indications or signs, place your trust only in Hashem.

This was not the only time the distinguished group of former leaders of the Justice Department traveled across the country on my behalf. As if the countless hours they spent advising our lawyers and *askanim* were not enough, they personally flew to meetings to appeal to DOJ officials and enlist support of political leaders to try and obtain justice for me and my family. It would be impossible to list them all, but the following is a small representative sample.

An *askan* from Detroit named Gary Torgow helped set up a meeting with Senator Carl Levin, a powerful Senator from Michigan and the chair of the Senate Armed Services Committee. At the meeting, which he attended along with Gary Apfel, Larry Thompson, and a former DOJ official named Makan Delrahim, they laid out the facts of the case. They made a strong impression on Senator Levin, but as people often do, he threw up his hands. "What can I do about it?"

Gary Apfel didn't accept that as an answer. "What makes me so sad is that that's what everyone says!" he cried out. "Everyone who hears the details of this case says it's a terrible injustice and a crying shame, but what can I do about it?!"

Hearing his thought reflected back at him, Senator Levin reconsidered and decided to get involved. He wrote a very forceful letter to the Department of Justice and Attorney General Holder demanding that the Attorney General investigate the case, and even went to the DOJ to meet Mr. Holder himself, something which is highly unusual.

His strong, open support—besides opening many doors—serves as a lesson for us, something to ponder when we face a challenge and want to throw up our hands and say, "There's nothing I can do about it."

Another meeting was organized by Howard Friedman, a former head of

AIPAC and a respected *askan*. The team went with him to Congressman Elijah Cummings, a highly respected and well-placed politician who headed the powerful Congressional Committee on Oversight.

As the Congressman heard the details about what had been done to me, he slumped lower and lower in his chair. "Why would the government *do* this?!" he blurted out when he'd had enough.

Before Gary had a chance to respond, Larry Thompson, a former Deputy Attorney General who was at the meeting, leaned in. "Congressman," he said, "I served in the DOJ. I have the greatest respect for the institution, but this was nothing more than blatant antisemitism."

The Congressional hearings that the *askanim* hoped would be held at that time never materialized, but the meeting did result in public support which was very helpful.

They even met with the Deputy Attorney General at the time, Jim Cole. That meeting was attended by Gary Apfel and Larry Thompson.[5]

When Mr. Cole interrupted Gary's presentation of the injustices of the case to say that twenty-seven years was only the low end of the Sentencing Guidelines, Gary lost it. Gary doesn't shout or wave his arms, but with the unmistakable intensity of quiet rage, Gary said to him, "I can't *believe* I'm sitting in the office of the Deputy Attorney General of the United States and hearing him justify a twenty-seven-year sentence of a first-time, non-violent offender by stating that it is the low end of the Guidelines…"

Larry put a hand on Gary's knee, and said, "Gary, let me try," and he turned to the aspects of the case he was supposed to present.

The meeting went very well and it seemed they had made a bit of a breakthrough. At that point, we had already discovered that the prosecution had withheld key information, a violation of my constitutional rights known as a *Brady* violation. As he walked them to the door, Mr. Cole was very reassuring. "We take *Brady* very seriously here," he said, as they parted. Yet again, nothing came of his assurances.

_____

5. Gary told me more than once that he considered it a tremendous privilege to work with legal luminaries like Louis Freeh, Philip Heymann, Larry Thompson, Charles Renfrew, and others of their caliber, like Professor Alan Dershowitz and former US Attorney General Michael Mukasey, who got involved later. In addition to their dedication to fighting this terrible injustice, spending hundreds and hundreds of hours *pro bono*, he outright marveled that these men, so accomplished and respected in their field, all possessed a deep humility.

It had long ago become clear that this judge wouldn't right the wrongs in my case. As we had with earlier attempts to appeal, we had filed a motion, along with the main filing, that the judge recuse herself and not sit in judgment on allegations of injustice with which she was so intertwined. Our motion retread familiar ground, primarily the *ex-parte* communications with the prosecutors which weren't disclosed by either judge or prosecutors, albeit under a different legal standard.

There were a few additional wrinkles, too. We had learned that her husband's law firm had, for a period of time, represented some of my father's Iowa-based companies, which was a problem for a number of reasons. He had access to information which he might have shared with her outside of the legal process. She may have been inclined to prove her objectivity by being extra strict or harsh with her husband's client. There were also possibly hard feelings in their household—her husband's firm had been let go and their replacement had sued them for fees.[6]

The facts behind these concerns had never been established in court, but that actually made her position worse. If these concerns were ever treated with the seriousness they deserved and given an evidentiary hearing, the judge could be called as a witness. A case where a judge might be called as a witness is another scenario in which judicial ethics demand a judge not sit in judgment.

The motion of recusal also pointed to another sign that her relationship with the prosecutor's office went beyond a normal working relationship. The judge had received a couple of worrying emails from people distraught about my ordeal and her role in it. The messages were forwarded to the authorities for investigation and it was properly assigned to the Southern District office, which was not connected to the case itself. The investigation was proceeding too slowly for the judge's taste, and, in frustration, she had reached out—not to the office investigating the letters, but to her friends in the Northern District office, the prosecutors in the case.

All in all, the recusal motion was a simple one, and it was based on facts and law with which the judge was very familiar, but her denial wasn't issued for two long years!

On one hand, this delay was a terrible injustice. The motion was concerning

---

6. Her husband was also discovered to have purchased stocks in privately operated prisons right before the raid and sold them at a handsome profit, although that didn't make it into the legal brief.

a claim that they had put me in a cage illegally, in violation of the Constitution. Every day the decision was put off was twenty-four hours in which a human being, an American citizen, was being imprisoned on what was claimed to be illegitimate grounds. A ruling on this matter should be of the utmost urgency.

On the other hand, this injustice neutralized a *different* injustice. In 1992, Congress passed a law which dictated that if a year has passed since the initial legal process was completed, an inmate can no longer file a 2255. An inmate might find irrefutable proof that his conviction was based on perjured testimony, but, if twelve months has already passed, it's just too bad. I never understood or got used to the idea that a claim of injustice has an expiration date.

Hashem works in wondrous ways. The judge's long delay in ruling on the recusal had the unintended consequence of giving my lawyers more time to formulate the motion fleshing out the appeal. More than that, this delay was open *hashgachah pratis*, because it was during this inexplicable delay that we miraculously found direct, compelling evidence proving our case, as I will detail next. If the judge had responded immediately, we would have been required to file our Merits Brief shortly thereafter, and our investigations would not have had the time which allowed them to turn up the evidence we needed.

A Legal Earthquake

Throughout the earlier appeals, from the district court all the way up to the Supreme Court, the arguments had focused on the inappropriate *ex parte* interactions between the judge and the prosecutors. It was a legitimate point, but we clearly weren't getting anywhere with it. We needed a new angle, and for that we needed new information. The jury interviews had been used against us, but other avenues of investigation were showing modest results.

One effort focused on getting to the bottom of the prosecution's impact on the sale of Agriprocessors. This was a key issue. As mentioned earlier, the basis for the twenty-seven-year sentence was the prosecutors' claim that the bank lost $27 million because of me. We knew that was not true—any loss that occurred was a result of the prosecutors' interference in the sale. If we could prove that, even without addressing any other aspect of the trial, the Guidelines sentence was *zero to six months*.

The team reached out to the bank to hear about their dealings with the prosecutors but they wouldn't talk. We had more success with potential bidders for the company. It wasn't just the ones we knew about at the time of the sentencing. Every single one we found told the same story: As soon as they expressed an interest, they were called into a meeting and intimidated by the prosecutors. Most were scared off and didn't even make a bid and even those who considered pursuing it further lowered their valuations of the company.

This was a powerful testimony, and was very effective with politicians, justice officials, and the public, but the judge had already rejected similar testimony. Adding new voices to our side of a previously debated argument wasn't going to count for much in a 2255 Motion. "What we need is an earthquake," I was told more than once, "something to shake up the whole landscape of the case."

Another effort was pursuing just such a potential earthquake. It was a long and circuitous road and the earthquake they found was not the one they set out to find, but Hashem's *hashgachah* guided them to exactly what the legal team needed to make their case.

The court-appointed trustee and his team had been right in the thick of things, torn between the prosecution and the bank. They'd had a front row seat to the decisions that were made, the communications around those decisions, and the impact they had on the financial health of the company and the ultimate repayment to the bank.

They were likely to have a wealth of useful information, but there was a problem. The raid and the subsequent legal prosecution had left me penniless, but there was still an open lawsuit against me on behalf of the trustees, which meant my lawyers weren't allowed to talk to them directly.

An accountant from Los Angeles named Brian Dror had been hired to examine the accounting related to the loss, which determined the sentence. For example, among other things, he found that the prosecution and the court had left a $10 million asset—the water treatment facility—off the balance sheet when calculating the loss. Brian knew the trustee, and he was so disturbed by the case, that he flew to New York on his own dime to meet him and find out what he knew.

He got detailed confirmation of the government's meddling not only in the sale of the company but in its daily operations, which resulted in major increases in expenses and loss of revenues and contributed to the loss. As a matter of fact, Brian learned that at the trustee's very first meeting with representatives of the US Attorney's office they told him "not to get the plant restarted or sold."

Brian laid this all out in a sworn affidavit to be filed with the 2255, but he felt there was more to be learned. He got the sense that the trustee had information he wasn't comfortable volunteering, but would disclose if he was under oath at a deposition. This would have been possible as part of the bankruptcy process, but that stage had already been completed and the bankruptcy lawyers weren't willing to get it reopened.

Gary and the team were put in contact with a lawyer from New York named Scott Steinberg and he was happy to help—*pro bono*! With him on board, they managed to negotiate a reopening of discovery in the bankruptcy case, in which they could compel people to share information, and Scott interviewed the trustee. None of the information was the bombshell we needed, but this was a critical step in the sequence of *hashgachah pratis* that led us directly to it.

This bankruptcy was preventing my lawyers from meeting with the trustee directly. Every earlier attempt to broker a resolution included a requirement that I falsely admit to wrongdoing, but I refused to make a *chillul Hashem* in that way. Scott Steinberg, who only came on board when he was needed for this interview, turned out to be Hashem's *shliach* in finally negotiating a resolution to this lawsuit. It was an eight-month game of chess, but in the end, with Hashem's help, he did it.

That was a good development and a *brachah* from Hashem on its own, but it also eliminated the prohibition on direct contact between my lawyers and the trustee, which was even better. By then, there was a specific thing we were looking for that was absolutely explosive.

When a bankruptcy is filed, the Department of Justice assigns an official, separate from the trustee appointed by the bankruptcy court, to monitor the situation and ensure the integrity of the bankruptcy process. The US Trustee for Agri's case was a man named Habbo Fokenna, and our team had a whistleblower report that he had sent an email to the parties in the case expressing concern about the prosecution's actions and their impact on the sale value of the company.

This would be a corroboration from no less an authority than the governmental watchdog in the case that the loss had been caused—and *knowingly* caused—by the actions of the prosecution, contrary to the testimony they had put on the stand during the sentencing and contrary to the judge's finding.

Although Mr. Fokenna had already retired, Gary and Steve reached out to him to request a copy of this email. He remembered the communication in question, but he no longer had the records we needed. They had tried every other way to find the email, without success. Now that the case in bankruptcy court had been settled, they were able to talk directly with the court-appointed trustee, who would surely have it. He would also be able to shed light on some of the areas we knew were questionable, and he might be able to tell us things we didn't even know that we didn't know.

The meeting was held in Los Angeles and our team was represented by Gary and Steve. Gary asked the trustee to start by telling him "the story of Agriprocessors"—which he did, over the course of the next five hours. Close to the start of this marathon story, he mentioned that, because of the possibility of criminal charges being leveled against the company, he had hired a law firm to advise him on that issue. They had only been involved for the first four or five weeks, and were little more than a footnote.

Toward the end of the meeting, five hours later, they got to the question of this email. The trustee also remembered it and, regretfully, he said that he also didn't have it. In a leap of logic and feat of memory that he attributes only to Hashem's guiding hand, Gary interjected, "Is it possible that the law firm might have it? The one you mentioned at the start of the story that you hired to advise on criminal matters?"

He didn't know for certain, but he willingly shared their contact information and reached out to them and gave them permission to cooperate with my lawyers.

"No," the other lawyers told them when they finally met, "we don't have that email, but when we checked our archives, we found some correspondence between the bank and the prosecutors. Would that be of interest?" It turned out to be of *significant* interest—it was the important half of a correspondence between the prosecutors and the bank, and its existence had been hidden from our lawyers. They hadn't even known to look for it.

In the documents that the prosecutors turned over to the defense, as they were legally required to do, they had included a message they'd sent to the bank informing them of their decision to reserve the right to initiate forfeiture proceedings should a potential buyer involve any Rubashkins in any capacity, including consulting. As far as this officially submitted record went, the correspondence ended there.

Omitted from the record, and now discovered by *hashgachah pratis*, was the bank's response, sent the very next day. In it, the bank's representative pointed out the harm this would do to efforts to sell the company, practically begging them to rethink this decision and avoid hurting the bank.

By hiding this response, the prosecutors had created the impression that the bank had no issue with their forfeiture decision. This made our insistence that it had caused the bank's loss look ridiculous. At the sentencing hearing, the prosecutors had even gone so far as to claim that no one had any issue with their threat of forfeiture.

The truth, as we now discovered, was that the bank had clearly communicated to the prosecutors that their actions would cause them financial loss—a support for our arguments from a most reliable source and a strong repudiation of the prosecutors' claims.

These were the first strong tremors of the earthquake we needed. This newest revelation showed that the prosecution violated my constitutional right to a fair trial by withholding evidence.

Then, almost as an afterthought, the lawyer who shared this email mentioned that he also had notes from some meetings with the prosecutors, if my lawyers wanted to take a look. When they looked through the notes, my lawyers were overjoyed. The notes were indisputable corroboration of everything we'd been saying from no less than the government's star witness. It was also a devastating indictment of the prosecutors.

This was the earthquake we needed! It didn't just reshape the landscape—it absolutely disintegrated the ground on which the whole travesty had been built.

The notes were a shorthand transcription of a meeting in the end of 2008 between the prosecutors and the trustee. The trustee was accompanied by his lawyers, one of whom was later the government's star witness on whose credibility the judge had absolved the government of any role in the loss.

At the sentencing hearing, they'd flat-out denied, through their witness, that any "no Rubashkins" policy had been applied, but the notes told a different story. At the meeting the notes transcribed, the Assistant US Attorney had explicitly and forcefully communicated exactly that policy: Any buyer of the plant would be prohibited from involving any Rubashkin, in any capacity. "No Rubashkins is very important to us—non-negotiable," the meeting notes quoted him as saying. "The problem," he went on, "is we don't have a seat at the table."

"We're going to set one up for you," the lawyer who would later be the star witness reassured him. "Are there any other non-negotiables?"

"No Rubashkin involvement from any standpoint," the prosecutor repeated.

The notes documented that the prosecutor was unwilling to rely on the assurances by the trustee's team that Rubashkins would be excluded. Instead, they insisted on claiming a seat in a proceeding that didn't include them by officially asserting a claim of forfeiture and holding that over the head of all potential buyers to ensure their compliance.

The trustee realized immediately the impact this would (and did) have on his ability to do his job and on his duty to the bank. He protested on the spot that this move "would kill off bidders" and "enormously hurt [his] ability to do his job [to maximize the value of Agriprocessors for sale purposes]." His and his team's protests and warnings of the inevitable loss didn't dissuade the prosecutor, and the trustee was instructed to inform all prospective buyers of this threat and how to avoid it.

These same prosecutors would stand in court sixteen months later and put questions to this same lawyer. In response to their questions, she testified under oath that there had been no such ban. She went on to insist that word on the street that there *was* such a ban was no more than "unreliable rumors" which certainly did not diminish the value of the company and create the bank's loss.

The openly miraculous discovery provided black-on-white contemporaneous lawyers' notes, which are accepted in court as evidence, that established without a doubt that not only was the witness lying, the prosecutor who was eliciting these lies *knew* she was lying, because the lie was about their own behavior!

The prosecutors entered that testimony into the record without revealing to the defendant or to the court that they knew it to be false and misleading. Then, they stood back and watched as the court relied on that witness, and presumably went home and celebrated their "victory" in obtaining a twenty-seven-year sentence on the strength of what they knew to be perjury about their own misconduct.

This was a clear and serious violation of my constitutional rights and of their duty as law enforcement officials. It was a textbook case of violation of the Fourteenth Amendment's right to due process both by what they call a *Brady* violation—in which prosecutors withhold evidence favorable to the defendant or damaging to the credibility of a witness—and also a *Napue* violation—in which prosecutors knowingly use false testimony.

It all added up to a very clear and compelling case of prosecutorial malfeasance.

If a motion laying all this out was filed and publicized, it would be a terrible embarrassment to the Department of Justice, in an entirely different league than what we'd known when the new US Attorney had been approached the first time, just over a year earlier. In light of these developments, the lawyers wanted to try negotiating one more time before they filed the motion. They thought that now the DOJ would surely be eager to avoid the embarrassment and would be open to a quick, negotiated resolution which would see me home without a lengthy and costly court battle.

Gary was sure that this was my ticket home, but when he explained that I would have to sign a non-disclosure agreement prohibiting any public discussion of what had happened, I didn't want to go along with it. The *chillul Hashem* they had caused would only be reversed if the story was told and the world saw through their facade. It also felt wrong to let them slink away without consequences or at least a public accounting after the suffering they had caused me and my family. Gary was having none of it. "I'll walk all the way from California to make you sign, if I have to!" he insisted. "I want to get you out of that gehinnom without delay. I'll take it on my shoulders." In the face of his insistence, I acquiesced.

Because of the nature of this offer, they didn't inform and enlist the long list of supporters in the legal community and academia, but the shocking revelations spoke for themselves. Steve Locher and Mathew McDermott met with the US Attorney and laid it all out for him.

The experts on our team were so confident that the discovery of this disgraceful behavior on the part of the prosecutors would finally spur the US Attorney to do the right thing, but after taking a few days to consider, he simply declined the offer to settle the matter out of court. Yet another roller coaster of encouragement followed by disappointment, yet another reminder: *Al tivtichu b'nidivim.* Even if it looks like there are natural reasons to take heart, place your trust only in Hashem.

Sometime during this protracted process, Gary Apfel was called to a meeting by his firm. They had granted permission for him to take on my case *pro bono*, and one of their other senior partners, Michael Schwartz, had also given of his time and expertise for free and helped tremendously, but it had been a year and a half and they wanted him back at work. That's eighteen months that Gary had put his career on hold to help a fellow Jew, well beyond the call of duty, but Gary wasn't finished.

Instead of accepting their decision, Gary negotiated an arrangement with them in which he resigned from the partnership to continue working on my case, staying on with them as outside special counsel. They accepted his offer. There are no words to properly describe such *ahavas Yisrael* and *mesiras nefesh*.

Forced to do it the long way, we moved forward with the 2255 Motion, laying out all the facts in our Merits Brief. In January of 2016, the judge finally ruled on our request that she recuse herself—denying it, of course—and setting a deadline of sixty days for the motion to be filed. The team filed a powerful brief, conclusively proving that I had been incarcerated in violation of my constitutional rights.

It was now undeniable that everyone involved knew the forfeiture threats would cause, and did cause, a loss to the bank. The notes from the meeting showed that the trustee knew and protested. The email from the bank showed that the bank knew and protested. In both cases, they had protested to the prosecutors, which meant that they knew the true impact of their actions, having heard from such important and knowledgeable sources as the court-appointed trustee and the bank in question.

Despite all of this, the prosecutors had purposely proceeded, against the will and the interests of the bank, to threaten every potential buyer with forfeiture.

To make things worse, the prosecutors had no legal authority to actually make the forfeiture they threatened, something we also pointed out in the brief. Their right to forfeit only covers property of the defendant and only assets which come from proceeds of a crime or which facilitated a crime. They had no right to take, as they threatened, "all corporate stock of Agriprocessors," essentially the company itself, which belonged to my father and not me, nor did that cover the product trademarks, which had nothing to do with the financial charges that they convicted me on.

The legal soundness of their claim didn't matter, because it was only a threat that they used to achieve something they knew was outside their legal powers. The notes quoted the Assistant US Attorney laying out very clearly why they needed to assert forfeiture—because without it, they had no way of controlling who bought the company. "[W]e don't have a legal leg to stand on," he had told the trustee. "Right now, until we [assert forfeiture as a threat], people are asking us to rely on the bankruptcy process and a promise that 'good faith [purchaser]' means what we need it to mean."

They had no authority to do what they wanted to do, which was to rewrite bankruptcy laws so they could exclude legally eligible buyers, so they used the leverage of (legally faulty) forfeiture to ensure a "seat at the table" at which they had no business sitting.

They had strenuously denied the existence of this effort, claiming that they were only preventing Rubashkins from surreptitiously repurchasing the company. The avalanche of affidavits from potential buyers,[7] testimony from the trustee himself, and even emails from the prosecutors, showed that this was a lie. They repeatedly refused to allow Rubashkins to help manage or even consult for the new owners.

"That would kill off bidders," the lawyer taking the notes had objected, and it had.

The trustee had said, "People are scared of you guys," and, as affidavit after affidavit testified under penalty of perjury, that fear resulted in fewer and lower offers to buy the company and a very real financial loss to the bank.

And it wasn't just the substance of their assertion of their right to forfeiture. They delivered it as an intimidating threat. As one affidavit put it, "The prosecutor was hostile and threatening."

One offer stood out among those for which we got affidavits—the offer by Soglowek for $40 million. It was an early bid which would have paid back the debt entirely, but the bank and trustee expected more and publicized it as the low bid to start off the auction. It was subsequently withdrawn, and with it went the repayment of the debt.

The prosecutors, bolstered by their star witness, had dismissed the idea that they had scared Soglowek away. The witness falsely testified that Soglowek

---

7. One of the potential buyers was told, under threat of forfeiture, "No one whose last name begins with 'R' could be involved in management," and, "The government would never approve any transaction if the Rubashkins were in any way involved."

A potential bidder testified that his group of investors didn't make a formal offer because they couldn't put together a management team after the prosecutor "forewarned us in no uncertain terms that if he [...] were to discover that any member of the Rubashkin family had either an equity interest or a management role [...] the Department of Justice would pursue this and we would be subject to prosecution."

The highest bidder during the initial auction in 2009 said he was forced to meet with prosecutors during the auction and they basically tried to scare him off: "He told me the business would have to 'start from scratch' and there could be no remnants of any connections to the Rubashkins. He said the US Attorney's Office would be 'watching [me]' and that it would not be easy to get funding or run the business."

had withdrawn their formal offer *before* meeting with the prosecutors. This meant they could not possibly have been to blame, and the bidder had simply lost faith in the business and backed out.

"Not true," said Soglowek himself in his affidavit. The withdrawal had nothing to do with the belief that $40 million was not a reasonable offer. The offer had actually been withdrawn *after* the meeting at which he'd been warned of the consequences if any member of the Rubashkin family had any ownership, management, or consulting role after their acquisition.

An affidavit from a business associate of his actually provided a firsthand account of the aftermath of that meeting. Soglowek had appeared frightened on his return from the meeting, and had immediately called his father in Israel to report back. He'd been deeply concerned about proceeding with the deal, telling his father, "Why do we need problems with the FBI and the American government?!"

The prosecutors knew they'd sabotaged the sale, and actively misled the court into blaming me.

This was also not the only way they'd caused the damage to the company that they attributed to me. We found an email from the bank to the trustee in which the bank said they were withdrawing financing critical to the functioning of the company because discussions with the prosecutors about their forfeiture threats had them worried. The prosecutors were obligated to inform us about those discussions and their impact—which would have strengthened our argument that they, not I, had caused the loss—but they again withheld the information.

Clearly, the court's finding on who was to blame for the loss was based on falsehood. The government's actions had definitely impacted the loss; the only question was by how much. The legal team hired a prestigious company to prepare a report that put it in dollars and cents. The report was written by one of the country's foremost experts in the areas of business valuation, a leading consultant and trainer for numerous Wall Street banks, like Bank of America, JPMorgan, and Citigroup.

The report took into account the bankruptcy and the bookkeeping issues, and concluded that if the company was sold without the prosecutors' interference, the sale would have sufficed to pay the debt entirely. The bank would have sustained *absolutely no loss at all*.

The newfound evidence both definitively discredited the government's key testimony about the loss and established the terrible financial damage caused by the prosecutors. The loss had been attributed to me falsely and in violation of the constitutional protections that ensure a fair and honest trial.

The lawyers still included the *ex parte* communications between the judge and prosecutors in the appeal, but this time, they focused on the prosecutors' violation of my constitutional rights by failing to disclose how extensive these meetings were. This gave the judge a way to rule that we were right without incriminating herself. That this was even a *consideration* shows how inappropriate it was that she was still sitting on this case.

On these and a number of other grounds, the lawyers asked that the sentence be fully overturned. In the event that the court wasn't persuaded by the overwhelming evidence that there had been constitutional violations by the prosecution, there was clearly enough to justify, at minimum, additional hearings where the truth could be discovered under oath.

The explosive revelations and the support of well-respected law professors, former prosecutors, and former judges made a real impact on the public. As those who were protective of the DOJ's reputation had feared, the substance of our motion was reported across the length and breadth of the country. Perhaps sensing the way the wind was blowing, media outlets which had never had a good word to say since the raid, and had followed the prosecution's lead in the tone of their reporting up to that point, suddenly pivoted to neutral and even positive coverage.

The 2255 Merits Brief was filed and the government filed their arguments in opposition, but the team still didn't give up on a negotiated solution. They still hoped they could bring the US Attorney to acknowledge that I was only in a place called prison due to their actions and agree to "time served," allowing me to return home.

He had turned down our offers to keep things quiet, and now that it was all in the open, we were free to reach out to an unprecedented group of former DOJ officials and judges, many who had previously expressed support. These new revelations shocked them all. The effort to gather these honorable signatories was led by Gary, Yaakov Weiss, Zvi Boyarsky, and others at Aleph. No less than 107 former senior Justice Department officials and former federal judges signed a letter to the Iowa US Attorney demanding he take steps to rectify the injustice. Among the signatories were former US Attorneys General, now including John Ashcroft, Michael Mukasey, and Stuart Gerson; former judges; and respected academics in the field of law.

Former Attorney General Mukasey's involvement came about as a result of the selfless efforts of Mr. and Mrs. Binyamin Philipson, a very special couple from Monsey who worked tirelessly to help me. They were also very supportive of my wife and children. They went with my wife to visit the Tosher Rebbe, to receive his *brachos* and his guidance. It was at his urging that they reached out to Mr. Mukasey, who went on to be a *shliach* for great *nissim*.

Others, including a previous Iowa US Attorney, wrote individual, personal letters. Louis Freeh, the former director of the FBI, emailed the Iowa US Attorney directly, insisting that he had "both a personal and professional obligation to rectify" the "severe miscarriage of justice."

Larry Thompson sent a letter echoing the sentiments of Mr. Freeh and adding some of his own thoughts, in very strong and direct language. "The reason Sholom Rubashkin has all this high-level support is because many former Justice officials and others believe he has suffered a great injustice. It is not because he is 'rich,' which I understand some in your office have indicated is the reason for all of this support. I know that Sholom's wife and children rely on charity to survive.

"Quite frankly," he went on, "I find all of this troubling because it is evidence of the stereotyping and bias that we believe has been underlying this case from the very beginning."

They didn't focus all their efforts on this one man. The same efforts and appeals were made to the DOJ at the national level, but efforts to even get a meeting were unsuccessful. Judge Renfrew and Professor Heymann—both former Deputy Attorneys General—bristled when they were turned away by some executive secretary, with the excuse that a meeting on an active case would violate long-standing DOJ policy. They had both been the second-in-command at DOJ in their time and they knew there was no such policy. Quite the contrary, it was part of the role of the central DOJ to keep itself informed on active cases and intervene where necessary.

By contrast, their efforts at meeting with political leaders from both parties were blessed by Hashem with tremendous success. For example, Roza Hindy went with Gary to meet Senator Orrin Hatch of Utah, a senior member on the Senate Judiciary Committee. He was very disturbed by the injustice in my case and he was also moved by my family's plight—especially the impact on Moishie. When the meeting was over, he told Roza Hindy, "Tell your mother I'll do everything to save your father."

The good Senator decided to go straight to the Attorney General at the time,

Loretta Lynch. He'd been a key supporter of hers during the confirmation process and he might have had some influence with her. Personal history aside, he was a member of the Judiciary Committee that oversees the DOJ and he was the second-highest-ranking official in the Senate.

Even *he* was denied the bare minimum of a meeting on the topic. He was very upset about the case and their unwillingness to even meet to discuss it, and he didn't leave it at that. He sent a strongly worded letter to the DOJ, writing that he was troubled by the case and urging "personal and careful attention to this matter" and requesting to be kept apprised of the steps taken to investigate it.

Sometime after the start of the Trump administration, which began half a year later, he even personally delivered a letter and a handwritten note to President Trump, laying out the injustice in my case and how much it meant to him personally, urging that it be corrected by presidential action. President Trump didn't hand the letter off to an aide. Instead, he put it into his own pocket and said, "I know this is important to you. I'll look at this more closely a little later."

Efforts in support of presidential clemency had been made alongside the legal and political efforts since the very beginning and they had intensified in the final two years of the Obama administration. Every outrageous action and argument by the prosecution, every dismissive and senseless decision by the courts, and every shocking discovery by the *askanim* gave our team more ammunition in their push to obtain a pardon or commutation.

Nothing came of their efforts during the Obama administration. In 2016, President Trump won election in a miraculous victory which stunned all the experts. Even before he was sworn in, the *askanim* began forging connections and making the case for clemency to anyone who would listen. Former Attorney General Michael Mukasey even sent a letter urging action on my behalf.

Presidential clemency is very rarely granted and most cases have no hope of even being considered. In terms of creating a *sibah*, if legal proceedings are the equivalent of working a day job, efforts to obtain clemency are like buying a lottery ticket.

Nonetheless, the *askanim* were seeing the hand of Hashem in the unprecedented support from the legal and political world. *Lev melachim v'sarim b'yad Hashem*—"The hearts of kings and ministers are in the hands of Hashem." Seeing that Hashem was opening up their hearts pushed the *askanim* to engage in this additional *sibah*, despite the slim chances it offered *al pi teva*.

To create a climate conducive to such an action by the President and remove as many obstacles as they could, Yaakov and Roza Hindy Weiss, along with the *askanim*, continued to meet with political leaders and respected legal experts, adding to the ranks of the supporters, building and increasing the volume of public support. Op-eds were published in prestigious papers criticizing the conduct of the prosecutors and the failure of the courts to rectify the injustice.

Hashem sent many messengers to further the efforts toward presidential clemency. One of these was Professor Alan Dershowitz, who had already helped privately in consultation and publicly as a signatory on some of the letters. At the end of a meeting at the White House to advise the President on policies related to Israel, the President asked him if there were any other issues he would like to raise. "Yes, Mr. President," he responded. "I'd like to discuss the case of a man named Sholom Rubashkin."

The President had actually already heard of my case, but he wanted Professor Dershowitz's take on it. Once the President had heard him out, he turned to his Chief of Staff and said, "John, please look into the particulars of this and keep me apprised. I think we should do something here."

It had been none other than Jared Kushner who had previously brought the case to the President's attention. Hashem had guided us to Jared six long years before, when no one could have imagined the position in which he would one day find himself.

Like Mordechai and Esther so long ago, *hashgachah pratis* had brought them close to the throne where they could intercede on my behalf, and they did so with tremendous self-sacrifice. To this day I'm not privy to everything they did for me, but I do know that both Jared and Ivanka spoke to the President multiple times about my case.

The White House reopened the clemency application that had been rejected by the Obama administration and this began an ongoing correspondence between those working for my release and the White House staff.

Without taking any money for their help, Professor Dershowitz served as a conduit to the President and his staff, and former Attorney General Michael Mukasey was in regular contact with the White House Counsel's office addressing whatever issues they raised. Their actions and the overall strategy and effort to secure clemency was coordinated by Gary Apfel, who also communicated directly with the White House Counsel's office and the White House staff.

They were assisted in their efforts by many people, including Dr. Daniel Feuer and Congressman Mark Meadows.

Amidst these efforts to create another conduit through which Hashem's *brachah* might flow, Hashem showed us clearly which of our actions were the true *hishtadlus*—our commitment to Hashem and His Torah and mitzvos.

Our efforts faced stiff opposition from high within the White House staff. One of the claims they wanted to use to dissuade the President from granting clemency was related to the immigration charges that had been leveled against me. Since opposing illegal immigration was a key issue for President Trump and I'd been accused of employing illegal immigrants, they argued that the President should not step in to help me.

Alan Dershowitz found out about this and brought it to Gary's attention. It was a big problem. Even if the President was inclined to help me, he would not want to give his opponents ammunition to attack him, which they had shown great willingness to do even on the flimsiest grounds.

The charges had never gone to trial and there was no way to show that they were baseless—or there *would* have been no way. *Baruch Hashem*, despite great pressure to plead guilty on "just" one charge to make the whole thing go away, I had insisted that the state child labor case go to trial in order to conclusively rebut this *chillul Hashem*. Little did I know at the time that this *mesiras nefesh* would be such a powerful assistance at such a pivotal stage.

When Gary realized that my exoneration in that case answered the challenge they faced, he gave former Attorney General Mukasey everything he needed to counter the opposition. He was able to show the White House Counsel that I'd been totally exonerated in the state case, which hinged on the same arguments, and this concern was dismissed.

All those involved also saw remarkable instances of open *hashgachah pratis*. As part of preparing the ground for potential clemency, people close to the President wanted to protect the President from political attack. This created another obstacle. They asked our team to solicit political support for such a move. Specifically, they wanted to see support from the Democrat party. This was no easy task. At an earlier stage, efforts to get a meeting with the central

DOJ hinged on getting bi-partisan support and despite every effort, the team couldn't get the Democrat signatory they needed.

Mindful that success is in the hands of Hashem, the team got to work. Yaakov and Roza Hindy reached out to politicians who were supportive of our past efforts and significantly expanded that group. Judge Renfrew, Professor Heymann, former Deputy Attorney General Thompson, and former Attorney General Mukasey were also great help in rallying politicians to support a potential clemency.

In seeking Democrat party support, Gary decided to go straight to the top. He began looking for connections to the House minority leader, Congresswoman Nancy Pelosi. First, Gary tried to find a connection through a *shliach* on the East Coast. That *shliach* had no contacts with the Congresswoman's office himself, but he referred Gary to the *shliach* in Pelosi's home state of California.

Always ready to help a fellow Jew in need, the *shliach* there put him in touch with someone he knew who had the necessary connections. Sadly, the man was unsympathetic and, when he heard why Gary was calling, he just hung up on him.

Undeterred, Gary called the *shliach* back and got contact information for a junior staffer. The staffer heard him out and was moved by the story, but he was too junior to offer anything concrete. He told Gary he'd pass the information along to his superiors and let him know what happened. Eventually, he got back to Gary with the message that, since Mr. Rubashkin is not one of the Congresswoman's constituents, they would regretfully decline to get involved.

Gary, to his credit, knew that his efforts were only a conduit for Hashem's *brachah*, and seeing all avenues cut off didn't discourage him and he maintained his trust in Hashem. Sure enough, shortly thereafter, without any additional *hishtadlus*,[8] he received a call directly from Congresswoman Pelosi's Washington office. It was her Washington counsel and he wanted to know more about the case. He really dug into the information Gary provided and promised an answer in a week or so. The end result was much more than quiet support of presidential clemency. Congresswoman Pelosi wrote a very strongly worded letter urging the President to act. This was a tremendous *brachah*, but there was still stiff opposition to overcome.

Although all of this was certainly encouraging, from the natural perspective,

---

8. Engagement in creating a *sibah*—referred to hereupon simply as "*hishtadlus.*"

there's nothing predictable about presidential clemency. I had been kept informed of the repeated obstacles and setbacks and I knew that this was a delicate, brittle process. Aside from the astronomically low odds of a given application being granted, even when there seems to be interest and everything seems to line up, the moment can pass and nothing can come of it.

There was a moment at the end of the Obama administration when a White House representative asked his contact on our team to get in touch and it seemed like they were going to issue a commutation, but when we got back to them, they said never mind. The moment had passed and the administration left office without doing anything about my case. There was also a strong feeling amongst my supporters that President Trump would grant clemency around Rosh Hashanah, September 2017, but nothing happened. The President was under constant attack and it was not inconceivable that he would decide to play it safe and not get involved.

I had seen enough cycles of encouragement and then disappointment to know that encouraging signs mean nothing. I chose to not even get on that roller coaster and held fast to the steady, true recognition that Hashem is the source of my salvation, be it through the courts or through the White House. The main thing was to trust in Hashem and do what we could to create the means through which His *brachah* could flow.

Motion Denied

Ten months after the 2255 Motion was filed, the judge gave her answer: Denied. After a hundred pages rehashing the history and the arguments of the case and laying out the relevant law, she dropped a bomb. With a flick of the wrist, she waved away every possible objection to the cruel and unjust sentence.

After more than six years of defending a twenty-seven-year sentence as not only reasonable but *magnanimous* by hiding behind the loss-driven Guidelines, the judge waved away the false and misleading testimony that had attributed that loss to me and absolved the US Attorneys of illegally withholding information and knowingly using false testimony—by saying it was…harmless.

How can shifting the blame for a $27 million loss to an innocent party—a loss for which the Sentencing Guidelines recommend twenty-seven years in prison—be harmless, you ask?! Simple. To paraphrase the judge: "I have the authority to arbitrarily pick a sentence which is sufficient but not greater than necessary for the purposes of justice. Even if you convinced me that the government impermissibly increased the loss, I would have still given you the exact same sentence anyway."

See? The perjury about who caused the loss is totally irrelevant because I only used it to defend a decision I could have made *without* justification. No harm done! A finer example of judicial logic has not been seen since the days of Sedom and Amora.

The biggest problem was that, strictly speaking, she was right. She *did* have the authority. It reminded me of an old story from Soviet Russia.

A *rav* was once arrested for officiating at Jewish weddings, managing a *mikvah*, and teaching *aleph-beis* to children—in short, counter-revolutionary activities. Before they carried out the verdict, they took a few minutes for a show trial. He was asked to respond to the charges against him and he responded by telling them a story:

A lion decided one night to have chicken for supper. The poor chicken was brought to him and the lion imperiously pronounced, loud enough for the assembled animals to hear: "Comrade Chicken! You are hereby sentenced to death for the crime of depriving the humans of sleep with your crowing."

"Your majesty," protested the chicken, "the humans benefit greatly from being awakened by my crowing! As a matter of fact, many humans acquire a chicken for that reason alone, so that we can wake them to start their day!"

The lion cleared his throat and tried again. "Comrade Chicken, you are hereby sentenced to death for the crime of thievery, for pecking the crumbs from the floors of the humans' huts."

"But your majesty," protested the chicken, "the humans benefit greatly from my actions! Their discarded crumbs would attract termites and other pests which would damage their homes. I am doing them a service!"

The lion cleared his throat and made one final pronouncement: "Comrade Chicken, you are hereby sentenced to death because I am strong and you are weak!"

Having made his point, the *rav* fell silent. What more was there to say? They had asked him for a response simply to perpetuate the lie of their system, not because anything he said might change the outcome. Reading the judge's ruling, I felt the same way. The United States of America vs. Sholom Rubashkin, as ridiculous a match-up as that is, wasn't even that. They pretended that the whole give-and-take over who was responsible for the loss was even *slightly* relevant only to maintain the illusion. Now that the show was over and no other avenue could be taken, she was ready to just come out and say: "Because I am strong and you are weak."

It's no wonder that people who lack *emunah* and *bitachon* are thoroughly destroyed by these legal decisions. The destruction of the illusion of justice has an explosive effect, psychologically and emotionally. The only thing that saved *me* is that I was *also* maintaining an illusion. Although I was working with lawyers and filing motions in court, I wasn't really trying to get *them* to let me out of a place called prison. I was really relying exclusively on Hashem, Who delivers the strong into the hands of the weak and the many into the hands of the few.

The motion was denied in full. She wrote an extensive—and outrageous—ruling with myriad legal details and technicalities which are not relevant to the purposes of this book and to which I will not subject you.[9]

She not only rejected our motion, she even went so far as to deny us authorization to appeal her decision, called a "Certificate of Appealability." I couldn't believe my ears when I was told that a single judge can rule on such an important question and also deny the ability to challenge the ruling!

We couldn't appeal a 2255 decision without a Certificate of Appealability. It's theoretically possible, although rare, to get one from the Appeals Court themselves, so we did our *hishtadlus*. The lawyers outlined for them the substantial arguments they'd made in the initial motion, showing that my constitutional right to a fair trial had been violated. We laid out the pivotal questions that had been decided based on testimony we could now prove was not only false, but *known* to be false by the prosecutors when they solicited it in court. We addressed all of the judge's legal arguments as well, and sat with our *Tehillims* while we waited for the response from the three-judge panel of the Eighth Circuit.

Six months later, they filed their response—request denied. They would not give me the right to appeal the judge's decision. What they were saying was that the only judge who would consider the question of whether I'd been incarcerated unconstitutionally would be the judge who had issued the

---

9. I'll only mention her ruling that at the 2255 level, a sentencing error is not enough of miscarriage of justice unless the sentence is more than the statutory maximum. Aside from the patent outrageousness of such a claim, even if legally correct, this became strong grounds for an appeal because it contradicts rulings in the Supreme Court and in other Courts of Appeal in other circuits.

original sentence—no review would be allowed! The lawyers explained the legal technicalities that were utilized to deny this review, but no one was able, or ever will be able, to explain why such an outcome is possible in a country that prides itself on a commitment to ethics, fairness, and justice.

There was one last *hishtadlus*, one last legal effort to be made. The initial trial had been lost; the appeal had been rejected at the district, appellate, and Supreme Court level; the constitutional challenge had been rejected at the district level; and the appeal of that rejection blocked at the district and appellate level. The only legal option left was to ask the Eighth Circuit to review the decision of their three colleagues. The other judges could decide to overrule the three-judge panel and allow me to appeal the rejection of the 2255 Motion, after all—either at a new panel of three judges or when all the circuit judges weigh in on the question.

That request was duly filed and I directed my hopes to the True Judge. *From where will my help come? My help will come from Hashem, the Maker of heaven and earth.*

CHAPTER THIRTY-TWO
The Big *Nes*

Aleph Teves

IT WASN'T OBVIOUS AT THE TIME, BUT HASHEM'S SALVATION AND THE END of my long ordeal began on Rosh Chodesh, *aleph* Teves, the seventh day of Chanukah.

It was a Tuesday, which was not a *"minyan* day" in Otisville, so I was *davening* in cell 307. *Davening* in a place called prison always takes effort. In order to *daven* with joy, you need to lift yourself up enough to see through the lie of your surroundings, and an even greater effort is required in order to properly sing Hallel, praising Hashem for His infinite kindness and miracles.

The Ba'al Shem Tov taught that a person is present not where his body happens to be, but where his thoughts and desires are. Standing in my *tallis* and *tefillin*, my thoughts and desires were very firmly in shul, with a *minyan* of *Yidden*. Since the rest of the *minyan* was only in my thoughts and desires, I led the *tefillos*. When I reached Hallel, I made the *brachah* with great joy and sang each part of the Hallel as we sing it in shul.

I finished saying, *"Hodu laHashem ki tov*—Offer praise to Hashem for He is good…" and as I proceeded to *"Min hameitzar karasi Kah*—From the straits I called to Hashem," I heard the counselor call me by name and instruct me to report to his office. I finished Hallel, took off my *tallis* and *tefillin*, and went as instructed.

Legal mail had arrived for me and he'd called me to pick it up and sign for it. I signed the paperwork and he handed me the envelope. It had been sent from the US Appeals Court, Eighth Circuit.

I had an envelope, but I was missing a phone call.

Out in the world of phones and emails, the lawyers were always informed as soon as a ruling was issued. In the past, I had always received a phone call from the lawyers well before the three or four days the mailman took to bring the official notification all the way to Otisville. It seemed odd to me that they hadn't called to explain the ruling and what it meant for our options going forward.

I opened the envelope right there in the office. A very short message was enclosed. The court was advising me that they had denied the last motion filed by my counsel, the request to overrule the panel and authorize our appeal of the judge's rejection of our constitutional challenge. There was no long-winded explanation or justification, just two short declarative sentences: The requested rehearing was denied. A rehearing by a different panel was denied.

I immediately understood the mystery of the missing legal phone call. This had been the last legal opening in the case. The ruling meant that, in legal terms, there was nothing else in the way of *hishtadlus* that could be done. The court had, with finality, dismissed clear evidence of perjury and prosecutorial misconduct, closing the case permanently. The paper said, "Denied," but what it really meant was, "As far as we're concerned, you're going to be in prison for the remainder of your twenty-seven-year sentence—more than eighteen years—and there is nothing you can do about it." My lawyers, led by a precious Yid with a big heart, couldn't bear to break the terrible news, perhaps fearing the emotional and psychological impact it would have.

I understood their concern. During my years in Otisville, I'd seen inmates receive similar news and the reactions were never pretty. They would either explode with rage, throwing things and roaring helplessly at a system deaf to the injustice of their case, or they would implode under the weight of their sorrow, retreating to their cells to drown in their tears or sink into the depths of silent depression.

Some managed to get through the initial emotions enough to try to rejoin the living, and they would make their way to the psych unit and seek professional help from the shrinks. These doctors could not alleviate their torment and usually just prescribed pills to cloud their minds and hearts enough to live with it.

Given all that, it was no wonder that my lawyers—brothers and friends that they'd become—were hesitant to share the news that the system which had put me in a cage had just thrown away the key. They were worried it would break me.

Not only were they wrong, they'd gotten it exactly backwards.

The legal process had been burdensome, filled with trickery, injustice, and false hopes. Nonetheless, it was the way to address my situation through natural means.

The Torah tells us that an opportunity in these matters is an obligation. When Hashem gives you a path forward, it's His way of telling you that it's your job to walk it. I had done so to the best of my abilities, while never forgetting from where my help would truly come. Now, mercifully, the path was closed. Hashem was telling me, "This is not for you to take care of. Place your faith and trust in Me and I will take care of this Myself."

It brought to mind a story of the Aleksander Rebbe. He and his father were staying in a remote cabin for health reasons. One night, he noticed tears falling from his father's eyes and asked him, "Tatteh, why are you crying?" His father explained that he was experiencing terrible pain and he felt that he would not live through the night, that he would pass away and be buried in this remote place, so far from his beloved chassidim and family.

"Tatteh," said the future Aleksander Rebbe, "I swear that you will recover." Reassured by this strong statement from his holy son, his father rested easier. The future Aleksander Rebbe then left the cabin and turned his eyes to the heavens, beseeching Hashem to heal his father. Sure enough, the pain subsided and his father regained his strength.

The next day, the father asked his son, "I appreciate your *emunah* and *bitachon*, but how did you have the certainty and confidence to swear?!"

His son responded simply, "I learned from my Rebbe, the *heilige* Ruzhiner, the meaning of a *pasuk* in *Tehillim*, *Ad anah Hashem tastir panecha...* The *pasuk* is usually translated as three questions: Until when, Hashem, will You ignore me forever? Until when will You hide Your face from me? Until when will I seek my own counsels, grief in my heart all day?

"The Ruzhiner taught me that the first two are questions a person asks when he faces a *tzarah*, but the third 'until when' is actually *the answer*.

"As long as a person has solutions to pursue, he may be left to work through those solutions, but when there are no solutions to pursue, there can be no concealment of Hashem's involvement, no barrier to a miracle. When I saw that we were in such a dire situation in such a remote place, a place with no doctor and no one to turn to, I knew that Hashem Himself would intervene and we would see a miracle."

I found myself in the same situation—which is why, taking my cue from the teaching of the Ruzhiner, I saw this as good news. There was no longer anything to be done. That meant that Hashem Himself would intervene and send a miraculous salvation.

When the time came, I went to the chapel to light the Chanukah menorah. I said the *brachos* and lit all eight candles, then I sang "*Haneiros Halalu.*" The last phrase lifted my spirits and, with *bitachon* in Hashem, I sang the words celebrating the miracles He had done for the Chashmona'im centuries ago, confident that He would also save me from *my tzarah* with great miracles and I would thank Him, "*For Your miracles, for Your wonders, and for Your salvations.*"

Although I had reached the right conclusion, these issues are never really closed for discussion. My *yetzer hara* still had some thoughts on the matter, and he had a standing nightly reservation for an attempted demoralization session after lights-out. Each night, when I closed my eyes, the thoughts would begin. First there were always objective thoughts—straightforward assessments of where things stood and what was the best way to proceed. From the perspective of *emunah* and *bitachon* those are fine, part of our obligation to take part in the natural processes.

Then, stealthily, the demoralizing or dispiriting thoughts were sprinkled in, taking advantage of my insincere acceptance of natural processes to make pessimistic predictions and counsel surrender. If I didn't pay attention, I would easily be dragged down these trails to despair and depression. However, if I *did* pay attention, there was an easy way to identify these thoughts for what they were; if the thought leads down to despair, it's from the *yetzer hara* and needs to be rejected. If it leads up to *bitachon* and *simchah*, follow that thought all the way up.

That night, the *yetzer hara* showed up right on schedule. I'd prepared for these moments and unfortunately had a lot of practice. I reviewed the words of *Sha'ar Habitachon*, which I knew by heart after all this time and practical use. As I went, I translated each concept into terms that explicitly applied to the situation I was facing. It took effort to reassert the reality as explained in Torah—that Hashem's help would come in the blink of an eye and this was not a loss at all. With Hashem's help, I succeeded. I quieted the *yetzer hara*, calmed my mind, and drifted off to sleep.

Beis Teves

I awoke early the next morning, Zos Chanukah, still experiencing the hard-earned clarity of the day before. I thanked Hashem for the news of the day before and looked forward with firm *bitachon* to the salvation I knew would now unfold.

At that time, Wednesday was a *minyan* day. We were, *baruch Hashem*, able to gather in the chapel to *daven*, read the *Krias HaTorah* for Chanukah, and say Hallel with a *minyan*. As I often did, I headed from *davening* to the computer room to read any correspondence that had arrived overnight.

One email that morning was from a very close friend whom I had never met—one of thousands I had heard from over the years. This particular friend was a Yid from England with whom I shared a warm and frequent correspondence. He would send emails full of encouraging words of *chizuk*, *divrei Torah*, and stories, along with his personal *brachos* and *tefillos* that Hashem would free me very soon.

About a week before Chanukah, he had sent me a long email with a *geshmake dvar Torah* of the Vilna Gaon along with a *brachah* that, "*Bayamim haheim, b'zman hazeh*," Hashem should perform the miracle I needed and free me in these days of Chanukah, just as Hashem had performed miracles for the Chashmona'im. This letter, so full of love, Jewish faith, and words of Torah and encouragement, refreshed and reinvigorated me, as these letters always did.

His latest email, which I received in the pre-noon hours of Zos Chanukah, had been sent after Yom Tov had already concluded in England. In his email, this precious Yid consoled me that although Chanukah had come and gone without my miracle, I should not lose heart and instead know that Hashem will make a *nes* for me and free me very soon.

Here's the email, dated Tuesday, December 19, 2017:

Dear Sholom,

I always write to you on Chanukah. This year I wrote eight days before Chanukah, as I explained in the letter, but I cannot allow traditions to fall away so I must write at least a short note to mark Zos.

My eight lights have just gone out and we are in darkness again, but very soon, long long long before next Chanukah, there should be a brilliant light in the world when justice is done [...] and Sholom can go home to his family.

Kol tuv,

Don

I wrote back. Chanukah was not yet over in New York and *b'ezras Hashem*, we would yet see Hashem's miracles:

B"H

Tayere Reb Don *sheyichye* :)

Happy Zos Chanukah :) Even though your eight lights have gone out physically, the illumination of Chanukah will be with you and me and the whole Klal Yisrael for the whole year :) *Kedushah* is a *nitzchi*[1] :) and it's the Chanukah lights which will bring the brilliant light you are talking about :) Thank you for your updated Chanukah message for this year and *b'ezras Hashem*, we will see great miracles from *Hashem Yisbarach* and I will be freed to *farbreng* with you whenever we want and face to face :)

May Hashem give you all His *brachos* and *hatzlachah* in everything you do :)

Sholom Mordechai Halevi ben Rifka *sheyichye* :)

Leaving the computer and turning to my handwritten correspondence, I decided to respond to a class from Vizhnitz Talmud Torah and their *rebbi*, Rabbi Nitzlich. The children had all written warm letters with words of *chizuk*, encouraging me to be strong in my *emunah* and *bitachon*. One note, written in Yiddish, read:

Reb Sholom Mordechai,

I feel very much for you. Strengthen yourself with *emunah*! Hashem is able to help in the last minute. Don't give up! You can still be freed!

Thank you,

Mechi

I wanted to connect with the purity of these children, so I sat down and wrote a few pages addressed to all of the children in the class. It was almost 2:30 p.m. by the time I finished. I never rushed to post letters early, because the mail wasn't picked up until after 9:30 p.m., but by *hashgachah pratis*, I decided to mail this letter before the 3:30 lock-in.

After dropping off the envelope, I headed back to cell 307 for the 3:30 lock-in and count. The cell was empty.

My cellmate had been complaining of an infection for a few days, but his

---

1. Enduring, eternal.

requests for medical attention had been ignored. The infection worsened to the point that he couldn't sleep at night due to the pain in his leg. I'd insisted that he go to medical sick call that morning, but when I returned to the cell after *davening* for the 10:30 a.m. count, he was still there. He hadn't been admitted to the infirmary.

Seeing the state of his leg, I had approached the officer in charge and told him that my cellmate was in terrible pain from a serious infection in his leg which was not being treated. I explained that he was not strong enough to fight for the medical attention he needed, but it was a life-and-death situation. I recognized the symptoms of a bad infection and I knew it needed immediate attention. The officer agreed to call for help and it seemed like they had finally come and taken him for the medical care he needed.

The lock-in began and the guard made the rounds, locking each cell from the outside with the—sadly familiar—sound of metal sliding on metal, ending with an emphatic thud. I was locked in for the next hour. Or so I thought.

I put the letters I'd been answering on a pile of other letters on the small table and opened my *Tehillim*, beseeching *Hashem Yisbarach*, "Please make the *nes* today, Zos Chanukah, *beis* Teves. *Beis* is for *bitachon* and I have complete *bitachon* that You will free me today!"

After a few *kapitlach*, I checked my watch to ensure that I washed for my meal before *shkiah*, linking Chanukah and its miracles with the rest of the year. I put some matzah and tuna fish on the table, washed my hands, and sat down for a Zos Chanukah *seudah*.

I had barely eaten enough to justify the *brachah* when the door suddenly swung open. It startled me. Cell 307 was quite far down the hallway and the guard unlocking the cells after the count always went from cell to cell in order. There were two other floors and a number of other cells on the third floor before he reached 307. I would always hear the noise of the keys jingling as he worked his way toward me, but this time, clearly, he had come straight to me. I didn't know what to make of it.

I looked up to see who it was and what he wanted. The guard at the door was the one whom I'd nicknamed "Good Shabbos" since he always greeted me with a humorous, "Good Shabbos!" regardless of the day of the week. He was a matter-of-fact sort of person who did his job professionally, without seeking to inflict additional pain or deriving vicious pleasure from his work.

"Rubashkin!" he said. He wasn't making any joking references that day and his demeanor was very stern. "Get out!" He tilted his head in the direction of the door to underline his command.

Being abruptly ejected from the cell with no explanation could have meant any number of things, most of them not good. I asked if this was a shakedown. "I've washed for a meal and it would be best if I didn't leave the room. I'll sit quietly and not interfere," I offered.

"No," he said, "you need to go downstairs and you'll be escorted from there."

My release was never far from my mind or my lips, so I asked, "Where am I going—home?"

He didn't immediately respond. After a pause, he evasively said, "You're changing your location."

I left the cell and began descending the stairs to the open area in the center of the barrack where I was to meet my escort. As I went down the stairs, his words replayed in my mind and I stopped mid-step. "You're changing your location," he had said. Wherever my new location might be, whether it was home or a stay in solitary, I would need my *tallis* and *tefillin*. I dashed back up the stairs and into cell 307 and grabbed my *tallis* bag. Already conspicuously late, I quickly headed back down the stairs. A guard was waiting to escort me.

The guard escorting me also refused to give me any information. We walked past the chow hall and barber "shop" and slowed near the lieutenant's office, where the assistant warden was standing, waiting for us. He fell in step with us and we continued walking, following the guard to the building which housed offices of the executive officers.

The assistant warden was unusually quiet. It was out of character. Only the day before, he'd come into the chapel and chatted with the Jewish inmates for quite a long time. Now he was very quiet. He kept staring at me when he thought I wasn't looking. It was clear that something out of the ordinary was going on, but he wouldn't tell me anything. "You'll be told when we get where we're going," was all he would say.

Where we were going, it turned out, was to one of the executive offices. After I was brought into the office, the warden herself came in. I didn't break the silence, and, for a while, neither did she. We stood silently for a few moments, the warden and assistant warden just looking at me with the most baffled look on their faces. Whatever they were about to say or do, it was obviously not something they did every day. They seemed to not know quite how to proceed.

I remained quiet and calm, telling myself that they would say what they had to say when they were ready.

Finally, the warden broke the silence. "Congratulations, Mr. Rubashkin." Mr. Rubashkin… I hadn't heard that basic title, a simple mark of respect, cross the lips of anyone in authority since I'd left the sentencing in Cedar Rapids, seven and a half years earlier. "The President of the United States of America has granted and signed your clemency petition. You're now a free man. You can go home."

Although they still didn't have the actual clemency decree, President Trump had instructed that I be released "with all due speed" so they had begun the process. The first step was removing me from the prison cell and informing me what had happened, which they had now done.

"*Hodu laShem ki tov ki l'olam chasdo!*" I exclaimed, my heart full and overflowing with gratitude and praise to Hakadosh Baruch Hu for this precious and miraculous gift. I felt so small and insignificant, unworthy of the infinite kindness Hashem was showing me.

As the reality of the moment fully sank in, the events of the last two days replayed in my mind. I marveled at the sequence of events, as clear and obvious a signature of Hashem scrawled across this news as a Yid can hope to see.

Little more than twenty-four hours earlier, I'd been given notice that the US Appeals Court, the highest court to which I had access, speaking for the most powerful nation on earth, had decreed that I would remain in chains for another eighteen years. Those who had been involved in putting me there no doubt celebrated the news of their total and final victory. There was no mistaking it. This *was* total and final victory by the rules of the game that they were playing. Checkmate.

I had taken the news as a Jew must, actively rejecting their claims of control. I knew that my involvement was only required when it was possible. Now that there was nothing to be done and I threw the burden on Hashem alone, it was a certainty, based on *emunah* and *bitachon*, that Hashem Himself would save me—and that is exactly what Hashem did, not twenty-four hours later.

Wonder of wonders, miracle of miracles! As soon as the door was slammed on our efforts and all the *hishtadlus* had ended, that's exactly when Hashem brought my salvation in the most miraculous way, through the President of the United States signing the document to free me. This was a real-life example of everything we had learned. A Yid is not subject to or under the control of nature, if only he rises above it with *emunah* and *bitachon*.

I looked up to see both the warden and her assistant watching me closely. It was important to me that they know that this was a Divine miracle, not a successful political maneuver. "Today is Chanukah," I told them, "and 2,200 years ago, the Jewish People were oppressed by the mighty Greek Empire. G-d loves the Jewish People and miraculously saved them on Chanukah all those years ago. I am Jewish. G-d loves me and miraculously saved me today."

The warden left the room and returned moments later with a copy of the commutation, which she read to me. Seeing the official letterhead and the signature of the President left a big impression on me. *How wondrous are the ways of Hashem and how great are the messengers through which He works!* I marveled to myself. Only one year into his presidency, the President of the United States of America, President Donald J. Trump, political leader of the free world, took the time to think about a Yid who was languishing in a place called prison and took action to set him free, returning him to his family and community.

He certainly deserves all the recognition and credit that a human being can receive for his actions. He had chosen to do this good thing and Hashem had chosen to do this through him, a sign that he is a person worthy of being a *shliach* of the goodness and kindness of Hashem Himself.

The warden interrupted my thoughts. "Who will be picking you up?" she asked.

"My wife," I responded simply. My wife lived about an hour away, in Monsey. She had moved there in order to be as close as possible so she could visit. Now she was close by and could pick me up before anyone else.

The warden's phone rang—it was the secretary with a call from my lawyer, Gary Apfel. She didn't know what the call was about, but a Mr. Apfel was on the phone, under orders from the White House to talk only with the warden. The warden put the phone on speaker, introduced herself, and informed Gary that they had already received the instructions relating to the presidential grant of clemency. "We immediately removed Mr. Rubashkin from his cell and he is standing here in my office. Would you like to speak to him?"

Gary said, "Yes!" She took the phone off speaker and handed me the handset. I had heard Gary's voice over the phone on countless occasions. We had spent hours learning and *davening* together during my legal calls, and, of course, discussing legal matters. This time he sounded very different and I'm sure I did too. His voice electric with excitement and trembling with emotion, he wished me a heartfelt, "Mazel tov!"

We had waited so long to share this call and have this conversation. "Tell my wife she should come pick me up," I told him. "*Baruch Hashem!*"

His happiness, excitement, and gratitude to Hashem was palpable despite the three thousand miles that separated us. "I'll call her the minute I hang up, Sholom!"

I suddenly realized that when "Officer Good Shabbos" had arrived so unexpectedly and literally drove me from the cell, he had done so in such great haste, like our forefathers leaving Mitzrayim, that I'd forgotten to make the proper *brachah acharonah*. Only about half an hour had passed, so I could still *bentch*, but the halachah is clear. I needed to go back to cell 307.

Without hesitation, I informed the warden that before I could leave prison, I needed to go back to the cell. "Why?" she exclaimed. "What for?!"

"I was in the middle of a meal at which I'd eaten bread," I explained. "Jewish Law dictates that I say the blessing after eating in the same place where I ate, returning to the place if necessary."

This might seem like an odd request, given that I'd just been allowed to leave after close to a decade behind bars, but it was specifically this attitude and this type of request that enabled me to survive all those years. From the first day I'd been thrown into the place called prison, I had realized that although it would be tempting to be less meticulous with the mitzvos given my circumstance, that was a temptation I must overcome.

To put it simply, when circumstances prevent a Yid from properly fulfilling a mitzvah, either the Yid will change or the circumstances will. By ensuring that I did not change and continued to keep every mitzvah to the fullest degree, I only left the option for the circumstances to change, allowing me to do the mitzvah and ultimately returning me home to my family.

The certainty of Hashem's presence, love, and involvement in my life—which is the heart of *emunah* and *bitachon*—naturally results in a commitment to fulfilling the mitzvos of Hashem, which are our means of connecting to Him, with the most loving meticulousness.

My stubborn insistence on staying connected to Hashem and keeping all the mitzvos fully and properly was what kept me safe and sane through eight and a half long years, raising me above the pain and limitations of the place called prison. Now, when Hashem was showing His love and miraculously freeing me, *of course* I needed to continue doing the mitzvos to the best of my ability. In this case, that meant going back to the cell one last time.

The warden refused, adamantly. I would not be allowed to return to the barrack. They had gone to great lengths to extract me from the cell at a time when all the inmates were locked down so they would not see me leaving. When a prisoner is released suddenly, the reaction of the other prisoners is intense, and could easily turn violent. Seeing someone else being freed magnifies the pain and bitterness the others feel over their own incarceration, which could lead to them taking out their anger on the personnel and the infrastructure. They're even liable to attack the newly freed prisoner, out of sheer, intense jealousy. There was no way she would allow me to go back.

With no other choice, the halachah is that I could say *Birkas Hamazon* where I was. I asked for water to wash my hands for *mayim acharonim*. They took me into a larger room where there was a water cooler and I took a cup of water, wet my fingertips and lips, and said *Birkas Hamazon*, thanking Hashem for His food that sustained me.

I had washed before Chanukah had ended, intentionally carrying it over into the year, and this was reflected in the *bentching*, during which I could now say, "*Al Hanissim.*" It's hard to describe the feeling of joy and gratitude with which I said the words thanking Hashem for the miracles He performed for our ancestors while I was actually living through a *nes*.

As I *bentched*, my erstwhile jailers sat nearby, completing all the paperwork relinquishing any claim they had to me and gathering my things from cell 307 for me to take home. The assistant warden went off to check on their progress and came back to report that it would take a few hours for them to collect all my things, partly because I had legal papers stored in the counselor's office and he had left for the day.

"Would you like to wait a few hours, or would you like to leave immediately?" he asked, somehow in earnest. I wasn't about to stay in Otisville for a single extra moment, and certainly not for a few meager possessions, and I told him so. He was pleased with my decision, because it meant he wouldn't have to stay overtime waiting along with me.

They brought in a few papers for me to sign. They then found a pair of black pants, a shirt, and a winter coat for me to wear, and I was escorted out of the office area through the hallway tunnel that leads out of prison. Each step I took was one step closer to freedom, and with each one I thanked *Hashem Yisbarach* anew for the *nes* He was performing for me.

I was brought into the front office waiting area, where my wife and children had so often waited to be allowed in to visit me. I was told to sit down and wait for my wife to pick me up. I didn't want to sit idly, so I looked in my *tallis* bag for something to learn and saw my little pocket edition of *Chovos Halevavos, Sha'ar Habitachon*.

I had received this small *sefer* while I was held without bail the first time, denied a basic right simply because I am a Jew, and I took great strength and encouragement from learning from it. So many years ago, when I was miraculously granted bail on *gimmel* Shevat, capping events that took place on *aleph* and *beis*, I'd understood the sign from Hashem. By strengthening my *aleph* and *beis*, my *emunah* and *bitachon*, my faith and trust in Him, I would experience my *gimmel*, my *geulah*, which would come from Him.

To express to my family that our salvation would come in the merit of our *emunah* and *bitachon*, I had often said, "I will walk proudly out of a place called prison holding my *Sha'ar Habitachon*."

Many times over the years, while being transferred from place to place or under certain circumstances in the places themselves, there had been a danger that this *sefer* would be confiscated, and each time Hashem's protective hand shielded it, displaying open Divine Providence.

I didn't have the forewarning or presence of mind to intentionally fulfill my prediction from all those years ago, but Hashem had seen to that as well. That morning, while reorganizing my locker, I had taken that specific *sefer* out and absentmindedly placed it into my *tallis* bag—unknowingly assuring that when I grabbed my *tallis* bag on the way out, I was fulfilling my words. That night, I walked out of the place called prison with my precious *Sha'ar Habitachon* in my hand.

I'd been sitting there for a while when a van pulled into the prison parking lot. I assumed it was the one my wife was driving so I stood up and approached the window, but it wasn't my wife. A few *Yidden* got out of the van, smiling from ear to ear and calling out, "*Baruch Hashem! Baruch Hashem!* Mazel tov!!" I found out later that these precious Jews were from the nearby community in Bloomingburg and they had rushed over to share their joy and gratitude to Hashem for making this great *nes* for me.

When the guards realized this was not the car picking me up and was instead just a well-wisher, they leapt into action, running out to the parking lot and driving the *Yidden* off with fierce shouting. Intent on preventing any *Yidden* from coming and greeting me, they called for reinforcements to stand in the parking lot and chase the Jews away.

I knew many of the guards only too well, and I knew which ones were anti-Semites who disguised their hatred in the regulations they were enforcing. Now, watching them chasing the *Yidden* away, I could see which guards were doing it to avoid a potential situation and a media circus, and which guards just enjoyed chasing *Yidden*. They were the ones yelling at these well-meaning people, threatening them with arrest and the like, instead of simply but firmly explaining that the parking lot was closed and not to be used that night—as is their approach when someone oversteps during a visit.

It was an ugly sight, and I turned away from the window so I wouldn't have to watch helplessly as they menaced my dear brothers. One of the guards in the room with me, hoping to defuse the situation, told me to sit near the back of the room where I would not be visible from the parking lot.

More time passed, and I began to wonder what was taking my wife so long to arrive. Having finally been released, I was impatient to leave that place behind forever. Before I had a chance to get too worked up about it, I caught myself. Here I was, getting impatient after waiting half an hour, when she had been patiently waiting for me for close to nine years! I was struck by the foolishness of the self-engrossed perspective that comes so naturally to us, where we notice only our own discomfort and overlook the greater discomfort and even pain of others, even of our spouse. I shook my head and laughed at myself, settling down to wait patiently for her arrival.

It was the end of the day, and a number of guards and officers were ending their shifts. One of them, a man relatively high in the hierarchy, stopped long enough to say, "Now that you're on the other side, I want to wish you mazel tov and happy Chanukah!"

I was struck by his preface. This moment was the first expression of humanity and empathy I had seen from this man, and he was explaining why: I was now on the other side. Society in general, and the prison staff in particular (with notable exceptions) don't see people in prison as human beings.

They're wearing khaki, which means they've violated some legal regulation. That, all on its own, means they've lost their humanity and they're no longer worthy of empathy. Their pain is not worth acknowledging and their achievements or victories not worth celebrating. It was only this moment, which gave me back my civilian clothes and brought me to the "other side," that brought me back to humanity, a person whose victory was worth celebrating.

To this guy's credit, at least he was able to reclassify me back into the family of humanity once I was freed. How many people issue a life sentence of ostracism on all levels to others who'd made an error in judgment, were ignorant of applicable regulations, or worst of all, were victims of unjust prosecution or conviction?

Gimmel Teves

Finally the moment came, the moment I had awaited for so long, clinging to my trust in Hashem. My wife came into the room—not to visit me as she had so many times before, but to pick me up and take me home!

She was carrying a hat box and my clothes. All those years, she had kept them in the trunk of her car so that when Hashem's salvation came, she wouldn't have to stop at home to pick them up. The day had finally come, and her trust had been rewarded. That day, she'd been in Brooklyn to speak at a *tefillah* assembly held by a girls elementary school. She had been on her way home, driving back to Monsey, when she received the call to come pick me up and she'd been able to drive straight over without taking the thirty-minute detour home to get my clothes.

I rushed into the washroom to put on the shirt, *kapote*, and hat. After eight and a half years in prison clothes, just putting on my *Yiddishe* clothing felt like coming home.

The guards watched slack-jawed as we walked together out the door of a place called prison, smiling and laughing. Our hearts were filled with gratitude and praise to *Hashem Yisbarach*, and we thanked Him with every step we took toward the family car which had never before held our entire family. I sat down in the passenger seat and fumbled with the seat belt. It had been a long time.

As we drove down the mountain on Two Mile Drive, we couldn't stop thanking Hashem for this great *nes*. We were each excitedly sharing our experience of the *nes* with each other—she was telling me how she found out that I was freed and where she was when she heard, and I was telling her all about the roller coaster of my last twenty-four hours in the place called prison.

As our car reached the bottom of the mountain, I noticed some seven vans parked on the side of the road. Seeing our van, the doors slid open and a dozen *Yidden* jumped out and ran over with excitement. Their love and joy were palpable. I didn't recognize any of them, but each and every one was greeting me as they would greet an only brother whom they hadn't seen in years. My heart filled with love and appreciation for these precious *Yidden* and their true *ahavas Yisrael* and for Hashem Who made us all part of such a special nation.

They wanted to dance right there, in middle of the road. I suggested that we get out of the street and pull into the gas station across the street, so we could dance in celebration and thanks to Hashem without interruption, which we did.

When we stopped to catch our breath, they invited me to come to their community in nearby Bloomingburg to eat something, use the *mikvah*, and *daven* Ma'ariv. I thanked them from the bottom of my heart, but explained that I had long ago resolved that, when my miracle happened, I would head straight to 770 to thank Hashem.

While we were speaking, another van pulled up and my son Yossi and son-in-law Yehuda jumped out. They ran over to me and we embraced and thanked Hashem together. They had brought along my son Moishie. He came out of the car and walked over, but this development was too big and too sudden for him to process. It was heart-wrenching to see him struggling to digest what was happening, not allowing himself to believe and accept that Tatty was finally coming home to stay.

Later in the evening, when he finally processed what had happened, his face lit up. He didn't stop smiling for the rest of the night, every once in a while bursting out in a happy laugh of celebration to himself, basking in the good news and the family's rejoicing.

We got back in the van and made our way south. My other children who lived in the region had all headed upstate when they heard the news, but we were, *baruch Hashem*, clear of the compound faster than they could make it there. We didn't want to wait any longer than necessary to be reunited, so we decided to meet up in Monsey and make our way to Brooklyn together from there.

Immediately after receiving the first phone call with the good news, my wife's phone had miraculously died. This gave her some alone time with Hashem as she drove up to Otisville and she had used that time to say Hallel and thank Him for His kindness. Now we had one more stretch of private time with Hashem for the one hour and fifteen minutes it took to drive to Monsey, and we used every moment.

As we neared our quiet, suburban street, we found the streets filled with *Yidden* who had come to congratulate me and celebrate the *nes* in person. Official accounts put the number at 3,500 to 4,000 people. Someone had brought a loudspeaker, and the assembled *Yidden* were dancing and saying *l'chaim* as they waited for my arrival.

I made it to the house with difficulty and addressed the crowd from the front steps, thanking them for their selfless dedication throughout my ordeal. Of course, I took that first opportunity to publicly thank Hashem for the great *nes*, and I pointed out that my salvation had occurred on *aleph, beis, gimmel*. I encouraged those present to place their trust in Hashem and they would surely see their own salvation as we await the final salvation of the *Geulah*.

The crowds of well-wishers waiting by our home in Monsey.

My son Getzel euphorically dancing on the roof of his van.

Rejoicing in Hashem's miracle. It was my first time in our Monsey home.

I had hoped to just stop at home long enough to gather with the family and continue on, but the many who had come were pressing forward, each hoping to have a moment to personally express their congratulations and their joy at the *nes*.

Volunteers came forward to keep things orderly and the house filled with *Yidden*. I stood in the packed kitchen as hundreds of *Yidden* filed by and wished me mazel tov, overflowing with love, joy, and celebration, some of them even reaching in for a hug or a kiss. The press of the crowd was intense but after years in prison, where these *Yidden* were a constant spiritual presence, I reveled in their physical presence. The well-wishers filed out the back of the house and things were moving in orderly fashion. The back porch couldn't support the weight of the masses filing through and collapsed, but, *baruch Hashem*, no one was hurt.

The generous people who run the Monsey Trails bus company offered us the use of one of their coach buses for the trip to Brooklyn. We gratefully accepted, and the family was able to sit together instead of splitting up into separate cars for the drive. I sat in the bus surrounded by my precious children and grandchildren.

The crowd sees us off as we depart for Brooklyn on the coach bus.

The good news had spread far and wide, and spontaneous celebrations were happening all over the world. When I could tear myself away from one of the constant phone calls, someone was always coming over to show me a video of the global outpouring of joy—an office full of *Yidden* dancing in a conference room; a single Jew on a flight dancing near an emergency exit; never-ending circles dancing in yeshivos and shuls in Russia, England, and France; *farbrengens* in Israel—and on and on it went.

The streets outside my father's office in Boro Park had been packed with well-wishers since the news first broke, and the streets outside my parents' home were likewise buzzing. I spoke to my beloved parents by phone and they were taking the hubbub with their characteristic humility. They were grateful for the outpouring of support and celebration, but mostly, they were just waiting to see their son, home at last. It was getting close to midnight and it was clear that, despite my resolution to head straight to 770, the mitzvah of *kibud av v'eim* demanded that I go see them first. A *rav* concurred, and we changed course.

Despite the late hour, there were still throngs of people filling the streets for more than a block around the house—men, women, and children. Official counts put the number at 12,000 *Yidden*. They tried to squeeze to the sides and clear the street itself so the bus could get through, but there were simply too many people. It was only with great difficulty that the bus was able to reach their street corner. We got off the bus and made the rest of the way on foot. Shomrim surrounded us to protect us from the excited crush of the crowds and we slowly made our way to the house.

The bus could not get through the throngs of people and
we walked from the corner to the house.

A solid wall of deafening, welcoming noise hit me as I walked through the familiar doorway. My sisters were waiting just inside, tears streaming from their eyes, and they ushered me into the jam-packed kitchen where my precious mother was waiting. Surrounded by the hubbub, she was sitting quietly by her kitchen table, the table at which she had been saying Tehillim for my freedom for all those years. Her heartfelt *tefillos* had finally been answered, and I walked into her kitchen and embraced her.

Her gratitude to Hashem was palpable and so was her gratitude to her fellow

The masses gathered in celebration of the great *nes*, as seen from my parents' front door.

The packed crowd inside my parents' house.

Jews. The first thing she told me was that throughout my ordeal, she had been constantly stopped on the street by people reassuring her that they were saying Tehillim and giving *tzedakah* in my *zechus*. She then shared her confidence that we would all go from this miraculous salvation to the miraculous salvation of Klal Yisrael with Mashiach. I spent some time with her and then made my way to the dining room, where my father was waiting.

The dining room was more densely packed than the kitchen had been. People were standing on chairs and benches, filling every square inch of the room. Many were part of the extended family, but I noticed others, some of whom had flown from across the country to participate in the celebration. I embraced my father, and turned to celebrate with the people in the room but immediately thought better of it. Thousands had gathered outside and I ought to go outside before I took a few moments with my family.

It wasn't easy getting out to the balcony. Shomrim, who had taken charge of keeping order and security, were a big help, and I eventually made it outside together with my father. A speaker system had been set up outside and the sea of *Yidden* were dancing to joyous music. When I came outside, the music fell silent, replaced with cheers and calls of mazel tov.

Someone passed me a microphone. As Yaakov Avinu had done when he was reunited with his son Yosef, I and all the assembled thanked Hashem by acknowledging His oneness and calling out together, "*Shema Yisrael, Hashem Elokeinu, Hashem echad!*"

With one heart and in one voice we cried out "*Shema Yisrael.*"

Thousands of *Yidden* called out the holy Shema together, filled with emotion. The sudden *nes* that had happened before their eyes inspired everyone to complete trust in Hashem and rejection of the false reality of nature, and all of that was expressed in their *Shema Yisrael*—it was a moment of pure, palpable *kedushah*. Everyone felt, witnessing such a clear expression of Hashem's love for His children, that Mashiach would come at any moment.

I spoke for a few minutes, pointing to the great *pirsumei nisa* that was happening. Hashem had shown that when Klal Yisrael comes together to *daven* for their fellow Jew, they will see miracles. If we unite with *ahavas Yisrael*, we can surely merit the *Geulah* we are all awaiting with Mashiach! I *bentched* those assembled with the words of the *Birkas Kohanim* and went back inside. The dancing resumed outside while I took a few moments to celebrate with my father and the many who had packed the house.

Next, we headed to 770. The crowd outside was still immense and the house was also holding many more people than any of its builders could have anticipated. The pressure was so great that the heavy wrought-iron railing on the front steps, which was anchored into the masonry, came loose, and quite a few people fell. By Hashem's kindness, aside from some scrapes and bruises, no one was hurt.

As we drove to Crown Heights, we were notified that the celebrations there, which had started as soon as the news came out some seven hours earlier, were still going full swing. The crowds were enormous and the energy was very high. The police wanted to know when we would arrive and from what direction, and we coordinated the safest way to proceed.

It was almost one in the morning by the time we pulled up to 770 Eastern Parkway. The service lane had been blocked because the large crowds made it impassable, so we stopped on the parkway itself. The bus was immediately swarmed. Getzel jumped out and clambered on top of the bus to command attention. He announced that I hadn't *davened* Ma'ariv yet and asked that the crowd move quickly and smoothly inside to thank Hashem through *davening* and afterwards, we would dance and celebrate together.

This helped, and instead of pushing through the crowd as we had in Boro Park, we were swept inside by the stream of celebrants. As I made my way down the steps and entered those familiar doors, I was overcome by a feeling of warmth and peace. The atmosphere around me was intense and electric, but in my heart, I felt a feeling of tranquility. I was home.

We were pushed to the front of the shul and we began a festive Ma'ariv. I was *zocheh* to be the *chazzan*. Hours earlier, the main *minyan* had sung the *tefillos* to the joyous tunes usually sung on Simchas Torah and we followed suit. After Ma'ariv, someone pushed a microphone into my hands. Full of emotion, I called out, "Sholom Mordechai is home! Sholom Mordechai is home! The *simchah* is great!" I made the *brachah*, *Matir Assurim*, blessing He who frees the imprisoned.

I had long ago prepared a *ma'amar* that I would repeat at the celebration of my miraculous release, which I always trusted that Hashem would grant at any moment. I took this opportunity to share a small part of it after Ma'ariv.

Now we were ready to dance! Looking up, I noticed that the musicians playing the joyous celebration music were the same musicians who had come

so many times to bring the joy of Yom Tov to the *Yidden* in Otisville. I waved to them and they smiled, unwilling to take their hands off their instruments and pause the music they had waited and hoped to play for so long.

The joy was intense. *Yidden* of every kind had converged on 770 and, despite the late hour, the dancing was full of energy and spirit. After about an hour, I realized that I had a promise to keep. My cousin, Sholom Duchman, had visited me many times over the years and one of the things we had discussed was his daughter, who needed a *shidduch*. These conversations had always ended with my heartfelt *brachos* and a promise that I would be by the engagement party. Believe it or not, she had become engaged a few days earlier, and her engagement was being celebrated that very night. I slipped out of 770 and went to fulfill my promise. Then I returned to 770 and rejoined the dancing.

We were still going strong when the clock hit three in the morning. My brother Moishie suggested that we go to the Ohel. We tore ourselves away from the celebration and boarded the bus to the Ohel.

It's customary to go to the *mikvah* before visiting the Ohel, so when we arrived in Queens, that was our first stop. It was my first opportunity to go to a proper *mikvah* in many years, and I left feeling purified and uplifted. I wrote a *pan* and entered the Ohel to express my deep gratitude and thanks to Hashem. As we waited for everyone to regroup in the tent near the Ohel, we broke into a spontaneous

Davening at the Ohel of the Lubavitcher Rebbe.

dance. The candles that had been lit during the day of Zos Chanukah were still burning, and we danced in their light to that last unending loop of joy at the end of "*Haneiros Halalu*"—*Al nisecha, v'al nifli'osecha v'al yeshu'asecha.* The menorah is lit in order to offer thanks and praise to Hashem's great Name for His miracles, for His wonders and for His salvations, and we danced in those early hours of the morning for the same reason.

It was close to seven in the morning by the time we made it back to Crown Heights. We made our way to the home of my brother Yossi, where I was going to stay while I was in Crown Heights. I put on my *tefillin* and said *Krias Shema* with the sunrise, as I had done in a place called prison, and lay down for some much-needed rest.

The very next day, or, more accurately, later that same day, would be the Thursday morning *Krias HaTorah*. I woke up two hours later and rushed to 770 to receive an *aliyah* and make *Birkas Hagomel*, thanking Hashem as halachah dictates. Many *Yidden* joined the *minyan* that morning especially to hear that *brachah* and *daven* together with me in thanks and praise to Hashem.

There were some formalities related to my release and ongoing probation which had to be handled, but the rest of the day was spent in praise of Hashem and celebration of His great *nes*. As the day drew to a close, we made our way back to Monsey—home. That night, I went to Ma'ariv in shul, like every other regular Yid. I stood and *davened* in shul with my son Uziel at my side for the first time in his life.

The days, weeks, and months that followed were full of both ecstatic celebrations and quiet moments of normalcy. I took time to visit the various communities which had played such a critical role in the miracle of my return home to my family. I was greeted warmly by the *admorim* and *roshei yeshivah* and expressed our heartfelt gratitude to them.

In those first weeks, I had the *zechus* to meet and thank many *admorim* and *gedolim* of Klal Yisrael and their *kehillos*. The *achdus* that Klal Yisrael had shown throughout my ordeal was on full display. I visited the *admorim* of Skver, Satmar, Bobov, Munkatch, Karlsburg, Skulen, Rachmastrivka, Gur, Belz, Boyan, Stutchin, Sanz-Klausenburg, Pupa, Forshay, Kopyczynitz, Toldos Aharon, Toldos Avraham Yitzchak, Sadigura, Slonim, Aleksander, Tzelem, Karole, Lelov, Sanz, Zvil, Novominsk, Rav Chaim Kanievsky, Rav Malkiel Kotler, Rav Yerucham Olshin, Rav Dovid Tzvi Schustal, Chief Rabbi Yitzchak Yosef, Rav Yisroel Meir Lau, Rav Shimon Baadani, Rav Dov Landa, Rav Berel Povarsky, Rav Yaakov Bender, Rav Eliyohu Brudny, Rav Dovid

Abuchatzeira, Rav Elimelech Biderman, Rav Shimon Galai, Rav Uri Zohar, Rav Yosef Chevroni, Rav Gershon Edelstein, Rav Tuvia Weiss, Rav Moshe Sternbuch, Rav Chaim Menashe Friedman, and others.

Even political figures in Eretz Yisrael wanted to use the opportunity to thank Hashem for His miracles and I met a few while I was there, including MK Meir Eichler, MK Uri Maklev, Mayor Moshe Leon of Yerushalayim, outgoing Bnei Brak Mayor Chanoch Zeibert, and incoming Mayor Avrohom Rubinstein.

I visited schools and shuls, trying to spend a few moments with whoever wanted to speak to me. This gave me the opportunity to meet many of my pen-pals, the precious children with whom I had exchanged so many letters full of Torah and *ahavas Yisrael*.

We all face challenges in our lives and the Torah teaches us how to rise to these challenges and how to *grow* from these challenges. I believe that a strong, widespread desire to know and internalize these Torah teachings were a big reason why my situation caught and held the attention of so many.

It was a common theme in all my correspondence from the very beginning, and these celebrations were no different. My message was always one of gratitude and praise to Hashem for His miracles, but also addressing how we could all strengthen our *emunah* and *bitachon* in order to see the *geulah* in whatever challenge we each face; *aleph, beis, gimmel*.

As time went on, the celebrations drew to a close, but the need for *Geulah* and the need to strengthen *emunah* and *bitachon* did not. I continued to travel wherever I was invited to talk, teach, and *farbreng* about *emunah* and *bitachon* and making them a reality in our lives. In the first year following my miraculous release, with Hashem's help, I was able to reach, in person, more than 100,000 people at over 500 different events.

Long ago, I had suspended my dreams of teaching in order to follow the very different path Hashem had set me on. It has been quite a journey, but Hashem has now put me in a position to return to my earlier ambition and focus full time on teaching Torah and *avodas Hashem*.

In the years since my release and in the time to come, until the coming of Mashiach, I have dedicated myself to sharing my story and the many lessons I've learned, helping *Yidden* discover and strengthen their *emunah* and *bitachon* and meriting Hashem's promise—their own personal *geulah* and our national *Geulah* with Mashiach Tzidkeinu, may it happen right now.

Meeting the Skulener Rebbe after my miraculous release. The joy was so great that the Rebbe spontaneously began dancing.

Meeting the Novominsker Rebbe, who had done so much on my behalf, and thanking Hashem together.

Celebrating with the Karlsburger Rav.

A special evening of appreciation was held for some of the prestigious supporters. Left to right: Rabbi Pinchos Lipschutz, me, former Attorney General Michael Mukasey, former Deputy Attorney General Larry Thompson, my lawyer Gary Apfel.

After our meal, we danced together in celebration. Pictured are former Attorney General Michael Mukasey, former Deputy Attorney General Larry Thompson, and my lawyer Gary Apfel.

Outside my home in Monsey that evening with Rabbi Zvi Boyarsky and former Deputy Attorney General Philip Heymann.

Celebrating a family *simchah* together with
my father and brothers—reunited again.

Celebrating with *askanim* from
the Klal Yisrael Fund.

After all the times he came
to bring *simchah* to Otisville,
Avraham Fried brought
simchah to thousands at the
first anniversary celebration.

A rally of thanks to Hashem held in Boro Park on the
first anniversary of my miraculous release.

Tzaddikim and *geonim*, leaders of many *kehillos* and *chatzeiros* of Klal Yisrael, thank Hashem for the great Zos Chanukah *nes*.

Many of them expressed a hope that a book would be written to publicize the story as an act of *pirsumei nisa* and *kiddush Hashem*. This is not a comprehensive compilation, since a picture could not always be taken.

Rav Dovid Abuchatzeira

Rebbe of Aleksander

Chacham Shlomo Amar, Chief
Rabbi of Jerusalem

Chacham Shimon Baadani of
Moetzes Chachmei HaTorah

Rebbe of Belz

Rav Aharon Mordechai Rokeach,
Belzer Rebbe's son (Credit: א.מ.ש.)

Rav Yaakov Bender, Rosh Yeshivah Darchei
Torah (Credit: Col-Itzik Roytman)

Rav Elimelech Biderman

Rebbe of Bobov-45 (Credit: JDN)

Dayan Aharon Dovid Dunner, Ra'avad of
London, and the Tchabe Rav (Credit: JDN)

Rav Gershon Edelstein, Rosh
Yeshivah of Ponovezh

Rebbes of Forshay and Kosson Hillcrest

Mekubal Rav Shimon Galai

Rav Chaim Kanievsky

Rebbe of Kopyczynitz

Rebbe of Kosson

Rav Malkiel Kotler, Rosh Yeshivah
Beis Medrash Govoha

Rabbi Yisroel Meir Lau, former Chief Rabbi
of Israel, and Rav Eliezer Sorotzkin

Rabbi Dovid Lau, Chief Rabbi of Israel

Rebbe of Lelov (Credit: JDN)

Rav Moshe Mordechai Lowy, Rav
of Agudas Yisrael Toronto

Rebbe of Machnovke Belz

Rebbe of Munkatch

Rav Yerucham Olshin, Rosh
Yeshivah Beis Medrash Govoha

Rav Ephraim Padwa, Ga'avad
of London (Credit: JDN)

Rav Berel Povarsky, Rosh
Yeshivah of Ponovezh

Rebbe of Pupa (Credit: JDN)

Rebbe of Rachmastrivka (Credit: Der Blick)

Rebbe of Radzin, Eretz Yisrael (Credit: JDN)

Rebbe of Sadigura *zt"l*

Rebbe of Sanz, Eretz Yisrael

Rebbe of Sanz-Klausenberg
(Credit: Der Blick)

Rebbe of Satmar, Rav Aharon Teitelbaum

Rebbe of Satmar, Rav Zalmen Leib
Teitelbaum (Credit: Der Blick)

Rav Dovid Schustal, Rosh Yeshivah
Beis Medrash Govoha

Rebbe of Skulen *zt"l* (Credit: Der Blick)

Rebbe of Skver (Credit: Der Blick)

Rav Yochanan Wosner,
Skver Dayan, Montreal

Rav Shmuel Eliezer Stern, Rav in Bnei Brak

Rav Moshe Sternbuch,
Ra'avad of Yerushalayim

Rebbe of Toldos Avraham Yitzchak

Rebbe of Toldos Yehuda Stutchin
(Credit: Der Blick)

Tzelemer Rav (Credit: JDN)

Rav Tuvia Weiss, Ga'avad of Yerushalayim

Rav Menachem Meir Weissmandl,
Nitra Dayan, Monsey (Credit: Der Blick)

Rav Chaim Meir Wosner *zt"l*,
Ga'avad of Zichron Meir

Chacham Yitzchak Yosef, Chief Rabbi of Israel

Rav Uri Zohar

Glossary

Y=Yiddish

A"h — abbreviation for *alav hashalom*—peace onto him; referring to a deceased individual

Achdus/achdusdig — unity/unified

Ahavas Yisrael — love for fellow Jews

Akeidah — the event during which Avraham was willing to sacrifice his son Yitzchak

Al netilas yadayim — blessing recited after ritual hand-washing

Al nisecha...v'al yeshu'asecha — upon Your miracles and upon Your salvation

Aleichem shalom — on you should be peace; a response to the greeting, "*shalom aleichem*"

Aleph — the first letter in the Hebrew alphabet

Aleph-beis — the Hebrew alphabet

Am Yisrael — the Nation of Israel

Amen! Yehei Shmei rabah... — Amen! May Your great Name... (part of the Kaddish prayer)

Amud — prayer lectern

Anshei Knesses Hagedolah — the Men of the Great Assembly

Anu ameilim v'heim ameilim... — we work (and get rewarded) and they work (and aren't rewarded); a comparison between those engaged in Torah studies and those engaged in trivial pursuits

Aravos — willow branches, one of the four species shaken on Sukkos

Aron — lit. box; here referring to the *aron kodesh*

Aron kodesh — lit. holy box; closet where Torah scrolls are kept

Asarah Harugei Malchus — ten Torah sages killed by the Roman king

Aseres Hadibros — the Ten Commandments

Askan (pl. askanim) — a Jewish activist

Askanus — activism on behalf of the Jewish community

Av beis din — the leading judge in a Jewish court

Aveilus, R"l — mourning, may G-d save us

Aveirah (pl. aveiros) — sin

Avodah — service

Avodah zarah — idol worship

Avodas Hashem — service of G-d

Avos — the Patriarchs

B'simchah — in a joyous state

Ba'al bitachon — one who is filled with trust in G-d

Ba'alei teshuvah — newcomers to religious observance

Bachur (pl. bachurim) — a young (unmarried) Jewish man

Badchan (Y) — Jewish comedian

Barchu — the opening word of the evening prayer service

Baruch Hashem — thank G-d

Bas Yisrael — Jewish daughter

Bedikas chametz — searching for leavened bread

Beis hora'ah — institution for guidance in Jewish law

Beis midrash — Jewish study hall

Bentch/bentched (Y) — to recite/recited grace after meals; to bless/blessed

Besamim — smelling spices

Bigdei Yom Tov — holiday clothing

Bimah — table used for the reading of the Torah scroll

Birkas Habanim — blessing for the children

Birkas Kohanim — priestly blessing

Bitachon — trust in G-d

Biur chametz — burning of the leavened bread

Brachah (pl. brachos) — blessing

Bris/bris milah — circumcision

Chaburah — group that gathers for Torah learning or other religious activities

Chachmah — wisdom

Chaf-beis — twenty-second

Chaf-hei — twenty-fifth

Chaf-tes — twenty-ninth

Chaf-vav — twenty-sixth

Chalav stam — ordinary milk, i.e. not milked under Jewish observation

Chalav Yisrael — milk that was milked under Jewish observation

Chametz/chametzdig — leavened bread/contaminated with leavened bread

Chas v'shalom — G-d forbid

Chasimah tovah — lit. a good seal; a wish for a good year

Chassan (pl. chassanim) — bridegroom

Chassidus — a distinct group of chassidim; chassidic studies

Chasunah — wedding

Chavrusa (pl. chavrusos) — study partner

Chazal — Talmudic Sages

Chazzan — cantor

Cheder (pl. chadarim) — Jewish boys school

Chein — favor

Cheirus — freedom

Chessed (pl. chassadim) — kind deed

Chillul Hashem — desecration of G-d's honor

Chillul Shabbos — desecration of the Sabbath

Chinuch — Torah education; child-rearing

Chizuk — encouragement

Chodesh — month

Chodesh HaGeulah — Month of the Redemption

Chol — non-holy; weekday

Chukim — Torah commandments for which the reasons are beyond human comprehension

Chuppah — wedding canopy

Churban — destruction (usually in reference to the Holy Temple)

Da'as Torah — opinion of a Torah scholar

Daf Yomi — study of a daily folio of the Talmud

Dalet kosos — four cups of wine at the Pesach Seder

Dalet minim — four species shaken on Sukkos

Daven/davened/davening (Y) — pray/prayed/praying

Dvar Torah (pl. divrei Torah) — a Torah thought

Ehrliche (Y) — honest

Eibeshter (Y) — G-d (lit. the One above)

Eishes chayil — wife of valor

Emunah — faith in G-d

Esrog — citron, one of the four species shaken on Sukkos

Eved Hashem — servant of G-d

Evyon — pauper

frum (Y) — religiously observant

Gabbai — sexton

Galus — exile

Gam zu l'tovah — this too is for the good

Gartel (Y) — belt worn during prayer by Jewish males of certain origins

Geirus — conversion to Judaism

Gelt (Y) — money

Gemachim — establishments that provide goods or services (for free or reduced prices) for the sake of engaging in kindness

Gemilas chessed (pl. gemilas chassadim) — the act of engaging in kindness

Geulah — redemption

Gezeirah (pl. gezeiros) — decree

Gimmel — third; the third letter of the Hebrew alphabet

Goldene medineh (Y) — golden land, a reference to America

Goy — non-Jew

Grammen (Y) — poetry usually recited in a sing-song chant

Gut voch (Y) — a good week

Hachnasas sefer Torah — celebration in honor of a new Torah scroll

Hadassim — myrtle branches, one of the four species shaken on Sukkos

Hadlakas neiros — candle-lighting

Haftorah — a portion of one of the Books of the Prophets read after the Torah reading

Haggadah (pl. Haggados) — book of liturgy recited at the Seder

Hakafah (pl. hakafos) — round of dancing in celebration of the Torah

Halachos — Jewish laws

Hashem yirachem — may G-d have mercy

Hashem Yisbarach — G-d, blessed be He

Hashgachah pratis — Divine Providence

Hashgachos — kosher certifications

Hashkafos — Torah outlook

Hataras Nedarim — a prayer recited before the start of the Jewish New Year in which one nullifies any vows made during the past year

Hechsher — kosher certification

Heilige (Y) — holy

Heter — a halachic dispensation

Hiddur (pl. hiddurim) — enhancement

Hiddur mitzvah — an enhancement in the fulfillment of a Torah commandment

Hishtadlus — efforts (usually in the realm of nature, see Chapter Thirty for an in-depth explanation)

Hisorerus — inspiration

Hodu laHashem — thanks to G-d

Hoshanos — bundle of willow branches

Im yirtzeh Hashem — G-d willing

Imahos — Matriarchs

K'das Moshe v'Yisrael — according to the law of Moses and the Sages of Israel

Ka'arah (pl. ka'aros) — Seder plate

Kabbalas ol — acceptance of a yoke, i.e. subservience

Kabbalas Shabbos — prayer ushering in the Sabbath

Kadosh — holy

Kallah — bride

Kapitel (Y) — chapter

Kapote (Y) — frock

Kapparos — a custom in which a prayer is said while money or an animal is offered in lieu of one's life

Karpas — a vegetable that is dipped into salt water as part of the Seder night ritual

Kashered/kashering — rendered/ rendering meat or utensils kosher

Kavanah — concentration, intent (generally used in regard to praying or performing a Torah commandment)

Kedushah — holiness

Kehillah — congregation; community

Keili — vessel

Kesubah — marital contract

Ketores — incense offered up in the Holy Temple

Kezeisim — a halachic measurement (the size of an olive)

Kibud av — the commandment to honor one's parents, one of the Ten Commandments

Kiddush Hashem — sanctification of G-d's honor

Kiddush Levanah — blessing recited to sanctify the new moon

Kinderlach (Y) — children

Kinos — lamentations recited on Tishah B'Av

Kittel (Y) — a white outer garment worn by men at distinct times such as Seder night and Yom Kippur

Kodesh — holy

Kohen (pl. kohanim) — Jewish priest, descendant of Aaron

Kol Nidrei — opening prayer of the Yom Kippur Eve services

Kollel — institute of learning for married men

Korban Pesach — Passover sacrifice

Kosher l'Pesach — kosher for Passover

Krias HaTorah — reading of the Torah

Krias Shema — recitation of the Shema prayer (in which one affirms one's faith in G-d)

Krias Yam Suf — the splitting of the Red Sea

L'havdil — lit. to differentiate; a term used when mentioning two incomparable entities

L'havdil bein chaim l'chaim — lit. to differentiate between the living (in this world) and the living (in the afterlife); a term used when mentioning both a deceased and a live individual

L'mehadrin min hamehadrin — in its most ideal form

L'shanah haba'ah b'Yerushalayim — next year in Jerusalem—words recited at the end of the Seder

Lechem mishneh — the two challah loaves used at religious meals

Licht bentching/licht tzindin (Y) — candle-lighting

Lichvod Shabbos — in honor of the Sabbath

Lichvod Yom Tov — in honor of the Jewish holiday

Litvish — Jews of Lithuanian descent

Lo aleinu — lit. not upon us; a phrase used when mentioning calamity

Lo sachmod — the prohibition to covet (one of the Ten Commandments)

Lulav — palm branch, one of the four species shaken on Sukkos

Ma'amar Chazal — a proverb of the Sages

Ma'asim tovim — good deeds

Machatzis hashekel — a half coin given in remembrance of the Jews' yearly contribution to the Holy Temple

Macher — hustler

Machlokes — dispute

Machzor (pl. machzorim) — holiday prayer book

Maggid — the recitation of the Passover Haggadah as part of the Seder ritual

Malkos — lashes

Maror — bitter herbs eaten at the Seder

Masechta (pl. masechtos) — Talmudic tractate

Mashal (pl. meshalim) — parable

Mashgichim — individuals tasked with overseeing the kosher status of food being prepared or served

Matanos l'evyonim — monetary gifts to the poor given on the holiday of Purim

Mattan Torah — the giving of the Torah at Sinai

Mazel — fortune

Mechallel Shabbos — desecrator of the Sabbath/to desecrate the Sabbath

Mechitzah — partition

Mechutan — the parent (or other close relative) of one's child-in-law

Mefarshim — commentaries

Melachah — lit. work; one of the thirty-nine actions that are forbidden on the Sabbath

Melamdim — Torah teachers of young children

Melaveh malkah — lit. escorting the queen; the meal eaten after the departure of the Sabbath

Menschlich (Y) — courteous

Mesiras nefesh — self-sacrifice

Mesivta — Jewish boys high school

Mesorah — tradition

Mi k'amcha Yisrael — Who is like Your nation, Israel

Middos/middos tovos — character traits/good character traits

Mikvah — pool for ritual immersion

Mikvah taharah — pool for ritual immersion used by women

Milchig/milchigs (Y) — dairy

Minhag (pl. minhagim) — custom

Minhag Yisrael — Jewish custom

Minyan (pl. minyanim) — a quorum of ten men (usually gathered for prayer)

Mishloach manos — two portions of food gifted to fellow Jews on the holiday of Purim

Mishpachah — family

Mitzvah d'Oraisa — a biblical commandment

Mitzvah goreres mitzvah — one good deed breeds another

Mitzvos d'Rabbanan — rabbinical commandments

Modeh Ani — lit. I thank; the prayer recited upon awakening

Mohel — one who performs a circumcision

Mussaf — supplementary prayer service recited on the Sabbath and festivals

Na'aseh v'nishma — we will do and we will hear

Nachas — pride or pleasure usually from one's children or students

Nachash — the original serpent

Nashim tzidkaniyos — righteous women

Ne'ilah — the closing prayer of the Yom Kippur services

Nefesh — (human) spirit

Negel vasser (Y) — ritual hand-washing performed upon awakening

Nes (pl. nissim) — miracle

Neshamah (pl. neshamos) — soul

Netilas yadayim — ritual hand-washing performed before eating bread

Nichum aveilim — consolation of mourners

Niggun (pl. niggunim) — a tune or a song

Nikur — the removal of forbidden veins and fats from meat

Nisayon (pl. nisyonos) — challenge

Nusach (pl. nuscha'os) — a particular text or style of prayer

Over — commit (in reference to a sin)

Panim chadashos — lit. a new face; a guest at a *sheva brachos* (see below) who hadn't attended any of the previous celebrations

Parnassah — livelihood

Parshah — weekly Torah portion

Parshas — the weekly Torah portion of

Paskened — ruled (in reference to halachic decisions)

Pasuk (pl. pesukim) — verse

Perach — treacherous (work)

Perek — chapter

Perush (pl. perushim) — commentary

Pesachdig — pertaining to Passover

Peyah (pl. peyos) — sidelock

Pidyon shvuyim — the redeeming of captives

Pirsumei nisa — the publicizing of a miracle

Poritz (Y) — wealthy non-Jewish landowner

Pushke (Y) — charity box

Rachmana litzlan — may G-d save us

Rachmanim bnei rachmanim — merciful ones, the children of merciful ones

Ratzon Hashem — G-d's will

Rav (pl. rabbanim) — rabbi

Rebbi — Torah teacher; leader of a chassidic sect

Refuah sheleimah — a complete recovery

Rofei kol basar — the Healer of all flesh, referring to G-d

Rosh kollel — the leader of a *kollel* (see above)

Rosh yeshivah (pl. roshei yeshivah) — the leader of an institution for Torah learning

Schach — covering made of branches or the like for the booths Jews dwell in on Sukkos

Sedarim — plural of (Passover) Seder

Sefer (pl. sefarim) — holy book

Sefer Torah (pl. sifrei Torah) — Torah scroll

Sefer'l — a term of endearment for a *sefer*

Segulah — a specific action one engages in in order to merit salvation

Selichos — early morning prayer services that begin several days before Rosh Hashanah

Seudah (pl. seudos) — religious meal

Seudas hamafsekes — the meal eaten before the fasts of Yom Kippur and Tishah B'Av

Seudas hoda'ah — meal of thanksgiving

Seudas Mashiach — meal of the Messiah

Seudas Shabbos — Sabbath meal

Seudas Yom Tov — holiday meal

Shabbos Kodesh — holy Sabbath

Shabbosdig — pertaining to the Sabbath

Shalom — peace

Shalom aleichem — peace be on you, a traditional greeting

Shamash — an auxiliary flame lit beside the menorah flames on Chanukah

Shamor es Yom haShabbos — guard the Sabbath day—one of the Ten Commandments

Shanah rishonah — the first year (of marriage)

Shas — the complete Talmud

Shechinah — Divine Presence

Shechitah — ritual slaughter

Shechted/shechting (Y) — slaughtered/slaughtering according to Jewish law

Shehakol — lit. that everything; a reference to the blessing recited on most foods

Sheitel (Y) — wig

Shelo asani goy — that I was not created a non-Jew

Shema koleinu — hear our voice

Shema Yisrael Hashem Elokeinu Hashem echad — Hear O Israel, Hashem is our G-d, Hashem is one

Shemiras einayim — the guarding of one's eyes from seeing impure sights

Shemiras halashon — the guarding of one's tongue from speaking evil

Shep (Y) — derive

Sheva brachos — the seven blessings recited at a Jewish wedding and at meals during the week that follows; the week following a wedding; festive meals served during that week

Sheva mitzvos Bnei Noach — the seven commandments that all of humanity is obligated to abide by

Shevarim — set of three short blasts from a ram's horn

Shevet — tribe

Shidduch — marital match

Shiur (pl. shiurim) — lecture

Shkiah — sunset

Shliach (pl. shluchim) — emissary, commonly used in reference to either an emissary carrying out the will of G-d or to a Chabad Jew involved in outreach

Shmuess (Y) — lecture

Shmurah matzah — unleavened bread that was made under supervision to ensure its kosher for Passover status

Shmutz (Y) — dirt, grime

Shochet (pl. shochtim) — individual who performs ritual slaughter

Shomer Torah u'mitzvos — one who observes all the Torah's commandments

Shtetl (Y) — village

Shtiebel (Y) — small (usually chassidic) synagogue

Shtreimelach (Y) — chassidic fur hats

Shulchan Aruch — Code of Jewish Law

Sichah — discourse

Siman Tov U'mazel Tov — a good omen and a good fortune—words of a song sung on happy occasions

Simchah (pl. simchos) — joy; a joyous occasion

Simchah goreres simchah — a joyous occasion breeds another joyous occasion

Simchas beis hasho'evah — the joyous celebration of the water-drawing at the Holy Temple; a celebration commemorating this

Simchas hachaim — joy of life

Simchas Yom Tov — joy of the festival

Sinas Yisrael — antisemitism

Siyata d'Shmaya — Divine assistance

Siyum (pl. siyumim) — celebration of the completion of a segment of Torah study

Sugya — Talmudic topic

Tallis — prayer shawl

Talmid chacham — Torah scholar

Tanna'im — Mishnaic Sages

Tatty (Y) — colloq. father

Tefillah (pl. tefillos) — prayer

Tefillin — phylacteries

Tekias shofar — the blowing of a ram's horn

Tekios — (sustained) blasts from a ram's horn

Teruos — staccato blasts from a ram's horn

Teshuvah — repentance; halachic response

Tikun Leil Shavuos — a study regimen compiled for the eve of Shavuos

Torah sheb'al peh — the Oral Torah

Toras Moshe — the Torah which we received from Moses

Treif/treife/treifus (Y) — non-kosher/non-kosher food

Tumah — impurity

Tza'ar ba'alei chaim — (causing) pain to live creatures

Tzarah (pl. tzaros) — calamity

Tzedakah — charity

Tzibbur — congregation; the Jewish public

Tzitzis/tzitzit — religious four-cornered garment with fringes

Tznius — modesty

V'Atah Hu Melech Keil chai v'kayam — and You (G-d) are King, a G-d that is live and enduring

V'higadita l'vincha — lit. and you shall tell your children; the obligation for a father to teach his children about the Exodus from Egypt

V'samachta b'chagecha — lit. and you shall rejoice in your holiday; the obligation to rejoice on the holiday of Sukkos

Va'ad — committee

Yahrtzeit (Y) — anniversary of death

Yasher koach — thank you

Yehi Ratzons — supplications (that begin with those words)

Yehi zichro baruch — may his memory be blessed

Yekkishe (Y) — Jews of German descent

Yerei Shamayim (pl. yirei Shamayim) — one who fears G-d

Yeshivah gedolah — lit. large institution for Torah learning; usually refers to a boys high school where Torah is studied

Yetzer hara — evil inclination

Yetzias Mitzrayim — Exodus from Egypt

Yiddelach (Y) — term of endearment for Jews

Yidden (Y) — Jews

Yiddishe (Y) — Jewish

Yiddishkeit (Y) — Judaism

Yiras Shamayim — fear of Heaven

Yisgadal v'yiskadash Shmei rabah — may (the honor of) His (G-d's) great name be increased and sanctified

Ym"s — abbreviation for *yimach shemo/shemam*—may his/their name be obliterated

Yotzei — to fulfill one's obligation

Yud — tenth; the tenth letter of the Hebrew alphabet

Yud-tes — nineteenth

Yungerman (pl. yungerleit) (Y) — young married man

Zaideh (Y) — grandfather

Zakai — innocent

Zechus — merit

Zei'ah shel mitzvah — the effort expended in fulfilling a commandment

Zerizus — alacrity

Zeroa — the shank bone on the Seder plate

Zeroa netuyah — an outstretched arm

Zman Simchaseinu — lit. time of our joy; another name for the Sukkos holiday

Zol zein gezunt — may s/he be healthy

Zt"l — abbreviation for *zecher tzaddik livrachah*—the memory of a righteous one should be blessed